THE OXFORD HANDBOOK OF

# PHILOSOPHICAL AND QUALITATIVE ASSESSMENT IN MUSIC EDUCATION

# THE OXFORD HANDBOOK OF

# PHILOSOPHICAL AND QUALITATIVE ASSESSMENT IN MUSIC EDUCATION

*Edited by*
DAVID J. ELLIOTT,
MARISSA SILVERMAN,
*and*
GARY E. McPHERSON

OXFORD
UNIVERSITY PRESS

Oxford University Press is a department of the University of Oxford. It furthers
the University's objective of excellence in research, scholarship, and education
by publishing worldwide. Oxford is a registered trade mark of Oxford University
Press in the UK and certain other countries.

Published in the United States of America by Oxford University Press
198 Madison Avenue, New York, NY 10016, United States of America.

Library of Congress Cataloging-in-Publication Data
Names: Elliott, David J. (David James), 1948– | Silverman, Marissa. | McPherson, Gary.
Title: The Oxford handbook of philosophical and qualitative assessment in music
education / edited by David J. Elliott, Marissa Silverman, and Gary E. McPherson.
Description: New York, NY : Oxford University Press, [2019] |
Series: Oxford handbooks | Includes bibliographical references and index.
Identifiers: LCCN 2019001334 | ISBN 9780190265182 (cloth : alk. paper) |
ISBN 9780190265205 (oxford handbooks online)
Subjects: LCSH: Music—Instruction and study—Evaluation.
Classification: LCC MT1 .O938 2019 | DDC 780.71—dc23 LC record
available at https://lccn.loc.gov/2019001334

1 3 5 7 9 8 6 4 2

Printed by Sheridan Books, Inc., United States of America

# Contents

# PART II.  METHODOLOGICAL PRACTICES

# PART III.  CREATIVITY

# Contributors

**Frank Abrahams** is professor of music education at Westminster Choir College of Rider University in Princeton, NJ. A native of Philadelphia, he holds degrees from Temple University and New England Conservatory. He has pioneered the development of a critical pedagogy for music education and has presented research papers and taught classes in the United States, China, Brazil, Taiwan, Hungary, Israel, Italy, Croatia, and the United Kingdom. He is senior editor of *Visions of Research in Music Education* and has been a member of the editorial board of the *Music Educators Journal*. With Paul Head, he is coauthor of *Case Studies in Music Education, Teaching Music through Performance in Middle School Choir*, and *The Oxford Handbook of Choral Pedagogy*. With Ryan John, he is coauthor of *Planning Instruction in Music* and *Becoming Musical*.

**Kenneth Aigen** is associate professor in music therapy at New York University. He has lectured internationally and authored numerous publications on Nordoff-Robbins music therapy, qualitative research, and music-centered music therapy. He is president of the Nordoff-Robbins Music Therapy Foundation and a trustee of Nordoff-Robbins International. He is a past president of the American Association for Music Therapy, is a recipient of the Research and Publications Award from the American Music Therapy Association, and was the scientific committee chairman for the Ninth World Congress of Music Therapy. Honors include the Research and Publications Award from the American Music Therapy Association and the Lindback Award for Distinguished Teaching from Temple University. His most recent book is *The Study of Music Therapy: Core Issues and Concepts*. His current research focuses on the everyday uses of music by adults on the autism spectrum.

**Julie Ballantyne** is associate professor in music education at The University of Queensland, Australia. An elected commissioner and chair (2017–2018) of the Music In Schools and Teacher Education Commission of the International Society of Music Education, her research, teaching, and other interests intersect around music teacher education, social justice in teacher education, and teacher identities. Ballantyne's recent project, www.musicteachersproject.com, utilized her experience in establishing online communities of practice to solve professional problems found in the field, and her work consistently aims to bridge gaps between universities and classrooms for music teachers. She has in recent years been awarded prizes and fellowships recognizing her efforts in designing quality learning in higher education. Having published more than forty refereed articles, book chapters, and conference papers, Julie remains inspired to do more in the area, with the hope of effecting change for the greater good.

**Adam Patrick Bell** is assistant professor of music education in the School of Creative and Performing Arts at the University of Calgary, Canada. He is the author of *Dawn of the DAW: The Studio as Musical Instrument* (2018), and has written several peer-reviewed articles and chapters on the topics of music technology in music education and disability in music education. Prior to his career in higher education, Bell worked as a kindergarten teacher, elementary music teacher, and support worker for adolescents with disabilities.

**Steven Bingham** is the music director at Santa Fe College in Gainesville, Florida. Bingham's duties include teaching music fundamentals; music appreciation, both on site and online; and directing three jazz ensembles: a big band and two jazz combos. His current international project is assisting in developing an inclusive community music program at the Notre Maison Orphanage in Port au Prince, Haiti. He has worked in the field of jazz inclusion for local K–12 and Santa Fe College based programs for students with disabilities, most recently in his rhythm and blues ensemble. Bingham has published extensively in the area of community music inclusion through his presentations at International Society for Music Education conferences in China, Greece, Brazil, and Scotland.

**John A. Carpente,** PhD, MT-BC, LCAT, is an associate professor of music therapy at Molloy College, founder and executive director of the Rebecca Center for Music Therapy, and founding director of the Center for Autism and Child Development at Molloy. He has twenty years of clinical and supervisory experience working in a variety of clinical settings serving children, adolescents, and adults with neurodevelopmental disorders. He is a founding member of the International Music Therapy Assessment Consortium and the creator of the Developmental Relationship-based Music Therapy model. In addition, he authored the internationally utilized assessment tool *Individual Music-Centered Assessment Profile for Neurodevelopmental Disorders* (IMCAP-ND). Dr. Carpente has published numerous book chapters and articles on improvisational music therapy with children with autism spectrum disorder. He has presented his work domestically and internationally and is frequently invited to guest lecture at various universities in the United States, Europe, and South America.

**Jian-Jun Chen-Edmund** is assistant professor of music education at the University of Minnesota Duluth. She teaches applied piano and graduate and undergraduate music education courses. She received her PhD in music education and served as adjunct assistant professor at the University of Florida. In 2007 she earned the Outstanding Academic Achievement Award from the UF International Center. Dr. Chen-Edmund earned her master of arts degree in music and music education at Teachers College, Columbia University, and a bachelor's degree in music performance at Fu Jen University in Taipei, Taiwan. She holds Orff Schulwerk and Kodály certifications. Dr. Chen-Edmund has presented research and conducted workshops regionally, nationally, and internationally. Her research areas of interest include Taiwanese indigenous folk music, connections between music instruction and language development, teacher education, and assessment in music education.

**Donald DeVito** is a music and special education teacher at the Sidney Lanier Center School in Gainesville, Florida. He was the 2011 National Council for Exceptional Children Teacher of the Year (special education) and a board member in 2014–2016 of the International Society for Music Education (which has members in over one hundred countries). DeVito publishes extensively and presents internationally on networking universities, schools, and community-based music programs for the benefit of children with special needs throughout the world. He is developing a music and special education program at the Notre Maison Orphanage for children with disabilities in Haiti and recently edited the first educational publication of the Haitian Teachers Association. Upcoming publications include chapters on music and special education in the *Handbook of Arts Education and Special Education* and *The Oxford Handbook of Technology and Music Education*.

**David Edmund** is assistant professor and chair of music education at the University of Minnesota Duluth. His research interests include pedagogy of musical creativity, music for exceptional learners, and music teacher artistry. He possesses certifications in the Orff-Schülwerk and Kodály approaches. Prior to his time at UMD, Edmund served on the faculty at the University of Florida, where he earned a PhD in music education. Edmund has presented research in East Asia, Europe, South America, and throughout the United States. He taught general music, choir, and beginning band for ten years in Florida elementary schools. Edmund earned the master of music education degree with jazz studies emphasis at the University of North Texas, where he performed in the One o' Clock lab band and directed the Six o' Clock. Dr. Edmund has toured and recorded with chamber winds, jazz, reggae, soul, pop, and rock ensembles.

**David J. Elliott** is professor at New York University. Prior to joining NYU, he taught at the University of Toronto for twenty-eight years. He is coauthor of *Music Matters: A Philosophy of Music Education* (2nd ed., 2015); author of *Music Matters: A New Philosophy of Music Education* (1995); editor of *Praxial Music Education: Reflections and Dialogues* (2005/2009); and coeditor of *Artistic Citizenship: Artistry, Social Responsibility, and Ethical Praxis* (2016). He has presented over three hundred papers and lectures in forty-four countries and is an award-winning composer/arranger (Boosey & Hawkes/ Hal Leonard).

**Martin Fautley** is director of research in the School of Education and Social Work at Birmingham City University in the United Kingdom. He was a classroom music teacher for many years. His main area of research is assessment in music education, but he also investigates understandings of musical learning and progression. He is the author of eight books, including *Assessment in Music Education* (Oxford University Press), and has written and published over fifty journal articles, book chapters, and academic research papers. He is coeditor of the *British Journal of Music Education*.

**John Finney** taught music in secondary schools in Southall, Worceste, and Basingstoke, England, before doing higher degree study at Reading University and joining the Music Department of Homerton College, Cambridge, in 1992. In 2001 the college was assimilated into the University of Cambridge, Faculty of Education, where John continued to prepare music graduates for secondary school music teaching as well as supervising higher degree study. In the role of teacher trainer John created a sustainable model of partnership working with music teachers throughout East Anglia. He retired in 2011. His research has focused on the analysis of classroom practice in relation to public policy, with particular attention to curriculum rationales, pedagogical innovation and change, and the problems of assessment. In addition to frequently publishing articles accessible to classroom music teachers evaluating and critiquing public policy, his major publications include *Rebuilding Engagement through the Arts: Responding to Disaffected Students* (with R. Hickman, M. Morrison, B. Nicholl, and J. Rudduck); *Masterclass in Music Education: Transforming Teaching and Learning* (with F. Laurence); and *Music Education in England 1950–2010: The Child-centered Progressive Tradition*, a critical commentary on ideas and practices that evolved during the second half of the twentieth century in England. From here his interest has focused on the possibility of developing an ethical approach to music education found at the heart of the relationship between the pupil and teacher and what is being learned, constructing relational knowledge and a music education with "human interest." John writes a weekly blog, *Music Education Now*, at jfin107.wordpress.

**Susan Hallam** is emerita professor of education and music psychology at the UCL Institute of Education. She was awarded an MBE in the 2015 honours list. She pursued careers as both a professional musician and a music educator before joining the Institute of Education, University of London in 1991. She joined Oxford Brookes as Professor of Education in January 2000 returning to the Institute of Education in January 2001. She has received research funding from the ESRC, DfE, the Scottish Executive, Calouste Gulbenkian Foundation, Nuffield Foundation, Performing Rights Society, the Christian Initiative Trust, CfBT, the Ministry of Defence, 4Children, EMI Sound Foundation, the Institute of Physics, SkillForce, and several Local Authorities for a range of projects relating to attendance at school, exclusion from school, behavior improvement, school-home links, ability grouping in primary and secondary schools, formative feedback in learning, instrumental music services, and the evaluation of various educational initiatives. In addition she has undertaken research in relation to pedagogy in secondary and higher education, text understanding and conceptions of argument of post-graduate students, homework, learning in music, and the effects of music on behavior and studying.

**Juniper Hill** is an ethnomusicologist with interests in music education and performance practice studies. A recipient of an Alexander von Humboldt, a Marie Curie, and two Fulbright Fellowships, she is professor and chair in ethnomusicology at the Julius Maximilian University of Würzburg. Her specializations include improvisation, creativity, pedagogy, revival, and intercultural exchange, on which topics she has conducted fieldwork in Finland, South Africa, the United States, and Ecuador. Her books include *The Oxford Handbook of Music Revival* (2014) and *Becoming Creative: Insights from Musicians in a Diverse World* (2018).

**Jillian Hogan** is a PhD student in developmental psychology in the Arts & Mind Lab at Boston College. She holds an MM in music education and a BM in clarinet performance from Boston Conservatory and has additional training in Montessori and Orff-Schulwerk approaches. In her research, she uses mixed methods to investigate what we learn through arts education and how those findings align with public perceptions. Her primary interest is the teaching and learning of habits of mind in visual art and music education, which is informed by teaching for six years in schools that specialize in gifted, inclusion, and autism spectrum disorder populations. She is an author of the book *Studio Thinking from the Start: The K-8 Art Educator's Handbook* (2018) (www.jillhoganinboston.com).

**Beatriz Ilari** is associate professor of music education at the University of Southern California (USC). Prior to her appointment at USC, she worked as associate professor of music education at the Federal University of Paraná in Brazil (2003–2010) and as the Lozano Long Visiting Associate Professor of Latin American Studies at the University of Texas in Austin. Her main research interests lie in the intersection of music, childhood, cognition, and culture. She is currently a research fellow at USC's Brain and Creativity Institute and a co-investigator on the Advancing Interdisciplinary Research in Singing initiative. She is currently on the editorial boards of the *Journal of Research in Music Education, Music and Science, Psychology of Music, Musicae Scientiae,* and *Research Studies in Music Education,* and the editor of *Perspectives: Journal of the Early Childhood Music and Movement Association.*

**Geir Johansen** is professor emeritus of music education and music didactics at the Norwegian Academy of Music in Oslo, Norway, holding a PhD in music education. He has contributed widely at international conferences and in international research journals. His research interests include all aspects of the sociology of music education, philosophical as well as empirical. Within this scope, his research interests are directed toward subject areas such as curriculum implementation, educational quality, identity, professions and professionalism, talent education, hidden curricula, and conservatoires in society. He teaches and supervises on the master's and PhD levels, and he frequently serves as a PhD defense opponent in Norway as well as abroad. Johansen is coeditor of the upcoming *Routledge Handbook on the Sociology of Music Education.*

**Kathryn Jourdan** is a performer, teacher, and researcher based in Edinburgh, Scotland. She freelances as a viola player with the Scottish Chamber Orchestra and teaches academic music, viola, and chamber music in the specialist setting of St Mary's Music School. In 2015 she completed a PhD in the field of the philosophy of music education with the dissertation "Through the Lens of Levinas: An Ethnographically-Informed Case Study of Pupils," supervised by John Finney in the Faculty of Education, Cambridge University. She is a member of the editorial boards of both the *British Journal of Music Education* and the *International Journal of Music Education* and continues to present and publish academic research. She is a board member of Sistema Scotland. She studied music at Clare College, Cambridge, completing postgraduate studies in viola and chamber music at the Royal Northern College of Music with Simon Rowland Jones and

Chris Rowland, where she was awarded the Bach and Leonard Hirsch prizes for solo and quartet performance. After five formative years in the city of Birmingham Symphony Orchestra under Simon Rattle's leadership, she played for three years in a London-based string quartet, training and then practicing as a secondary music teacher back in Cambridge, inspired by the outreach and education work in inner-city Birmingham in which she had taken part as a member of CBSO.

**Alexis Anja Kallio** is a postdoctoral research fellow in music education at the Sibelius Academy, University of the Arts Helsinki, Finland. Her research interests include music education for social justice; reflexive approaches to teaching, learning, and research; and pedagogical ethics in diverse education contexts.

**Sidsel Karlsen** is professor of music education at the Norwegian Academy of Music and docent at the Sibelius Academy, University of the Arts Helsinki, Finland. She has published widely in international research journals and is a frequent contributor to international anthologies and handbooks. Her research interests include cultural diversity in music education, the interplay between formal and informal arenas for music learning, and the social and cultural significance of music festivals. Currently she is one of two PIs for the research project Global Visions through Mobilizing Networks: Co-developing Intercultural Music Teacher Education in Finland, Israel and Nepal (funded by the Academy of Finland 2015–2019). She also works within the project of The Social Dynamics of Musical Upbringing and Schooling in the Norwegian Welfare State (funded by the Research Council of Norway 2018–2022).

**Alexandra Kertz-Welzel** is professor and department chair of music education at Ludwig Maximilian University in Munich (Germany). She obtained her PhD in musicology from Saarland University in Saarbruecken (Germany), as well as master's degrees in music education, German studies, philosophy, piano, and harpsichord. From 2002 to 2005 she was visiting scholar and lecturer in music education at the University of Washington in Seattle (USA). With research interests in international music education, philosophy of music education, music education policy, community music, and children's musical cultures, she has regularly presented at national and international conferences. She is author and editor of several books and a frequent contributor to leading journals in music education. Her new book, *Globalizing Music Education: A Framework* was published in 2018 by Indiana University Press. She is currently chair of the International Society for the Philosophy of Music Education and co-chair of the ISME Commission on Policy.

**John Kratus** is currently retired and living in Florida. He is professor emeritus from Michigan State University, where he was chair of music education. He has presented his ideas at conferences in Ireland, Scotland, the United Kingdom, Sweden, Germany, Austria, Greece, Egypt, Japan, China, Indonesia, Canada, and the United States. In 2004 Kratus was contracted by the US Department of Defense to provide in-service education to the music teachers working in schools on military bases around the world. He was a keynote speaker at the CMS/NASM conference on "Music in General Studies" in 2007 and at the CMS Summit on twenty-first-century music school design in 2016. His articles have appeared in most of the world's major music education journals. Kratus has served as chair of the Special Research Interest Groups in Creativity, Philosophy, and Popular Music Education, and he is currently on the editorial boards of the *International Journal of Music Education* and the *Journal of Popular Music Education*.

**Janice Krum** has taught kindergarten through fifth-grade general music for thirteen years in the Michigan Public School system, most recently in Northville Public Schools. She previously taught in Lake City Area Schools. Janice holds both bachelor's and master's degrees in music education from Michigan State University. Her particular interests are in early childhood music and the development of audiation in children.

**Roger Mantie** is associate professor in the Department of Arts, Culture and Media at University of Toronto Scarborough. His work emphasizes connections between schooling and society, with a focus on lifelong engagement in and with music and the arts. He is co-editor of the Oxford Handbook of Technology and Music Education (2017) and the Oxford Handbook of Music Making and Leisure (2016). Learn more at rogermantie.com.

**Gary E. McPherson** studied music education at the Sydney Conservatorium of Music before completing a master's of music education at Indiana University, a doctorate of philosophy at the University of Sydney, and a licentiate and fellowship in trumpet performance through Trinity College, London. He is the Ormond Professor and director of the Melbourne Conservatorium of Music and has served as national president of the Australian Society for Music Education and president of the International Society for Music Education. His research interests are broad and his approach interdisciplinary. His most important research examines the acquisition and development of musical competence and motivation to engage and participate in music from novice to expert levels. With a particular interest in the acquisition of visual, aural, and creative performance skills, he has attempted to understand more precisely how music students become sufficiently motivated and self-regulated to achieve at the highest level.

**Nasim Niknafs**, the recipient of the Connaught New Researcher Award, Faculty Mobility Grant, and OMEA's Agha Khan Initiative, is an assistant professor of music education at the Faculty of Music, University of Toronto. Nasim's interdisciplinary research engages with equity and politics of contemporary music education, cultural studies, popular music education, and anarchism and activism in music education. Her selected publications have appeared in academic journals and books such as *Action, Criticism, and Theory for Music Education; Music Education Research; Bulletin of the Council for Research in Music Education; The Ashgate Research Companion to Popular Music Education;* and *Punk Pedagogies*. At the university level, Nasim has taught courses such as Politics of Sound and Music Making, Multimodal Approaches to Music Teaching and Learning, Cultural Perspectives in Music Education, and Advanced Topics in Research in Music Education. Nasim holds degrees from Northwestern University, New York University, Kingston University, London, and University of Art, Tehran.

**Bryan Powell** is assistant professor of music education and music technology at the John J. Cali School of Music at Montclair State University. Prior to joining MSU, Bryan served as the Director of Higher Education for Little Kids Rock, and the Interim Director of Amp Up NYC, a partnership between Little Kids Rock and Berklee College of Music. Bryan is a founding principal editor of Journal of Popular Music Education and also serves as the Executive Director of the Association for Popular Music Education. Bryan is the current Chair for the NAfME Popular Music Education SRIG and is an International Affiliate for Musical Futures.

**Andrew Reid** is a curriculum manager in Queensland, Australia. He has many years' experience in significant educational change, including development, implementation, and assessment of curriculum and educational programs from preparatory years to the senior years of secondary education. He is immediate past president of The Australian Society for Music Education (ASME) Queensland Chapter and was co-convener of the 2011 ASME National Conference "Making Sound Waves: Diversity, Unity, Equity." He is regularly engaged as an adviser for music and arts curriculum and assessment initiatives, including as advisory panelist for the development of The Australian Curriculum: The Arts—Music. He has developed and presented curriculum and assessment professional capacity building in primary, secondary, and tertiary settings. Reid's broadening educational management portfolio includes large-scale curriculum change in primary and secondary education at the system level. Andrew is passionate about ensuring every child has access to quality curriculum, teaching, and learning.

**Lauren Kapalka Richerme** is assistant professor of music education at Indiana University, where she teaches undergraduate and graduate courses on music education foundations, philosophy, and sociology. Her research interests include poststructuralist philosophy and education policy, and her work has been published in the *Journal of Research in Music Education; Bulletin of the Council for Research in Music Education; Philosophy of Music Education Review; International Journal of Music Education; Music Education Research; Arts Education Policy Review; Journal of Music Teacher Education; Music Educators Journal;* and *Action, Criticism, and Theory for Music Education.* Her book *Complicating, Considering, and Connecting Music Education,* in which she proposes a Deleuzian-inspired philosophy of music education, will be available through Indiana University Press. Prior to her university teaching, she taught high school and middle school band and general music in Massachusetts. She holds degrees from the University of Massachusetts Amherst, Harvard University, and Arizona State University.

**Karen Salvador** is assistant professor of music education at Michigan State University. Previously, she coordinated the music education programs at the University of Michigan–Flint, and she has also taught early childhood music, elementary general music, drama and choir in Michigan and New Zealand. Dr. Salvador's research pertains to how music educators meet individual student needs, particularly in early childhood and elementary grades. This research extends into music teacher education, exploring both program practices for music educator preparation and also the lived experiences of music educators who are working to become more inclusive and responsive. Dr. Salvador is a co-facilitator for the Society for Music Teacher Education's Area for Strategic Planning and Action on Cultural Diversity and Social Justice, and is President-Elect of the National Association for Music Education's North Central Division.

**Andrea Schiavio** is currently postdoctoral researcher at The Centre for Systematic Musicology of The University of Graz, Austria, and honorary research fellow at the Department of Music of the University of Sheffield, UK, from which he received his PhD in 2014. After his doctoral studies he served as postdoctoral researcher at the Cognitive and Systematic Musicology Lab of the Ohio State University (USA) and at the Department of Psychology of Boğaziçi University Istanbul, Turkey. In 2017 he lectured at The University of Music and Performing Arts Graz, Austria. His work combines empirical and theoretical research at the crossroads of music psychology, cognitive (neuro)science, and philosophy of mind. In his writings he defends a "4E" approach to music cognition, one that conceives of music as an embodied, embedded, extended, and enactive phenomenon.

**Iman Bikram Shah** is principal of the Nepal Music Center, Kathmandu. His work in recent years, as a team member of the Curriculum Development Center and the National Center for Education Development (NCED), has focused on introducing music education programs in Nepal and developing Nepal's first music teacher education.

**Megan M. Sheridan** is assistant professor of music education at the University of Florida, where she teaches courses in undergraduate and graduate music education. She has taught elementary general music in public and private schools. Dr. Sheridan is Kodály certified and currently serves as chair of the National Conference Choir Committee for the Organization of American Kodály Educators. She has also completed Orff-Schulwerk Level I training. Her research interests include pedagogical practices in elementary general music, children's vocal development, music for children with special needs, and qualitative research methods. She frequently presents her research and gives workshops at schools and conferences in the United States and abroad.

**Marissa Silverman** is associate professor at the John J. Cali School of Music, Montclair State University, NJ. A Fulbright scholar, her research agenda focuses on dimensions of music philosophy, artistic interpretation, community music, and interdisciplinary curriculum development. Dr. Silverman is author of *Gregory Haimovsky: A Pianist's Odyssey to Freedom* (University of Rochester Press) and coauthor of the second edition of *Music Matters: A Philosophy of Music Education*. She is coeditor of *Community Music Today* (Rowman & Littlefield) and *Artistic Citizenship: Artistry, Social Responsibility, and Ethical Praxis*.

**Gareth Dylan Smith** is the manager of program effectiveness at Little Kids Rock and president of the Association for Popular Music Education. He is founding coeditor of the *Journal of Popular Music Education*; lead editor of the *Routledge Research Companion to Popular Music Education* (2017) and *Punk Pedagogies in Practice* (2017); coeditor with Roger Mantie of *The Oxford Handbook of Music Making and Leisure* (2016); and coauthor with Hildegard Froehlich of *Sociology for Music Teachers: Practical Applications*

(2nd ed., 2017). His research interests include drumming and drummers, popular music, identity, eudaimonism, auto-ethnographic research methods, and embodiment in performance. He plays drums with V1, Oh Standfast, the Eruptörs, and Stephen Wheel.

**Johan Söderman** is a professor in child and youth studies at the University of Gothenburg and reader in music education at Lund University. Söderman was previously a visiting scholar at Teachers College, Columbia University, and is currently a board member of the Swedish Council for Popular Adult Education. Söderman's research interests regard community music, social mobilization/social movements, nonformal/informal learning, and popular adult education within the fields of cultural studies and music studies. Söderman has published articles for journals such as *Music Education Research*, *British Journal of Music Education*, *Finnish Journal of Music Education*, and *International Journal of Community Music*. He has also published several books, such as *Hip Hop Within and Without the Academy* (with Karen Snell) and *Bourdieu and Sociology of Music Education* (with Pamela Burnard and Ylva Trulsson-Hofvander).

**Brent C. Talbot** is associate professor and coordinator of music education at the Sunderman Conservatory of Music at Gettysburg College. He is also artistic director of the Gettysburg Children's Choir and the founding director of Gamelan Gita Semara. His teaching and scholarship, informed by his many travels as well as his experiences as a school music educator, examine power, discourse, and issues of social justice in varied settings for music learning around the globe. He is the editor of *Marginalized Voices in Music Education* (2018) and author of *Gending Raré: Children's Songs and Games from Bali* (2017) and *Finding a Way* (2012). Brent serves on the editorial board of the *Bulletin of the Council for Research in Music Education* and is the associate editor of *Action, Criticism, and Theory for Music Education*. For more go to www.brentctalbot.com.

**Vilma Timonen** is a lecturer in folk music and doctoral researcher in the music education department at the Sibelius Academy, University of the Arts Helsinki, Finland. Vilma's collaborative action research, involving music educators in Nepal and Finland, focuses on envisioning future music teacher education through intercultural learning.

**Danielle Shannon Treacy** is a doctoral researcher in the music education department at the Sibelius Academy, University of the Arts Helsinki, Finland. Her work focuses on collaborative learning and the ethical and methodological deliberations that are involved in intercultural music teacher education policy, practice, and research.

**Lauri Väkevä** is vice rector of research and doctoral education at University of the Arts, Helsinki and professor in music education at Sibelius Academy of University of Arts, Helsinki. A coauthor of three books, he has also published book chapters and articles in peer-reviewed journals and presented numerous papers at international conferences in the fields of music education, musicology, music history, and popular music studies.

**Janelize van der Merwe** received BMus and MMus degrees from the Northwest University School of Music in Potchefstroom, South Africa. She is currently a lecturer in music education at Northwest University and a doctoral fellow in music education at

New York University. She teaches music education and community music courses at undergraduate and graduate levels at NWU. She is also an active community musician and manager of the Musikhane Community Music Engagement Programme. Musikhane provides students at the Northwest University School of Music with unique, critical-service learning opportunities. Students engage with various sectors of the community, including vulnerable children, the elderly, and schoolteachers through participation in Musikhane. Her research interests focus on ethical considerations in music education and community music, particularly informed by an ethic of care.

**Dylan van der Schyff** is a postdoctoral research fellow in the Faculty of Music at the University of Oxford. His scholarship draws on recent developments in embodied cognitive science to explore questions related to how and why music is meaningful for human beings; a special focus is given to developing possibilities for thought and action in practical areas such as performance and music education. His published work appears in journals that cover a broad spectrum of fields in the sciences and humanities, including, *Frontiers in Neuroscience*; *Phenomenology and Practice*; *Psychomusicology: Music Mind and Brain*; *Phenomenology and the Cognitive Sciences*; *Frontiers in Psychology*; *Action, Criticism, and Theory for Music Education*; and *Interference: A Journal of Audio Culture*. Van der Schyff is also an experienced music educator and performer, appearing on well over one hundred recordings that span the fields of jazz, free improvisation, experimental, and "new music."

**Lise C. Vaugeois**, PhD, lives in Thunder Bay, Ontario, where she works as a musician, composer, scholar, and activist. She is concerned with the development of pedagogical spaces in which educators and students can explore social, political, and philosophical issues together with questions of public meaning making, community development, and social and material change. She teaches professional year and graduate courses at the Faculty of Education, Lakehead University.

**Hakim Mohandas Amani Williams**, a native of Trinidad and Tobago, is an associate professor of Africana studies at Gettysburg College, where he is also the director of peace and justice studies and an affiliate of the Education, Globalization Studies, and Public Policy Departments. He received his doctorate in international educational development and peace education from Teachers College, Columbia University. He is an associate editor of *Anthropology and Education Quarterly*. His research and teaching interests are school violence, educational inequity, mediation, negotiation and conflict resolution, education for social change, postcolonialism, masculinities, human rights, and restorative justice. He was a visiting scholar at the Advanced Consortium for Cooperation, Conflict and Complexity at the Earth Institute and is one of the recipients of the inaugural Emerging Scholar Award from the African Diaspora Special Interest Group of the Comparative and International Education Society.

**Ellen Winner** is professor and chair of psychology at Boston College and senior research associate at Project Zero, Harvard Graduate School of Education. She directs the Arts and Mind Lab, which focuses on cognition in the arts in typical and gifted children as well as adults. She is the author of over one hundred articles and three books—*Invented Worlds: The Psychology of the Arts* (1982); *The Point of Words: Children's Understanding of Metaphor and Irony* (1988); and *Gifted Children: Myths and Realities* (1996)—and coauthor of *Studio Thinking: The Real Benefits of Visual Arts Education* (2007) and *Studio Thinking 2: The Real Benefits of Visual Arts Education* (2013). Soon to appear are *Studio Thinking for Elementary Schools* and *How Art **Really** Works*. She received the Rudolf Arnheim Award for Outstanding Research by a Senior Scholar in Psychology and the Arts from APA Division 10 in 2000.

# PART I

## FOUNDATIONAL CONSIDERATIONS

# CHAPTER 1

# PHILOSOPHICAL AND QUALITATIVE PERSPECTIVES ON ASSESSMENT IN MUSIC EDUCATION

*introduction, aims, and overview*

DAVID J. ELLIOTT, MARISSA SILVERMAN, AND GARY E. McPHERSON

THE *Oxford Handbook of Philosophical and Qualitative Assessment in Music Education* (OHAME) gathers a wide range of international philosophical and qualitative researchers, teachers, and community musicians across various areas within music teaching and learning to clarify, (re)conceptualize, and critique current perspectives on a wide range of issues concerning assessment, evaluation, and measurement in or for music and music education. The central aim of the OHAME is to broaden and deepen understandings and critical thinking about the problems, alternatives, spaces, and places, as well as practical strategies that music educators at local, regional, and global levels may want to consider, acknowledge, reject, employ, develop, and deploy to improve various aspects of music teaching and learning.

## ASSESSMENT MATTERS IN CONTEXT

Across various domains in the field of education, "assessment" is a reality that is as commonplace, complex, and value laden as "music." However, in contrast to more than twenty-five hundred years of philosophical considerations of many dimensions of the nature and values of education, music, and music education, critically reasoned concepts of assessment, evaluation, and measurement in or for music education are rare. Instead, a great deal of discourse concentrates on the means and methods that teachers, groups of teachers, administrators, and collaborative student groups can or should employ to make formative and summative assessments of students' "success" in achieving the short- and long-term aims, goals, and objectives of curricula; in measuring students' musical development in minute ways; and in designing and implementing "national standards," (and so forth) as the first steps on the path to creating assessment regimes.

Thus, school music teachers—because they are often weighed down by heavy, top-down "orders" to test (test, test) their students—well-meaning administrators, policy-makers, and "assessment experts" are prone to overlook much more fundamental issues and questions, which should come long before issues of assessment. For example: How can or should assessment, evaluation, and measurement contribute to music students' pursuit or attainment of the deepest values or "goods" that active music making (in all available forms) has the potential to offer? Concomitantly, what might these values be? Should scholars develop or have critically reasoned concepts of the nature and values of musics and education before they adopt any assessment regime? Could it be that assessment, evaluation, and measurement procedures have the potential to compromise students' joy in learning music and developing enough motivation to pursue lifelong music making? Indeed, it is one thing to achieve musical ability and meet "standards"; it is quite another to be disposed to make music when schooling is over, to feel an inner need or a "passionate obsession" for music making and listening. Psychologists define a passionate obsession as "a strong inclination toward a self-defining activity that one loves and finds important, and in which one invests a substantial amount of time and energy" (Elliott & Silverman, 2015).

Related to these questions, if teachers, administrators, and others fail to continuously challenge taken-for-granted definitions, aims, and processes of assessment, what detrimental effects can many school systems' single-minded occupation with "assessment-ism" have on music students' self-identity, emotional health, well-being, and sense of safety and security; students' musical joy, which should be at the heart of every music teaching-learning episode; and music teachers' own joy, satisfaction, resilience, and dedication to empowering students' musical growth, creativity, and self-efficacy?

## ASSESSMENT AND VALUES OF MUSIC AND MUSIC EDUCATION

We just emphasized that critically reasoned concepts of the value of music and music education should precede or accompany the application of assessment processes. This opens the way for a huge discussion that is beyond the scope of this chapter. But four major points deserve attention.

(1) Current music education advocacy claims in some nations wag the dog of assessment methods and the design of aims, goals, and standards. Primary among these is the claim that music making and listening contribute to the improvement of academic achievement scores, contributing to advocates' ultimate goal of marketing music education as a means of making a living, as opposed to making a life. For example, teachers have been told that "music makes you smarter," "school music raises math scores," and "music educates feeling" (Reimer, [1970] 1989, 2003). But as explained elsewhere (Elliott & Silverman, 2015), serious scholars have published numerous studies that forcefully challenge these claims.

Ellen Winner has devoted her long career to supporting and improving school arts programs through copious scientific research on relationships between the arts and intelligence, thinking, and creativity. Winner has written more than one hundred articles and four books on the "invaluable habits of mind that arts education teaches us" (Winner quoted in Wu, 2013, p. 2). In the process, she has criticized the bogus claims of arts advocates. For example, Winner states, "there is NO definitive evidence that music improves math" (p. 3). Her research team studied "mathematicians' self-reported musicality" (p. 3) and compared them to people in other fields: "We asked over 100 PhDs in math...to self-report on all kinds of measures of their musicality. And guess what we found? No difference" (p. 3). People in other fields "are just as likely to report being musical (including playing an instrument) as people in mathematics" (p. 3).

After a large meta-analysis of correlation studies, Glenn Schellenberg (2006) concluded that even if music lessons correlate with improved math abilities, this does not mean that music causes improvement in math abilities. It may only mean that "children with high IQs (who perform well in a variety of test settings) are more likely than other children to take music lessons" (p. 458). Likewise, Eugenia Costa-Giomi (2012) argues that there is "not a single study" supporting the claim "that classical music improves young children's cognitive development" (p. 21). Like Schellenberg, Costa-Giomi acknowledges that even though there seems to be "a strong relationship between music participation and academic achievement,...the causal nature of the relationship is questionable" (p. 24). Why? Because what advocacy writers usually fail to understand is that statistical correlations do not necessarily mean that music instruction produces (or causes) achievement gains. In fact, the situation may be the other way around, because "it is known that students who choose to participate in the arts are more academically inclined than students who choose not to do so" (p. 24). In addition, research does not support the claim that musical participation might improve academic achievement, because "it's difficult to disentangle the true effects of music instruction from the effects of many other variables," such as a student's capacity to concentrate during music teaching and learning interactions; her family's income; the social dimensions of her musical experiences in her band, rock band, choir, and so forth; and the positive emotional effects she experiences during her teacher-student interactions "that mediate participation, persistence, and success in learning music. This is why we must be cautious in our assertions about the long-term intellectual benefits of music instruction" (Costa-Giomi, 2012, p. 28). This is also why it makes no sense to tie music students' musical achievement to their scores on standardized math and reading scores, as many administrators in the United States are doing.

What about claims that "music makes you smarter?" Although early research by Frances Rauscher suggested that listening to ten minutes of Mozart's music improved test scores on spatial reasoning, many researchers have not been able to replicate this study. In addition, Schellenberg (2015), who has conducted many studies on the relationships among music, spatial reasoning, math abilities, and IQ, found that the "Mozart Effect" may help some people do better on tests of spatial reasoning, but this is not always the case, and it's not unique to music. What seems to propel improved performance on cognitive measurements is being in a state of positive emotional arousal, which can result from many forms of stimulation during the time it takes to complete cognitive tests (Wu, 2013, p. 4). For example: "It turns out that if they [test takers] prefer to listen to a Stephen King story, and you let them listen to a Stephen King story, they also do better and rate themselves as more positively aroused. This is entirely consistent with what many cognitive psychologists have shown: that being in a state of positive arousal [or flow experience] improves performance on cognitive tests" (Winner cited in Wu, 2013, p. 4).

And what about the long-standing claim of "aesthetic music educators" (e.g., Reimer, 1970/1989) that music listening and music making are valuable because "music education is the education of feeling" (Reimer, 2003, p. 90)? The first question we need to ask is: What is an "educated feeling?" If such things, dispositions, or processes exist, how could we assess whether a person possesses or is developing educated feelings through music education? And if music educates people's feelings, does this mean that professional and amateur music makers and listeners become kinder, more compassionate, or more ethical than other people? If so, how do we account for the fact that many professional and amateur musicians and listeners are not necessarily kind, compassionate, or ethical? Consider the great German conductor Herbert von Karajan. Despite being a superb musician who could easily excel on all types of musical assessments, or "national music standards," he was generally not an ethical person because he voluntarily served as Hitler's official conductor (see Elliott & Silverman, 2015, p. 21). And what about the murderous Soviet dictator Joseph Stalin, who loved music, attended concerts and operas frequently, and wrote concert reviews? In short, there are many examples of unkind, unethical, and pernicious music lovers. And there's no qualitative, quantitative, or pragmatic evidence to support the theoretical claim that music listening, music making, or school music "educates feelings."

(2) Let us return to the idea that education is the process of preparing students to earn a living, because this theme flows from the dominant political and educational ideology of the last thirty years in many Western countries. The name of this ideology is *neoliberalism* (discussed in more detail later in the chapter). Many contemporary political, economic, and educational scholars furnish lucid criticisms of the meanings and the tragic effects of neoliberalism.

For one thing, neoliberal politicians, policymakers, and administrators past and present have been very successful in cutting the arts and other "unprofitable" subjects from school curricula (see Elliott & Silverman, 2015). Why? At first glance, neoliberalism seems benign because it seems to make financial sense to many people in our globalized world. Moreover, neoliberals have been masterful in conveying and marketing their ideology as nothing more than a common-sense, socially beneficial "reform" movement aimed at improving the lives of all citizens by "making trade between nations easier" and facilitating "the [global] movement of goods, resources and enterprises in a bid to always find cheaper resources, to maximize profits and efficiency" (Shah, 2010). In other words, a core premise of neoliberalism is that the "free market," which many incorrectly associate with democracy, should be allowed to determine all aspects of government policy-making and economic, political, and social life.

However, to ensure that the free market has unfettered "free rein" to determine prices, incomes, and so forth, neoliberals (usually the wealthiest members of Western societies) aggressively pressure governments to reduce or cease funding to as many social services as possible, notably education, healthcare, water and electrical services, and similar public goods. Neoliberals seek to privatize as many dimensions of public life as possible in order to reap a continuous stream of profits from the public sector. Among many effects of neoliberal policies is the gradual demise of "public and community good" and the rise of virulent individualism and rabid capitalism. As philosopher and historian Philip Mirowski (2013) explains, neoliberals have largely succeeded in camouflaging their agenda as "progress" and a "natural and inexorable state of mankind," when in fact it's actually a right-wing movement driven by economic and political fundamentalists who want to erase "distinctions among the state, society, and the market" and subordinate society to the market. As a result, says Henry Giroux (2012), "the democratic mission of public education is under assault by a conservative right-wing reform culture in which students are viewed as human capital in schools that are to be administered by market-driven forces." Not surprisingly, corporate leaders, local business leaders, and hedge fund managers in the United States "now sit on school boards across the country doing everything in their power to eliminate public schools and punish unionized teachers who do not support" the privatization of public schools, evaluation processes, curriculum development, and so forth (Giroux, 2012). Thus the administration of American schools is gradually becoming the domain of "managers" trained in accordance with "best business practices," not school principals educated as educators. Schools and universities are being reconceived, reconfigured, and branded as businesses and corporations that are better equipped to raise the "standards" of education, teaching, and learning. Neoliberals argue that education can only be "reformed" by adopting and imposing on schools the corporate forms of assessment, evaluation, and profit-driven measurements that dominate American business, which of course place little value on arts education.

Indeed, the educational sociologist Michael Apple (2001) argues that "for all too many of the pundits, politicians, corporate leaders, and others, education is a business and should be treated no differently than any other business" (pp. 1–2). Richard Colwell (2004) concurs and adds that in the minds of politicians and marketplace educators, testing subject matter is the key to winning control of the curriculum and securing the long-term and short-term values and interests of, say, American business (p. 18).

Need we say more about the contemporary values and ethics of American business? These days, if not always, "business ethics" is an oxymoron. Notably, "accountability" comes from the lexicon of business, in which "success" means financial profit, not personal growth and human development (Noddings, 2007, pp. 38–39). Indeed, *education* is (or should be) concerned with *responsibility*, not financial and test-score bean counting. Education should be about governments, administrators, parents, and teachers *acting ethically and responsibly* for students. It should not be controlled by the accounting mentality of government and school administrators who are not in minute-by-minute contact with students as individuals. In short, *"business" has no business being in schools and classrooms!*

There are many other spin-offs of the default "philosophy" of neoliberalism. For example, thousands of teachers are leaving or have already left the profession. This is due in part to the onerous chores and controls that come with accountability and assessment-ism. Indeed, and in spite of the best efforts of many teachers, schools and school boards are much more focused on "student control through testing" than on education.

(3) So what can be said about the relationship among musical values, music education, and assessment? We review here basic points of a praxial philosophy of music education—which is admittedly difficult to assess in conventional, summative ways—that are clearly present in various processes of formative assessments and holistic approaches to education. We postulate that the more teachers, administrators, and others keep the main themes of a praxial philosophy (Elliott & Silverman, 2015) in mind while developing curricula and assessment strategies, the more likely it is that students will reap the deepest values of music education.

To Aristotle, praxis meant active reflection and reflective action for the positive transformation of people's everyday lives and situations. But praxial music education (Elliott, 1995; Elliott & Silverman, 2015; Elliott, Silverman, & Bowman, 2016; Regelski, 2005) also includes a focus on (1) the why-what-how-where-when of effective, democratic, and civic education in, about, and through music performing, improvising, composing, arranging, and conducting/leading music musically, regardless of the media and technologies utilized; and (2) empowering people to make and listen to music for their own and others' experiences of meaningfulness, happiness, self-worth, and musical satisfaction.

Praxial music education is guided by an informed and ethical disposition to act rightly—musically, socially, ethically, communally, and so forth—with continuous concern for protecting and advancing human creativity. Praxial school music teachers should integrate several kinds of thinking and doing for the purpose of achieving musically and socially just, down-to-earth, humanly worthwhile results. So praxis is inherently social; it includes a deep concern for human personhood (Chappell, 2011; Elliott & Silverman, 2015, pp. 153–191), social-cultural communities, social capital, and all forms of identity formation: personal, musical, cultural, gendered, spiritual, and so forth. Praxial music teaching requires "the virtue of caring for those served, and, thus, of being prudent or care-full in decisions and actions that affect their well-being" (Regelski, 2012, p. 297).

Thus, music does not have one value; it has numerous values, depending on the ways in which it is conceived and used by people engaged in specific musical style communities. For example, when music education is thoughtfully guided—when we teach people not only in and about music, but also through music—we achieve what Aristotle and many other philosophers have considered the highest human values: a "good life" of well-being, flourishing, virtue, and happiness for the benefit of oneself and others. The Greeks summarized all these values in one term, *eudaimonia*, which is the ultimate aim of praxis and a central aim of a praxial philosophy of music education.

In summary, a praxial philosophy of music education emphasizes (1) that music making should include active reflection and critically reflective action dedicated to supporting and advancing human flourishing and well-being, the ethical care of others, and the positive transformation of people's everyday lives; and (2) that each instance of music should be conceived, taught, and learned as a social praxis—as a fusion of people, processes, products, and ethical "goods" in specific social-cultural contexts. Praxial means that a full understanding of the nature and significance of music and music education involves far more than an understanding of "elements" or pieces of music alone. Music, as a diverse social praxis, involves many intertwined dimensions.

Discussions of assessment in music education rarely, if ever, begin, proceed, or end with such ideas in mind. This is often why assessment concentrates so heavily on verbal knowledge *about* music and on technical musical skills, at the expense of the development of students' full human flourishing and their holistic personhood.

(4) When scholars and music educators speak and write about "music education," they often assume that it is a unitary phenomenon. Not so in this volume. Our contributors are well aware of the danger of doing so because, among other things, a one-dimensional approach confounds the meanings of and actions we take in the name of teaching, learning, and assessing.

Compare how common it is today to hear people talk in terms of "musics" because there are a massive number of different musical styles, musical-style communities, musical practices, or what we prefer to call musical praxes; a musical praxis conveys the idea that music making and learning are carried out with a constant concern for the ethics of music making (see Elliott & Silverman, 2015; Regelski, 2016).

Likewise, there are massive variations in the ways musics are taught and learned at all levels of formal and informal "education" worldwide. So why is it that writing and talking about education omits to take account of the *extraordinary differences* in the ways teachers teach thinking and doing in all "subjects," including "musics," in vastly different global situations at preschool, elementary, middle school, secondary, university, and conservatory levels; in community music contexts; and so forth, ad infinitum?

In short, and as odd as it may seem, there is no such "thing" as education; in reality, we are involved in the global phenomenon of EDUCATIONS. Thus, depending on where teachers live and teach, their activities in terms of assessment are "flashpoints" in a universe of possibilities, practices, and challenges—including what assessment, evaluation, and measurement mean.

# DEFAULT PHILOSOPHIES OF ASSESSMENT

Despite the complexities involved in what we have just outlined, and as we stated previously, there are relatively few critically reasoned and comprehensive concepts of assessment, let alone full-blooded philosophies of assessment. Instead, *"default* philosophies" of assessment (Elliott, 2010) in or for music teaching and learning are frequent.

A default philosophy arises from a lack of careful thinking and an absence of democratic dialogue (Gunzenhauser, 2003). Default philosophies grow and feed on unexamined assumptions. We often fail to notice them because they sneak up on us; before we know it, we are "saluting standards," surrendering to oppressive pressures to evaluate students according to cookie-cutter measurement regimes, and so forth, rather than challenging these default ways of thinking and doing. Thus, default philosophies morph into the "common sense" of global societies, worldwide educational institutions, and national and international music education and community music practices.

Of course, educational improvement is an unquestionably important aspect of education, and assessments are necessary companions of improvement. More broadly, educational assessment is a logical extension of what we do in all aspects of our lives. Whether we do it consciously or not, we continuously judge ideas, actions, people, and situations. This is just a necessary part of making our way in the world. Moreover, since a great deal of our students' learning is informal and nonformal, we have a responsibility to help them develop their *personal* assessment strategies so that they may better navigate our "Googleized," "Twittered," "YouTubed," and "Fake News" environments. These potentially harmful aspects of students' worlds are ever present in all forms of media, including music. So how can or do the processes of assessing music students help empower them to critique and resist social injustices through music making and listening—for example, collaborating on composing, sharing, and giving each other constructive, informal feedback and feed-forward (discussed later in the chapter)—in relation to the songs they create about what they witness in their schools or on the Internet? Several authors in this volume discuss or critique related processes.

While we are on the topic, it is useful to note that many educators or music educators make a simple distinction between two different forms of assessment—*formative* and *summative*—that some scholars are reluctant to accept (e.g., Carr, 2003, pp. 153–54). Other educators view formative and summative assessment across a wide continuum of possibilities. For example, as coeditor Gary McPherson argues, formative assessment should involve giving students both moment-to-moment feed-back and *"feed-forward"* about how well they are doing. McPherson notes that students crave more feedback, not less, because even some formative assessments can involve unconscious, hurtful criticism.

From this perspective, during in-class and in-action processes of *formative* assessment, teachers may include a variety of cues and "languages" (e.g., words and gesture) to educate their students about the quality of their efforts in the moment. Teachers *guide* (not control) students by targeting their attention to key details of their tasks, by adjusting their actions, and by cueing them to reflect critically about their actions and understanding. As Jack Nelson, Stuart Palonsky, and Kenneth Carlson (2004) write: "Assessment programs should focus on the individual student and examples of what they actually have produced" (p. 362). In contrast, as most teachers understand clearly, *summative* forms of assessment usually require us to step back from our students and their efforts in order to examine, test, judge, and otherwise reduce their work and understandings to numerical grades or brief verbal reports. Sadly, summative assessing diverts teachers' attention away from interacting with students both empathetically and with an "ethic of care" (see, e.g., Noddings, 2007; Silverman, 2012; Elliott & Silverman, 2015) and reframing "assessment-ing" toward the goal of achieving more holistic and *transformative* "educations" for both students and teachers, as we discuss in more detail later in this chapter.

In stark contrast, some "assessment experts," corporations, and institutions that design and apply assessment tools commonly assert or protest that they, too, are committed to serving education. An arguable point. Indeed, as the eminent educational historian Diane Ravitch (2010) says, it seems that "assessment strategies" and evaluative measures rule supreme because (for one thing) many educators are convinced that the importance and classification of "subjects" are boosted when they are "objectively assessed." In the same vein, it seems that neoliberal school systems—which often view students, teachers, administrators, and school boards as commodities and "currencies"— often assign power, rank, identities, and school funding according to various measurements that range from socially unjust to radically unjust practices.

The tensions that accompany the long-standing dualisms mentioned above have intensified dramatically in recent years due to the increased use of summative assessment by politicians, policymakers, and school administrators. In jurisdictions where testing has become an obsession (e.g., many parts of the United States), teachers and students spend most of their time preparing for "objective" tests that have little or nothing to do with significant learning, "deep understanding," or learning to learn. As Joel Spring (2017) points out, "for students, high-stakes tests might determine promotion between grades or graduation from high school" (p. 186). Needless to say, however, the emotional consequences of high-pressure testing range from anxiety, to fear, to trauma for students and teachers alike. Nelson, Palonsky, and Carlson (2004) note: "No teacher wants his or her students to perform poorly on standardized achievement tests, and no school administrator wants his or her school to rank below others in the state or district" (p. 361).

Indeed, the negative side effects of "objectively" assessing students can impact different educators in different ways, including artistically, ethically, practically, and emotionally. Nelson, Palonsky, and Carlson (2004) assert: "Testing alone cannot convey to students, parents, college admissions officers, or anyone else adequate information about individual achievement and ability" (p. 362). For example, some educators enjoy the privilege of working in schools where principals view formative and summative assessments as two complementary aspects of a much larger enterprise: the holistic, *educational* enterprise of the school. The emphasis in these schools is on individual student progress, safety, support, collaboration, human flourishing, intrinsic motivation, and self-efficacy. Thus, these transformative administrators view and support educators as trustworthy professionals who continuously work to improve their understanding of assessment and therefore evaluate their students' work ethically, with care, and in a fully educational manner.

Problematic situations occur when administrators decide (for a variety of political and personal reasons) to enforce strict forms of summative assessment on all subjects in a school. In these cases, teaching begins to resemble the worst kind of "education"—that is, training—in which tiny bits of verbal knowledge and simplistic skills are "examined" out of their normal and natural contexts of use and enjoyment.

When a "mis-educative" teacher, administrator, or school overemphasizes summative assessment at the expense of educational matters and feed-forward formative assessment, then music "learning" is reduced to training students' technical, notational, and aural skills or stuffing learners' heads with abstract concepts about music. In such cases, music education becomes purely subject centered, rather than a continuous and harmonious process of integrating learner and subject experiences, which is what *eudaimonic teaching, learning, and assessment* includes, and much, much more besides (Elliott & Silverman, 2015). Training, says Peter Abbs (1994), "invariably involves a narrowing down of consciousness to master certain techniques or skills. These...are known in advance and can be unambiguously imparted by the trainer and assimilated by the learner. What is transmitted is functional and predetermined, a set of skills matching a set of operations" (p. 15).

Abbs states that training transmits skills related tightly to perpetuating the status quo: "It seeks to shape behaviors to pre-specified ends. Education, on the other hand, involves 'an opening out of the mind that transcends detail and skill and whose movement cannot be predicted'" (p. 15). What education should do is take "the student beyond the status quo into what is not fully known, fully comprehended, fully formalized. Education is the expression and development of a primary impulse for truth, a deep epistemic instinct that we inherit as part of our biological nature" (p. 16).

Spring (2006) agrees. Citing an example given by the National Council of Teachers of Mathematics, a past president remarked: "It isn't a question now of what is best for the children, but who's going to win." Spring concludes: "The struggle can best be described as being between those advocating teaching math through conceptual understanding, mental computation and estimation, and cooperative work and those favoring traditional methods of memorization, paper-and-pencil computations, and drill and practice" (p. 205).

As Nelson, Palonsky, and Carlson (2004) put it, "every teacher knows that testing drives the curriculum: What is tested is taught" (p. 361). Some even argue that the *very last* thing educational "reformers"—that is, neoliberal, marketplace "educators"—really want is thoughtful students with the abilities and dispositions to think critically and creatively. Indeed, if we examine the way high-stakes testing has changed schools into input-output "measurement factories," then it's plain to see that such accountability measurements are about business-type accounting, conformity, and obedience.

In the minds of marketplace, neoliberal policymakers and "educators" and conservative politicians, summative assessment is the key to winning control of the American curriculum and in the process securing the long- and short-term values and interests of American business (Colwell, 2004, p. 18). In short, conservative business and political leaders want top-down control of schools so they can control and *manage* the future of the marketplace and protect "traditional" values. In contrast, truly *educational* educators want control of the curriculum for the purpose of providing all children with a *balanced* curriculum for their complete development, which includes students' academic, social, cultural, physical, artistic, and emotional selves.

Summarizing to this point, it seems fair to say that while most teachers see assessment as a means of supporting their students' growth and development, many administrators, school boards, and test designers do not. As Nelson, Palonsky, and Carlson (2004) state: "Everyone in education knows that, too often, newspapers report results of statewide testing in much the same way they report basketball standings. 'We're Number One' or 'County Schools Lowest in State' are not uncommon headlines in many local newspapers. To avoid such invidious comparisons, schools gear instruction to the test" (p. 361).

Accountability, high-stakes testing, measurement, rubrics, validity, reliability, and so on are both the foundations and symptoms of today's default philosophy of "education as assessment-ism," as opposed to (say) praxialism, pragmatism, and many other critically reasoned philosophies of education and music education. Given the primacy of today's "assessment-ism" and its corollaries, which often put measurable data and behaviors first and educational aims in "last place," the tail is now wagging, tripping, and strangling the dog. The goals and technologies of assessment-ism have taken over our professional discussions, and they dominate our ways of thinking about curriculum development, teacher education, and instructional strategies, not to mention our fundamental educational ideals. Thus, the priorities, creativity, and independence of our best teachers and researchers have been largely curtailed.

Furthermore, as Colin Wringe (2015) notes, while it seems justifiable that teachers plan lessons with a set of objectives in mind, plan out classroom activities to achieve those objectives, and build assessment activities for the sake of understanding whether or not students are progressing as critically reflective thinkers and doers, "what is important is not that these things should be done," but that teachers, in conversation with and knowing their students' various needs, "identify *appropriate* objectives, choose *stimulating* materials, *motivating* activities and *searching* assessment tasks" (pp. 28–29; emphasis in original). Wringe also notes that the ability to engage in such educational practices is not accomplished through "compliance," but is rather *a habit of mind* "based on qualitative judgments" (pp. 28–29; emphasis in original). This kind of "educatorship" (Elliott, 1995; Elliott & Silverman, 2015) is best developed over time, not conditioned by following fearful governmental mandates or caving in to default "philosophies" of assessment-ism.

# ALTERNATIVES

How might we link assessment to education in responsible, ethical, and reasonable ways? First, we must get back to basics; we must put critical thinking about the nature and value of "capital E educations" back at the center of our concerns. As we said previously about the relationships among assessment, a praxial music education, and *eudaimonia*, Aristotle, John Stuart Mill, John Dewey, Nel Noddings, Jane Roland Martin, and many others have argued persuasively that the purpose of education is to nurture personal growth by igniting students' critical and creative thinking in classrooms and community situations that emphasize mutual care, connectedness, empathy, full human flourishing, and democratic interactions. Education is—or should be—about learning how to solve human and educational problems in environments that value mutual discussion, expression, intrinsic motivation, intersubjectivity, respect, and self-efficacy. Yes, skills and facts have a central place in these processes. However, these aspects of education should be thoughtfully conceived and ethically applied for the purposes of students' personal, intellectual, musical, and care-full growth.

As Noddings (2007) points out, "standardized tests almost never serve this function" (p. 69). Besides, standardized tests require a clinical environment in which teachers are forced to pepper students with short bursts of test questions and narrow tasks within a controlled number of minutes or hours. The results of such "assessments" tell us nothing important about what students really understand or how they can apply their understandings critically and creatively. In other words, it is one thing to "school" students; it is quite another thing to deepen their growth as knowing and compassionate human beings.

In contrast to testing and "assessment-ist schooling," a truly *educational* classroom is a social situation in which there is time for the acquisition of skills, knowledge, understandings, habits of mind and heart, and emotional sensibilities through transformative teacher-student interactions and peer work. Music classrooms are a paradigmatic example: "Collaboration on a standardized test is called 'cheating'; in the classroom it is valued and praised" (Fulcher & Davidson, 2007, p. 414). Working toward shared goals through mutual efforts is vital; joint products lead to learning from and with others, as well as the development of students' awareness of ethical and intersubjective responsibilities. In these situations, teachers and students participate in assessment, with the result that assessments are not only formative but also *transformative*: "Transformative learning involves participation in constructive discourse" (Mezirow, 2000). That is, when students engage in dialogue and exchange, they come to understand and act on their own clarified purposes, feelings, and values. To us, "transformative assessment" should be at the heart of teaching and learning musical creativity.

Noddings (2007) reminds us that some people are good test takers, "but many bright creative people are not good test-takers and children develop at different rates" (p. 68). She also points out what teachers already know very well: there is a huge disparity across, say, the United States in terms of teacher education programs, teaching competencies, school facilities, and funding, not to mention fundamental linguistic, social, and racial disparities. These conditions will take decades to remedy. More broadly, many scholars emphasize the central irony of American education today: even though the United States is a democracy, coercive, top-down, cookie-cutter assessments are the battle cry of the majority of politicians and educational policymakers.

In summary, due to a lack of vigilance among teachers, parents, professional organizations, and policymakers, assessment-ism has overtaken what is most important in formal education settings. Sam Hope (2006) makes the point eloquently: "A manic focus on assessment, accountability, and status usually appears when vision is lacking or faltering in terms of content, intellect, individual mind, and spirit. When our vision turns to power and control of the achievement of empty things, [then] assessment, accountability, and status become masters and not servants. If vision is centered on the humanistic and spiritual... evaluation and assessment are servants and assistants in achieving the vision."

## PREMISES, AIMS, AND ASSUMPTIONS

Why *philosophical* and *qualitative* perspectives on assessment in or for music education? While there are numerous quantitative research projects that investigate assessment in or for music education, which are certainly important, they typically do not help us understand the fundamental conceptual nature of and assumptions about assessment and evaluation across global contexts, as this volume does—which in turn shape and drive why and how students, and their actual and potential creativities, are harmfully or ethically impacted. In addition, quantitative research projects that examine assessment and evaluation tend to begin with a priori assumptions that assessment and evaluation are inherently valuable for music teaching and learning. Thus, it was important for us to "step back" from these assumptions and ask the authors in this volume to question the potentials and pitfalls of music education assessment practices and procedures, to expose the "rights and wrongs" of existing sites of assessment.

Three basic premises guided our selection of contributors to this project, three fundamental convictions about the nature of music and music education that we were confident our participants' contributions would help illuminate.

The first of these is that *musics are made by and for people*, and musical values are not universal but style, community, and context dependent. All forms of music and music making—regardless of media or the particular "messages" or meanings they embody or convey—are social endeavors and encounters. Musics are made by and for people living in real worlds involving conflicts large and small. As such, they are also and invariably embodiments of people's political and ideological beliefs, understandings, and values, personal and collective. Musical endeavors are rich human actions replete with human significance and, by extension, ethical responsibilities. Because of this, all forms of music education assessment practices must consider the "human" dimensions of music teaching and learning.

These social considerations are not incidental, subsidiary, or artistically extrinsic; on the contrary, they are fundamental to the meanings, values, and broadly human significance of musical endeavors, and they should be at the forefront of people's thinking about the roles of assessment in or for music education. Music making, sharing, taking, and experiencing are richly personal, corporeal, cognitive, emotional, gendered, perceptual, social, and more. Central to the meanings and import of all kinds of music are the ways these dimensions relate to the individual circumstances, dispositions, and needs of persons living with and for other persons. While every individual is unique, everyone is also a member of a vast, multidimensional, ecological human network. Thus, assessment in music education *must never be reduced*—as it is so often today—to *simplistic* notions and practices of formative and summative assessments, not to mention *simplistic* tests of musical skills and verbal knowledge about music history. When such thinking and doing occur, then teachers are engaging in—or are being forced to engage in—educational malpractice.

Our intrapersonal and interpersonal experiences of music—our individual and shared feeling and thinking; our teaching and learning; everything we conceptualize, do, or desire—stem from our status as beings who possess, undergo, enact, and "perform" our individual and collective personhoods (Elliott & Silverman, 2015). Musical actions and interactions are fundamental to the creation of our individual and collective human identities. Musical "assessing" gone wrong can destroy all the values or "goods" that music and music education have to offer. Unfortunately, many scholars and music teachers are a long way from creating forms of assessment that can even begin to assess students' growth toward attaining many of the most important musical values.

Our second premise can be traced to the work of John Dewey and to the many scholars and arts practitioners who, as he did, stress the need to integrate art making and art engaging (whether by amateurs, professionals, or teachers) with personal and community life. The arts, urged Dewey, should not be placed on an "aesthetic pedestal," consigned to consumption or contemplative gratification by connoisseurs in concert halls, art galleries, theaters, or museums. It is a profound mistake to regard art as merely composed of entities whose significance is unconnected to everyday experience or ordinary life (Elliott, Silverman, & Bowman, 2016).

In *Art as Experience* (1934), Dewey states his opposition to canonizing artists' creations as untouchable objects that exist to be worshipped—mysterious "things" with otherworldly or godlike status, "masterworks" of high art. Against this Romantic, late eighteenth- and early nineteenth-century view, Dewey believed that art emerges from and is continuous with everyday human experience. When art and art making are separated from or elevated above everyday life—as self-sufficient entities, valued solely for their beauty—they are stripped of their power to make meaningful social differences. "When an art product once attains classic status," Dewey asserts, "it somehow becomes isolated from the human condition under which it was brought into being and from the human consequences it engenders in actual life-experience" (1934, p. 1).

Social and practice-based perspectives like Dewey's show us that the arts in general, and music specifically, do not consist exclusively or even primarily of "works," nor do they necessarily take the form of "fine art." Music and its values are numerous, diverse, dynamic, and invariably grounded in social experience. Music's values are not intrinsic or self-contained, but are functions of its service to various human needs and interests. In other words, such values emerge from the effectiveness with which music is "put to work" for the realization of a variety of overlapping and interwoven human "goods." So the notion that music exists for its intrinsic value—for musical elements and form alone, which are too often the focus of testing music students—is not just misguided, but seriously misleading (Bowman, 2013). The values of musics, like all values, are a function of what they are good *for*, the uses to which musics are put. These concepts and principles should be kept in mind in thinking philosophically and qualitatively about music education assessment and evaluation. Can scholars and music educators develop curricula and authentic forms of assessment that enable students to integrate art making and art engaging with personal and community life? Better understandings of concepts and practices of "artistic citizenship" (Elliott, 2012; Elliott, Silverman, & Bowman, 2016) may lead to answers.

Of course, not all contributors to the OHAME agree with every detail of our philosophical perspectives, which is why we invited them to contribute to this volume.

# FUNDAMENTAL QUESTIONS

As we noted previously, in framing this project we invited contributors across various domains in music teaching and learning to share their research; practical projects and strategies; experiences; and insights as researchers, music educators, and music makers across the world. We deliberately left open the meaning of *assessment* in order to allow a range of interpretations and perspectives to emerge. The result is, we hope, an engaging collection of essays, richly suggestive in their range and scope.

More specifically, contributors to the OHAME asked and answered questions such as the following:

- What are the natures, scope, aims, and purposes of music education assessment, feedback, and evaluation?
- What kinds of understandings and abilities do school and community music teachers or facilitators need to develop and implement appropriate and innovative assessment and feedback strategies?
- What does *evaluation* mean? Why and how do we differentiate among assessment, feedback, and evaluation in the domains of school and community music and in formal, informal, and nonformal music teaching and learning?
- What historical factors contribute to understanding relationships between assessment and feedback and the "why, what, how, who, where, and when" of music

teaching and learning in different contexts worldwide? How can answers to these questions activate and guide the evolution of music teaching and learning assessment and feedback procedures?

- What relationships exist between assessment and feedback and worldwide music curricular demands, choices, and policies?
- How can educators implement music assessments without compromising the natures and values of specific musics, educative teaching, and artistic practices?
- What actual and potential roles do musical and educational technologies have in or for assessment and feedback in music education and community music contexts?
- How do governmental policies affect assessment and feedback processes in music teaching and learning settings?
- How should we evaluate assessment and feedback in music teaching and learning?

The contributors to this volume offer diverse, sometimes divergent, but invariably fascinating perspectives on these issues. Such richness and diversity are exactly what we hoped would emerge from this project.

Ultimately, the questions, discussions, and actions that are explained, implied, and activated by the authors in the OHAME will be the measure of this book's significance. We leave it to readers, then, to carry these conversations forward—to *critically* assess the themes and ideas offered by the chapters in this volume. Although we cannot know precisely the form such ideas may eventually assume, it is our hope that they will involve continuous critical dialogues among music educators and community musicians who engage with conceptual, practical, and ethical matters of assessment.

# OVERVIEW OF THE BOOK

We conclude this introductory chapter with a brief survey of the contributions comprising this volume.

In the first section of the OHAME, "Foundational Considerations," Lise C. Vaugeois investigates what might seem to be disparate themes: evaluation as a form of ranking, ongoing colonial processes that maintain internal hierarchies of who counts as human, and structures of formal schooling that produce obedient subjects. As Vaugeois shows, many young people, systemically labeled as "at risk," not only reject this label; they also reject the role that schooling plays in preparing them to become part of dominant social, political, and economic structures.

Kathryn Jourdan and John Finney begin their chapter with the foundational assertions that music making is an ethical encounter (Bowman, 2001) and an exercise in hospitality (Higgins, 2006). From these starting points, the authors examine what an ethical practice in music education might look like through the philosophical writings of

Emmanuel Levinas. They examine thinking tools drawn from Levinas's *Totality and Infinity* (1969), which includes concepts of "practices of facing" and of "putting a world in common." Jourdan and Finney's conceptual lens enables them to investigate Levinas's radical openness—the breaking of "infinity" into "totalizing" practices—and consider what this might mean for assessment in music education.

Andrea Schiavio explores a possible alternative to traditional evaluative measures in music classes. He argues that an approach based on phenomenological philosophy, which is inspired by recent developments in cognitive science, may shed new light on learning and help educators reconsider grading systems. Schiavio reframes cognitive *phenomena*—learning described as a measurable event based on "information process-ing"—in terms of *cognitive ecosystems*: learning understood as a negotiating and trans-formative activity codetermined by diverse embodied and ecological factors connected in recurrent fashion. Accommodating this shift, according to Schiavio, helps to trans-form assessment practices into more open and flexible systems that appreciate coopera-tive learning and phenomenological reflections.

In drawing on critical pedagogy (as described by Paolo Freire, Henry Giroux, and bell hooks), Brent C. Talbot and Hakim Mohandas Amani Williams investigate the impor-tance of interrogating injustices via Critical Pedagogy in order to teach students to transform their local and global social conditions. According to the authors, learning to perceive the social, political, and economic contradictions in our worlds often leads to multiple forms of resistance in and out of our music classrooms. In terms of music education, this leads to a questioning of the kinds of assessment strategies that can therefore inspire social consciousness and transformation.

Lauri Väkevä proposes that C. S. Peirce's and John Dewey's views on perception and experience hold important consequences for qualitative assessment in music education. According to Väkevä, Peirce understood engagement in the world as having interpreta-tive potentials, and that these potentials possess meanings that are contingent upon dimensions of our personhood. Relatedly, Dewey transformed phenomenological experiences into habits of action that can be interpreted as meaningful in certain con-texts. In combination, according to Väkevä, Peirce's and Dewey's views suggest that developing contextual aesthetic judgment could be an important strategy for qualitative assessment in music education. In addition, Väkevä argues that qualitative assessment concerns both ethical and aesthetic matters. Putting his ideas into a specific context, Väkevä investigates the new Finnish National Core Curriculum for Basic Education and suggests ways to approach qualitative assessment that are conducive to achieving its cognitive, aesthetic, ethical, and political goals.

Finally in this first section, Lauren Kapalka Richerme examines four measurement-related themes from Gilles Deleuze's writings and explores how these themes might inform concepts and practices of assessment in various music teaching and learning contexts. The first theme suggests that each group of connective relations, what Deleuze terms a "plane of immanence," demands its own forms of measurement. Second, Deleuze emphasizes varieties of measurement. Third, those with power, whom Deleuze terms the "majority," always set the standard for measurement. Fourth, Deleuze derides continuous assessment. According to Richerme, Deleuze's writings suggest that assessments in music education, which are created for one musical practice or style, should not transcend their own "plane of immanence"; a variety of nonstandardized assessments is desirable; the effects of measurement on "minoritarian" musical practices must be examined carefully; and it is essential to ponder the potentials of unmeasured music making.

In the second section of the OHAME, "Methodological Practices," Karen Salvador and Janice Krum argue that standardized, high-stakes teacher evaluation reduces music teacher effectiveness, particularly with regard to inclusion and cultural responsiveness. They provide a brief review of the literature regarding music teacher evaluation, marginalized populations in school music education, and equitable and inclusive practices in the music classroom. Following this, Salvador and Krum use fictionalized vignettes to illustrate their analyses of the cognitive dissonances and perverse incentives inherent in music teacher evaluation and how they manifest themselves across three categories: (1) contributing to the gap between theory and practice; (2) misusing measurement tools; and (3) forcing teachers to remain in the status quo, unable to stray from formulaic "markers of effectiveness" to take the risks necessary for the creative, innovative work of inclusion and cultural responsiveness. The chapter concludes with specific suggestions for music teachers who wish to resist these effects of teacher evaluation.

Susan Hallam considers whether summative assessment systems in music determine not only what is taught but also what learners learn. Hallam proposes that the most appropriate way of enhancing learning is to ensure that summative assessment procedures are authentic and possess real-world relevance that supports the teaching and learning process to ensure that learners are motivated and see the relevance of what they are learning. This might take many forms, says Hallam, depending on musical genre, communities of practice, and the wider cultural environment.

John Kratus engages with sociologist George Ritzer's concept of "McDonaldization." According to Kratus, Ritzer's thoughts about McDonaldization have been applied to such disparate fields as education, religion, social work, and journalism. Kratus's chapter shows how the dehumanizing principles of McDonaldization—which include efficiency, calculability, predictability, and control—have influenced music education practices. His chapter concludes with a means for opposing the McDonaldization of music education.

Jillian Hogan and Ellen Winner note that music making requires "habits of mind," or dispositions potentially useful outside of the music room. They report a preliminary analysis of the habits of mind that they systematically observed and thematically coded in twenty-four rehearsals of six public high school music ensembles: band, choir, and orchestra. They discuss how authentic assessments of habits of mind in the music classroom may require novel methods, including the development of classroom environments that foster additional levels of student agency.

Donald DeVito, Megan M. Sheridan, Jian-Jun Chen-Edmund, David Edmund, and Steven Bingham present multiple case studies of assessment in music teaching and learning that have taken place at the K–12 Sidney Lanier Center School for students with varying exceptionalities in Gainesville, Florida. The authors ask: How do we move beyond assessment for the purposes of evaluating teacher proficiency and student performance outcomes and, instead, consider assessment for understanding student musical experiences and preferences for the purpose of promoting lifelong musical engagement?

John Carpente and Kenneth Aigen critique existing music therapy assessment tools. They point out that the field of music therapy has a tendency to consider only nonmusical areas of functioning and overly narrow examinations of functional areas in isolation. According to the authors, an alternative, music-centered perspective may be fruitful in remedying the deficiencies of the predominance of existing music therapy assessment tools. They describe one assessment tool—the Individual Music-Centered Assessment Profile for Neurodevelopmental Disorders (IMCAP-ND)—to illustrate a music therapy assessment that looks at functional areas within music and within the context of a coactive music therapy relationship.

Finally in this section, Frank Abrahams discusses integrative assessment strategies for music education framed by the writing of Paulo Freire. Freire suggests that teaching and learning are a partnership—teacher and student together—and that learning takes place only when both are transformed. According to Abrahams, the most important aim of music education is to promote musical agency among students and teachers. Such agency and transformative potentials foster the acquisition of what Freire labeled a critical consciousness. Only if and when assessments in music education help teachers and students transform their worlds can they be deemed valuable contributions to music teaching and learning.

In the third section of the OHAME, "Creativity," Juniper Hill suggests that assessing creative work is exceptionally challenging, especially in culturally diverse learning environments in which students and educators may not hold the same musical values. For example, says Hill, an instructor aiming to teach proficiency within a specific style may unintentionally give feedback that devalues a student's personal creative expressions, which in many cases reflect diverse musical heritages. Such devaluing feedback can inhibit individual creative development, stifle innovation, and perpetuate sociocultural power imbalances. In her chapter, Hill provides examples from jazz, classical, and traditional musicians in Cape Town and Helsinki to illustrate how and why idiomatic boundaries are enforced, how musical value judgments can perpetuate social inequalities, and how negative feedback can inhibit individual creative development. Hill emphasizes the personal, social, and cultural importance of embracing musical diversity and the value of permitting and supporting developing musicians to go beyond idiomatic conventions in their creative work. Strategies are discussed for how music educators might better support individual creative development and social justice.

Adam Patrick Bell examines how music technology in, for, and as music education should be assessed in teaching and learning contexts. Commencing with an explanation of the concept of the "personal best" in the context of running, Bell suggests that an approach to assessment that incorporates self-assessment and peer assessment ought to be used in music education settings. Bell proffers that peer feedback and self-feedback are synergistic strands of a "feedback loop" that learners must enter in order to experience an authentic and complex learning environment, and that summative assessment can and should be a natural outgrowth of formative assessment. Ultimately, the aim of this approach is to construct a context in which learners at all levels and of all abilities can engage in meaningful experiences with music technology while providing a framework to evaluate the quality of the learning that has taken place from multiple perspectives.

Dylan van der Schyff explores the challenging question of curriculum and assessment for music improvisation pedagogy. He begins by offering a critical review of standard approaches to improvisation pedagogy and argues that such approaches often neglect the processes of discovery and collaboration, which "free" approaches afford. He then discusses the challenges that free improvisation presents to traditional modes of practice and assessment in music education. Next he considers reasons improvisation cannot be taught and assessed according to standardized models, and argues that it is not something that can be inculcated in students, but rather is a fundamental disposition that should be nurtured. This perspective is then examined in relationship to very recent developments in "enactive cognitive science," in which "living cognition" is explored as a "4E" phenomenon: as fundamentally embodied, embedded, enactive, and extended. Van der Schyff suggests that cognition may be understood as an improvisational process, even at the most fundamental levels.

Bryan Powell and Gareth Dylan Smith discuss the commoditized relationships among music education, higher education, and popular music. From these perspectives, they investigate contexts for a set of subcultural practices and look through lenses of authenticity before exploring a canon and specific repertoire in popular music education. Powell and Smith highlight examples of assessment practices in particular popular music education contexts and the ideologies and philosophies that consciously or unconsciously undergird these. Following this, they present a model of assessment derived from working with undergraduate students across disciplines, which they see as one possible broad, inclusive approach to establishing a philosophy of assessment for popular music education.

To complete this third section of the OHAME, Roger Mantie and Beatriz Ilari provide a view of music assessment predicated on the belief that "the *what*" of assessment in P–12 music education should include understandings and attitudes about music and culture not typically ascertainable through traditional music assessment practices. Through the use of six vignettes, the authors examine ways that children's drawings, as a projective technique of visual representation, might be used to expose and discern, or assess, children's thinking, understandings, and attitudes about music and culture. They argue that the multimodality of drawing and talking in response to musical prompts offers rich potential for informing instruction that better accounts for the lifeworlds of children.

In the final section of this volume, "International Perspectives," Martin Fautley discusses how national curriculum content and assessment in England have been subverted by performativity and accountability requirements. These requirements have had the effect of moving music teaching and learning in secondary school music classes away from a focus on musical content and music making and toward meeting the demands and requirements of an accountability system. According to Fautley, this puts schools in the position of having to second-guess what they think the English inspection regime (Ofsted) will want to see in relation to its pseudo-positivist attainment data, which devalues the musicality of the assessments undertaken by classroom teachers. As Fautley notes, England operates its public school music education with a focus on what might be termed "generalist" classroom teaching and learning for all students. This has an impact on the ways in which assessment can be undertaken.

Danielle Shannon Treacy, Vilma Timonen, Alexis Anja Kallio, and Iman Shah suggest that because music classrooms may be conceptualized as meeting places for difference, music education policy and practice are required to contend with various, and at times conflicting, musical and cultural values and understandings. In Nepal, say the authors, this situation has intensified due to a music education curriculum adopted by the Ministry of Education in 2010 that guides music teaching and learning for 75 national districts and more than 125 caste/ethnic groups within a rapidly globalizing society. Assessment plays a key role in framing the knowledge and pedagogical approaches deemed desirable in Nepali music education, and it serves as a way of appraising certain values over others, which is especially important if the profession intends to uphold democratic ideals; ethically engage with difference; and imagine *ends not yet in view*, which may encourage reflection upon the inclusive and exclusive processes of assessment that frame *whose* ends in view count, and in what ways.

Janelize van der Merwe explores the concept of assessment in music education through the lens of care ethics by (1) providing an overview of "care" as practice, disposition, and relation; (2) discussing personhood through the lens of care ethics; (3) examining "assessment as care" and understandings of "relationship" as developed by Carol Gilligan and Nel Noddings and examining concepts of care ethics and "self-fulness" as developed by Marissa Silverman; and (4) exploring and applying these concepts in the context of the South African Grade 10 to 12 IEB (Independent Education Board).

Sidsel Karlsen and Geir Johansen explain that the Norwegian compulsory school formal curriculum implemented in 1993 and 2006 consists of two separate parts. The older core curriculum provides guidelines for the broad aims of education and for their cultural and moral foundations. The latter are anchored in the humanist *Bildung* tradition, which emphasizes the holistic development of the human being. The newer curriculum part, named Knowledge Promotion, consists of individual syllabi for all subjects, including music. The first page of the music syllabus mirrors values expressed in the core curriculum; the later part is an operationalization of a positivist-oriented ends-means approach to music education. The authors explore this multi-ideological split and pursue two major questions: What are the consequences of ends-means related assessment criteria that shape the context of music teaching and learning? What other assessment criteria exist that would align better with the *Bildung* and progressive education foundations of the curriculum?

Andrew Reid and Julie Ballantyne note that assessment should be synonymous with effective learning, reflect the intricacies of each subject area, and align with equitable opportunities for all students to achieve. These challenges are made difficult in circumstances in which educational and musical contexts are highly heterogeneous, such as in Queensland, Australia, but the official assessment system often demands standardization. Reid and Ballantyne discuss the design and implementation of large-scale curricula as experienced in secondary schools in Queensland. Among several other issues, they also discuss the provision of supportive networks and mechanisms to foster autonomy for a diverse range of music educators and contexts.

Johan Söderman explains that while the Swedish concept of *bildning* (*Bildung* in German) cannot be directly translated into English, its meaning lies somewhat close to *education*. *Bildning*, according to Söderman, has a wider meaning and originates with philosopher Immanuel Kant's enlightenment ideals of human emancipation. In the Swedish context, the concept of *bildning* historically connects to the democratization process of Swedish society and the struggle for social justice over the last 150 years. During this struggle, says Söderman, advocates of holistic *bildning* ideals have recurrently directed strong criticism at the formal school system and its "cramming culture" (or "teaching for the test") and elitist ideals. In contrast, learning through a *bildning* perspective should be characterized by the enjoyable, motivationally, and voluntary aspects of learning, as epitomized in music. Music and *bildning* can thus be regarded as intertwined. This chapter highlights how standardized assessment procedures contradict the holistic ideals of *bildning*.

Nasim Niknafs examines music education assessment issues inherent in the Iranian context. Not having official state-sanctioned public music education, Iranian youth, specifically rock and alternative musicians, follow a self-organized and anarchistic path of music making. Expertly navigating pathways between acts of music making and the unpredictable situations of daily life, they become adept and creative in finding new ways to propagate their music and develop the rules and tools of their profession. Meanings attached to assessment in these circumstances are continuously redefined and overshadow the quality of the music being created. Therefore, assessment becomes a local form of activism that countervails the top-down, summative model. Assessment in urban Iranian music education can be categorized as (1) do-it-yourself (DIY) and do-it-with-others (DIWO), (2) interactive and decentralized, (3) local anarchism, and (4) lifestyle. Niknafs concludes that assessment in music education should aim for a proactive and embodied approach.

Finally, Alexandra Kertz-Welzel notes that while some problems related to assessment are internationally similar, concepts of and approaches to assessing music making and listening vary dramatically in different regions and nations of the world depending on the circumstances/characteristics of a specific assessment culture, the aims of education, teachers' and administrators' concepts of the nature and values of musics and music education, teachers' individual teaching philosophies, and various "schooling cultures" in respective countries. By utilizing approaches from comparative music education, philosophy, and sociology of music education, this chapter scrutinizes global similarities and differences and proposes new approaches to assessment.

## References

Abbs, P. (1994). *The educational imperative: A defense of Socratic and aesthetic learning*. London: Falmer Press.

Apple, M. (2001). *Educating the right way: Market, standards, god, and inequality*. New York: RoutledgeFalmer.

Bowman, W. (2001). Music as ethical encounter: The Charles Leonhard Lecture, School of Music, University of Illinois, Urbana-Champaign. *Bulletin of the Council for Research in Music Education, 151*, 11–20.

Bowman, W. (2013). The ethical significance of music-making. *Music Mark: The UK Association for Music Education, 3*(Winter), 3–6.

Carr, D. (2003). *Making sense of education: An introduction to the philosophy and theory of education and teaching*. New York: RoutledgeFalmer.

Chappell, T. (2011). On the very idea of criteria for personhood. *Southern Journal of Philosophy, 49*(1), 1–27.

Colwell, R. (2004). A peak at an international perspective on assessment. In P. Shand (Ed.), *Music education entering the 21st century* (pp. 59–70). Nedlands, Western Australia: International Society for Music Education.

Costa-Giomi, E. (2012). Music education and intellectual development in children: Historical, research, and educational perspectives. Conference Proceeding, Anais Do II Simpom 2012—SIMPÓSIO BRASILEIRO DE PÓS-GRADUANDOS Em MÚSICA, 21. Retrieved from http://www.seer.unirio.br/index.php/simpom/article/viewFile/2601/1929

Dewey, J. (1934). *Art as experience*. New York: G. P. Putnam's Sons.

Elliott, D. J. (1995). *Music matters: A new philosophy of music education*. New York: Oxford University Press.

Elliott, D. J. (2010). Assessing the concept of assessment: Some philosophical reflections. In T. Brophy (Ed.), *The practice of assessment in music education* (pp. 367–80). Chicago: GIA Publications.

Elliott, D. J. (2012). Music education as/for artistic citizenship. *Music Educators Journal, 99*(1), 21–27.

Elliott, D. J., & Silverman, M. (2015). *Music matters: A philosophy of music education*. New York: Oxford University Press.

Elliott, D. J., Silverman, M., & Bowman, W. (Eds.) (2016). *Artistic citizenship: Artistry, social responsibility, and ethical praxis*. New York: Oxford University Press.

Fulcher, G., & Davidson, F. (2007). Tests in life and learning: A deathly dialogue. *Educational Philosophy and Theory, 40*(3), 408–17.

Giroux, H. A. (2012). Can democratic education survive in a neoliberal society? Truthout, October 16. Retrieved from https://truthout.org/articles/can-democratic-education-survive-in-a-neoliberal-society/

Gunzenhauser, M. G. (2003). High-stakes testing and the default philosophy of education. *Theory into Practice, 42*(1), 51–59.

Higgins, L. (2006). *Boundary-walkers: Contexts and concepts of community music* (Doctoral dissertation). University of Limerick, Limerick, Ireland.

Hope, S. (2006). *Oral report to the executive director: 2*. Presented at the meeting of the National Association of Schools of Music, Chicago, Illinois.

Mezirow, J. (2000). *Learning as transformation: Critical perspectives on a theory in progress*. San Francisco, CA: Jossey-Bass.

Mirowski, P. (2013). The thirteen commandments of neoliberalism. Utopian. Retrieved from
    http://www.the-utopian.org/post/53360513384/the-thirteen-commandments
Nelson, J. L., Palonsky, S. B., & Carlson, K. (2004). *Critical issues in education: Dialogues and
    dialectics* (5th ed.). Boston: McGraw-Hill.
Noddings, N. (2007). *When school reform goes wrong.* New York: Teachers College Press.
Ravitch, D. (2010). *The death and life of the great American school system: How testing and
    choice are undermining education.* New York: Basic Books.
Regelski, T. (2005). Music and music education: Theory and praxis for "Making a Difference."
    *Educational Philosophy and Theory, 37*(1), 7–27.
Regelski, T. (2012). Ethical dimensions of school-based music, In W. Bowman & A. L. Frega
    (Eds.), *Oxford handbook of philosophy in music education* (pp. 284–304). New York: Oxford
    University Press.
Regelski, T. (2016). *A brief introduction to a philosophy of music and music education as social
    praxis.* New York: Routledge.
Reimer, B. (1970/1989). *A philosophy of music education.* Upper Saddle River, NJ: Prentice Hall.
Reimer, B. (2003). *A philosophy of music education: Advancing the vision* (3rd ed.). Upper
    Saddle River, NJ: Prentice Hall.
Schellenberg, G. E. (2006). Long-term positive associations between music lessons and IQ.
    *Journal of Educational Psychology, 98*(2), 457–68.
Schellenberg, G. E. (2015). Music and non-musical abilities. In G. McPherson (Ed.),
    *Child as musician: A handbook of musical development* (pp. 149–76). New York: Oxford
    University Press.
Shah, A. (2010). A primer on neoliberalism. Global Issues, August 22. Retrieved from http://
    www.globalissues.org/article/39/a-primer-on-neoliberalism#Neoliberalismis
Silverman, M. (2012). Virtue ethics, care ethics, and "The Good Life of Teaching." *Action,
    Criticism, and Theory for Music Education, 11*(2), 96–122.
Spring, J. (2006). *American education* (12th ed.). Boston: McGraw Hill.
Spring, J. (2017). *American education* (18th ed.). New York: Routledge.
Wringe, C. (2015). Learning to teach and becoming a teacher: *Techne* and *phronesis.*
    In R. Heilbronn & L. Foreman-Peck (Eds.), *Philosophical perspectives on teacher education*
    (pp. 23–37). West Sussex, UK: John Wiley & Sons, Ltd.
Wu, D. (2013). Entrepreneurship in research: Ellen Winner on why we need the arts.
    *Entrepreneurship Review* (March 6), 2. Retrieved from http://miter.mit.edu/ellen-winner-
    on-why-we-need-the-arts/

# CHAPTER 2

# INSTITUTIONAL MUSIC EDUCATION AND RANKING AS A FORM OF SUBJECTIFICATION

*the merits of resistance and resilience*

## LISE C. VAUGEOIS

In this chapter I take up what might appear to be disparate themes: evaluation as a form of ranking; ongoing colonial processes that in order to maintain their force are dependent on an internalization of hierarchies of who counts as human; and structures of formal schooling as processes of subjectification that produce docile, obedient subjects. I want to generate "thoughts of the outside"[1] by taking seriously the rejection of evaluation practices and associated priorities of authorized schooling by "abjected" young people pursuing music learning in "abject spaces."[2] These are young people, often characterized as "at risk" within the school system, who through their actions not only reject the label of "at risk" but also reject the idea that they should pursue education in order to become part of dominant social, political, and economic structures, which they have more often than not experienced as hostile and oppressive. By exploring the fault lines made visible by looking from the outside at existing dominant educational frameworks, I hope to draw attention to structural relations of power that are not as easily seen from within dominant locations.

The "thoughts of the outside" began for me with experiences working in, or observing, programs for youth in sites of abjection, that is, in programs for homeless, street-involved, or incarcerated youth. These experiences unsettled my notions of what matters in education and, more specifically, what matters in music education. In these settings I was struck by how taken-for-granted values and disciplining forces enacted in authorized education settings were delegitimized or "made strange."[3] Here students rejected the role of the teacher to plan and then pass judgment on their learning. They expressed their autonomy by pursuing music learning on their own terms, according to their own priorities, demonstrating both resistance and resilience. The question for me then became: What boundaries and what issues might become visible if I considered these expressions of resistance and resilience in abjected sites of learning as central, rather than marginal, and considered these in counterpoint to normalized practices within authorized sites of schooling?

This chapter is organized into seven sections. In this introductory section I explore the place of ranking in authorized settings versus the absence of formal ranking in abject settings; define the inside and outside for the purposes of this chapter; and point to the insufficiently acknowledged, but inevitable, positioning of some people on the outside. I follow this with a theoretical grounding in concepts of power in the construction of the self and then take up the ubiquity of ranking in school settings. From here I introduce the reader to the "outside" (abject) sites of music learning and what appear to be very different goals and priorities. The next two sections explore the historical production of inside/outside subjectifications created through politically strategic uses of ranking—that is, the construction of "worthy" and "unworthy" categories of the human. This is followed by activist/intellectual voices addressing the merits of the "outside"; finally, I offer my concluding thoughts about ranking as a strategy of population management that normalizes categories of who counts as fully human.

# DISCIPLINING PRACTICES AND THE PRODUCTION OF INSIDE VERSUS OUTSIDE SOCIAL LOCATIONS

The teaching and learning of *music*, rather than other subject areas, offers a particularly rich and important area of consideration. In learning to sing or play an instrument, disciplining the body and measuring the success of this discipline through repeated engagements with forms of ranking are woven together with pleasure as complementary processes to achieve levels of mastery. In abject settings, pleasure and learning are also closely woven together; however, pressure to conform to rules of comportment, pace of learning, timetables, repertoire, style, and other externally determined parameters for making music are absent, as is, most notably, the routine of being ranked by external judges. It was this lack of interest in external validation that first struck me as significantly different from my experiences with music teaching and learning in authorized settings—or what I refer to here as "inside" settings. In my role teaching music educators on a faculty of education, for example, I have observed an overwhelming concern with grades. Whereas for students the concern is that grades be as high as possible, often regardless of what has actually been learned, for administrators the concern is that the grade average be no higher than 79 percent so that the faculty cannot be accused of "grade inflation." In comparing the intense engagement with grading in this institutional setting with music learning in "abject" settings where grading is not a consideration, I came to question whether the large amount of mental space taken up with the discipline of ranking might be doing more "work" than simply giving feedback on a student's learning. Specifically, I began to wonder whether the intense concern with evaluation as ranking might constrain imaginative possibilities; leave learners with a lack of resilience when notions of the self are tied to external validation; keep learners (and teachers) focused on obedience to existing systems; and keep us engrossed in individual goal setting, as a result leaving us less able to notice contradictions between claimed conditions of equality and actual material conditions for differently situated populations.

I have set up a dividing line between these sites of learning—inside versus outside—as a means of exploring competing notions of what counts in education and, specifically, in music education; however, I am not suggesting that in practice music teaching and learning falls neatly on either side of this divide, nor am I suggesting that music educators do not routinely pursue multiple creative approaches to teaching music in support of the needs and interests of their students, because many do. Instead, what I am looking to bring forward through this exploration is a genealogy of practices of ranking and how these might impact our understandings of who we are, how we are positioned socially and economically, and how we understand the systems that structure our lives.

The assumption that undergirds this chapter is that hierarchies of who counts as fully human structure people's lives very differently depending on how they are positioned as subjects. For example, the positionality of those who experience their lives as wealthy, as white, and middle class, versus those who experiences themselves as racialized and "dangerous" or colonized and "abject," signify vastly different life possibilities in settler colonial states such as Canada, the United States, South Africa, and Australia. In Thunder Bay, Canada, for example, where I currently live, the racism experienced by young people coming from remote First Nations[4] communities to attend high school is relentless and life threatening. Here, young people leaving their communities for the first time in their lives discover that they are unwelcome "foreigners," subject to verbal and physical attacks from the moment they arrive in the city. This is nothing these students have "asked for"; it is a consequence of colonial dispossession and the racism developed to justify it. Tragically, nine of these students from First Nations communities have died in suspicious circumstances since 2010.[5] Seven were found dead in local rivers; the deaths were classified by police as "indeterminate" with "no evidence of foul play"—this in spite of numerous reports of other young First Nations people narrowly escaping beatings and attempted drownings.[6] For students obliged to come to Thunder Bay for a high school education, it is thus a place of danger in which exposure to physical and psychological oppression is a daily occurrence. The sense of being on the outside of a system intended to destroy their culture, values, and very being, is thus palpable and well founded.

The potential deadliness of anti-black racism is also well documented and quite routine, even in a city, such as Toronto, that advertises itself as a model multicultural city.[7] This is apparent in the high numbers of black people "carded" (the practice of collecting personal information to create a "known to police" database), constant surveillance in black-dominated neighborhoods, the arbitrary stopping and searching of black people by police, and the number of unarmed black people killed during encounters with the police (Anderson, 2016; Cole, 2015; Davis, 1998; Maynard, 2017). The ubiquitous occurrence of such encounters in the United States and Canada has led to the urgent organizing efforts of the Black Lives Matter movement (see https://blacklivesmatter.com/). Indigenous activists continue to organize through the Idle No More movement for these reasons as well as the need to fight for land claims and settler adherence to treaty obligations (see http://www.idlenomore.ca/). Indeed, for people who are on the wrong side of the divide between those who are considered meritorious and those considered disposable, hierarchies of who counts as human are a matter of life and death. My assumption in this chapter is thus that hierarchies of who counts as fully human—which developed during the slave trade, the expansion of empire through projects of colonization, and throughout the growth of capitalism—continue to profoundly shape people's lives and, in this instance, young people's relationships to mainstream schooling.

# THEORETICAL ORIENTATION

To frame my analysis, I draw on the work of Michel Foucault to consider how we come to understand ourselves as certain kinds of "subjects." The modernist concept of the "subject," or "individual," is based on the notion that the autonomous individual has an essential nature that exists outside of historical circumstance. In contrast, Foucault (1980) argues that external conditions and relations of power constitute a significant part of how we come to understand "the truth" about who we are and our place in the world. Based on Foucault's concept of subject formation, I draw attention to ranking as a form of subjectification, meaning a relation of power that shapes how people come to understand who they are in relation to others. I am interested in how ritualized forms of assessment—that is, ranked grading—might function as a means to "educate feeling," building emotional associations with experiences of approval, disapproval, valorization, or rejection in association with projects of music learning. In the case of evaluation as ranking, I suggest that there is a rupture between an *inside*— that is, the roles of assessment within highly regulated and controlled school settings— and an *outside* in programs for street-involved, homeless, and incarcerated youth that reveals relations and rituals of power that are otherwise taken for granted. Power, as articulated by Foucault (1982), "is less a confrontation between two adversaries than a question of government, a way in which the conduct of individuals or groups may be directed" (p. 221). "Neither consensus nor violence constitutes the basic nature of power: it is rather a total structure of actions brought to bear upon possible actions; it incites, it induces, it seduces, it makes easier or more difficult; in the extreme it constrains or forbids absolutely; it is nevertheless always a way of acting upon an acting subject or acting subjects by virtue of their acting or being capable of action. A set of actions upon other actions" (p. 220).

In formal music education settings,[8] examples of factors shaping the range of possible actions are timetables, class sizes, physical space, repertoire and instruments, the frequency of classes, the extent to which the curriculum is predetermined, and the imposition of consequences if certain criteria are not met. Each of these examples represents a structurally constraining element that governs possible actions by teachers and students and thus what actions and routines come to be seen as normal.[9] As actions upon other actions, we can recognize disciplining practices that shape experience and thought in particular directions, representing paths of least resistance. Ranking, as a form of evaluation, is one such disciplining practice that represents "acting upon actions" by creating conditions that reward certain behaviors and punish others. Notably, it is not discipline per se that is either "good" or "bad," but the ways in which disciplining processes, and the discourses that sustain them, become difficult to recognize *as disciplining processes* when they are part of taken-for-granted structures. It should be noted that I am not arguing against giving learners rigorous feedback, nor am I making a case against structured learning. Rather, my project here is to note the routinization and internalization of grading as a form of discipline that sustains particular relations of power. My project is thus not to dismiss any and all forms of ranking as automatically negative, but rather to draw attention to some of the historical roots and contemporary outcomes of ranking practices that might otherwise go unnoticed.

Foucault (1977) describes the evolution of "disciplinary practices" as a consequence of the development of concerns about maximizing the use value of members of definable populations, combined with notions of the "art of the human body" (p. 137). In contrast to earlier monastic concepts of discipline, the disciplines of modernity entail attention to the body that is to be "manipulated, shaped, trained, which obeys, responds, becomes skilful and increases its forces" (p. 136). Discipline in its modernist manifestation is thus "not about law" but about "normalization." It is about using reason to determine "truths" about the nature of human beings in their relationships with each other and with the nonhuman world (p. 106). Through disciplining practices and the proliferation of classificatory scientific projects, all is discovered to be "relational" (p. 146); although discipline increases the "forces of the body," leading to different levels of skill mastery, Foucault notes that the development of various disciplining procedures also comes to embody new relations of power. Domination is achieved not necessarily through overt uses of force but through disciplining procedures that produce "subjected and practiced bodies, 'docile' bodies" (p. 138). The markers of privilege and affiliation that once indicated status in modernist frameworks "are increasingly replaced—or at least supplemented by—a whole range of degrees of normality indicating membership in a homogenous social body but also playing a part in the classification, hierarchization and the distribution of rank" (p. 184). Schools are emblematic of systems of classification and ranking, but how does a child become acclimated to being classified, ranked, and placed within a hierarchy of presumed merit?

# RANKING AND CONSTRUCTIONS OF THE SELF

From very early during the period when children begin to attend formal schools in North America, they learn to associate learning with being ranked. Grading is a primary mechanism that keeps students focused, not only on learning, but also on gaining external approval for what they do. For those who see themselves reflected in school curricula, who enjoy school and invest in the idea that they can, and likely will, attain good grades, succeeding within the system offers a certain exalted status—especially among teachers and other students who excel within the school context. For those who resist or do not function well within the disciplining frameworks of formal schooling, however, lower status is the inevitable consequence, at least in terms of institutional ranking. For while some students might gain status amongst their peers as renegades, in institutional terms, these are noncompliant, problem students. With the addition of high-stakes testing and competition among schools for funding based on test scores, there is now even more pressure to valorize those students who do well on standardized tests and censure or even expel those who do not. Indeed, as documented in Elliott and Silverman (2015), free market and privatization movements, under the banner of neoliberalism, are subjecting music education programs to the relentless measurement practices previously limited to subjects such as math and English. Within neoliberal structures, a school's competitive ranking impacts funding as well as the culture of schools and the priorities administrators find themselves obliged to pursue. Ranking within and among schools, through the vehicle of standardized testing, is argued to be a means to ensure accountability by ostensibly demonstrating the degree to which students have learned what they are mandated to learn and the degree to which teachers have taught what they are mandated to teach. Participating in annual music competitions, a practice that predates neoliberal pressures, has also been part of many school music programs and is a common rite of passage for those aspiring to careers as classical musicians. In some traditional music education settings, there is also a hierarchy of types of music, with classical Western music being the most exalted, and non-Western and popular musics being progressively lower on the scale; in some forms of Western ensemble music, there are clearly delineated hierarchical roles that become closely associated with people's identities and sense of worth. Here again, I do not want to suggest there is never any useful purpose for ranking, nor do I want to dismiss the teaching done by music educators that deliberately steps outside of ranking systems. Indeed, I am not trying to attach permanent meanings to any given practice; however, what I do want to note is that ranking practices inevitably pervade all sites affected by decisions regarding the distribution of resources, thus determining the extent to which subject areas, activities, and people (as individuals or as members of identifiable populations) are recognized as deserving of institutional support (Au, 2016; Barrera, 2016; Graham & Neu, 2004). In other words, whether or not we accept rationales for how something is ranked, people, places, and things are placed in *relation* to each other on a scale of deserving and undeserving—a practice argued to be a necessary part of educational decision-making.

With the pressure to achieve the highest possible place in these hierarchies, gaining a competitive advantage and lessening the fear of not having the financial resources to survive is a powerful motivator; however, it is crucial to note that the system requires disadvantage in order to sustain the desirability of advantage. The fact that some teachers resist subjecting their students to standardized testing, risking their jobs in the process (Chen, 2014), provides further evidence that ranking practices are closely bound with contests over relations of power.

To be clear, I am not suggesting that people are equally gifted or that there are not differences in effort or accomplishment among individuals. Nevertheless, I want to point out the seductiveness of believing oneself to be special and thus deserving of special privileges. Like advantage and disadvantage, the corollary of believing in privilege is believing, also, that others should have less. It is a philosophical and psychological framework that easily slips into the unquestioned assumption that material inequality is due to the failure of individuals to work hard enough, normalizing vast inequalities in the distribution of resources and leaving systemic causes of inequality out of consideration.

To place this normalized practice of seeing oneself as a ranked person in a different context, consider for a moment the political challenge if large numbers of people believed that everyone merits a reasonable standard of living, meaningful work, safe and healthy working conditions, an absence of systemic violence, and perhaps enough leisure time to be able to live a full life. If such a view were the norm, an expectation of relative equality would be created—an expectation that might unite people from multiple backgrounds to work together to achieve a shared political goal. A central part of education in Western contexts would necessarily include deconstructions of the rationales and results of colonial and slave-based economies, as well as detailed studies of labor wins and losses in battles for workers' rights, civil rights battles, and other battles to achieve greater equality. With individuals habituated to being assigned a rank from the first moment of authorized schooling, however, young people internalize the experience that relative equality, or recognizing and valuing the gifts of each member of the school body, is not the expected outcome of schooling, in spite of the constant circulation of pedagogical and political discourses that claim that fairness and equality are societal ideals. One might expect that such contradictions would be the cause of cognitive dissonance; however, they are not generally recognized as conflicting goals.

## A View from the Outside (Part 1)

Over a number of years I have led or visited music programs for young people in which many of the standard practices of formal education have been absent, including teacher-led ensembles, grading, learning about the canon of Western music, and performing the music of other composers. In music learning sites for homeless, street-involved, or incarcerated youth, the taken-for-granted values and disciplining forces contained in authorized music education settings are made "strange" because these particular structures and disciplining forces have no meaning in these contexts. While these young people are subjected to many constraints and societal disciplines that shape their lives, there is an ironic freedom from external directives, including ranking, in terms of their music learning and music making that contrasts with what is generally (though not always) normed within the constraints of school music education.

The three music programs I refer to here are SKETCH: Working Arts for Street Involved and Homeless Youth (see http://sketch.ca/) and "Beatz to Da Streetz"[10] (both based in Toronto), and a program for incarcerated youth based in Thunder Bay, Ontario.[11] What initially stood out to me in each of these settings was the gap between my school-based, white middle-class musical training and expectations and the musical interests of the mostly racialized[12] young people in these programs. At SKETCH, for example, the range of musical styles embraced by the studio's young learners did not contain any of the forms of music I had experienced in my university music program. In fact, when a group of university-trained music educators visited the music studio at SKETCH in 2008, the long list of genres identified by the studio mentor were outside the practice of all but one member of our teacher group. Fortunately, in some university settings the preparation of music educators now includes experience with a broad range of musical genres.[13] Nevertheless, the gap between what counts as useful knowledge in the SKETCH program and the standard classical music background that is still, to my knowledge, a prerequisite for attaining a university degree in music education, is significant (Koza, 2008).

A second notable difference between the experiences of our group of music educators and the knowledge valued by the young people at SKETCH was that our professional practices were focused mostly on the study and performance of institutionally sanctioned composers, while the students' interests were in learning to write, perform, and record their own original music. Here again, there are music educators who have been supporting students in creating their own music for some time (Friesen, 2009; Lashbrook & Mantie, 2009); however, becoming skilled in pedagogies that support student creativity is not yet a standard requirement for music education degrees, thus leaving a significant gap between what these students value and institutional expectations.

A third difference was the amount of money required to learn the instruments common to the professional educators versus the financial accessibility of the music the students at SKETCH were pursuing. (This contrast brings to mind Bourdieu's [1984, 1993] critique of "musical tastes" and an association with the most labor-intensive and costly forms of musical production as a means to rationalize and sustain class distinctions.) In order to further their learning, students work with mentors and peers and compare recordings of their own work with professional recordings that provide models for their musical goals.[14] While such listening and modeling may also be part of some school music classes, formal testing or evaluation as a form of ranking and group-based teaching and learning are foreign to the culture at SKETCH.

My second example of music learning in an abject setting draws on my experience working with incarcerated youth in Thunder Bay. While some of the mostly First Nations young people I met in this context thrived on the social aspect of group hand-drumming, the young people with strong musical ambitions were not interested in the group program. My "authority" as a qualified "music teacher" was irrelevant. Indeed, insofar as I was offering group-based programming, any requirement to attend the scheduled "music sessions" was a hindrance to these more ambitious music learners, given their limited access to "free" time. These individual young people—a guitarist in one case and an aspiring rap artist in another—were driven to make their own music, with no need or interest in linking their learning with any kind of external approval or authorizing process. In common with many of us who pursue music with a passion, becoming a skilled musician is central to how these students come to identify themselves. However, what is different between the urgency with which these students (on the outside) learn and the passion brought by those learning music in schools (on the inside) is that the students in this place of incarceration are entirely responsible for their own learning. They may seek help from other musicians, but they are not part of a system with built-in support, on the one hand, or systems of ranking, on the other.

In school music programs, a significant portion of teaching and learning is teacher directed and generally includes time dedicated to appreciating the music of composers of the Western canon. This is not to dismiss the musical experiences available through the Western canon or to suggest that those who learn music in school settings are not motivated to learn to make their own music. What is different here is that getting a grade, preparing for a career in music, or otherwise seeking an authorized form of approval for their efforts is not part of their motivation. Indeed, in these otherwise abject settings, I witnessed young people taking charge of their learning and ferociously protecting their goals and interests from external judgment. What is relevant to these students is not a grade but finding resources to support their learning. I'm sure that music educators see students with this kind of single-minded drive in their classes as well; however, my point is not to say that this mindset is unique to "outside" sites of music learning but rather to note that other institutional aspects of music education are absent and undesired in these settings.

My third example of music learning in abject conditions is Beatz to Da Streetz (B2DS), a program developed for young, mostly black, mostly street-involved youth who use their original music to "speak truth to power," talking back to police and talking back to a white, middle-class world that fails to acknowledge the race- and class-based structural violence profoundly affecting their lives. As in SKETCH, students were mentored by musicians able to support their interests and also able to appreciate the systems they were fighting. While profoundly personal, the original music of B2DS also directly challenged their experiences with social and economic injustice.

Learners in each of these settings do not necessarily have access to analyses that might help them gain a deep understanding of the systems of oppression that shape their lives, but they do know that what they learn in school and what they need to know in order to survive and keep their souls intact do not necessarily coincide. Formal music schooling, when grounded in middle-class values of civilizational aspiration, rarely accommodates challenges to the legitimacy of these civilizing claims (Vaugeois, 2014). While some music educators may bring a radical critique of these values to their music teaching, the institutional forms of state-mandated education remain grounded in colonial, capitalist relations, rooted in race, class, and gender hierarchies that are rarely identified as such from within school settings (Curtis, 1988, 1992). In addition, multicultural and diversity programs that are not grounded in analyses of systemic oppression often do more to mask than expose systems of power (Bradley, 2008; Hess, 2013). Thus, marginalized students frequently reject participation in formal schooling because they do not trust that the system is intended to benefit them.

In his book *I Won't Learn from You*, Herbert Kohl (1994) describes a number of contexts in which students choose not to learn because what is being taught pushes up against values the students feel the need to be protect. Of particular relevance to this discussion are those students who refuse to learn because they perceive that school structures, and what is being taught, are in direct opposition to their well-being. The following passage exemplifies a kind of resilience that protects such students from subsuming their experiences into narratives that erase their reality:

> The [school's] program is a very confusing system. There's nobody to explain it to you. They just, you know, like pat you on the back. People tell me if you don't go along with the program, you'll mess up your whole life.
>
> I say then, well, to hell with my life. You have to take some kind of stand. Everything you learn is lies."
>
> It's their education. Not mine.
>
> It's their history. Not mine.
>
> It's their language. Not mine.
>
> You name it. It's theirs. Not mine.
>
> A white teacher, he has not lived the life. He cannot relate any of the things to me. So I'm bored. (Paul quoted in Kohl, 1994, p. 30)

"Paul" is describing his refusal to allow his mind to be colonized by the values and practices normalized within a particular authorized school system. He is not an "at-risk" student so much as a young person expressing resistance to a system that rarely acknowledges its part in maintaining systemic oppression.

The reader should not mistake my respect for the independence of mind and resilience shown by these learners as romanticizing the lives of young people who have been incarcerated; who do not have safe homes to return to; or who are routinely exposed to combinations of racism, poverty, sexual exploitation, police violence, and lateral violence often endemic to the lives of people positioned as targets of systemic oppression. Nevertheless, as an outsider to authorized narratives about what matters in life and who is "worthy" or "unworthy," the young man quoted by Kohl, like the young people learning music in the abject sites I have described, demonstrates resilience and an assertion of self that rejects the need for institutional approval. There is an independence and creativity evident among students in these outside settings that I found quite striking. I shift my attention now to a history, or genealogy, of power in relation to the development of authorized music education settings.

# CAPITALISM, COLONIZATION, AND THE MIRAGE OF MERITOCRACY

Returning to the production of an inside versus an outside, in the context of empire building and the extraction of wealth through colonial expansion, a new version of hierarchical levels of human worth and entitlement emerged in Western countries through the expansion of empire and "accumulation through dispossession" in the form of settler colonialism. The slave trade, another key mechanism used to amass power and wealth in colonial and European states, was also a process of acquisition through dispossession—in this case, acquiring the use of the bodies of slaves not only to provide forced labor but to reproduce an enslaved workforce through master-slave sexual relations (Wynter, 2003). Intrinsic to such projects are dividing practices that assign different levels of humanity to different kinds of people. A particularly successful strategy deployed to keep underclasses of people within the colonial state from taking up common cause with other exploited groups was to offer slightly higher status to populations now identified as White. This strategy encouraged White people to invest in maintaining whatever advantage was on offer in order not to fall (or be pushed) any lower in the hierarchy (McWhorter, 2004; Wynter, 2003).[15] In countries linked to European projects of colonization, Whiteness[16] and the assumed supremacy of educated White men (legally identified as the highest markers of human merit [Harris, 1993]) are central to legitimizing hierarchies of authority and entitlement while also legitimizing forms of violence against those further down the scale—people who invariably have something those at the top of the hierarchy desire to possess (e.g., land, labor, women's bodies). Linking notions of civilizational advancement with rationales for the dispossession, enslavement, and oppression of different peoples has hinged on notions of hierarchical merit. By the nineteenth century, rationales for hierarchies of meritorious versus disposable bodies were based on identifiable raced and gendered markers. As Ann Laura Stoler (1995) notes: "Race [was] the organizing grammar of an imperial order in which modernity, the civilizing mission and the 'measure of man' were framed. And with it, 'culture' was harnessed to do more specific political work; not only to mark difference, but to rationalize the hierarchies of privilege and profit, to consolidate the labor regimes of expanding capitalism, to provide the psychological scaffolding for the exploitative structures of colonial rule" (p. 27).

Culture, as both a marker and maker of subjectivities, distinguishes the identities of colonizers from those they are colonizing. The idea of culture as advancement works primarily to assert the superiority of the dominant group by creating categories of the "meritorious" versus the "unevolved" while reinforcing colonial claims of entitlement. "Culture was imbricated both in the means and the ends of colonial conquest, and culture was invented in relationship to a variety of internal colonialisms.... Culture became fundamental to the formation of a class society, and to developing discourses of race, biology, and nationality" (Dirks, 1992, p. 4). Cultural rankings, like categories of class, race, gender, and able-bodiedness, were used as a means to categorize and divide people in terms of their place in colonial/capitalist projects and to rationalize dispossession and the vastly unequal distribution of resources—all the while using notions of cultural superiority to claim these actions as morally justified (Stoler, 1989, 1995). While Enlightenment philosophers were expounding on notions of equality "among men," endless legitimations of domination and hierarchical worthiness coexisted comfortably within the same philosophical orientations by defining some people as fully evolved and others as less evolved, less than fully human, and therefore legitimately dominated by their "betters" through whatever force necessary (Gilroy, 2000; Goldberg, 1993). Through these processes of accumulation through domination and the discourses developed to create moral justifications for violent and oppressive relationships,[17] notions that hierarchical relationships are the rational outcome of objective standards of measurement are normalized through a variety of discursive and material processes. For example, people whose European forebears immigrated to countries such as Canada, the United States, Australia, New Zealand, and South Africa as settler colonials learn a heroic narrative—a romanticized story of difficult but noble adaptation to a foreign and dangerous environment that valorizes the position of settler colonials and delegitimizes the lives of those they displaced. Colonization, in these narratives, is a worthy and exciting project to bring civilization to the dark corners of the earth (Fanon, 1963; Kipling, 1899/1929). The connection to the business of extracting and exporting resources for the primary benefit of owners and shareholders is secondary in these narratives, although where capitalism is identified as key to the structure of the nation, it is identified as a primary source of "human progress" and civilization (Gordon, 2010). Indeed, narratives of exaltation woven through our respective nation-building myths, and corresponding narratives of abjection for those conceived of as outside the national "family," continue to reinforce categories of "us versus them" while obscuring the structures of violence used to maintain, and enhance, existing relations of power.

## Histories of Ranking Practices in Schooling

Writing about the development of centrally controlled public education in Upper Canada,[18] education historian Bruce Curtis (1988) argues that public education was never intended to produce a society free of a class system, but rather to produce a populace comfortable with existing hierarchies: "Educational practice would resolve the contradiction between the formal equality of citizenship and the social subordination of the mass of the population demanded by bourgeois civilization. It would create social subjects who enjoyed and actively embraced their social subordination, who experienced subordination as equality and liberty" (p. 106). While many educators are committed to equity and fairness and to discovering and meeting the needs of their individual students, I often wonder if our education system, with its institutional controls, built-in rewards and punishments, and focus on individual accomplishment, does not do more to teach us to conform while remaining ignorant of the system of which we are a part. Recalling the words of the Brazilian educator Paulo Freire (2000): "Education either functions as an instrument which is used to facilitate integration of the younger generation into the logic of the present system and bring about conformity or it becomes the practice of freedom, the means by which men and women deal critically and creatively with reality and discover how to participate in the transformation of their world" (p. 34).

My concern is that habituating ourselves to ranking practices also habituates us to the notion that those who have so much more must merit their dominance. When we learn that social and economic relations are the sum of individual actions in what we are repeatedly told is a fundamentally fair system, we are often unable to see the effects of structures, institutions, and economic and political forms of power that are designed to shape the trajectory of whole populations. The fundamental inequality that is built into the system remains largely unspeakable and, for those living with relative privilege, the built-in, unearned hierarchies of the system are largely unnoticed. Within modernist philosophies, advantage and disadvantage are reduced to the characteristics of individuals, or individual families, without acknowledging the political uses of group identities (race, gender, and class being only three examples) or considering the systems that produce such different positionalities. Notably, as evidence of systemic inequality, recent United Nations reports have cited both the US and Canadian governments for allowing extreme levels of poverty to exist in the midst of countries producing so much wealth (Kent, 2017; Nuttall, 2016; Pilkington, 2017).

Egerton Ryerson's successful campaign to achieve centralized control of education in Ontario, Canada, established a paternalistic relationship between the state and its citizens and institutionalized the notion of a multiyear regimen of discipline to which all young people (at least in sites of public education) would be subject (Curtis, 1988, pp. 22, 205).[19] Ryerson, like other proponents of the educational state, understood education to be a process of subjectification, a process based on the "subject-shaping" management of action (Curtis, 1988, p. 16; Sangster, 1897). Curtis describes the social tensions that Ryerson hoped to ameliorate through compulsory education: "Educational practice would resolve the contradiction between the formal equality of citizenship and the social subordination of the mass of the population demanded by bourgeois civilization. It would create social subjects who enjoyed and actively embraced their social subordination, who experienced subordination as equality and liberty" (p. 106). Ryerson believed that music had an important role to play in public education, subject formation, and the management of populations.[20] "For Ryerson, vocal music was an important avenue to the faculties, since all students enjoyed it, and its enlistment in educational endeavours could connect morality with pleasure.... [V]ocal music would train students to 'worship God in the family' and in the 'public sanctuary,' and by 'furnishing the young people with interesting moral songs,' the educator could 'displace in their social amusements many of at least a questionable character.' Vocal music would allow the transformation of the leisure of students into a period of instruction. Music could then 'refine and humanize' students" (Curtis, 1988, p. 106).

Ryerson's notion that an engagement in particular forms of music could contribute to producing particular kinds of subjects was not unique. Britain's John Hullah worked tirelessly to bring "choralism" to the British working classes as a means to "initiate pupils into principles of order," contain worker dissent, and produce subjects loyal to the British Empire (Olwage, 2005, p. 27). Similar to the brass band movement established in British mining towns, Hullah established choral programs and competitions as a means to focus energies away from worker rebellion toward pursuits that, it was hoped, would contain and redirect rebellious energies. Music was thus brought into the service of enjoining lower classes to adopt bourgeois ideals (Campbell, 2000; Olwage, 2005).

It is not my intention to reduce the effects of these approved musical activities exclusively to goals of population management. Musical engagements may have served to strengthen lower-class solidarity in ways not foreseen by the architects of these projects. As musicians and music educators, we see that music making can have a range of effects on individual and group well-being—aspects that are taken up at length by music education philosophers.[21] Nevertheless, even though a range of experiences emerge from music making within formal, authorized settings, we need to recognize that music education is not only influenced by local and structural conditions; it also embodies political projects that need to be recognized as such.[22]

In earlier eras, when the competing interests of capitalists and workers were more clearly understood as being in opposition to each other (Harvey, 2010), the disciplining structures developed in the process of developing musical norms were also recognized as political moves with hoped for political outcomes. Influential Canadian musician and music educator Sir Ernest MacMillan, for example, argued that conservatory exams and local, regional, and national competitive music festivals would help to create "a culture of aspiration," providing models of "good" culture and showing people where they stood in relation to others. Maria Tippett (1990) describes the multiple purposes envisioned by the originators of the music and drama festivals:

> According to two of its most enthusiastic supporters—Arthur Collingwood and Ernest MacMillan—the music festival was "a healthy stimulus to the music students, [and] an ideal public forum for the competent teacher," for it encouraged playing "the right kind of music in the right way" and gave "the student a sense of proportion, showing him where he stands in relation to others." And besides, while all this was happening for the student performer, the audience was "being educated in the art of listening to music" and thereby "developing a critical taste" towards what it heard. (p. 56)

This statement expresses the assumed supremacy of Western classical music, the sense of the "rightness" of the colonial project as expressed in musical "standards," and the goal to create a "culture of aspiration" among the mixed populations (and classes) of original inhabitants and newcomers. The masses are to be encouraged to recognize hierarchies of merit not only in terms of musical accomplishment, but also in terms of musical forms of expression.[23] As Nicholas Dirks (1992) argues, "in certain important ways, culture was what colonialism was all about. Cultural forms in newly classified 'traditional' societies were reconstructed and transformed by and through colonial technologies of conquest and rule, which created new categories and oppositions between colonizers and colonized, European and Asian, modern and traditional, West and East, even male and female" (p. 2).

Taking up the contemporary moment, we have new variations on an older theme: improving the self by attaining more and more credentials that certify the self as worthy and "job ready" even as there are fewer and fewer stable, full-time jobs available, whether in music education or other fields (Gerster, 2018; Kalleberg, 2011; Vosko, 2005). As a continuation of the disciplining of populations, contemporary credentialism, like evaluation as ranking, is one of a number of disciplining practices that directs people toward self-improvement and away from noticing shared conditions. In a system that now requires more formal schooling to do work previously done without the need for particular credentials, one outcome is that students go deeply into debt in order to acquire degrees. In spite of the recruiting claims of learning institutions, however, it should be clear, especially to those teaching in institutions of higher learning, that those with the highest possible academic credentials—for example, holders of PhDs—often wind up working as the low-waged, precarious sessional instructors who now provide the bulk of teaching that sustains universities and colleges (Baker, 2017).

In another example, education students are now strongly encouraged to pursue master's degrees; however, even with these additional degrees, graduates can expect years of precarious, part-time employment while they work their way up the supply lists or leave the country to teach overseas. In the current economic context, their high grades, proven skills, and multiple credentials do not necessarily equate with monetary success, stability, or security. One question then is how well prepared "successful students" are in terms of the emotional and psychological resilience they will need to cope with a system that does not deliver what it claims to offer. The resilience and resistance demonstrated by music learners in Beatz to Da Streetz and SKETCH, for example, reflect an awareness that learning to be obedient to the demands of the system will not help them become any less abject within a social and economic system built on domination and white supremacy (Abdel-Magied, 2017). These forms of resilience, and the critical questioning that accompany them, are not as readily accessible to those who, having functioned reasonably well within authorized systems of schooling, have internalized the idea that our ranked society is based on "just" systems of merit.

Here I recall Foucault's (1977) words about discipline: "Discipline increases the forces of the body (in economic terms of utility) and diminishes these same forces in political terms of obedience" (p. 138). In an economy of constructed scarcity in which the means of production, the profits gained from the dispossession of populations formerly living on desired resources, and the "surplus value" extracted from the labor of working people are all controlled by a small number of extremely wealthy and powerful people. Thus, focusing all of one's energies on "self-improvement" becomes an exercise in political docility—a subjectification that I refer to elsewhere as "terminal naivety" (Vaugeois, 2014, pp. iii, 214).

We are living in a time of acute anxiety in which fears of economic, ecological, and civilizational collapse are part of the daily news. And while there is a growing distrust of core institutions and fears that young people will have much more difficult lives than their parents, the notion of meritocracy, with corollary notions of deserving and undeserving populations, continues to hold a central place in public discourse. For example, white supremacist movements openly claim that racialized people (whether refugees, immigrants, or workers) are responsible for economic inequality and that feminists and other challengers to patriarchal order are responsible for social collapse—a powerful, if terrible, expression of meritocracy not far from the rationales of the colonial and slave trade eras. Such White supremacist, antifeminist, anti-immigrant movements do, however, reflect a sense that the current system is not fair. Unfortunately, the strategy of inciting hatred of identifiable "others" works as well now as it did in the past to create "enemies" in order to distract from the inequalities enforced by interests far more powerful than immigrants, refugees, or activists struggling to achieve greater equality.

Within this context of distrust of core institutions, Karen Stote's (2015) description of the historical context of colonial era immigration is noteworthy:

> For many, the move to this side of the ocean was not necessarily by choice. State and private interests were also busy expropriating the lands and resources of Europe and in many respects, they employed policies and practices similar in form to those wielded on Aboriginal peoples to do so. A primary motivation for the mass transference of people from one continent to another in the nineteenth and early twentieth centuries was indeed to relieve the state from the responsibility of dealing with the aftermath of these practices on the peoples of Europe. Some individuals and families came unwillingly, and countless others were enticed with the promise of a better life. Once here, settlers were given the opportunity to work as servants to a state which had so recently dispossessed them, and to aid in the continued creation of wealth by dispossessing the original inhabitants of these lands. (p. 2)

In this passage, Stote draws attention to the similarities in practices of dispossession experienced by many European immigrants drawn into projects of colonization that, from their origins to today, continue to be dependent for their moral validity on having settler colonial populations thoroughly saturated in notions of their racial, civilizational, and cultural superiority (Black & Lost People Films, 2010; Maynard, 2017; Razack, 1998; Thobani, 2007); as we have seen, the dividing and ranking practices so necessary to projects of capital accumulation have also been intrinsic to the development of schooling for the masses.

In an economy of constructed scarcity in which the means of production, the profits gained from the dispossession of populations located on desired resources, and the "surplus value" generated by workers are held by fewer and fewer people, and in which governments are unwilling for ideological reasons, or unable for political reasons to use taxation and regulation to redistribute resources equitably across the entire population, failing to recognize how populations have been pitted against each other in pursuit of wealth and power leaves people unable to make sense of the current historical moment—and vulnerable to the most violent forms of divide-and-conquer politics.

# A View from the Outside (Part 2)

Given the foundational inequalities of the political and economic structures shaping people's life possibilities, it is not surprising that a number of activists and intellectuals from marginalized populations challenge the idea that making existing educational structures more "inclusive" will resolve any of the fundamental conditions of inequality embedded in our system. For example, while Indigenous academic and activist Leanne Betasamosake Simpson (2012) notes that Indigenous education is chronically start underfunded and that provincial curricula (in Canada) do not "meet the needs of our nations or our students," she argues that rather than finding ways to adapt to the existing colonial education system, Indigenous peoples should instead follow the model of the Akwesasne Freedom School (which has adopted a total Mohawk immersion curriculum) and start "putting our energy into building the educational experiences we want for our children"—that is, outside of the colonial education system and embracing significantly different structures and values.

In a similar line of thinking, activist and scholar Angela Davis (2017) makes the case that trying to be accepted within a system that is designed to dispose of those designated as abject will lead to a shallow victory:

> We always use as our standard, those who are at the centre of the structures we want to dismantle! But why would women want to become equal to men? Why would Black people and Latinos, and Muslims and Arabs want to be equal to White people? Why would the LGBT community want to become equal in the context of heteropatriarchy?
>
> We have to be aware of the extent to which assimilationism always tends to reign. You [can't] solve racism by integrating Black people and people of color into a white supremacist society without thinking about what it is we need to do to transform that society.

Here, Davis suggests that becoming part of the existing system will not change the destructive relationships upon which the system is based.

I quote Simpson and Davis to introduce the idea that systems and practices that are assumed to be right and normal are not necessarily seen as desirable by those on the margins of those systems. From these outside perspectives, it is the larger social structures within which education and music education have particular roles that are the problem—not the students from racialized and/or impoverished communities who are so often identified as being "at risk." If schooling is embedded in particular structures and belief systems that rank who counts as human and allow inequality, oppression, and deprivation to persist within the illusion of a just society, from the perspective of these authors, achieving "inclusion" is not a radical enough change to achieve justice.

Cynthia Wesley-Esquimaux (2009), in writing about pre-contact Indigenous societies, presents another alternative to hierarchically based systems of social organization:

> The old social systems of Aboriginal people were cooperative and autonomous, peace-centred and ritual-oriented, and based on ideas of complementarity and intercon-nectedness. (p. 17)

> Social benefits, as well as social responsibilities, were, in principle, also the same for both sexes. Those societies, in which the centrality of women to the social wellbeing of the entire community was never questioned, were also characterized by an equal distribution of goods, with the welfare of children and elders being of paramount importance. (p. 22)

In Esquimaux's descriptions, an alternative worldview is introduced that values the gifts each person brings to the community. Complementarity, respect of self, and respect toward others are central tenets along with an equal distribution of resources. I present this alternative to ranked forms of social organization to suggest that the normalization of inequality is not based on human nature but rather on systems of social organization sustained by discourses that rationalize the unequal distribution of resources. In standard forms of Western education, we do not spend a lot of time considering alternative values or forms of social organization; rather, we learn that ranking is a necessary part of learning and a normal and accepted part of the social, political, and economic structures that shape our lives.

Likewise, Indigenous scholar Glen Coulthard (2014) argues that having one's culture "recognized" will not result in "reconciliation," as it does not challenge existing relations of power. Coulthard recommends recovering communitarian values rather than trying to fit into a system based on inequality and the limitless exploitation of resources. He calls for the goal of developing "grounded normativity," by which he means reinforcing "land-connected practices and longstanding experiential knowledge" that inform and structure "ethical engagements with the world" and "relationships with human and nonhuman others" (p. 406). These views from the "outside" suggest a kind of creativity and imaginative freedom to envision profoundly different approaches to life and learning that falls well outside of existing educational structures.

# Concluding Thoughts

In Western discourse outside of the school context, humans are categorized into "First World" versus "developing world," civilized versus primitive, higher status knowledge laborers versus lower status manual laborers, migrant workers versus workers entitled to citizenship and legal protection, and so forth. While it is not always apparent on the surface that constructed categories of the human are the subtext that normalizes identities assumed to be entitled to a "good life" and identities of disposability, these divisions are framed as natural outcomes of the characteristics of specific populations— a rationale that continues to justify slaughter as somehow necessary to "progress."

I have used "evaluation as ranking" as an entry point to consider effects of ranking practices assumed to be normal and necessary to the education process. By exploring the priorities of young people who develop their musical subjectivities in abject settings, the normalization of ranking practices embedded in formal structures of schooling is brought to the foreground and placed within the context of historical actions intended to cement particular relations of power in place. The viewpoints of racialized intellectuals who challenge the philosophical and practical framework of the existing system serve to further highlight alternatives difficult to see within education systems based on systems of classification and the ranking of human worthiness.

My contention is that habituation to ranking practices and the failure to notice related strategies of population management keep people from recognizing processes of dehumanization that further function to keep them from recognizing their common cause. Western discourses and economic structures are a long way from recognizing the values of complementarity and interconnectedness that Wesley-Esquimaux (2009) and Coulthard (2014) identify as integral to Indigenous concepts of social life, including education, and a world in which a respectful sharing of the means of life occurs will never be possible if it cannot first be imagined. At the very least, I believe it is incumbent upon educators to ask whether reward versus punishment, exaltation versus abjection, and notions of civilized versus uncivilized need to be inextricably bound to concepts of education. Music has tremendous power to heal. Yet wielded as a "civilizing force," it also has tremendous power to exclude and oppress. In our obedience to authorized expectations and unchallenged oppositions between an "inside," with its normalized representations of worthy and unworthy, and an "outside," with its energy of creative resistance, there is an ever-present danger that musical engagements produce musical skills but politically docile subjects—a subjectification to which the resilient and independent music learners in abject settings offer a profound challenge. As fears over economic and environmental collapse increase, we cannot afford to accept categories of worthy and unworthy human beings constructed as if they were the intrinsic characteristics of particular populations. The view from the outside presented by marginalized music learners and activists from marginalized communities challenges much more than the role of ranked grading in formal music education; it challenges our assumptions about what matters in education and in life and demands that we recognize the political strategies that work so dangerously well to keep us from recognizing our common cause.

## Notes

1. Foucault (1970).
2. The term "abjection" came into wide usage based on the work of Julia Kristeva. In her psychoanalytical work, Kristeva expands the meaning of the word beyond "the state of being

cast off" to an inescapable relationship between the self and that which is cast from the self (1995, p. 1).

3. In Foucault's text "What is an Author?," he notes particular discursive functions and identities associated with the concept of the "author." I suggest that the "teacher function" likewise "performs a certain role with regard to narrative discourse, assuring a classificatory function" which define[s], differentiate[s] [it] from and contrasts [it] to others (Foucault, 1998, p. 210).

4. Remote First Nations communities are designated on maps as "Indian Reservations." In Canada, the preferred terms to represent the people whose ancestors lived in this part of the world prior to European contact are First Nations, Métis, and Inuit. In the United States, the term American Indian is used. In Australia, Indigenous peoples are referred to as Aboriginal. In this chapter I use the terms First Nations and Indigenous. It should be noted, however, that the term "Indigenous" is currently being questioned by activists and intellectuals.

5. http://www.cbc.ca/interactives/longform/news/deep-water-indigenous-youth-death.

6. http://aptnnews.ca/2017/05/31/evidence-from-first-nation-student-who-survived-thunder-bay-river-attack-resurfaces-following-eye-witness-claim/.

7. https://www1.toronto.ca/wps/portal/contentonly?vgnextoid=dbe867b42d853410VgnVC M10000071d60f89RCRD.

8. Elliott and Silverman (2015) make an important distinction between the concept of schooling and education, as does Jorgenson (Jorgensen, 2003); however, for the purposes of this chapter, I use the terms interchangeably—not because I refuse to acknowledge the distinction but because governments and other advocates of standardized testing make the claim that standardized testing is necessary for a quality education system (see http://www.eqao.com/en).

9. Andy Hargreaves writes about the crushing of creativity for both teachers and students that is the result of the normalization of enforced standardized teaching and testing (Hargreaves, 2003, pp. 82–90).

10. The final showcase was on November 29, 2011 (https://twitter.com/b2ds?lang=en). "Beatz to da Streetz is a youth-led arts program that aims to provide a safe and supportive space for youth ages 16–24. The program leverages the powerful connection between young people and music to promote opportunities for creative expression and self-discovery, building life skills opening access to professional mentorship, education and income generation for marginalized youth ages 16–24" (https://www.reverbnation.com/b2ds).

11. This took place at William W. Creighton Youth Services (http://www.creightonyouth.com/) and was sponsored by the Community Arts and Heritage Project of Thunder Bay (http://cahep.ca/).

12. Racialized, meaning designated as a not-white, and therefore not fully human, identity. This term also applies to white-appearing young people otherwise marked as abjected outsiders.

13. University of Lethbridge, for example, has a very strong "world music" program, open to music students as well as community members from outside the university (Wasiak, 2013). N.B.: There are important critiques of using the term "world music" to designate non-Western forms of music; however, taking up these critiques is beyond the scope of this chapter.

14. In fact, this learning style is advocated by Lucy Green (2014) in her teacher's guide to informal music teaching and learning and is being taken up in some university music education programs under the name "Musical Futures" (see, e.g., http://www.music.uwo.ca/outreach/music-education/musical-futures-workshop.html).

15. Interestingly, the "blue eyes, brown eyes" experiment with grade 3 children undertaken by Jane Elliott in 1968 demonstrates the seduction of privilege in shifting understandings of self and behaviors toward people now identified as "other" in an experiment that only took two days to show dramatic effects (Peters, 1985).

16. I capitalize Whiteness and White here to indicate the constructedness of these categories in the same way that Black and Indian are constructed to represent peoples as intrinsically deserving of higher or lower status.

17. These include concepts such as Manifest Destiny, terra nullius, and the Doctrine of Discovery (General Synod of the Anglican Church of Canada, 2001).

18. Upper Canada was an earlier designation of what is now known as the province of Ontario.

19. I am referring here to public and some private forms of education that are governed by provincially mandated curricula and conceptualized according to middle-class values. Educational institutions that cater to the children of elite classes are structured to replicate class advantage (Gaztambide-Fernandez, 2009). Ruling class institutions are a different manifestation of the same economic project, but they are not included in the analysis offered in this chapter. Ryerson was also an advocate of the industrial and later residential schools that were intended to prepare Indigenous children to become servants and laborers for middle- and upper-class Whites (Curtis, 1988).

20. Music education historian George Trowsdale counts eighty-five references to the importance of music education for "the masses" in Ryerson's writings (Countryman, 1981, p. 9).

21. There are too many to mention here, but Bennett Reimer (2003), David Elliott (1995), David Elliott and Marissa Silverman (2015), Estelle Jorgenson (2003), and Elizabeth Gould (Gould, 2012) count among philosophers of music education.

22. Elliott and Silverman (2015) make the same case for recognizing the political implicatedness of music education practices.

23. The expectation that music would inculcate particular expectations and an acceptance of existing social relations in the United States is well documented in numerous sources (Campbell, 2000; Gustafson, 2009; Popkewitz & Gustafson, 2002).

## REFERENCES

Abdel-Magied, Y. (2017, September 26). I tried to fight racism by being a "model minority"— and then it backfired. *Teen Vogue*. Retrieved from https://www.teenvogue.com/story/fight-racism-model-minority-yassmin-abdel-magied

Anderson, C. (2016). *White rage: The unspoken truth of our racial divide*. New York: Bloomsbury.

Au, W. (2016). Meritocracy 2.0: High-stakes, standardized testing as a racial project of neoliberal multiculturalism. *Educational Policy*, 30(1), 39–62.

Baker, K. J. (2017, February 21). The contingent campus—Adjunctification and the growth of the academic "precariat." Retrieved from http://www.politicaltheology.com/blog/the-contingent-campus-adjunctification-and-the-growth-of-the-academic-precariat-kelly-j-baker/

Barrera, J. (2016, January 26). Cindy Blackstock: Ottawa believed First Nation children were "not worth the money". Retrieved from http://aptnnews.ca/2016/01/26/cindy-blackstock-ottawa-believed-first-nations-children-were-not-worth-the-money/

Betasamosake Simpson, L. (2012). *As we have always done: Indigenous freedom through radical resistance* (3rd ed.). Minneapolis: University of Minnesota Press.

Black, C. (Director), & Lost People Films (Producer). (2010). *Schooling the world* [Film]. Retrieved from http://www.filmsforaction.org/watch/schooling-the-world-2010/

Bourdieu, P. (1984). *Distinction: A social critique of the judgement of taste*. Cambridge, MA: Harvard University Press.

Bourdieu, P. (1993). *The field of cultural production*. New York: Columbia University Press.

Bradley, D. (2008). Oh, that magic feeling! Multicultural human subjectivity, community, and fascism's footprints. *Philosophy of Music Education Review, 17*(1), 56–74.

Campbell, G. J. (2000). "A higher mission than merely to please the ear": Music and social reform in America, 1900–1925. *The Musical Quarterly, 84*(2), 259–86.

Canada, General Synod of the Anglican Church of. (2001). Doctrine of discovery and terra nullius. Retrieved from http://www.anglican.ca/gs2001/rr/presentations/terranullius.html

Chen, M. (2014, April 7). Why are teachers and students opting out of standardized testing? *The Nation*. Retrieved from https://www.thenation.com/article/teachers-and-students-opt-out-defy-testing-machine/

Cole, D. (2015, April 21). The skin I'm in: I've been interrogated by police more than 50 times—all because I'm black. *Toronto Life*. Retrieved from https://torontolife.com/city/life/skin-im-ive-interrogated-police-50-times-im-black/

Coulthard, G. S. (2014). *Red skin, white masks: Rejecting the colonial politics of recognition* (Vol. foreword by Taiaiake Alfred). Minneapolis: University of Minnesota Press.

Countryman, J. C. (1981). *An analysis of selected songs series textbooks used in Ontario schools, 1846–1965*. (Unpublished MMus thesis). University of Western Ontario, London, ON.

Curtis, B. (1988). *Building the educational state: Canada West, 1836–1871*. London, ON: The Althouse Press.

Curtis, B. (1992). *True government by choice men? Inspection, education, and state formation in Canada West*. Toronto, Buffalo, London: University of Toronto Press.

Davis, A. Y. (1998). Race and criminalization: Black Americans and the punishment industry. In J. James (Ed.), *The Angela Y. Davis reader* (pp. 61–73). Malden, MA: Blackwell.

Davis, A. Y. (2017). Words from Angela Davis on assimilationism, white feminism, toxic masculinity and intersectionality, the prison industrial complex and more. Festival: Women of the World. Retrieved from https://www.southbankcentre.co.uk/whats-on/festivals-series/women-world-2017

Dirks, N. B. (1992). Introduction: Colonialism and culture. In N. Dirks (Ed.), *Colonialism and culture* (pp. 1–25). Ann Arbor: University of Michigan Press.

Elliott, D. J. (1995). *Music matters: A new philosophy of music education*. New York: Oxford University Press.

Elliott, D. J., & Silverman, M. (2015). *Music matters: A philosophy of music education* (2nd ed.). New York: Oxford University Press.

Fanon, F. (1963). *The wretched of the earth*. Constance Farrington (Trans.). New York: Grove Press.

Foucault, M. (1970). *The order of things*. London: Tavistock Publications.

Foucault, M. (1977). *Discipline and punish: The birth of the prison*. Alan Sheridan (Trans.). New York: Vintage Books.

Foucault, M. (1982). The subject and power. In H. L. Dreyfus & P. Rabinow (Eds.), *Michel Foucault: Beyond structuralism and hermeneutics* (pp. 208–226). Chicago: University of Chicago Press.

Foucault, M. (1998). What is an author? In J. D. Faubion (Ed.), *Aesthetics, Method, and Epistemology* (pp. 205–22). New York: The New York Press.

Freire, P. (2000). *Pedagogy of the Oppressed*. New York: Continuum.

Friesen, D. (2009). That teacher pedestal: How alternative methods challenged my concept of the teacher role. In E. Gould, J. Countryman, C. Morton, & L. R. Stewart (Eds.), *Exploring social justice. How music education might matter* (pp. 253–60). Toronto: Canadian Music Educator's Association.

Gaztambide-Fernandez, R. (2009). *The best of the best: Becoming elite at an American boarding school.* Cambridge, MA: Harvard University Press.

Gerster, J. (2018, August 21). Engineer? Teacher? Sorry, that doesn't guarantee job security anymore. Retrieved from https://globalnews.ca/news/4399615/professional-jobs-increasingly-precarious/

Gilroy, P. (2000). *Against race: Imagining political culture beyond the color line.* Cambridge, MA: Belknap Press of Harvard University Press.

Goldberg, D. T. (1993). *Racist culture: Philosophy and the politics of meaning.* Cambridge, MA: Blackwell.

Gordon, T. (2010). *Imperialist Canada.* Winnipeg, MB: Arbeiter Ring.

Gould, E. (n.d.). Music education-becomings: Subjectivity as resistance. May Day Group: Action Ideals.

Gould, E. (2012). Uprooting music education pedagogies and curricula: Becoming-musician and the Deleuzian refrain. *Discourse: Studies in the Cultural Politics of Education, 33*(1), 75–86.

Graham, C., & Neu, D. (2004). Standardized testing and the construction of governable persons. *Journal of Curriculum Studies, 36*(3), 295–319.

Green, L. (2014). *Hear, listen, play! How to free your students' aural, improvisation, and performance skills.* London: Oxford University Press.

Gustafson, R. I. (2009). *Race and curriculum: Music in childhood education.* New York: Palgrave Macmillan.

Hargreaves, A. (2003). *Teaching in the knowledge society: Education in the age of insecurity.* New York: Teachers College Press.

Harris, C. I. (1993). Whiteness as property. *Harvard Law Review, 106*(8), 1707–91.

Harvey, D. (2010). *The enigma of capital and the crises of capitalism.* New York: Oxford University Press.

Hess, J. (2013). Performing tolerance and curriculum: The politics of self-congratulation, identity formation, and pedagogy in world music education. *Philosophy of Music Education Review, 21*(1), 66–91.

Jorgensen, E. R. (2003). *Transforming music education.* Bloomington: Indiana University Press.

Kalleberg, A. L. (2011). *Good jobs, bad jobs: The rise of polarized and precarious employment systems in the United States, 1970s–2000s.* New York: Russell Sage Foundation.

Kent, M. (2017, August 13). Canada's record on racial discrimination under scrutiny at UN. Retrieved from http://www.cbc.ca/news/world/canada-racial-discrimination-un-1.4244297

Kipling, R. (1899/1929). The white man's burden: The United States & the Philippine Islands, 1989. In *Rudyard Kipling's Verse: Definitive Edition.* Garden City, NY: Doubleday. (Found at History matters: The U.S. survey course on the web).

Kohl, H. (1994). *"I won't learn from you!" The role of assent in learning.* New York: The New Press.

Koza, J. E. (2008). Listening for whiteness: Hearing cultural politics in undergraduate school music. *Philosophy of Music Education Review, 16*(2), 145–55.

Kristeva, J. (1995). *Powers of horror: An essay on abjection.* New York: Columbia University Press.

Lashbrook, S., & Mantie, R. (2009). Valuing subjugated experience: The One World Youth Arts Project. In E. Gould, J. Countryman, C. Morton, & L. R. Stewart (Eds.), *Exploring social justice: How music education might matter* (pp. 2–22). Toronto: Canadian Music Educator's Association.

Maynard, R. (2017). *Policing black lives: State violence in Canada from slavery to the present.* Halifax, NS, & Winnipeg, MB: Fernwood Publishing.

McWhorter, L. (2004). Sex, race, and biopower: A Foucauldian genealogy. *Hypatia, 19*(3), 38–62.

Nuttall, J. J. (2016, March 8). UN tells Canada to clean up its act on inequality, social rights. Retrieved from https://thetyee.ca/News/2016/03/08/UN-Tells-Canada-Clean-Up-Inequality/

Olwage, G. (2005). Discipline and choralism: The birth of musical colonialism. In A. J. Randall (Ed.), *Music, power, and politics* (pp. 25–46). New York: Routledge.

Peters, W. (1985). A class divided [Television series episode]. In W. Peters (Writer and Producer), *Frontline*. PBS.

Pilkington, E. (2017, December 15). A journey through a land of extreme poverty: Welcome to America. *The Guardian.* Retrieved from https://www.theguardian.com/society/2017/dec/15/america-extreme-poverty-un-special-rapporteur

Popkewitz, T. S., & Gustafson, R. (2002). Standards of music education and the easily administered child/citizen: The alchemy of pedagogy and social inclusion/exclusion. *Philosophy of Music Education Review, 10*(2), 80–91.

Razack, S. H. (1998). *Looking white people in the eye: Gender, race, and culture in courtrooms and classrooms.* Toronto: University of Toronto Press.

Reimer, B. (2003). *A philosophy of music education: Advancing the vision* (3rd ed.). Upper Saddle River, NJ: Prentice Hall.

Sangster, J. H. (1897). *Progress in education: The system of today compared with that in vogue half a century ago: Dr. Sangster's able address at the Normal School jubilee celebration* [Microform]. Retrieved from https://archive.org/stream/torontojubileeooschouoft/torontojubileeooschouoft_djvu.txt

Stoler, A. L. (1989). Making empire respectable: The politics of race and sexual morality in 20th-century colonial cultures. *American Ethnologist, 16*(4), 634–660.

Stoler, A. L. (1995). *Race and the education of desire: Foucault's history of sexuality and the colonial order of things.* Durham, NC: Duke University Press.

Stote, K. (2015). *An act of genocide: Colonization and the sterilization of Aboriginal women.* Halifax & Winnipeg: Fernwood Publishing.

Thobani, S. (2007). *Exalted subjects: Studies in the making of race and nation in Canada.* Toronto: University of Toronto Press.

Tippett, M. (1990). *Making culture: English-Canadian institutions and the arts before the Massey Commission.* Toronto, Buffalo, London: University of Toronto Press.

Vaugeois, L. C. (2014). *Colonization and the institutionalization of hierarchies of the human through music education: Studies in the education of feeling* (PhD dissertation, University of Toronto). Retrieved from http://hdl.handle.net/1807/43747

Vosko, L. F. (2005). *Understanding labour market insecurity in Canada.* Montreal: McGill-Queen's Press.

Wasiak, E. B. (2013). *Teaching instrumental music in Canadian schools.* Don Mills, ON: Oxford University Press.

Wesley-Esquimaux, C. C. (2009). Trauma to resilience: Notes on decolonization. In G. G. Valaskakis, M. D. Stout, & E. Guimond (Eds.), *Restoring the balance: First Nations women, community, and culture* (pp. 13–34). Winnipeg: University of Manitoba Press.

Wynter, S. (2003). Unsettling the coloniality of being/power/truth/freedom. *The New Centennial Review, 3*(3), 257–337.

# CHAPTER 3

# AN ETHICAL CONSIDERATION OF ASSESSMENT IN MUSIC EDUCATION THROUGH THE LENS OF LEVINAS

## KATHRYN JOURDAN AND JOHN FINNEY

> To pass a judgement on the value of a thing and/or a person, and thereby contribute to maintaining or generating new values, involves a responsibility on my part towards the Other and in the context of the world we share.
>
> —Martine Beauvais (2011)

RECENT notions of music making as ethical encounter (Bowman, 2001; Elliott & Silverman, 2015; Regelski, 2016) and as the practice of hospitality (Higgins, 2007) have taken forward Small's (1998) relationship-oriented conceptualization of musicking. These provide the starting point for finding an ethical underpinning for music education in the work of French Jewish philosopher Emmanuel Levinas, whose thinking has in recent years become influential across a wide spectrum of social science disciplines including education, where it provides a profound challenge to the "managerial" outlook of standardization and assessment prevalent in British educational practice and characteristic of global policy initiatives by bodies such as the Organisation for Economic Co-operation and Development (OECD).

*Totality and Infinity*, Levinas's (1969) first major work, written after many years as a teacher, and its exhortation "to look into the face of the Other" yield two valuable conceptual tools: "practices of facing" and "putting a world in common."[1] Looking through the lens of Levinas opens up questions concerning "totalizing" practices in assessment, arising from current discourses of "performativity" in the United Kingdom (Ball, 2003; Lyotard, 1984). This chapter asks what it might mean instead for assessment in music education to allow for the breaking in of "infinity," representing a radical openness toward pupils' music making and their own responses as musicians. In seeking to uncover pupils' "practices of facing" and evaluate how they have "put a world in common," we might begin to capture rich learning in the classroom.

# Observations from a Music Classroom

The following three vignettes are drawn from classroom observations of second-year students in a Scottish high school, and the fourth item is from an interview with one thirteen-year-old class member (Jourdan, 2015).

(i) A class of thirteen-year-olds is given a listening task as a lesson opener. Using a CD of examples from the exam board, with extracts of music from contrasting genres and cultural expressions, their music teacher poses questions. An extract from the show *Riverdance* is played, and pupils are asked which instruments they can hear. The tone is one of warm affirmation of pupils by the teacher. She keeps a fast pace, demanding that they retrieve knowledge from past lessons and glean helpful information from displays around the room. The tone is supportive, and there is a sense of expectancy.

Almost all the girls in the class, sitting apart from the boys, respond to the music by dancing in their seats. A frisson goes around the room as the castanets enter, and two girls at the far table pretend to play them, hands held high in the air. Yet the task at hand is now to identify "which sort of music this is," choosing from a selection of "concepts" specified by the exam board. Most pupils suggest "folk" as they enjoy and identify with the "Celtic" sounds underlying the music's foreground. "It's the rhythm they make in Latin America," the teacher corrects, insisting on upholding the neat categorization into which the exam board had squeezed this track. I empathize with the slightly dazed, deflated response to this outcome prevalent among the class. They have enjoyed the music. Some have responded physically and with pleasure, feeling that this was in some way "their music," but they have reached the "wrong" answer. Their responses must be corralled into one of the exam board's own categorizations. The pupils' openness to and encounter with the music has been shut down prematurely. The required answer is quite clear, it seems (Jourdan, 2012, p. 382).

(ii) The class are playing back their "mash-ups" on Garageband. Pupils use the computer software to take extracts from different songs by favorite bands downloaded from the Internet and manipulate them using various kinds of sonic transformation. Kirsty calls across the class to the boy who was preparing to present his work, "Liam, play them your ending. That's really cool!" Kirsty has already heard Liam's version, as pupils share their in-process work with one another, and has identified the most striking section of his remaking of a favorite song. I am interested that Kirsty is so eager for Liam to receive praise from the class, and that she makes some effort to make sure he is recognized for his work. Liam is not a close friend of Kirsty's and is from time to time fairly disruptive to the class lessons, but he gives an impression of vulnerability rather than aggression. I am intrigued that Kirsty almost takes on the role of teacher in this situation, and Liam seems to grow in stature through her intervention and affirmation.

(iii) The class reach their seats, and the student teacher instructs them to take out their planners. The learning objective is to find out about the music of Java. The lesson moves quickly into an introduction: finding where Java might be. Coffee provides the first clue. South America and Africa are suggested; yes, coffee does come from these areas, too. Ms. H guides the class nearer to China, and someone offers "Indonesia."

The class is fairly interested, but their attention is really drawn in when the first extract of music is played. They listen closely. Ms. H talks about the different instruments used in the Gamelan orchestra. Pupils' interest is aroused particularly in the "gongs." These are unusual, new to pupils. It's easy to draw the conclusion here that pupils are very eager to embrace learning experiences of unfamiliar, distant musical forms.

Concentration deepens as two more extracts are played, and Ms. H gives some background information to guide their interpretation of the scene on video. She explains about the elders playing the gongs, the most respected having charge of the most revered instruments.

Amez's engagement is fascinating today; Stephen does his best to distract him, but he persists in entering fully into an engagement with this new learning experience. "They look depressed," he observes. "No, they're not depressed," Ms. H responds. It would be interesting to take this further: respect, concentration, the solemnity of ritual.

He asks, "Is that not rude, Miss, that the older man playing the gong sometimes falls asleep. Is it not rude while everyone's playing?" He's not sending this up. He's really entering the situation imaginatively, I think. Again, points for development. "An older man could teach a younger one to do it." He's raising rich points for learning, for encountering the Other here. These are fundamental questions about how this music operates in this place as part of this tradition. It affects the way people relate to each other. Amez is sensitive to this.

(iv) "You shouldn't just scrape the top off music. You should go down into it and see where it came from and that—it gives you a better understanding and different views of what's happening" (from interview with Tom).

In the course of a discussion of learning about the blues, Tom senses that rich contextualization resists (totalizing) practices of abstraction and reduction. His words suggest a "scraping off" of other people's music to use elsewhere (as our own?) without a closer engagement. He goes on to explain why he values encounters with other people's music: "Sometimes you get a different perspective of the country—it makes you think differently about them, and you can find out about what they've done in history."

Tom's perspectives reveal a sensitivity to place, to story, and to meaning in the music he hears from more distant communities of musicians around the world. In example iii, Amez wonders about the social meanings of an unfamiliar musical event and practices of music making. Yet there isn't time to explore his questions, as the lesson is targeted at fulfilling objectives shaped by public exam assessment criteria. In the second example Kirsty has learned to make judgments based on her own hierarchy of musical value and recognizes in Liam's work something worthy of note. Her public affirming of his musical work not only builds up his confidence, contributing to a supportive atmosphere among the class that facilitates the sharing of work, but also begins to lay out pointers for evaluating, for valuing each other's work.

These examples, drawn from classroom observation, build a picture of pupils' valuing of music making, of evaluating in the music classroom, which contrasts sharply with some of the assessment practices that shape the way in which their school music making will finally be examined. The first example, set against the rest, reveals a dissonance between the experiences of young people composing, performing, and thinking and talking about music in the classroom in a holistic manner, paying attention to ethical relating with one another and with the distant Other whose music they encounter, and the public examinations in music, which demand that their music making and learning be squeezed into narrow categories, "scraping off the top" and not giving value to, or space for, richer, wider perspectives.

# ASSESSMENT: FROM ACCOUNTABILITY TO RESPONSIBILITY?

While assessment in school education has traditionally been linked to notions of accountability, this is now taking on new significance in the light of international policy-making priorities in education. Music educator Pam Burnard (2011) writes that it is well established now that "standards" in education are one of the key drivers of teaching and learning: "Schools and teachers are living with, and in, a climate of increasing accountability, league tables, politically-driven targets, and high-stakes tests" (p. 22).

Focusing on the consequences within the music classroom, Burnard observes: "It is increasingly apparent that the system, tasks and methods that music teachers use for summative assessment often constrain their capacity to reinforce and communicate a holistic view of quality in their daily music classroom practice and interactions with students" (2011, p. 29). Implicit here is the suggestion that in fulfilling the requirements to ever more effectively assess pupils' achievement and to find ways of continually improving their performance, teachers have to work against their own professional values and ways of valuing pupils' music making and learning in their musical work. Burnard (2011) writes that the development of an audit and surveillance culture has led school leaders to make greater demands on teachers: "The focus on performance targets, delivering better results, raising standards, benchmarks, and accountability is related to the discourse of performativity.... In the United Kingdom, the dominant model of schooling is a 'high performance' one—for the most part, students are valued to the extent that their attainments contribute to the school's organisational performance. The pressure under which both pupils and teachers seek to improve performance and raise standards is immense and can ... undermine the purpose, aspirations, and justification of the school" (p. 26; see also Fielding, 2007).

Performativity used in this sense is rooted in Jean-François Lyotard's development of the term as referring to the political and bureaucratic mechanisms of control, which drive toward the achievement of goals in increasingly efficient ways. The discourse of performativity requires teachers to fulfill externally applied edicts and commands without allowing for the exercise of individual or ethical judgment (Burnard, 2011, p. 28). Central to its functioning is the translation of complex social processes into simple figures or categories of judgment (Ball, 2003, p. 217). Knowledge that is seen as complex and not easily assimilated is quickly abandoned. It is not difficult to see how the exam board would therefore seek to force "musical styles" into apparently clearly delineated categories, as illustrated in example i.

Burnard (2011) suggests that rather than promoting innovative, fresh approaches in which pupils are allowed to develop ideas freely into musical forms, the pressures of performativity might emphasize the acquisition of skills through the manipulation of materials, tools, and musical-cognitive processes to produce particular musical outcomes (p. 27). The prioritizing of the increasingly efficient achievement of goals in terms of learning outcomes may limit the range of musical responses pupils are able to make. Conceptions of "musical knowing" may become narrow and constrained, in which only those aspects of musical knowledge that are easily packaged up, assessed, and lacking in nuance or complexity are permitted in the music curriculum.

The present culture of accountability within education in Britain ultimately makes "relationships of responsibility" impossible (Biesta, 2004, p. 250). The older conception of "accountability," in contrast with the newer "managerial" notion, was associated with responsible action. Biesta turns to Bauman's articulation of postmodern morality, in which his idea of "responsibility" takes central place. Influenced by the philosophy of Emmanuel Levinas, Bauman (1993) holds that being responsible is our human condition, "the first reality of the self" (p. 13). Levinas uses the idea of "proximity" to express the unique quality of the moral relationship, not concerned with physical closeness but understood as a "suppression of distance," an attentiveness to the Other, "the state of permanent attention come what may. Responsibility never completed, never exhausted, never past" (Bauman, 1993, p. 88).

# THINKING TOOLS FROM LEVINAS

The thinking of Emmanuel Levinas, rooted in his practice as a teacher, has become influential on an increasingly wider range of commentators and scholars, including now those within the education research community. Levinas began his philosophical process within the phenomenological method inherited from Edmund Husserl and Martin Heidegger, but his first major work, *Totality and Infinity* (1969), is a critique of Heidegger and Husserl, in fact of the whole sweep of Western philosophy, in order to reposition ethics as "first philosophy," prior to ontology. Western philosophy has been preoccupied with the "totality" of Being, at the expense of what is other than or outside of Being, transcendent, exterior, infinite—the Other.[2] Levinas uses the term "ethics" not in a traditional sense, as a code of morality or moral decision-making, but rather as a relation of responsibility to the Other.

Who is Levinas's Other? The concept of the "other" has long been used to articulate the formation of "self" in opposition to the "other": the self needs the "other" in order to define itself. Georg Hegel was among the first to introduce the idea of the "other" as a constituent of self-consciousness, discussed in chapter 4 of his *Phenomenology of Spirit*. The "other" has been used in social science research to denote those outside a social grouping, those who in some way do not fit in, who are excluded; French psychoanalyst Jacques Lacan was instrumental alongside Levinas in coining contemporary usage of the "Other" as "radically other," different, unknowable.

Levinas takes a foundationalist ethical position; for him there is nothing more fundamental to human existence than the ethical. Ethics has a particular *and* a universal reach. Levinas's ethics is not concerned with "morality" as traditionally conceived. His conception of ethics is in "encounter" with the Other, where the Other calls the self into question:

> A calling into question of the same...is brought about by the other. We name this calling into question...by the presence of the Other ethics. The strangeness of the Other, his irreducibility to the I, to my thoughts and my possessions, is precisely accomplished as a calling into question of my spontaneity, as ethics.... The welcoming of the other by the same, of the Other by me, is concretely produced as the calling into question of the same by the other, that is as the ethics that accomplishes the critical essence of knowledge. (Levinas, 1969, p. 43)[3]

Ethics, says Levinas, describes what happens when, through the encounter with another, my existence is disturbed as my whole self is put into question, breaking open the "totality" of self and enabling the possibility of "coming to know."

Levinas prioritizes ethics over ontology, positing ethics as "first philosophy" prior to ontology and making a powerful critique of the "totalizing" habits of Western philosophy throughout its history: "A philosophy of power, ontology is, as first philosophy which does not call into question the same, a philosophy of injustice.... *Being* before the *existent*,[4] ontology before metaphysics, is freedom...before justice. It is a movement within the same before obligation to the other" (Levinas, 1969, pp. 46–47). Encountering another provided an opportunity to make him or her "the same," to treat that person as if he or she were merely what I understand him or her to be. Categorizing others has led inexorably to many terrors and atrocities against the Other, to imperialist domination, to tyranny, and especially, in Levinas's experience, to the Shoah.

Levinas insists that ethics is "first philosophy," reorienting philosophical priorities set by Aristotle in his *Metaphysics* when the Greek philosopher called ontology the "first philosophy." Before all else, before any understanding of the world, I am responsible for the Other, the other person, for You. This orientation will govern everything else that follows in our human experience. Everything we do, says Levinas, should be governed by this standard.

Levinas's relational conception of education throws a certain light upon the cultures of standards, accountability, and performativity. From his perspective the educational experience will not be a "standard" one in any way, as each encounter between pupils and teacher is dependent on the *responsibility* of the one and the *responsivity* of the other. There could hardly be a more "accountable" milieu for learning than the one Levinas sets before us, in which "coming to know" emerges from the encounter between pupils and teacher.

The richness and openness of Levinas's conception of education stands in stark contrast to a tightly controlled regime of testing, which promotes a reduced and impoverished model of knowledge in the name of accountability. He offers a way of "encountering the Other" that not only reorients relations in the classroom and beyond, but also breaks open narrow models of knowledge shaped by the demands of the standards, accountability, and performativity narratives and offers an ethical basis for pupils and teacher together to encounter the other in an infinitely rich conception of music education. As we "look into the face of the Other," we glimpse Infinity, a profound notion of alterity or openness to the Other that draws back the boundaries of our conceptions of knowledge.

# TOTALITY OR INFINITY: ETHICAL KNOWING

Philosopher of education Paul Standish (2008) elucidates Levinas's distinction between Totality and Infinity, articulated in the latter's essay of 1957, "Philosophy and the Idea of Infinity" (Levinas, 1987), as he describes the two directions the philosophical spirit can take:

> In the first, the thinker maintains a relation distinct from him, other than him. It involves a movement that must lead us beyond the nature that surrounds us and towards a beyond: it goes towards the stranger in a kind of perfectionism towards the divine. This is heteronomy itself. Levinas identifies this thinking in terms of a relation to *infinity*. In the second, the thinker freely assents to propositions that are then incorporated in such a way that his nature is preserved: it thereby brings into the same what was other. It moves towards a kind of autonomy in which nothing irreducible would limit thought. Disparate and diverse events are incorporated into a history; this might be seen as "the conquest of being by man over the course of history" (Levinas, 1987, p. 48). This is a thinking in terms of *totality*. (p. 58)

Levinas questions the kind of freedom, within the frame of *totality*, in which too strong a faith in autonomy and mastery is rooted. His conception of freedom is on the realization of one's responsibility out of prior obligation (p. 58).

Levinas sets his face-to-face, asymmetrical ethical encounter within a spectrum of orientation commencing with Totality at one end—the ideologies with which we make sense of the world, the drive to subsume the experience of another so that he or she is colonized and homogenized—and Infinity at the other, representing an unlimited openness to the Other seen as a glimpse of the infinite. Levinas (1969) writes: "Teaching is not a species of a genus called domination, a hegemony at work within totality, but is the presence of infinity breaking the closed circle of totality" (p. 171). Adopting this view requires us to engage critically, to resist any premature closure of thought and remain profoundly open. The consequences for education of adopting this outlook of radical openness are far-reaching. Knowledge is no longer seen as entirely contained within a specific context, but as infinitely open to new possibilities, which lie beyond the scope of our present understanding.

So Levinas reorients our outlook. As I turn my face, with humanity, toward those who are different from me, my own self is called into question: "The calling into question of the I, coextensive with the manifestation of the Other in the face, we call language" (Levinas, 1969, p. 171). He writes: "To speak is to make the world common, to create commonplaces. Language does not refer to the generality of concepts but lays the foundation for a possession in common" (p. 76). The relation to the Other does not just happen at an abstract level but is grounded in language, which Levinas presents as, at its first impetus, ethical.

Philosopher of education Paul Standish's view, following Levinas, is that the content of the *curriculum* may be seen as a form of relation to the Other: "Subjects are language to the extent that they are ways of thinking and reasoning about the world that have passed down through the generations, where this thinking and reasoning essentially is language" (Standish, 2008, p. 63). Formal education, Standish seems to suggest, has been responsible for violence toward the Other in models of learning that emphasize mastery of the subject under study. In this Levinasian orientation, "The pupil is less the owner of their own learning than as one possessed by it, less master of the subject matter than being in its service" (p. 65).

Following Levinas's assertion that "to see the face is to speak of the world,"[5] that language is an offering to the world, the means through which things receive a name and become concepts, "a first action" (Levinas, 1969, p. 174), Standish insists that it is through what he calls the "language of the curriculum" that the learner is brought face to face with the Other. Standish's writing takes Levinas's thinking into the classroom and elucidates the role of the teacher in "going before" pupils and bringing them to an encounter at which they may look into the face of the Other and be drawn more deeply into the infinity of their curriculum subject, and in the context of this study, into the infinity of music making.

# Practices of Facing

Toward the end of his book *Self and Salvation*, which involves a rich discussion of Levinas's thought in dialogue with Paul Ricoeur and Eberhard Jüngel, theologian David Ford (1999) considers the "practices of facing" in the lives of two contemporary saints. Above all, this is what Levinas calls us to as educators, "practices of facing," learning to look into the face of the Other and to respond to the ethical call we perceive there, to bring pupils into an encounter with the infinity of the Other, and to pass on to our pupils habits of "facing" as they learn to hear the voice of another. What might these practices of facing look or sound like in the music classroom?

Levinas's thinking offers us a re-envisaging of music education in which his "ethics as first philosophy" underpins our understanding. Prior to any ways of conceptualizing how music education functions is the primary orientation outward, toward the Other, and the first ethical impulse to reach out and "put a world in common." This requires a radical openness to the infinity of music making as a practice and music as a discipline, a subject, and a curriculum area. This "ontological basis" generates a plurality of epistemological approaches that enable and explore different aspects of music making, but that all spring from the initial ethical impetus of music making as "putting a world in common."

As pupils build up experiences of listening, performing, and composing, they develop musical fluency in playing, listening to, and talking about music through which aesthetic sensitivity can grow, which enables them to embrace arresting moments of intensification, allowing them to perceive the *face* or the *voice* of the Other and to linger and be responsive. This both involves a musical response in which new sounds and devices are encountered, embraced, and explored, and opens up possibilities for an ethical response—a reorientation and a "being changed"—having the potential to develop into something richer perhaps than the notion of what curriculum documents have sometimes termed "cultural understanding." Below we suggest "practices of facing" for teachers and pupils in the music classroom:

# Teachers

- Take on a role of "master," having "gone before," and leading pupils into an encounter with the face of the Other through music making, and to discern the voice of the Other in (unfamiliar) musical expressions and within "musical works."
- Draw pupils deeper into the infinity of music, using the "language of the curriculum," which opens up learning rather than closing it down.

- Embrace complexity, resist early closure, and allow time for pupils to explore unexpected pathways into deeper learning, responding with flexibility to follow new turnings.
- Introduce contextually rich, complex material that keeps offering fresh insights and challenges.
- Allow themselves to be changed by the encounter.
- Seek the face of each pupil and respond in responsibility and responsivity to the ethical call they find there.
- In a committed stance, become a conduit for, mediate, and become inextricably bound with pupils' experience of learning.

# Pupils

- Learn to discern the face of the Other, to hear his or her voice, and to respond in an ethical relationship of "proximity," reducing distance yet cherishing difference.
- Learn to stay in the encounter, resisting the desire for easy answers with which to close down learning.
- Develop a committed engagement, allowing themselves to be changed, even transformed, by the encounter.
- Develop musical fluency—a "living language within a tradition"—not just "learning the catechism" (Katz, 2012).
- Develop *aesthetic sensitivity* through practices of listening, composing, honing, practicing, and performing
- Learn to be responsible for and responsive to each other as they play, compose, listen, craft, and discuss together, leading each other into deeper engagement, facility, and sensitivity.

# Toward a Levinasian Conception of Assessment?

So how might the experiences of the pupils mentioned at the outset of the chapter be richer if we were to follow the thinking of Levinas? What sort of assessment might be envisaged? How might practices of evaluation of pupils' music making create a space for the valuing of the aesthetic and ethical sensitivity discussed here, which grounds the pursuit of technical and expressive skill? What might it mean for assessment to be reoriented so that pupils are not masters of their knowledge, but in its service? How might exam boards deal with an infinity of outcomes, rather than prescribe easily assessable bites of musical knowledge? This chapter opens up these questions and sets out a case for acknowledging that a fresh, ethically grounded approach is required, yet these questions go beyond the scope of this chapter and require further research. Two strands are drawn out in conclusion as pointers to a reorientation in evaluative practices in music education.

## A Living Language—Not Just *Learning the Catechism*

As a teacher and teacher trainer, Levinas considered the learning of ancient Hebrew in the context of a Jewish education to be of vital importance for enabling pupils to enter into "living conversations that keep the text dynamic rather than static." He contrasted the *static* catechism he saw as being taught within Catholic schools to the *opening up* of the text that occurs when the original language is learned, allowing "multiple voices and interpretations to emerge" (Katz, 2012, p. 214). If pupils within the music classroom are encouraged to develop a *musical fluency* in performing, listening, and composing while being attentive "to the relationships created between people, sounds and places" and learning the "common tongue of musicking" (Odendaal et al., 2014, p. 173), as well as an accompanying *fluency in talking together about* and finding meaning in music making, then music's *infinity* of social, political, historical, aesthetic, emotional, and spiritual meanings will open up to them ever more deeply.

Means of evaluating this sort of rich learning that recognize depth and do not insist on empty abstraction or narrowly prescribed responses must be found. In example ii of the classroom observations, Kirsty acknowledges Liam's endeavor and achievement, building up his confidence as a musician while making aesthetic evaluations based on her own criteria derived from her response to his particular work. She engages with her classmate in a committed way that sees his musical work in the terms she had developed through her own music making, leading him and the rest of the class into a deeper appreciation of his music, while taking on an ethical responsibility for him.

## Avoiding Early Closure: Questions That *Open Up* Rather Than *Close Down*

The pupils in example i, who were faced with categorizing an excerpt from an examination type question set by the exam board, experienced the "violence" that Levinas described as resulting from "totalizing" practices. Their recognition of this music as in some sense "theirs" and their joyful, embodied responses to it were closed down by the assertion of the "correct" label. Yet the excerpt might have yielded whole worlds of musical exploration and also discovery of what had occurred as one culture's musical expressions had met another's. Instead pupils were crestfallen and sensed they had "failed." Similarly, when listening examination questions require checking off multiple-choice boxes, they leave no room for another response that might be equally valid in a wider musical context. Both Amez (example iii) and Tom (example iv) reveal a curiosity and a thirst for a deeper engagement within a richer context of learning, going well beyond the reductive labeling of style and period. They want to explore meaning in a much wider and deeper sense. This is an ethical question. Forms of musical knowing that shut down learning and disallow alternative interpretations are doing violence to the pupil.

# ALLOWING FOR "THE PRESENCE OF INFINITY BREAKING THE CLOSED CIRCLE OF TOTALITY"

The examples from classroom observation and pupil interviews outlined in this chapter reveal instances in which the nature of musical knowing has been shaped by assessment processes higher up in the school, so that public examinations dictate first- and second-year curricula (S1 and S2 for twelve- and thirteen-year-olds in Scotland). The exam board's drive toward the standardization of assessment processes between examination subjects and an ever-increasing pressure for more efficient ways of assessing and marking have led to an intolerance for complexity and the corralling of rich musical knowledge and experience into narrow categories that become meaningless, alienating pupils from their own lived musical encounters in the classroom.

A wealth of riches has been brought to light in terms of pupils' resourcefulness in subverting these totalizing practices and in their agential actions in encountering the Other despite school structures. The challenge from this Levinasian reorientation is to rethink assessment to celebrate these abilities/capacities, such as Kirsty's perception, analysis, and intentionality when commenting on Liam's mash-up, or Tom's desire for a deeper engagement with music making, in which superficiality is eschewed in a richer contextual setting. These are complex and unquantifiable parameters that rely on the professional judgment of deeply engaged class music teachers, who in their "practices of facing" and "putting the world in common" will be "doing no violence" to pupils.

## NOTES

1. There are some parallels between the thinking of Emmanuel Levinas and that of Martin Buber. They knew each other as associates and friends, and Levinas was undoubtedly influenced by the older philosopher, but his "ethics as first philosophy" goes radically further than Buber does; for instance, for Levinas the relation of self to the Other is one of unending responsibility, whereas for Buber the I-Thou relationship is always reciprocal.
2. "Being" is a term established by Heidegger. Levinas's use of it is an answer to Heidegger's development of the term in his own philosophy.
3. Alfonso Lingis, Levinas's translator, notes that with the author's permission he has translated *autrui*, the personal other, the *you*, with a capital—Other—while *autre* remains "other" (Levinas, 1969, p. 24).

4. Levinas deliberately employs terms used in the writings of Heidegger, whose pupil Levinas was but whose thinking he turned against when Heidegger's philosophy became associated with Nazi ideology. Levinas sought to "go beyond" Heidegger's thinking in order to reorient Western philosophy.
5. "The presence of the Other, or expression, source of all signification, is not contemplated as an intelligible essence, but is heard as language, and thereby is effectuated exteriorly" (Levinas, 1969, p. 297).

# REFERENCES

Ball, S. J. (2003). The teacher's soul and the terrors of performativity. *Journal of Education Policy*, 18(2), 215–18.

Bauman, Z. (1993). *Postmodern ethics*. Malden, MA: Wiley-Blackwell.

Beauvais, M. (2011). Assessment: A question of responsibility. UNIVEST. Retrieved from http://dugi-doc.udg.edu/bitstream/handle/10256/3592/Beauvais_en.pdf?sequence=2

Biesta, G. (2004). Education, accountability, and the ethical demand: Can the democratic potential of accountability be regained? *Education Theory*, 54(3), 233–50.

Bowman, W. (2001). Music as ethical encounter. The Charles Leonhard Lecture, School of Music, University if Illinois, Urbana-Champaign. *Bulletin of the Council for Research in Music Education*, 151, 11–20.

Burnard, P. (2011). Creativity, performativity, and educational standards: Conflicting or productive tensions in music education in England? In P. G. Woodford (Ed.), *Rethinking standards for the twenty first-century: New realities, new challenges, new propositions*. Studies in music from the University of Western Ontario, 23. London, ON: University of Ontario.

Elliott, D. J., & Silverman, M. (2015). *Music matters: A philosophy of music education* (2nd ed.). New York: Oxford University Press.

Fielding, M. (2007). The human cost and intellectual property of high performance schooling: Radical philosophy, John MacMurray and the remaking of person-centred education. *Journal of Educational Policy*, 22(4), 383–409.

Ford, D. F. (1999). *Self and salvation: Being transformed*. Cambridge, UK: Cambridge University Press.

Higgins, L. (2007). Acts of hospitality: The community in community music. *Music Education Research*, 9(2), 281–91.

Jourdan, K. (2012). Towards an ethical music education? Looking through the lens of Levinas. *Music Education Research*, 14(3), 381–99.

Jourdan, K. (2015). *Through the lens of Levinas: An ethnographically-informed case study of pupils' "practices of facing" in music-making* (Unpublished doctoral thesis). University of Cambridge.

Katz, C. E. (2012). Turning toward the Other. In S. Davidson & Diane Perpich (Eds.), *Totality and Infinity at 50* (pp. 209–26). Pittsburgh, PA: Duquesne University Press.

Levinas, E. (1969). *Totality and infinity: An essay in exteriority*. A. Lingis (Trans.). Pittsburgh, PA: Duquesne University Press.

Levinas, E. (1987). Philosophy and the idea of infinity. In A. Lingis (Trans.), *Collected philosophical papers* (pp. 109–26). Dordrecht, Netherlands: Martinus Nijhoff.

Levinas, E. (1988). The paradox of morality, an interview conducted by T. Wright, P. Hughes and A. Ainley. In R. Bernasconi & D. Wood (Eds.), A. Benjamin & T. Wright (Trans.), *The provocation of Levinas: Rethinking the Other* (pp. 168–80). London: Routledge.

Lyotard, J. F. (1984). *The postmodern condition. A report on knowledge.* G. Bennington & B. Massumi (Trans.). Manchester, UK: Manchester University Press.

Odendaal, A., Knakkene, O. T., Nikkanen, H. M., & Vakeya, L. (2014). What's with the K? Exploring the implications of Christopher Small's "musicking" for general music education. *Music Education Research, 16*(2), 162–75.

Regelski, T. A. (2016). *A brief introduction to a philosophy of music and music education as social praxis.* New York: Routledge.

Small, C. (1998). *Musicking—The meanings of performing and listening.* Hanover, NH: Wesleyan University Press.

Standish, P. (2008). Levinas and the language of the curriculum. In D. Egea-Kuehne (Ed.), *Levinas and education: At the intersection of faith and reason* (pp. 55–66). Abingdon, UK: Routledge.

CHAPTER 4

..................................................................................................

# THE PRIMACY OF EXPERIENCE

*phenomenology, embodiment, and*
*assessments in music education*

..................................................................................................

## ANDREA SCHIAVIO

ASSESSMENT practices in music education usually take a variety of different forms, from informal methods, such as observations and subjective impressions, to more formal measurements based on structured performance tasks (Barkley, 2006). Generally speaking, it is often assumed that music teachers consider assessment a positive tool to enhance learning (Hill, 1999). One reason for this belief is that grading systems may help to motivate and "discipline" students (Carter, 1986), thus improving both their musical and nonmusical skills. As reported by Russell and Austin (2010), however, a number of contrasting elements are currently making it difficult to engage in a much-needed renewal of the techniques and concepts that lie at the heart of assessment practices. For example, while the number of music students is growing, this does not always result in more teaching time being available to dedicate to them (Tracy, 2002), giving rise to problematic situations for grading practices (Kotora, 2005).

Among such problematic situations, a core issue emerges when trying to provide assessments of musical abilities "away from narrow definitions, which tend to be associated with assessment models derived from formal music education, and toward broader, more open definitions, often associated with traditional, vernacular, popular and other 'world' music learning practices" (Green, 2001, p. 201). In other words, it may be argued that in current music education environments—in order to monitor the progress of many students—we rely too heavily on formalized methods, ignore more personalized or situated approaches, and thus often risk objectifying human musicality. Such concerns have been shared by a number of authors (Elliott, 1995; Elliott & Silverman, 2015; Small, 1998), suggesting that too often various important aspects of one's musical life—including the development of personal preferences, compositive abilities, and informal playing—are downplayed (see the chapter by van der Schyff in this volume). As "most music teachers in schools—public and private music schools—are trained in Classical music, and school music curricula have typically favored Classical music" (Regelski, 2009, p. 4), it comes as no surprise that Western classical music is considered a superior form compared to more informal traditions. And since classical music has been associated with formalized assessment methods, it could be argued that its popularity among teaching settings has contributed to creating a tension between "subjective" and "objective" strategies adopted by teachers to grade their students, whereby the latter are privileged.

In this chapter I maintain that to implement new and improved assessment practices, one should go beyond such a dichotomy. In doing so, I draw on recent conceptual tools that have emerged in cognitive sciences and philosophy of mind and explore their application to the domain of music. In particular, I consider the possibility that a more phenomenologically oriented framework, enriched with insights from so-called embodied and enactive approaches to cognition (Gallagher, 2005; Thompson, 2007; Varela, Thompson, & Rosch, 1991), may inspire a more balanced methodology to conduct assessments in music education and situate them in a broader context beyond grading decisions only. This last point resonates with warnings from Noddings (1999, 2012), who asks teachers to "enrich their teachings and offer multiple opportunities for students to make connections with the great existential questions as well as questions of current social life" (Noddings, 1999, p. 215).

The relevance of phenomenology for music research is well established (see later discussion on the phenomenological body; see, e.g., Ferrara, 1984, 1986; Holmes & Holmes, 2013). Traditionally, however, this perspective has been accompanied by a general anti-objectivistic stance, which resulted in the development of qualitative research methods (see Bresler, 1994, 1995a, 1995b) often thought to be in open contraposition with quantitative research. In fact, it may be argued that the primacy of experience posited by phenomenologists goes even deeper than such contraposition of "objective" and "subjective" (Schiavio & Høffding, 2015). Within the context of music education, then, a detailed study of experience may provide the tools necessary to consider pedagogical settings, norms, and theories from a "situated" point of view, one that admits no discontinuities between "inner" experience and "outer" world. In other words, as phenomenology posits no objective distinction between the world and us because we *are* fundamentally already in the world (Heidegger, 1962; Merleau-Ponty, 1945), its adoption could help us explore music education from a different perspective. In this view, the traditional separation of mind, world, and body—subjective, abstract, experience versus objective, physical objects—may not hold up anymore, as these categories all play together to co-constitute our cognitive life in a meaningful and creative way (Thelen, 2000). I return to this issue later in the chapter. For now, it should be noted that I am not implying that *qualitative* research is mistaken, or that it does not provide necessary answers for my investigations. Rather, my main interest is to show that phenomenology (linked, as I show, with recent developments in cognitive science) may help to explore the possibility of an experience-based approach to music education and assessments, without generating an unsolvable tension with other (*quantitative*) methodologies. For example, by integrating first- and third-person perspectives to explore human experience in a holistic way (Colombetti, 2014; Schilbach et al., 2013; see also Varela, 1996), modern (critical) neuroscience aims to face such a challenge using insights from phenomenology, theoretical research in embodied cognition, and tools from traditional experimental methodologies (Slaby, 2015; Slaby & Gallagher, 2015). A number of scientists thus see phenomenology as a useful tool to understand and interpret new discoveries and to inform empirical research more generally. Although I do not explore this in detail, I suggest that the new conceptual tools this work introduces can be similarly developed in line with interdisciplinary scholarship in music education. As a result, it may help researchers and music teachers to shed new light on assessment studies.

In the next section of the chapter, I focus on the phenomenology of the body to show how a deeper understanding of our concrete "embodied" activities can shape new ways to study music education and musical experiences. In the third section the issue of integrating "subjective" and "objective" categories is given main relevance, drawing in particular from the recent reorientation in the cognitive sciences that have given rise to an "embodied approach" to cognition. If educators want to integrate *living* and *lived* experiences as valuable sources for assessments, then exploring such an approach is fundamental. It is also expected that conceptual clarifications of the main embodied concepts—such as bodily self-regulation, action-perception coupling, and intersubjective interaction—not only will help us investigate assessment studies from a new perspective, but will also provide new insights that are relevant to the philosophy and praxis of music education.

In the concluding section I briefly discuss assessment research in music pedagogy through the principles just discussed, hoping to show how traditional methodologies may be inadequate when describing (and trying to generate precise predictions concerning) various aspects of one's musical life. As I argue, a mixed approach rooted in phenomenology and embodied cognition, which fosters open communication, descriptive reflections, and intersubjectivity, may provide a more effective supporting framework for music assessment practices. In sum, I hope to encourage music researchers and scholars to go beyond the subjective-objective dichotomy briefly presented here to provide some initial insights for the development of new and fruitful ways to understand and redefine musical education and assessment practices in a way that is more ecologically valid and closer to what musical experience really entails.

# THE PHENOMENOLOGICAL BODY

Phenomenology is a philosophical tradition that sees *experience* as the main source of significance of our "being-in-the-world" (see Gallagher & Zahavi, 2008). As such, phenomenological research is interested in understanding the structures of consciousness through a detailed analysis of what first-person experience entails. Scholars working within this tradition are usually concerned with how experience manifests itself and with what determines experiential activity. Is there only "conscious" experience, for example? With regard to this issue, Heidegger (1962) famously invites us to consider activities such as walking, which do not require any kind of (thematic or focused) awareness. Indeed, usually we just walk; we do not think about walking or create a propositional statement in our minds about such activity. But we nevertheless *experience* our walking in certain ways: we move with and around other persons, we reach the concert hall we wanted to go, and we do so while we can explicitly think about totally unrelated situations, songs, objects, persons, and so forth (see Johnson, 2007). Similar observations were made by Husserl (1989), who maintained that our perceptual activity allows us to be only *implicitly* aware of the multiplicity of things happening at the margins of our attentive processing. This means that "intentionality"—that is, the "aboutness" of our mental activity—comes in different shades and forms.

But while it is obvious that we experience things in different ways, it is not so obvious that *extraneural* and *nonorganic* factors may take an active part in constituting such experience (Colombetti, 2014). By "extraneural" categories, I mean the body and its dynamic sensorimotor activities. Indeed, immersed in the bodily based dynamics of action, we walk and experience walking through our bodies, as if we *offload* our cognitive processes into them. In a sense, we think through our bodies and are led by them in walking; the body, in other words, offers an extraordinary combination of factors that shape our behavior, thoughts, and mental life more generally. Consider for example the fascinating work by Susan Goldin-Meadow (2003). Her research captures how human gestures convey information that is inseparable from speech and cognitive processes. She has explored their role in the acquisition and development of skills (Goldin-Meadow, 2014). Visuospatial thinking, indeed, may display the potential to change thoughts in listeners and speakers, offering a unique tool to reach an understanding of problems not yet evident from speech.

When it comes to "nonorganic" factors, good examples can be found in how unanimated objects may help us achieve certain cognitive tasks (Clark & Chalmers, 1998); tools, instruments, and other ecologically embedded props can therefore be considered as *participating* in—and *co-constituting*—our mental life (see also Anderson, Richardson, & Chemero, 2012). A blind man, for example, can use his cane to explore the environment as if it were part of his body. The cane becomes "incorporated" (Merleau-Ponty, 1945), as it provides a unique way to make sense of the environment immediately. Cognition—at least in a certain sense—*extends* through the artifact into the world without any inferential mediation. In the case of music, this idea can be explored using the following vignette. Imagine a musician who is asked to improvise a short piece of music in order to familiarize herself with the features of a particular instrument (say, a new guitar with a different kind of strings than what she is used to). How would her experience change when shifting from the concrete exploration of the instrument—its actual playing—to a theoretical study of the nuances of the guitar, such as the reading of a review written by another performer? We would expect her creativity to be somehow boosted by her sensorimotor engagement with the guitar (Menin & Schiavio, 2012). Playing with sounds, touching the strings, discovering promising techniques—these may indeed provide the amateur with a new range of possibilities that only her concrete experience with the instrument could afford. In a sense, her creativity is distributed across her brain (e.g., contributing in generating predictions about the sounds), her body (e.g., developing certain actions specific for the determination of a preferred sound), and the guitar (e.g., displaying certain physical features that could be acted upon by the amateur). It can thus be argued that this network consisting of brain, body, and guitar *constitutes* the performer's creative experience. The guitar, in this vignette, is not only a tool that could just be "represented" in the head, or a simple object "out there"; it is rather a meaningful web of complex and rich affordative structures that becomes part of the learner's embodied cognitive system thanks to her bodily power of action.

Generally, we could say that bodily activity shapes the way in which we make sense of the world without necessarily recruiting high-level forms of cognition (Hutto & Myin, 2013). The phenomenological and biological dimensions of the body, indeed, are not just mediators between an objective reality "out there" and our inner realms of experience. Rather, experience itself may be considered an emerging property of the interactive dynamics involving brains, bodies, and environment—a property that cannot be captured by a rigid distinction between "subjective" and "objective" sensibilities. This is best understood when considering that perceiving through our bodies, and acting and being open to the constantly changing demands and perturbations of the environment in which we are embedded, is the condition for the possibilities of mental operations, not the other way around. From birth we are immersed in the changing dynamics of the world's openness, and we constantly negotiate meaning with it from the very beginning of our lives. In light of these observations, it may be argued that positing boundaries between "objective" and "subjective" as two distinct categories may not be the best solution. Consider the following passage:

> I can therefore take my place, through the medium of my body as the potential source of familiar actions, in my environment conceived as a set of manipulanda and without, moreover, envisaging my body or my surrounding as objects in the Kantian sense [i.e. as the objects of a Newtonian "scientific" universe]. There is my arm seen as sustaining familiar acts, my body as giving rise to determinate action having a field or scope known to me in advance ["practically" known, by the body itself], there are my surroundings as a collection of possible points upon which this bodily action may operate.
> (Merleau-Ponty, 1945, p. 105, quoted in Keat, 1982, p. 8)

Our bodies provide us with an immediate, noninferential access to the world. This primacy of bodily based experience is now also well understood by modern neuroscience, which has been increasingly integrating the body and its sensorimotor dynamics into the study of cognitive processes more broadly (e.g., Rizzolatti & Sinigaglia, 2008).

Several recent contributions in music education are in line with such embodied perspectives (Borgo, 2007; Elliott & Silverman, 2015; Karlsen, 2011; Regelski, 2016; Schiavio & Cummins, 2015; van der Schyff, 2015; Westerlund, 2002). The roles of the body and technology are, accordingly, increasingly emerging as a constitutive part of teaching and learning music (Desmet, Nijs, Demey, Lesaffre, & Leman, 2012; Nijs, Coussement, et al., 2012; Nijs, Moens, et al., 2012). This resonates, for example, with the *praxial* approach to music education first developed by Elliott (1995) and further expanded by a number of other scholars in a variety of ways (Bowman, 1998, 2004; Regelski, 1998). Such approaches see music as not just something to be acquired and practiced to achieve a particular goal (i.e., its "consumption"). Instead, here music becomes something dependent on a number of other *experiential* aspects defined by our complex ethical and social ways of "being-in-the-world" (Elliott & Silverman, 2015). Looking beyond mere practical engagement and consumption, this framework represents a turning point in music education. Indeed, as Westerlund and Juntonen (2005) remind us, "music has been widely [...] accepted as a matter of cognitive understanding, or special intelligence, instead of flesh-and-blood experience in which there is a continuum between various aspects of experience" (pp. 114–15). A praxial approach to music education is thus a welcome alternative to previous traditional approaches, as it develops a more holistic view of experience that embraces the complexity of life and mind (Thompson, 2007). Its relevance for assessment practices, however, remains largely unexplored.

In the following sections, therefore, such an alternative view is taken into consideration with regard to assessment studies. First, however, I briefly consider how approaches that focus on the relevance of the living body in or for cognition integrate neuroscientific, psychological, and phenomenological insights that may help to expand musical research in new ways (Magee & Stewart, 2015; Reybrouck & Brattico, 2015; Schiavio & Altenmüller, 2015). Indeed, research by Leman (2007), Reybrouck (2005), Krueger (2009, 2014a, 2014b), Pelinski (2005), and many others has contributed to a new embodied account of music cognition that has drastically changed the way in which human musicality is understood (Schiavio, 2012, 2014). Conceiving of the body as a source for meaning making that is *not* separated from—but instead is dynamically continuous with—higher level cognitive processes and the world around us, such contributions provide a valid alternative to traditional perspectives on musical experience. Such "traditional" perspectives are often based on cognitive models that may downplay the body and its meaning for cognition. More specifically, because these older approaches often reduce music cognition to brain (or mental) mechanisms acting on incoming signals from the world "out there," they usually omit the living human body of the listener. Instead, embodied approaches make clear how sensorimotor contingencies such as, for example, musical expertise (Lahav, Saltzman, & Schlaug, 2007), gestures (Acitores, 2011), bodily feelings (Krueger, 2011), and intersubjective interactions (Moran, 2014), among others, can shape our musical experience *directly*. In the next section I explain in more detail how this could be so by introducing the "enactive" paradigm, which pushes the embodied thesis even further. In addition, such a perspective may allow us to apply phenomenological and embodied concepts, which are central to this discussion of assessment practices, without remaining committed to a subjective-objective dichotomy.

# BEYOND "OBJECTIVE" AND "SUBJECTIVE"

To problematize the foundations of assessment studies in music education and explore a way to rethink and implement such practices beyond the phenomenological concerns raised in the previous section, it is necessary to examine the explanatory power of moving beyond notions of "objective" and "subjective" in more detail. Doing so, however, is a tricky business; it requires embracing three main principles at the base of the embodied approach to cognition—self-regulation, sensorimotor coupling, and intersubjective interaction—which in recent years have helped a growing number of researchers develop conceptual tools to understand cognition and life in a general sense (Varela et al., 1991). Silverman (2012) explored some of the embodied and enactive notions discussed later in this chapter in the broader context of care ethics, selfhood, and education, providing an important contribution that anticipates many of the issues the present chapter wants to raise. In this section I aim to complement her work and extend the discussion to the context of assessment studies, going even deeper by emphasizing phenomenology and embodiment—through the three main principles already mentioned—as fundamental categories to conceptualize, describe, and possibly reform such practices.

*Self-regulation* is an important aspect of our lives, with particular regard to our own bodies and to the way they are involved in exchanging energy and co-creating information with the world (Colombetti, 2003). As living systems, indeed, the degree of complexity of our biological structures plays a fundamental role in regulating and controlling the thermodynamic processes required to maintain the organism's life and constant openness to the world (Thompson, 2007). The workings of such complex interacting networks of chemical, neural, emotional, and metabolic activities, it has been argued, are not hierarchically organized in a top-down/bottom-up fashion (Kelso, 1995), but are rather dynamic and realized through mechanisms involving the entire living system (Varela, 1979; Weber, 2001). In this sense, no real boundaries between *subjective* and *objective* aspects of life seem to be relevant for such self-regulatory processes to take place. By responding to the perturbation of the environment, we basically engage in a meaningful coupling with the world on different levels and timescales.

Music, as a human activity, is a particular type of such brain-body-world interplay (Schiavio, 2012, 2014). With this in mind, the focus on self-regulation may become an interesting aspect of the way in which music is taught. Excellent work in this direction has been conducted by McPherson (2012) and colleagues (McPherson, Nielsen, & Renwick, 2014; see also McPherson & Zimmerman, 2011; Kupers, van Dijk, van Geert, & McPherson, 2015). Adopting theoretical tools such as dynamic system models and insights from qualitative research, such studies investigate autonomy, self-determination, and self-regulations occurring between students and teachers bidirectionally. For assessment practices, the lessons we can draw from such work are multilayered. Music learning should not focus on the improvement of a given behavioral output only. Rather, as an activity rooted in the dynamics of action, it deals with the complex web of interactions among worldly conditions (e.g., the music teachers), the brain (e.g., by giving rise to particular neural settings apt to regulate certain music-related movements, judgments, representations, and anticipations), and the body (e.g., in developing adequate muscular support to perform music). As such, grading strategies should address intra- and inter-individual changes on different timescales, including dyadic interactions with the teacher, the instruments, and (eventually) peers. Integrating insights from different views and inspiring open dialogue between students and teachers, self-regulative aspects of musical learning may be taken into consideration in improving assessment systems.

Consider now the second principle of the embodied paradigm, *sensorimotor coupling*. This concept helps capture how living systems act in and perceive the world they inhabit. In particular, a number of scholars argue that the mastery of particular sensorimotor skills actively shapes perceptual experience (O'Regan & Noë, 2001a, 2001b). In this view, the body becomes fundamental in providing us with the tools necessary to make sense of the world; through its neural, emotional, and muscular, activity, we participate in co-constituting the environment by negotiating meanings and patterns of embodied actions. The world shows up in certain ways for us, depending on our degree of biological complexity, without necessarily recruiting sophisticated (high-level) cognitive processes:

> It takes no thought or intellectual skill to know that to bring the item off to the left better into view, you must turn your head to the left…, [or] when you hear a sound as being on the left you don't need to think about which way to turn your head in order to orientate toward the sound.…You do need to think about how to maneuver a couch to squeeze it through a small passage. But you do not need, in the same way, to think about how to maneuver your body to squeeze it through the doorway. Just perceiving the doorway as having certain spatial qualities is perceiving it as enabling, requiring, or permitting certain kinds of movements with respect to it.
>
> (Noë, 2004, p. 89)

Such claims have been variously endorsed also within the musical domain. For example, drawing from recent empirical and theoretical work in neuroscience (Bangert & Altenmüller, 2003), development (Gerson, Schiavio, Timmers, & Hunnius, 2015; Phillips-Silver & Trainor, 2005), and musicology (Clarke, 2005; Reybrouck, 2006), a number of today's scholars advocate an embodied approach to music experience (see Matyja & Schiavio, 2013). As Krueger (2011) elegantly puts it:

> Sensorimotor knowledge consists in the practical understanding that modulations of bodily movement and attentional focusing affect sensory change. For instance, when we perceive a visual scene, movements of the head or body change the way that occluded objects (e.g., part of a bush obscured by a tree standing in front of it) gradually reveal themselves as I move closer to or around them. We possess similar knowledge of how bodily movements and attentional modulations shape the

character and content of musical experience. Rudimentary sensorimotor knowledge is thus the implicit, practical understanding that, as an embodied agent, I possess the sensorimotor skills needed to secure experiential access to different features of my world by using my body in different ways. Being sensitive to the sensorimotor contingencies governing my relation to perceptual objects is what it means to be a "skilled" perceiver. (p. 12)

Sensitivity to such patterns of actions—governing musical experience—is apparently left behind in traditional grading systems. A detailed account of movements, actions, and expressive gestures may instead inspire a richer understanding of how learners acquire and develop musical skills, thus providing an apt counterpoint to more *objectivist* approaches to assessments in music education (see also Laroche & Kaddouch, 2014). Indeed, a description of such embodied activity may be elaborated in a dialogical way among students and teachers (Duckworth, 1996, 1997, 2001), opening up new phenomenological accounts of how certain movements lead to richer musical and learning experiences (van der Schyff, 2015; see also van der Schyff's chapter in this volume). Indeed, grading systems should take advantage of the actual reflexive, interactive, and embodied experiences of students (Brookfield, 1987; Dewey, 1938/1991), thus becoming more flexible, fluid, observational, and open to constructive interactions with students and peers. Of course, expecting students to flourish in a classroom poses a challenge to the codification of the single individual's musical parameters often associated with assessment practices (see Bruner, 1996).

This leads us to the third principle of the embodied paradigm: *intersubjective interaction*. Developments in recent years have brought forth a radical reconsideration of the cognitive processes in play during social interactions (De Jaegher & Di Paolo, 2007). From a traditional focus on how a single individual would *react* to a particular event, recent embodied accounts tend to emphasize the concrete—gestural, coordinated, emotional, and so forth—dynamics of interactions as the main explanatory unit (De Jaegher, 2009). Intersubjectivity, it is argued, is not simply reducible to a stimulus-response model, but requires a more nuanced approach, which takes into consideration what happens in real time among individuals as the interaction unfolds (Moran, 2014). This kind of dynamic coupling may reveal how positing boundaries between *internal* states of the agent and *external* features of the world cannot fully capture the actual cognitive complexity of living beings. When applied to pedagogical contexts, this idea may sound radical. How could we ensure the development of individual skills and understandings if teachers emphasized interactive contexts and collaborative praxis outside formal tuitions? Stated differently, how could we enhance learning experiences without studying the single unit, meaning the learner? Such concerns may be challenged when considering music learning itself as a participatory event irreducible to the individual's mental or physiological state (Schiavio & Cummins, 2015). A learner is not a "black box" with no connections with the world in which he or she is embedded. He or she is in fact already historically, physically, socially, and culturally "present" to his or her world, a world that should be accounted for when engaging in musical classes. From this it could be argued that learning music—flourishing as individual musical identities and engaging in meaningful and exploratory musical practices—is fundamentally an intersubjective activity, because the meanings enacted across such a range of practices are distributed in a phenomenologically rich social environment that cannot be ignored.

In this view, the focus on intersubjectivity should be embedded within musical grading practices. Green (2001) describes how learners can "assess themselves throughout the learning process, in relation to their progression measured against their own past and projected performance, that of their peers and that of the models they are copying" (p. 209). While she is mostly concerned here with informal learning among popular musicians, an implementation of such a model in classrooms may depend on a number of variables concerning the style of music and the ability of the teachers to provide a safe environment in which open communication among peers is ensured. Introducing new transformational and flexible learning modalities (e.g., peer-to-peer learning) should thus be reflected by appropriate grading systems that do not decontextualize the learners from their active, meaningful, and participatory involvement with music. Beyond their ability to respond "correctly" to given demands associated with standardized grading scales, music learners should be concerned with negotiating open and dialogical communication with teachers and peers.

# RETHINKING ASSESSMENTS?

The domain of musical learning has been resonating for years with a very traditional model of skills development, the one suggested by psychologists Fitts and Posner (1967). For them, three stages are required to learn a particular (musical) skill: (1) the *cognitive* stage, in which conscious attention is required; (2) the *associative* stage, at which the activity is refined; and (3) the *autonomous* stage, when the skill becomes automatic (quoted in Rink, 2002, pp. 104–5). Here, learning to play an instrument is described as cognitive ability that depends on how the single individual processes adequate information "in the head" before putting it into practice through actions. As such, "paper and pencil" assessments may be useful to monitor the progressive development of such information, as it slowly becomes automatic. However, as we have seen, this may not be the whole story. Skill development should be understood as an emergent property of the learner's sense-making ability to interact with the world, a learner who enacts a meaningful repertoire of actions in constant adaptation with the changing environment and its properties. In this sense, learning occurs as the musical activity unfolds and is thus best described in nonlinear, dynamic, and interactive terms. Such methodological insights and conceptual tools—emerging from phenomenological philosophy, observational practices, and shared and open communication between students and teaches—may provide a valuable resource to revise traditional assessment practices. The adaptive flexibility between students and teachers (described, for example, by the ability to engage with the needs of each student) is thus rooted in a critically reflective approach that goes beyond standard curricula. In particular, the revitalization of established music learning practices through relational and cooperative music praxis may help transform pedagogical environments in places of "salience" (Elliott & Silverman, 2015). Students should be encouraged to develop their musical skills together without the worry of being judged on the basis of their musical "outcome." Through participatory musical activities with teachers and peers, open questions can be posed, and aspects of music and culture can be discussed. This rich experiential context promotes a sense of shared responsibility that decenters the focus from the individual to the collectivity (Schiavio, van der Schyff, Gande, & Kruse-Weber, 2018), stimulating new possibilities for meaning making and assessment. By reshaping grading systems in light of such a mixed approach, the development of the learner, his or her enjoyment, personal preferences, and musical choices will be enhanced—as the relevance of phenomenology across a vast range of domains (van Manen, 2014) and embodied perspectives on music cognition (Reybrouck, 2005) seem to confirm. Going beyond codified pedagogies and assessment practices may also deepen teachers' understandings of the transformative possibilities of music for the lives of the students, enacting relational autonomy rather than conformity.

Embracing the open and reflective communication described here can help students enjoy their musical experiences more and more and help teachers develop more appropriate tools to foster a phenomenological attitude in music classes (van der Schyff, 2016). Developing such transformative, open, and adaptive attitudes may facilitate the shift from most consumption-based approaches to music education to a pedagogy that emphasizes the flexible properties and processes emerging from the growing awareness of each student's own musical potential. Such awareness, as I have argued, may emerge in the complex interactive dynamics fostered by phenomenological insights, and further reform the grading systems currently adopted by music schools. Taking exams throughout a period of tuition, for example, could compromise the reflective and world-making potentials through which phenomenologically inspired learners can examine the structure of their directed experience. This is different from judging retrospectively a particular style of performance—which often happens in current assessment practices— where no agentic attitude seems to be promoted. A context-based educational system can replace or, better still, integrate assessment practices with a more nuanced approach based on exploring body-kinetic and intersubjective interactions (Sheets-Johnstone, 1999, 2010, 2012), which goes well beyond the reification of musical skills.

Taken together, the rejection of the subjective-objective dualism, and an awareness of embodied principles of bodily self-regulation, sensorimotor coupling, intersubjective interactions, and the resources stemming from a phenomenological enquiry, provide the tools we need to reframe traditional notions of "cognitive-musical phenomena"— including music learning described reductively as a measurable "information-processing" event. Together with these factors, and viewed as *cognitive ecosystems*, music learning can be understood as an open and flexible activity codetermined by diverse embodied and ecological factors connected in recurrent fashion (Hutchins, 2014). As the latter notion implies, traditional forms of assessment may fail to capture such rich webs of interactivities, thus downplaying the world-making potential of the learners and the capacity of teachers to foster in students a phenomenological and creative attitude.

I have suggested that a more nuanced approach to formative and summative music assessments—one rooted in open communication, reflectiveness, and direct descriptions and cooperation between students and teachers—may inspire a much-needed reconsideration of and challenge to long-standing notions of musical abilities as "measurable" categories. While the development of such new music assessment approaches goes beyond the limitations of this chapter, I imagine that a mixed approach of interviews, self-reports, and open questionnaires may inspire a move toward this way of music learning, enhancing the development of knowledge sharing through embodied action and open interactivity.

## ACKNOWLEDGMENTS

I am grateful to Dylan van der Schyff, Eugenia Costa-Giomi, and the editors of this volume for their useful comments and suggestions. I also thank Ryosuke Yokoe for proofreading the manuscript. Any remaining error is only mine. This work is supported by a Lise Meitner Postdoctoral Fellowship granted by the Austrian Science Fund (FWF), project number M2148.

## REFERENCES

Acitores, A. P. (2011). Towards a theory of proprioception as a bodily basis for consciousness in music. In D. Clarke & E. Clarke (Eds.), *Music and consciousness: Philosophical, psychological, and cultural perspectives* (pp. 215–30). New York: Oxford University Press.

Anderson, M. L., Richardson, M. L., & Chemero, A. (2012). Eroding the boundaries of cognition: Implications of embodiment. *Topics in Cognitive Science, 4,* 717–30.

Bangert, M., & Altenmüller, E. (2003). Mapping perception to action in piano practice: A longitudinal DC-EEG study. *BMC Neuroscience, 4*(26). doi:10.1186/1471-2202-4-26

Barkley, M. (2006). *Assessment of the national standards for music education: A study of elementary general music teacher attitudes and practices* (M.M. dissertation). Wayne State University, Michigan (Publication No. AAT 1439697).

Borgo, D. (2007). Free jazz in the classroom: An ecological approach to music education. *Jazz Perspectives, 1*(1), 61–88.

Bowman, W. (1998). *Philosophical perspectives on music.* New York: Oxford University Press.

Bowman, W. (2004). Cognition and the body: Perspectives from music education. In L. Bresler (Ed.), *Knowing bodies, moving minds: Toward embodied teaching and learning* (pp. 29–50). Dordrecht, The Netherlands: Kluwer Academic Press.

Bresler, L. (1994). Zooming in on the qualitative paradigm in art education: Educational criticism, ethnography, and action research. *Visual Arts Research, 20*(1), 1–19.

Bresler, L. (1995a). Ethnography, phenomenology, and action research in music education. *Quarterly Journal of Music Teaching and Learning, 6*(3), 6–18.

Bresler, L. (1995b). Ethical issues in qualitative research methodology. *Bulletin of the Council for Research in Music Education, 126,* 29–41.

Brookfield, S. D. (1987). *Developing critical thinkers: Challenging adults to explore alternative ways of thinking and acting*. San Francisco, CA: Jossey-Bass.

Bruner, J. (1996). *The culture of education*. Cambridge, MA: Harvard University Press.

Carter, K. G. (1986). The status of vocal/general music programs in Oklahoma elementary schools. *Dissertation Abstracts International, 47*, 3349.

Clark, A., & Chalmers, D. (1998). The extended mind. *Analyses, 58*(1), 7–19.

Clarke, E. F. (2005). *Ways of listening: An ecological approach to the perception of musical meaning*. Oxford: Oxford University Press.

Colombetti, G. (2003). Complexity as a new framework for emotion theories. *Logic and Philosophy of Science, 1*(1), 1–16.

Colombetti, G. (2014). *The feeling body: Affective science meets the enactive mind*. Cambridge, MA: MIT Press.

De Jaegher, H. (2009). Social understanding through direct perception? Yes, by interacting. *Consciousness and Cognition, 18*(2), 535–42.

De Jaegher, H., & Di Paolo, E. A. (2007). Participatory sense-making: An enactive approach to social cognition. In *Phenomenology and the Cognitive Sciences, 6*(4), 485–507.

Desmet, F., Nijs, L., Demey, M., Lesaffre, M., & Leman, M. (2012). Assessing a clarinet player's performer gestures in relation to locally intended musical targets. *Journal of New Music Research, 41*, 31–48.

Dewey, J. (1938/1991). *Logic: The theory of inquiry*. In J. A. Boydson (Ed.), *John Dewey: The Later Works, 1925-1953* (Vol. 12, pp. 1–527). Carbondale, IL: Southern Illinois University Press.

Duckworth, E. (1996). The having of wonderful ideas. In E. Duckworth (Ed.), *The having of wonderful ideas and other essays on teaching and learning* (pp. 1–14). New York: Teachers College Press.

Duckworth, E. (1997). *Teacher to teacher: Learning from each other*. New York: Teachers College Press.

Duckworth, E. (2001). *Tell me more: Listening to learners explain*. New York: Teachers College Press.

Elliott, D. J. (1995). *Music matters: A new philosophy of music education*. New York: Oxford University Press.

Elliott, D. J., & Silverman, M. (2015). *Music matters: A philosophy of music education* (2nd ed.). New York: Oxford University Press.

Ferrara, L. (1984). Phenomenology as a tool for musical analysis. *Musical Quarterly, 70*(3), 355–73.

Ferrara, L. (1986). Music in general studies: A look at content and method. *College Music Symposium, 26*, 122–29.

Fitts, P. M., & Posner. M. J. (1967). *Human performance*. Belmont, CA: Brooks/Cole Publishing.

Gallagher, S. (2005). *How the body shapes the mind*. New York: Oxford University Press.

Gallagher, S., & Zahavi, D. (2008). *The phenomenological mind*. New York: Routledge.

Gerson, S., Schiavio, A., Timmers, R., & Hunnius, S. (2015). Active drumming experience increases infants' sensitivity to audiovisual synchronicity during observed drumming actions. *PLoS ONE, 10*(6), e0130960.

Goldin-Meadow, S. (2003). *Hearing gestures. How our hands help us think*. Cambridge, MA: Harvard University Press.

Goldin-Meadow, S. (2014). Widening the lens: What the manual modality reveals about language, learning, and cognition. *Philosophical Transactions of the Royal Society B, 369*(1651), 1–11.

Green, L. (2001). *How popular musicians learn: A way ahead for music education.* London and New York: Ashgate Press.

Heidegger, M. (1962). *Being and time.* New York: Harper and Row.

Hill, K. W. (1999). A descriptive study of assessment procedures, assessment attitudes, and grading policies in selected public high school band performance classrooms in Mississippi. *Dissertation Abstracts International, 60,* 1954A.

Holmes, P., & Holmes, C. (2013). The performer's experience: A case for using qualitative (phenomeno-logical) methodologies in music performance research. *Musicae Scientiae, 17*(1), 72–85.

Husserl, E. (1989). *Ideas pertaining to a pure phenomenology and to a phenomenological philosophy.* [Second Book: *Studies in the Phenomenology of Constitution*]. Dordrecht, The Netherlands: Kluwer.

Hutchins, E. (2014). The cultural ecosystem of human cognition. *Philosophical Psychology, 27*(1), 34–49.

Hutto, D., & Myin, E. (2013). *Radicalizing enactivism: Basic minds without content.* Cambridge, MA: MIT Press.

Johnson, M. (2007). *The meaning of the body: Aesthetics of human understanding.* Chicago: University of Chicago Press.

Karlsen, S. (2011). Using musical agency as a lens: Researching music education from the angle of experience. *Research Studies in Music Education, 33*(2), 107–21.

Keat, R. (1982). *Merleau-Ponty and the phenomenology of the body.* Unpublished manuscript, University of Edinburgh. Retrieved from http://www.russellkeat.net.

Kelso, S. (1995). *Dynamic patterns.* Cambridge, MA: MIT Press.

Kotora, E. J. (2005). Assessment practices in the choral music classroom: A survey of Ohio high school choral music teachers and college choral methods professors. *Contributions to Music Education, 32,* 65–80.

Krueger, J. (2009). Enacting musical experience. *Journal of Consciousness Studies, 16*(2–3), 98–123.

Krueger, J. (2011). Doing things with music. *Phenomenology and the Cognitive Sciences, 10*(1), 1–22.

Krueger, J. (2014a). Affordances and the musically extended mind. *Frontiers in Psychology, 4*(1003), 1–12.

Krueger, J. (2014b). Emotions and the social niche. In C. von Scheve & M. Salmela (Eds.), *Collective emotions* (pp. 156–71). New York: Oxford University Press.

Kupers, E., van Dijk, M., van Geert, P., & McPherson, G. E. (2015). A mixed-methods approach to studying co-regulation of student autonomy through teacher–student interactions in music lessons. *Psychology of Music, 43*(3), 333–58.

Lahav, A., Saltzman, E., & Schlaug, G. (2007). Action representation of sound: Audiomotor recognition network while listening to newly acquired actions. *Journal of Neuroscience, 27,* 308–14.

Laroche, J., & Kaddouch, I. (2014). Enacting teaching and learning in the interaction process: "Keys" for developing skills in piano lessons through four-hand improvisations. *Journal of Pedagogy, 5*(1), 24–47.

Leman, M. (2007). *Embodied music cognition and mediation technology.* Cambridge, MA: MIT Press.

Magee, W. L., & Stewart, L. (2015). The challenges and benefits of a genuine partnership between music therapy and neuroscience: A dialog between scientist and therapist. *Frontiers in Human Neuroscience, 9,* 223. doi:10.3389/fnhum.2015.00223

Matyja, J., & Schiavio, A. (2013). Enactive music cognition. Background and research themes. *Constructivist Foundations, 8*(3), 351–57.

McPherson, G. E. (2012). Using self-regulation to unlock musical success. In A. Mornell (Ed.), *Art in motion II* (pp. 225–40). Frankfurt am Main, Germany: Peter Lang Internationaler Verlag der Wissenschaften.

McPherson, G. E., Nielsen, S., & Renwick, J. (2014). Self-regulation interventions and the development of music expertise. In H. Bembenutty, T. Cleary, & A. Kitsantas (Eds.), *Applications of self-regulated learning across diverse disciplines: A tribute to Barry J. Zimmerman* (pp. 355–381). Charlotte, NC: Information Age Publishing.

McPherson, G. E., & Zimmerman, B. J. (2011). Self-regulation of musical learning: A social cognitive perspective on developing performance skills. In R. Colwell & P. Webster (Eds.), *MENC handbook of research on music learning* (Vol. 1). New York: Oxford University Press.

Menin, D., & Schiavio, A. (2012). Rethinking musical affordances. *AVANT: Trends in Interdisciplinary Studies, 3*(2), 202–15.

Merleau-Ponty, M. (1945). *Phenomenology of perception*. London: Routledge.

Moran, N. (2014). Social implications arise in embodied music cognition research which can counter musicological "individualism". *Frontiers in Psychology, 5*(676). doi:10.3389/fpsyg.2014.00676

Nijs, L., Coussement, P., Moens, B., Amelynck, D., Lesaffre, M., & Leman, M. (2012a). Interacting with the Music Paint Machine: Relating the concepts of flow experience and presence. *Interacting with Computers, 24*, 237–50.

Nijs, L., Moens, B., Lesaffre, M., & Leman, M. (2012b). The Music Paint Machine: Stimulating self-monitoring through the generation of creative visual output using a technology-enhanced learning tool. *Journal of New Music Research, 41*, 79–101.

Noddings, N. (1995). *Philosophy of education*. Boulder, CO: Westview Press.

Noddings, N. (1999). Response: Two concepts of care. *Philosophy of Education Archive*, 36–39.

Noddings, N. (2012). The caring relation in teaching. *Oxford Review of Education, 38*(6), 771–81.

Noë, A. (2004). *Action in perception*. Cambridge, MA: MIT Press.

O'Regan, J. K., & Noë, A. (2001a). A sensorimotor approach to vision and visual consciousness. *Behavioral and Brain Science, 24*(5), 939–73.

O'Regan, J. K., & Noë, A. (2001b). What it is like to see: A sensorimotor theory of visual experience. *Synthèse, 129*(1), 79–103.

Pelinski, R. (2005). Embodiment and musical experience. *Trans. Revista Transcultural de Música, 9*. Retrieved from http://www.redalyc.org/articulo.oa?id=82200914

Phillips-Silver, J., & Trainor, L. J. (2005). Feeling the beat: Movement influences infants' rhythm perception. *Science, 308*(5727), 1430.

Regelski, T. (1998). The Aristotelian bases of praxis for music and music education as praxis. *Philosophy of Music Education Review, 6*(1), 22–59.

Regelski, T. (2009). Curriculum reform: Reclaiming "music" as social praxis. *Action, Criticism & Theory for Music Education, 8*(1), 66–84.

Regelski, T. (2016). *A brief introduction to a philosophy of music and music education as social praxis*. New York: Routledge.

Reybrouck, M. (2005). A biosemiotic and ecological approach to music cognition: Event perception between auditory listening and cognitive economy. *Axiomathes: An International Journal in Ontology and Cognitive Systems, 15*(2), 229–66.

Reybrouck, M. (2006). Music cognition and the bodily approach: Musical instruments as tools for musical semantics. *Contemporary Music Review, 25*(1/2), 59–68.

Reybrouck, M., & Brattico, E. (2015). Neuroplasticity beyond sounds: Neural adaptations following long-term musical aesthetic experiences. *Brain Science, 5*, 69–91.

Rink, J. (Ed.). (2002). *Music performance: A guide to understanding.* Cambridge, UK: Cambridge University Press.

Rizzolatti, G., & Sinigaglia, C. (2008). *Mirrors in the brain: How our minds share actions and emotions.* Oxford: Oxford University Press.

Russell, J. A., & Austin, J. R. (2010). Assessment practices of secondary music teachers. *Journal of Research in Music Education, 58*(1), 37–54.

Schiavio, A. (2012). Constituting the musical object: A neurophenomenological perspective on musical research. *Teorema, 13*(3), 63–80.

Schiavio, A. (2014). Action, enaction, inter(en)action. *Empirical Musicology Review, 9*(3–4), 254–62.

Schiavio, A., & Altenmüller, E. (2015). Exploring music-based rehabilitation for Parkinsonism through embodied cognitive science. *Frontiers in Neurology, 6*(217). doi:10.3389/fneur.2015.00217

Schiavio, A., & Cummins, F. (2015). An inter(en)active approach to musical agency and learning. In R. Timmers, N. Dibben, Z. Eitan, R. Granot, T. Metcalfe, A. Schiavio, & V. Williamson (Eds.), *Proceedings of the International Conference on the Multimodal Experience of Music 201.* Retrieved from https://www.dhi.ac.uk/openbook/chapter/ICMEM2015-Schiavio

Schiavio, A., & Høffding, S. (2015). Playing together without communicating? A pre-reflective and enactive account of joint musical performance. *Musicae Scientiae, 19*(4), 366–88.

Schiavio, A., van der Schyff, D., Gande, A., & Kruse-Weber, S. (2018). Negotiating individuality and collectivity in community music: A qualitative case study. *Psychology of Music.* doi:10.1177/0305735618775806

Schilbach, L., Timmermans, B., Reddy, V., Costall, A., Bente, G., Schlicht, T., et al. (2013). Toward a second-person neuroscience. *Behavioral & Brain Sciences, 36*, 393–414.

Sheets-Johnstone, M. (1999). *The primacy of movement.* Amsterdam, The Netherlands: John Benjamins.

Sheets-Johnstone, M. (2010). Thinking in movement: Further analyses and validations. In J. Stewart, O. Gapenne, & E. A. Di Paolo (Eds.), *Enaction: Toward a new paradigm for cognitive science* (pp. 165–82). Cambridge, MA: MIT Press.

Sheets-Johnstone, M. (2012). Fundamental and inherently interrelated aspects of animation. In A. Foolen, U. Lüdtke, T. Racine, & J. Zlatev (Eds.), *Moving ourselves, moving others: Motion and emotion in intersubjectivity, consciousness and language* (pp. 27–56). Amsterdam, The Netherlands: J. Benjamins.

Silverman, M. (2012). Virtue ethics, care ethics, and "the good life of teaching". *Action, Criticism, & Theory for Music Education, 11*(2), 96–122.

Slaby, J. (2015). Critical neuroscience meets medical humanities. *Medical Humanities, 41*(1), 16–22.

Slaby, J., & Gallagher, S. (2015). Critical neuroscience and socially extended minds. *Theory, Culture and Society, 32*(1), 33–59.

Small, C. (1998). *Musicking: The meaning of performing and listening.* Middletown, CT: Wesleyan University Press.

Thelen, E. (2000). Grounded in the world: Developmental origins of the embodied mind. *Infancy, 1*(1), 3–28.

Thompson, E. (2007). *Mind in life: Biology, phenomenology, and the sciences of mind.* Cambridge, MA, and London: Harvard University Press.

Tracy, L. H. (2002). Assessing individual students in the high school choral ensemble: Issues and practices. *Dissertation Abstracts International, 63*(09), 3143.

van der Schyff, D. (2015). Music as a manifestation of life: Exploring enactivism and the "eastern perspective" for music education. *Frontiers in Psychology, 6*, 345. doi:10.3389/fpsyg. 2015.00345

van der Schyff, D. (2016). From Necker cubes to polyrhythms: Fostering a phenomenological attitude in music education. *Phenomenology and Practice, 10*(1), 4–24.

van Manen, M. (2014). *Phenomenology of practice*. Walnut Creek, CA: Left Coast Press.

Varela, F. (1979). *Principles of biological autonomy*. Boston: Kluwer Academic.

Varela, F. (1996). Neurophenomenology: A methodological remedy for the hard problem. *Journal of Consciousness Studies, 3*(4), 330–49.

Varela, F., Thompson, E., & Rosch, E. (1991). *The embodied mind*. Cambridge, MA: MIT Press.

Weber, A. (2001). Turning the inside out: Natural forms as expression of intentionality. *Sign Systems Studies, 29*(1), 153–68.

Westerlund, H. (2002). *Bridging experience, action, and culture in music education*. Helsinki: Sibelius Academy.

Westerlund, H., & Juntonen, M.-L. (2005). Music and knowledge in bodily experience. In D. J. Elliott (Ed.), *Praxial music education: Reflections and dialogues* (pp. 112–22). New York: Oxford University Press.

# CHAPTER 5

# CRITICALLY ASSESSING FORMS OF RESISTANCE IN MUSIC EDUCATION

## BRENT C. TALBOT AND HAKIM MOHANDAS AMANI WILLIAMS

Knowledge emerges only through invention and re-invention, through the restless, impatient, continuing, hopeful inquiry human beings pursue in the world, with the world, and with each other.

—Paulo Freire, *Pedagogy of the Oppressed*

IN this chapter we[1] explore the question: What do critical forms of assessment look like in music classrooms that use critical pedagogy and embrace resistance to foster conscientization? We begin with an overview of critical pedagogy—in which we explain phrases key to our argumentation, such as "teacher-student," "problem-posing education," and "learning and teaching as praxis"—followed by a fleshing out of the term *conscientization* (consciousness raising), which we characterize as one of the main goals of our teaching and of assessment. We follow this with a conceptualization of resistance as having voice and agency and a theorization of indexicality as a powerful tool for assessing resistance as transformation. All of these discussions provide the necessary scaffolding for our explorations of the synergies among assessment, critical pedagogy, and music education. We then interrogate traditional assessment before pivoting to a bulleted list of examples of co-constructed and co-enacted formative assessments that can be used in classrooms to evaluate notions of resistance. Assessment of a critical pedagogy in music education—one centered on the dialectical, co-constructive, student-centered, problem-posing, praxial approach to learning music—is therefore presented as an integral part of an ongoing inquiry in and about the world.

We write of critical assessment not necessarily as a negation of traditional forms of assessment but to widen the parameters of what is currently deemed intellectually acceptable and scientifically robust. Indeed, whereas David Kahl (2013) notes that "many critical educators tend to view assessment as inherently negative" (p. 2617), we are not of that orientation. We believe assessment is pivotal in and for music teaching and learning. However, we are avowedly of the belief that the logics of traditional assessment are insufficient in the face of fast-changing educational landscapes, whose topographies are being deeply restructured by fascinating social, political, economic, and cultural influences. We echo Patricia Broadfoot's (2009) sentiments:

> For many, the certainties of modernism have been replaced by post-modern doubts about the possibility of progress. Recognition of the fallibilities of science has brought with it an increased recognition of the importance of diversity and subjectivity. Changes in the nature of work, globalisation, the information revolution and the increasingly social nature of contemporary challenges also suggest different priorities for education systems. (p. vii)

Impelled by Freirean thought, one such priority that we posit is that many of the processes and ends of education should equip both teachers and students to see the inequities and oppressions of our world and to craft and implement radically differentiated ways of being. Assessment can and must play a major role in these processes, but not to the extent that it becomes the proverbial tail wagging the dog. That is, the core of education must not be assessment as a teleological end, but rather assessment as an open-ended process of inquiry. Whatsoever we, as educators, deem to be ends—in whatever spheres we work—we should strive to see "ends" not as discrete entities per se but as parts of a continuum: "Ends become a part of a process, one stage in a continuum. Dewey actually preferred to use the term 'ends-in-view' to capture this sense of process. This term keeps our attention on the ends of the particular task at hand and reminds us that ends are always provisional and changing throughout the course of educational experiences. Thus, ends-in-view are deliberately open ended" (Hildreth, 2011, p. 34). When assessment is conceived as a compartmentalized, self-constituted entity, it can reify the trope of assessment-and-learning as objectively knowable and apolitical. In contrast, assessment within a critical pedagogical framework provides a different perspective—one that is agential, co-constructive, and political.

## CRITICAL PEDAGOGY: AN OVERVIEW

Critical pedagogy developed as an educational response to injustices, inequalities, and oppressive power relations found in the world. In his seminal work *Pedagogy of the Oppressed*, the radical educational theorist and practitioner Paulo Freire (1970) presents a *liberating*[2] and *humanizing* perspective of learning, a process of overcoming oppression that is rooted in a *love for the world*. He outlines key concepts of learning that have shaped the discourses and practices of education over the past forty years. These include

- a *dialogical* approach to inquiry that is rooted in the situations of the learner and teacher who, together, *in the world, with the world, and with each other*, co-construct and co-produce knowledge;
- the hyphenated term *teacher-student*, which is meant to capture a more interdependent and equitable learning relationship;
- *problem-posing* and narrative-based learning that is connected to the lived experiences of students, as opposed to the *banking method* of learning, in which knowledge is *deposited* in the student;
- learning as a form of *praxis*, a process of *conscientização*, in which the human subject experiences and *reflects* upon the *limit-situations* that challenge understanding and then works with others to develop plans of *action* that address issues emerging from the social, political, and economic disparities impacting our communities; and
- a *political* perspective on learning, in which learners and teachers become conscious of how power operates and then engage in various forms of *resistance* to *transform* the conditions in which power is used to oppress.

Freire's work is based on his own educational practices for improving literacy in Brazil in the 1960s and 1970s. These practices involve *naming* situations to be critiqued in order to reveal the systems of oppression. This *decoding* is a point of departure that contributes to the development of a set of *generative themes* by which learners collaboratively determine their own pedagogical needs and the manner in which they will meet those needs. Working as an *investigating team*, learners identify the *nuclei of contradictions* that influence and shape their lives. Through their *restless, impatient, continuing*, and *hopeful inquiry in the world*, learners take steps to become more critically aware of their situations and how to change their conditions, a process Freire termed *conscientização*, or *conscientization*—a key term/notion for the argument of this chapter with direct relevance to assessment in music classrooms.

# CONSCIENTIZATION

Conscientization, as postulated by Freire (2005), refers to critical consciousness. Freire theorized conscientization as a self-reinforcing feedback loop of reflection and action in which neither is useful without the other (Freire, 1970). To Freire, *activism* is action without constant and deliberate reflection, and *verbalism* is reflection without action. Activism and verbalism are both untethered from a critical historicity and, in that respect, are apolitically constituted and not aimed at radical social transformation, a cornerstone of conscientization. Such critical consciousness calls for *perceiving the social, economic and political contradictions in the world*, as well as a purposeful, constant striving to upend the inequities emergent therefrom. This synergy—between reflection and action—is how Freire defines *praxis* (Freire, 1970).

Conscientization has been operationalized into the varied theories and practices of critical pedagogy that followed Freire's seminal work.[3] These theories[4] examine and promote practices in education and music education[5] that have the potential to transform oppressive institutions or social relations. Linked to the aforementioned political nature of education, Ira Shor (1992) contends that "a curriculum that avoids questioning school and society is not, as is commonly supposed, politically neutral … *not* encouraging students to question knowledge, society, and experience tacitly endorses and supports the status quo" (p. 12). Shor adds that beyond the in-class texts, "politics reside not only in subject matter but in the discourse of the classroom, in the way teachers and students speak to each other. The rules for talking are a key mechanism for empowering or disempowering students. How much open discussion is there in class? How much one way 'teacher talk'? Is there mutual dialogue between teacher and students or one-way transfers of information from teacher to students?" (p. 14). This highlights yet another tenet of Freirean critical pedagogy: the dialogic nature of co-constructed knowledge, wherein power is continually inverted and renegotiated, producing teacher-qua-student and student-qua-teacher (Freire, 1970). This dialectical nature of education aims to dismantle the banking concept/model of education (which sees students as mere repositories of knowledge from the teacher to be regurgitated later) and replace it with a problem-posing model of education (which is generative and reflexive) (Freire, 1970).

The yin and yang of problem-posing pedagogy—as evinced by the seemingly antagonistic dyads of reflection and action and of teacher and student—beckon a certain reflexivity, one that is essential for navigating the tensions that surely emerge in these dialectical relationships. Regarding reflexivity, Victoria May Door (2014) states that "one aspect of Freire's concept of conscientization is that individuals develop a deepening awareness of both the socio-cultural world and their own potential for transforming that world … about deepening awareness of self in the world, in the context of consistency of thought and action … [so that] our own actions [do not] perpetuate the very cycle from which we hope to escape" (p. 89). She adds that "[b]eing critically reflexive therefore does not imply self-interested introspection, but involves looking to our own judgement and behaviour as well as to the nature of the systems in our particular institution" (p. 97). Therefore, when conscientization is the modus operandi of the learning environment, music learners see knowledge as a process of inquiry, not mere facts to be memorized. Learners see knowledge as power—a tool for transforming our world and the conditions in which we live. Conscientization, or critical consciousness as Thomas Regelski (2005) points out, "leads people to take ownership of their own history, empowering them to realize their own individual and collective interest through the freedom and wherewithal to change their social and individual selves" (pp. 14–15). Through conscientization, learners understand that to overcome the social, political, and economic contradictions of our world we must (1) *name* and *decode* how power and knowledge operate within systems of oppression, (2) *reflect* how we participate in and contribute to these systems and how these systems operate upon us, and (3) *act* and *resist* in both small and large ways in order to transform our world.

# RESISTANCE

Critical pedagogues strive to co-construct the aforementioned learning environment with students. In challenging students to apprehend the social, economic, and political contradictions of our world, cognitive dissonances necessarily abound. We welcome these because the ontological perturbations that are the result of our varied praxes must perhaps first emanate from within intellectual and epistemological ruptures. Maria Martinez Serrano, Mark O'Brien, Krystal Roberts, and David Whyte (2015) note that "Critical Pedagogy approaches to learning are not an 'easy option' and do require an attitudinal shift by the students and tutors, as well as a resource commitment. For students from educational backgrounds where didactic teaching has been the norm, notions of autonomous learning and co-learning with the teacher can be difficult" (p. 16). As teacher educators, we believe in challenging the status quo in and out of our university classrooms. We wish to both resist (and work against oppressions in our worlds) and model this resistance. At the heart of this resistance is the notion of voice. Voice being integral to our conceptualization of resistance is not divorced from action; in fact, we deem voice *as* action and actions-qua-resistances as expressions and extensions of voice.

**Theorizing voice.** Voice has been theorized by many sociolinguists to reveal processes of being systemically muted, marginalized, or silenced and to show how voice is both limited and empowered through the form and function of our language use. As Jan Blommaert (2005) indicates, "[t]he issue of voice is an eminently social issue...it is about function, and function is affected by the social 'values'—in a politico-economic sense—attributed to particular linguistic resources" employed (pp. 68–69). Blommaert draws upon John Gumperz (1982) and writes: "Language differences play an important positive role in signalling information as well as in creating and maintaining the subtle boundaries of power, status, role, and occupational specialization that make up the fabric of our social life. Assumptions about value differences associated with these boundaries in fact form the very basis for the indirect communicative strategies employed in key gatekeeping encounters" (pp. 6–7).

As critical pedagogues interested in opening up more inclusive spaces for learning, we examine with students how these boundaries and codes shape our abilities to speak and music. We consider what value, meaning, and function of our language and music are prevented or accepted as we move from one social, cultural, political, and economic space to another. As Blommaert (2005) points out: "Whenever discourses travel across the globe, what is carried with them is their shape, but their value, meaning, or function do not often travel along. Value, meaning, and function are a matter of uptake, they have to be *granted* by others on the basis of their real or potential 'market value' as a cultural commodity" (p. 72). The same can be said as we travel from home communities to school communities within the same geographic region. As students and teachers often come from differing backgrounds, the "market value" of our language is often muted, marginalized, or dismissed as it travels from our home lives to our school settings.

Another way to look at this is that while performing language (Hymes, 1996), speakers display "orientations towards *orders of indexicality*—systemically reproduced, stratified meanings often called 'norms' or 'rules' of language" (Blommaert, 2005, p. 73). These norms or rules index certain identity markers, such as class, race/ethnicity, gender, and sexuality, and have also been theorized by educational sociologist Basil Bernstein (1990) as *codes*. Language and code switching is common for almost every person in some capacity and is a matter of indexicality (Talbot, 2013). Alessandro Duranti (2007) sums up: "Indexicality ties language usage firmly to social and cultural practices. To say that words are indexically related to some 'object' or aspect of the world out there means to recognize that words carry with them a power that goes beyond the description and identification of people, objects, properties, and events. It means to work at identifying how language becomes a tool through which our social and cultural world is constantly described, evaluated, and reproduced" (p. 19).

John J. Gumperz (2001) indicates that our conversations are filled with indexes— signs that have some kind of existential relation with what they reference. For example, Duranti (2007) explains "that an expression like *this table* includes an imaginary arrow to something recognizable, most likely something perceptually available to both the speaker and the addressee" (p. 18). Indexes rely on context and become complicated when we consider linguistic resources in conversations that employ more than one type of language or identity. As Duranti indicates, "in bilingual communities, where language switching is a daily affair, the choice of a particular language over another may index one's ethnicity or a particular political stance toward the relation between language and ethnicity" (p. 18). The same can be said about music. To choose a particular music over another may index a cultural or political stance. To say that language or music is indexical (Talbot, 2013), then, is to say that what a word or piece means is context dependent. As Betsy Rymes (2003) points out: "How words are used can create new relevant contexts, and whether any of this meaning-making potential is realized at all, is dependent on the kinds of interactions people have around those words. Furthermore...indexical meaning accrues through multiple interactions (Ochs & Schieffelin, 1984)." The way meanings are indexed over the course of a single interaction and in repeated, patterned interactions influences how people understand (and create new understandings for) both words and events" (p. 126).

**Voice and agency.** In any music classroom setting, the indexes of power, knowledge, status, and control continually develop meaning as participants interact more and more throughout the year. Many of these indexes come preprogrammed from the socialization process of early schooling years. The rules and norms of schooling carry indexes toward a history and culture of schooling that values a hierarchical and authoritative structure modeled on factory production and efficiency that serves the economic and political interests of the upper class. Thus, argues Bernstein, when we think of having *voice* in the classroom, we must make a distinction between "the voice" and "the message." Drawing from the work of Madeleine Arnot and Diane Reay (2007) on "pedagogic voice," Gary Spruce (2015) describes their differences, noting that what is often " 'heard' is not 'the voice' but 'the message'—a message that reflects and sustains the power relationships of the pedagogical context within which the voice is formed" (p. 292). This theorization positions voices in most classrooms as lacking agency; that is, they are not "independently constructed 'voices,' but are rather 'the messages' created by particular pedagogical contexts" (Arnot & Reay, 2007, p. 317). Spruce (2015) explains further:

> Consequently, for some children, their experience of school is one in which they are aware of the power relationships and frameworks within which they find themselves, though they are unable to articulate the expected or required messages that enable them to be heard—they are in effect muted, marginalized, and potentially alienated. But this muting, marginalization, and alienation are masked by the illusion that consultation and the elicitation of the student voice inevitably realize and release principles and frameworks of equity, democratic engagement, and social justice...the messages that are heard in schools (particularly within strongly framed and classified pedagogical contexts) are from those voices that have been successfully enculturated into the dominant discourses. Thus the potential for the student voice to disrupt hierarchies and power relationships through democratic engagement with the processes of music education is negated, as the messages that are heard are only those that project the school's legitimated text. (pp. 292–293)

The theorizations of Bernstein, Arnot and Reay, and Spruce specifically focus on the notion of student voice, but as critical pedagogues we suggest that their concepts also apply to teacher voice, because teachers are also bound by the codes, norms, and rules of language as they too travel between spaces in and out of schools. Critical pedagogy thrives on this multiplicity of voice: the individual, the co-constructed, the questioning, the afraid, the uncertain, the inspired. As Henry Giroux (2011) states, critical pedagogy asserts that we can engage our own "learning from a position of agency and in so doing can actively participate in narrating [our] identities through a culture of questioning that opens up a space of translation between the private and the public while changing the forms of self- and social recognition" (p. 14). Thus, in classrooms that employ critical pedagogy, teachers and students work together to liberate voices from the codes, rules, and norms of oppression that are embedded in our language. We use indexicality as a tool to *name* and consider how these codes operate, then we reappropriate and use them as a means for navigating spaces, resisting oppression, and changing the conditions in which we operate. This resistance is the foundation for our work and our transformation in the world.

**Resistance.** Resistance takes many forms in our classrooms.[6] Different kinds of resistances often emerge: the conservative student who admonishes the supposed liberalism and academic overreach of critical pedagogy, the apathetic student for whom our political interest in liberation is a bore, and the self-professed radically progressive student who thinks that critical pedagogy has already been co-opted by larger institutional forces. But we do not necessarily perceive all of these as *resistance* per se; some may just actually be oppositional behaviors. We desire a classroom for all types of behavior, but there is a distinction between resistance (as we wish to operationalize it in this chapter) and mere oppositional behavior. Our notion of resistance is scaffolded on a Girouxian understanding:

> Resistance must be viewed from a theoretical starting point that links the display of behavior to the interest it embodies, going beyond the immediacy of behavior to the interest that underlies its often hidden logic, a logic that also must be interpreted through the historical and cultural mediations that shape it.... [T]he ultimate value of the notion of resistance must be measured not only by the degree to which it promotes critical thinking and reflective action but, more importantly, by the degree to which it contains the possibility of galvanizing collective political struggle.
>
> (Giroux, 1983, p. 291)

We concur that, in contextualizing resistance, there ought to be a type of metacognitive grasp (by both students and teachers) of the historical and cultural mediations that shape it. This is not to say that students must at all times be comprehensively aware of the historical and cultural mediations that feed their oppositional behaviors to our practices, pedagogies, and praxes (we are aware of the automaticity with which our subconscious guides us in the world). But this is why reflexivity is of such import; reflexivity and meta-cognition go hand in hand in this mightily political project of teaching and learning for liberation. Resistance, then, is operationalized here as a spectrum, one in which opposi-tional behaviors to our goals of conscientization are acknowledged and not sidelined (no matter how uncomfortable they make us at times), but also as the epistemological and ontological resistances that we, with our students, dialectically co-construct and co-enact against the status quo and the inequities that it reinforces.

These constitutive elements of conscientization—praxis (reflection + action), co-construction of knowledge, inversions of power, problem-posing education, and reflexivity—coupled with resistance and the tool of indexicality, all have direct bearing on assessment. If we are to answer Door's (2014) ethical call for consistency in our practice, then we must tend to the not-too-easy challenge of postulating assessments congruent with the ethos of critical pedagogy. This leads us to consider the following question: What do critical forms of assessment look like in music classrooms that use critical pedagogy and embrace resistance to foster conscientization? Before we get at this ques-tion, however, we must first look at what we mean by assessment and how it connects to a critical pedagogy in music education.

# ASSESSMENT, CRITICAL PEDAGOGY, AND MUSIC EDUCATION

Assessment has many purposes in education and comes in many forms. While the rhet-oric and practices around educational accountability have intensified, we agree with Randy Elliot Bennett and Drew H. Gitomer (2009) that "there is a fundamental problem with the system as currently implemented" (p. 45). We are most certainly not opposed to rigor, accountability, and reflection in our practices, all marshaled toward constant interrogations, articulations, and tweakings of the linkages between aims and inputs on the one hand and outcomes and impact on the other. But in an era in which teachers, students, and educational managerialists are increasingly stressed by the politically charged top-down approach to high-stakes testing, it is imperative to impugn the prevailing testing culture and the significant consequences it has on our lives.

Freire averred that education is not neutral. In that same vein, we believe that "there is no cultural neutrality in assessment or in the selection of what is to be assessed" (Gipps & Stobart, 2009, p. 111). Since "theories are historical, social and, hence ideological products of the manifold social and political forces of the time of their making and use" (Kress, 2009, p. 27), we view assessment as "a socially embedded activity that can only be fully understood by taking account of the social and cultural contexts within which it operates" (Gipps & Stobart, 2009, p. 106). This critical take on assessment impels us to consider what Gunther Kress (2009, p. 27) asks:

1. Whose interests count in terms of curriculum and learning: those of the authority or those of the learner?
2. How can we assess learning expressed in modes other than those that are dominant in formal educational settings?
3. Whose interests rule?

These questions demonstrate our explicit aim of conjoining assessment and critical pedagogy to unmask the oft-unacknowledged role that power and political interests play.

While we acknowledge the difficulty in crafting creative and critical assessments to match creative and critical pedagogies, we agree with Patrick Griffin (2009) that "nothing is too hard to measure" (p. 184). In the pursuit of better comprehending and rendering its evaluability and assessability, we note the perils of hyper-instrumentalizing something as seemingly amorphous as critical pedagogy itself and thereby puncturing its avowedly revolutionary zeal.

However, Serrano et al. (2015, p. 18) present three succinct ways in which assessment and critical pedagogy can be merged:

1. Forms of assessment that allow the structure of learning to be defined by student learners' lived reality, rather than a predetermined or designed structure.
2. Forms of assessment that encourage students to be "free learners," able to challenge the physical and ideological structure of their pedagogical environment and relationships.
3. Forms of assessment that move students to action and involvement in the world in ways that promote and further the causes of social justice and democracy.

This is not meant to be an exhaustive list of possibilities, because a flexible array of pedagogies begets a flexible array of assessments. As Mary Breunig (2005) states, "if multiple 'ways of knowing' and multiple sources of knowledge are valued, then multiple methods of assessment and evaluation must also be considered" (p. 115). But within Serrano et al.'s (2015) suggestions are several core notions of critical pedagogy: student centeredness, agency, social justice, and action in the world. Regarding the relevance of this to music education, Frank Abrahams (2005) writes:

> Unlike the popular approaches of Orff or Kodaly, Critical Pedagogy does not advocate a particular body of repertoire, or specific teaching procedure. Instead, it is a view that provides teacher and student with a flexible pedagogy. For music education, this pedagogy questions, challenges, and empowers students to experience *our* (i.e. the teacher's) music, and their teachers to understand *their* (i.e. the student's) music as integral parts of a collective reality. Critical pedagogy suggests that music, as part of our cultural past, present and future, has the power to liberate students and their teachers from present stereotypes about music and musicians, and encourages critical thinking, critical action, and critical feeling. It places music into a social, political and cultural context that results in a connection of what Freire calls "word," which in our case is the music, to "world." (p. 8)

This co-constructedness of the classroom—and the dialecticism that informs it—is indeed pivotal to our praxis, and it too must help shape assessment both discursively and technically. This dialecticism between music teachers and students can be fostered and evaluated in terms of formative assessment. Martin Fautley (2015) states: "True formative assessment, that which involves teacher and student in a dialogue about the music produced, and has as its primary aim to develop the music that the student has produced, is very different from the formative use of summative assessment, where the student is told what grade they have scored in a test, and this is then used to provide a target for the student to aim at next time a test is given" (pp. 514–515).

We wholeheartedly agree with Fautley's injunction that the application of assessment needs to shift the primary focus from summative assessment to one on "developing learning and achievement through formative assessment…in order to truly develop music education for all pupils" (p. 519). This, therefore, is "assessment for social justice as it involves learners in becoming agentive in the processes of their own learning, and although interventionist to some extent, it is personalized purposefully so that the learning journey is negotiated, not imposed" (p. 523). So what does a critical pedagogy model look like in music education, and how does assessment work in such a space?

# CRITICAL PEDAGOGY FOR MUSIC EDUCATION

Abrahams (2005) proposed a model of critical pedagogy for music education oriented around four questions borrowed from Jurgen Habermas (1982): (1) Who am I? (2) Who are my students? (3) What might they become? (4) What might we become together? He connects these questions to four domains of music: *experiencing, connecting, creating,* and *performing*. These are then sequenced through eight lesson steps that are flexible in nature: (1) honoring the students' world, (2) sharing the experience, (3) connecting their world to the concept, (4) dialoguing together, (5) practicing the concept, (6) connecting word to world, (7) assessing transformation, and (8) acknowledging transformation. This sequence model is unlike traditional lesson plans, in that it is flexible and relies on the teacher's expertise as "music education connoisseur": one "who knows from instinct and experience when it is appropriate to go with the flow, or when it is time to move on" (p. 10).

Like Abrahams, we perceive a potent synergy between music education and critical pedagogy. We mobilize the synergy toward engendering conscientization, ergo assessments must be, so to speak, conscientizational: participatory, problem posing, reflexive, and not overly prescriptive. They must be developed in conjunction with students and must connect to the overall goals of a critical music pedagogy: using and creating music as a means to perceive contradictions in the social, economic, and political conditions of the world and taking reflective action to change the conditions in which we live. Social justice is the foundation of any critical pedagogue's work, and for music educators who use critical pedagogy, music is the medium in which we act. Together, through music, we resist—as transformative action—the injustices of the world. And if resistance is at the heart of what we do as critical pedagogues, how then do we assess it? We return to our guiding question: What do critical forms of assessment look like in music classrooms that use critical pedagogy and embrace resistance to foster conscientization?

## Critical Forms of Assessment

Premised on the theoretical work around multiple intelligences (Gardner, 2011), we feel compelled to use a wide array of critical assessments in our classrooms because varied assessments are necessitated by the very presence of student diversity and by the fact that there is no singular assessment that will capture all that we (teachers and students) wish to capture. Kahl (2013), in conceptualizing "preassessment," suggests that "the process of conscientization should begin before [we engage with] course material" (p. 2618). Though we have professional and ethical responsibilities as teachers to set the intentions and goals of the courses in which students enroll, we regularly provide space and invite students throughout the semester to propose alterations to our syllabi, including the types of creative projects we design and assess together. Students and teacher vote on proposed changes through a democratic process. This is intended to immediately set the tone that our classroom—and the documents that regulate the expectations—are spaces that belong to each person and are aimed at co-creating a learning community.

Students are expected to revise and resubmit all work throughout the semester, turning the focus of assessment on a formative process rather than a summative product. As Fautley (2015) states: "Central to the notion of good formative assessment is that quality is developed by personal human interaction between teacher and student. At the heart of this is the notion of *feedback*, or, as some would put it, *feed-forward*. This takes place in the moment, as music making is proceeding, and while the process is still unfolding. Doing this renders the *process* of musicking significant" (p. 514).

So what does this actually look like? In this section we offer a bulleted list of examples of critical assessments we use in a number of our courses,[7] with an attendant explanation of how each indexes resistance and the greater notion of *conscientization*—that is, reflexivity, problem- posing/promoting critical thinking, praxis [reflection + action], co-construction, inverting power relations/hierarchies, perceiving contradictions in the world, and so forth.

- *Responsive suite.* This is presented as a set of options (reflective journaling, blogging, and recorded chats) from which students may choose. In our classes, students do readings and listen to musical selections suggested by both teacher and students around questions that emerge from class interactions. Participants offer their own substantive interrogations of these readings and musical selections by writing in reflective journals, posting on the class blog, or engaging in further discussions outside of class that are recorded and uploaded to the course content management site. Participants respond to each other's posts and pose questions that problematize or offer possible plans of action to address various topics or issues. These questions, additional materials, and action plans are then revisited during subsequent class sessions. Embedded in these activities are opportunities to express disagreements one may not have felt comfortable articulating in the larger group setting or opportunities to further extend and contribute to the perspectives and plans of actions presented in class. These assessments are antithetical to banking education and encourage students to bring their own voice to bear on the material. They are also encouraged to merge this with their own educational histories and experiences. [reflexivity, problem posing/promoting critical thinking, perceiving contradictions]

- *Found object ensemble.* Working in teams can be an asset and is a much-needed skill. Students bring outside materials and have opportunities to facilitate part of the class teaching, learning, and composition sessions. These include musical recordings of pieces they wish to perform using instruments they make out of objects found from home. Throughout the project, students consider the following questions: What is music? What is culture? What is our relationship to music as humans? How does music contribute to our humanization? This project connects to life outside of school and honors our individual identities while co-constructing a reflective classroom identity. By promoting collaboration as the dialogic modus operandi of the class, this project promotes student agency and challenges the competitiveness and rugged individualism so prevalent in American educational systems. As they create, reflect, and perform, students learn skills in negotiating interpersonal dynamics in group settings.

    [inverting power relations/hierarchies, co-construction, perceiving contradictions]

- *Musicals for social change.* Working as a class, students write, compose, and produce a thirty-minute musical focused on creating awareness of an issue they wish to change in our community. They have wide latitude in selecting the topic and implementing a plan to achieve their goal. Students assign each other various roles for writing, composing, performing, filming, and editing the musical. They are asked to create an original plot that includes an antagonist and protagonist and must compose original music, including: solos, chorus, and small group numbers. As a group, students can either put on a live production of the musical or film and edit it in "real-life" settings. Students organize and promote either a live performance or a screening of their film in the local community. Throughout, and at the end of, the semester, students are asked to submit evaluations of their project, which reflect a charting of their project's successes and challenges, all linked to key notions of social justice. This iterative process represents the feedback loop of reflection and action.

  [reflexivity, problem posing/promoting critical thinking, praxis, co-construction, perceiving contradictions in the world]

- *Constructive controversy.* This is used in conflict resolution/mediation training in which the teacher presents a controversial issue to be discussed, and students are asked to choose which side they vehemently support. They are then asked to convincingly argue for the opposite side by composing a new or arranging an established protest song; this encourages students to step into the "other" perspective that is so often easily/readily demonized. Through this project, participants examine the historical roots of particular songs, such as "La Cucaracha," "This Land Is Your Land," and "Mississippi Goddam," and explore their origins, ways in which these songs have been appropriated to articulate agendas, and how their meanings have changed over time. As students engage with this material and think about opposing views, they develop awareness of how individuals and groups use music as a tool to promote political, economic, and cultural interests. This kind of role-playing is often a challenge for students because they recognize how deeply wedded we sometimes are to our own perspectives/opinions/beliefs, and it can lead to a discussion about notions of resistance and voice. This process of stepping into the "other's shoes" is not meant to dissuade students of their perspective, but to deepen tolerance and augment nuance. Constructive controversy requires active listening because we ask students to paraphrase the arguments of the opposing side. We ask the opposing side if the other side paraphrased them well, and this presents an opportunity for students to see how adept (or not) they are at active listening. At the end of the activity we give feedback on the process to each side.

  [reflexivity, problem posing/promoting critical thinking, co-construction, perceiving contradictions in the world]

- *A class session without the teacher.* We ask students to choose and lead a warm-up, lead a rehearsal, or teach a music activity at which the teacher is not present. We then ask all students to use the tool of indexicality—learned throughout the semester—to assess the experience, identifying and reflecting on power dynamics, hierarchy, autonomy, and teacher-student relationships. They are asked to reflect upon whether new hierarchies emerged and whether students' engagement and linguistic markers shift without the teacher present. They consider the following questions: What are the roles and responsibilities of the various participants in ensemble settings? How is repertoire chosen, what types of repertoire are chosen, and who decides? What are the components of the rehearsal, and why? How is the music learned, and what are the media and structures of delivering content? How does one convey musical meanings? How does a group convey musical meanings? How do we provide space to create, embrace, and express our identities?

[reflexivity, problem posing/promoting critical thinking, co-construction, inverting power relations/hierarchies]

# CONCLUSION

We view assessment of critical music pedagogy as *conscientizational*; that is, assessment is developed in conjunction with students to be participatory, problem posing, reflexive, and not overly prescriptive. To assess from a critical music pedagogical perspective means to consider and evaluate specific ways in which our knowledge has been transformed. As Giroux (2011) reminds us: "Critical pedagogy becomes a project that stresses the need for teachers and students to actively transform knowledge rather than simply consume it...to connect classroom knowledge to the experiences, histories, and resources that students bring to the classroom...to link such knowledge to the goal of furthering their capacities to be critical agents who are responsive to moral and political problems of their time and recognize the importance of organized collective struggles" (p. 7). In short, students and teachers use music together to *resist* the injustices of the world. Resistance is at the heart of our praxis as critical music pedagogues. Resistance is to have voice, to have agency to "call people in," to dialogue, to reflect and act in order to transform the conditions in which we live. Resistance is the manifestation of Freire's notion of *conscientização*.

A critical music pedagogy uses formative assessments (Fautley, 2015) to evaluate resistance by examining the shifts in indexical meanings. As Giroux (2011) reminds us, "resistance must be viewed from a theoretical starting point that links the display of behavior to the interest it embodies, going beyond the immediacy of behavior to the interest that underlies its often hidden logic, a logic that also must be interpreted through the historical and cultural mediations that shape it" (p. 291). Drawing upon tools presented by Blommaert (2005), Hymes (1996), and Rymes (2003), we see indexicality as a theoretical and methodological tool that promotes pedagogic voice (Bernstein, 1990) among students (Arnot & Reay, 2007; Spruce, 2015) and teachers. As teachers and students co-construct knowledge through projects that challenge and shift our positionalities and perspectives, we use formative assessment throughout, placing the focus on the process of our development. We create spaces within each project to reflect upon our growth as individuals and as a group, identifying and examining the indexes that point to our beliefs and the shifts of indexical meanings that display this growth and the transformation of knowledge.

Critical forms of assessment in music classrooms—those that embrace resistance and foster conscientization—are embedded in the very types of critically minded, creative projects we have described here. In other words, the project as process *is* the assessment itself. These projects are not the traditional forms that assess the "objectively knowable material" presented in textbooks to be "transferred" to students through memorization teaching. Instead, they are dynamically responsive and dialectically constituted, problem-posing projects that engage students and teacher from a position of agency tied to the lived experiences and conditions of our communities. Through these musical projects we perceive the contradictions in the world, reflect on our participation in these contradictions, and co-create ways to address these contradictions. In reference to the epigraph, critical assessment becomes our inquiry in the world, with the world, and with each other.

## NOTES

1. Brent teaches courses in music and education, and Hakim teaches courses in education and Africana studies, at Gettysburg College.
2. All italicized words are key terms used by Freire in *Pedagogy of the Oppressed*.
3. We are also aware that Freire's practice was enacted in a very particular space, and we remain cognizant of this challenge of its cross-pollinative employment: "The places of learning to which latter day Critical Pedagogy has sought to enter are established [educational] institutions, with established ways of doing things (cultural norms, rules, protocols and hierarchies) that have been established over centuries. Critical Pedagogy by definition seeks to establish an alternative set of norms that are not necessarily compatible with the established culture of [our own institutions]. The danger that follows from this dilemma (of a sub-dominant culture entering an established culture) is that the latter will always be able to co-opt the former" (Serrano, O'Brien, Roberts, & Whyte, 2015, p. 4).
4. Ira Shor's (1992) conceptualization of *radical educational practice* positions the teacher as the mediating figure between outside authority and the student. Henry Giroux's concept of *emancipatory authority* (Giroux, 1994, 162–63) legitimates teachers' and students' own critiques of oppression and hierarchy in the schooling system and links it to democratic struggles. He saw students and teachers as *border crossers* who work at the interfaces of different cultural landscapes, revealing and negotiating the tensions of identity and representation that these create in the classroom (Giroux, 1994, 141–52). Joe Kincheloe's concept of *bricolage* advocates that educational material should be drawn from many sources, perspectives, and methodologies, with the aim of transforming the classroom into a place where previously suppressed voices are heard. bell hooks's (1994) *engaged pedagogy* transgresses gender, race, and class segregation, building teaching as part of the community rather than as an isolated act. For hooks, to choose not to break down oppressive structures of hierarchical education is not to be neutral, but to offer political support to existing inequalities. Peter McLaren's (1995, 1997) *revolutionary pedagogy* is a Marxist approach

influenced by the guerrilla insurrectionist philosophy of Che Guevara, which explicitly links educational practice to social activism for change.

5. As Juliet Hess (2017) documents, "A significant body of literature in music education in the 1990s centered on tenets of Freirian pedagogy.... With this focus...Music educators thus acknowledge students' histories and experiences and make room in the institution for students not only to speak, but name the world, and dissent from dominant discourse" (pp. 173–74).

6. We incorporate critical pedagogy in all of our classrooms, but explicitly teach and model it in three classes: Social Foundations of Music Education, Education for Social Change, and Secondary Music Education Methods.

7. These assessments are a combination of the various forms we use in our respective contexts.

## References

Abrahams, F. (2005). The application of critical pedagogy to music teaching and learning. *Visions of Research in Music Education, 6*. Retrieved from http://www.rider.edu/~vrme

Arnot, M., & Reay, D. (2007). A sociology of pedagogic voice: Power, inequality and pupil consultation. *Discourse: Studies in the Cultural Politics of Education, 28*(3), 343–58.

Bennett, R. E., & Gitomer, D. H. (2009). Transforming K-12 assessment: Integrating accountability testing, formative assessment and professional support. In C. Wyatt-Smith & J. J. Cumming (Eds.), *Educational assessment in the 21st century: Connecting theory and practice* (pp. 43–62). Dordrecht, The Netherlands: Springer.

Bernstein, B. (1990). *Class, codes and control.* Vol. IV, *The structuring of pedagogic discourse.* London: Routledge.

Blommaert, J. (2005). *Discourse.* Cambridge, UK: Cambridge University Press.

Breunig, M. (2005). Turning experiential education and critical pedagogy theory into praxis. *Journal of Experiential Education, 28*(2), 106–22.

Broadfoot, P. (2009). Signs of change: Assessment past, present and future. In C. Wyatt-Smith & J. J. Cumming (Eds.), *Educational assessment in the 21st century: Connecting theory and practice* (pp. v–xi). Dordrecht, The Netherlands: Springer.

Door, V. (2014). Critical pedagogy and reflexivity: The issue of ethical consistency. *International Journal of Critical Pedagogy, 5*(2), 88–99.

Duranti, A. (2007). *Linguistic anthropology.* New York: Cambridge University Press.

Fautley, M. (2015). Music education assessment and social justice. In C. Benedict, P. Schmidt, G. Spruce, & P. Woodford (Eds.), *The Oxford handbook of social justice in music education* (pp. 513–24). New York: Oxford University Press.

Freire, P. (1970). *Pedagogy of the oppressed.* New York: Continuum.

Freire, P. (2005). *Education for critical consciousness.* New York: Continuum International Publishing Group.

Gardner, H. (2011). *Frames of mind: The theory of multiple intelligences.* New York: Basic Books.

Gipps, C., & Stobart, G. (2009). Fairness in assessment. In C. Wyatt-Smith & J. J. Cumming (Eds.), *Educational assessment in the 21st century: Connecting theory and practice* (pp. 105–18). Dordrecht, The Netherlands: Springer.

Giroux, H. (1983). Theories of reproduction and resistance in the new sociology of education: A critical analysis. *Harvard Educational Review, 53*(3), 257–93.

Giroux, H., & McLaren, P. (1994). *Between borders: Pedagogy and the politics of cultural studies.* New York: Routledge.

Giroux, H. (2011). *On critical pedagogy.* New York: Continuum.

Griffin, P. (2009). Teachers' use of assessment data. In C. Wyatt-Smith & J. J. Cumming (Eds.), *Educational assessment in the 21st century: Connecting theory and practice* (pp. 183–208). Dordrecht, The Netherlands: Springer.

Gumperz, J. (1982). *Discourse strategies.* Cambridge, UK: Cambridge University Press.

Gumperz, J. (2001). Contextualization and ideology in intercultural communication. In A. Di Luzio, S. Günthner, & F. Orletti (Eds.), *Culture in communication* (pp. 35–53). Amsterdam, The Netherlands: John Benjamins.

Habermas, J. (1982). A reply to my critics. In J. Thompson & D. Held (Eds.), *Habermas: Critical Debates* (pp. 219–83). London: Palgrave.

Hess, J. (2017). Critiquing the critical: The casualties and paradoxes of critical pedagogy in music education. *Philosophy of Music Education Review, 25*(2), 171–91.

Hildreth, R. W. (2011). What good is growth? Reconsidering Dewey on the ends of education. *Education & Culture, 27*(2), 28–47.

hooks, b. (1994). *Teaching to transgress: Education as the practice of freedom.* New York: Routledge.

Hymes, D. (1996). *Ethnography, linguistics, narrative inequality: Towards an understanding of voice.* London: Taylor and Francis.

Kahl, D. (2013). Critical communication pedagogy and assessment: Reconciling two seemingly incongruous ideas. *International Journal of Communication, 7,* 2610–30.

Keesing-Styles, L. (2003). The relationship between critical pedagogy and assessment in teacher education. *Radical Pedagogy, 5*(1). Retrieved from http://www.radicalpedagogy.org/radicalpedagogy.org/The_Relationship_between_Critical_Pedagogy_and_Assessment_in_Teacher_Education.html

Kincheloe, J. (2004). The knowledges of teacher education: Developing a critical complex epistemology. *Teacher Education Quarterly, 31*(1), 49–66.

Kincheloe, J. (2008). Critical pedagogy and the knowledge wars of the twenty-first century. *International Journal of Critical Pedagogy, 1*(1), 1–22.

Kress, G. (2009). Assessment in the perspective of a social semiotic theory of multimodal teaching and learning. In C. Wyatt-Smith & J. J. Cumming (Eds.), *Educational assessment in the 21st century: Connecting theory and practice* (pp. 19–42). Dordrecht, The Netherlands: Springer.

McLaren, P. (1995). *Rethinking media literacy: A critical pedagogy of representation.* New York: Peter Lang.

McLaren, P. (1997). *Revolutionary multiculturalism: Pedagogies of dissent for the new millennium.* New York: Westview Press.

Ochs, E., & Schieffelin, B. (1984). Language acquisition and socialization: Three developmental stories. In R. Shweder & R. Levine (Eds.), *Culture theory: Essays on mind, self, and emotion* (pp. 276–320). Cambridge: Cambridge University Press.

Regelski, T. A. (2005). Critical theory as a foundation for critical thinking in music education. *Visions of Research in Music Education, 6.* Retrieved from http://www.rider.edu/~vrme

Rymes, B. (2003). Relating word to world: Indexicality during literacy events. In S. Wortham & B. Rymes (Eds.), *Linguistic anthropology of education* (pp. 121–50). Santa Barbara, CA: Praeger Publishers.

Serrano, M., O'Brien, M., Roberts, K., & Whyte, D. (2015). *Assessing critical pedagogy: "Non-traditional learning" and module assessment.* London: University of Liverpool and The

Higher Education Academy. Retrieved from https://www.liverpool.ac.uk/media/livacuk/cll/reports/assessing_critical_pedagogy_non-traditional_,learning_and_module_assessment.pdf

Shor, I. (1992). *Empowering education: Critical teaching for social change*. Chicago: University of Chicago Press.

Spruce, G. (2015). Music education, social justice, and the "student voice": Addressing student alienation through a dialogical conception of music education. In C. Benedict, P. Schmidt, G. Spruce, & P. Woodford (Eds.), *The Oxford handbook of social justice in music education* (pp. 285–301). New York: Oxford.

Talbot, B. C. (2013). Discourse analysis as potential for re-visioning music education. *Action, Criticism, and Theory for Music Education*, 12(1), 47–63. Retrieved from http://act.maydaygroup.org/articles/Talbot12_1.pdf

CHAPTER 6

··································································································

# EVALUATION FOR EQUALITY

*applying a classical pragmatist perspective*
*in qualitative assessment in finnish*
*general music education*

··································································································

## LAURI VÄKEVÄ

IN a classic textbook, Hirst and Peters (2011/1970) defined education as "the development of desirable qualities in people" (p. 19). Were we to agree with this definition, it would seem to be important to be able to judge what desirable qualities are and how they can be developed. In turn, this would seem to require a more general level of reflection on what qualities are and how they can be judged.

Such reflections are by no means irrelevant to how educators, music educators included, should approach educational assessment strategies. Of the multiple approaches to assessment, qualitative assessment has proven to be the most challenging, especially in educational systems that base their evaluative practices on standardized methods of collecting and analyzing quantitative data, informed by what Angela Barrett, Rita Chawla-Duggan, John Lowe, Jutta Nikel, and Eugenia Ukpo (2006) call "the economist view of education" (p. 2). This view highlights the quality of schooling, focusing on measuring the efficiency and accountability of the educational system rather than finding out how education can develop desirable qualities in students (p. 1). Such preference reflects, but also sustains, the common distinction made between assessment and evaluation, in which the former concerns the student's learning and the latter the efficacy of the learning programs (Booth, 2009, p. 168).[1]

Despite the challenges of qualitative assessment, a number of educational theorists (e.g., Eisner, 1996, 2002, 2007; Hickman, 2007; Murphy & Espeland, 2007; Russell & Zembylas, 2007) have argued that it is the best choice for art subjects because of its qualitative substance. Similar arguments have also appeared in the music education literature (e.g., Swanwick, 1988, pp. 4, 35ff., 152, 2002, p. 105; Elliott, 1995, pp. 230–34, 282;

Brophy, 2000; Colwell, 2002, 2010; Woodford, 2005, p. 62; Mills, 2005, pp. 176ff.; Murphy, 2007; Philpott, 2007, pp. 209–10; Jorgensen, 2003, p. 66; Booth, 2009, p. 168; Fautley, 2010; Burnard & Fautley, 2015). Examining this literature, there are several interpretations of what "quality" means. Such semantic diversity no doubt reflects the everyday use of the word. For instance, the *Oxford English Dictionary* describes quality as "the nature, kind, or character (of something)," "the standard or nature of something as measured against other things of a similar kind," and "the degree of excellence possessed by a thing" (OED, 2016). This raises philosophical questions regarding the scope of qualitative assessment: Is it viable to talk about quality as "the nature, kind, or character" when the goal is to adjudicate? Does not assessment always require comparison? Can we compare without standards of excellence?

In this chapter[2] I propose that we can draw productive consequences for developing a notion of qualitative assessment in music education from Charles Sanders Peirce's and John Dewey's philosophical views on how qualities operate in experience. In the next two sections I provide a reading of how Dewey reinterpreted Peirce's notion of qualities in his naturalistic pragmatist characterization of "esthetic" or "consummatory" experience. I then discuss more specific possibilities of applying a Deweyan notion of qualities in educational assessment. Next, using Dewey's theory of (e)valuation as a frame of reference, I provide a conceptual sketch of how such notions can inform qualitative assessment in art subjects. In the last section I relate this discussion to the new Finnish Core Curriculum for Basic Education (OPS, 2014a, 2014b, 2014c), especially regarding assessment in music.

## PEIRCE AND DEWEY ON QUALITIES

In contemporary philosophy, qualities are usually referred to as properties that can be predicated on objects. However, in the classical pragmatist tradition, qualities received more substantial treatment. This reading originates from Peirce's work on "phaneroscopy," his description of "the collective total of all that is in any way or in any sense present to the mind" (Peirce, 1904/CP 1.284[3]). Peirce (1904/CP) described his first category of "phanerons" as follows:

> Among phanerons there are certain qualities of feeling, such as the color of magenta, the odor of attar, the sound of a railway whistle, the taste of quinine, the quality of the emotion upon contemplating a fine mathematical demonstration, the quality of feeling of love, etc. I do not mean the sense of actually experiencing these feelings, whether primarily or in any memory or imagination. That is something that involves these qualities as an element of it. But I mean the qualities themselves which, in themselves, are mere may-bes, not necessarily realized.... That mere quality, or suchness, is not in itself an occurrence, as seeing a red object is; it is a mere may-be. Its only being consists in the fact that there might be such a peculiar, positive, suchness in a phaneron. (p. 1.304)

Peirce is pointing out how qualities are revealed to the reflective consciousness. While qualities cannot be known as such, combined with things of the second category (i.e., "facts"), they can produce entities of the third category of phanerons, or "signs." Because all "thought is of the nature of the sign" (Peirce, 1906/CP, p. 5.553), qualities belong to the "functional organization of the mind," which means that they also have a role in learning (Määttänen, 1993, p. 105; Chiasson, 2005).

Dewey used Peirce's notion of how qualities are incorporated in experience as a basis for constructing a naturalistic pragmatist theory of aesthetic or "consummatory" experience.[4] Culminating in *Art as Experience* (Dewey, 1934/LW, p. 10[5]), this theory brought qualities from the shade of logical possibility to the spotlight of human activity, suggesting that when experience has run its course, it is united by a particular quality, making it "*an* experience"—a specific situation that "stands out as an enduring memorial" (p. 43).

Dewey also argued that art is about experiencing such particular qualities. Here it is beneficial to remember that Dewey, along with other classical pragmatists, defined experience as an active relationship between the experiencer and what one experiences. In *Art as Experience*, Dewey characterized experience as "the everyday events, doings, and sufferings" (Dewey, 1934/LW, p. 9). Experience shows itself as a dynamic process in which an organism strives to maintain its balance. In such conditions, energy becomes continually transformed as "the live creature" coordinates its activity to the vicissitudes of its environment (p. 9). In a phase of equilibrium a harmonic unity is achieved that can be experienced as "consummation" rather than "cessation" (p. 42). This unity "rounds out" *an* experience by providing it an "esthetic" quality (p. 322).

While aesthetic judgments can emerge in all areas of life, Dewey developed a more precise concept of art-based aesthetic experience that can also be applied to music (see Jackson, 2000, p. 36). The arts can be understood as specific sets of inquiries that find their subject matter in qualities. Because of this function, the arts allow experiences that meet exceptionally well the three criteria that define consummatory experiences: completeness, uniqueness, and emotional impact (p. 36). It is in the arts that one can experience qualities to the max, as artistic products and performances communicate by expressing themselves through the artist's medium (Dewey, 1934/LW, pp. 10, 110–11).

Perhaps the most controversial corollary of this argument is that a work of art is not what the artist produces, but rather "what the product does with and in experience" (Dewey, 1934/LW, p. 9). From this standpoint, musical work does not equal the composition, nor even a performance. It is the pervasive quality that makes any work of art *an* experience. Dewey's naturalistic approach reveals that for the arts to fulfill their aesthetic potential, one does not have to assume a contemplative, distanced, reflective, or critical standpoint. The pervasive quality can simply be enjoyed as such. Yet this does not prevent one from focusing on connections between the pervasive quality and other qualities, enriching one's experience through interpretation. The point is that such inquiries do not leave the qualities untouched, but change our relationships with them by showing them in new light, as they are transformed to signs. For Dewey, this possibility of finding relations between qualities constitutes the basis of art criticism (p. 328).

# CONTEXTUALIZING CLASSICAL PRAGMATIST
# DISCOURSE ON QUALITIES

What is the point of positing qualities as entities that cannot be known? To understand the logic beneath this view it is useful to study the broader questions discussed by Peirce, Dewey, and other classical pragmatists (most notably William James).

In pragmatism studies, there has been an ongoing debate whether, in his later period, Dewey followed Peirce in maintaining how things are, or whether he kept to a Jamesian view about how things present themselves in experience (see, e.g., Bernstein, 1971, pp. 200ff.; Mounce, 1997). This tension can also be observed in Dewey's metaphysics, which can be interpreted both as "metaphysics of existence" and "metaphysics of experience" (Alexander, 1987, Chapter 3). It can be argued that it was on the question of "realism"— that is, whether knowledge refers to something "out there"—that Peirce and Dewey most fundamentally disagreed. Peirce judged Dewey's epistemology to be a "normative science," stating that it "does not concern itself in the least with what actually takes place in the universe" (Peirce, 1904/CP, p. 8.239). Peirce also suggested that Dewey's epistemological perspective cannot "see that anything is so very false," thus falling into the trap of antirealism (Peirce, 1904/CP, p. 8.241).[6]

Yet Dewey did not deny the connection between knowledge and reality (Dewey, 1911/ MW 6, pp. 103ff.; see also Boisvert, 1988, pp. 73ff.; Shook, 2000, pp. 45ff.; Hildebrand, 2003, pp. 26ff.; Putnam, 2010, p. 43). The point is that entities can only be judged to be objects of knowledge when they make their way into experience; otherwise, they are just "things," or immediate qualities (Dewey, 1911/MW, pp. 6, 108). Moreover, the relationship between the knower and the known is dynamic: the object of knowledge does not remain untouched by experience but is changed by it, and this process transforms the knower as well. If knowledge transforms its object, it makes no sense to grant the epistemic judgment to any particular kind of intellectual activity. This explains why Dewey did not have much use for the kind of realist concept of truth that Peirce esteemed. At most, argued Dewey, truth can be taken as "warranted assertibility," indicating that "all special conclusions of special inquiries are parts of an enterprise that is continually renewed" (Dewey, 1938/LW, pp. 12, 16–17).[7]

Dewey was acutely involved with developing philosophical views on ethics, aesthetics, political philosophy, and of course, education. Naturalistic pragmatism anchored Dewey's ideas on what he took to be the most important study object of philosophy: "the problems of men [sic]" (Dewey, 1917/MW, pp. 10, 46). Dewey's interpretation of the practical value of philosophy was partly inspired by James, who famously took truth to be "cash value" of an idea and encouraged the philosophical community to accept its practical bearings as signs of its ultimate meaningfulness (James, 1907, p. 31; see also James, 1975/1909). This was an interpretation that Peirce, as a realist, could not accept.

What seemingly inspired Dewey to study Peirce was the shared interest in overcoming the metaphysical distinction between nature and experience, accompanied by skepticism toward epistemological dualisms that stemmed from interpreting the necessary elements of knowledge as having existence prior to it—a reading that Dewey called "the error of intellectualism" (Dewey, 1912–1913/MW, pp. 7, 267) and "the fallacy of selective emphasis" (Dewey, 1925/LW, pp. 1, 32). For Dewey, this notion either ends up with a concept of reality independent of the knower or with a concept of knower independent of reality. This duality already vexed Dewey in his early philosophical writings, in which he attempted to solve it by absolving both the knower and the known of the spiritual absolute (see, e.g., Dewey, 1883/EW, pp. 1, 19ff.; see also Shook, 2000; Good, 2006). For the mature Dewey, a more feasible alternative was to be found from postulating that the knower and the known are parts of the same adaptive scheme. It was Peirce whom Dewey credited for introducing the idea to philosophy:

> I am quite sure that [Peirce], above all modern philosophers, has opened the road which permits a truly experiential philosophy to be developed which does not, like traditional empirical philosophies, cut experience off from nature, a road which if followed leads out of the impasse into which Locke's "ideas" and the contemporary theory of sensa and of essences alike conduct philosophy.
> (Dewey, 1935/LW, pp. 11, 94)

Dewey saw getting rid of such dualisms as a principal strategy for paving the way for a "truly experiential" approach that could "recover" or "reconstruct" philosophy by showing that both experience and knowledge are outgrowths of natural processes (Dewey, 1935/LW, pp. 11, 94; see also Dewey, 1917/MW, pp. 10, 3ff., and 1920/MW, pp. 12, 77ff.).

For Dewey, grasping the function of qualities in experience was a key element in philosophy's reconstruction. Acknowledging that experience has a qualitative dimension and recognizing "the inability of classical metaphysics to provide an adequate... description of experience" (McDermott in Dewey, 1987/LW, pp. 11, xiii). Dewey judged the main obstacle in the way of philosophy's recovery to be the modernist understanding of knowledge as a correspondence relation between the subject and the object, wherein the subject provides the qualitative dimension. According to Dewey, this understanding was drawn from a long history of looking at epistemic relation in terms of "the act of vision," in which things are thought to be "seen" in the mind's eye (Dewey, 1929/LW, pp. 4, 19). When this perspective was used to argue for the fundamental role of representations in knowledge, the epistemologists ended up in a cul-de-sac: they now had to depend on the idea of representation when making assumptions about knowing. This led into the paradox that the real objects of knowledge were left outside knowledge. Thus, epistemologists were left with two options: either they had to postulate something exterior to the mind that guarantees that representations represent external reality, or the mind had to be assumed to have an active role in constructing reality as phenomena.

It can be argued that Dewey took Peirce's (and James's) classical pragmatism(s) further in the path of naturalism by claiming that all knowledge is an outgrowth of natural interactions. This also pertains to the mind, which Dewey saw as "the power to understand things in terms of the use made of them" (Dewey, 1916/MW, pp. 9, 38).

Whereas Peirce feared that such radical naturalization leads philosophy to the dangerous path of losing its focus on what is truly real, Dewey settled on constructing a pluralist account of experience and used this construction to develop normative ideas of what we can know and how we should live.

Dewey's mature philosophy painted a metaphysical image of life in which qualities permeate everything we do, think, know, and enjoy. Whereas Peirce wanted to arrive at an aerial view of how qualities, facts, and signs partake in knowing, Dewey focused on understanding how qualities appear in and complete human experience. This ambition also drove his naturalized aesthetics: not to present another philosophy of art, but to argue that our communications with the world and each other are permeated by qualities.

## Evaluating Qualities

Dewey's vision of what is ethical was based on a notion that to be fully human necessitates communication. This idea also connects Dewey's ethics to his educational philosophy (see Dewey, 1916/MW, pp. 9, 7). In Dewey's vision, sharing experience helps individuals to grow, as they learn how to coordinate their interests. The more complex the social life becomes, the more challenging such coordinations become. However, this does not mean that synchronizing ways of life is pointless. On the contrary, continual forming, testing, and warranting value judgments through deliberation, or making "ordinary judgments upon what it is best or wise to do," is a necessary condition for both individual and social growth (Dewey, 1922/MW, pp. 14, 132).

To draw a line between his naturalistic ethics and views that take moral values as given, Dewey called the outcomes of ethical deliberation "evaluations"[8] (e.g., Dewey, 1925/LW, pp. 2, 78, 1938/LW, pp. 12, 125). In this connection, "to evaluate" simply means making informed choices among values. As a noun, "evaluation" can be understood to refer to a value that has proved its worth in some ethical inquiry. As outcomes of such inquiries, evaluations trigger meaning-relations by suggesting that some ways of acting are more preferred than others. Thus, they have a degree of generality. However, this does not mean that they point at absolute values. As outcomes of inquiries, evaluations are always situational, which means that they are as fallible as scientific theories.

At the core of evaluation is an ability to respond to novel circumstances by grasping their emergent qualities as values. Evaluation becomes a requisite when previously acquired habits do not work anymore. We find ourselves in an "incomplete" situation in which some of the constituent qualities no longer appear to hang together coherently (Dewey, 1915/MW, pp. 8, 15). A disruption of habitual activity forces us to "stop, look, and listen" (Dewey, 1916/MW, pp. 9, 110) in the interest of perceiving new value potentials among the situation's qualities. An important part of such perceiving is "dramatic rehearsal," in which possible ways of solving the problem are imagined and possible consequences anticipated (Dewey, 1908/MW, pp. 5, 292–93, 1932/LW, pp. 7, 275; see also Fesmire, 2003). In problematic situations that are predominantly ethical because they involve moral qualities (e.g., tensions between personal interests), we need to be able to rehearse our ethical imagination, identifying and investigating the value of possible solutions from several standpoints. Even more important, ethical deliberation requires a readiness to reflect critically on one's own values. This does not mean that one cannot have moral principles; however, it does mean that they should be recognized as outcomes of previous inquiries, warranted to a degree by their situational value (Dewey, 1932/LW, pp. 5, 275–83).

Dewey made an analytic distinction between two phases of value judgment: valuing and (e)valuation (Dewey, 1939/LW, pp. 13, 195). As discussed previously, "evaluations" can be seen as outcomes of ethical inquires; they are new habits of action. In turn, when we merely "value" something, we operate on the courtesy of our previously acquired habits that make us respond to it as having certain valence; that is, we experience it immediately as good or bad. This experience is the first step of evaluation, as what is immediately valued presents itself as a quality that can be interpreted as a sign in some context of ethical inquiry, to paraphrase Peirce's terms. As Dewey (1915/MW) put it: "To term the thing good or evil is to state the fact (noted in recollection) that it was actually involved in a situation of organic acceptance or rejection, with whatever qualities specifically characterize the act" (pp. 8, 26). From Dewey's standpoint, experience is energetic throughout, meaning that both valuing and evaluation should be seen as active processes (pp. 8, 26). Yet only evaluation can conclude the ethical judgment. When one reflects on a quality, investigating its potential meaning as a value, one considers "whether it is good and how good it is," asking "how it, as if acted upon, will operate in promoting a course of action" (pp. 8, 26). This reflects the classical pragmatist understanding of how meanings are arrived at in inquiry. According to Peirce's famous pragmatist maxim, to find out what something means, we need to operate on it, anticipating what kinds of consequences it would have when operated upon and testing such operations in ways that take us closer to universal judgments concerning its behavior in similar conditions in the future (Peirce, 1902/CP, p. 5.2). For Peirce, such tests, when guided by the logic of experimental science, are the best ways to "fix belief" (Peirce, 1877/CP, pp. 5.375–377). In fact, he took them as the only reliable way to arrive at the "final interpretant," or an interpretation that can approximate universal validity (Peirce 1909/CP, p. 8.314). This explains why Peirce draws on categorical differences among qualities, facts, and signs. In his system, categories fulfill different logical functions, and it is only signs that can claim a metaphysical status of "intellectual interpretants" that point at "ultimate reality" (Peirce, 1907/CP, p. 2.431).

For Dewey, qualities are just things experienced immediately (Dewey, 1930/LW, pp. 5, 243). For instance, when one is startled by a scream in a quiet neighborhood in the middle of the night—or, applied to musical situations, when one encounters a surprising harmonic or rhythmic event within otherwise conventional musical texture—one is grasped by a particular emotional quality as a function of a problematic situation. For Dewey, this initiative encounter is just as important as any other part of this experience and any consequences one might arrive at in studying the situation. When the situation is inquired into, and a conclusion is arrived at, the immediate quality is transformed: one now knows how to relate to the situation in a practical way (e.g., by calling for help, closing the window, or enjoying the composer's or performer's novel vision). Instead of presenting a metaphysical problem, such transformation of qualities is perfectly on a par with Dewey's naturalistic philosophy, which portrays the world as a complex network of intertwining events that reveal themselves as meaningful through inquiries (Dewey, 1925/LW, pp. 1, 63ff.). It is on the basis of our abilities to commit inquiries on such events, experienced as qualities, that we can structure this phenomenological manifold and turn it into a system of signs; and it is only through inquiry that we can arrive at agreement on how to draw the coordinates of our intertwined lives— including their artistic dimensions.

# Evaluating Qualities in (Art) Education

Dewey (1916/MW) saw education as a laboratory "in which philosophical problems become concrete and tested" (pp. 9, 338–39). This insight was based on his observation that education has a dual role in modern society. On the one hand, it is a place where new idea(l)s can be fashioned; on the other hand, it should represent and transmit existing idea(l)s.

To bridge the dichotomy between school and society was an important goal of Dewey's philosophy of education. For Dewey (1902/MW), this dichotomy reflects the modernist pedagogical discourse that separates the child from the curriculum, establishing logical distinctions that bifurcate experience and nature, knower and the known, value and fact, and individual and society (pp. 2, 274). The most apposite way to bridge all such dualisms is to focus on experience, understood as a dynamic field of interactions where new qualities constantly emerge and can be interpreted as values in some social-cultural context. In the same reading, experience can be understood as a method of learning, for it is from experience that learning has to launch and back to it that it must refer in order to make a difference.

Dewey's insistence that curriculum should be synchronized with students' experience established coordinates for mapping out the meaningfulness of education from both the individual's and society's standpoint. It also suggested how to reconstruct educational ideas of assessment. From a Deweyan standpoint, evaluation, understood as making value judgments, is as important in education as in other fields of human life. In a pedagogical context evaluation presents its worth primarily as a way to support learning. This does not mean that we cannot compare the outcomes of learning to the standards set out by society. Yet it means that those standards should be understood more as "ideals" that one can "choose" and "identify...with" than as something that controls one's judgment (Dewey, 1908/MW, pp. 5, 13; see also Herrick, 1996).

In Dewey's far-reaching vision, evaluation concerns the whole society, not just assessment of learning. As a naturalistic philosopher, Dewey wanted to situate evaluation in human life in a way that proves the organic connection among qualities, facts, and values in experience. From the standpoint of today's educational theory, Dewey's theory of evaluation supports holistic, authentic, sustainable, and formative assessment. Dewey also anticipated contemporary discourses on the limits of educational assessment when he took a stand against testing achievement in specific areas of learning in the interest of classificatory and selective purposes (Simpson & Jackson, 2001). While piecemeal assessment may be effective from the standpoint of developing standardized criteria that help teachers and administrators compare learning outcomes, when used exclusively such procedures fail to take notice of the wholesome nature of learning as qualitative transformation of experience. It is for the needs of further learning that one learns, and it is against this guiding value that assessment should be balanced. The ultimate problem of piecemeal assessment is that it fails to recognize particular qualities that emerge from the situational background of experience. Each learning process is unique, not in the sense that individuals learn alone, but in the sense that their learning is based on a continuum of situations bound together by particular qualities. To detect particular qualities and to turn them into values is to expand one's semiotic reach in society, which equals growth.

All learning processes thus incorporate unique experienced qualities that can be evaluated. While it may be useful to assess students' achievements for diagnostic needs, to hang all hopes of educational evaluation on such procedures is to fail to see evaluation as a continuous process of qualitative judgment. While teachers can (and hopefully do) belong to the functional organization of students' experience in pedagogical situations, they cannot dictate how learning serves students' growth. To keep assessment authentic requires humility and respect for the qualitative uniqueness of the learning process.

To grasp the difference between Dewey's holistic view of evaluation and the more analytical approaches of assessment, it might be useful to review Ralph Tyler's ideas on how educational evaluation should reflect educational objectives in the context of curriculum development. Tyler (1969/1949) famously argued that educational objectives should reflect three value horizons: "the learners themselves," "contemporary life outside the school," and "suggestions…from subject specialists" (pp. 11ff.). Setting of objectives should also be informed by philosophy of education and psychology of learning. While philosophy can offer tools for "drawing out values" from experience, psychology can help us to understand how such values can be best realized in learning (Kridel & Bullough, 2007, p. 78). In this way, curriculum designers can focus on what is most crucial: selecting and organizing students' learning experience (Tyler, 1969/1949, pp. 50ff.).

Tyler also argued that "preliminary checks" of learning do not suffice to provide "adequate appraisal[s] of the learning experiences planned for curriculum and instruction" because "they are not highly precise statements of the exact conditions to be met in providing for the learnings desired" (1969/1949, p. 111). "A more inclusive check" is needed (p. 112). Such a "check" is provided by evaluation proper, or summative assessment, which Tyler understands as the "process for determining the degree to which [certain desirable] changes in behavior are actually taking place" p. 112). Thus, Tyler makes assessment a matter of behavioral study.

The wide application of Tyler's ideas in the second half of the twentieth century testified to the power of thinking about evaluation in terms of behavioral objectives. However, according to Brooks (2012), for historical reasons, behavioristic views on evaluation soon became primary guidelines of assessment. In the United States this development was triggered by the post-Sputnik federal curriculum reform, which led to a "divorce" between curriculum theory and evaluation theory and to an increasing "devotion" of the latter to scientific testing and measurement (p. 2). This ideal has maintained a strong position in the global educational economy through the present time.

Yet as Brooks (2012) also observes, alternative voices have been raised during the decades of educational measuring and testing. Already in 1969, curriculum theorist Paul Klohr argued for the importance of recognizing the limitations of "scientific thinking" in assessment, encouraging the theorist to recognize that "undefined, primitive entities will precede the formulation of curriculum design data language" (Klohr, quoted in Brooks, 2012, p. 3). Sharing a similar conviction, some scholars began to reconceptualize the relation between curriculum and evaluation theory, aiming at revitalizing qualitative evaluation as a basis for educational assessment.

Elliot Eisner's work is especially relevant in this connection, as it takes us back to the topic of arts education and helps us to clarify the role of qualitative assessment, or evaluation, as a creative approach. In the late 1960s, Eisner argued that "some of education's most significant aims may not result in measurable outcomes" (cited in Brooks, 2012, p. 3). Instead of basing assessment on clearly specified and measurable objectives, Eisner proposed focusing on "expressive" objectives that allow for "self-discovery, originality, and inventiveness" (p. 3; see also Eisner, 2005, Chapters 2 and 3). This proposal was motivated by Eisner's way of "looking at problems and opportunities with an eye towards their aesthetic qualities" (2005, p. 1). The key concepts that Eisner used to describe qualitative assessment were appropriated from the art world. "Connoisseurship" marks an ability to discern "[q]uestions of authenticity, value, merit, … meaning and significance," whereas "criticism" points at the capability to "reeducate the perception of the work at hand" (p. 2). Together, connoisseurship and criticism can guide educational evaluation toward respecting "teaching as an art form" (p. 2). Evaluating teaching as an art form (an idea that reflects back to Dewey) is to reveal "qualities of classroom life" through a process that is analogous to narrative studies and other qualitative approaches in contemporary educational research (Eisner, 2005, p. 2; see also Eisner, 1998, 2004). Instead of subsuming qualities to measurable variables, then, Eisner envisioned an art-based approach to assessment that involves evaluation as an integral part of the creative process of drawing out values.

Eisner's work shares Dewey's interest in reconceptualizing "the ways in which we think about teaching, school structure, educational aims, pedagogical practices, and educational evaluation" (2005, p. 3). Eisner saw an integral connection between assessment and politics; the modernist reliance on achievement standards and accountability measures can be seen as a reflection of politically driven ideological assumptions about what education is and what it should be (p. 3; see also Fautley, 2010). One challenge for critical evaluation theory is to find alternatives to the prevailing policies and ideologies. As an alternative, Eisner (2005) suggested that "academic fields would do quite well to try to look more like the arts when the arts are well taught" (p. 6), and that studying "thinking in the arts" can "re-frame our conception of what education might try to accomplish" (2004, p. 2).

The link between education and art was also very central in Dewey's thinking. One could perhaps even say that it was the most important thread running through his mature philosophy (Alexander, 1987; Väkevä, 2004, 2007, 2012). Against this interpretation, there seems to be a certain productive logic guiding Dewey's decision to focus on naturalization of logic, ethics, and aesthetics in his major later works and to bring them together in his metaphysics. I conclude this section with an attempt to provide an aerial view of this logic.

Dewey's theory of inquiry (1938/LW, p. 12) can be understood as an elaboration of the Peircean notion that thinking is a form of intelligently controlled action that aims at new habits. In turn, Dewey's ethics and value theory (Dewey, 1932/LW, p. 5, 1939/LW, pp. 13, 192–251) shows how new habits are arrived at when valuings are transformed into evaluations. Together, these theories can be taken as statements of the central role of criticism in human life, where "criticism" should be understood as "control of the course of events so that it may yield... objects that are stable and that tend toward creation of other values" (Dewey, 1925/LW, pp. 1, 9). Note here that Dewey connects the outcomes of an inquiry and the values that arise from that inquiry. The difference between an intellectual idea and a value is not in their function but in the perspective from which they are observed: from the standpoint of science, the "stable" objects show themselves as facts; from the standpoint of ethics and value theory, they show themselves as evaluations.

Moreover, the "stable objects" incorporate "esthetic" qualities, meaning that they can be enjoyed immediately as such (Dewey, 1934/LW, p. 10). Again, the difference between ethical and aesthetic inquiry is a matter of perspective. These two approaches of evaluation are united in Dewey's naturalistic vision of how experience emerges from nature, revealing qualitative possibilities as values. Art, understood as a general mode of inquiry, grants us a chance to enjoy values in the full scope. To the degree that educational evaluation can be understood as an artistic effort, rather than just an assessment of artistic outcomes, it can partake in this project where values are drawn out from qualities.

# EVALUATING QUALITIES IN MUSIC EDUCATION: THE FINNISH CORE CURRICULUM FOR BASIC EDUCATION

It can be argued that music presents an especially tough case for assessment because it affords multiple interpretations of what the assessor should focus on. At least three reasons for this can be pointed out: (1) musical practices are so diverse that it is difficult to find criteria for excellence without privileging certain culture-specific standards; (2) Western approaches to musical assessment have traditionally emphasized product-centered and summative judgments that do not do justice to the holistic process of musical learning; and (3) even if there were universally comparable standards for assessing musical learning, it is difficult to deny that as an art form, music makes its impact largely in aesthetic experience, where judgments of value are based on qualities.

Despite such difficulties in the way of musical assessment, it can be argued that we need some standards of excellence to develop our curricula and instructional programs. While this challenge has been met in different ways in different educational systems and cultures (see Brophy & Abrahams, 2010), there seems to be global agreement that assessment standards have to reflect the qualities and values of music as an "art form" (e.g., Swanwick, 1988, pp. 4, 35ff.; Colwell, 2002, 2010; Mills, 2005, pp. 176ff.; Philpott, 2007, pp. 209–10; Booth, 2009, p. 168). This makes assessment dependent on how one defines music as art. From the Deweyan standpoint, one might argue that artistic quality gets different interpretations in different situations, and we have to accept that evaluation is contextual as a matter of fact. This might necessitate developing different value standards for different institutional forms of music education. I end this chapter by reflecting on what kinds of conditions the new Finnish Core Curriculum for Basic Education (OPS, 2014a, 2014b, 2014c) provides for assessment in the general music classroom. I hope that this short discussion will illuminate how Deweyan ideas of evaluation fit the egalitarian and democratic spirit of present-day Finnish comprehensive schools, especially regarding qualitative assessment in music.

In recent years the Finnish comprehensive school system has received high praise because of its high rankings on the Programme for International Student Assessment (PISA) tests.[9] This success has caused educationalists from around the world to investigate Finland's system. Often these observers have taken notice of the quality of Finnish teacher education and the democratic school culture, which appears to have avoided the pitfalls of testing, competition, and administrative accountability (see Sahlberg, 2014).[10]

The school system in Finland was developed by focusing on the possibilities to "develop everyone's potential" (Gross-Loh, 2014) and to promote "equity, equality and justice"[11] in Finnish society (OPS, 2014a, 2014b, p. 18). The comprehensive school is seen as a "learning community" in which "human rights" and "participation" are secured for all pupils (OPS, 2014a, 2014b, p. 28). The underlying values listed in the curriculum are the "uniqueness of each pupil and right to a good education"; "humanity, general knowledge [*sivistys*][12] and ability, equality and democracy"; understanding "cultural diversity as a richness"; and recognizing "the necessity of a sustainable way of living" (OPS, 2014a, 2014b, pp. 15–16). The concept of learning that the core curriculum endorses sees the pupils "as active actors" who "learn to set goals to and solve problems both independently and together with others" (OPS, 2014a, 2014b, p. 17). A pupil's ability to reflect on her "learning, experiences and emotions" is taken as a key to "[p]ositive emotional experiences, the joy of learning," and creativity (OPS, 2014a, 2014b, p. 17). Learning is also recognized to be diverse, situational, and "cumulative," in the sense that it requires "long-term and persistent practice" (OPS, 2014a, 2014b, p. 17).

When discussing assessment, the Core Curriculum echoes these views: "The interests, appraisals, working approaches and emotions, as well as their experiences and ideas of themselves as learners, influence [the pupils'] learning process and motivation. The self-image, self-efficacy and self-esteem of the pupils influence the goals they set for their actions. Encouraging guidance received during the learning process reinforces the pupils' trust in their potential. Giving and receiving versatile positive and realistic feedback are a key part of interaction that both supports learning and expands the pupils' interests" (OPS, 2014a, 2014b, p. 17). In this light, assessment in Finnish comprehensive schools should primarily serve a pupil's learning and the development of her reflective abilities. This is in line with The Finnish Basic Education Act (Basic Education Act 628/1998), which states that assessment must "guide and encourage learning and to develop the pupil's capability for self-assessment" (§22). Assessment is thus not seen primarily as an administrative mechanism that guarantees the quality of the educational system, but rather as a pedagogical means in developing a "culture of assessment" that is permeated with "supporting atmosphere," driven by "dialogical and interactive" practices that support the pupil's participation and "understanding of [her] personal learning processes" and aim to support the pupil's "progress throughout the learning process" (OPS, 2014a, 2014c, p. 47). Such a culture is made possible by "versatile," "fair, and ethical assessment" procedures (OPS, 2014a, 2014c, p. 47). Pupils should also be encouraged to give feedback to each other and to the teacher as a basis for developing their capabilities in self-assessment. In addition, the culture of assessment should support the school's cooperation with the home, provide tools for self-assessment for the teachers, and help with pedagogical differentiation (OPS, 2014a, 2014c, p. 47).

Clearly the ideal of assessment in Finnish comprehensive schools deviates from the scientific model. While assessment should be based on the objectives of the Core Curriculum (further specified in the local curricula), "the pupils and their achievements" should not "be compared to those of other pupils," and "the assessment shall not focus on the pupil's personality, temperament, or other personal characteristics" (OPS, 2014a, 2014c, p. 48). Rather, assessment should be tailored to the age, abilities, and developmental stage of the pupil and provide guidance, rather than adjudication. In other words, the Core Curriculum puts a strong emphasis on formative assessment and portrays summative assessment mainly as a diagnostic tool.

This general rationalization of assessment in the Finnish core curriculum seems to be in sync with Dewey's views of the role of evaluation in education. From Dewey's perspective, education should create conditions favorable for every individual's lifelong learning as a member of the democratic community. The Core Curriculum also reflects the egalitarian values of the Finnish educational system: respecting the uniqueness of every person involved in the system should be the primary concern of administration, teaching, and assessment. In line with this, assessment in Finnish comprehensive schools should be understood as part of an ongoing process of evaluative judgment that provides a basis for equality, equity, and social justice by maintaining sensitivity about the qualitative differences among learners, learning situations, and learning processes.

Are there any indications in the Core Curriculum that these values should guide assessment in music? This question could be approached by observing the sections that describe "transversial competence" (OPS, 2014a, 2014c, p. 20). Such competence is learned to support "growth as a human being"; to impart abilities "required for membership in a democratic society and a sustainable way of living"; and to "encourage the pupils to recognize their uniqueness and their personal strengths and developmental potential, and to appreciate themselves" (OPS, 2014a, 2014c, p. 20). The transversial competence is structured among seven "multidisciplinary modules" (OPS, 2014a, 2014c, p. 20):

(1) "thinking and learning to learn";
(2) "cultural competence, interaction, and self-expression";
(3) "taking care of oneself and managing day life";
(4) "multiliteracy";
(5) "ICT competence";
(6) "working life competence and entrepreneurship"; and
(7) "participation, involvement and building a sustainable future."

These modules are also recognized in the definitions of subject-based purposes, goal areas, and content areas.

The subject-specific curriculum in music lists five goal areas for three grade groups or educational stages (grades 1–2, 3–6, and 7–9): (1) "participation," (2) "making music[13] and creative production," (3) "cultural understanding and multiliteracy," (4) "safety and well-being in music," and (5) "learning-to-learn skills in music." In addition, the curriculum lists four content areas for all grade groups: (1) "making music together[14]"; (2) "components of music"; (3) "music in the pupil's life, community, and society"; and (4) "repertoire" (OPS, 2014a, 2014c, pp. 141–42). The assessment guidelines for the specific grade groups are as follows:

- In grades 1–2, the pupils should be given "feedback and…opportunities to assess their own and their group's action so that it encourages them to try out…and practice the skills to be learned." Special attention is to be given to "development of co-operation skills and skills in making music." Assessment should be based on "versatile demonstrations of skills and competence." The key object areas to assess in grades 1–2 are musical "co-operation skills" and "understanding the basic concepts[15] of music through musical activities" (OPS, 2014a, 2014c, p. 143).
- In grades 3–6, the teacher should again provide the pupils encouraging guidance in rehearsing "musical skills and understanding as well as holistic growth and cooperation skills" (OPS, 2014a, 2014c, p. 264). The purpose of the assessment is to "guide every pupil to perceive music concepts[16] and develop her action as a group member in relation to sounding musical whole" (OPS, 2014a, 2014c, p. 264). At the end of the sixth grade, the pupils should be given verbal or numeral marks based on the national assessment criteria. All other summative assessments should be based on local curricula (OPS, 2014a, 2014c, p. 265).

- In grades 7–9, the pupils are to be given "realistic, but supportive and encouraging feedback" that helps them "to increasingly perceive musical composition and performance as well as musical expression and different meanings of music." Feedback is especially important when assessing work "connected to the creative production of music and to music technology." The final assessment of music applies national criteria to judging how the pupil has reached the goals of the mandatory syllabus. The pupil receives a numeric mark based on her progress in relation to the assessment criteria (OPS, 2014a, 2014c, p. 264).

The assessment criteria in music seem to be in line with the general guiding values and goals of the transversial competence of the Core Curriculum. In all grades, the pupils are expected to learn thinking and learning skills; how to cooperate; how to participate in a variety of practices; how to take care of themselves, others, and their environment; and how to assess their own learning in musical contexts. These areas are assessed during and after teaching, with an emphasis on formative assessment.

How are qualities to be focused on in assessment? Here it might be advisable to use the adjective "aesthetic" as a point of reference. The word appears in several places in the Core Curriculum: when discussing the value basis,[17] in the general section that describes the transversial competencies,[18] and in two sections recounting how transversal competencies should be learned in the grade groups.[19] However, in the subject-specific section of music the focus appears to be on assessing hands-on musicking and the kind of musical understandings that can be reported verbally. The term "aesthetic" is mentioned twice in the music curriculum for grades 1–2. The description of purpose states that "the pupils' creative musical thinking and aesthetic and musical understanding [should be] promoted by providing them with opportunities to compose and perform musical ideas and use their imagination and creativity both independently and together with others" (OPS, 2014a, 2014c, p. 141). "Aesthetic" also appears in the goal area of "cultural understanding and multiliteracy," which states that the pupil should learn to "enjoy the aesthetic, cultural, and historical diversity of music" (OPS, 2014a, 2014c, p. 142). In addition, "aesthetic" appears twice in the subject-specific music curriculum for grades 3–6, which states that "creative and aesthetic thinking associated with sound and music" should be "promoted by creating situations where the pupils may plan and implement different musical or multidisciplinary art projects" (OPS, 2014a, 2014c, p. 263). The term makes yet another appearance in connection with the goal area of "cultural understanding and multiliteracy," in which the pupil is to be guided "to explore his or her musical experiences and the aesthetic, cultural, and historical diversity of music" and assessment is to be based on how she can report them (OPS, 2014a, 2014c, p. 266). The term "aesthetic" does not appear at all in the sections describing subject-specific goals, contents, and assessment criteria for grades 7–9.

It seems that according to the Core Curriculum, assessment in music in Finnish comprehensive schools is to focus mainly on practical and linguistic skills, perhaps reflecting the idea that observations of hands-on musicking and written or verbal reports of musical experience are the most convenient entry points to musical learning.

It is interesting to compare this approach to one of the key objectives of the music curriculum, which is to help the pupils grasp "multiple meanings of music" (OPS, 2014a, 2014c, p. 141). The electronic version of the Core Curriculum elaborates these meanings as follows:

> Music arises emotions that are often different compared to the feelings experienced… on a daily basis. Music is used to transform mood and alertness, to inspire action, and to help one to concentrate. In addition to regulating one's own emotions, music can be used in sharing expression and distributing feelings. The meaningfulness of music relates strongly to both experiencing the selfhood and to social interaction. Self is always built in relationship with other people and surrounding cultures. Therefore it is important to understand different cultures and…their musics. In specific, music has an immense meaning…in youth, when one constructs one's own identity in relation to the peer group. (OPS, 2014b)

In turn, the electronic document clarifies the meaning of "aesthetic thinking and understanding" as follows:

> Aesthetic thinking or understanding in music are related to observation of [its] aesthetic value, [viz.], the beauty value of music and how one responds to it. One needs aesthetic thinking when listening, producing, and interpreting music. Children learn aesthetic thinking and artistic making when they practice musical performing or interpretation of musical pieces. Originating in musical perceptions, aesthetic thinking is a multimodal and versatile process, where acoustic structures are coordinated and revalued e.g. in order to achieve or to find better musical interpretation. Through musical listening experiences, the pupils learn how aesthetic thinking and ideals of beauty emerge in different eras, different cultures, and music's different styles.
> (OPS, 2014b)

Thus, while the Core Curriculum recognizes the value of aesthetic experience in learning music, it does not provide much guidance in how the qualitative aspect of such experience could be recognized in assessment, apart from hands-on musicking and reports on how the student can conceptualize her perceptions. Of course from the Deweyan standpoint as discussed in this chapter, to assess experience is in itself an aesthetic process. This means that we can only experience qualities that our students experience by organizing learning environments that are conducive to artistic communication. As art, music offers one way to share qualitative experience. Apart from recognizing the value of learning by doing and the role of reflection in learning, it is important to guarantee that the uniqueness of each learner, learning situation, and learning process is recognized. To the degree that we can accept Dewey's claim that all evaluation is dependent on how qualities are transformed into values, we can perhaps presume that good assessment cultures in music education are built on respecting qualitative differences in how music is experienced. In light of the guiding ideals of the Finnish comprehensive school, such respect could be also seen as key to the realization of equality and other basic values of democratic societies. When examined from the more general standpoint of the role of evaluation in music education, the pragmatist view discussed in this chapter suggests a pluralist approach that respects a variety of musical experiences as possible sources of artistic growth and finds such experiences permeated with values. Yet the processes of transforming qualities into values are not restricted to artistic situations; they are at the heart of a democratic way of life, implying a political role for evaluation in all contexts.

## Notes

1. Another way to make a distinction between assessment and evaluation is to say that assessment is formative and evaluation is summative. However, the clearest distinction between these terms relates to different approaches of judging educational phenomena. From this perspective, assessment involves determining a variable's position against some predecided measure, whereas evaluation refers more generally to reflecting on the educational phenomena in terms of some value dimension (cf. Murphy & Espeland, 2007).

2. This research has been undertaken as part of the ArtsEqual project funded by the Academy of Finland's Strategic Research Council from its Equality in Society program (project no. 93199).

3. All Peirce references are to *The Collected Papers of Charles Sanders Peirce* (Peirce, 1994). The individual documents' dates are provided with each citation (e.g., Peirce, 1904/CP 1.284).

4. The qualifier "naturalistic pragmatist" refers here to a philosophical view that understands experience as an emergent function of natural processes without reducing it to physical events. When discussing aesthetics, Dewey commonly uses the word "esthetic" instead of "aesthetic," but a common interpretation is that he does not make a difference between the two uses.

5. I use the standard procedure in referring to Dewey's *Collected Works* (Dewey, 1996), in which the abbreviation (EW for *The Early Works*, MW for *The Middle Works*, and LW for *The Later Works*) is followed by the volume number and page number. The individual works' dates are also provided with each citation (e.g., Dewey, 1934/LW, p. 10).

6. Peirce's letter was a follow-up to his review (Peirce, 1904/CP, pp. 8.188–.190) of Dewey's *Studies in Logical Theory* (Dewey, 1903/MW, pp. 2, 293–375).

7. While Dewey credited Peirce as the originator of the idea of the fallibility of knowledge, Peirce himself had more faith in scientific inquiry as a way to reveal, at least potentially, what is real "independent of the vagaries of me and you" (Peirce, 1868/CP, p. 5.311). Interestingly, Peirce (1909/CP, p. 1.27n) described a realist as someone who believes that "the property, the character, the predicate, [e.g.] hardness, is not invented by men, as the word is, but is really and truly in the hard things and is one in them all, as a description of habit, disposition, or behavior"; in this sense, there is not a fundamental difference between his and Dewey's metaphysical views.

8. Dewey used different terms to mark what is here called "evaluation" or "evaluations" (Gouinlock, 1972). I follow Anderson (2014) in making a difference between "evaluation" and "valuation," where the latter can be understood as a general signifier that refers to the whole evaluation process.

9. In 2000, Finland was the top-scoring nation in PISA (Sahlberg, 2014, p. 34). In all fairness, Finnish PISA results have been declining lately (OKM, 2013; PISA, 2015).

10. While PISA results do not measure achievement in the art subjects, some commentators have remarked that the arts seem to play a vital role in Finnish schools. This observation has occasionally changed to amazement when the visitor in question has been told that Finland also has a publicly funded system of extracurricular art education. On the Finnish art education system, see, for example, OKM (2010). The Finnish music education system is described in Rikandi (2010).

11. All quotes are from the electronic English version of the Finnish Core Curriculum for Basic Education (OPS, 2014a). I have also added the original reference to the Finnish text.

12. The Finnish concept *sivistys* would be easier to translate as the German *Bildung* than to the English "general knowledge and ability." According to the dictionary of The Finnish Board of Education, *sivistys* can also be translated as "education" (OPH, 2016). However, the term also has more extensive semantic overtones that go back to German educational discourse of the nineteenth century, which emphasized the dynamic interaction between the individual and society. One source for becoming familiar with this discussion and its connections to classical pragmatist tradition is Siljander, Kivelä, and Sutinen (2012).

13. The original Finnish word is *musisointi* (lit. "musicking"), and it is defined as involving "singing, playing instruments, listening, moving, improvising, and composing" (OPS, 2014a, 2014c, 142; cf. Elliott, 1995, the probable source of the Finnish reference).

14. The original Finnish phrase is *miten musiikissa toimitaan* (lit. "how one acts in music").

15. "The basic concepts" of "sound (and music)" are defined in the Finnish electronic edition of OPS (2014b) as "pitch, duration, volume, and [tone] color." All translations from the Finnish electronic edition (OPS, 2014b) are mine.

16. According to the electronic edition of the core curriculum (OPS, 2014b), "the music concepts" are "rhythm, tempo, melody, harmony, form, timbre, and dynamics."

17. "The perspectives of ethics and aesthetics guide the pupil to think about what is valuable in life" (OPS, 2014a, 2014c, p. 16).

18. The students are to be "guided to act in a manner that promotes aesthetic values in their environment action and to enjoy their various manifestations" (OPS, 2014a, 2014c, p. 21) and to "discuss and reflect ethical and aesthetical questions" when developing "multiliteracy" (OPS, 2014a, 2014c, p. 22).

19. For grades 1–2 "the development…of ethical and aesthetic thinking" should be "supported with…songs" and "different art forms" (OPS, 2014a, 2014c, p. 141); for grades 7–9 "[t]he arts deepen ethical and aesthetic thinking by stirring emotions and creating new inventive ideas" (OPS, 2014a, 2014c, p. 282).

## REFERENCES

Alexander, T. (1987). *John Dewey's theory of art, experience, and nature: The horizons of feeling.* New York: State University of New York Press.

Anderson, E. (2014). Dewey's moral philosophy. In E. Zalta (Ed.), *The Stanford encyclopedia of philosophy.* Retrieved from http://plato.stanford.edu/archives/spr2014/entries/dewey-moral/

Barrett, A., Chawla-Duggan, R., Lowe, J., Nikel, J., & Ukpo, E. (2006). *The concept of quality in education: A review of the international literature on the concept of quality in education.* EdQual Working Paper No 3. EdQual RPC. Retrieved from http://www.edqual.org/publications/workingpaper/edqualwp3.pdf/at_download/file.pdf

Bernstein, R. J. (1971). *Praxis and action: Contemporary philosophies of human activity*. Philadelphia: University of Pennsylvania Press.

Boisvert, R. (1988). *Dewey's metaphysics*. New York: Fordham University Press.

Booth, E. (2009). *The music teaching artist's bible: Becoming a virtuoso educator*. New York: Oxford University Press.

Brooks, N. (2012). Restoring the relationship of "e-valuation" and curriculum. *The Journal of the American Association for the Advancement of Curriculum Studies, 8*, 1–13.

Brophy, T. (2000). *Assessing the developing child musician: A guide for general music teachers*. Matrlesham, UK: Boydell & Brewer.

Brophy, T., & Abrahams, J. (2010). *The practice of assessment in music education: Frameworks, models, and designs*. Chicago: GIA Publications.

Burnard, P., & Fautley, M. (2015). Assessing diverse creativities in music. In M. Fleming, L. Bresler, & J. O'Toole (Eds.), *The Routledge international handbook of the arts and education* (pp. 254–67). London: Routledge.

Chiasson, P. (2005). Peirce's design for thinking: An embedded philosophy of education. *Educational Philosophy and Theory, 37*(2), 207–26.

Colwell, R. (2002). Assessment's potential in music education. In R. Colwell & C. Richardson (Eds.), *The new handbook of research on music teaching and learning: A project of the Music Educators National Conference* (pp. 1128–57). New York: Oxford University Press.

Colwell, R. (2010). Many voices, one goal: Practices of large-scale music assessment. In T. S. Brophy (Ed.), *The practice of assessment in music education: Frameworks, models, and design* (pp. 3–17). Chicago: GIA.

Dewey, J. (1996). *The collected works of John Dewey: The electronic edition*. Larry A. Hickman (Ed.). Charlottesville, VA: InteLex Corporation.

Eisner, E. W. (1996). *Cognition and curriculum reconsidered*. London: Paul Chapman Publishing.

Eisner, E. W. (1998). Does experience in the arts boost academic achievement? *Arts Education Policy Review, 100*(1), 32–40.

Eisner, E. W. (2002). *The arts and the creation of mind*. New Haven, CT: Yale University Press.

Eisner, E. W. (2004). What can education learn from the arts about the practice of education? *International Journal of Education & the Arts, 5*(4), 1–12.

Eisner, E. W. (2005). *Reimagining schools: The selected works of Elliot W. Eisner*. London: Routledge.

Eisner, E. W. (2007). Interlude: Assessment and evaluation in education and the arts. In Liora Bresler (Ed.), *International handbook of research in arts education* (pp. 423–26). Dordrecht, The Netherlands: Springer.

Elliott, D. J. (1995). *Music matters: A new philosophy of music education*. New York: Oxford University Press.

Fautley, M. (2010). *Assessment in music education*. Oxford: Oxford University Press.

Fesmire, S. (2003). *John Dewey and moral imagination: Pragmatism in ethics*. Urbana, IL: Indiana University Press.

Good, J. A. (2006). *A search for unity in diversity: The "permanent Hegelian deposit" in the philosophy of John Dewey*. Lanham, MD: Lexington Books.

Gouinlock, J. (1972). *John Dewey's philosophy of value*. New York: Humanities Press.

Gross-Loh, C. (2014, March 17). Finnish education chief: "We created a school system based on equality." *The Atlantic*. Retrieved from http://www.theatlantic.com/education/archive/2014/03/finnish-education-chief-we-created-a-school-system-based-on-equality/284427/

Herrick, M. J. (1996). Assessment of student achievement and learning, what would Dewey say? A "Recent" interview with John Dewey. *Journal of Career and Technical Education, 13*(1). Retrieved from https://ejournals.lib.vt.edu/JCTE/article/view/510/701

Hickman, R. (2007). Wipped-fancying and other vices: Re-evaluating assessment in art and design. In T. Rayment (Ed.), *The problem of assessment in art and design* (Vol. 4, pp. 77–88). Chicago: Intellect Books, The University of Chicago Press.

Hildebrand, D. L. (2003). *Beyond realism and antirealism: John Dewey and the neopragmatists.* Nashville, TN: Vanderbilt University Press.

Hirst, P. H., & Peters, R. S. (2011/1971). *The logic of education.* London: Routledge.

Jackson, P. W. (2000). *John Dewey and the lessons of art.* New Haven, CT: Yale University Press.

James, W. (1907). *Pragmatism: A new name for some old ways of thinking; Popular lectures on philosophy.* New York: Longmans, Green & Co.

James, W. (1975/1909). *The meaning of truth.* Cambridge, MA: Harvard University Press.

Jorgensen, E. R. (2003). *The art of teaching music.* Bloomington: Indiana University Press.

Kridel, C., & Bullough, R. V., Jr. (2007). *Stories of the eight-year study: Reexamining secondary education in America.* Albany, NY: State University of New York Press.

McDermott, J. (1987). The later works, 1925-53: John Dewey. In J. Boydston (Ed.), *Essays, Reviews, Miscellany, and The Public and Its Problems* (Vol. 11, pp. 1935–1937). Carbondale, IL: Southern Illinois University Press.

Mills, J. (2005). *Music in the school.* Oxford: Oxford University Press.

Mounce, H. O. (1997). *The two pragmatisms: From Peirce to Rorty.* London: Routledge.

Murphy, R. (2007). Harmonizing assessment and music in the classroom. In L. Bresler (Ed.), *International handbook of research in arts education* (pp. 361–88). Dordrecht, The Netherlands: Springer.

Murphy, R., & Espeland, M. (2007). Prelude: Making connections in assessment and evaluation in arts education. In L. Bresler (Ed.), *International handbook of research in arts education* (pp. 337–40). Dordrecht, The Netherlands: Springer.

Määttänen, P. (1993). *Action and experience: A naturalistic approach to cognition.* Annales Academiae Scientiarum Fennicae, Dissertationes Humanarum Litterarum 64. Helsinki, Finland: University of Helsinki.

OED. (2016). "Quality." In *Oxford English Dictionary.* Retrieved from http://www.oed.com. ezproxy.uniarts.fi/view/Entry/155878?rskey=4xz5rq&result=1&isAdvanced=false#eid

OKM. (2010). *Arts education and cultural education in Finland* (Policy Analysis Reports of the Ministry of Education and Culture 2010, 2). Retrieved from http://www.minedu.fi/export/sites/default/OPM/Julkaisut/2010/liitteet/okmpolo22010.pdf?lang=fi

OKM. (2013). *PISA 2012: Proficiency of Finnish youth declining.* Retrieved from http://www.minedu.fi/OPM/Tiedotteet/2013/12/pisa.html?lang=en

OPH. (2016). *Opetushallinnon sanasto* [Dictionary of educational administration]. Retrieved from http://www03.oph.fi/sanasto/

OPS. (2014a). *National core curriculum for basic education 2014.* Helsinki, Finland: Finnish Board of Education.

OPS. (2014b). *Perusopetuksen opetussuunnitelman perusteet 2014* [National core curriculum for basic education]. Helsinki, Finland: Opetushallitus. Retrieved from http://www.oph.fi/download/163777_perusopetuksen_opetussuunnitelman_perusteet_2014.pdf

OPS. (2014c). *Perusopetuksen opetussuunnitelman perusteet 2014* [National core curriculum for basic education]. Helsinki, Finland: Opetushallitus. Retrieved from https://eperusteet. opintopolku.fi/#/fi/perusopetus/419550/vuosiluokkakokonaisuus/428780/oppiaine/466343

Peirce, C. S. (1994). *The collected papers of Charles Sanders Peirce* (Electronic ed.). C. Hartshorne, P. Weiss, & A. Walter Burks (Eds.). Charlottesville, VA: InteLex Corporation.

Philpott, C. (2007). Creativity and music education. In C. Philpott & G. Spruce (Eds.), *Learning to teach music in the secondary school: A companion to school experience* (pp. 119–34). London: Routledge.

PISA. (2015). PISA 2015: Finnish youth still at the top despite the drop. Retrieved from http://okm.fi/OPM/Tiedotteet/2016/12/PISA2015.html?lang=fi&extra_locale=en

Putnam, R. A. (2010). Dewey's epistemology. In M. Cochran (Ed.), *The Cambridge companion to Dewey* (pp. 34–54). Cambridge, UK: Cambridge University Press.

Rikandi, I. (Ed.) (2010). *Mapping the common ground: Philosophical perspectives on Finnish music education*. Helsinki: BTJ Finland.

Russell, J., & Zembylas, M. (2007). Arts integration in the curriculum: A review of research and implications for teaching and learning. In L. Bresler (Ed.), *International handbook of research in arts education* (pp. 287–312). Dordrecht, The Netherlands: Springer.

Sahlberg, P. (2014). *Finnish lessons 2.0: What can the world learn from educational change in Finland?* New York: Teachers College Press.

Shook, J. R. (2000). *Dewey's empirical theory of knowledge and reality*. Nashville, TN: Vanderbilt University Press.

Siljander, P., Kivelä, A., & Sutinen, A. (Eds.). (2012). *Theories of Bildung and growth: Connections and controversies between continental educational thinking and American pragmatism*. Rotterdam, The Netherlands: Sense.

Simpson, D. J., & Jackson, M. J. B. (2001). John Dewey and educational evaluation. In J. L. Kincheloe & D. K. Weil (Eds.), *Standards and schooling in the United States: An encyclopedia* (Vol. 1, pp. 419–28). Santa Barbara, CA: ABC Clio.

Swanwick, K. (1988). *Music, mind and education*. London: Routledge.

Tyler, R. W. (1969/1949). *Basic principles of curriculum and instruction*. Chicago: University of Chicago Press.

Väkevä, L. (2004). *Kasvatuksen taide ja taidekasvatus: Estetiikan ja taidekasvatuksen merkitys John Deweyn naturalistisessa pragmatismissa* [The art of education and art education: The significance of aesthetics and art education in the naturalistic pragmatism of John Dewey]. Acta xUniversitatis Ouluensis. E, Scientiae rerum socialium 68. Oulu, Finland. Retrieved from http://herkules.oulu.fi/isbn9514273109

Väkevä, L. (2007). Art education, the art of education and the art of life: Considering the implications of Dewey's later philosophy to art and music education. *Action, Criticism & Theory for Music Education*, 6(1). Retrieved from http://act.maydaygroup.org/articles/Vakeva6_1.pdf

Väkevä, L. (2012). Experiencing growth as a natural phenomenon: John Dewey's philosophy and the Bildung tradition. In P. Siljader, A. Kivelä, & A. Sutinen (Eds.), *Theories of Bildung and growth: Connections and controversies between continental educational thinking and American pragmatism* (pp. 261–80). Rotterdam, The Netherlands: Sense.

Woodford, P. (2005). *Democracy and music education: Liberalism, ethics, and the politics of practice*. Bloomington: Indiana University Press.

CHAPTER 7

.......................................................................................................

# COULD THERE BE DELEUZIAN ASSESSMENT IN MUSIC EDUCATION?

.......................................................................................................

### LAUREN KAPALKA RICHERME

IN this philosophical inquiry I examine four themes from Gilles Deleuze's writings as they relate to measurement and consider how these themes might inform concepts and practices of assessment in various music teaching and learning contexts. The first theme suggests that each group of connective relations, what Deleuze terms a "plane of immanence," demands its own forms of measurement. Second, Deleuze emphasizes varieties of measurement. Third, those with power, or what Deleuze terms the "majority," always set the standard for measurement. Fourth, Deleuze derides continuous assessment. His writings suggest that music educators consider that assessments created for one musical practice or style should not transcend their own "plane of immanence," that a variety of nonstandardized assessments are desirable, that the effect of measurement on "minoritarian" musical practices must be examined carefully, and that it is essential to ponder the potential of unmeasured music making.

## INTRODUCTION AND CURRENT CONTEXT

.......................................................................................................

French philosopher Gilles Deleuze (1925–1995) is generally categorized as a "poststructuralist" writer.[1] The poststructuralist movement, which began in France in the 1960s, also encompasses the work of Jacques Derrida, Michel Foucault, Julia Kristeva, and Jean-François Lyotard. Broadly speaking, these authors aimed to counter structuralism, a movement whose adherents treated difference as superficial and argued that overarching systems and structures underlie all aspects of human culture (Belsey, 2002).

Deleuze spent the majority of his career teaching at the University of Paris VIII in Vincennes. Drawing inspiration from the works of Lucretius, Hume, Spinoza, Nietzsche, and Bergson, he reimagined ontological investigations as creative processes leading toward openness rather than as searches for clarity and limits (May, 2005). Deleuze wrote both alone and with Félix Guattari (1930–1992), a political activist and practicing psychoanalyst who trained with the French psychoanalyst and philosopher Jacques Lacan. In music education, Elizabeth Gould has offered a sustained exploration of Deleuze's work, using it to investigate issues including feminism, heteronormativity, social justice, and creativity (e.g., Gould, 2005, 2006, 2007a, 2007b, 2009, 2011, 2012). Music educators have yet to examine in detail the possibilities that Deleuze's work might hold for educational assessment.

The practice of assessment can take many forms, including formal, informal, formative, and summative, and it can involve materials and practices ranging from tests to portfolios to rubrics to descriptive feedback. Authors of contemporary American education and arts education policies, including the Every Student Succeeds Act (2015) and current drafts of the Music Model Cornerstone Assessments (National Association for Music Education, 2016), tend to emphasize the adoption of formal, summative assessment practices. The current pervasiveness of such rhetoric necessitates multiple philosophical investigations of the nature of assessment and its outcomes. As noted at the outset, I base my investigation on Deleuze's writings.

Deleuze's emphasis on ongoing differing and imaginative possibilities may at first glance appear incompatible with overarching, codified assessments. Indeed, Deleuze (1990/1995) writes negatively about "forms of continuous assessment," noting the problems of bringing business practices into every level of education (p. 182). He also criticizes societies' increasing use of ongoing assessments as a form of control, mourning the "continual monitoring of worker-schoolkids or bureaucrat-students" (p. 175). These writings suggest that Deleuze would shun the forms of assessment prevalent in contemporary education discourse.

While Deleuze does not offer further insight into the practice of assessment, he posits a more nuanced explanation of measurement. Many educational authors note the interconnection of measurement and assessment (e.g., Miller, Linn, & Gronlund, 2009; Reynolds, Livingston, & Willson, 2009). Payne (2003) summarizes: "Assessment = Measurement + Evaluation" (p. 9). The interconnection of measurement and assessment also appears in education policy documents. For example, the authors of the American Common Core State Standards website assert that the standards will enable "the development and implementation of common comprehensive assessment systems to measure student performance annually that will replace existing state testing systems" (Common Core, 2015, p. 2). Similarly, writers of the current drafts of the Model Cornerstone Assessments intend the assessments to "provide formative and summative means to measure student achievement of performance standards in the National Core Music Standards" (e.g., National Association for Music Education, 2015, p. 1). Deleuze's assertions about measurement may therefore offer insights applicable to music education assessment.

# PLANES OF IMMANENCE

Deleuze addresses the processes of measurement and assessment indirectly through his concept of "planes of immanence," which plays a central role in his metaphysics. Deleuzian scholar James Williams (2005) explains *immanence* as the process of emphasizing connectivity between relations. While Deleuze uses immanence primarily as a way of explicating his own philosophical processes, immanence in music making might include the interplay of notes in a melody or the changing interactions on a marching band field. In each case, the connectivity involves a process—the motion between notes or among band members—rather than connectivity between stagnant entities or identities.

Offering further explanation, Deleuze and Guattari (1980/1987) contrast immanence with transcendence. Williams (2005) summarizes that while immanence involves "a relation 'in' something," transcendence involves "a relation 'to' something" (p. 126). Immanence involves the relations *in* a melody or *in* a marching band show; transcendence involves how a melody relates *to* another melody or how a marching band show relates *to* another show. These statements demonstrate that immanent relationships do not exist in isolation; the motion within a melody or marching band show involves not a single relationship but diverse, evolving ones. The multitude of "relations in" forms what Deleuze and Guattari (1991/1994) term a "plane of immanence." They explain: "When immanence is no longer immanent to something other than itself it is possible to speak of a plane of immanence" (p. 47). The multitude of connective relations within a melody constitute a plane of immanence that differs from the plane of immanence constituted by a marching band show.

In addition to the continually changing connections within a single plane of immanence, Deleuze and Guattari (1991/1994) assert that the planes themselves form relationships as ideas from one plane transpose into others. They argue: "In any concept there are usually bits or components that come from other concepts, which corresponded to other problems and presupposed other planes" (p. 18). Rather than being closed off from each other and from other aspects of life, planes of immanence transform as concepts flow between them and connect with situations and events.

Deleuze and Guattari (1980/1987) explain that individual authors lay out planes of immanence by emphasizing divergent movements and interactions. For example, they contrast the plane of immanence laid out by Heinrich von Kleist—a German poet, novelist, and dramatist—with those laid out by his contemporaries, including Goethe and Hegel. Specifically, Deleuze and Guattari argue that Kleist's emphasis on speed and slowness differs from Goethe's and Hegel's emphases on "harmonious development of Form and a regulated formation of the Subject, personage, or character" (p. 268). Kleist's plane of immanence exists and develops differently from those of Goethe and Hegel and cannot be subsumed by them.

How might the concept of planes of immanence relate to assessment? Deleuze and Guattari's examples of individual authors' planes of immanence suggest that one could not evaluate different authors' writings based on the exact same criteria. To assess Kleist primarily on his form or Goethe and Hegel primarily on their fluidity would not do justice to each writer's unique contributions. The evolving relations *in* Kleist's plane of immanence deserve more attention than how Kleist's plane of immanence relates *to* Goethe's or Hegel's plane of immanence. When individuals do make comparisons between planes of immanence, they need not aim for transcendence by asserting a hierarchy between them; rather, like Deleuze and Guattari's aforementioned observations about differences among Kleist, Goethe, and Hegel, they might celebrate the uniqueness of each plane of immanence.

The concept of planes of immanence has a clear connection to acts of musical creation. To assess students' compositions or improvisations using others' planes of immanence does not do justice to their unique individual contributions. As such, teachers and students might emphasize the evolving relations *in* a single student's plane of immanence rather than comparing those practices *to* either other students' planes of immanence or those of professional musicians. Such action leads not to immobile judgments of transcendence but to changing assessments that integrate with students' evolving experiences. This does not mean that individuals might never compare their own or others' musical creations to those of peers or respected composers or improvisers; highlighting immanence does not mean that assessments should never involve explorations of transcendence. Yet given that contemporary educational rhetoric foregrounds transcendence by assessing students primarily in relation to standards or to their peers, focusing on immanence serves as a counter to such practices.

Deleuze and Guattari's conception of planes of immanence may also hold implications for musical practices such as performing and listening. For example, Deleuze and Guattari (1980/1987) explain the flux within a plane of immanence that occurs when playing a piece by Chopin:

> Even a rubato by Chopin cannot be reproduced because it will have different time characteristics at each playing. It is as though an immense plane of consistency of variable speed were forever sweeping up forms and functions, forms and subjects, extracting from them particles and affects. (p. 271)[2]

These statements suggest that evaluating a performance of an existing work necessitates considering how it adheres to the characteristics set out within its plane of immanence while simultaneously troubling that plane of immanence, evoking new combinations and possibilities. One can therefore critique both a performer of a Chopin piece who completely disregards the plane of immanence that Chopin created and a performer who, by attempting to replicate exactly another's performance, neglects to set Chopin's plane of immanence into motion. Similarly, it is problematic for listeners to assess music on planes of immanence not set out by its performers or creators or to assess their endeavors on how well the performers mimic past listening experiences. In short, assessments consistent with Deleuze's writings thus require a balance of respecting existing planes of immanence while concurrently innovating within them.

Given that concepts flow between planes of immanence and connect with problems and experiences outside of such planes, individuals can never completely limit their assessments to the plane of immanence at hand. A listener or performer familiar with particular hip-hop or bluegrass planes of immanence cannot completely exclude those understandings when he or she tries to evaluate a gamelan performance. While planes of immanence offer a means of conceptualizing the need and importance of not applying assessment criteria appropriate in one context to a contrasting musical endeavor, even if individuals try to make such distinctions, they will likely lack complete control over the process. As such, although Deleuze's concept of planes of immanence offers a way of conceptualizing the need for assessments appropriate for specific music practices, it also serves as a reminder of the limits of such action.

## VARIETIES OF MEASUREMENT

Measurements within a single plane of immanence, however, are not without potential limitations. Deleuze and Guattari (1980/1987) problematize situations in which single "units of measurement" serve to unify the continual differing of existence (p. 8). For example, in referring to Christian doctrine and ritual they write: "Church power has always been associated with a certain administration of sin possessing a strong segmentarity (the seven deadly sins), units of measure (how many times?), and rules of equivalence and atonement (confession, penance)" (p. 218). In such situations, church leaders measure individuals' sinfulness by considering how many times they have committed various sins, ultimately converting their measurements into a penance of equivalent magnitude. The church's power derives in part from the priest's or minister's authority to equate units of sin with units of penance.

While music educators clearly do not deal directly with measuring morality, they do equate measured units with specific grades or other indicators of progress. For instance, a teacher may decide that missing three problems on a music theory exam or scoring a four out of five on a performance rubric equates to a grade of "B." Such designations are in part arbitrary; while one teacher might mark three missed problems a "B," another might deem the same result an "A-." Once teachers make such distinctions, however, single units of measure translate directly into consequential outcomes. While formal assessments often necessitate such action, Deleuze offers an alternative focal point.

Instead of emphasizing how a particular measurement quantifies the quality under investigation, Deleuze and Guattari (1980/1987) highlight diverse forms of measurement. They write, "We do not have units of measure, only multiplicities or varieties of measurement" (p. 8). While Deleuze and Guattari obviously acknowledge the existence of units of measure elsewhere in their writing, their emphasis on varieties of measurement focuses attention away from segmentation and toward diversity. This distinction between solidified divides and variability relates to Deleuze and Guattari's concepts of striated spaces and smooth spaces.

Striated spaces involve walls and enclosures that restrain movement and variation, separating items and ideas into predefined, closed locations (Deleuze & Guattari, 1980/1987). Deleuze and Guattari (1980/1987) directly equate striated spaces with measurement, asserting that "to striate" is "to measure magnitudes" (p. 484) and that striated space "is canopied by the sky as measure and by the measurable visual qualities deriving from it" (p. 479). Applying such thinking to education, I posit that striated spaces occur when units of measurement divide musical practices. Teachers can segment a student's composition into categories within a rubric and a student's performance into a list of check pluses, checks, and check minuses next to various musical skills. Such action striates or bounds students' musical actions and understandings into distinct units of measure.

In contrast, Deleuze and Guattari (1980/1987) posit that smooth spaces lack limitations, foregrounding growth and motion and allowing constant flows, alterations, and diversification. Events, affects, and intensities, rather than stable properties, fill smooth spaces. Emphasizing a variety of measurements contributes to the formation of smooth spaces that highlight the diverse and evolving nature of musical and educative practices. As such, divergent measurements provide a more nuanced and complicated understanding of a student's work and development, avoiding the limitations of single units of measure.

In *Educational Life-Forms: Deleuzian Teaching and Learning Practice*, David Cole (2011) provides specific examples of how educators might use a variety of measurements when teaching various subjects. Cole's four lesson plans include subjects, objectives, procedures, and outcomes, each of which he separates into four strands: life, epiphanies, the virtual, and affect. Take, for instance, Cole's sample English literature lesson plan centering on Frankenstein's monster. The "life outcomes" of this plan involve drawing a scientific diagram of the monster and how he was given life. The "epiphany outcomes" include creating a detailed character sketch of Victor Frankenstein as well as a historical timeline of man-made inventions and their consequences. The "virtual outcomes" necessitate noting a mind map of the ways in which the monster has been represented and debating the ethics of the monstrous, while the "affective outcomes" entail creative writing about the monster and his creator, including poetry, letters, and reflections (p. 112).

Similarly, music educators might consider "life outcomes" by, for example, interrogating how everyday endeavors such as work or play constitute "life" in various places, perhaps performing, creating, and listening to music designed to express or to function in integration with such activities. They might also focus on "virtual outcomes" by debating the ethics of different forms of musical engagement or brainstorming how they might make concerts or other musical events more ethical. This vast range of possible outcomes made possible by utilizing a variety of measurements exemplifies a smooth space.

In addition, Cole's (2011) examples demonstrate that teachers need not select varieties of measurement at random, simply seeking diversity for the sake of diversity. Rather, they might choose measurements connected to meaningful material circumstances, ranging from the problems and possibilities of innovation to ethical considerations about deviations from norms. Deleuze and Guattari (1991/1994) argue that philosophical concepts should address pertinent problems: "A concept lacks meaning to the extent that it is not connected to other concepts and is not linked to a problem that it resolves or helps to resolve" (p. 79). Likewise, music educators could consider how their musical practices and accompanying measurements might relate to contemporary dilemmas ranging from discrimination based on qualities such as race, class, and sexual orientation, to environmental debates such as fracking and global warming, to issues such as immigration and gun violence. Relating varieties of measurement to such problems can inform students' understandings and actions in ways that extend beyond the classroom, allowing them to engage with and create additional smooth spaces.

While Deleuze and Guattari (1980/1987) imply a favoring of smooth spaces over striated ones, they ultimately posit their integrated nature, asserting: "Smooth space is constantly being translated, transversed into a striated space; striated space is constantly being reversed, returned to a smooth space" (p. 474). Similarly, teachers and students may include a variety of different measurements, but they cannot completely escape the units of measurement inherent to each. The smooth spaces of diverse measurements ultimately return to the striated space of units of measure. So the question is not whether or not music educators can have units of measure *or* varieties of measurement, but how long teachers and students remain in the striated space of quantified measurement results before seeking out the smooth space of different measurements. Yet simply including diverse measurements does not negate the power-laden nature of measurement practices. Who determines both the units of measure and the varieties of measurement as well as the resulting evaluations of those measurements necessitates further attention.

# MAJORITIES AND MEASUREMENT STANDARDS

According to Deleuze, majorities always set standards for measurement. Further explication of this position necessitates clarification of Deleuze's distinction between majorities and minorities. Deleuze (1990/1995) explains that size or quantity does not distinguish majorities from minorities; minorities may be bigger or more numerous than a majority. Instead, "what defines the majority is a model you have to conform to: the average European adult male city-dweller, for example. . . . A minority, on the other hand, has no model, it's a becoming, a process" (p. 173). This assertion reveals how power plays out in majority-minority relationships. In Deleuze's late twentieth-century Europe, the "average European adult male city-dweller" held more power than various other subgroups, including females, citizens of rural communities, children, and the elderly. Deleuze and Guattari (1980/1987) directly acknowledge the relationship between influence and majority status: "Majority assumes a state of power and domination, not the other way around" (p. 105).

This place of power enables majorities to serve as homogeneous constants to which others, always heterogeneous subsystems, exist in opposition. As Deleuze and Guattari (1980/1987) explain: "Majority implies a constant, of expression or content, serving as a standard measure by which to evaluate it" (p. 105). In other words, in addition to possessing the power to determine measurement criteria, majorities serve as the dominant norm that minorities find themselves positioned against. For example, Gloria Ladson-Billings (1998) explains: "Whites are exempted from racial designations and become 'families,' 'jurors,' 'students,' 'teachers'" (p. 11). While news reporters may note that five members of a jury were black, without further clarification, one assumes the remaining members to be white. The consistency of the majority enforces a standard of measurement from which minorities, in this case black jurors, deviate.

While qualities such as race and gender clearly affect music teaching and learning, since this chapter specifically aims to address the measurement and assessment of musical practices, I now apply Deleuze and Guattari's assertions about majorities and minorities to such endeavors. In many formal teaching and learning settings, Western classical music continues to represent the "majority" and thus defines the standard of measurement. Although contemporary music education often includes practices and repertoire beyond the Western canon, the language of Western classical music still permeates many measurements and their corresponding assessments.

Take, for example, the use of popular music in formal music education settings. While Lucy Green's (2002) extensive study of popular musicians demonstrates the central role of aural learning in such music making, bands, orchestras, and choirs often learn and perform popular music using notation. It follows that playing tests or other performance measures related to this music making will frequently rely on the language of the "majority"—Western classical music—to evaluate this minoritarian musical practice. Similarly, while writers such as Carlos Abril (2006) and Mary Goetze (2000) have asserted the need for sensitivity to the original context and instructional methods when learning non-Western musical practices, teachers regularly utilize Western terminology such as form, timbre, and intonation when engaging with such music making. This discourse serves as a part of not only pedagogy but also informal and formal measurements and assessments. For example, a choir learning a South African song may evaluate their performance as "out of tune" by Western classical standards even if native singers do not perceive certain fluctuations in pitch as such. In these instances, the "majority" serves as the standard of measurement that minimizes and subjugates minoritarian musical practices.

Another current example of the language indicating the "majority" status of Western classical music can be found in the drafts of American Music Model Cornerstone Assessments. Take, for instance, the Grade 5 Creating Model Cornerstone Assessment (National Association for Music Education, 2015). While the authors of this assessment do not strictly limit students to composing in a Western classical style, they imply that Western classical music serves as the "majority" by, for example, asking students to select three elements from various columns, including "rhythmic," "form," and "expressive." Under the heading of "expressive," the table lists items such as "Dynamics (*p, mp, mf, f* )," "Tempo (*largo, andante, allegro, presto*)," and "Articulation (*legato/staccato*)"

(p. 7). Such language clearly illustrates the majoritarian status of Western classical traditions. While students need not select anything from the "expressive" column and hence have freedom to create music without considering such terms, the mere existence of this discourse sets the standard of measurement from which any minoritarian practices necessarily deviate. While the authors of this and other Music Model Cornerstone Assessments do not advocate that teachers dismiss minoritarian forms of music making, they reinforce Western classical music as the norm and thus powerful "majority."

In problematizing the ways in which Western classical music serves as the "majority" in many contemporary formal teaching and learning settings, I am not arguing that such music making lacks value. While Deleuze implies the benefits of emphasizing the unique contributions and becomings of "minorities," such as striated and smooth spaces, he acknowledges the interconnected nature of majorities and minorities. To make minoritarian practices majoritarian would still result in the unequal power relationships from which Deleuze ultimately sees no complete escape. Yet Deleuze favors an ongoing challenging of the "majority" in order to jar its stagnation and homogeneity. As such, music educators need not view either Western classical music's majoritarian position or the language surrounding measurement and assessment documents such as the Model Cornerstone Assessments as inevitable or immobile. Given that the "majority" sets the standards for measurement, making music without measurement or assessment may provide "minority" musical practices spaces in which to flourish absent constant reminders of their secondary status.

## "Rhythm Without Measurement"

Writing specifically about music, Deleuze and Guattari (1980/1987) posit the possibilities of "rhythm without measurement" (p. 364). They elaborate that rhythm without measurement "relates to the upswell of a flow, in other words, to the manner in which a fluid occupies a smooth space" (p. 364). Contrasting what one typically thinks of as a fluid measurement apparatus—perhaps a beaker or measuring cup—with this image of an open and evolving space illustrates how measurements stagnate the objects and qualities under investigation, while not measuring affords freedom and new possibilities.

Deleuze and Guattari relate the idea of "rhythm without measurement" to specific musical experiences. Using the example of Boulez's compositions, they suggest a preference for music that lacks or upsets clear metric patterns. Given Deleuze and Guattari's conception of existence as constituted by difference and differing, this challenging of standardization applies not only to certain types of music but to life in general. While music educators may consider the possibilities of incorporating musical practices that resist regularity, they may also experiment with unmeasured musically educative experiences more broadly.

Drawing on Deleuze's ideas, Gould (2009) explains how women working in music education at the university level face systemic inequalities: they are hired, promoted, tenured, and compensated at lower rates than their male counterparts. For Gould, challenging the status quo involves rejecting the "inflexible and unending requirements" of the contemporary university system, instead reimagining it as a community that values the unique attributes and practices females bring to music teaching and learning (p. 137). She writes: "The task begins by changing relations, preferring ambiguity to clarity, contingency to certainty, potentiality to stability" (p. 138). While Gould does not negate the need for moments of clarity, certainty, and stability, she posits a reversal of emphases, in which ambiguity, contingency, and potentiality become primary and important in their own right.

Through overarching initiatives such as the Common Core State Standards and their accompanying assessments, policymakers have accentuated clarity, certainty, and stability while subjugating or excluding other qualities. Music education leaders have propagated this view. For example, authors of the Conceptual Framework that accompanies the 2014 American National Core Arts Standards write: "What is chosen for assessment signals what is valued.... What is not assessed is likely to be regarded as unimportant" (State Education Agency Directors of Arts Education, 2014, p. 15). In contrast, Gould (2009) challenges educators to value that which is not currently assessed, to make spaces for qualities such as ambiguity, contingency, and potentiality without regard to how or even if one might measure them.

Music teaching and learning that embraces "rhythm without measurement" might begin by setting off time and maybe even physical space free from measurement and assessment. Rather than conceiving of such moments as a deviation from the norm of assessment-driven practices, teachers might treat them as valuable and worthy of sustained attention. This does not mean that teachers might never move along prepared trajectories toward preplanned assessments; however, they might perceive such instances as secondary to music making emphasizing qualities, perhaps including emotion, uncertainty, ethics, and social interactions, that resist or even defy existing summative assessment measures. While some arts education leaders want assessments to "anchor the curriculum" (State Education Agency Directors of Arts Education, 2014, p. 15), teachers and students emphasizing "rhythm without measurement" prefer to spend the majority of their time afloat imagining and experimenting with the possibilities of nonmeasured music making.

# DELEUZIAN ASSESSMENT IN MUSIC EDUCATION

Thus far, this philosophical inquiry has examined how teachers and students might conceive of measurements as immanent rather than transcendent and has emphasized varieties of measurement rather than units of measure. I have investigated the relationship between majoritarian, power-laden norms and measurement and posited the possibilities of refraining from measurement. This chapter now returns to the opening question: Could there be Deleuzian assessment in music education?

Combining the four aforementioned ideas—planes of immanence, varieties of measurement, majorities and measurement standards, and rhythm without measurement—reveals that because measurement ultimately enables and reinforces hegemonic relationships and inhibits emphasizing ongoing differing, formal assessments completely consistent with Deleuze's writings cannot exist. Yet his thinking can still inform music education measurement and assessment practices. In this section I offer possible implications for each of these four ideas individually and then posit a conception of assessment inspired by their integration.

Deleuze's writings about planes of immanence suggest two implications for music education assessment practices. First, if music educators and students acknowledge that there does not exist a single transcendent musical ideal to which all musical practices should conform, then those designing assessments need to consider the plane or planes of immanence to which the given musical practices belong. While such action may at first appear straightforward, consider, for example, the teacher who asks orchestra students to perform a transcription of a popular tune and evaluates their rhythm and intonation. Students familiar with the original tune may deviate from notated rhythms in order to mimic the nuances of a live recording of the song as well as vary the intonation of certain pitches in ways consistent with the subgenre to which it belongs. To measure and evaluate a student based on adherence to notated pitches and Western classical standards of intonation places the popular song on a different plane of immanence than the one its creators, performers, and listeners intended. Furthermore, to assess a student's performance of a popular tune solely on characteristics such as rhythm and intonation neglects details such as tone and inflection that distinguish subgenres of popular music from each other and from other musical styles.

The same goes for musical practices such as composing and improvising. When students create music, they each lay out their own plane of immanence to which their practices belong. While students may at times benefit from attempting to work within the planes of immanence laid out by various composers, improvisers, and performers, allowing them to invent their own planes of immanence enables them to develop unique styles not bounded by the endeavors of others. In terms of assessment, such action might mean asking students to create the criteria by which they or others evaluate their own individual creations as well as facilitating music learning spaces not directly impacted by measurement. By focusing on individual planes of immanence rather than transcendence, music educators and students can refrain from assessing musical practices through criteria not applicable to them and from limiting, misunderstanding, or dismissing musical practices that occur on unfamiliar planes of immanence.

Second, without neglecting the plane of immanence to which a given musical practice belongs, music educators and students might consider how they can create assessments that emphasize variation rather than reproduction or replication. This doesn't mean eliminating all assessments that address replication; evaluating the accurate reproduction of given rhythms or pitches, for instance, certainly has its place in music teaching and learning. Yet music educators and students might complement such assessments with ones highlighting diversity and divergent practices. For example, teachers might assess how students add articulations, phrasing, dynamics, or inflections to an existing piece of music in order to offer a different way of expressing and communicating its content while still demonstrating an understanding of the musical style or genre to which it belongs. Such actions honor specific planes of immanence while highlighting that music making involves more than just replication.

This emphasis on divergence within planes of immanence shares similarities with Deleuze and Guattari's foregrounding of multiple forms of measurement. Drawing on such thinking, music educators and students might consider various ways in which they can measure and subsequently assess a single musical endeavor. These actions might include using different types of assessments, such as rubrics, written feedback, checklists, portfolios, and artistic responses. They might also include utilizing diverse assessors, including self-assessments as well as those of peers, teachers, amateur and professional musicians, and other adults, perhaps through a combination of in-person and virtual interactions. Music educators and students could also challenge themselves to create new, previously unimagined types of measurement and assessment. Such actions enable the collection of rich, divergent information that honors the complexity of musical practices and the educative process.

Advocating for varieties of measurement doesn't mean that music teaching and learning should center on assessment. Instead, a thorough assessment of a single musical endeavor using multiple forms of measurement may provide enough detailed information about students' growth that it can free teachers and students to have time for other practices. Rather than focusing on units of measure by constantly assessing musical practices through a single type of assessment over time, music educators and students can select a couple of significant musical events that they assess through multiple measures, devoting their remaining time to unmeasured musically educative endeavors.

Even using multiple measures, however, does not eliminate the hegemonic nature of measurement and ultimately assessment. Since majorities always set the standard for measurement, minoritarian practices can never articulate their full value within those standards. Therefore music educators and students need to consider carefully what their measurements and assessments exclude and subjugate as well as examine the effects of measurement on "minoritarian" musical practices. They might ask: What musical practices are setting the standard of measurement in my teaching and learning? What power structures do these practices hide and reinforce? What alternative musical practices do my assessments minimize or relegate? What musical practices do students and community members consider majoritarian and minoritarian, and how might their perceptions inform the learning within my classroom? What would happen if other musical practices became the majoritarian ones in various teaching and learning scenarios?

In order to fully honor minoritarian musical practices as well as diverse musical becomings more broadly, music educators and students might also consider the possibilities of unmeasured music making. For example, music educators cannot easily measure and assess students' learning of how to express their emotions through music, use music as a means of understanding and altering their evolving subjectivities, or engage in musical social justice endeavors. Yet such experiences can have a profound impact on students' lives and thus do not deserve secondary status in comparison to endeavors facilitating clear measurements and assessments. Music teaching and learning without measurement involves trusting in the experience of growth rather than demanding quantifications of it.

In addition, musically educative endeavors undertaken without the prospect of measurement enable teachers and students to wander along divergent paths, to explore and at times fail without fear of consequences. In these instances, choosing *not* to measure and assess music learning serves as an act of defiance, an undermining of the majority's measurement standards. Through such practices, minoritarian ways of making music and becoming through music can flourish, and teachers and students can celebrate previously unimagined potentials for music education.

Combining these four ideas enables an envisioning of music teaching and learning that relies on immanence rather than transcendence, highlights variations within specific planes of immanence, and emphasizes varieties of measurement. By not eliminating assessment completely, such action enables music educators to meet the needs of the current education policy climate. Yet this Deleuzian-inspired vision of music education also necessitates acknowledging the normative, oppressive nature of any measurement and thus giving equal if not more weight to music teaching and learning not directly resulting in measured experiences. Doing so celebrates the diversity and complexity that contribute to the meaning and value of musical experiences and may empower music educators to embrace their own and students' musical becomings without the limits of preplanned paths and stagnant endpoints. While music educators cannot necessarily craft assessments that completely align with Deleuze's writings, they can use his work as inspiration for reimagining their assessment practices and celebrating musically educative endeavors that occur absent assessment.

## NOTES

1. The term "poststructuralism" was not used by the writers themselves but rather subsequently applied to their work by American academics (Poster, 1988).
2. While Deleuze and Guattari use both the terms "plane of consistency" and "plane of immanence" to refer to the same idea in their earlier writings, they favor "plane of immanence" in their later work.

## REFERENCES

Abril, C. R. (2006). Music that represents culture: Selecting music with integrity. *Music Educators Journal*, 93(1), 38–45.

Belsey, C. (2002). *Poststructuralism: A very short introduction*. New York: Oxford University Press.

Cole, D. R. (2011). *Educational lifeforms: Deleuzian teaching and learning practice*. Rotterdam, Netherlands: Sense Publishers.

Deleuze, G. (1990/1995). *Negotiations: 1972–1990*. M. Joughlin (Trans.). New York: Columbia University Press.

Deleuze, G., & Guattari, F. (1980/1987). *A thousand plateaus: Capitalism and schizophrenia*. B. Massumi (Trans.). Minneapolis: University of Minnesota Press.

Deleuze, G., & Guattari, F. (1991/1994). *What is philosophy?* H. Tomlinson & G. Burchell (Trans.). New York: Columbia University Press.

Every Student Succeeds Act, Pub. L. No. 114–95, S. 1177 (2015).

Goetze, M. (2000). Challenges of performing diverse cultural music. *Music Educators Journal*, *87*(1), 23–35 + 48.

Gould, E. (2005). Nomadic turns: Epistemology, experience, and women university band directors. *Philosophy of Music Education Review*, *13*(2), 147–64.

Gould, E. (2006). Dancing composition: Pedagogy and philosophy as experience. *International Journal of Music Education*, *24*(3), 197–207.

Gould, E. (2007a). Social justice in music education: The problematic of democracy. *Music Education Research*, *9*(2), 229–40.

Gould, E. (2007b). Thinking (as) difference: Lesbian imagination and music. *Women and Music: A Journal of Gender and Culture*, *11*(1), 17–28.

Gould, E. (2009). Women working in music education: The war machine. *Philosophy of Music Education Review*, *17*(2), 126–43.

Gould, E. (2011). Feminist imperative(s) in music and education: Philosophy, theory, or what matters most. *Educational Philosophy and Theory*, *43*(2), 130–47.

Gould, E. (2012). Uprooting music education pedagogies and curricula: Becoming musician and the Deleuzian refrain. *Discourse: Studies in the Cultural Politics of Education*, *33*(1), 75–86.

Green, L. (2002). *How popular musicians learn: A way ahead for music education*. Burlington, VT: Ashgate Publishing Company.

Ladson-Billings, G. (1998). Just what is critical race theory and what's it doing in a nice field like education? *International Journal of Qualitative Studies in Education*, *11*(1), 7–24.

May, T. (2005). *Gilles Deleuze: An introduction*. Cambridge, UK: Cambridge University Press.

Miller, D., Linn, R. I., & Gronlund, N. E. (2009). *Measurement and assessment in teaching* (10th ed.). Upper Saddle River, NJ: Pearson.

National Association for Music Education. (2015). Music model cornerstone assessment: Artistic process; Creating 5th grade general music. Retrieved from http://www.nafme.org/wp-content/files/2014/11/Music_MCA_Grade_5_GenMus_Creating_2015.pdf

National Association for Music Education. (2016). Student assessment using Model Cornerstone Assessments. Retrieved from http://www.nafme.org/my-classroom/standards/mcas-information-on-taking-part-in-the-field-testing/

Payne, D. A. (2003). *Applied educational assessment* (2nd ed.). Toronto, ON: Wadsworth.

Poster, M. (1988). *Critical theory and poststructuralism: In search of a context*. Ithaca, NY: Cornell University Press.

Reynolds, C. R., Livingston, R. B., & Willson, V. (2009). *Measurement and assessment in education* (2nd ed.). Upper Saddle River, NJ: Pearson.

State Education Agency Directors of Arts Education. (2014). National Core Arts Standards: A conceptual framework for arts learning. Retrieved from http://www.nationalartsstandards.org/content/conceptual-framework

Williams, J. (2005). Immanence. In A. Parr (Ed.), *The Deleuze dictionary* (pp. 125–27). Edinburgh: Edinburgh University Press.

# PART II

## METHODOLOGICAL PRACTICES

# CHAPTER 8

# MUSIC TEACHER EVALUATION, TEACHER EFFECTIVENESS, AND MARGINALIZED POPULATIONS

*a tale of cognitive dissonance
and perverse incentives*

KAREN SALVADOR AND JANICE KRUM

Educational equity is increasingly being conceptualized as opportunities for all students to be held equally accountable to the same high-stakes test, despite unequal resources and opportunities to learn. Teacher preparation is increasingly being conceptualized as a training and testing problem to ensure that all teachers have basic subject matter knowledge and the technical skills to work in schools devoted to bringing pupils' test scores to certain minimum thresholds. And preparing young people to live in a democratic society is increasingly being conceptualized as efficiently assimilating all school children into mainstream values, language, and to the economy, and preserve the place of the United States as the dominant power in a global society.

—Marilyn Cochran-Smith

THE Every Student Succeeds Act (ESSA, 2015) does not explicitly mandate teacher evaluation. However, ESSA requires that states evaluate teacher quality and effectiveness for reports regarding factors such as educational equity. Moreover, the United States Department of Education's (USDoE) negotiated rulemaking regarding the Higher

Education Act (USDoE, 2016), or HEA, mandates state-determined measures of student outcomes that meaningfully differentiate among teachers in order to measure educator preparation program effectiveness. In the rulemaking, USDoE (2016) specifically indicates that "states that received ESEA [Elementary and Secondary Education Act] flexibility or a Race to the Top grant may well have a head start in implementing systems for linking academic growth data for elementary and secondary school students to individual novice teachers, and then linking data on these novice teachers to individual teacher preparation programs" (§ 612.5, p. 35). This language underscores the fact that those who already had ESEA waivers—forty-two states, Puerto Rico, and the District of Columbia—already are heavily invested in systems for evaluating teacher quality.[1] Therefore, HEA, ESSA, and resources already devoted to teacher evaluation systems combine with persistent rhetoric around eliminating "bad teachers" to guarantee the continuation of systematic state-mandated teacher evaluation programs despite the lack of a specific national mandate.

While teacher evaluation ostensibly is intended to increase teacher effectiveness and improve educator preparation programs,[2] in this chapter we argue that standardized, high-stakes teacher evaluation actually reduces music teacher effectiveness, particularly with regard to inclusion and cultural responsiveness. We begin with a brief critical review of the literature regarding music teacher evaluation, marginalized populations in school music education, and equitable and inclusive practices in the music classroom. Then we use fictionalized vignettes to illustrate our analysis of the philosophical dissonances and perverse incentives inherent in music teacher evaluation and how they manifest in three broad categories: (1) contributing to the gap between theory and practice, creating dissonance between teachers' philosophies and classroom practices by inappropriately driving curricular and instructional decision making, including assessment of student learning; (2) misusing measurement tools originally intended for teacher development as punitive high-stakes evaluations, eroding the expert status of music educators and rendering them impotent as agents of change; and (3) forcing teachers to remain in the status quo, unable to stray from formulaic "markers of effectiveness" to take the risks necessary for the messy, creative, innovative work of equity, inclusion, and cultural responsiveness. We conclude the chapter with specific suggestions for music teachers who wish to resist these effects of teacher evaluation on their instruction.

# MUSIC TEACHER EVALUATION

Teacher evaluation in American schools is not new. Consistently over the last century, different groups have championed a number of methods to improve the quality of teaching, including various evaluation schemes (Shaw, 2016b). However, within the last decade high-stakes teacher evaluation, particularly using "big data" metrics such as value added measures (VAMs), has become increasingly common. These evaluations are primarily focused on "objective[3]" measures of student growth such as standardized tests. Unfortunately, many districts evaluate music educators on the basis of a VAM that includes children they do not teach and/or include only student growth metrics from "tested" subjects such as math and English (Shaw, 2016b). States and school districts used data from VAMs inappropriately to such a degree that both the American Statistical Association (ASA, 2014) and the American Educational Research Association (AERA, 2015) issued statements on the (mis)use of VAMs in education.

Problems with VAMs and other high-stakes teacher evaluation systems resulted in lawsuits because teacher effectiveness ratings affect teacher pay, tenure, and even employment status. Essentially, tools that were intended to improve teacher effectiveness are instead being used to rank, rate, and punish teachers.

Many states and districts have moved away from evaluating music teachers by using VAMs based on standardized test scores. Instead, they evaluate music educators based on student growth in music, often using some form of student learning outcomes (SLOs). However, even when music teachers are evaluated based on the progress of students they actually teach, problems persist with high-stakes teacher evaluation. Shaw (2016c) found that burnout and stress in music teachers resulted from increased anxiety and workload associated with teacher evaluation. Particularly at the secondary level, ensemble directors often feel pressured to use large group performance metrics such as festival/contest ratings, which have well-documented issues with reliability and validity (e.g., Bergee & McWhirter, 2005; Bergee & Platt, 2003; Hash, 2013; Howard, 2012; Price, 2006). Moreover, even "authentic" and improvement-focused teacher evaluation tools involving more holistic measures of performance such as classroom observations can be problematic. For example, compliance requirements and evaluation paperwork take teachers' time away from teaching (Network for Public Education, 2016). Also, "emphasis on improving test scores...has overwhelmed every aspect of teachers' work, forcing them to spend precious collaborative time poring over student data rather than having conversations about students and instruction" (p. 2). Perhaps most disturbingly, high-stakes teacher evaluation is having a negative effect on teacher conversations with supervisors and colleagues, is associated with bias against veteran educators, and has "coincided with a precipitous drop in the number of Black educators in 9 major cities" (p. 2).

In this chapter we specifically reference the 5D+ Teacher Evaluation Rubric (University of Washington Center for Educational Leadership, 2012) because it is commonly used and is similar to other familiar evaluations (e.g., The Framework for Teaching; danielsongroup.org, 2013). This rubric consists of the descriptors "Unsatisfactory," "Basic," "Proficient," or "Distinguished" for teacher behaviors in five dimensions, which are divided into thirteen subdimensions, for a total of thirty-seven indicators. While we acknowledge that different models may result in different specific points of analysis, we assert that the overall cognitive dissonances and perverse incentives we describe are present anytime a system (district, state) standardizes and adopts a single teacher improvement model and applies it across all grade levels and subject areas for high-stakes evaluative purposes. Therefore, although we used examples from 5D+ in this chapter, we are not asserting that this particular tool is somehow worse than any other tool. Instead, 5D+ provides specific language that allows us to explore problematic aspects of administrator-conducted, rubric-based teacher evaluation systems in general, particularly in how they impact educators who are attempting the "messiness" of equity work (Hess, 2017).

# Defining Teacher Effectiveness

Agreeing on a definition of *teacher effectiveness* could simplify discussions regarding the improvement of teacher evaluation systems. Scholars conceptualize teacher effectiveness in a variety of ways, including teacher qualifications (e.g., quality of teacher preparation, advanced degrees), teacher dispositions (e.g., caring, fairness, enthusiasm), instructional practices (e.g., instructional delivery, student assessment, learning environment), and impacts on student learning (e.g., increased test scores, project-based evidence) (see Stronge, Ward, & Grant, 2011 for a review). Despite this variety of potential lenses, researchers examining effective teaching for the purposes of creating standardized teacher evaluation frameworks usually identify teachers as research participants on the basis of their students' standardized test scores. The implied logic is that good teachers raise student test scores, so researchers identify these teachers and describe their behaviors, dispositions, and classroom environments; teacher effectiveness for all teachers is then evaluated on the basis of these findings.

This logic is predicated on two faulty premises. Good teaching does not necessarily equate to higher standardized test scores, because other factors affect student achievement, including (but not limited to) parental involvement, socioeconomic status, parental education level, language difference (ELL), and ability difference/disability (Jeynes, 2005, 2007; Menken, 2008; Tienken et al., 2017; White et al., 2016). The American Statistical Association (2014) concluded that in-school factors (teachers, class sizes, resources, budgets) accounted for only 1–14 percent of variation in standardized test scores. The second faulty premise is that "the few subjects that are tested are the only, or even best, indicators of good education" (Amrein-Beardsley & van der Wateren, 2015, p. 28). That is, because music is not a tested subject, and the goals, processes, and pedagogies in music are different from those in tested subjects, definitions of effective teaching derived from studying characteristics of teachers who raise standardized test scores may not be applicable or appropriate for evaluating music educators.

Research that seeks to define music educator effectiveness is rare (Edgar, 2012; Forrester, 2015). The National Association for Music Education does not offer a definition, and community expectations often focus on large-group musical performances, which are the visible outcome of instruction, rather than on the effectiveness of instructional practices or the impact of instruction on individual student learning. For the purposes of this chapter, we propose the following components as a starting point for a definition. Effective music educators

- immerse students in musicking, in ways that are developmentally appropriate and suitable for the class context (e.g., fifth-grade musicking is different from pre-K musicking or musicking in a high school orchestra, songwriting class, show choir, mariachi ensemble, etc.);
- are caring and equitable, actively seeking to include all students in music;
- create inclusive and welcoming learning environments that sustain the cultures of the students they teach;
- respond to individual needs, working with each student to facilitate participation and learning; and
- engage in ongoing musical and pedagogical study that allows them to facilitate meaningful and responsive music instruction for their students.

In addition, Scott Edgar (2012) suggested the importance of effective communication with administrators, families, and other stakeholders, and Salvatore Vascellaro (2011) and Steven Demarest (2015) proposed that willingness to venture outside of school walls may also be critical for effective instruction.

# MARGINALIZED POPULATIONS IN MUSIC EDUCATION

## Diversity in Schools in the United States

The school-aged population in the United States is rapidly diversifying. As a proportion of the total US student population, white student enrollment is decreasing, while the proportion of African American students remains steady, and the proportions of Latino[4] and multiracial enrollment are rising (Kena et al., 2016). Much diversity in US schools is not well described by these census categories. For example, students are becoming increasingly open about their sexual preferences and gender presentation (Mitchell, Ybarra, & Korchmaros, 2014). Nearly one in four children under the age of eight has an immigrant parent, a number that has steadily increased from 13 percent in 1990 and is projected to continue growing (Fortuny, Hernandez, & Chaudry, 2010). Although 43 percent of these parents come from Mexico, the remainder hail from countries all over the world. Thus, home language, religion, and other cultural influences are also increasingly varied in schools. Of the total student population in the United States, 9.3 percent are English Language Learners (ELLs) (Kena et al., 2016). Students are also increasingly diverse with regard to abilities, as rates of provision of special education services rose to 13 percent of all US students in 2013–2014 (Kena et al., 2016).

However, data that indicate sustained increases in a variety of indicators of overall US student diversity obscure the reality in individual schools. For example, immigrant families are predominantly clustered in California, Texas, New York, Florida, Illinois, and

New Jersey (Fortuny, Hernandez, & Chaudry, 2010), and specific groups of immigrants tend to cluster in specific metropolitan areas, such as the Somali population in Minneapolis (Marohn, 2016). Moreover, although census categories indicate increasing racial diversity in student populations as a whole, individual schools are increasingly segregated. This segregation is obvious:

> 80% of Latino students and 74% of black students attend majority nonwhite schools, and 43% of Latinos and 38% of blacks attend intensely segregated schools (those with only 0-10% of white students). . . . Fully 15% of black students and 14% of Latino students, attend "apartheid schools" . . . where whites make up 0 to 1% of the enrollment. (Orfield, Kuscera, & Siegel-Hawley, 2012, p. 9)

Moreover, "almost all intensely segregated minority schools, but very few all-white schools, are associated with concentrated poverty" (p. 52).

## Diversity in School Music Education

In this rapidly diversifying and yet increasingly segregated school landscape, groups of students who are marginalized in the broad scope of US education are also marginalized in terms of their access to music instruction. Karen Salvador and Kristen Allegood (2014) found that schools with intensely segregated school populations were less likely to offer any music instruction at all, indicating that structural access is an issue for some marginalized populations. Even in schools that offer music classes, Kenneth Elpus and Carlos Abril (2011) found that "certain groups of students, including those who are male, English language learners, Hispanic, children of parents holding a high school diploma or less, and in the lowest SES [socioeconomic status] quartile, were significantly under-represented" (p. 128). In addition, students who receive special education services are less likely to participate in school music programs (Hoffman, 2011). Indeed, structural access—a program being present in a school—is only the first step for student access to music instruction, as social and cultural factors impact whether students take part in music education in their schools (Butler, Lind, & McKoy, 2007), and a lack of cultural responsiveness among music teachers likely reduces student participation and retention in music programs (Lind & McKoy, 2016).

# EQUITY AND INCLUSION IN
# THE MUSIC CLASSROOM

Rhetoric among some music educators, music teacher educators, and music education researchers includes the notion that all people can learn and grow in and through music, and thus that all students can benefit from and should be entitled to music education. Equitable and inclusive practices are natural outgrowths of this rhetoric, but educational structures and instructional practices do not always live up to these ideals. For example, structural deficits in the provision of music instruction—namely, that some schools do not offer any music instruction at all—present major roadblocks to equity in school music education. In schools that do offer music education, the literature suggests that equitable and inclusive instructional practices include but are not limited to the following interrelated/overlapping recommendations:

- Restore or add voices silenced by the omission of specific historical and cultural influences and materials from the traditional canon of music education literature and pedagogy (Hess, 2015; Kindall-Smith, McKoy, & Mills, 2011; Kruse, 2016; Shaw, 2016a).
- Adapt instructional practices and materials to meet individual learning needs of all students, including students with individual education programs (IEPs) (Darrow, 2015; Hammel & Hourigan, 2011; offer entry points to music classes for all students at all levels, Hourigan, 2015).
- Ameliorate the effects of class difference on structural and sociological access to music instruction (Bates, 2011, 2014; Wright & Davies, 2010).
- Democratize music learning as social practice and foreground high-status creative projects (Allsup, 2003; Burnard, 2008; Green, 2009).
- Implement culturally responsive pedagogy/teaching (Gay, 2010; Kelly-McHale, 2015; Lind & McKoy, 2016).

Equitable and inclusive music instruction would therefore vary by context and would require music educators to (1) focus more on individual student progress and interests, (2) listen and be responsive to students and families, (3) be flexible and try new things, (4) change repertoire and curriculum, and (5) learn alongside their students. In the following sections we illustrate how standardized high-stakes teacher evaluation creates cognitive dissonances and perverse incentives for all music teachers, particularly for those who wish to incorporate these more inclusive and equitable practices.

# Philosophical Dissonances and Perverse Incentives

Vignettes 1–4 (Boxes 8.1–8.4) are prototypical retellings of stories we have heard from practicing teachers in Michigan and around the country. We selected these stories because they illustrate common situations that we have repeatedly witnessed or been told about.

## Theories on Music Teaching and Learning vs. K–12 Standardized Rubric

The main cognitive dissonance captured in the first vignette (Box 8.1) is that best practices in early childhood music instruction are not necessarily the same as the teacher behaviors

## BOX 8.1 VIGNETTE 1: MS. L IN MICHIGAN

*Ms. L teaches over seven hundred students a week in three K–5 elementary schools. She sees each of her classes once a week for fifty minutes. One kindergarten class has twenty-four students, three of whom speak no English at home, and limited English at school. One student has moderately severe autism spectrum disorder (ASD) and is mainstreamed during music time from the self-contained ASD classroom. Based on her preparation regarding developmentally appropriate practices (DAP) for early childhood music instruction, Ms. L's goal for the first nine weeks of kindergarten music is to fully immerse her students in a rich musical environment. She guides the five-year-olds through experiences that focus on the elements of music through movement, singing, chanting, and playing instruments. Ms. L does not expect "correctness" or compel participation. Students are welcome to observe or to participate, because DAP assumes that children will join activities when they are ready. Students use these immersive experiences to teach themselves how to coordinate their movement, breath, singing, and chanting. Ms. L deliberately uses few words—even singing and chanting songs without words, because this is helpful to her ELL students and to her student with autism, and it helps the other children focus on musical rather than verbal content. Instead of giving verbal directions, she models movements and uses props, vocalizations, instruments, and facial expressions to engage the children.*

*When one of Ms. L's three different building principals comes for an unannounced fifteen-minute observation, he sees children pretend to paint polka dots and swirls with scarves while Ms. L and some of the students sing a melody without words. He hears children say, "bah-bah" and create sirens and animal noises individually and in groups in response to Ms. L's playful vocalizations. He does not hear Ms. L state learning goals or give verbal feedback. He does not see anything that resembles his vision of instructional guidance, questioning, student talk, or assessment. He rates Ms. L "unsatisfactory" for many indicators on her teacher evaluation.*

described by indicators on teacher evaluation rubrics. This dissonance is summed up in a question we've heard from many teachers: Should I persist in using DAP for my five-year-old students even if that means I do not score well on my evaluation? Although music educators who specialize in early childhood instruction might commend Ms. L's application of DAP (e.g., Salvador & Corbett, 2016), her principal rates her as "unsatisfactory" on many 5D+ indicators (see Box 8.1). For example, according to indicators P4 and P5, a teacher who is proficient or distinguished would verbally and visually state learning targets, check for student understanding of what the targets are, and reference the targets throughout instruction. A proficient or distinguished teacher would make success criteria for the learning targets clear to students, and students (even five-year-old students) would refer to the success criteria and use them for improvement. However, best practices in music education in general—and early childhood music instruction in particular—intentionally privilege *making* music over *talking about* music. That is, music educators recognize that children can be taught to parrot words and phrases about music, but unless they are immersed in making music, even children who fluently use words about music are not necessarily proficient in the aural and physical (moving, singing, playing, listening) skills of musicking.

## Student Engagement and Assessment for Student Learning

Ms. L also would be unsatisfactory in most areas of dimension 2, "Student Engagement," and dimension 3, "Assessment for Student Learning." The student engagement dimension indicates that Ms. L's work with kindergarten students should include (among other things) opportunities for students to engage in "quality talk" and student-to-student talk and questioning, and that she should frequently ask questions that deepen students' understanding. Ms. L's administrator would not have observed any of this. However, an observer familiar with early childhood music instruction would likely understand that movements, chanting, and other vocalizations (such as sirens and animal noises) can be seen both as "questions" and as responses. Such an observer would also see that students often engage one another in movement, chanting, or vocalization "talk," and that immersion in active music making reflects a high level of student engagement.

With regard to "Assessment for Student Learning," 5D+ indicates that a proficient teacher creates frequent opportunities for students to assess their own learning in relation to success criteria or learning targets. However, Ms. L knows that these students are not ready to self-assess. How can a child self-assess singing abilities or beat competence when he or she is still developing both? Student lack of awareness regarding pitch matching ability and/or the ability to move accurately with beat is common in early childhood music instruction. A teacher's use of immersive experience to guide students toward matching pitch and moving with beat is more productive than asking a child to self-evaluate something he or she may not accurately perceive.

## Criteria Regarding Classroom Culture

In the 5D+ system, as implemented in Ms. L's district, evaluators perform fifteen-minute unannounced "walk-throughs." During a walk-through, an administrator writes a script of what he or she observed and then "codes" the script into the 5D+ dimensions and indicators for summative evaluation. The teacher has twenty-four hours following the walk-through to provide detailed planning documents, analysis of the teaching interactions, and reflection. During these walk-throughs, one dimension the administrator evaluates is "Classroom Environment and Culture." Three different administrators each observe Ms. L, twice in each of her three buildings. This creates challenges for a variety of reasons: the administrators do not coordinate, so she is sometimes observed all six times in the last six weeks of school, the observations are inconsistent with one another, and there is no system for the three administrators to arrive at a final rating. Furthermore, Ms. L teaches six grade levels, and the administrators do not coordinate to decide if they are going to try to see each grade level, which might show advancement in music learning over time; or one grade level, which might show progress toward learning targets for the year; or one class, which is not possible, but might justify comment on climate and culture. Ms. L is held to the same standards for classroom climate and culture as other teachers in her buildings who work with twenty-five students all day, every day, in a room that they do not share with other teachers. Ms. L learns her building assignments at the beginning of each school year (sometimes with only a few days' notice), so she does not even teach the same seven hundred students every year. Each building in which she works has a different culture and set of expectations, and Ms. L has to learn these anew each time she is reassigned. While classroom environment and culture are certainly important factors in teaching, evaluating Ms. L on the same criteria as the other elementary teachers is absurd.

---

### BOX 8.2 VIGNETTE 2: MR. B IN MICHIGAN

*Mr. B wants to help each student in his high school orchestra develop independent practice habits and better playing technique. He designs an online "practice journal," which involves students playing an assigned excerpt onto Google Voice at least once each week, along with submitting a journal entry with a self-evaluation and a description of strategies the student applied to get the "best take" that he or she sent. Mr. B plans to use these recordings and journals to give individual feedback and to inform his instruction of individual students and of the group. Mr. B also plans to vary the excerpt assignments to challenge students who are advanced and scaffold for students who are struggling. He plans to make equipment available in practice areas before and after school and during lunch for students who cannot do this assignment from home. In addition to his formative use of the recordings and journal entries, Mr. B will use a rubric to rate each student's first excerpt and last excerpt as measurement data to calculate student growth for his teacher evaluation. However, his administrator insists that assessments of student growth must use a "true pre-post design" and be "objective." When Mr. B asks for clarification, he learns that the administrator believes that an objective measurement must be a pencil-and-paper task with right or wrong answers that anyone could grade. Together, they decide to use a vocabulary test in which students write definitions for commonly used musical terminology, to be given in identical format at the beginning of the year and the end of the year.*

---

## Ease and "Objectivity" vs. Best Practice in Student Growth Measures

Best practices suggest that assessment of music learning should be formative—for feedback purposes—and not necessarily for evaluation. Assessment should be frequent, specific to the context, developmentally appropriate, and as authentic as possible to the musical goals of the individual and the class (Henry, 2015; Kastner & Shouldice, 2016; Russell, 2014). Therefore, in a high school orchestra class, students can and should be assessed on their playing skills, and such an assessment should be of an individual student, playing music that is at an appropriate level of challenge, and applying strategies the student has have learned in class. Data from such an assessment would likely comprise a recording (audio or video) scored with a rubric and/or with a self-evaluation. However, vignette 2 (see, Box 8.2) captures a commonly reported perverse incentive of high-stakes, standardized teacher evaluation: the incentive to focus on what is easy to measure rather than what is important in music teaching and learning. This incentive simultaneously devalues what music teachers do (i.e., guide students in making and creating music), while also encouraging music teachers to view measurement of student growth as an extra "hoop" to be "jumped through" rather than something that could improve teaching and learning.

Another perverse incentive highlighted in this vignette is that the administrator's insistence on a specific assessment format (true pre-post) and delivery (pencil and paper) will take instructional time away from more authentic and educative musical experiences. Specifically, the time spent giving a pretest that all students are intended to fail and the time spent drilling vocabulary, definitions, and spelling will not be spent playing, listening, singing, self-assessing, and collaborating—making music. Furthermore, requiring that all teachers conform to one kind of evaluative growth measure under-mines and devalues the teachers' expertise in their pedagogical content area. Insistence on pencil-and-paper and true pre-post testing is also common at the elementary level, where the issues raised may be more egregious, because elementary music teachers have more limited time with students, typically only once or twice per week (as in vignette 1), and also because pencil-and-paper tests are more likely to measure early elementary students' reading and writing skills than their musical understanding.

## Discussion: Theory and Practice

The vignettes in this section present two specific examples of ways that standardized teacher evaluation can influence instruction in ways that do not align with best practices in music education. In both cases, instructional changes related to teacher evaluation could also further disadvantage students who are already marginalized in music teaching and learning settings. For example, several indicators on the teacher evaluation rubric focus on students verbalizing music learning targets and conceptual information. This is not developmentally appropriate practice in music instruction for kindergarten children who do not share common musical experiences. For a kindergarten child who also has an intellectual disability, has a speech or language disorder, or speaks English as a second language, an insistence on specific verbal responses can create a barrier to participation. However, young students, including those with disabilities and those who do not speak English, can often participate in music making as a bridge or induction into the vocabu-lary and concepts of music, which they will gradually begin to use as music instruction continues over the course of elementary school. That is, teacher evaluation indicators regarding "quality talk," student-to-student talk, a teacher's use of questioning, and stu-dents' ability to talk about learning goals and success criteria do not support best practice in early childhood music, but might be appropriate measures of effective instruction when fourth- or fifth-grade students are working in small groups to compose music.

Ms. L's overall instruction would rate poorly because of her choice to teach based on what she believes are best practices for young children and because of things that she cannot change about her job assignment. Similar dissonances abound in a variety of music teaching and learning contexts because it is unrealistic to expect that one rubric could be equally applicable in all teaching and learning settings and with all ages of students. Instruction can and should be different in early childhood music or a songwriting class or a marching band. Each way of musicking has its specific processes, including pedagogical practices, and products, including standards for quality (Elliott & Silverman, 2015, p. 105). It is also unrealistic to think that an evaluator who is not familiar with the philosophy and practices of a content area (let alone a specific musical praxis) would be able to interpret teaching and learning interactions without being welcomed into those philosophies and practices through discussion, observation, and participation.

Dogmatic insistence on true pre-post pencil-and-paper tests of student growth also disadvantages students who already are marginalized in music education. Similar to the focus on verbalizing previously described, pencil-and-paper tests are likely to disadvantage ELLs and students with IEPs, who may be progressing well with their music making and might perform differently on authentic measures of their music making. In addition, if a student whose parents have lower levels of education or who perceive that they are a "nonmusical" family fails a pretest (that by design all students were supposed to fail), such a student might attribute this failure to a lack of potential, ability, or "talent" for music and as further proof that school music is not for "a kid like them" (Salvador, 2014).

It is interesting to note that 5D+ and other teacher evaluations encourage using multiple forms of assessment that can be applied for instructional purposes (i.e., not as a stand-alone measurement activity). Moreover, teacher evaluation rubrics do not make assertions about assessment formats or modes of delivery. Yet in talking with music teachers, administrator insistence on true pre-post pencil-and-paper tests is a common complaint. It seems likely that some administrators want measurements they (and other stakeholders such as parents) can read and interpret despite their lack of music content knowledge and pedagogical content knowledge.

Interference in appropriate use of classroom assessment also takes other forms. As part of accountability measures for student growth and teacher evaluation, it is becoming increasingly common for districts to design common grade-level assessments in elementary schools and common course assessments in secondary schools (e.g., a single district-wide, end-of-semester assessment for all Algebra I courses). Because music teachers are often grouped K–12 for district professional development, we spoke with several teachers who had been required to create a common assessment for all music classes K–12 (both performing groups and nonperforming classes). Because the music teachers' grade-level and subject area colleagues in math and English were doing district-wide assessments, music K–12 needed a similar standardized growth measure, regardless of how obviously ridiculous this idea is.

# MISUSE OF MEASUREMENT TOOLS

---

### BOX 8.3  VIGNETTE 3: MS. T AND SADIE IN MICHIGAN

*Sadie is a student with Down syndrome who loves to sing in high school choir. She is an enthusiastic member of the group and functions well in rehearsals with the assistance of an assigned student "buddy." Sadie's buddy has worked with the special education teachers to learn about Sadie's needs. For example, Sadie does not read music; in fact, her IEP goals include working on functional reading skills so that she can read simple directions in her native language (English). Because of Sadie's difficulties with reading and decoding symbols, Sadie learns her choir music by ear. This strategy is effective after additional practice with her buddy. However, in rehearsal Sadie often loudly sings before she has learned the notes or words to a piece, even when the rest of the group is sight-singing. Ms. T, the director, decides not to take Sadie to choral festival, even though Sadie really wants to go. Ms. T tells the students and Sadie's parents that this exclusion is out of concern for Sadie, that she would be uncomfortable in this high-pressure, unfamiliar setting. However, the decision also arose out of a conversation in which Ms. T's administrator said her teacher evaluation scores would be negatively affected if she did not continue her predecessor's tradition of earning top ratings at state festival. Sadie's exuberance and excitement would likely result in lower festival scores for the group because of criteria regarding stage decorum and the likelihood that Sadie would loudly and inaccurately sing during sight-singing.*

## (Mis)Use of Solo or Group Festival Ratings

Although the Individuals with Disabilities Education Act (1990) guarantees a free and appropriate education to students with disabilities, and the Americans with Disabilities Act (1990) protects people from discrimination on the basis of disability, stories like the one in vignette 3 (Box 8.3) are common. This is because festival/contest ratings are sometimes used as a proxy for music teacher effectiveness, even if they are not specifically described on the evaluation rubric. We have heard many teachers say, "Festival is *our* MStep" (Michigan's annual standardized test of student achievement in tested areas). Emphasis on festival ratings results in a perverse incentive for teachers to exclude students who have disabilities.

Moreover, if we want to be more inclusive and equitable in our practices, we need to provide multiple entry points to music instruction (Hourigan, 2015). Valuing festival ratings at the high school level also creates a perverse incentive for teachers to refuse to teach beginners—to exclude students from music instruction because they don't yet know how to play or sing. Furthermore, festival ratings often reflect factors that would disadvantage smaller schools and schools with fewer resources, such as some rural or inner-city schools (Bergee & McWhirter, 2005; Hash, 2013; Howard, 2012). Use of festival ratings as an indicator of teacher effectiveness also creates cognitive dissonance, because group festival ratings are not valid as measures of individual student growth. Some teachers use solo and ensemble ratings as indicators of student growth, but students who score well at solo and ensemble typically take private lessons, which disadvantages students from lower income families (and teachers from lower SES school districts). In addition, festival "required lists" and criteria for evaluation require a focus on repertoire and practices in the Western classical canon, silencing or excluding voices and musics that might resonate with marginalized populations of students (Kindall-Smith, McKoy, & Mills, 2011; Kruse, 2016). Although teacher evaluation rubrics may not specifically address festival ratings, community and administrator expectations and the competitive nature of secondary programs could mean lower ratings on related indicators; the perverse incentive to exclude students, play easier material, or not go to festival may be present with or without teacher evaluation.

---

### BOX 8.4 VIGNETTE 4: MR. C IN MICHIGAN

*Mr. C teaches general music and band K–12 in an impoverished rural community. His evaluation observations are split between two administrators: the secondary school principal, who is also the district's athletic director, and the K–6 principal, who taught first grade prior to becoming an administrator. His two evaluators are inconsistent in their ratings of his teaching. The secondary school evaluator is unsatisfied with the II and III ratings that Mr. C's band of twenty-three seventh- to eighth-grade students earned at festival. Mr. C sees this band of mixed ability students for ninety minutes two to three times a week (an A–B block schedule). The secondary administrator also contends that the marching band doesn't sound or look the way he thinks it should at halftime or in parades. However, Mr. C has deliberately chosen to make marching participation voluntary because many students struggle to get transportation to and from after-school practices, games, and parades. Mr. C's K–6 evaluator is particularly critical of his classroom management.*

*For professional development, Mr. C went to observe a colleague who routinely receives "distinguished" ratings on her teacher evaluations. She teaches seventh- and eighth-grade band in an upper middle-class suburban middle school. Here, the seventh- and eighth-grade bands each have sixty to seventy-five players, and she sees these students daily for fifty-five minutes in groups of about twenty-five to thirty. Her eighth-grade band just earned straight "I" (superior ratings) at state-level contest for its fifth consecutive year. The school's instruments are in good repair, but most students purchase or rent their own instruments, and more than half of the band members study privately. Mr. C leaves the observation feeling depressed, knowing that he and his students are not competing on a level playing field, at contests or regarding teacher evaluation.*

## Misuse of Teacher Evaluation Itself

The 5D+ rubrics and online materials include the saying: "Helping educators understand what good teaching looks like" (University of Washington Center for Educational Leadership, 2012). Leaving aside the obvious (and offensive) assertion that educators might not know what good instruction looks like, the statement is problematic in that it implies (1) that good teaching looks the same at all grade levels and in all content areas and (2) that an evaluator would not need content knowledge or pedagogical content knowledge to evaluate teaching in various subjects or at different developmental levels. Philosophical dissonances abound, as music teachers who understand educational assessment know that any assessment is only valid for a specific use. Nevertheless, high-stakes teacher evaluation systems use materials that were intended to help teachers to reflect on and improve their instruction to instead rank and rate teachers. Because the potential ramifications of a low score are dire, many teachers give in to a perverse incentive to outsmart the rubric rather than engage in deep reflection and improvement. This perverse incentive is summed up by the question: Is the goal to move up on the rubric, or to become a better music teacher? The drive to outsmart the system is common enough that the National Association for Music Education recently blogged about an article and national conference presentation detailing "Universal Techniques for Top-Notch Observations" (Potter, 2016).

Teacher evaluation systems also disadvantage "specials teachers" such as music educators. It is common for teachers such as Ms. L and Mr. C (see Boxes 8.3 and 8.4) to teach in two or three buildings with different administrators and to have five to seven hundred students in six or eight different classes/grade levels to plan for and teach each week. Due to the nature of their schedules, music teachers are often evaluated by several administrators, who see dissimilar content and instruction and give inconsistent ratings and feedback on what they see. We spoke with many music teachers who were told that they cannot achieve at "distinguished" level because of what they teach. We assert that this dissonance arises both because teacher evaluation rubrics cannot reflect best practices for all music teaching and learning settings and because music teachers are often evaluated by administrators who do not know enough about what they are observing to offer accurate evaluations or helpful feedback.

Finally, teacher evaluations are not equitable measures across settings. Differences in school climate from district to district and even building to building could affect a teacher's scores. Lower scores on teacher evaluations have repercussions, including lower pay in a district or state that offers differential pay for highly effective ("distinguished") teachers and on a teacher's ability to maintain licensure in a district or state that requires a certain number of "proficient" ratings. A teacher in a district or building in which the overall climate results in more challenges for classroom management and student engagement will not score as well on indicators pertaining to student engagement and classroom environment and culture. This presents a perverse incentive for teachers to improve their evaluation scores by moving to a district where student behavior is not impacted by the stressors of generational poverty or the trauma of community violence. This directly undermines the equity issues that teacher evaluation systems are supposed to be addressing. This perverse incentive is not unique to music educators, but bears examination in the context of this chapter. Marginalized groups of students (i.e., those in impoverished rural and some urban schools) experience high rates of teacher turnover, are left with the least experienced teachers, and are sometimes taught by uncertified substitute teachers who do not know from day to day if they will be called back to teach. Such schools often cut music programs if they cannot find a music teacher who will persist despite low pay, high stress, and the uneven playing field for teacher evaluation. When music teachers like Mr. C move on to districts like the one he visited, students who are already marginalized are further disadvantaged.

## Forced Stagnation in the Status Quo

Thus far we have focused on the music education status quo, describing situations in general music, orchestra, choir, and band. However, if music education is going to be inclusive of diverse populations, we may need to consider other ways that people are musical. Standardized, high-stakes teacher evaluation privileges certain musics and musical practices and discourages the creativity, risk-taking, and experimentation that could result in more inclusive, more responsive, more individualized music teaching and learning. Consider the stories in boxes 8.5–8.7, which are not prototypical like the preceding vignettes, but describe specific lived experiences of individual music teachers. All three have been condensed and edited from personal communications.

---

**BOX 8.5 VIGNETTE 5: SARAH IN MINNESOTA**

*After twelve years teaching band, I took a new position in a high school that offered Beginning Band, an entry-level class for students who wanted to learn a band instrument. The goal of Beginning Band was for students to advance to Concert Band the following semester. Typically, out of about twenty students, half would continue into Concert Band. In the past, Beginning Band was primarily white students from the United States, but the year I started my new job coincided with an influx of "newcomers"—students who had been here in the United States for less than a year.*

*On my first day of school, I saw many skin colors and many hijabs in first hour Beginning Band. My attendance paperwork indicated that fifteen of the seventeen students were English Language Learners, and of those fifteen, ten were "level one," meaning limited to no English proficiency. I decided to show the students pictures of traditional band instruments and*

*(Continued)*

*videos of people playing those instruments. The students seemed unimpressed with the flutes, clarinets, or saxophones, but one of them pointed to a picture of a guitar with a look of excitement in her eyes. "Taas waxaan u ciyaari karaa?" ["Can I play this?"] I looked at her, and at some of the other students, who were grinning with excitement. They wanted to play guitar. "Bands" in their home countries always had a guitar-like instrument. Besides, the translator had arrived and was starting to explain that some of the students were hesitant to play an instrument that went inside their mouths for religious/cultural reasons. At first I was at a loss, thinking: "This is band class. What should I do? These students are eager to make music, but their concept of music making is not what our music department does."*

*I decided to take a chance. My first hour "Beginning Band" became a guitar class, which then morphed into a songwriting class. It has been an amazing experience to learn alongside these students, as they use guitars and songwriting to learn English, get to know each other, express their thoughts and feelings about being "newcomers," and make music.*

## BOX 8.6 VIGNETTE 6: BRUCE IN MICHIGAN

*After finally finishing my music education degree at age thirty-two, I was hired for my first job as a full-time music teacher at an inner-city charter high school. I had just completed my student teaching in a traditional high school band program. Imagine my surprise when I discovered that there were no band instruments at my school and no students who wanted to play them! I knew I was also going to teach Music Appreciation, but since I was hired for a position with the title "Band Director," and band was one of the classes on my schedule, I just assumed that there would be band instruments and kids who wanted to play them.*

*I have been a percussionist in all kinds of bands since high school (funk, heavy metal, bluegrass, jazz... whatever gigs I could land), and I also had a private studio where I taught drums, acoustic and electric guitar, bass, keyboard, and voice. I brought my guitars, drums, and sound equipment to the school and scrounged for students who were willing to come try music with me. In addition to my equipment, and some donations, a few students brought instruments from home, and some sang, and some rapped, and I arranged music for them. I'd describe the music on our first concert as R&B/motown/hip-hop/jazz-ish. We were exploring the material that is sampled in songs the students are listening to. Now that the students know me better, I am bringing in other kinds of music.... Next year we are starting a drumline, and I wonder if some of the non-band students will want to step with us. I am also doing a donors choose project to get some DJ equipment... and I've ditched the history book we used for Music Appreciation to turn the class into something more participatory. I'm not sure what that will be, but I want it to reflect more of what my students know as music.*

*It's really **really** hard work. I have no budget. And do you know what [my mentor teacher from student teaching] said to me? "Don't worry, after two years there you'll have enough experience to get a REAL job."*

## BOX 8.7 VIGNETTE 7: CLAIRE IN KANSAS

*I teach K–5 general music at a high-poverty elementary school in small-town Kansas where almost all the kids are Hispanic. They are predominantly Mexican… first, second, even third generation with some more recent immigrants. I grew up in an upper middle-class suburb of a metropolitan center, went to a selective music program at a huge university, and student taught in an affluent suburban school. When I first got here, I had no idea what I was getting myself into. I didn't know how to deal with the culture shock, let alone the challenges of being a first-year educator. I was just like, "OK they're Mexican.… I'll do some songs in Spanish."*

*Gradually, I realized that I was afraid to try to connect with the students and their families. I didn't know what I was doing, and I didn't want to make mistakes. I would never ask my colleagues, kids, or families for ideas or help—even for something like making sure I'm saying lyrics correctly. I was afraid to look ignorant or say the wrong thing. So I only did a few token songs with Spanish lyrics. I mostly felt like, "I'm this perfect, trained musician, so I'm going teach what I know."*

*But I had an "aha moment" over one summer.… I don't have to be perfect. It is more important for me to get to know my kids and their families than it is that I seem on top of everything. My kids are going to make mistakes, and I need to model for them that mistakes are part of learning. We are going to learn from each other. And ever since I started working on myself… it's made my experience this year a thousand times better than my last four years of teaching. We have this big Cinco de Mayo celebration, where the whole school is involved. In the past, I chose some horrid songs, because I didn't know what I was doing. So this year I actually started planning early, did some research, pulled out a bunch of material, and had my older kids listen to everything and help me pick what was most appropriate for the celebration. Next year, I think we might even write some of our own Cinco de Mayo music.*

*Learning all this stuff from my kids and their families, in front of my students and colleagues, or in front of an administrator observing, has been very scary and very challenging. But it's also been a huge learning opportunity. Actually using my students' knowledge, so I'm more aware of **their** culture and meeting **their** needs… has really helped me build better connections with my kids. And they are more willing to share and to create with me. It's been amazing.*

Each of these teachers encountered a music teaching/learning situation he or she did not expect and responded by creating a new-for-him/her approach to reach the students. These vignettes reflect promising attempts-in-process to be equitable and inclusive by focusing more on individual student progress and interests, listening and being responsive to students and families, being flexible and trying new things, changing repertoire and curriculum, and learning alongside students. Each is an exemplar of some possible combinations of the bullet points suggested in the section.

However, in each case, aspects of instruction could cause failing ratings on standardized high-stakes teacher evaluations. Sarah abandoned the planned curriculum and goals for "Beginning Band." If she were evaluated on her ability to teach that particular set of learning outcomes to her students (e.g., 5D+ indicators P1 and P2), she would fail.

Bruce's band could not participate in band festival because of instrumentation, performance practices, and repertoire. If his school wanted to use large-group festival ratings as a measure of his effectiveness, he would fail. Claire's students are responding to her interest in their lives and culture by talking more about musical—and nonmusical—things that are important to them. For example, several students were inconsolable because they had relatives, including parents, who were planning to leave the country because they were undocumented. Claire led the group in discussing how their classroom community could understand and support one another. On a standardized teacher evaluation, such "off-topic" engagement would likely be scored as poor classroom management (e.g., 5D+ indicator CEC4). In addition, Sarah, Bruce, and Claire all taught classes filled with mistakes, missteps, and confusion, because they were creating something they had never done before. With humility and a focus on their students, each persevered and came back the next day with new ideas for what might work. However, teachers are usually evaluated on the basis of their subject area expertise and on being able to plan and control exactly what happens in a given lesson (e.g., 5D+ indicators CP1, CP2, CP3, CP4). Therefore, when teachers facilitate and even learn alongside their students, that does not measure as proficient or distinguished on widely used teacher quality metrics—although many education theorists and music education researchers would recommend this practice (e.g., Demarest, 2015; Green, 2009; Vascellaro, 2011). Standardized high-stakes teacher evaluation seems to ignore the real-life aspects of teaching; a well-designed lesson can go well or poorly. Student engagement and management can vary even in a master teacher's classroom. Student interest is not always predictable—and learning experiences that are different from what we expected are sometimes the most powerful.

We spoke with many teachers who want to be more inclusive and equitable in their instruction. Most were afraid to try to change their practices because of a combination of concerns, including worry about doing or saying the "wrong things" and concerns regarding community expectations that are based on the status quo. Teachers also expressed anxiety about poor scores on standardized, high-stakes teacher evaluation if they were to embrace the possibly messy work of change. The consequences of low scores can include punitive "improvement plans," job reassignment, changes in pay, and even termination. It is difficult to think of a set of systems that could more efficiently discourage the creativity, risk-taking, and experimentation inherent in creating a more equitable, more inclusive, more responsive, more individualized music teaching and learning practice.

# THOUGHTS FOR THE FUTURE

Although "[m]ost VAM studies find that teachers account for about 1% to 14% of variability in test scores, and that the majority of opportunities for quality improvement are found in system-level conditions" (ASA, 2014, p. 2), and despite a professional consensus that no more than 6 percent of teachers are below standards (Danielson, 2016), most teachers now work within high-stakes and potentially punitive standardized teacher evaluation systems. As demonstrated here, these evaluation systems do not always reflect best practices in the status quo of music teaching and learning; can result in further marginalization of populations that are already disadvantaged in music education; and serve to stifle attempts to move beyond the status quo to more equitable, inclusive, culturally responsive music instruction. Furthermore, the materials, professional development, and time spent on evaluation procedures and documentation cost money and take time that could theoretically be spent improving access to music education. Most important, we are troubled by how some high-stakes teacher evaluation systems devalue the complex science and art of education by supplanting the specialized expertise and judgment of professional educators with reductionist rubrics, as though teaching were a set of behaviors that could be checked off a list. In this spirit, we offer the following suggestions for teachers who wish to resist the effects of teacher evaluation on their practices and profession.

## Reclaim Professional Learning

Research indicates that teachers in general are more anxious and overwhelmed and feel less supported as a result of teacher evaluation processes (Network for Public Education, 2016). Music teachers specifically are suffering burnout that they attribute to changes in teacher evaluation and student assessment (Shaw, 2016c). Of particular concern are reports that evaluation is contributing to poor relationships among teachers and bad work climates in schools (Network for Public Education, 2016): "Of all the lessons of teacher evaluation in the current era, perhaps this one is the most important: that we not adopt an individualistic competitive approach to ranking and sorting teachers that undermines the growth of learning communities which will, at the end of the day, do more to support student achievement than dozens of the most elaborate ranking schemes ever could" (Darling-Hammond, 2013, p. 2). Thus, one path forward is to (re)claim professional learning community (PLC) time for the music education "team." In many districts, work related to high-stakes standardized teacher evaluations now takes up much of the time and energy of PLCs, and professional development is often geared toward teacher evaluation and related work such as standardizing student growth measures. However, improvements in teaching practice are more likely to emerge from Wenger's (1998) notion of a community of practice, in which people with a shared passion come together in person or electronically to get better at what they do.

In this spirit, the Network for Public Education (2016) study on the impact of teacher evaluation recommends that "teacher collaboration not be tied to evaluation but instead be a teacher-led cooperative process that focuses on [teachers'] own and their students' learning" (p. 3). Reclaiming professional learning time might result in a virtuous cycle. Music teachers sharing stories about their work toward becoming more inclusive and inquiring together on topics of mutual interest may reignite an atmosphere of trust and curiosity. An atmosphere of trust and curiosity could, in turn, create the conditions for risk-taking and creativity that might lead to more equitable, inclusive, and responsive teaching—and to improvements in student learning.

## Advocate for Music Educators with Your Administration

Based on the situations described in this chapter, we suggest, for the short term, that music educators advocate for the following local policy changes. First, teacher evaluation processes should reflect the overall competence of professional educators. Such a system would allow for beginning and novice educators to work closely, over a period of several years, with mentor teachers who have significant teaching experience, content knowledge, and pedagogical content knowledge in music. These interactions would primarily consist of observation, self-assessment, and dialogue, that could be guided by a tool for teacher improvement, as long as it was used for the novice teacher's personal growth and professional growth, not for assigning a score or checking off boxes. After a set number of years, the novice would be inducted as a professional educator. Second, the evaluation of professional educators should primarily revolve around ongoing professional learning and could take place in the PLCs described above. This collaborative inquiry into student learning and teacher self-improvement should include peer observation and perhaps peer evaluation, with elements of self-assessment, reflection, and peer dialogue. Such interactions would meet both of the conflicting purposes of teacher evaluation systems, "effectively measuring teacher performance and providing feedback to help them improve. Peer Assistance and Review (PAR) programs, in place in dozens of districts across the country, have shown that this dual purpose is possible" (Papay, 2012, p. 138). Third, music teacher evaluators should have adequate teaching experience, content knowledge, and pedagogical content knowledge in music to understand what they are seeing and to provide useful feedback: "[E]valuators must be well trained, knowledgeable about effective teaching practices as defined in the standards, and able to analyze observed practices to determine how well teachers are meeting these standards. The importance of developing high-quality evaluators and the challenges they will face must not be underestimated.... Effective evaluators must be willing to provide tough assessments and to make judgments about the practice, not the person. They must also be expert in providing rich, meaningful, and actionable feedback to the teachers they evaluate" (Papay, 2012, p. 135).

The Measures of Effective Teaching project concluded that administrators should not only be trained on the evaluation instrument; they should be required to "demonstrate their accuracy by scoring videos or observing a class with a master observer" (Cantrell & Kane, 2013, p. 20). This study also recommended two forty-five-minute observations by an administrator, combined with one forty-five-minute peer evaluation and three fifteen-minute peer evaluations by different peers to increase reliability. Papay (2012) also supported peer evaluation, citing "several districts across the country [that] have experimented quite successfully with identifying expert peers to serve as evaluators" (p. 135).

Finally, any evaluation process of a music educator must include a discussion of teaching assignment/context. The National Association for Music Education's Opportunity to Learn Standards (National Association for Music Education, 2015) include sections on curriculum and scheduling, staffing, materials and equipment, and facilities that could provide some context for this conversation. This discussion could lead to goal setting that acknowledges the numerous and real ways that music instruction is different from other subjects, not only in its methods and outcomes but also in the expectations placed on the instructors in terms of teaching in multiple location(s), availability and quality of materials, student/teacher ratios, and so forth. This goal setting should also highlight the importance of student growth measures that are also student learning experiences and/or that are authentic to the goals of the students and the practices of the class. We hope that the cognitive dissonances and perverse incentives outlined in this chapter also provide fertile ground for discussions in PLCs and with mentors and evaluators.

## Engage in Policy Work in Local, State, and National Government

Unfortunately, many practicing teachers might read the preceding suggestions and think: "That is just not realistic in the climate at my school." The effects of teacher evaluation on instruction described in this chapter are symptoms and consequences of larger issues in our educational landscape. Teachers who care about equity, inclusion, and justice in education must consider the ways that structures in our educational system contribute to marginalization. As Sarah, Bruce, and Claire experienced, music education curricula are sometimes not aligned with the wants and needs of students. It is not only teacher evaluation, but also the goals and processes of music education that require interrogation. Music educators' selection of student learning outcomes and student growth measures can contribute to marginalization.

Music educators must also interrogate the larger structures both from the historical legacy of education and from current politics and policy, which position teacher evaluation as a part of the larger neoliberal education reform agenda (Cochran-Smith, Piazza & Power, 2013; Costigan, 2013). Working to adjust music teacher evaluation systems could be compared to rearranging deck chairs on the *Titanic*, when perhaps the real need is for music educators who wish to be more equitable and inclusive to engage in policy work aimed at dismantling neoliberal education agendas in favor of more student-centered or critical pedagogies. Working for the small gains of adapting the language and practices of high-stakes teacher evaluation in order to "get along" or "make it work" is an acquiescence to neoliberal systems and serves to further reduce educator professionalism and autonomy. We assert that for music education to be equitable, inclusive, and just, it must be context dependent and flexible to respond to the interests, abilities, and cultures of the students. As Audre Lorde (1983) reminds us, "the master's tools will never dismantle the master's house" (p. 94). Thus, following Dunn (2017), when music teaching and learning are reduced to rubric-measurable tasks such as those on 5D+, we "need to find new tools. . . . Until those revolutionary tools exist, and until we work together to create them, then we must revolt against the dominant tools in place" (p. 13). Engagement with musicking can be a source of empowerment and emancipation for students and teachers.

# FINAL THOUGHTS

Neither assessment of student growth nor reflective practices geared toward instructional improvement are problematic in and of themselves. Indeed, reflective practice based on authentic formative assessment of student learning is one hallmark of an expert teacher. However, Campbell's Law "hypothesizes that the more a given social indicator is used to monitor a social process the more likely it is that the indicator and the process it is intended to monitor will become distorted" (Shaw, 2016b, p. 7). At this time in history, standardized, high-stakes teacher evaluation (indicator) and practices in teaching and learning (process) are a perfect illustration of Campbell's Law. Therefore, the suggestions we have made for music teachers, PLCs, and evaluators will only work to the degree that they remain contextual, flexible, individualized, and geared toward dialogue; otherwise, we just trade one tool of marginalization for another. With regard to the effects of music teacher evaluation on marginalized populations, we encourage music educators to start dialogues in their PLCs and with their evaluators about pathways to more inclusive and equitable music instruction. When we all raise our voices, we will be powerful.

*Postlude: After thirteen years of teaching (and just after we submitted this chapter), coauthor Janice Krum left for a position outside public education. She wrote: "I loved to teach children, but my profession has been tragically changed. Standardized evaluation systems are forcing teachers not to look at the learning of their students first, but rather to stay within the status quo, check off the boxes, and work solely toward a rating for fear of administrative reprisal— the ultimate perverse incentive. This was the ethical line that I could not cross. Students are an after-thought of these systems, and teachers are being asked to question their professional ethics in order to keep their jobs. We must continue to speak out toward inclusivity for all students and advocate for the return the profession to its teachers." This cautionary tale illustrates the reality teachers face and the reason that focusing on getting through evaluations and having conversations with administrators and other music teachers is not enough. The systemic effects of high-stakes teacher evaluation are part of our current teacher shortage and are playing into the hands of those who would make teaching into a low-skilled, low-wage job, rather than a career for a highly skilled professional. Thus, we reiterate our assertion that we all—within and outside the system—must engage critically regarding neoliberal education reforms, to create an education system that is just, equitable, empowering, and emancipatory for students and for teachers.*

## NOTES

1. As of November 9, 2015, the following states did not have ESEA waivers, which are officially termed "ESEA Flexibility": California, Illinois, Iowa, Montana, Nebraska, North Dakota, Vermont, and Wyoming (USDoE, n.d.). At that time, Iowa and Wyoming had flexibility requests under review. Washington state previously had an ESEA waiver, but Secretary of Education Arne Duncan revoked it in 2014 (Klein, 2014). Principle 3 of the ESEA Flexibility Policy Document (USDoE, 2012) states:

   > To receive this flexibility, an SEA and each LEA must commit to develop, adopt, pilot, and implement, with the involvement of teachers and principals, teacher and principal evaluation and support systems that: (1) will be used for continual improvement of instruction; (2) meaningfully differentiate performance using at least three performance levels; (3) use multiple valid measures in determining performance levels, including as a significant factor data on student growth for all students (including English Learners and students with disabilities), and other measures of professional practice (which may be gathered through multiple formats and sources, such as observations based on rigorous teacher performance standards, teacher portfolios, and student and parent surveys); (4) evaluate teachers and principals on a regular basis; (5) provide clear, timely, and useful feedback, including feedback that identifies needs and guides professional development; and (6) will be used to inform personnel decisions. An SEA must develop and adopt guidelines for these systems, and LEAs must develop and implement teacher and principal evaluation and support systems that are consistent with the SEA's guidelines.

   That is, any state granted ESEA flexibility (and those that have applications under review) must have systematized guidelines for teacher evaluation that local education agencies are required to follow. Therefore, nearly all states have these systems in place.

2. In this chapter we argue this claim at face value, by asserting that teacher evaluation systems are not effective ways to improve teaching and learning, particularly for students who are already marginalized by education systems. However, the claim is problematic, because teacher evaluation systems are likely also about power and control (Webb, Briscoe, & Mussman, 2009).

3. The notion of "objective" teacher assessment on the basis of student growth measures is problematized in the literature (see Papay, 2012). This chapter focuses on standards-based observational teacher evaluation methods, so we do not discuss this debate further here.

4. In this chapter "Latino" refers to ethnic heritages originating in Latin America, and "Hispanic" refers to people who speak Spanish.

## REFERENCES

Allsup, R. E. (2003). Mutual learning and democratic action in instrumental music education. *Journal of Research in Music Education, 51*(1), 24–37. doi:10.2307/3345646

American Educational Research Association. (2015). AERA statement on use of value-added models (VAM) for the evaluation of educators and educator preparation programs. *Educational Researcher, 44*(8), 448–52.

American Statistical Association. (2014). ASA statement on using value-added models for educational assessment. Retrieved from https://www.amstat.org/asa/files/pdfs/POL-ASAVAM-Statement.pdf

Amrein-Beardsley, A., & van der Wateren, D. (2015). Measuring what doesn't matter: The nonsense and sense of testing and accountability. In J. Evans & R. Kneyber (Eds.), *Flip the system: Changing education from the ground up* (pp. 25–38). New York: Routledge.

Bates, V. C. (2011). Sustainable school music for poor, white, rural students. *Action, Criticism, and Theory for Music Education*, 10(2), 100–27.

Bates, V. C. (2014). Rethinking cosmopolitanism in music education. *Action, Criticism, and Theory for Music Education*, 13(1): 310–27.

Bergee, M. J., & Platt, M. C. (2003). Influence of selected variables on solo and small-ensemble festival ratings. *Journal of Research in Music Education*, 51(4), 342–53. doi:10.2307/3345660

Bergee, M. J., & McWhirter, J. L. (2005). Selected influences on solo and small-ensemble festival ratings: Replication and extension. *Journal of Research in Music Education*, 53(2), 177–90. doi:10.2307/3345517

Burnard, P. (2008). A phenomenological study of music teachers' approaches to inclusive education practices among disaffected youth. *Research Studies in Music Education*, 30(1), 59–75. doi:10.1177/1321103X08089890

Butler, A., Lind, V. R., & McKoy, C. L. (2007). Equity and access in music education: Conceptualizing culture as barriers to and supports for music learning. *Music Education Research*, 9, 241–53. doi:10.1080/14613800701384375

Cantrell, S., & Kane, T. (2013). Ensuring fair and reliable measures of effective teaching: Culminating findings from the MET three-year study. Retrieved from http://www.edweek.org/media/17teach-met1.pdf

Cochran-Smith, M. (2004). *Walking the road: Race, diversity, and social justice in teacher education*. New York: Teacher's College Press.

Cochran-Smith, M., Piazza, P., & Power, C. (2013). The politics of accountability: Assessing teacher education in the United States. *The Educational Forum*, 77(1), 6–27. Retrieved from http://dx.doi.org.libproxy.umflint.edu/10.1080/00131725.2013.739015

Costigan, A. T. (2013). New urban teachers transcending neoliberal educational reforms: Embracing aesthetic education as a curriculum of political action. *Urban Education*, 48(1), 116–48. doi:10.1177/0042085912457579

Danielsongroup.org. (2013). Framework for teaching. Retrieved from https://www.danielson-group.org/framework/

Darling-Hammond, L. (2013). *Getting teacher evaluation right*. New York: Teacher's College Press.

Darrow, A. A. (2015). Ableism and social justice: Rethinking disability in music education. In C. Benedict, P. Schmidt, G. Spruce, & P. Woodford (Eds.), *The Oxford handbook of social justice in music education* (pp. 204–20). Oxford: Oxford University Press.

Demarest, A. (2015). *Place-based curriculum design: Exceeding standards through local investigations*. New York: Routledge.

Dunlop Velez, E. (2016). *The condition of education 2016* (NCES 2016-144). Washington, DC: US Department of Education, National Center for Education Statistics. Retrieved from http://nces.ed.gov/programs/coe/pdf/coe_cge.pdf, http://nces.ed.gov/programs/coe/indicator_cgg.asp, http://nces.ed.gov/programs/coe/indicator_cce.asp, http://nces.ed.gov/programs/coe/indicator_cgf.asp

Dunn, A. H. (2017). Refusing to be co-opted: Revolutionary multicultural education amidst global neoliberalisation. *Intercultural Education*, 28(4), 1–17. doi:10.1080/14675986.2017.1345275

Edgar, S. (2012). Communication of expectations between principals and entry-year instru-
    mental music teachers: Implications for music teacher assessment. *Arts Education Policy
    Review, 113*(4), 136–46.

Elliott, D. J., & Silverman, M. (2015). *Music matters: A philosophy of music education* (2nd ed.).
    New York: Oxford University Press.

Elpus, K., & Abril, C. R. (2011). High school music ensemble students in the United States:
    A demographic profile. *Journal of Research in Music Education, 59*, 128–45. doi:10.1177/
    0022429411405207

Every Student Succeeds Act (ESSA). (2015). Pub. L. No. 114–95 § 114 Stat 1177. Retrieved from
    https://www.congress.gov/bill/114th-congress/senate-bill/1177/text

Forrester, S. H. (2015). *Music teacher knowledge: An examination of the intersections between
    instrumental music teaching and conducting.* (Unpublished doctoral dissertation), University
    of Michigan.

Fortuny, K., Hernandez, D. J., & Chaudry, A. (2010). *Young children of immigrants: The leading
    edge of America's future* (Brief No. 3). Urban Institute (NJ1). Retrieved from http://files.eric.
    ed.gov/fulltext/ED511771.pdf

Gay, G. (2010). *Culturally responsive teaching: Theory, research, and practice.* New York:
    Teachers College Press.

Green, L. (2009). *Music, informal learning, and the school: A new classroom pedagogy.* London:
    Ashgate Publishing, Ltd.

Hash, P. M. (2013). Large-group contest ratings and music teacher evaluation: Issues and
    recommendations. *Arts Education Policy Review, 114*(4), 163–69. doi:10.1080/10632913.2013.
    826035

Hammel, A., & Hourigan, R. (2011). *Teaching music to students with special needs: A label-free
    approach.* New York: Oxford University Press.

Henry, M. L. (2015). Assessment in choral music instruction: Overcoming challenges and dem-
    onstrating excellence. In A.-L. Santella (Ed.), *Oxford handbooks online: Scholarly research
    reviews.* doi:10.1093/oxfordhb/9780199935321.013.101

Hess, J. (2015). Decolonizing music education: Moving beyond tokenism. *International Journal
    of Music Education, 33*(3), 336–47. doi:10.1177/0255761415581283

Hess, J. (2017). Troubling whiteness: Music education and the "messiness" of equity work.
    *International Journal of Music Education, 36*(2), 128–44. doi:

Hoffman, E. (2011). *The status of students with special needs in the instrumental musical ensem-
    ble and the effect of selected educator and institutional variables on rates of inclusion* (PhD
    dissertation). University of Lincoln-Nebraska. Retrieved from http://digitalcommons.unl.
    edu/cgi/viewcontent.cgi?article=1045&context=musicstudent

Hourigan, R. (2015). Understanding music and universal design for learning: Strategies for
    students with learning differences in the 21st century. In H. Russell & C. Conway (Eds.),
    *Musicianship-focused curriculum and assessment.* Chicago: GIA.

Howard, S. A. (2012). The effect of selected nonmusical factors on adjudicators' ratings of high
    school solo vocal performances. *Journal of Research in Music Education, 60*(2), 166–85.
    doi:10.1177/0022429412444610

Jeynes, W. H. (2005). A meta-analysis of the relation of parental involvement to urban ele-
    mentary school student academic achievement. *Urban Education, 40*(3), 237–69.

Jeynes, W. H. (2007). The relationship between parental involvement and urban secondary
    school student academic achievement: A meta-analysis. *Urban Education, 42*(1), 82–110.

Kastner, J., & Shouldice, H. (2016). Assessment in general music education from early child-hood through high school: A review of literature. In *Oxford handbooks online: Scholarly research reviews*. doi:10.1093/oxfordhb/9780199935321.013.99

Kelly-McHale, J. (2015). Democracy, canon, and culturally responsive teaching. In L. DeLorenzo (Ed.), *Giving voice to democracy in music education: Diversity and social jus-tice in the classroom* (pp. 216–34). New York: Routledge.

Kena, G., Hussar W., McFarland J., de Brey C., Musu-Gillette, L., Wang, X., Zhang, J., Rathbun, A., Wilkinson-Flicker, S., Diliberti M., Barmer, A., Bullock Mann, F., & Kindall-Smith, M., McKoy, C. L., & Mills, S. W. (2011). Challenging exclusionary paradigms in the traditional musical canon: Implications for music education practice. *International Journal of Music Education, 29*(4), 374–86. doi:10.1177/0255761411421075

Klein, A. (2014, April 24). Arne Duncan revokes Washington state's NCLB waiver. *Education Week*. Retrieved from http://blogs.edweek.org/edweek/campaign-k12/2014/04/washington_state_loses_waiver_.html

Kruse, A. J. (2016). "They wasn't makin' my kinda music": A hip-hop musician's perspective on school, schooling, and school music. *Music Education Research, 18*(3), 240–53. doi:10.1080/14613808.2015.1060954

Lind, V., & McCoy, C. (2016). *Culturally responsive teaching in music education: From under-standing to application*. New York: Routledge.

Lorde, A. (1983). The master's tools will never dismantle the master's house. In C. Moraga & G. Anzaldua (Eds.), *This bridge called my back: Writings by radical women of color* (pp. 94–101). New York: Kitchen Table Press.

Marohn, K. (2016, January 24). Fact check: Somali student numbers. *St. Cloud Times*. Retrieved from http://www.sctimes.com/story/news/local/immigration/2016/01/24/fact-check-somali-student-numbers/79062702/

Menken, K. (2008). *English learners left behind: Standardized testing as language policy*. Clevedon, U.K.: Multilingual Matters.

Mitchell, K. J., Ybarra, M. L., & Korchmaros, J. D. (2014). Sexual harassment among adolescents of different sexual orientations and gender identities. *Child Abuse & Neglect, 38*(2), 280–95. doi:10.1016/j.chiabu.2013.09.008

National Association for Music Education. (2015). Opportunity to learn standards. Retrieved from http://www.nafme.org/wp-content/files/2015/01/OTL-draft-Jan-2-2015.pdf

Network for Public Education. (2016). Educators on the impact of teacher evaluation. Retrieved from http://networkforpubliceducation.org/wp-content/uploads/2016/04/NPETeacherEvalReport.pdf

Orfield, G., Kuscera, J., & Siegel-Hawley, G. (2012). E pluribus…separation: Deepening double segregation for more students. Los Angeles, CA: Civil Rights Project UCLA. Retrieved from http://escholarship.org/uc/item/8g58m2v9

Papay, J. (2012). Refocusing the debate: Assessing the purposes and tools of teacher evaluation. *Harvard Educational Review, 82*(1), 123–41. doi:10.17763/haer.82.1.v40p0833345w6384

Potter, D. (2016). Universal techniques for top-notch observations. Music in a Minuet Archives. Retrieved from http://www.nafme.org/universal-techniques-top-notch-observations/

Price, H. E. (2006). Relationships among conducting quality, ensemble performance quality, and state festival ratings. *Journal of Research in Music Education, 54*(3), 203–14. doi:10.2307/4151342

Russell, J. (2014). Assessment in instrumental music. In *Oxford handbooks online: Scholarly research reviews*. doi:10.1093/oxfordhb/9780199935321.013.100

Salvador, K. (2014). Identity and transformation: Reclaiming an inner musician. In C. Randles (Ed.), *Music education: Navigating the future* (pp. 215–32). New York: Routledge.

Salvador, K., & Allegood, K. (2014). Access to music education with regard to race in two urban areas. *Arts Education Policy Review, 115*(3), 82–92. doi:10.1080/10632913.2014.914389

Salvador, K., & Corbett, K. (2016). "But I never thought I'd teach the little kids": Secondary teachers and early grades music instruction. *Music Educators Journal, 103*(1), 55–63. doi:10.1177/0027432116655199

Shaw, J. T. (2016a). "The music I was meant to sing": Adolescent choral students' perceptions of culturally responsive pedagogy. *Journal of Research in Music Education, 64*(1), 45–70. doi:10.1177/0022429415627989

Shaw, R. D. (2016b). Arts teacher evaluation: How did we get here? *Arts Education Policy Review, 117*(1), 1–12. doi:10.1080/10632913.2014.992083

Shaw, R. D. (2016c). Music teacher stress in the era of accountability. *Arts Education Policy Review, 117*(2), 104–16. doi:10.1080/10632913.2015.1005325

Stronge, J. H., Ward, T. J., & Grant, L. W. (2011). What makes good teachers good? A cross-case analysis of the connection between teacher effectiveness and student achievement. *Journal of Teacher Education, 62*(4), 339–55.

Tienken, C. H., Colella, A., Angelillo, C., Fox, M., McCahill, K. R., & Wolfe, A. (2017). Predicting middle level state standardized test results using family and community demographic data. *RMLE Online, 40*(1), 1–13.

University of Washington Center for Educational Leadership. (2012). 5D+™ rubric for instructional growth and teacher evaluation (version 2). Retrieved from http://info.k-12leadership.org/hs-fs/hub/381270/file-1144787717-pdf/

US Department of Education (USDoE). (2016). 34 C.F.R. Parts 612 and 686: Teacher preparation issues. Retrieved from http://www2.ed.gov/documents/teaching/teacher-prep-final-regs.pdf

US Department of Education (USDoE). (2012, June 7). ESEA flexibility. Retrieved from https://www2.ed.gov/policy/elsec/guid/esea-flexibility/index.html

US Department of Education (USDoE). (n.d.). Index page for ESEA flexibility. Retrieved from https://www2.ed.gov/policy/elsec/guid/esea-flexibility/index.html

Vascellaro, S. (2011). *Out of the classroom and into the world: Learning from field trips, educating from experience, and unlocking the potential of our students and teachers.* New York: The New Press.

Webb, P. T., Briscoe, F. M., & Mussman, M. P. (2009). Preparing teachers for the neoliberal panopticon. *The Journal of Educational Foundations, 23*(3/4), 3.

Wenger, E. (1998). *Communities of practice: Learning, meaning, and identity.* Cambridge, UK: Cambridge University Press.

White, G. W., Stepney, C. T., Hatchimonji, D. R., Moceri, D. C., Linsky, A. V., Reyes-Portillo, J. A., & Elias, M. J. (2016). The increasing impact of socioeconomics and race on standardized academic test scores across elementary, middle, and high school. *American Journal of Orthopsychiatry, 86*(1), 10.

Wright, R., & Davies, B. (2010). Class, power, culture and the music curriculum. In R. Wright (Ed.), *Sociology and music education* (chapter 3). Oxfordshire, UK: Ashgate Publishing.

# CHAPTER 9

# THE INFLUENCE OF ASSESSMENT ON LEARNING AND TEACHING

*using assessment to enhance learning*

SUSAN HALLAM

THERE have long been debates about whether it is appropriate to assess performance and creative outcomes in the arts. Musicians are subject to informal assessment throughout their working lives. Whatever the nature of their portfolio careers, their work will be assessed through audience reactions, sales of recordings, the comments of music critics, offers of employment, contracts or commissions, evaluations of teaching, and so on. Although this assessment is informal, it has a major impact. If it is negative, it can destroy a musician's career. If it is positive, it can raise one's status and prospects. Alongside this external, summative assessment, musicians need to constantly evaluate their own work, developing self-assessment skills to be able to improve their performance or in some cases make decisions about changes in the direction of their careers. This form of assessment, designed to improve task performance, is known as *formative assessment*.

Summative assessment evaluates what has been learned by a particular point in time. While for professional musicians, summative assessment tends to be informal, in education systems it is formal and usually graded in some way. It is the most common way of verifying attainment and awarding qualifications, which means that it can have a critical impact on the individual's future and in some cases that of his or her teacher or institution. Summative assessment is controversial in music because to a great extent the assessment of performance, improvisation, or composition is based on subjective judgments.

Formative assessment occurs when feedback from learning activities is used to inform future learning and teaching (Black & Wiliam, 1998a). In music, in its simplest form, formative assessment consists of the aural feedback received by performers as they are playing, which enables them to assess their ongoing performance and make adjustments as necessary. These may be immediate if they are in a performing situation or may lead to changes in the technical or musical approach adopted in the preparation stage. Musicians can also take advantage of recent developments in personal recording techniques, for instance on mobile phones, to support their assessment of their progress, as this enables them to adopt an audience perspective. Formative assessment also includes comments and guidance offered by teachers or peers on how to improve and can be undertaken by learners to assist teachers in enhancing their pedagogy (Black & Wiliam, 1998a, 1998b). In the literature, summative and formative are usually considered separately, although summative assessment can be used formatively, for instance when comments received on a composition or performance are discussed to set future goals.

In this chapter, taking account of the research evidence, which has mainly focused on Western music, frequently classical music, I discuss how the summative assessment of musical outcomes, in schools and higher education, determines not only what is taught but also what learners learn, because learning outcomes that are not assessed are typically not given priority by teachers or learners. I outline what we know about how to optimize learning by aligning aims and processes with the criteria for summative assessment. I consider the various approaches to the summative assessment of performance, composition, and improvisation; its subjective nature; and the factors that may affect it. The importance of formative assessment for learning is addressed, as well as how peer and self-assessment can contribute to that process. Finally, I argue that learning and motivation can best be enhanced by ensuring that summative assessment procedures are authentic and have real-life relevance.

## SUMMATIVE ASSESSMENT

Summative assessment has a very powerful effect on learning and teaching. Graded instrumental examinations frequently determine much of what is taught in instrumental lessons. What is taught in school music lessons frequently focuses on what will be assessed in national assessment systems. The impact of summative assessment is so powerful that Elton and Laurillard (1979) suggest that if educators or policymakers want to change what is taught and learned, they should change the assessment system. As John Biggs and Philip Moore (1993) note, "[T]he assessment tail wags the educational dog" (p. 391). Furthermore, as Richard Snow (1990) states, "[T]ests drive instruction to concentrate only on what these tests seem to measure" (p. 455). This effect is described as "backwash" and can be cognitive or affective (Biggs & Moore, 1993). Cognitive backwash refers to the strategies used for preparing for the assessment, while affective backwash refers to the impact on emotions, attitudes, and motivation. Learning outcomes that are not assessed tend to be viewed as unimportant.

The importance of the relationship of the assessment procedures adopted, the aims of learning, and processes of teaching and learning is stressed by Biggs (1996). He suggests that to optimize the impact of assessment, these three factors should be aligned. Alignment means that assessments are connected with learning outcomes, the current level of expertise of the learner, and those required in the institution. In music the most appropriate way of achieving these ends and ensuring meaningfulness for students is to ensure that assessment procedures are authentic and have real-life relevance. Authentic assessment strategies are closely related to real-world situations; in music, typically, these include performance, improvisation, and composition.

# SUMMATIVE ASSESSMENT OF MUSICAL PERFORMANCE

Learners can use summative assessments to improve future performances. However, this is not a straightforward process. Overall, the evidence suggests that assessments of musical performances are not reliable (e.g., Wringley, 2005; Wapnick, Ryan, Lacaille, & Darrow, 2004). Judges do not give the same grades when they are presented with the same performance twice (without being informed) (Fiske, 1978), and there is high variability even when they are assessing performance on the same instrument using the same assessment protocol (Ciorba & Smith, 2009). In a study investigating the perceptions and judgments of performance made by three professional musicians and six young performers, David J. Elliott (1987) found considerable variation across assessments, although some performances commanded more consensus than others. In the area of technical skills—in which one might have expected to find the most agreement—there was a large measure of disagreement even among the three professional judges. Professional musicians have also been shown to experience difficulties explaining how they perceive individual performances (Wrigley & Emmerson, 2013).

Unsurprisingly, students express concerns about the subjective nature of summative assessment processes (Hay & McDonald, 2008), and many find the experience stressful and potentially damaging (Booth, 2009). Musical performance is very personal, and young musicians increasingly develop their own interpretations and individuality as they progress toward professional careers (Wesolowski, 2012). The subjective nature of assessment can act to undermine their confidence in relation to this process. A further issue is the extent to which young people find performance rewarding. For some it is an exhilarating and joyful experience (Howe & Sloboda, 1991), but for others any pleasure derived from it is minimal because of stage fright. Performance anxiety is an issue for a significant proportion of musicians, novices, and experts, at all ages (see Papageorgi, 2007), and negative summative assessment can contribute to increasing anxiety.

Taken together, the evidence raises questions about what, if anything, students can learn from the summative assessments they receive. Students need to be able to make judgments about the validity of assessments and which elements, if any, are relevant to their future careers. Evaluating the feedback they are given is a challenge that they will continue to face throughout their careers as they receive informal feedback from audiences, critics, and the level of commercial success they achieve.

Many factors influence the summative assessment of performance in institutional or other formal contexts. These include

- the purpose of the assessment (high or low stakes);
- the genre of the performance;
- whether the performance is of individuals or groups and, if the latter, whether the assessment will be at group or individual level and how this will be undertaken;
- the performance environment (informal, formal);
- the reliability and validity of the assessment process; and
- the characteristics of the assessors.

The assessors also face the challenge of distinguishing between the music (the composer's intentions, as indicated in the score) and performers' use of expression as they evaluate technique and interpretation (Thompson, 2009).

Assessors are influenced by a range of factors that are not directly related to the performance. These include

- the physical attractiveness, gender, and race of performers (Elliot, 1995; Davidson & Coimbra, 2001);
- the order of performance in competitions (Flores & Ginsburgh, 1996);
- preconceptions about performers (Duerksen, 1972);
- whether performers play from memory (Wapnick et al.,1993);
- the stage manner and dress of performers (Platz & Kopiez, 2013; Davidson & Coimbra, 2001);
- the way in which performers interact with the audience (Wapnick, Mazza, & Darrow, 1998); and
- the facial expression, body movements, and gestures of performers (Davidson & Correia, 2002; Kokotsaki, Davidson, & Coimbra, 2001; Thompson, Graham, & Russo, 2005).

Some of these factors are beyond the control of performers, but some elements are under their control, including whether they play from memory; their stage manner and dress; their interactions with the audience; and their facial expressions, body movements, and gestures. To be successful they need to take account of each of these, as all contribute to the aesthetic and perceptual experience of listeners (Thompson, 2009).

A major controversy in the assessment of performance is whether the criteria adopted should be holistic or detailed. This is important, as the type of criteria determine the extent to which the feedback is useful. There is variability in the extent to which assessment is holistic; includes elements that support a holistic approach; or involves detailed checklists of specific criteria for each instrument family, including musical and technical approaches (Stanley et al., 2002). Holistic approaches have been argued to be as reliable as, or more reliable than, criterion-defined scales (Webster & Hickey, 1995), and some teachers have suggested that detailed, specific instrument criteria detract from the assessment of the holistic elements of performance (Stanley & Brooker, 2002). However, not all of the evidence supports this assertion (Thompson & Williamon, 2003). Assessors themselves frequently acknowledge that there are discrepancies between their global and analytic appraisals. This suggests that there is a need for assessment to include holistic and criteria-based methods (McPherson & Thompson, 1998; Stanley & Brooker, 2002).

Where approaches are designed to support holistic assessment, they may include musical elements, command of instrument, and presentation (Ciorba & Smith, 2009). The musical attributes of performance can include phrasing, balance, articulation, rubato, and dynamic range (Thompson, 2009; Boyle, 1992). Some systems have been devised for individual instrument groups based on rating scales, which have been validated through factor analysis (Bergee, 1993; Abeles, 1973; Wapnick, Flowers, Alegant, & Jasinskas, 1993; Zdinski & Barnes, 2002). These focus on different instrument groups, and the items included are instrument relevant. The advantage of performance dimensions being assessed at this level is that performers are given very detailed information, which can support them in improving (Latimer, Bergee, & Cohen, 2010). This suggests that there are advantages in assessment being undertaken by specific instrumental specialists, particularly in relation to technique. However, nonspecialists can make an important contribution to assessing musical outcomes and may bring fresh ideas and approaches.

At university levels, where the marks (or grades) awarded affect degree outcomes, some institutions have adopted multidimensional assessment rubrics to try to address the subjective nature of assessment. For instance, in one university the dimensions of assessment (musical elements, command of instrument, presentation) were derived by a panel of performance experts, who also outlined the various levels of achievement within each dimension, from basic to advanced levels. Scores were given for each scale dimension, written comments were provided, and a final grade was given (Ciorba & Smith, 2009). This level of scrutiny provided guidance for the students going forward as they began to develop their professional careers.

# SUMMATIVE ASSESSMENT OF COMPOSITION AND IMPROVISATION

The challenges faced in providing objective assessment, whether formative or summative, in relation to performance are amplified when composition and improvisation are assessed. Assessment of composition and improvisation typically takes account of novelty, but also the extent to which the music created makes an appropriate and valuable contribution to the field. This is problematic in that what is considered appropriate and valuable is highly subjective in the arts. Indeed, there have long been debates over whether there is any value at all in undertaking formal assessment of contemporary creative endeavors. This view is legitimized by the frequent disagreements among professional music critics and the way that the value of musical outputs is frequently not recognized until after the death of the musician. Overall, the assessment of creative musical activities is subjective and depends on the assessor's personal preferences and level of expertise (Hickey, 2001).

These issues are particularly challenging in educational contexts. Composition is typically assessed through its performance, which in some musical traditions creates the further problem of differentiating between the performance and the composition. Assessment of composition is usually supported by the use of a range of criteria (e.g., Amabile, 1982, 1996; Auh & Walker, 1999; Hickey, 2001; Kratus, 1994; Leung, Burnard, Jeanneret, Leung, & Waugh, 2012). These may include originality, fluency, flexibility, appropriateness, elaboration, and novelty (Webster, 1994, 2002). Checklists have also been developed to assess improvisation skills, including elements such as first impression, originality, imaginativeness, instrumental fluency, musical syntax, general impression, and final appraisal (Hassler & Feil, 1986; McPherson, 1993). While the use of checklists may appear to add more rigor to the assessment process, their completion remains subjective and therefore problematic. Feedback given in relation to improvisation needs to take account of the particular genre within which the improvisation is being developed. Within that framework, issues relating to the appropriateness of the style, the development of ideas, the use of different sound textures (melodic, rhythmic, harmonic, dynamic), expressive qualities, the extent to which the improvisation is structured, originality, imagination, and effectiveness may all be considered.

An alternative to assessing individual compositions or improvisations is assessing the creative process that the musician has adopted (Cain, 2015). There are three main ways of assessing compositional processes: think aloud or retrospective interviews (e.g., Barrett, 1996; Nilsson & Folkestad, 2005), the exploration of "flow" during the process (e.g.; Seddon & O'Neill, 2003), and the observation of the process with systematic coding of behaviors (e.g., Kratus, 1989). Some research has focused on the development of measures of creative thinking in music (e.g., Webster, 1990). Recently, ways of assessing the creative musical skills of those with no previous musical training have been developed (e.g., Barbot & Lubart, 2012). Understanding the processes involved in creativity can be extremely useful for learners. Those participating in creative activities need to be able to monitor progress and critically evaluate the developing creative product. Self-criticism is central to creativity in the long term. The most creative individuals set personal goals, negotiate the relationship between global and specific parameters, experiment and constructively criticize their work, and, while demonstrating an optimistic outlook and internal locus of control, are more critical of their work than are their peers.

One response to dealing with some of the difficulties in assessing the creative outputs outlined here is a proposal to adopt a system of negotiated assessment. This is based on a series of interviews between teachers and pupils in which they agree on the evaluation

(Pupil Assessment Conversations with Teachers, PACT) (Ross & Mitchell, 1993). This system clearly has benefits for both learners and teachers, as they can discuss process and outcomes. However, it is time consuming and is unlikely to have sufficient credibility to be accepted as accredited evidence of specific levels of attainment.

# ASSESSORS

Some research has focused on the role of assessors and the way in which their characteristics may impact outcomes. One focus has been their level of musical expertise. For instance, Pope (2013) explored the ratings given by seventy-eight preservice band, choral, and orchestra teachers who self-reported their academic status as lower (n = 39) and upper (n = 39) classmen. Participants assigned ratings to performers' interpretation, musicianship, dynamics, balance/blend, and other factors on a seven-point Likert-type scale. There were differences between the groups in the ratings. Upper classmen assigned more favorable ratings than lower classmen, while preservice choral teachers gave the least favorable ratings and preservice orchestra teachers the most favorable.

Similar differences have emerged in relation to composition. Evaluations of ten-year-old children's music compositions showed that there was most agreement among those involved in teaching music, followed by the children (in seventh and second grades), with the least agreement among professional composers. The more specialized the assessors of composition are, the more specific structural characteristics of the music they seem to take into account (Seddon & O'Neill, 2001). Assessment of musical activities carried out by teachers inevitably depends on their level of expertise. At primary level, where many teachers lack even moderate levels of musical expertise, it is not surprising that they have difficulty in carrying out assessments (Hallam et al., 2009). In the United Kingdom, the Office for Standards in Education (Ofsted) (2009) reported that of the forty-seven primary schools in which assessments carried out by primary school teachers were evaluated in detail, the practice in ten schools was judged as good or outstanding and in sixteen was judged as inadequate. Beston (2004) found that teachers tended to prefer to use composition-specific criteria rather than less quantifiable measures, for instance, creativity.

There are also issues relating to the genre in which assessment takes place, as each has its own stylistic conventions. Expertise in one area of music does not necessarily transfer to others, so it may be difficult for a Western classically trained examiner to assess jazz or the performance of music from other cultures. Similarly, assessing improvisation needs to be based on different criteria than other types of performance.

There is clearly a need for assessors to be trained (Toohey, 1999). Reliability seems to be higher when there are a greater number of assessors (Bergee, 2003). In addition, where there is more than one judge, the level of agreement between them can be assessed using statistical methods (e.g., Leung, Wan, & Lee, 2009).

# FORMATIVE ASSESSMENT

While summative assessment can be useful in guiding future learning, formative assessment is crucial in supporting ongoing learning (Black & Wiliam, 1998a). Formative assessment is at the heart of much music tuition. Music teachers spend the majority of their time highlighting how performance or composition can be improved through commenting, instructing, and asking questions. These strategies assist the teacher in identifying the student's level of understanding while also shaping learning behavior (Kennell, 2002). Music is privileged in comparison with many subject domains in that the sounds produced by learners provide immediate feedback to teacher and learner. This is the case whether teaching is at the individual, small, or large group level, although the smaller the group the more detailed the feedback available to the teacher about the performance of each individual.

For formative feedback to be effective, teacher and learner must have clear and shared goals and expectations. The feedback must provide high-quality, detailed information to learners about their progress, errors that they may be making, and what still needs to be improved (Hallam, 1998). Research based on observations of instrumental lessons has shown that teachers spend a great deal of time pointing out errors, highlighting details of the task, and reducing its complexity to make it manageable. Time spent in demonstration supports the development of representations of what is to be learned, but this constitutes a much smaller element of lessons. Learners typically spend the majority of lesson time playing (Kennell, 2002). The goal of formative assessment should be to enable learners to work independently and develop critical skills so that they can objectively reflect on and evaluate their work, identifying areas for improvement while also recognizing their achievements. Teacher modeling of evaluative and learning processes is important in this respect.

The type of formative feedback given by teachers tends to change as the learner develops musical expertise. To support early motivation to engage with music, teachers should be relatively uncritical, encouraging, and enthusiastic. As students progress, the relationship with the teacher changes from one of liking and admiration to respect for their expertise. At this point constructive criticism is valued (Sosniak, 1990; Manturzewska, 1990).

Pupil-teacher relationships are crucial in providing an appropriate environment for feedback to be given and acted upon. In instrumental teaching, the master-apprenticeship model has historically been dominant, with the teacher giving feedback to the learner. In this relationship, the teacher has held the power (Nerland, 2007). Potentially, this can undermine the developing autonomy of the learner (e.g., Creech & Hallam, 2010; Gaunt, 2011), essential for those who aspire to become professional musicians or engage in music making throughout the lifespan. Helena Gaunt and Heidi Westerlund (2013) suggest that in higher education, learning needs to be collaborative, with teachers and students working as colearners bringing their ideas and experiences to the learning situation. However, if this relationship is dysfunctional, it is not always easy for learners to change it or extricate themselves from the situation.

Formative assessment is particularly important in creative musical activities, although it is also problematic in that teachers have to take care not to impose their musical values on what is being produced. One solution to this is to focus on the process of teacher support. In a study of four secondary school teachers, Martin Fautley (2004) found that two teachers adopted what appeared to be a "laissez-faire" approach, not interfering in the composing process immediately, preferring to address issues in a postcomposing plenary session or in the structure of the next composing task. This meant that pupils were able to work in a relatively uninterrupted fashion. Other teachers adopted a stop and question approach, leading or challenging students in their thinking or practice. Analysis of when teacher intervention occurred was based on nine stages:

1. Initial confirmatory (pupils discuss the task).
2. Generation (ideas are produced).
3. Exploration (ideas are explored and potentialities investigated).
4. Organization (ideas are explored and ordered).
5. Work-in-progress performance (formally requested by the teacher; undertaken informally by the group).
6. Revision.
7. Transformation/modification.
8. Extension and development.
9. Final performance.

The majority of teacher interventions were related to the organization phase, in which concerns focused on pupils meeting the requirements of the task as set, followed by the generation phase and the requirement for a performance of work in progress. The teachers did not focus on musicality or aesthetic concerns, reflecting awareness of the complex issues arising from assessing creative work.

## PEER ASSESSMENT

Peer assessments, whether formal or informal, are increasingly being recognized as having a crucial role to play in the development of self-evaluation skills. Typically, peer assessments are formative, although in higher education they have sometimes contributed to summative assessment.

The evidence from a range of informal learning contexts has demonstrated the effectiveness of group working, not only in developing independent learning and self-assessment, but also in promoting a range of transferable skills (e.g., Green, 2002; Kokotsaki & Hallam, 2007). It supports learners in developing critical skills that they can apply to their own learning (Blom & Poole, 2004; Daniel, 2004; Lebler, 2008b;

Searby & Ewers, 1997). Even young children are able to assess the compositions of their peers, although their assessments do not consistently match those of their teachers (Hickey, 2001). Initially students find the process challenging, but the more frequently they engage with the process, the greater value they derive from it (Searby & Ewers, 1997).

In higher education students are increasingly involved in the summative assessment of their peers, in which typically they are issued with guidelines and agreed criteria. These might relate to the extent to which performance is convincing, is technically assured, is informed by a sense of style, communicates the music in a way that demonstrates understanding, and displays individuality. This can result in more objective assessment and encourage learners to prepare more thoroughly for performance (Hunter & Ross, 1996).

# Self-Assessment

Knowledge of results is necessary for all learning. Without feedback there is no means of improving. When musicians practice or perform, they receive multisensory feedback in relation to the music that they are producing. The most important feedback is aural, relating to the sounds that they are making, but they will also experience kinesthetic feedback (related to movement, e.g., muscle use, finger patterns); visual feedback (from their place in the written notation and in some cases from what they can see of their instruments); and emotional feedback, which may be related to emotions conceptualized in the music or their response to the quality of their performance (Hallam, 2014).

In its simplest form, self-assessment involves responding to feedback received from the sounds created. When new skills are being acquired, performance of the individual components of the activity require individual checking. This is known as closed-loop control. The closed loop refers to feedback between the execution of an individual action being used to check the match between intention and action. If there is a match, the next individual action can be executed. Behavior under closed-loop control is halting, slow, and variable. As skills become well learned through practice, the need for this level of feedback is eliminated. The skilled performer instigates an action and does not check that each individual action matches the initial intention. This is known as open-loop control and reflects the development of automaticity in skills. The performer still responds to naturally occurring feedback but at a meta, conscious level to take account of the current situation (Hallam, 2014).

As individuals learn or create a new piece of music, they need to be able to respond to its naturally occurring feedback. In the case of an existing piece of music this will only be possible if they already have an internal representation of what they are trying to achieve. To be able to evaluate progress, current performance must be compared to the mental representation of what is being aimed for. For novices this can be challenging (Hallam, 2001a, 2001b). When creating new music learners also need to have some conceptualization of what they are aiming for, although this may lack detail and be relatively abstract.

Metacognitive skills (knowledge concerning one's own cognitive processes and products or anything related to them) are crucial for using feedback effectively. Learners and creators need to be able to recognize personal strengths and weaknesses, have a range of musical strategies and know when to apply them, and be able to monitor progress toward a goal. They need to adopt a cyclical approach: recognizing a problem, using strategies to address it, self-evaluating, and then taking further action as necessary (Hallam, 2001a, 2001b). Developing self-assessment skills in students has been shown to develop stronger listening skills that feed into their practice and performance (Goolsby, 1999). Scott (2012) refers to this type of process as "self-reflective formative assessment."

In supporting the development of self-assessment, in the United Kingdom some schools have developed assessment criteria with students so that they can judge the extent of their progress and ultimately their level of success. An example is provided in table 9.1. Another approach has been to develop contracts between teachers and students that lead to shared responsibility (Andrews, 2004). The role of the teacher is to articulate outcomes and provide activities and modes of presentation, while the students select activities in consultation with the teacher and contribute to the assessment through self-evaluation.

Table 9.1 A Format for Students to Self-Evaluate Their Progress within the UK National Curriculum for Music

| National Curriculum Level 4<br>Pupils identify and explore the relationship between sounds<br>and how music reflects different intentions. | No | Not Sure | Yes |
|---|---|---|---|
| Can you use sound to create a piece of music that sounds as you intended? | | | |
| Can you play and hold your part in a group? | | | |
| Can you read simple musical notation? | | | |
| Can you play simple tunes by ear? | | | |
| Do you know how your part fits with other players? | | | |
| Do you know what a good performance sounds like? | | | |
| Do you know how to structure your musical ideas? | | | |
| Can you improvise melodies and rhythms when playing in a group? | | | |
| Can you evaluate your performance? | | | |
| Do you know how to improve your work? | | | |
| Do you know how to help others improve their work? | | | |
| Do you know how to describe different pieces of music using musical terms? | | | |

*(Continued)*

## Table 9.1 Continued

| | No | Not Sure | Yes |
|---|---|---|---|
| National Curriculum Level 4<br>Pupils identify and explore the relationship between sounds and how music reflects different intentions. | No | Not Sure | Yes |

Do you know how to compare different pieces of music?

Do you know how to evaluate different pieces of music?

| | No | Not Sure | Yes |
|---|---|---|---|
| National Curriculum Level 5<br>Pupils identify and explore musical devices and how music reflects time and place. | No | Not Sure | Yes |

Can you play sections of music from memory?

Can you play sections of music using notation?

Can you use different types of notation?

Do you know when to take the lead in a group?

Do you know when to play a solo in a group?

Do you know when to provide rhythmic support to others in the group?

Can you improvise rhythms and melodies within a clear structure?

Can you compose music for different occasions?

Do you know how to improve your own work?

Do you know how to help others improve their work?

Can you identify musical structures and specific musical devices?

Can you recognize different types and genres of music and music from different cultures?

Can you explain and compare different elements in music?

Can you describe why music is composed and performed for different occasions or audiences?

| | No | Not Sure | Yes |
|---|---|---|---|
| National Curriculum Level 6<br>Pupils identify and explore the different processes and contexts of selected musical genres and styles. | No | Not Sure | Yes |

Can you play expressively?

Can you adjust your playing so that your part fits sensitively within a group?

Can you improvise and compose in different styles and genres?

Can you use chords and other harmonies?

Can you use a range of different rhythms?

Can you use different notations?

Can you plan, revise, and improve your work?

Can you help others plan, revise, and improve their work?

Can you develop your musical ideas to achieve the effects that you want?

Can you recognize different styles and genres of music?

Do you understand the traditions of the music that you compose, play, and listen to?

Can you compare, analyze, and evaluate different pieces of music?

Are you able to discuss how music relates to where and when it is created and performed?

| National Curriculum Level 7 | No | Not Sure | Yes |
|---|---|---|---|
| Pupils discriminate [among] and explore musical conventions in, and influences on, selected genres, styles, and traditions. | | | |

Can you perform in a range of different styles, genres, and traditions?

Can you make an important contribution to your group and support the work of others?

Can you compose something that is original in a particular style?

Can you generate, develop, abandon, or adapt ideas when you are composing or performing?

Can you recognize and tell the differences among different styles, genres, and traditions of music?

Can you evaluate and criticize a range of music?

Can you explain and talk about how musical conventions are used?

Can you demonstrate your understanding of how music is linked to its context?

| National Curriculum Level 8 | No | Not sure | Yes |
|---|---|---|---|
| Pupils discriminate [among] and exploit the characteristics and expressive potential of selected musical resources. | | | |

Can you perform, improvise, and compose extended pieces of music in a range of different styles, genres, and traditions?

When composing, improvising, and performing, do you take account of direction and shape in relation to rhythm, melody, and overall form?

Do you take account of musical expression when composing, improvising, and performing?

Can you play by ear and from a range of different notations?

Can you differentiate among a wide range of genres, styles, and traditions; discuss their characteristics and historical and geographical backgrounds; and critically evaluate them?

Can you critically evaluate pieces of music challenging musical conventions?

In higher education, assessment is increasingly seen as an important element in learning and as encouraging independence in students (Harrison, Lebler, Carey, Hitchcock, & O'Bryan, 2013). Institutional systems need to be developed to support this (Jorgensen, 2000) and help students to evaluate and critique their own instrumental practice and performances. Assessment procedures should be authentic and useful to students as they move toward entry into the music profession (Lebler, 2008a).

Recent technological developments are particularly useful in supporting self-evaluation. Video and audio recording makes it possible for performers and composers to assess their work from an audience perspective. Young people are increasingly making use of technology (Hallam et al., 2012; Zhukov, 2015). Where composition is part of the curriculum in secondary schools, young people can record their progress more easily, facilitating development (Ofsted, 2009). Ryan Daniel (2001) found that students who were required to evaluate a video of a public performance developed stronger critical assessment skills and insights. Most reported that this helped them identify their errors more clearly than at the time of performance and helped them to identify difficulties and address them. It also enabled them to take an audience perspective, although in some cases it increased anxiety levels (Daniel, 2001). Similarly, Kelly Parkes (2010) evaluated the use of performance rubrics developed for assessing performance in exams in one-to-one lessons. Recording lessons, using the exam rubrics to self-assess and critique, and reflecting in an online journal helped students understand their improvement, providing ongoing feedback and helping them to take responsibility for their learning. Video feedback is direct and combines visual and auditory senses. It has the advantage that it can bypass the interpersonal communication between teacher and learner, which can sometimes be biased (Baker-Jordan, 1999). Recordings also help to address distortions in perception, which occur when students are actually performing (Gordon, 2006).

## IMPLICATIONS FOR EDUCATION

To learn successfully depends on responding to feedback. For young children, in performance the feedback provided from the sounds they produce needs to be augmented by the teacher until they have developed aural templates against which they can compare their own performances. As expertise develops, musicians become more adept at responding to natural feedback. However, what the performer hears differs from what the audience hears. Teachers therefore need to provide this perspective and also support learners in developing self-evaluation skills. This may be through providing models of what is to be learned and how to go about learning, demonstrating critical listening and evaluation processes, utilizing recordings of practice and performances, and setting up opportunities for peer evaluation. For learners to successfully continue engagement with music when they are no longer involved in formal education, they have to develop self-evaluation skills. Recent technological developments mean that it has never been easier to evaluate performance or creative work from an audience perspective.

There will always be controversy in the arts about the relevance of formal assessment and the extent of its subjective nature. Similarly, there will always be disagreements about whether summative assessment should be based on holistic or itemized assessment procedures. While the outcomes in terms of grading may be similar, having detailed criteria is more likely to benefit learners, providing them with clear guidance about how to improve. The more authentic the assessment procedures, the more likely they are to support developing professional careers and lifelong learning.

## References

Abeles, H. F. (1973). Development and validation of a clarinet performance adjudication rating scale. *Journal of Research in Music Education, 21*, 246–55.

Amabile, T. M. (1982). Social psychology of creativity: A consensual assessment technique. *Journal of Personality and Social Psychology, 43*, 997–1013.

Amabile, T. M. (1996). *Creativity in context*. Boulder, CO: Westview Press.

Andrews, B. W. (2004). Musical contracts: Fostering student participation in the instructional process. *International Journal of Music Education, 22*(3), 219–29.

Auh, M., & Walker, R. (1999). Compositional strategies and musical creativity when composing with staff notations versus graphic notations among Korean students. *Bulletin of the Council for Research in Music Education, 141*, 2–9.

Baker-Jordan, M. (1999). What are the pedagogical and practical advantages of "three or more" teaching? *Pedagogy Saturday, III*, 22–23.

Barbot, B., & Lubart, T. (2012). Creative thinking in music: Its nature and assessment through musical exploratory behaviors. *Psychology of Aesthetics, Creativity, and the Arts, 6*(3), 231–42.

Barrett, M. (1996). Children's aesthetic decision-making: An analysis of children's musical discourse as composers. *International Journal of Music Education, 28*, 37–62.

Bergee, M. J. (1993). A comparison of faculty, peer and self-evaluation of applied brass jury performances. *Journal of Research in Music Education, 41*(1), 19–27.

Bergee, M. J. (2003). Faculty interjudge reliability of music performance evaluation. *Journal of Research in Music Education, 51*(2), 137–50.

Beston, P. (2004). Senior student composition: An investigation of criteria used in assessments by New South Wales secondary school music teachers. *Research Studies in Music Education, 22*(1), 28–41.

Biggs, J. B. (1996). Enhancing teaching through constructive alignment. *Higher Education, 32*, 1–18.

Biggs, J. B., & Moore, P. J. (1993). *The process of learning*. Englewood Cliffs, NJ: Prentice Hall.

Black, P., & Wiliam, D. (1998a). Inside the black box: Raising standards through classroom assessment. *Phi Delta Kappan, 80*(2), 139–49.

Black, P., & Wiliam, D. (1998b). Assessment and classroom learning. *Assessment in Education, 5*, 7–75.

Blom, D., & Poole, K. (2004). Peer assessment of tertiary music performance: Opportunities for understanding performance assessment and performing through experience and self-reflection. *British Journal of Music Education, 21*(1), 111–25.

Booth, E. (2009). *Music teaching artist's bible: Becoming a virtuoso educator*. New York: Oxford University Press.

Boyle, J. (1992). Evaluation of music ability. In R. Colwell (Ed.), *Handbook of research on music teaching and learning*. New York: Schirmer.

Cain, M. (2015). Participants' perceptions of fair and valid assessment in tertiary music education In D. Lebler, G. Carey, & S. D. Harrison (Eds.), *Assessment in music education: From policy to practice* (pp. 87–106). New York: Springer.

Ciorba, C. R., & Smith, N. Y. (2009). Measurement of instrumental and vocal undergraduate performance juries using a multidimensional assessment rubric. *Journal of Research in Music Education, 57*(1), 5–15.

Creech, A., & Hallam, S. (2010). Interpersonal interaction within the violin teaching studio: The influence of interpersonal dynamics on outcomes for teachers. *Psychology of Music, 38*(4), 403–21.

Daniel, R. (2001). Self-assessment in performance. *British Journal of Music Education, 18*(3), 215–26.

Daniel, R. (2004). Peer assessment in musical performance: The development, trial and evaluation of a methodology for the Australian tertiary environment. *British Journal of Music Education, 21*(1), 89–110.

Davidson, J. W., & Coimbra, D. C. C. (2001). Investigating performance evaluation by assessors of singers in a music college setting. *Musicae Scientiae, 5*(1), 33–53.

Davidson, J. W., & Correia, J. S. (2002). Body movement. In R. Parncutt & G. E. McPherson (Eds.), *The science and psychology of music performance* (pp. 237–52). New York: Oxford University Press.

Duerksen, G. L. (1972). Some effects of expectation on evaluation of recorded musical performance. *Journal of Research in Music Education, 20,* 268–72.

Elliott, C. A. (1995). Race and gender as factors in judgments of musical performance. *Bulletin of the Council for Research in Music Education, 127,* 50–55.

Elliott, D. J. (1987). Assessing musical performance. *British Journal of Music Education, 4*(2), 157–84.

Elton, L. B. R., & Laurillard, D. (1979). Trends in student learning. *Studies in Higher Education, 4,* 87–102.

Fautley, M. (2004). Teacher intervention strategies in the composing processes of lower secondary school students. *International Journal of Music Education, 22*(3), 201–18.

Fiske, H. E. (1978). *The effect of a training procedure in music performance evaluation on judge reliability.* Brantford, ON: Ontario Educational Research Council Report.

Flores, R. G., & Ginsburgh, V. A. (1996). The Queen Elisabeth musical competition: How fair is the final ranking? *The Statistician, 45*(1), 97–104.

Gaunt, H. (2011). Understanding the one-to-one relationship in instrumental/vocal tuition in Higher Education: Comparing student and teacher perceptions. *British Journal of Music Education, 28*(2), 159–79.

Gaunt, H., & Westerlund, H. (2013). *Collaborative learning in higher music education: Why, what and how?* Surrey, UK: Ashgate.

Goolsby, T. (1999). Assessment in instrumental learning: How can band, orchestra and instrumental ensemble directors best assess their students' learning? Here are some evaluation tools and techniques to consider. *Music Educators Journal, 86*(2), 31–50.

Gordon, S. (2006). *Mastering the art of performance: A primer for musicians.* New York: Oxford University Press.

Green, L. (2002). *How popular musicians learn: A way ahead for music education.* Aldershot, UK: Ashgate Publishing Ltd.

Hallam, S. (1998). *Instrumental teaching: A practical guide to better teaching and learning.* Oxford: Heinemann.

Hallam, S. (2001a). The development of metacognition in musicians: Implications for education. *The British Journal of Music Education, 18*(1), 27–39.

Hallam, S. (2001b). The development of expertise in young musicians: Strategy use, knowledge acquisition and individual diversity. *Music Education Research, 3*(1), 7–23.

Hallam, S. (2014). The role of feedback. In W. F. Thompson (Ed.), *Music in the social and behavioural sciences: An encyclopedia* (Vol. 1, pp. 461–64). Los Angeles, CA: SAGE Reference.

Hallam, S., Burnard, P., Robertson, A., Saleh, C., Davies, V., Rogers, L., & Kokatsaki, D. (2009). Trainee primary school teachers' perceptions of their effectiveness in teaching music. *Music Education Research*, 11(2), 221–40.

Hallam, S., Rinta, T. Varvarigou, M., Creech, A. Papageorgi, I., & Lani, J. (2012). The development of practising strategies in young people. *Psychology of Music*, 40(5), 652–80.

Harrison, S., Lebler, D., Carey, G., Hitchcock, M., & O'Bryan, J. (2013). Making music or gaining grades? Assessment practices in tertiary music ensembles. *British Journal of Music Education*, 30, 27–42.

Hassler, M., & Feil, A. (1986). A study of the relationship of composition improvisation to selected personality variables. *Bulletin of the Council for Research in Music Education*, 87, 26–34.

Hay, P., & MacDonald, D. (2008). (Mis) appropriations of criteria and standards-referenced assessment in a performance based subject. *Assessment in Education: Principles, Policy and Practice*, 15(2), 153–68.

Hickey, M. (2001). An application of Amabile's consensual assessment technique for rating the creativity of children's musical compositions. *Journal of Research in Music Education*, 49, 234–44.

Howe, M., & Sloboda, J. (1991). Young musicians' accounts of significant influences in their early lives, 2: Teachers, practising and performing. *British Journal of Music Education*, 8(1), 53–63.

Hunter, D., & Ross, M. (1996). Peer assessment in performance studies. *British Journal of Music Education*, 13(1), 67–78.

Jorgensen, H. (2000). Student learning in higher instrumental education: Who is responsible? *British Journal of Music Education*, 17(1), 67–77.

Kennell, R. (2002). Systematic research in studio instruction in music. In R. Colwell & C. Richardson (Eds.), *The new handbook of research on music teaching and learning* (pp. 243–56). Oxford: Oxford University Press.

Kokotsaki, D., Davidson, J., & Coimbra, D. (2001). Investigating the assessment of singers in a music college setting: The students' perspective. *Research Studies in Music Education*, 16, 15–32.

Kokotsaki, D., & Hallam, S. (2007). Higher education music students' perceptions of the benefits of participative music making. *Music Education Research*, 9(1), 93–109.

Kratus, J. (1989). A time analysis of the compositional processes used by children ages 7 to 11. *Journal of Research in Music Education*, 37, 5–20.

Kratus, J. (1994). Relationships among children's music audiation and their compositional processes and products. *Journal of Research in Music Education*, 42, 115–30.

Latimer, M. E., Bergee, M. J., & Cohen, M. L. (2010). Reliability and perceived pedagogical utility of a weighted music performance assessment rubric. *Journal of Research in Music Education*, 58(2), 168–83.

Lebler, D. (2008a). Perspectives on assessment in the learning of music. In D. Bennett & M. Hannan (Eds.), *Inside, outside, downside up: Conservatoire training and musicians' work* (pp. 181–93). Perth, Australia: Black Swan Press.

Lebler, D. (2008b). Popular music pedagogy: Peer learning in practice. *Music Education Research*, 10(2), 193–213.

Leung, C. C., Wan, Y. Y., & Lee, A. (2009). Assessment of undergraduate students' music compositions. *International Journal of Music Education*, 27, 250–68.

Leung, S., Burnard, P., Jeanneret, N., Leung, B. W., & Waugh, C. (2012). Assessing creativity in music: International perspectives and practices. In G. McPherson & G. Welch (Eds.), *The Oxford handbook of music education* (Vol. 2, pp. 389–407). New York: Oxford University Press.

Manturzewska, M. (1990). A biographical study of the life-span development of professional musicians. *Psychology of Music, 18*(2), 112–39.

McPherson, G. (1993). Evaluating improvisational ability of high school instrumentalists. *Bulletin of the Council for Research in Music Education, 119*, 11–20.

McPherson, G., & Thompson, W. (1998). Assessing music performance: Issues and influences. *Research studies in Music Education, 10*(June), 12–24.

Nerland, M. (2007). One-to-one teaching as cultural practice: Two case studies from an academy of music. *Music Education Research, 9*(3), 399–416.

Nilsson, B., & Folkestad, G. (2005). Children's practice of computer-based composition. *Music Education Research, 7*(1), 21–37.

Office for Standards in Education (Ofsted). (2009). *Making more of music: An evaluation of music in schools 2005/2008.* London: HMSO.

Papageorgi, I. (2007). *Understanding performance anxiety in the adolescent musician* (Unpublished doctoral thesis). Institute of Education, University of London.

Parkes, K. A. (2010). The use of criteria specific performance rubrics for student self-assessment: A case study. In T. S. Brophy (Ed.), *The practice of assessment in music education: Frameworks, models and designs* (pp. 453–58). Chicago: GIA Publications.

Platz, F., & Kopiez, R. (2013). When the first impression counts: Music performers, audience and the evaluation of stage entrance behavior. *Musicae Scientiae, 17*(2), 167–97.

Pope, D. A. (2013). Influence of primary performance area, education level, and performance quality on pre-service music teachers' ratings of string orchestra performances. *String Research Journal, IV*, 55.

Ross, M., & Mitchell, S. (1993). Assessing achievement in the arts. *British Journal of Aesthetics, 33*(2), 99–112.

Scott, S. (2012). Rethinking the roles of assessment in music education. *Music Educators Journal, 38*, 31–35.

Searby, M., & Ewers, T. (1997). An evaluation of the use of peer assessment in higher education: A case study in the School of Music, Kingston University. *Assessment and Evaluation in Higher Education, 22*(4), 371–83.

Seddon, F. A., & O'Neill, S. A. (2001). An evaluation study of computer-based compositions by children with or without prior experience of formal instrumental tuition. *Psychology of Music, 29*(1), 4–19.

Seddon, F. A., & O'Neill, S. A. (2003). Creative thinking processes in adolescent computer-based composition: An analysis of strategies adopted and the influence of instrumental music training. *Music Education Research, 5*, 125–37.

Snow, R. E. (1990). New approaches to cognitive and conative assessment in education. *International Journal of Educational Research, 14*, 455–74.

Sosniak, L. A. (1990). The tortoise and the hare and the development of talent. In M. J. A. Howe (Ed.), *Encouraging the development of exceptional skills and talents* (pp.149–64). Leicester, UK: The British Psychological Society.

Stanley, M., & Brooker, R. (2002). Examiner perceptions of using criteria in music performance assessment. *Research Studies in Music Education, 18*, 43–52.

Thompson, S., & Williamon, A. (2003). Evaluating evaluation: Musical performance assessment as a research tool. *Music Perception: An Interdisciplinary Journal, 21*(1), 21–41.

Thompson, W. F. (2009). *Music, thought, and feeling: Understanding the psychology of music.* New York: Oxford University Press.

Thompson, W. F., Graham, P., & Russo, F. A. (2005). Seeing music performance: Visual influences on perception and experience. *Semsiotica, 156*(1–4), 177–201.

Toohey, S. (1999). *Designing courses for higher education*. Buckingham, UK: Open University Press.

Wapnick, J., Flowers, P., Alegant, M., & Jasinskas, L. (1993). Consistency in piano performance evaluation. *Journal of Research in Music Education, 41*, 282–92.

Wapnick, J., Ryan, C., Lacaille, N., & Darrow, A. (2004). Effects of selected variables on musicians' ratings of high-level piano performances. *International Journal of Music Education, 22*(1), 7–20.

Wapnick, L., Mazza, J. K., & Darrow, A. A. (1998). Effects of performer attractiveness, stage behaviour, and dress on violin performance evaluation. *Journal of Research in Music Education, 46*(4), 510–21.

Webster, P. (1990). Creativity as creative thinking. *Music Educators Journal, 76*, 22–28.

Webster, P. (1994). *Measure of creative thinking in music-II (MCTM-II): Administrative guidelines*. Unpublished manuscript, Northwestern University, Evanston, IL.

Webster, P. R. (2002). Creative thinking in music. In T. Sullivan & L. Willingham (Eds.), *Creativity and music education* (pp. 16–33). Edmonton, AB: Canadian Music Educators' Association.

Webster, P. R., & Hickey, M. (1995). Rating scales and their use in assessing children's composition. *The Quarterly Journal of Music Teaching and Learning, 6*(4), 28–44.

Wesolowski, B. (2012). Understanding and developing rubrics for music performance assessment. *Music Educators Journal, 38*, 36–42.

Wrigley, W. J. (2005). *Improving music performance assessment* (Unpublished doctoral thesis). Griffith University.

Wrigley, W. J., & Emmerson, S. B. (2013). Ecological development and validation of a music performance rating scale for five instrumental families. *Psychology of Music, 41*(1), 97–118.

Zdinski, S. F., & Barnes, G. V. (2002). Development and validation of a string performance rating scale. *Journal of Research in Music Education, 50*, 245–55.

Zhukov, K. (2015). Challenging approaches to assessment of instrumental learning. In D. Lebler, G. Carey, & S. D. Harrison (Eds.), *Assessment in music education: From policy to practice* (pp. 55–70). New York: Springer.

.....................................................................................................................

# CHAPTER 10

# THE MCDONALD'S
# METAPHOR

*the case against assessing standards-based
learning outcomes in music education*

.....................................................................................................................

## JOHN KRATUS

ORTHODOXY suggests that the first step in the assessment of music learning is to specify the desired learning outcomes (McMillan, 1997). In a previous generation, these outcomes were called "behavioral objectives," easily observable and measurable indications of student learning (Madsen & Yarbrough, 1980). In our currently more "enlightened," postbehavioral times, we refer to learning outcomes as "standards." In this chapter I make the case that a standards-based approach for assessing student success or failure in school music is detrimental to student learning.

This chapter begins with an extended food metaphor, which seems fitting as the author is in the sixth and seventh week of a diet as this is being written. Next is a brief, edited history of assessment in American music education and a critique of the process. The chapter concludes with an alternative means for assessing success and failure in school music.

## McDonald's Gold Standard

.....................................................................................................................

The golden arches of the McDonald's Corporation are widely known around the world. The restaurant chain was founded in 1948 by brothers Richard and Maurice McDonald, who developed a "Speedee Service System" for preparing hamburgers quickly and inexpensively (Martin, 2010). In essence, the McDonald brothers adapted Henry Ford's assembly line model for manufacturing automobiles to the preparation of fast food.

Ray Kroc, a restaurant equipment salesman, was so impressed by the McDonald's operation that he eventually bought the company's assets in 1961. Today the company operates over thirty-six thousand fast-food restaurants in 120 countries (McDonald's, n.d.).

McDonald's maintains uniformity among its restaurants by adhering to a strict gold standard, that ensures, for example, that a Big Mac tastes the same in every McDonald's restaurant. Barbara Booth is McDonald's director of sensory science, charged with enforcing the gold standard. She writes: "Every single menu item, from our World Famous Fries to the Fruit 'N Yogurt Parfait, has a 'taste profile.' That's basically a description of each of our Menu offerings—how it should look, taste, smell, feel, and sound. [It is a] system we use around the world to make sure our products are up to our high standards" (Team GHR, 2012). The standards that Booth describes are designed to maintain uniformity, not necessarily quality.

Maintaining "high standards," even a "gold standard," in food preparation does not inevitably produce beneficial results for consumers. Morgan Spurlock's 2004 film *Supersize Me* documented his experience eating three meals a day for one month at various McDonald's restaurants (Spurlock, 2005). Over the course of the month, Spurlock gained twenty-five pounds (eleven kg); developed heart palpitations; suffered from headaches, depression, and lethargy; and lost muscle mass and sex drive. The physical and psychological damage Spurlock endured to make his film was not diminished by the fact that every Big Mac he ate looked, tasted, and smelled the same.

The point I am making, quite obviously, is that simply maintaining strict standards, whether in fast food or in music education, does not guarantee a positive outcome. Eating a quarter pounder with cheese every day does not necessarily satisfy the body's need for nourishment, even though the burgers are made according to exacting standards. Learning to identify the names of the instruments of the orchestra does not necessarily satisfy students' musical needs, even though that standard may be part of a required curriculum. But there is a deeper level to this metaphor.

In 1983 sociologist George Ritzer coined the word "McDonaldization," which he describes as "the process by which the principles of the fast food restaurant are coming to dominate more and more sectors of American society as well as of the rest of the world" (Ritzer, 2008, p. 1). Since that time, Ritzer's concept of McDonaldization has been applied to such disparate areas as higher education (Hartley, 1995; Hayes & Wynward, 2002), religion (Drane, 2012), social work (Dustin, 2016), journalism (Franklin, 2005), and tourism (Weaver, 2005). McDonaldization has become a worldwide phenomenon.

In the book *The McDonaldization of Society*, Ritzer (2008) describes four features of McDonaldization: efficiency, calculability, predictability, and control. These characteristics evolved over the years from the McDonald brothers' "Speedee Service System" that Ray Kroc so admired. Ritzer's thesis is that the ubiquity of McDonald's restaurants enabled these same principles to permeate many facets of society in the United States and around the world. In the following section, I explain the four dimensions of McDonaldization and their manifestation in music education.

# McDonaldization
# and Music Education

**Efficiency.** When Ray Kroc visited one of the original McDonald's in San Bernardino, California, he was impressed by the efficiency of offering a limited menu of only hamburgers, cheeseburgers, French fries, and milk shakes. He also noted that "the burgers were…all fried the same way" (Kroc, 1977, p. 8). The purpose of offering a limited menu produced in identical ways was to streamline the procurement and preparation of food. Diversity of the menu and individually prepared meals were sacrificed for speed and productivity. Customers interested in healthier food, such as fresh fruit, or slower food, such as beef stew, had to go elsewhere. To further improve efficiency, a procedure such as preparing a hamburger was broken down into its most basic component parts, and each part of the task was systematized in a strict sequence to maximize efficiency. For example, the length of time that a hamburger cooks on the griddle is identical at all McDonald's restaurants.

Has music education adopted the efficiency of McDonaldization? Certainly. At the secondary level, prospective music students have their choice of participating in either band or choir, and occasionally orchestra. It does not matter that this limited menu of musical offerings has little connection to the musical lives of adolescents outside of school or after graduation. Large ensembles are an especially efficient use of an instructor's time, in that one music teacher can work with fifty or more students at a time. Students interested in learning to play guitar or compose beats, taught in classes with a much less efficient teacher-student ratio, often must pursue their interests outside of school. (It should be noted that the culpability for the limited menu of offerings in school music does not lie with the teachers. They can only teach what they have been taught.) The emphasis on efficiency also affects the type of music making taught in schools. One of the primary reasons that elementary music teachers give for not teaching composition is that there is "not enough time" (Strand, 2006). Regarding pedagogical techniques, McDonald's systemized and sequential approach to efficiently making hamburgers is replicated in the Orff approach, the Kodály method, and Gordon's learning theory, all of which carefully sequence discrete component parts (e.g., so-mi) in the development of students' music literacy.

**Calculability.** The second dimension of McDonaldization is calculability, which is the use of quantifiable outcomes rather than subjective judgments of quality as a measure of achievement. Some readers may be old enough to remember when the large illuminated signs outside of every McDonald's restaurant announced how many million (or billion) hamburgers the chain had sold. The signs did not promote the quality of the hamburgers, only the number sold. Presumably, potential consumers would think that billions of hamburgers would only have been sold if the burgers were good. Quantity was used to imply quality.

Ultimately, there is a trade-off between quantity and quality. A restaurant chain, even one with thirty-six thousand locations, is not going to sell billions of fairly inexpensive hamburgers if each burger is lovingly prepared by a Cordon Bleu–trained chef. To compensate for mediocre quality, McDonald's and other restaurant chains increase portion size by offering large and extra-large versions of their primary menu items: a double burger instead of a single, extra-large fries instead of regular fries. The customer drives off with a full belly but is not well fed. In this case quantity becomes a substitute for quality.

Education has certainly fallen prey to McDonaldization in its emphasis on assessing quantifiable learning outcomes to imply or substitute for quality. Children are required to take multiple high-stakes tests during their school years. The percentage of students who "pass"—however that is defined—is often published in local newspapers as a measure of the success of the school. In Australia, for example, the test results from every school in the country are published on the website MySchool (Polesel, Rice, & Dulfer, 2013). Learning, in many classes, becomes a matter of studying to take the test. Other calculable measures of student achievement, such as grade point averages and standardized test scores, greatly influence college admission decisions. Students' educational prospects and schools' reputations are reduced to numbers.

In two important ways, calculability is embedded in music education practices. The quality of large ensemble performances in the United States is rated by judges using Roman numerals from I to V, with I being the highest score, and with most scores given being either a I or a II. The scores are based on the performance from a limited, prescribed repertoire, using a set of unchanging criteria, much like McDonald's gold standard. It is difficult to imagine any other school subject assigning a single number to assess the combined achievement of a group of fifty or more students. Calculability also figures prominently in terms of student participation. Because secondary music education is an elective subject, the number of students music teachers can recruit and retain in their ensembles becomes a measure of quality of the ensembles and thereby a measure of the quality of their teaching. More students enrolled or more hamburgers sold: quantity implies or substitutes for quality.

**Predictability**. When customers walk into a McDonald's, they have every reason to expect that the Big Mac they order will be the same as the last one they ate. The ingredients in a Big Mac, which was introduced in 1967, are identical fifty years later. McDonald's management prides itself on that predictability, and customers have come to rely upon the sameness. The uniformity of McDonald's extends to the look of the restaurants, the ordering procedures, and even the scripted interaction with employees: "Do you want fries with that?" Predictability is comforting, but, as Ritzer (2008) points out, it has a downside: a tendency to turn everything—consumption, work, management—into mind-numbing routine" (p. 98).

There is certainly a place for predictability in music education. Ensemble classes typically begin with warm-ups, and elementary general music classes often begin with the singing of a familiar song. Students come to expect the familiarity. But the regularity of procedures can also lead to boredom and a dulling of the daily learning experience.

Furthermore, predictability has a stifling effect on innovation. For example, the standard instrumentation for concert bands has remained the same since the early twentieth century. As musical tastes and technology have evolved over the past one hundred years, the school band has remained frozen in time and out of step with contemporary musical experiences. School concerts today sound much as they did in 1967, when the Big Mac was introduced.

**Control**. The fourth dimension of McDonaldization is control of humans through technology, rules, regulations, and techniques. At McDonald's, a simple procedure such as making French fries is reduced to a series of nine steps: "(1) Open the bag of (frozen) fries. (2) Fill the basket until it is half full," and so on (Newman, 2007, p. 44). Ray Kroc was concerned that employees, left to their own judgment, would overcook or undercook fries, so fryers have buzzers that tell employees when to remove the basket of fries. Computerized systems tell managers how many hamburgers they will need to prepare at lunchtime. The substitution of rules and standard procedures for worker expertise is dehumanizing but necessary for McDonaldization to take root. Ritzer (2008) writes that "people are the greatest threat to predictability. Control over people can be enhanced by controlling processes and products, but control over processes and products also becomes valued in itself" (p. 128). In a work environment, regulations become a replacement for individual employees' skill and contextual knowledge. In a learning environment, control delegitimizes each teacher's expertise and each student's unique desire to learn.

Music educators have increasingly been subjected to this type of control. Mandated curriculum guides and standards developed by government agencies, professional organizations, and school districts dictate the learning that should take place in various grades and instructional settings. Ensemble teachers are told which pieces are "acceptable" for contest and festival adjudication and what criteria are to be judged. General music textbook series come with teachers' editions that recommend step-by-step lesson plans for each learning activity in the students' books, much like the McDonald's instructions for making French fries. Organizations that provide accreditation for collegiate music programs (e.g., National Association of Schools of Music) mandate strict guidelines for the preparation of collegiate musicians, including preservice music educators. All of these restrictions have the effect of limiting curricular initiatives and controlling outcomes. The professionalization of the profession is sapped by control exerted by those who would standardize music education.

In turn, students in music classes and ensembles are strictly controlled. The music they make is not their music; it is music given to them by their teachers in elementary classrooms and secondary ensembles. The way students perform the music is also controlled by teachers, who often believe it is their duty to correct mistakes and strictly obey the composer's intentions. Thus, music teachers and students are controlled by a system that regulates procedures and content and minimizes creativity and individual initiatives.

In recent years McDonald's and other fast-food restaurants have offered slightly greater flexibility in menu offerings, albeit within a façade of alternatives among limited choices. For example, many McDonald's locations now offer breakfast items all day rather than only before 10:30 a.m. The incremental changes still allow for McDonaldization's efficiency, calculability, predictability, and control. If a customer asked for a medium-rare burger, that request would not be honored. Similarly, music education has offered alternative electives within a limited range of menu options. For example, the choir director may offer various options to the mixed choir ensemble: show choir, men's and women's choirs, madrigal choir, and gospel choir. But all of these options provide the efficiency, calculability, predictability, and control of a teacher passing out music to a large number of students and leading them in rehearsals toward a concert.

To summarize, the four characteristics of McDonaldization are efficiency, calculability, predictability, and control. These qualities work in tandem to reduce error and produce a predetermined result, whether it be a satisfied customer or a musically educated student. The process is a rational one in that it is logical and consistent. The next section of this chapter discusses the unintended consequences of rationality and its effects on humans.

# RATIONALITY AND HUMANIZATION

McDonaldization is a rational process designed to sell more food faster, thereby maximizing corporate profits. Rationality results in actions based on reason and facts, rather than on whim. McDonald's adopted efficiency, calculability, predictability, and control as a rational means to maximize profits. Music education applied similar means as a rational means to maximize student learning. Rationality is logical. The problem with rationalization is that it is acontextual (Habermas, 1984); that is, it does not take into consideration unique differences in various situations, and it is overly prescriptive of human behavior (Etzioni, 1988). As a consequence, rationality can lead to irrational results.

One of McDonald's rational decisions that resulted in an unintended outcome is the introduction of the drive-thru window, which was meant to speed up the process of ordering and buying fast food (Ritzer, 2008). It is rational to assume that if customers could purchase and pick up food without leaving their cars, that would decrease the time for them to receive their food, and McDonald's would sell more food (and make more profit) faster. That would improve efficiency. The problem is that McDonald's found that drive-thru windows were too successful in attracting patrons who did not want to leave their cars. The average wait time for customers ordering from the drive-thru line was longer than the time it took customers to park their cars, go inside the restaurant, and order their food. Drive-thru windows may be convenient for some customers, but from McDonald's standpoint they were not more profitable and efficient for the corporation.

An example of rationality in music education having unintended consequences is the large ensemble. From a rational standpoint, the large ensemble is an efficient means for one teacher to engage a great many students simultaneously. The large ensemble is certainly the most prominent venue for music learning in middle schools and high schools.

But at what cost? As Williams (2011) points out, the overwhelming presence of large ensembles in many secondary schools has limited opportunities to develop new music classes that might attract those students who do not wish to perform in a traditional band, orchestra, or choir. Students participating in school ensembles rarely continue performing after high school, because the opportunity to make music with sixty or so musicians under the direction of a conductor is rarely available outside of schools. Individual differences among students' interests and ability levels are sublimated to the needs of the ensemble. Music teachers, who often pride themselves on directing sixty or eighty or one hundred students at one time, have the impossible task of educating those students at more than a superficial level. It is notable that high school calculus teachers or world history teachers do not aspire to teach sixty or more students in a class as a measure of their worth.

It should be noted that there are significant philosophical arguments for why the art of music should not be subjected to McDonaldization. Some of the most thoughtful persons in music education have authored powerful rationales for the values of music education (Allsup, 2016; Elliott & Silverman, 2015; Jorgensen, 2003; Reimer, 2002), and none of these rationales has anything to do with efficiency, calculability, predictability, or control. Simply put, the dehumanizing aspects of McDonaldization act to minimize subjectivity, creativity, individuality, and expressiveness, all the human qualities that an education in music seeks to instill.

Another problem with McDonaldization when applied to music education is that the qualities of efficiency, calculability, predictability, and control are not the reasons young people choose to engage in music. In recent years, researchers have studied the ways that children and young adults make use of music in their everyday lives. They have found that music is beneficial in that (1) it serves to develop psychological and sociological identity (Kubrin, 2005; MacDonald, Hargreaves, & Miell, 2002), (2) it is used for mood regulation (Saarikallio & Erikkia, 2007), (3) it is an expression of the self (Juslin & Laukka, 2003), and (4) it acts as a connection to other people (Hays & Minichiello, 2005; Laiho, 2004). All of these benefits require children and young adults to engage in music meaningfully, but none of these uses entails efficiency or even a high level of proficiency in music performance.

Susan Hallam (2010) published in the *International Journal of Music Education* an extensive review of the empirical evidence on the role of active musical engagement in intellectual, social, and personal development of children and young people. She found that the development of music skills may transfer to other areas such as literacy, creativity, concentration, self-confidence, social skills, self-discipline, and relaxation, but that a high level of musical proficiency was not necessary for these benefits to occur. She further found that the effects of music on personal and social development only occur if it is learned through an enjoyable and rewarding experience.

Efforts to rationally maximize student learning by maintaining and measuring high standards may be turning students away from music education. As one who for decades has taught college music students who are not music majors and interviewed prospective music majors, I can attest that a large number of potential music majors choose not to major in music because, they say, they love music too much. Nearly all adolescents love music, but only a small fraction of them choose to enroll in large ensembles. Perhaps the rest love music too much.

The following section provides a brief history of assessment and standards in American music education and concludes with a rationale for why students' progress in achieving educational standards should not be used as a measure of the quality of a school's music program.

# ASSESSMENT, STANDARDS, AND MCDONALDIZATION

The assessment of music performance has been with us for a very long time, certainly before the first set of golden arches went up. Twenty-six hundred years ago in ancient Greece, the Pythian Games, the forerunner of our modern Olympic Games, included music contests as well as athletic contests. Instrumental and vocal performances were judged by senior musicians. The winners, rather than receiving a gold medal, got an apple (Remijsen & Clarysse, n.d.).

Assessment of student musicians in the United States can be traced to the School Band Contest of America, held in Chicago in 1923 (Fay, 1925; Gordon, 1956; Holz, 1962; Maddy, 1957). The contest was created and sponsored by the Band Instrument Manufacturers Association as a means to promote its members products to the education market. The contest was an advertising bonanza for the Band Instrument Manufacturers, with front-page headlines in newspapers across the country, and further contests were planned. The instrument manufacturers did not want to appear to have a commercial motive. So they arranged for the National Music Supervisors Conference, the forerunner to the National Association for Music Education, to hold annual national band contests, as well as band contests in every state. That is where the emphasis on competition and quasi-professional performance standards for secondary music students came from, and it led to contests, festivals, and all-state ensembles.

The Band Instrument Manufacturers had correctly foreseen that schools would be eager to transform music education into another means of interscholastic competition, much like sports. To accomplish those ends, music classes needed to become *efficient* rehearsals for performances, the quality of ensembles was *calculated* with judges' ratings, the *predictability* of performances was enhanced by rehearsing the same few pieces over and over to minimize error, and *control* was established by professional organizations that dictated repertoire and standard instrumentation and by teachers in the classroom. In effect, this rational process was McDonaldization before McDonald's.

Prior to that time, the aims of school music in the United States were quite different. Music was meant to be personally satisfying and life enriching, and amateur music making was fostered in music classes. It was not a programmatic goal of school music programs to help students achieve high standards in music performance. Early in the twentieth century, the influential music educator James L. Mursell (1936) wrote: "[Music education] should be organized deliberately to produce palpable practical results in pupils' lives both now and later on. We may perhaps state its most characteristic and basic aim in terms of use as follows: The music program should aim at the promotion of active and intelligent musical amateurism" (p. 10). A historical example should illustrate my point. Instrumental ensembles began to appear as after-school activities at the end of the nineteenth century. By 1921, 10 percent of the students in the Los Angeles Public Schools performed in a school orchestra, and about half of these orchestras were taught during the school day. Thanks to historian Edward Bailey Birge (1928/1966), we know what the typical school orchestra looked like. A typical school orchestra had about fifteen members. (High schools were much smaller back then.) The only string instrument played was the violin, because violas, cellos, and basses were too rare and expensive. About half the student orchestra members played the violin. The other instruments in a typical orchestra were piano, drum set (not percussion), trumpets, saxophones, clarinets, trombones, and bells (yes, bells, as in a bell choir). With this instrumentation, two things become readily apparent. First, there was no attempt to copy the instrumentation of professional orchestras. Performances of marches, waltzes, hymns, and overtures had to be arranged by the music teacher or the students for the unique instrumentation of the school orchestra. Second, music educators of the time must have encouraged anyone with an interest in instrumental performance to join the orchestra. The emphasis of the instrumental programs would have been on inclusion, according to students' diverse musical interests and backgrounds, rather than on quasi-professional performance norms.

The modern movement in assessment of school music in the United States received a boost from the federal Goals 2000 law in 1994, which required that students meet world-class standards in a variety of subjects, including the arts. The arts education community of music, dance, theater, and visual arts responded by creating the National Standards, a guide to what every American should know or be able to do in the arts (Consortium of National Arts Education Associations, 1994). By doing so, the leadership of the arts education community joined the educational communities of eight other subjects, including English, mathematics, and science, in the "world-class" learning that should occur at various grade levels.

As a result of the creation of these standards, all states developed tests of English, mathematics, and later science, which were administered to students at various grade levels. The quality of education in a school was then measured by the percentage of students receiving passing scores on the tests. In other words, the success of a school's educational programs was determined by the success of its students in passing state-mandated tests. Music was not included in this testing, as a reflection of music's lower status as an important school subject.

Although Congress has defunded Goals 2000—after not reaching any of its goals— and its follow-up No Child Left Behind, the assessment movement spurred in the

1990s has continued to gather strength. Many states are now requiring proof of annual progress in students meeting musical goals as a means to assess the success or failure of a school music program. Some states have suggested using easily calculable contest ratings of ensembles as a measure of success.

There are three problems with using measures of students' musical performance to determine a music program's success. The first stems from the primary reason given for educational reform in the late twentieth century: economic security, both domestic and international (National Commission on Excellence in Education, 1983). Domestic economic security means jobs. One can make the case that students who meet certain high standards in reading, writing, math, and science have an employment advantage in certain fields. But can one establish that the students who meet the highest level of music standards will get employment using what they have learned? Maybe, but there simply are not enough jobs there. According to data from the US Bureau of Labor Statistics, less than .1 of 1 percent of American adults make a living as performing musicians (US Department of Labor, 2016). That means that in the average school less than 1 of every 1,000 students will eventually be employed as a performer. If we focus music standards on domestic economic security, we are shortchanging 999 of every 1,000 children. Rather than contribute to economic security, as do many other school subjects, music is a humanizing subject, as described previously.

International economic security means maintaining an educated workforce to compete with US global trading partners. One can make the case that students who meet certain high standards in reading, writing, math, and science can create a workforce that will enable US companies to compete worldwide. But I am unaware of any geopolitical advantage for developing the world's best bassoonists.

The second reason measures of students' musical performance should not be used to determine a music program's success is that music is an elective subject. Even though most states do have some sort of one-year arts requirement, it is ridiculously easy for students to be exempt from it with classes such as "auto repair," "cooking," and "French." So rather than assess students' performance in classes that are taken over a period of years by all students—such as reading, math, and science—educators would be assessing subject knowledge in an area in which the large majority of students have at most a single year's instruction.

Furthermore, since music is an elective subject, if music students' performance was used as a measure of the quality of a music program, then it would be to the music teachers' advantage to limit enrollment in these elective classes and ensembles to only the top-performing students. The likely effect of assessing students' performance in elective music classes would be to place greater limits on the number of students in those classes. For example, if a performance rating of a school band is used to determine the quality of the band program, then it is less likely that a band teacher would welcome novice eleventh graders or special education students into the band and thus place a high rating at risk. In addition, it would be unlikely that a teacher would develop a new, experimental class such as popular music ensemble or songwriting.

A third reason for not using students' performances to assess quality harkens back to the original National Standards, which were designed to be "world-class" standards. The world has changed in twenty-two years, and "world-class" music education standards do not necessarily lead to the highest level of performing musicians. Consider the world-class Musical Futures program in the United Kingdom (Musical Futures, 2017) or the popular music education taught in Scandinavian schools (Karlsen, 2010). These programs inspire inclusion and student creativity, not perfect performances.

The 2014 US National Standards in Music (National Association for Music Education, 2014) assess music solely in terms of an individual's musical achievement in creating, performing, responding, and connecting, which are all musical and rational outcomes of music education. Other models of assessment utilize a socially based and more holistic framework. For example, the five U S National Standards for K–12 Physical Education (Society of Health and Physical Educators, 2014) ask students to demonstrate "responsible personal and social behavior that respects self and others" and learn "the value of physical activity for health, enjoyment, challenge, self-expression and/or social interaction." Among the four criteria in the music assessment rubric for Musical Futures Australia (Musical Futures, n.d.) is "Explore & Express Ideas," with levels of "sometimes positive," "involved thoughtful follower," "shares ideas, supports the team," and "leader, fair negotiator." These standards assess learning as something more than an individual's achievement.

To summarize, music's relation to assessment is different from that of other school subjects, because students' musical proficiency is not linked to economic security; music is an elective, not required, subject; and "world-class" standards in music are not the same as "high performance" standards in music.

The measurement of learning outcomes based on prescribed standards is a perfect example of rationalization. The logic of defining the learning standards that all students should achieve, measuring those standards, and using the resulting measurements as indications of success or failure is a clear case of McDonaldization in practice: The process is *efficient*, because the standards outline a limited menu of musical behaviors, broken down into sequentially learned steps (i.e., *so* and *mi* before *la*). The process is *calculable*, because quantitative measures are used to determine the extent to which the specified standards have been met (i.e., ease of measurement rather than assessment of quality). The process is *predictable*, because the standards apply equally to all students in every school (i.e., conventional rather than diverse). The process is *controlling*, because all teachers, regardless of circumstance, teach the same standards, and all students, regardless of desire, learn the same standards (i.e., uniformity rather than individuality).

As previously discussed, rationality comes at a cost: the dehumanization of McDonaldization undermines the reason for teaching music to children. And yet music educators need some valid criteria for determining whether their music programs are effective in meeting students' needs. If they don't use the students' own musical performance as a criterion, what would they use?

# RESISTING MCDONALDIZATION
## IN MUSIC EDUCATION

Here I return to the McDonald's metaphor one last time. Ritzer (2008) admits that many people are comforted by a McDonaldized society that is efficient, predictable, and uncluttered by too many choices. McDonald's is a profitable company with many satisfied customers worldwide. Similarly, many high school students are satisfied by the procedural rigors and limited choices of marching band or mixed choir. However, humanistic music educators understand that the children in their care are not "sopranos" or "saxophones" producing a concert product. They are individuals with unique needs and ideas and desires. Ritzer suggests that the effort to mitigate the worst excesses of McDonaldization are ennobling and worth the effort (p. 208).

I suggest an alternative to McDonald's gold standard, which specifies ingredients and procedures for making the items on McDonald's menu. When applied to music education, these standards can be dehumanizing. In keeping with the restaurant metaphor, I suggest that assessment of school music programs should be more congruent with standards upheld by local health departments. Health departments do not regulate menus, cooking procedures, or ingredients. Rather, they ensure that the food served in restaurants is healthy and safe and that restaurants are nondiscriminatory.

In applying similar criteria to music education, I suggest six criteria for assessing school music programs. The music teachers in each school or district would be responsible for determining the evidence to be used to determine whether or not a criterion had been met. Here are the criteria:

1) Music learning should be **sustainable,** that is, learning that extends beyond the school day and beyond the school years. Whatever it is that is taught, it should be of sufficient depth and interest to be used in later life.
2) Music learning should be **socially responsible and inclusive**; that is, the programmatic offerings should be diverse and relevant enough to attract a cross section of the school's population.
3) Music learning should take advantage of both **global and local** resources; that is, make use of the Internet and local musicians.
4) Music learning should be **individually expressive**; that is, it should acknowledge and encourage each student's unique muse.
5) Music learning should be **collaborative**; that is, students should have the opportunity to work with each other, not only under the direction of their teacher.
6) Music learning should be **life affirming**; that is, it should bring meaning and joy to students' lives.

If a music program can meet these criteria, then it would be considered successful. The criteria are specific but flexible enough to apply to music programs in small, rural schools or large, urban schools. It would not matter whether a school had an award-winning marching band or not, as long as the criteria were met. Examples of music programs that exemplify these criteria already exist in many schools: the creative approach of Musical Futures and the Modern Band approach of Little Kids Rock. Both approaches are expanding rapidly across the educational landscape and providing models for a new resurgence of music education.

An interesting epilogue to this story is that the past may well serve as prologue to the future. The school orchestras of one hundred years ago, with their violins, drum sets, and bells, were inclusive and allowed anyone to perform. The creativity and individualization of those ensembles could serve as a model for contemporary music education.

## REFERENCES

Allsup, R. E. (2016). *Remixing the classroom: Toward an open philosophy of music education.* Bloomington, IN: Indiana University Press.

Birge, E. B. (1928/1966). *History of public school music in the United States.* Reston, VA: Music Educators National Conference.

Consortium of National Arts Education Associations. (1994). *National standards for arts education.* Reston, VA: Music Educators National Conference.

Drane, J. (2012). *The McDonaldization of the church.* Macon, GA: Smyth & Helwys.

Dustin, D. (2016). *The McDonaldization of social work.* London: Routledge.

Elliott, D. J., & Silverman, M. (2015). *Music matters: A philosophy of music education* (2nd ed.). New York: Oxford University Press.

Etzioni, A. (1988). Normative-affective factors: Toward a new decision-making model. *Journal of Economic Psychology, 9,* 125–50.

Fay, J. W. (1925). State and national high school and grammar school band contest: 1925. *Music Supervisors' Journal, 11*(3), 46–49.

Franklin, B. (2005). McJournalism: The local press and the McDonaldization thesis. In S. Allen (Ed.), *Journalism: Critical issues* (pp. 137–50). Milton Keynes, UK: Open University Press.

Gordon, E. B. (1956). The birth of the school bands and orchestras. *Music Educators Journal, 43*(2), 34–45.

Habermas, J. (1984). *The theory of communicative action.* Volume 1, *Reason and the rationalization of society.* Cambridge, UK: Polity Press.

Hallam, S. (2010). The power of music: Its impact on the intellectual, social and personal development of children and young people. *International Journal of Music Education, 28,* 269–89.

Hartley, D. (1995). The "McDonaldization" of higher education: Food for thought? *Oxford Review of Education, 21,* 409–23.

Hayes, D., & Wynyard, R. (2002). *The McDonaldization of higher education.* Westport, CT: Bergin & Garvey.

Hays, T., & Minichiello, V. (2005). The meaning of music in the lives of older people: A qualitative study. *Psychology of Music, 33*(4), 437–51.

Holz, E. A. (1962). The schools band contest of America (1923). *Journal of Research in Music Education, 10,* 3–12.

Jorgensen, E. R. (2003). *Transforming music education.* Urbana: Indiana University Press.

Juslin, P. N., & Laukka, P. (2003). Emotional expression in speech and music. *Annals of the New York Academy of Sciences, 1000*(1), 279–82.

Karlsen, S. (2010). BoomTown music education and the need for authenticity—informal learning put into practice in Swedish post-compulsory music education. *British Journal of Music Education, 27,* 35–46.

Kroc, R. (1977). *Grinding it out.* New York: Berkeley Medallion Books.

Kubrin, C. E. (2005). Gangstas, thugs, and hustlas: Identity and the code of the street in rap music. *Social Problems, 52,* 360–78.

Laiho, S. (2004). The psychological functions of music in adolescence. *Psychology of Music, 13*(1), 47–63.

Maddy, J. E. (1957). The battle of band instrumentation. *Music Educators Journal, 44*(1), 30–35.

Madsen, C. K., & Yarbrough, C. (1980). *Competency-based music education.* Englewood Cliffs, NJ: Prentice-Hall.

Martin, R. (2010). Design thinking: Achieving insights via the "knowledge funnel." *Strategy & Leadership, 38*(2), 37–41.

MacDonald, R. A., Hargreaves, D. J., & Miell, D. (Eds.). (2002). *Musical identities* (Vol. 2). Oxford: Oxford University Press.

McDonald's. (n.d.). About us. Retrieved from https://www.mcdonalds.com/us/en-us/about-us.html

McMillan, J. H. (1997). *Classroom assessment: Principles and practices for effective instruction.* Needham Heights, MA: Allyn & Bacon.

Mursell, J. L. (1936). Principles of music education. In G. M. Whipple (Ed.), *The thirty-fifth yearbook of the National Society for the Study of Education, part 2: Music education* (pp. 1–16). Bloomington, IL: Public School Publishing.

Musical Futures. (2017). Musical Futures: It's the way we learn. Retrieved from https://www.musicalfutures.org

Musical Futures. (n.d.). Assessment rubric. Retrieved from https://www.musicalfuturesaustralia.org/store/p26/Assessment_Rubric_%28with_spreadsheet%29.html

National Association for Music Education. (2014). 2014 music standards. Retrieved from https://nafme.org/wp-content/files/2014/11/2014-Music-Standards-PK-8-Strand.pdf

National Commission on Excellence in Education. (1983). *A nation at risk.* Washington, DC: US Department of Education.

Newman, J. (2007). *My secret life on the McJob: Lessons from behind the counter guaranteed to supersize any management style.* New York: McGraw-Hill.

Polesel, J., Rice, S., & Dulfer, N. (2013). The impact of high stakes testing on curriculum and pedagogy: A teacher perspective from Australia. *Journal of Education Policy, 29,* 640–57.

Reimer, B. (2002). *A philosophy of music education: Advancing the vision.* Englewood Cliffs, NJ: Prentice Hall.

Remijsen, S., & Clarysse, W. (n. d.). Ancient Olympics: The Pythian games. Retrieved from http://ancientolympics.arts.kuleuven.be/eng/tb002en.html

Ritzer, G. (2008). *The McDonaldization of society* (5th ed.). Thousand Oaks, CA: SAGE.

Saarikallio, S., & Erkkilä, J. (2007). The role of music in adolescents' mood regulation. *Psychology of Music, 35,* 88–109.

Society of Health and Physical Educators. (2014). Grade-level outcomes for K-12 physical education. Retrieved from https://www.shapeamerica.org/standards/pe/upload/Grade-Level-Outcomes-for-K-12-Physical-Education.pdf

Spurlock, M. (2005). *Don't eat this book.* New York: G. P. Putnam's Sons.

Strand, K. (2006). Survey of Indiana music teachers on using composition in the classroom. *Journal of Research in Music Education, 54,* 154–67.

Team GHR. (2012, September 9). The gold standard. [Web log post]. Retrieved from http://teamgrh.blogspot.com/2012/09/the-gold-standard.html

United States Department of Labor. (2016, May). *Occupational employment and wages: 27-2042, Musicians and singers.* Retrieved from https://www.bls.gov/oes/current/oes272042.htm

Weaver, A. (2005). The McDonaldization theory and cruise tourism. *Annals of Tourism Research, 32,* 346–66.

Williams, D. A. (2011). The elephant in the room. *Music Educators Journal, 98*(1), 51–57.

# CHAPTER 11

## HABITS OF MIND AS A FRAMEWORK FOR ASSESSMENT IN MUSIC EDUCATION

JILLIAN HOGAN AND ELLEN WINNER

EVERYONE faces challenges. But not everyone responds to the same challenge in the same way. How we respond is governed by our habits of mind, our thinking dispositions. Imagine three people in a room with a jigsaw puzzle to solve. The first person industriously gets to work and formulates a plan that allows her to get from start to finish. She lays down the corners, then the borders, and fills in the middle. We can surmise that the pursuit of organization and order seems to be a cognitive umbrella that governs her choices. She has the skill to get organized, sees a puzzle as a useful opportunity to be organized, and chooses to go ahead and make a plan. The second person responds differently, with irritation, questioning the need to complete the puzzle. She never begins the task. We can surmise that the desire to question authority seems to be governing her choices. The third person leisurely inspects the puzzle. She takes a moment to smell the cardboard of the box and slowly takes out each puzzle piece, looking at and feeling each one. This person's behavior suggests a different cognitive umbrella: she seems governed by the habit of mindfully noticing sensory information. In new situations, she defaults immediately to slowing down and attentively taking in the sights, sounds, and smells of the setting.

We all have developed habits of mind that guide our behaviors. In the activities of a musician, we can infer many thinking routines that are a result of engaging in music making, automatic trains of thought that do not require a great deal of prompting to elicit. Wondering "Am I in tune?" and asking "How should I fix it?" are pervasive, habitual ways of thinking for a skilled musician. We do not see professional orchestra conductors touching their earlobes, frantically trying to signal that the chord should be tuned. That behavior is more likely to be seen in high school conductors, whose students are still developing the habit of mind of listening for intonation. Similarly, longtime musicians do not receive lengthy lectures about arriving at 7:00 p.m. for the 8:00 p.m. concert or about preparing for rehearsal by bringing a pencil, as we sometimes hear from school music teachers. Rather, seasoned musicians have a disposition of thought that has them wondering, "Am I ready? For the next performance? For the next rehearsal? For the next entrance?" By the time musicians have reached an amateur level, there is a thorough understanding that music making requires persistence. They enter the practice room and rehearsal space with a general understanding that to make progress, they will need to work hard, even when things are difficult. This isn't a new discovery every time they begin music making, but rather an underlying habit of mind that motivates their behavior.

For practiced musicians, habits of mind like these are nearly automatic. They don't require a great deal of conscious thought; they are readily accessible. In this chapter we argue that music education helps instill a number of discipline-specific habits of mind, and that these are useful to musicians at all levels. While the vast majority of music students do not aim to be professional musicians, they nonetheless can benefit from broad thinking dispositions that are a result of participation in music making. Arguably, these are the most cogent and important benefits for amateur musicians. These habits of mind are of great importance to music making and music understanding, but they have not typically been considered when assessment frameworks in music are developed. Since we believe all students can benefit from calling attention to and valuing habits of mind used by musicians, we argue in this chapter that music assessment should include an assessment of musical habits of mind.

## Conceptions of Thinking

In using the term "habit of mind" we are referring to generalizable ways of thinking that are big and broad, not necessarily specific to the music domain. Examples of domain-specific skills include recognizing the images on a microscope slide (biology), drawing in linear perspective (visual art), knowing fingerings for guitar chords (music), and demonstrating proper form for a basketball free throw (athletics). By describing something as a habit of mind, we imply a more general and generalizable ability. Habits of mind are ways of thinking that could potentially be used outside of the domain in which they are observed. Categorization, for example, is a habit of mind that might be taught in biology class but could be deployed in many disciplines, including the arts, language learning, and history.

Another way of thinking about habits of mind is that they are cognitive patterns that support dispositional thinking (Perkins & Tishman, 2001; Perkins, Jay, & Tishman, 1993). Dispositional thinking is a way of describing abilities beyond just the use of skills.

D. N. Perkins and others consider three aspects of dispositional thinking: ability, sensitivity, and inclination. Take the example of categorization. A child may have the *ability* to sort nonliving from living things in a science class but may not notice when this is called for. Noticing when this is called for requires *sensitivity* to situations in which the ability to categorize might be useful. When a child uses her ability to sort living from nonliving things as a way of deciding if something is compostable or not, she is showing sensitivity to the opportunity to use this ability. *Inclination* refers to the motivation to use categorical thinking as opposed to some other strategy, such as guessing whether or not the object is compostable. When using a lens of thinking dispositions, teachers ask not only the skill-based question, "Can the student do this?" They also probe behaviors and attitudes with questions such as, "Does the student know when to do this?" (asking about sensitivity) and "Will the student do this?" (asking about inclination). We consider the terms "habit of mind" and "thinking disposition" to be synonymous and use both interchangeably here.

Habits of mind are broad enough to make their utility applicable to more than one discipline. However, cultivating one particular habit of mind in one discipline does not necessarily mean that habit of mind will transfer to another discipline (Detterman & Sternberg, 1993; Perkins & Salomon, 1989). The study of transfers of habits of mind between disciplines is one for continued and future research.

# HABITS OF MIND

A focus on habits of mind in school curricula is not new. The teaching of habits of mind, or similar concepts called by different names, is noted in general education (Boyes & Watts, 2009a, 2009b; Costa & Kallick, 2013; Fletcher, Najarro, & Yelland, 2015; Ritchhart, Church, & Morrison, 2011; Root-Bernstein & Root-Bernstein, 2013; Tishman, Jay, & Perkins, 1993, 1995). The teaching of habits of mind is also noted in distinct subject areas: math education (Cuoco, Goldenberg, & Mark, 1996; Goldenberg, 1996; Goldenberg & Mark, 2015), special education (Burgess, 2012), science education (Calik & Coll, 2012; Steinkuehler & Duncan, 2008), higher education (Berrett, 2012; Wineburg, 2003), teacher education (Borko, Liston, & Whitcomb, 2007; Diez & Raths, 2007; Dottin, 2009), and medical education (Epstein, 2003; Lunney, 2003). Most of these are lists of habits of mind that are created "top-down"; that is, they derive from literature reviews or beliefs about the kinds of habits central to a particular discipline. A few frameworks have been built "bottom up," on the basis of systematic observation of teaching in specific disciplines.

Because we know of no literature that specifically puts forth a framework of habits of mind or thinking dispositions in music education, we first examine resources in general education and other disciplines in order to illustrate what we believe to be possible within the domain of music education.

## Habits of Mind in General Education

Some of the most prolific resources about habits of mind are those by Arthur Costa and Bena Kallick (2000, 2008, 2009). They have developed a top-down list of sixteen habits of mind (e.g., striving for accuracy, managing impulsivity, gathering data through all the senses, finding humor), now adopted by schools around the world. Costa and Kallick (2008) aimed to create a list of dispositions that help students become critical producers— rather than reproducers—of knowledge. They define habits of mind as "broad, enduring, and essential lifespan learnings that are as appropriate for adults as they are for students" (p. xvii), a definition consistent with our own vision. Their books describe various strategies for formatively and summatively assessing such habits of mind, including school report card redesigns that reflect progress with each habit of mind; lists of concrete behaviors that serve as evidence of thinking within a habit of mind; tools for helping students monitor their thinking progress and set goals; and rubric, portfolio, performances, and journal examples. A quick search engine query reveals many blogs and resources that teachers have developed for using and assessing habits of their own minds in their classrooms—evidence that using thinking as a fundamental guide for learning in the classroom is possible.

## Habits of Mind for Creative Education

Habits of mind in creative education are addressed theoretically (Booth, 2009, 2012) and in terms of assessment in schools (Lucas, 2016; Lucas, Claxton, & Spencer, 2014; Spencer, Claxton, & Lucas, 2012). Booth argues that his top-down list of twenty habits of mind for creative engagement includes attitudes and processes that occur within the flow state of creative activity. These habits include inquiring skillfully, persisting, observing intentionally, going back between parts and wholes, and self-assessing. Booth notes that while creative engagement is often seen in the arts, creativity is not limited to the arts and can be seen in any discipline. These habits become routine and automatic. They do not require conscious control because they are ingrained. Using them helps learners achieve flow. Bill Lucas, Guy Claxton, and Ellen Mary Spencer developed an assessment tool that captures five broad dispositions (inquisitive, persistent, imaginative, collaborative, and disciplined), each with three subdispositions. Teachers in various disciplines, and teaching at different grade levels, have used this tool, ranking each student's progression from novice to advanced within each of the fifteen subdispositions. Teachers found this assessment tool not only useful but also feasible for giving formative feedback, and students reported that the accompanying self-report was accessible.

## Habits of Mind in the Arts

The habits of mind put forth in *Studio Thinking: The Real Benefits of Visual Art Education* (Hetland, Winner, Veenema, & Sheridan, 2007, 2013) were developed bottom up, through systematic observation of high-level teaching in the visual arts. Five teachers in arts-based high schools were observed, videotaped, and interviewed over the course of a school year. The aim was to code teachers' behaviors into the teaching of habits of mind. Teaching of eight broad habits of mind was observed: develop craft, persist, envision, express, observe, reflect, stretch and explore, and understand art worlds. Because this list of dispositions was created from data within classrooms, these habits of mind are ones that teachers are likely to already be teaching. In fact, many visual arts teachers report that having a list of such dispositions resonates with their current teaching and provides them with language to discuss the value of their discipline (Hogan, Hetland, Jaquith, & Winner, 2018). Thus this framework was not put forward as a mandate for how teachers should teach, but rather was offered as a way of illuminating ways of thinking already present within the authentic practice of the discipline. And if these ways of thinking are authentic, they should be assessed.

The Studio Thinking framework has been adopted in the visual arts curricula and assessment practices by school districts across the world. Teachers report that this list of habits of mind provides them with concepts and terms with which to speak to administrators, parents, and students about the importance of what they do. Now, in addition to assessing technical skills such as color mixing or shading or perspective drawing, teachers are discussing and assessing students' ability to persist through technical challenges, envision a plan for creating and completing an artwork, and critically reflect upon their own progress.

Visual arts teachers are putting these kinds of habits of mind at the forefront of their teaching, making them explicit to students, and making them a part of ongoing formative assessment. For example, many teachers try to help students become aware of the habits they are using and thereby become more metacognitive in their art-making practice. Teachers hang signs on the wall noting each habit of mind, use the first five minutes of class to discuss a famous artwork whose creation exemplifies a particular studio habit of mind, review strategies for becoming skilled in a particular studio habit of mind, and provide students with feedback on how well they are exhibiting studio habits of mind. Other strategies include asking students to discuss studio habits of mind in artist statements written after the completion of a work and "exit tickets," in which students reflect on which habits of mind they employed during the course of the class. Visual arts teachers have developed rubrics to capture progression within the development of each habit of mind, and these can be completed by the teacher as well as the student (Hogan, Hetland, Jaquith, & Winner, 2018).

## Habits of Mind in Music Education

We argue here that music teachers should follow the example of visual arts teachers by teaching for and assessing musical habits of mind. We have brought the approach used by Lois Hetland et al. (2007, 2013) to the high school music ensemble classroom (Hogan & Winner, 2015). In short, we have developed, bottom up through systematic observation, a catalog of habits of mind that are already present within high school ensemble classrooms. Our method was to code the teaching behaviors of six public high school ensemble teachers in twenty-four videotaped rehearsals.

We describe our findings in the following sections, with an awareness of the current environment of disagreement about the aims and potential reform of music ensemble education (Allsup, 2012; Allsup & Benedict, 2008; Elliott & Silverman, 2015; Fonder, 2014; Heuser, 2011, 2015; Regelski, 2013; Thibeault, 2015; Williams, 2007, 2011). Here we adopt two different perspectives: that of empirical researchers observing what we see and that of critical commentators. The aim of the study was to investigate and identify those broad, potentially transferable habits of mind that are already present in typical high school ensemble teaching—ensembles in which the conductor-teacher does most of the talking and group decision-making. We believe that reporting what we observe will shed light on the thinking that is occurring (mostly through modeling) in teacher-directed, large ensembles. At the same time, as critical commentators we wholeheartedly support emancipatory arguments for the democratization of music education, increasing student-centered and social practices, and making music education more relevant to diverse populations—ideas fundamental to practices such as informal music learning (Green, 2002, 2009).

It is our hope that an identification of the habits of mind being taught in traditional music ensemble classrooms will help teachers of all music education approaches make the teaching of these habits of mind more explicit. At the same time, we also aim to call attention to authentic and important musical habits of mind that we do not see when we observe what actually goes on in typical ensemble music classrooms. Thus our work may also be useful in thinking not only about how best to assess, but also about how best to teach and how to best structure any possible reforms.

Our preliminary findings suggest that teaching behaviors used in the course of rehearsals can be categorized into eight habits of mind, five of which were seen with high levels of frequency and three of which were seen with more moderate levels of frequency. Habits of mind taught with high levels of frequency were evaluate (decide what needs to be better), listen (really listen, not just hear), imagine (use imagery and inner hearing), persist (focus and "stick to it"), and set goals and be prepared (think toward the future). The three less frequently observed habits of mind were participate in community (show accountability to the musical group), express (find and show meaning), and notice (critically observe through the eyes and body).

As mentioned previously, it is important to know not only what is being taught in music classrooms but also what is not being taught. In our study, there were two habits of mind that we consider important but that were not observed being taught: use creativity (engage in novel and useful thinking) and appreciate ambiguity (recognize that musical problems have more than one correct answer). Arts advocates often claim that arts education teaches students to think creatively and to recognize that problems have more than one correct answer (Davis, 2008; Eisner, 2002), and 97 percent of the American public believes that playing an instrument helps a child or teenager develop creativity (NAMM, 2009). While we did not observe music teachers trying to instill these two habits of mind despite systematically looking for them, we believe these habits can and should be taught in all music classes.

A notable difference emerged between the coding processes in visual arts and ensemble music. In visual arts classes, students were directly engaged in practicing the habits of mind being taught. They were nearly always active participants in the thinking disposition. This happened when teachers asked questions to lead students to their own thoughts rather than giving explicit directions for improvement. In ensemble music rehearsals, the conductor-teacher did not engage the students in this way, instead giving the students explicit directions about what to do. Was the conductor-teacher the only one doing the thinking, or did the students implicitly model this example? We cannot know, but we can say that the students rarely stated any decisions or evaluations. We recognize that other types of music classes, not large secondary school ensembles, may be more likely to emphasize these habits of mind or to teach them in a way that is more active on the part of students. Perhaps environments such as general music classes, popular music ensembles, jazz groups, and dedicated composition and songwriting classes are more natural settings for such activities. However, we believe teachers of high school ensembles can continue to build upon the habits of mind we've documented here and grow to both include additional habits of mind and become more student centered and informal in their practice. Models for reconceptualizing traditional ensembles are becoming more available to assist teachers (Abrahams, Rafaniello, Vodicka, Westawski, & Wilson, 2017; Clements, 2010; Colquhoun, 2017; Heuser, 2015).

## Musical Habits of Mind

The ten habits of mind we have identified in our study are consistent with our definition of a habit of mind; they are big, broad, and potentially useful outside of the music room. We can also think of them in terms of the framework of D. N. Perkins, Eileen Jay, and Shari Tishman (1993): they encompass a skill, an awareness of when to use the skill, and an inclination to do so. Furthermore, these thinking dispositions are already either inherent in the process of authentic school music making or on the minds of practicing music teachers, as evidenced by their presence in the literature, discussed later in the chapter. But by drawing attention to the concept of habits of mind, teachers may be encouraged to make these more explicit in their teaching and to develop ways of assessing them. In what follows, we go into more detail about each of the habits we observed being taught.

Habits of mind are nonlinear. They are complex cognitive routines, and though they develop through systematic practice, they do so over time and in idiosyncratic ways. The list of possible habits of mind used for assessment in the classroom is presented alphabetically here. We make no claims for the importance of one habit of mind over another or any kind of developmental progression. Rather, it is our claim that thinking dispositions work together simultaneously, the boundaries separating one disposition from another are not always clear, and they are often fuzzy.

# Habits of Mind Observed in Music Classrooms

## Evaluate (Decide What Needs to Be Better)

The general music classroom, the ensemble rehearsal, and the individual practice session all incorporate forms of evaluation. In our data, teachers were often the modelers of the evaluation process, pointing out errors and making suggestions for their improvement, but we know there were additional opportunities for students to take greater part in the evaluation process. While there is considerable discussion about music teacher modeling in regard to skills, such as the demonstration of beautiful tone quality or correct rhythm (Dickey, 1992; Haston, 2007; Polk, 2006), there is far less discussion about music educators using modeling to teach thinking behaviors such as evaluating. We suggest that the continual modeling of evaluating out loud by the teacher is of equal or greater importance as the modeling of skills. Even more important, we hope to see further research on how teacher modeling of student evaluation can improve students' self-evaluation so that students can become active participators in all musical evaluations.

While teachers can and should model the skill of evaluating a piece of music, doing so does not fully cultivate a habit of mind in the three-part definition of Perkins, Jay, and Tishman (1993), which includes skill, sensitivity, and inclination. While students may, for example, have the skill to identify something to make measure six better, they may not have the sensitivity to know that measure six is a good place to focus some attention or the inclination to make improvements at all. In fact, research by Perkins and colleagues suggests that when presented with problems that require dispositional thinking, students do quite well in demonstrating the skill to solve problems. However, only about 10 percent of the time were students able to demonstrate the sensitivity to find those problems (Ritchhart & Perkins, 2005). Thus, while students may learn from teacher modeling how to evaluate their playing, they do not naturally intuit when to evaluate themselves. Teachers must therefore provide opportunities for them to do so.

The development of independent practicing skills has been stressed in music education (Byo, 2004; Hart, 2014; Miksza, Prichard, & Sorbo, 2012; Prichard, 2012). Teachers regularly create practice charts, logs, forms, and reflection prompts in order to focus students' attention during music making (Johnson, 2009; Oare, 2011). The aim of these activities is to create musicians who are able to monitor their performance and then take appropriate steps, through evaluating, toward refining that performance. When students are encouraged to troubleshoot problems in their music on their own, they practice not just the skill of evaluating, but also the sensitivity and inclination to do so. This process can provide valuable assessment information for teachers as they consider how each student is progressing toward thinking like an authentic musician.

Throughout daily life, we frequently encounter situations that require evaluation. From troubleshooting why the freezer isn't keeping the ice cream cold enough to concluding whether a posting on social media is reliable or not, people constantly demonstrate the skill to examine information, the sensitivity about when to examine that information and assign value to it, and the inclination to do so.

## Express (Find and Show Meaning)

Expression in the music classroom is taught both verbally and nonverbally through musical works. Consider the role of the ensemble conductor-teacher. One of her aims is to help convey intended emotional messages through the performance of the group. She may choose to do this nonverbally, through the shape, force, speed, and articulation of her gestures. She may also choose to do this verbally; for example, "play cheerfully," "play like a stormy day," "play like you are fearful." Consider how a general music teacher can help his second-grade students sing a lullaby. By prompting with questions about phrasing, dynamics, and articulations, he is helping students convey expressive emotionality in music.

Teachers can use students' abilities to recognize and convey expressive messages in music for assessment. By allowing students the opportunity to work in small groups to make musical choices about interpretation; giving homework assignments to mark up a score with dynamic, tempo, or other expressive markings (as suggested by Byo, 2014); or assigning composition work with the guideline of having an expressive message, teachers are teaching and can assess the way students express through music.

Expression is something we value throughout the course of a student's school day, including language arts classes and foreign language instruction. The ability to identify a message to convey and craft a meaningful way in which to portray it is paralleled in writing essays, completing geometry proofs, and articulating a winning basketball strategy.

## Imagine (Use Imagery and Inner Hearing)

Imagining includes the ability to call up pictures, sounds, smells, feelings, and moods. Music teachers frequently ask their students to imagine, and we separate these instances as happening through both metaphorical and literal means. A teacher may invite students to imagine they are singing for the queen of England, playing a baby to sleep, or any other situation that helps set the mood, genre, or spirit of the piece. In general music settings, students may have a chance to imagine during exploration activities, fundamental to the Orff-Schulwerk approach (Frazee & Kreuter, 1987), or by devoting time to exploratory musical centers, as described by Stevens (2003). The results of these imaginative explorations can be documented by the teacher, in student reflections, or by in-group sharing. In referring to literal imagining, we mean the process of "audiation" (Gordon, 2003)—that is, "singing in one's head" tones and rhythms that have been heard before or something created in the moment. A direction to play a passage with shorter articulations may result in a band student audiating the passage before playing it. A general music student may audiate the steps of the folk dance he is learning after being taught using Phyllis Weikart's (2006) "say, say and do, whisper and do, think and do" approach. While theories of audiation in music making have been challenged in recent years by more holistic and complex theories, such as Elliott and Silverman's (2015) 4E-concept of musical personhood, the emphasis teachers placed on subdividing, giving time to play something "in one's head," or questions about how a passage might sound from outside of the ensemble and from an audience perspective, which emerged during our coding process, required students to use their inner hearing in an imaginative way.

While this habit of mind could be assessed by Edwin Gordon's (1986) Music Aptitude Tests, assessing in this manner is unlikely to capture all the parts that are encompassed within a habit of mind. The use of this measure would not reveal whether a student knows when it is a good time to be using inner hearing. For this, we must assess in vivo or retrospectively, within the context of actual music making.

The habit of mind of imagining is used in many disciplines. Architects and engineers imagine new buildings and products before they are reality, while dancers and athletes imagine their bodies moving through space, and archaeologists and historians imagine a world before the time in which they live.

## Listen (Really Listen, Not Just Hear)

In many ways, listening is the aural counterpart to observing. While Hetland et al. (2013) describe observing as "really seeing, not just looking," listening can be thought of as "truly listening, not just hearing." In a world full of sounds, music teachers aim to engage children in "ear cleaning" (Schafer, 1976 in Campbell & Scott-Kassner, 2013), in which students eliminate the distractions of aural pollution in order to reflect on and attend only to musical sounds. Students in music classes are regularly asked to listen to themselves and the group critically. Judgments that students are asked to independently make about their own sounds include focused aural attention to subtleties in intonation, balance, timbre, pitch and rhythm accuracy, articulations, and the musically expressive interpretation of the score as a whole. Students are regularly encouraged to listen not only to their own sounds, but to how their sounds match the sounds of those around them. For example, questions such as "Are my standmate and I playing that note the same length?" are ones that conductor-teachers encourage students to be asking of themselves; if they don't, conductor-teachers ask them for the students.

Listening is recognized in the literature as an important part of teaching music (Byo, 1990; Elliott & Silverman, 2015; Huenink, 2012; Townsend, 2003).

Listening happens concurrently when we evaluate a performance, persist in recreating a specific sound, imagine a place where this piece might be played, or observe whether or not a peer's playing is following the conductor. Because music making is impossible without listening, and comprehensive listening education can happen simultaneously within active music making (Elliott, 1997; Elliott & Silverman, 2015), this habit of mind is ubiquitous within the music classroom. It should be assessed in ways that reflect the active, authentic music making that occurs in those classrooms, which may include integration with another habit of mind.

Common statements by elementary classroom teachers, such as, "get your listening ears on," or "stop, look, and listen," confirm that listening is important throughout one's day, particularly in following directions, communicating with others, and synthesizing spoken information. Some researchers argue for the human connection that listening provides and advocate for its systematic teaching in general education (Wolvin, 2012; Wolvin & Coakley, 2000).

## Notice (Critically Observe Through the Eyes and Body)

Students in music classes, particularly those that involve group performance, need to look closely, specifically at the gestures of the conductor-teacher or the group leader. Eye contact, facial movements, and gestures, from the tip of a finger to the entire body, are just some of the ways that the conductor-teacher conveys important information to students mid-piece. Phrases such, "Look up here!," "Eye contact!," and "Follow the stick!" (referring to the baton) were all common utterances by conductor-teachers in our data, and they encourage close and frequent critical observation. In less teacher-centered environments, such as garage bands and chamber ensembles, a focus on observing one another is equally or more important.

In addition, teachers in our study consistently called attention to students' bodies—for posture, fingerings, bowings, breathing, and so on. They also designed warm-up activities specifically aimed at focusing students' attention on their bodies, and they periodically asked students to check their posture.

The ability to critically notice also holds value outside of the artistic realms. The eye contact and facial observation taught in music ensembles are comparable to the systematic teaching of social and communication skills in other domains or with exceptional populations (Cappadocia & Weiss, 2011; Palmer, 2011). In addition, critical observation plays an important role in analyzing the results of scientific experiments and mathematical data. Those in the medical sciences frequently critically observe in order to find abnormalities and form diagnoses. Awareness of one's body can help with the maintenance of: a positive state of mind, one's health and well-being, and one's direction of movement through complex crowds and tight spaces.

# Participate in Community (Be Accountable to the Musical Group)

The formed community and individualized culture of the school music ensemble are well documented in the literature (Adderly, Kennedy, & Berz, 2003; Bartolome, 2013; Morrison, 2001; Parker, 2014) and were present in our sampled high school classes. Music ensembles in high schools are different from other classes in the school day in the way students refer to them. While one "takes" a math class, another is "in" the orchestra (Morrison, 2001). Sarah Bartolome (2013), Mary Kennedy (2002), and Adderly, Kennedy, and Berz (2003) describe students' perceptions of ensembles as collective experiences. Students report learning to think of the group before oneself and valuing the opportunity to be with like-minded individuals. Sarah Morrison (2001) believes ensemble teachers serve as "culture bearers," passing on values, traditions, and accepted practices to a younger generation. Acts of culture bearing can vary widely on the part of the conductor-teacher, from ordering band jackets and organizing group field trips, to modeling the conversational manner of musicians, to assigning orchestra buddies, to pairing younger and older students as stand partners. When ensemble teachers hold students to high standards of musicality and for commitment and accountability to the group, they are helping to teach students to work for the good of the entire group. Teachers can document these culture-promoting practices formally, such as assigning new students older ensemble buddies or giving jobs to make sure set up and strike down are completed. Or they can be documented more informally, such as noting the student who volunteers to give up her spot on a prized classroom instrument in an Orff Schulwerk arrangement so that a better balance can be achieved, or the high school senior who volunteers to wake up extra early to help drive freshmen to the orchestra competition on time.

Having the ability, awareness, and inclination to work with others and for the good of the group is acknowledged to be a valuable habit of mind. The Partnership for 21st Century Skills (n.d.) cites both interacting effectively with others and working effectively in diverse teams as necessary life skills for current students. Furthermore, mental health professionals advocate for a systematic emphasis on group belonging in the education of adolescents, and this subject is prevalent in the literature (Allen & Bowles, 2012; Faircloth & Hamm, 2011; Tillery, Varjas, Roach, Kuperminc, & Meyers, 2013).

# Persist (Focus and "Stick to It")

We use group engagement with "persist" because students are most likely to persist when they are engaged. Music making is an activity that lends itself to deep engagement, as described in the flow process articulated by Mihaly Csikszentmihalyi (2011) and first applied to music education by David J. Elliott (1995). The playing of a musical instrument is acknowledged in the literature to require perseverance, discipline, and persistence (Costa-Giomi, Flowers, & Sasaki, 2005; Pitts, Davidson, & McPherson, 2000), and teachers play a large role in encouraging students to continue on an instrument (Davidson, Sloboda, & Howe, 1995; Woody, 2001).

Music teachers cultivate in their students the twin habits of engaging and persisting in a number of ways. In woodshedding a piece of music, the band teacher continually asks for "one more time," modeling that a piece can always be better, even moments before a performance. Choir teachers who stress body and posture awareness are asking for the complete engagement and attention of their students. The orchestra teacher who has her students hold chords over and over to distinguish subtle changes in intonation is requiring sustained perseverance. The nature of the music ensemble rehearsal in schools—beginning a piece that is difficult enough to require continued practice and seeing that piece through until it is polished enough for public performance—can be viewed as one long exercise in persisting through challenges. This persistence can be documented in any number of ways for assessment purposes: through student reflection, recorded practice sessions archiving student persistence, or teacher rubrics documenting effort through composition or small group activity challenges. In addition, teachers who model constant engagement are teaching their students how to engage deeply. Bakker (2005) found a positive relationship between the flow music teachers reported in their work day and the flow experiences reported by their students.

Persistence is likely mediated by the positive rewards that music provides, including emotional investment (Gabrielsson, 2010; Mas-Herrero, Marco-Pallares, Lorenzo-Seva, Zatorre, & Rodriguez-Fornells, 2013; Schellenberg, 2003). It is easy to look at these benefits and assume that all musical experiences lead to engagement through the intrinsic motivation that results from positive emotion. And perhaps for many students these positive emotions are enough to maintain engagement no matter the music education setting. However, practices present in some traditional music ensembles, such as auditioned seating, scored festivals, and relentless standards for perfection from a conductor-teacher (sometimes accompanied by shaming for not reaching the goal), may be motivating students through extrinsic means (Ryan & Deci, 2000; Kohn, 1999). If students are to become independent amateur or professional musicians beyond their years in school, they should be aware of their motivations for participating in music, and those should be intrinsic—without the need for medals and ribbons, and simply for the cognitive, emotional, social, and spiritual well-being music making can provide.

The ability to persist is useful in all areas of life, not only in the music room. The presence of grit and deep persistence over time predicts future success (Duckworth, Peterson, Matthews, & Kelly, 2007), and self-discipline is a better measure of academic performance than is IQ (Duckworth & Seligman, 2005). In addition, the occurrence of flow, achieved through deep engagement in an activity, is argued by Csikszentmihalyi (2011) to increase happiness in life.

## Set Goals and Be Prepared (Think toward the Future)

Traditionally, the ensemble rehearsal can be conceptualized as a series of segments, each devoted to a particular performance goal (Duke, 1994, 1999; Worthy, 2003). These goal-setting behaviors were fundamental to the rehearsals in our data set, in which students were continually challenged to meet a new goal. According to K. Anders Ericsson, Ralf Krampe, and Clemens Tesch-Romer (1993), deliberate (goal-oriented) practice is a key component in becoming a musician (at an amateur or a professional level), and this behavior was commonplace in the traditional music ensembles we observed. To refer to a piece as "done" is not compatible with musical vernacular. Instead, musicians are continually setting goals to make improvements. Students are taught to set goals that encompass increasingly minute details in terms of musicality, expressivity, tone, and other musical elements. When conductor-teachers model this process with their classes, they are teaching the habit of goal setting and preparedness.

Similarly, musicians must always be prepared for the next thing. This might be having one's bow up to play as soon as the conductor takes the podium, bringing a pencil to rehearsal, arriving for warm-up early enough before the performance, or being prepared to watch the conductor for the starting downbeat. Authentic music making always includes being prepared for what is coming next. Assessment practices in music education should aim to capture this habit of mind and thereby call students' attention to this in a focused manner.

Goal setting and preparedness is important in many arenas. This forward-thinking orientation is used by travel agents and event planners, who are always ready with a plan B; by shift leaders, who set reasonable production goals for their staff; and by medical assistants, who prepare the emergency room with all needed equipment for the incoming patient.

# HABITS OF MIND NOT OBSERVED

## Appreciate Ambiguity (Recognize Problems with More Than One Correct Answer)

As mentioned, arts education theorists have argued that the arts enable students to see that multiple perspectives can be correct and valid, and that there is frequently more than one correct answer to a question (Davis, 2008; Eisner, 2002). And as mentioned, we did not see this kind of understanding being cultivated. While playing or singing in a group, there is an understanding that certain creative liberties on the part of each performer must be sacrificed in order to create a cohesive interpretation. In most cases, both professionally and in school ensembles, the conductor decides all aspects of these interpretations. But ensemble classrooms need not be this way. Giving students creative liberties to explore possible musical interpretations allows them to practice authentic music making. This would also reinforce a habit of mind fundamental to musical literacy: a recognition that there are multiple ways of conveying, experiencing, or understanding the same phenomenon.

Certain adaptations can be made to ensemble classes to emphasize this habit of mind, such as the integration of chamber groups. In addition, composition or general music classes may emphasize this habit of mind more than we see in traditional ensemble classrooms.

How might the recognition of multiple ways of thinking about a problem be generalized? Clearly there are multiple ways of interpreting data in science and multiple ways of interpreting historical events, and the recognition of multiple points of view is a critical skill for empathy.

## Use Creativity (Engage in Novel and Useful Thinking)

When we conceptualize creative thinking in the classroom, we rely on the most commonly used definition: allowing students to think about solutions that are both novel and useful.

In our study (Hogan & Winner, 2015), we saw very little evidence that high school students in large ensembles use any kind of creative thinking. Composition-based and general music classes are likely to provide more opportunities for students to gain experience making creative musical decisions. But we believe that opportunities to make creative decisions can and should be incorporated into ensemble classes, in which case creative decision-making could be assessed.

The claim that students need greater opportunities to develop creative thinking is very common (The Partnership for 21st Century Skills, n.d.), and developing novel and useful ways to accomplish processes and products is relevant in nearly every discipline, from medicine, design, architecture, marketing, and hairstyling to fashion design.

# ASSESSING MUSICAL HABITS OF MIND

It is important to repeat that each of these broad habits of mind encompasses skills, and that these skills may, on their own, be fairly easy to assess. However, by identifying these abilities as habits of mind, we are interested in calling attention not just to the skill, but also to the awareness of when to use the skill and to the motivation to do so. While these two components may be more difficult to assess, they are important qualities that help students make practical use of these ways of thinking until they truly are habits: patterns of thinking that can be accessed immediately and without teacher direction, rather than a capability that a student can demonstrate but only at the teacher's request. For example, teachers could design a task assessing the ability to observe a conductor: Can a student distinguish a ⅝ beat pattern from a ⅞ beat pattern by watching a video of a conducting pattern? But a more authentic assessment would place a student in an ensemble with her instrument and determine whether she knows that the measure that switches from ⅝ to ⅞ is an important time to watch the conductor. This would also show that the student is motivated enough to stay with her section that she will do so. Teachers can use videotapes to record rehearsals and watch these student behaviors in context.

For many of these proposed habits of mind, authentic assessment may need to happen in ways that are not fully congruent with the large ensemble tradition. Assessment may be easier to accomplish with the integration of chamber groups, unusual homework assignments, more use of composition activities, dedication to reflection activities, use of student conductors so that the teacher can make written observations about sections, and generally more opportunities for students to make individual musical decisions. However, the prevalence of these habits of mind in the music education literature shows they are already relevant to the thinking of music educators.

In fact, the US National Core Arts Standards (2014) employ habits of mind in the category called "anchor standards." Each of the eleven anchor standards is an example of a habit of mind that is useful inside and outside the arts. For example, one "conveys meaning" in many different places and ways—through writing essays, by monitoring one's body language, through creating a dance, and so on. Many of the anchor standards also map directly onto the habits of mind we have observed and described here. Anchor standard 6, "convey meaning through presentation of artwork," is very similar to what we describe as "express," while anchor standard 5, "develop and refine artistic work," is nearly synonymous with "goal setting."

In an editorial in the *Music Educators Journal*, NAfME president Glenn Nierman (2015) mentions dispositions such as working together toward common goals, flexibility, and risk taking, and he draws connections among these dispositional ways of thinking in music and the process orientation of the new National Standards. In addition, the National Association for Music Education (NAfME) modified its advocacy strategy in 2014 in order to include broad ways of thinking. Rather than focusing narrowly on in-the-[testing]-bubbles messages about arts education, such as the idea that music improves academics (which has little concrete support; see reviews by Winner & Cooper, 2000; Winner, Goldstein, & Vincent-Lacrin, 2013), the "Broader Minded" movement includes ways of thinking that go "beyond the bubbles" to assess habits such as grit, decision-making, reflection, and communication (National Association for Music Education, 2015).

While using these broad ways of thinking for advocacy is another avenue to encourage discussion about habits of mind, including these concepts in classes, with students, and for curriculum and assessment purposes is even more important. It is encouraging that NAfME and the National Standards have included broad ways of thinking in their recent publications and statements. But these declarations are not the result of bottom-up research that tells us what is actually going on in music education classrooms. We believe further research that examines the kinds of habits of mind being taught in a variety of music classes—from general music to iPad ensembles to guitar class—is needed. In addition, studies that investigate whether students are learning habits of mind that are being taught and that document assessment practices for these habits of mind are also important next steps.

# CONCLUSION

The act of music making is complex and multifaceted. When music educators focus solely on assessing musical technique, they are shortchanging the important ways of thinking that are developed through music making. While some music educators may acknowledge the habits of mind documented here, we argue that these should be put at the forefront of curricular and assessment discussions in all music education environments. Instead of viewing the inclusion of habits of mind as an external mandate, unrelated to or piled on top of the important work that music educators are already doing, the inclusion of habits of mind should be seen as illuminating the thinking that is already occurring in classrooms. At the same time, to capitalize on the development of certain habits of mind, some reforms and flexibility may be needed by music teachers. Fortunately, there are several successful frameworks in various disciplines that can help guide music educators, and the inclusion of habits of mind in the new National Core Arts Standards can help make the discussion of habits of mind in music education more commonplace. It is important that standards, frameworks, and assessment tools that are developed be a result of research that critically and systematically takes into account what teachers are already emphasizing in their classrooms, while still challenging teachers to make music making a more authentic, democratic, and relevant process for students.

## REFERENCES

Abrahams, F., Rafaniello, A., Vodicka, J., Westawski, D., & Wilson, J. (2017). Going green. In F. Abrahams & P. Head (Eds.), *The Oxford handbook of choral pedagogy* (pp. 65–86). New York: Oxford University Press.

Adderly, C., Kennedy, M., & Berz, W. (2003). "A home away from home": The world of the high school music classroom. *Journal of Research in Music Education, 51*(3), 190–205.

Allen, K., & Bowles, T. (2012). Belonging as a guiding principle in the education of adolescents. *Australian Journal of Educational & Developmental Psychology, 12,* 108–19.

Allsup, R. E. (2012). The moral ends of band. *Theory into Practice, 51*(3), 179–87.

Allsup, R. E., & Benedict, C. (2008). The problems of band: An inquiry into the future of instrumental music education. *Philosophy of Music Education Review, 16*(2), 156–73.

Bakker, A. B. (2005). Flow among music teachers and their students: The crossover of peak experiences. *Journal of Vocational Behavior, 66*(1), 26–44.

Bartolome, S. (2013). "It's like a whole bunch of *me*!": The perceived values and benefits of the Seattle Girls' Choir experience. *Journal of Research in Music Education, 60*(4), 395–418.

Berrett, D. (2012). Habits of mind: Lessons for the long term. *Chronicle of Higher Education A, 1*, A4.

Booth, E. (2009). *The music teaching artist's bible: Becoming a virtuoso educator.* New York: Oxford University Press.

Booth, E. (2012). The habits of mind of creative engagement. Retrieved from http://ericbooth.net/the-habits-of-mind-of-creative-engagement/

Borko, H., Liston, D., & Whitcomb, J. A. (2007). Apples and fishes: The debate over dispositions in teacher education. *Journal of Teacher Education, 58,* 359.

Boyes, K., & Watts, G. C. (2009a). *Developing habits of mind in elementary schools.* Alexandria, VA: ASCD Publishing.

Boyes, K., & Watts, G. C. (2009b). *Developing habits of mind in secondary schools.* Alexandria, VA: ASCD Publishing.

Burgess, J. (2012). The impact of teaching thinking skills as habits of mind to young children with challenging behaviours. *Emotional and Behavioural Difficulties, 17*(1), 47–63.

Byo, J. (1990). Teaching your instrumental students to listen. *Music Educators Journal, 77*(4), 43–46.

Byo, J. L. (2004). Teaching problem solving in practice. *Music Educators Journal, 91*(2), 35.

Byo, J. L. (2014). Applying score analysis to a rehearsal pedagogy of expressive performance. *Music Educators Journal, 101*(2), 76–82.

Çalik, M., & Coll, R. K. (2012). Investigating socioscientific issues via scientific habits of mind: Development and validation of the scientific habits of mind survey. *International Journal of Science Education, 34*(12), 1909–30.

Campbell, P., & Scott-Kassner, C. (2013). *Music in childhood: From preschool through the elementary grades.* Boston: Cengage Learning.

Cappadocia, M., & Weiss, J. (2011). Review of social skills training groups for youth with Asperger syndrome and high-functioning autism. *Research in Autism Spectrum Disorders, 5*(1), 70–78.

Clements, A. (Ed.) (2010). *Alternative approaches in music education: Case studies from the field.* Lanham, MD: Rowman & Littlefield Education.

Colquhoun, S. (2017). Informal learning from a band director's perspective. *Media Journal in Music Education, 1.* Retrieved from http://hosted.usf.edu/mjme/

Costa, A., & Kallick, B. (2000). *Habits of mind: A developmental series.* Alexandria, VA: Association for Supervision and Curriculum Development (ASCD) Publishing.

Costa, A. L., & Kallick, B. (2008). *Learning and leading with habits of mind: 16 essential characteristics for success.* Alexandria, VA: ASCD Publishing.

Costa, A. L., & Kallick, B. (Eds.) (2009). *Habits of mind across the curriculum: Practical and creative strategies for teachers.* Alexandria, VA: ASCD Publishing.

Costa, A. L., & Kallick, B. (2013). *Dispositions: Reframing teaching and learning.* Thousand Oaks, CA: Corwin Press.

Costa-Giomi, E., Flowers, P. J., & Sasaki, W. (2005). Piano lessons of beginning students who persist or drop out. *Journal of Research in Music Education, 53*(3), 234–47.

Csikszentmihalyi, M. (2011). *Flow: The psychology of optimal experience.* New York: Harper Perennial Modern Classics.

Cuoco, A., Goldenberg, E. P., & Mark, J. (1996). Habits of mind: An organizing principle for mathematics curricula. *Journal of Mathematical Behavior, 15*(4), 375–402.

Davis, J. (2008). *Why our schools need the arts.* New York: Teachers College Press.

Davidson, J. W., Sloboda, J. A., & Howe, M. J. (1995). The role of parents and teachers in the success and failure of instrumental learners. *Bulletin of the Council for Research in Music Education, 127,* 40–44.

Detterman, D. K., & Sternberg, R. J. (1993). *Transfer on trial: Intelligence, cognition, and instruction.* New York: Ablex Publishing

Dickey, M. R. (1992). A review of research on modeling in music teaching and learning. *Bulletin of the Council for Research in Music Education, 113,* 27–40.

Diez, M. E., & Raths, J. D. (2007). *Dispositions in teacher education.* Charlotte, NC: Information Age Publishing.

Dottin, E. S. (2009). Professional judgment and dispositions in teacher education. *Teaching and Teacher Education, 25*(1), 83–88.

Duckworth, A. L., Peterson, C., Matthews, M. D., & Kelly, D. R. (2007). Grit: Perseverance and passion for long-term goals. *Journal of Personality and Social Psychology, 92*(6), 1087–1101.

Duckworth, A. L., & Seligman, M. E. (2005). Self-discipline outdoes IQ in predicting academic performance of adolescents. *Psychological Science, 16*(12), 939–44.

Duke, R. A. (1994). Bringing the art of rehearsing into focus: The rehearsal frame as a model for prescriptive analysis of rehearsal conducting. *Journal of Band Research, 30*(1), 78–95.

Duke, R. A. (1999). Measures of instructional effectiveness in music research. *Bulletin of the Council for Research in Music Education, 143,* 1–48.

Eisner, E. (2002). *Arts and the creation of mind.* New Haven, CT: Yale University Press.

Elliott, D. J. (1995). *Music matters: A new philosophy of music education.* New York: Oxford University Press.

Elliott, D. J. (1997). Continuing matters: Myths, realities, rejoinders. *Bulletin of the Council for Research in Music Education, 132,* 1–37.

Elliott, D. J., & Silverman, M. (2015). *Music matters: A philosophy of music education* (2nd ed.). New York: Oxford University Press.

Epstein, R. M. (2003). Mindful practice in action (II): Cultivating habits of mind. *Families, Systems, & Health, 21*(1), 11.

Ericsson, K. A., Krampe, R. T., & Tesch-Römer, C. (1993). The role of deliberate practice in the acquisition of expert performance. *Psychological Review, 100*(3), 363.

Faircloth, B., & Hamm, J. (2011). The dynamic reality of adolescent peer networks and sense of belonging. *Merrill-Palmer Quarterly, 57*(1), 48–72.

Fletcher, J., Najarro, A., & Yelland, H. (Eds.). (2015). *Fostering habits of mind in today's students.* Sterling, VA: Stylus.

Fonder, M. (2014). Another perspective: No default or reset necessary—Large ensembles enrich many. *Music Educators Journal, 101*(2), 89–89.

Frazee, J., & Kreuter, K. (1987). *Discovering Orff: A curriculum for music teachers.* London: Schott & Company Limited.

Gabrielsson, A. (2010). Strong experiences with music. In P. N. Juslin & J. A. Sloboda (Eds.), *Handbook of music and emotion* (pp. 547–74). Oxford: Oxford University Press.

Goldenberg, E. P. (1996). "Habits of mind" as an organizer for the curriculum. *Journal of Education, 178*(1), 13–34.

Goldenberg, E. P., & Mark, J. (2015). *Making sense of algebra.* Portsmouth, NH: Heinemann.

Gordon, E. (1986). *Manual for the primary measures of music audiation and the intermediate measures of music audiation: Music aptitude tests for kindergarten and first, second, third, and fourth grade children.* Chicago: GIA Publications.

Gordon, E. (2003). *Learning sequences in music: Skill, content, and patterns; A music learning theory.* Chicago: GIA Publications.

Green, L. (2002). *How popular musicians learn: A way ahead for music education.* London: Ashgate Publishing, Ltd.

Green, L. (2009). *Music, informal learning and the school: A new classroom pedagogy*. London: Ashgate Publishing, Ltd.

Hart, J. T. (2014). Guided metacognition in instrumental practice. *Music Educators Journal, 101*(2), 57–64.

Haston, W. (2007). Teacher modeling as an effective teaching strategy. *Music Educators Journal, 93*(4), 26–30.

Hetland, L., Winner, E., Veenema, S., & Sheridan, K. (2007). *Studio thinking: The real benefits of visual arts education*. New York: Teachers College Press.

Hetland, L., Winner, E., Veenema, S., & Sheridan, K. (2013). *Studio thinking 2: The real benefits of visual arts education*. New York: Teachers College Press.

Heuser, F. (2011). Ensemble-based instrumental music instruction: Dead-end tradition or opportunity for socially enlightened teaching. *Music Education Research, 13*(3), 293–305.

Heuser, F. (2015). Pipe dreams, ideals and transformation in music education: Lessons from the field. *Research Studies in Music Education, 32*(4), 215–31.

Hogan, J., Hetland, L., Jaquith, D., & Winner, E. (2018). *Studio thinking from the start: The K-8 art educator's handbook*. New York: Teachers College Press.

Hogan, J., & Winner, E. (2015, August). *Ensemble habits of mind: What is actually taught in high school music ensembles? Preliminary results*. Poster presented at American Psychological Association conference, Toronto, Ontario.

Huenink, J. (2012). Sing it, hear it, play it! Ear training for middle school students. *Teaching Music, 10*(1), 56–61.

Johnson, D. (2009). More than just minutes: Using practice charts as tools for learning. *Music Educators Journal, 95*(3), 63–70.

Kennedy, M. A. (2002). "It's cool because we like to sing:" Junior high school boys' experience of choral music as an elective. *Research Studies in Music Education, 18*(1), 22–36.

Kohn, A. (1999). *Punished by rewards: The trouble with gold stars, incentive plans, A's, praise, and other bribes*. New York: Houghton Mifflin Harcourt.

Lucas, B. (2016). A five-dimensional model of creativity and its assessment in schools. *Applied Measurement in Education, 29*(4), 278–90.

Lucas, B., Claxton, G., & Spencer, E. (2014). Progression in student creativity in school: First steps towards new forms of formative assessments. *Contemporary Readings in Law and Social Justice, 6*, 81.

Lunney, M. (2003). Critical thinking and accuracy of nurses' diagnoses. *International Journal of Nursing Knowledge, 14*(3), 96–107.

Mas-Herrero, E., Marco-Pallares, J., Lorenzo-Seva, U., Zatorre, R. J., & Rodriguez-Fornells, A. (2013). Individual differences in music reward experiences. *Music Perception: An Interdisciplinary Journal, 31*(2), 118–38.

Miksza, P., Prichard, S., & Sorbo, D. (2012). An observational study of intermediate band students' self-regulated practice behaviors. *Journal of Research in Music Education, 60*(3), 254–66.

Morrison, S. (2001). The school ensemble: A culture of our own. *Music Educators Journal, 88*(2), 24–28.

NAMM Foundation. (2009). New Gallup survey by NAMM reflects majority of Americans agree with many benefits of playing musical instruments. Retrieved from http://www.namm.org/news/press-releases/new-gallup-survey-namm-reflects-majority-americans

National Association for Music Education. (2015). Broader minded. Retrieved from https://nafme.org/broader-minded-beat-how-much-does-talent-matter/

National Core Arts Standards: A Conceptual Framework for Arts Learning. (2014). Retrieved from http://www.nationalartsstandards.org/content/conceptual-framework

Nierman, G. E. (2015). From the president's keyboard: Strategic priorities—Focusing on standards and student dispositions. *Music Educators Journal, 102*(1), 10.

Oare, S. (2011). Practice education: Teaching instrumentalists to practice effectively. *Music Educators Journal, 97*(3), 41–47.

Palmer, E. (2011). *Well-spoken: Teaching speaking to all students.* Portland, ME: Sternhouse Publishing.

Parker, E. (2014). The process of social identity development in adolescent high school choral singers: A grounded theory. *Journal of Research in Music Education, 62*(1), 18–32.

The Partnership for 21st Century Skills. (n.d.). Life and career skills. Retrieved from http://www.p21.org/our-work/resources/for-educators

Perkins, D. N., Jay, E., & Tishman, S. (1993). Beyond abilities: A dispositional theory of thinking. *Merrill-Palmer Quarterly, 39*(1), 1–21.

Perkins, D. N., & Salomon, G. (1989). Are cognitive skills context-bound? *Educational researcher, 18*(1), 16–25.

Perkins, D. N., & Tishman, S. (2001). Dispositional aspects of intelligence. In J. Collick, S. Messick, & U. Schiefele (Eds.), *Intelligence and personality: Bridging the gap in theory and measurement* (pp. 233–57). New York: Psychology Press.

Pitts, S. E., Davidson, J. W., & McPherson, G. E. (2000). Models of success and failure in instrumental learning: Case studies of young players in the first 20 months of learning. *Bulletin of the Council for Research in Music Education*, (146), 51–69.

Polk, J. A. (2006). Traits of effective teachers. *Arts Education Policy Review, 107*(4), 23–29.

Prichard, S. (2012). Practice makes perfect? Effective practice instruction in large ensembles. *Music Educators Journal, 99*(2), 57–62.

Regelski, T. A. (2013). Re-setting music education's "default settings". *Action, Criticism, and Theory for Music Education, 12*(1), 7–23.

Ritchhart, R., Church, M., & Morrison, K. (2011). *Making thinking visible: How to promote engagement, understanding, and independence for all learners.* Malden, MA: John Wiley & Sons.

Ritchhart, R., & Perkins, D. N. (2005). Learning to think: The challenges of teaching thinking. In K. Holyoak & R. G. Morrison (Eds.), *The Cambridge handbook of thinking and reasoning* (pp. 775–802). Cambridge: Cambridge University Press.

Root-Bernstein, R. S., & Root-Bernstein, M. M. (2013). *Sparks of genius: The thirteen thinking tools of the world's most creative people.* New York: Houghton Mifflin Harcourt.

Ryan, R. M., & Deci, E. L. (2000). Intrinsic and extrinsic motivations: Classic definitions and new directions. *Contemporary Educational Psychology, 25*(1), 54–67.

Schafer, R. M. (1976). *Creative music education: A handbook for the modern music teacher.* New York: Schirmer Books.

Schellenberg, E. G. (2003). Does exposure to music have beneficial side effects? In I. Peretz & R. J. Zatorre (Eds.), *The cognitive neuroscience of music* (pp. 430–48). Oxford: Oxford University Press.

Spencer, E., Lucas, B., & Claxton, G. (2012). *Progression in creativity: Developing new forms of assessment.* Newcastle, UK: Creativity, Culture and Education, and Centre for Real-World Learning.

Steinkuehler, C., & Duncan, S. (2008). Scientific habits of mind in virtual worlds. *Journal of Science Education and Technology, 17*(6), 530–43.

Stevens, S. (2003). Creative experiences in free play. *Music Educators Journal, 89*(5), 44–48.

Thibeault, M. D. (2015). Music education for all through participatory ensembles. *Music Educators Journal, 102*(2), 54–61.

Tillery, A., Varjas, K., Roach, A., Kuperminc, G., & Meyers, J. (2013). The importance of adult connections in adolescents' sense of school belonging: Implications for schools and practitioners. *Journal of School Violence, 12*(2), 134–55.

Tishman, S., Jay, E., & Perkins, D. (1993). Teaching thinking dispositions: From transmission to enculturation. *Theory into Practice, 32,* 147–53.

Tishman, S., Perkins, D., & Jay, E. (1995). *The thinking classroom: Learning and teaching in a culture of thinking.* Needham Heights, MA: Allyn & Bacon.

Townsend, A. (2003). Stop, look, listen! For effective band rehearsals. *Teaching Music, 10*(4), 22–25.

Weikart, P. S. (2006). *Teaching movement & dance: A sequential approach to rhythmic movement.* High/Scope Foundation.

Williams, D. A. (2007). What are music educators doing and how well are we doing it? *Music Educators Journal, 94*(1), 18–23.

Williams, D. A. (2011). The elephant in the room. *Music Educators Journal, 98*(1), 51–57.

Wineburg, S. (2003). Teaching the mind good habits. *Chronicle of Higher Education, 4,* 11–49.

Winner, E., & Cooper, M. (2000). Mute those claims: No evidence (yet) for a causal link between arts study and academic achievement. *Journal of Aesthetic Education, 34*(3–4), 11–75.

Winner, E., Goldstein, T., & Vincent-Lacrin, S. (2013). *Art for art's sake? The impact of arts education.* Paris: OECD Publishing.

Wolvin, A. (2012). Listening in the general education curriculum. *International Journal of Listening, 26*(2), 122–28.

Wolvin, A., & Coakley, C. (2000). Listening education in the 21st century. *International Journal of Listening, 14*(1), 143–52.

Woody, R. H. (2001). Learning from the experts: Applying research in expert performance to music education. *Update: Applications of Research in Music Education, 19*(2), 9.

Worthy, M. D. (2003). Rehearsal frame analysis of an expert wind conductor in high school vs. college band rehearsals. *Bulletin of the Council for Research in Music Education, 156,* 11–19.

# CHAPTER 12

......................................................................

# ALTERNATIVE
# ASSESSMENT FOR
# MUSIC STUDENTS
# WITH SIGNIFICANT
# DISABILITIES

*collaboration, inclusion, and transformation*

......................................................................

DONALD DEVITO, MEGAN M. SHERIDAN,
JIAN-JUN CHEN-EDMUND, DAVID EDMUND,
AND STEVEN BINGHAM

How do we move beyond assessment for the purposes of evaluating teacher proficiency and student performance outcomes to instead consider assessment for understanding student musical experiences and preferences for the purpose of promoting lifelong musical engagement? In this chapter we examine three distinct music education approaches that have been taken at the K–12 Sidney Lanier Center School for students with varying exceptionalities in Gainesville, Florida. Megan Sheridan illustrates inclusion and assessment using the Kodaly approach, David Edmund and Jian-Jun Chen-Edmund examine creative lessons developed for exceptional learners in a general music setting, and Steven Bingham and Donald DeVito illustrate adaptive jazz inclusion and performance for public school and university students with disabilities. This collaborative development in qualitative music assessment has taken place through the following:

1. Developing methods of communicating our recognition of student engagement and affective responses during inclusive engagement in public school music education settings, specifically in Kodaly-based music instruction, K–12 general music classes, and secondary jazz ensembles.

2. Using students' interests and engagement as a means of curriculum development and assessment in inclusive public school music settings.

3. Building collaborative relationships with parents and the community for post-school lifelong music learning.

# SECTION 1

It is not uncommon for music educators of young children to ascribe to a specific approach to teaching, such as Kodaly, Orff, or Dalcroze. These approaches to music teaching give music educators a set of tools and a framework in which to develop and implement music learning experiences. Common among the various approaches is the concept of active music making as a means to musical engagement and literacy. It is easy to envision active music making and skill building in a typical music classroom with typically developing children. However, it may be more challenging to envision how a music educator might adapt one of the previously named approaches for an inclusive class with children who have intellectual and/or developmental challenges. Regardless of a child's intellectual capacity or physical challenges, he or she has the capacity to make music and gain musical understanding.

This section is a description of how the Kodaly approach was implemented in an inclusive music setting at a public school that serves children with a wide range of behavioral, developmental, and intellectual needs and how it led to opportunities for alternative assessment in music. For context, a brief overview of the Kodaly approach is given, followed by descriptions of the types of assessment utilized in typical Kodaly-based music settings.

## The Kodaly Approach

The Kodaly approach, developed by Zoltán Kodály during the mid-twentieth century in Communist Hungary, is not a defined method with set teaching techniques that must be used verbatim. Rather, it is an approach that brings together several key tenets that guide a music educator's pedagogical choices. Teachers who teach according to the Kodaly approach believe the following:

- Music learning must begin with the voice.
- Music literacy (and musical independence) is the right of all people.
- Aural skills must be developed through a cappella singing in a sound-to-symbol approach.
- Music education must be rooted in music from the child's mother tongue.
- High-quality music must be used.
- Music concepts should be sequenced in a developmentally appropriate manner (Choksy, 1981; Sinor 1997).

Much of Kodály's writings, and the writings of his followers, focus on music education for children in primary school. This is likely due to the fundamental belief that music education should begin very early in the child's life. However, this does not mean that the approach cannot be implemented in secondary music classrooms. Shea Clay (2009), Lois Choksy (1988), Franklin Gallo (2010), and Michael Houlahan and Philip Tacka (2015) have described ways in which the approach can be modified to suit the needs of older students. In addition, the Organization of American Kodály Educators now offers a series of sessions at its annual conference for teachers in secondary choral programs. These advances in the development of the Kodaly approach informed the pedagogical decisions made during the lessons described later in this chapter.

## The Kodaly Approach in a Special Needs Classroom

There are no specific methods that Kodaly-based teachers are expected to adhere to; thus there is an aspect of freedom found in true Kodaly-based teaching. Teachers are able to design learning experiences for their students in a manner that is most appropriate for and meets the needs of each individual student; they can therefore include multiple means of assessment. This is especially important for students with special needs, who may not be able to engage with music in the same manner that their typically developing peers can. In a Kodaly-based classroom, students with special needs are given opportunities to engage with music in multiple ways, represent their knowledge in multiple ways, and access multiple means of action and expression (Hourigan, 2015),[1] which leads to opportunities for alternative assessment.

The Kodaly approach offers flexibility for music teachers when designing music learning experiences for all students. Once a teacher understands that it is a philosophy or approach, not a method, he or she may find that it can be very useful when working with all students, regardless of ability or disability. Using the six tenets outlined previously, Megan Sheridan implemented a series of music lessons that were designed to enable students with special needs to engage with music from the American folk tradition through singing and playing instruments while building music literacy skills.

On seven Fridays in the fall semester of 2016 and one Monday in January 2017, Sheridan implemented Kodaly-based lessons in a class of thirteen to twenty high-school-aged students at Donald DeVito's school. Sheridan is Kodaly certified, and she designed and executed the lessons after consulting with DeVito about the knowledge and abilities of the students. Each lesson lasted between fifteen and thirty minutes, and on some occasions undergraduate and graduate students from the local university accompanied and assisted Sheridan in the lessons.

The overarching objectives of the lessons included the following:

1. Students will be able to sing part or all of the selected song material to the best of their ability.
2. Students will be able to play a unique rhythmic ostinato in time to accompany each song.

3. Students will be able to make a musical decision among playing the beat, playing the ostinato, or improvising during the free-form sections of the songs.
4. Students will be able to add expressive qualities while playing the djembes and following a conductor.
5. Students will understand that folk songs from around the world are passed down through an aural/oral tradition.

The expectations for the students varied according to each student's ability. For example, a student who has hydrocephalus and is a very capable musician was expected to be able to sing the songs in their entirety by the end of the lessons; another student, who uses a communication device and has limited motor control, was expected to produce vocal sounds in specific parts of the songs. It was important to modify expectations because each student had unique abilities and challenges, and doing so allowed us to support all the students in their musical growth.

Song material for the lessons was selected after Sheridan observed DeVito working with the students on several occasions. The students were accustomed to engaging with a wide range of genres, including folk music from around the world. Therefore, it was deemed that traditional American folk music would be appropriate and meaningful for this group of students. Sheridan selected two American folk songs, "Stewball" and "Dinah" (with additional verses), as the song material for these lessons. For this discussion, we focus on the process through which "Stewball" was taught. Although these specific songs might appear in some elementary curricula, they can be used in lessons for students of all ages. One of the most important aspects of designing music lessons for students with special needs is the absolute necessity to select material that is appropriate for their chronological age (Adamek & Darrow, 2010). In this situation, the students were between the ages of fifteen and twenty-one; therefore, folk songs such as "Twinkle, Twinkle Little Star" and "Rain, Rain Go Away" were not appropriate because of their lyrical content, even though the musical content may have been appropriate.

"Stewball" is an American folk song with British roots that tells the story of a racehorse named Stewball. It was recorded by Lead Belly in the early part of the twentieth century. The song has a number of verses, but for the purposes of these lessons, only the first verse and refrain were used. The verse is in a call and response form:

Verse 1

| *Way out* | | *mm-hm* |
| *California* | *mm-hm* | |
| *Where Stewball* | | *mm-hm* |
| *Was born* | *Was born* | |
| *All the jockeys* | *mm-hm* | |
| *In the country* | *mm-hm* | |
| *Said he blew there* | *mm-hm* | |
| *In a storm* | *In a storm* | |

Refrain
*Well, you can bet on old Stewball,*
*And you might win, win, win.*
*Yes, you can bet on old Stewball,*
*And you might win.*

The Kodaly approach emphasizes the use of singing as a means for musical understanding, and the call and response form, with the response being "mm-hm" in most places, enabled access for all students and encouraged singing and the use of voice. For the purposes of these lessons, an adjustment was made to the lyrics:

Verse 1

| | |
|---|---|
| *Way out* | *mm-hm* |
| *California* | *mm-hm* |
| *Where Stewball* | *mm-hm* |
| *Was born* | *mm-hm* |
| *All the jockeys* | *mm-hm* |
| *In the country* | *mm-hm* |
| *Said he blew there* | *mm-hm* |
| *In a storm* | *mm-hm* |

Refrain
*Well, you can bet on old Stewball,*
*And you might win, win, win.*
*Yes, you can be on old Stewball,*
*And you might win.*

The "mm-hm" response was used throughout the verse. This consistency in the response allowed for more students to more readily learn the song and immediately engage with music.

When "Stewball" was introduced to the students, they were first given a brief background and introduction to the song, including that it was a folk song from the United States and that it was about a racehorse named "Stewball." Some students shared that they had seen horse races on TV, which resulted in a very brief discussion about the way a racehorse moves (it runs fast). Prior to singing the song, Sheridan informed the students that they had a part to sing as a response to whatever she sang. Sheridan sang the "mm-hm" (ascending minor third) and had the students echo it several times. Then Sheridan sang the call and response verse. The remainder of "Stewball" (call and refrain) was taught through immersion, in which the teacher sings the song multiple times and students join in as they are able. Some students were able to sing the entire song after only a couple of lessons.

Another goal of the Kodaly approach is to transfer musical knowledge learned through singing to instruments. As soon as the students were comfortable with the "mm-hm," Sheridan guided them in transferring the rhythm of "mm-hm" to a djembe or tubano, on which they played the rhythm while singing. This exercise allowed for assessment of students' rhythmic skills (playing in time), vocal skills, and ability to adjust their playing so as not to drown out the singing.

In the next lesson, after a review of the song, a new ostinato was introduced to the students:

♩   ♫

Go, Stewball!

The students were not presented with the traditional notation; rather, they were shown iconic notation. Because the ostinato was reminiscent of a cheer, one large picture of pompoms was used to represent the quarter note, and two smaller pictures of pompoms were used to represent the eighth notes. This addition of iconic notation allowed for all students to process the ostinato kinesthetically, aurally, and visually.

At this point the students had been introduced to all of the material for the song "Stewball." Over the course of the remaining lessons, the class worked to build a larger piece of music out of the song and ostinato. An introduction consisted of all students playing and speaking the ostinato, starting soft and slow, then progressively getting louder and faster while following a conductor. Then they sang the song, playing on each "mm-hm." To end, the students were given the option of playing the beat, playing the ostinato, or improvising. The students were required to watch the conductor for a cue to stop.

Assessment of students' musical skills and understanding took place throughout the lessons with an eye to assessment that is "done for" and "done by" the students (Scott, 2012, p. 32). Throughout the lessons, students were asked to evaluate their playing: Were they playing too loudly? If so, how could they fix it? Were they maintaining a steady beat? Were they making appropriate musical choices? Because the students were required to self-evaluate and determine solutions, we were able to guide them in constructing their own understandings of their music making and to improve their music skills through constructive assessment. Students were actively involved in the "learning process ... as problem solvers," which led to more purposeful assessment (Scott, 2008, p. 8).

The flexibility of the Kodaly approach allows music educators to design musical experiences that can be readily differentiated to meet the learning needs of students with varying abilities and disabilities. In addition, and most important, it gives teachers the freedom to assess students in ways that are most appropriate for each child, which is commonly found in methods other than verbalization or written responses. Students with special needs are able to show their understanding through music choices and performance (Adamek & Darrow, 2010; Mazur, 2004).

## Case Study: Elijah Thomas

This past school year Elijah Thomas,[2] a student with a rare form of cerebral palsy, seizure disorder, speech language impairments, and physical needs that require the use of a wheelchair and communication device to program his comments and questions became a member of our music ensemble. Elijah and his grandmother requested that he have the opportunity to communicate his experience with assessment in one of several case studies in this chapter. Typically, communication devices for our students outside of music are utilized with visual aids to communicate "I am hungry, yes and no" or "I need to use the bathroom." In music, questions for students are provided through visual aids to communicate: "I am interested in…" or "Tell me more about…" or "I prefer this music or activity." Elijah is able to use a single finger to utilize a device on his wheelchair to communicate his own perspectives on assessing the lesson, indicating how his needs and interests were met.

At one point the students were learning to sing is "I Got Rhythm." for the Florida Music Educators Conference performance with Sheridan and her University of Florida students. Sheridan asked Elijah to program his communication device for the final phrase of the song, "Who could ask for anything more?," which would give him a final solo for the song. Elijah communicated through his device that he liked this opportunity to have a solo, but also wanted to use his own voice during the songs "Stewball" and "Dinah" and in the other parts of "I've Got Rhythm." In class, rehearsals commenced by going back and forth, word by word, with the class singing each word and Elijah singing back in a call and response pattern that allowed him the time to phrase each word. The song was done in an a cappella format for this accommodation. The sequence would follow: "Who" (Who), "Could" (Could), "Ask for" (Ask for), "Any-Thing" (A-Ny-Thing), "More." Elijah enjoyed the access to an inclusive setting created with the University of Florida students in our ensemble and in the conference performance, which included more than one hundred audience members who sang along on the final song. Elijah specifically utilized the communication device for the purpose of communicating assessment, interests, feedback, and questions regarding each phase of the trip. "Awesome" was communicated verbally when he saw the skyline of downtown Tampa from the charter bus and was reminded that the performance venue would soon be reached.

As this case study illustrates:

1. Sometimes the opportunity to communicate using one's own voice and not a communication device is preferred.
2. Assessment can take many forms, including students' assessment through feedback on the experience and level of services they are receiving. Elijah asked for help, asked for an increase or decrease in assistance in an activity, expressed thanks when his interests and preferences were recognized, and discussed his assessment of music by comparing past middle school and high school experiences with his current ones.
3. Students with special needs value inclusion, as well as the opportunity to perform in out-of-school and out-of-district experiences. Having a wheelchair-accessible bus arranged for Elijah before he requested it went a long way toward assuring his value as a member of the ensemble.

4. Out-of-school and out-of-district activities help to provide experiences that can lead to lifelong learning after students graduate. Elijah entered the transition program after his music performances. This school training had him working off campus, going to a job site and learning to navigate a county bus transportation system. He returned in time for his music classes, and lessons now turned toward his instrument of interest after graduation, the guitar. Planning for lifelong learning in music through the students' assessment and communication of their experiences rather than just the teacher's assessment of student learning is an important component of services for music students with disabilities.

5. Student preference in the method of performance should be taken into account and is valued by the students.

6. In the percussion part of Elijah's performance, he was given a tall conga or snare on a stand that could be turned at an angle for him to readily access with the hand he could use for gross and fine motor activities, such as keeping the beat on a drum or using a finger to type his needs on his communication device.

# SECTION 2: GENERAL MUSIC EDUCATION

## Using Students' Interests and Engagement as a Means of Curriculum Development and Assessment in Inclusive Public School Music Settings

*Musical Creativity and Response: A Model for Alternative Assessment*

This segment of the chapter is an illustration of a collaborative project among David Edmund, Jian-Jun Chen-Edmund, and Donald DeVito. The collaboration was initiated with a week-long residency, during which the Edmunds shared musical creativity lessons with DeVito's students, who have moderate to severe physical, intellectual, and behavioral exceptionalities. This project illustration consists of a description of the collaboration, reviews of qualitative modes of assessment, and the implementation of a model for alternative assessment.

In January 2016 the Edmunds visited the Sidney Lanier Center to share musical improvisation, composition, and musical response lessons. Throughout the week, more than three hundred photos and nearly two hundred videos of student interactions were gathered and analyzed. Photos and videos were distilled into a limited number of episodes, each representing a different form of musical interaction. For example, one episode involved a sixth-grade student with special needs. The student was engaged in an improvisation activity on the piano, which developed from incoherent striking of the keys to a spontaneous, rhythmic ostinato, performed in conjunction with Jian-Jun's accompaniment of a jazz/gospel selection.

Video episodes were shared with music education professionals during multiple private sessions in order to elicit additional interpretations regarding the impact of music and musical creativity on students with exceptionalities. The framework of this work employs Wayne Bowman's (2009) suggestion that narrative inquiry should involve co-constructed meanings from the perspectives of the researcher, participants, and reader (or in this case, observers). The piano improvisation video episodes are described in greater detail in the following subsections.

## Semistructured Interviews as Alternative Assessment

Lesley Farmer (2004) cites the benefits of reflection as a mode of critical inquiry. Further, narrative feedback may be employed by the researcher/educator to provide student feedback and inform instructional modification. Sheila J. Scott (2012) explains that formative assessment may guide instruction while meeting individual needs. In the current project, reflection constituted a means for assessment. Students gained insight regarding their own experiences and musical progress when provided with opportunities for meaningful reflection.

After creativity-based lessons were done, student self-reflection took place in the form of semistructured student interviews. Individuals and groups were asked two guiding questions: (1) What did you learn today? and (2) What did you enjoy most about today's class? In some cases, interview items were altered to adapt to the students' responses. For example, fourth graders with behavioral needs experienced multisensory approaches to music making that involved instrumental improvisation (i.e., drums, keyboard, mallet percussion) and creative movement. When asked question 2, one student responded more generally about the love of music. When asked, "*What* do you love *most* about music?" the student explained, "It's just my thing. Music is just somethin' I was born with. When I was like three, I sang Rudolph the Red-nosed Reindeer with my Mom. *I've just always been musical.*"

When asked question 1, another fourth grader with behavioral needs initially claimed, "nothin'...I already knew it all." Upon a moment's consideration, the student followed up with a poignant response: "I learned how to jump inside a beat without thinkin'." Such alternative assessments provide responses that are not only intriguing; they offer the music educator authentic feedback regarding the ways that these particular students learn and enjoy music.

## COIM: A Model of Qualitative Assessment for Students with Exceptionalities

In addition to Bowman's (2009) inclusion of external constituents in narrative inquiry, we employ the National Research Council's (2001) Assessment Triangle model, which involves cognition, observation, and interpretation (COI). Here, *modification* is included

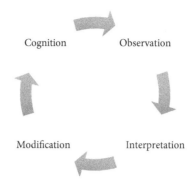

Cognition          Observation

Modification       Interpretation

FIGURE 12.1 COIM model of qualitative assessment. Adapted from the National Research Council (2001).

as a method of closing the assessment loop (see figure 12.1). The project focuses on cognitive function while students create and respond to music. Students with various exceptionalities engage in musical creativity, whether as creators (high-functioning students) or responders, where music provides a stimulus for interaction. Photo, video, and field notes serve as artifacts for observation. Analysis of the artifacts, by both the coauthors and other members of the music education community, constitute a means for interpretation. Suggestions for modification may then be developed for future lessons and projects, in order to optimize achievement by students with exceptionalities.

Here we elaborate on the previously mentioned episode involving a sixth grader with special needs. This student (referred to as "Rose") has a tendency to play musical instruments very aggressively. She explores every sound variable associated with each instrument: often guitar, drum set, and piano. She approaches instrumental performance with a penchant for rhythmic intensity, often creating her own fast, syncopated fragments. Rose does not merely depress piano keys; she strikes them with forceful intent, rarely avoiding a single key on the instrument. During one lesson, Chen-Edmund showed Rose the placement of "G" on the piano. Rose proceeded to locate each G and then selected two adjacent Gs in the upper register, with which she created a rhythmic ostinato. This recognition was a new form of cognition for Rose and one step in the process of guiding her away from her tendency toward incoherent music making to the development of self-made music with a greater sense of structure.

Next, Chen-Edmund performed an accompaniment to the tune "Mo Better Blues," in the key of G. Video analyses showed a new facial expression on Rose, from the instant the piano sounded. Her expression indicated curiosity about the potentials of the instrument, a curiosity we had not previously observed (as if to express, "I had no idea the instrument could do *that!*"). After a single chorus of the song, Chen-Edmund invited Rose to join in with her G-octave ostinato. Rose aptly matched her rhythmic pattern with the four-beat metric and four-measure phrase structure of the song. The contrast between striking keys aggressively and nonsensibly only five minutes before and performing a spontaneously created, syncopated rhythm pattern on a tonic pitch was remarkable; this was achieved by working in conjunction with the performance of Chen-Edmund's accompaniment.

Observations (step two in the COIM model) of Rose's video episode provided the team with opportunities to reflect upon aspects of instructional effectiveness within a given lesson. Sharing this episode with other music teacher professionals, from elementary to secondary and higher education, offered multiple interpretations (step three in the COIM model) of how musical meaning and structure were achieved. Observations and interpretations offered insights for instructional modifications that may take place in the future. For example, the lead author experienced the opportunity not only to witness the episode live, but also to elicit feedback during sessions in which interpretive feedback was offered. Combining his own knowledge and experience of Rose's musical/ learning style with interpretive feedback from others, the lead author has been able to provide additional structured, creative musical experiences. Rose's success on piano and other instruments has progressed to an extent that she was selected to participate as musical equipment manager at a session in a state music education conference in January 2017. This ongoing collaboration involves musical creativity and response for students with varying exceptionalities. We continue to share our work with members of the music teaching community and our college students. Ultimately, we hope to serve as a model of qualitative/alternative assessment strategies within the creating and response modes. This model will be continually adapted, with the purpose of best enhancing the teaching and learning of musical creativity and response for students with exceptionalities.

## Case Study: Emotional Needs

Instructing middle school students with significant emotional needs may include individualized education plan (IEPs) specifically designed to have students "ask for help" in all situations to parallel the importance of this interaction when they are feeling the strongest impact of depression. The setting of this case study is DeVito's middle school class of students with special needs. The classroom was set up with piano keyboards, guitars, drum kit, African percussion, and microphones and speakers for singing. The students were empowered to determine the curriculum among these choices and then to adapt and innovate through collaboration with their classmates and teacher. The student in this example selected guitar and wanted to begin with a song by Pink Floyd. When asked if the song was school appropriate, he replied, "Of course, it's Pink Floyd." The student came to class with an iPod (ancient technology compared to today), yet vinyl records and music of the 1960s to 1980s were his primary areas of interest. He went through the more than five hundred songs that he claimed he had, and his next request was "Take It to the Limit" by the Eagles.

DeVito very quickly agreed and picked up on this selection to reinforce the opportunity to add the coping skills of the lyrics to his curriculum. Teacher and student related the lyrics to the latter's own personal situation. The ideas of (a) trying one more time even though one is all alone; (b) being a dreamer; (c) not seeming to settle down; (d) still coming back, running back for more when there is nothing to believe in; and (e) asking to be shown a sign and taking it to the limit one more time were significant to him.

The acoustic guitar and the chord patterns and tabs, which would help the student to play the accompaniment sequence of the harmony, were taught. He played along with the recording and practiced at home as well. Having him perform this for students in the school was not an appropriate goal because it was best presented as a personal experience for the student.

Note the following conclusions:

1. Related to the case study, assessment of student musical performance is not always intended to be shared with others and can be deeply personal to the student. In this case, the physical skills of playing the chords on the guitar (something that could also be accommodated through a jazz-style fake book) resulted in musical engagement with the student. Ideally, for students who are particularly shy or experiencing distress, an individual electronic speaker and electro/acoustic guitar would be ideal, with headphones as we have in this scenario. This allows the student to practice on his own, which in this case provided the needed time for the student to rehearse in class without necessarily being heard by others.

2. Center-based instruction is often provided in the general education classroom (e.g., a science lab class), in which students go from one activity to the next to learn the steps needed to come to a completed project and thus a complete understanding of a topic or concept. In music, centers do not involve the necessity of dividing a class into four or five stations and having them rotate. The teacher can have a class doing one activity and provide an opportunity for a few students with special needs to have a station to practice and develop on their own. Returning to the remainder of the class for whole group instruction can be determined based on the teacher and the specific needs of the students. This helps to overcome difficulties for the student who is feeling depressed and is sitting with her head down, not wanting to engage with an entire class or in a large group setting.

## SECTION 3: SECONDARY JAZZ ENSEMBLES

### Santa Fe College Jazz Band Inclusion

Over the last decade, collaboration has taken place among the students at the Sidney Lanier Center, students with disabilities at Santa Fe College, and the Santa Fe College Jazz Band. All of this is accomplished through emphasizing inclusion. How? Santa Fe College adults with disabilities engage in ensemble participation through the use of adaptive instrumentation and drum circles. A sense of community through musical interaction and communication is demonstrated by allowing participants of all ages (middle school through adult) to perform in a group setting. Engagement is adapted musically so as to promote successful and meaningful relationships and connections through the inclusionary process of an ensemble performance. The desire of the individual to be included is provided for in a holistic manner, and observable musical growth is assessed in the most accommodating and accessible setting possible.

The first collaborative concerts of the Sidney Lanier School students with the Santa Fe College Jazz Band occurred at the University of Florida homecoming dance, as well as at a swing dance at the historic Thomas Center in Gainesville, Florida, a Valentine's Day dance, and other community events. The musical selections included "Street Music" by Fred Sturm, a slow blues number; "Tiger of San Pedro" from Hanna Labarbara, a Latin piece; "Jazz Police," a rock tune by Gordon Goodwin; and "For Once in My Life" by Ron Miller and Orlando Murdenan, a slow, easy ballad. The Sidney Lanier students utilized djembes in the performances to provide balance with the jazz band. The students performed in the front row of the ensemble with DeVito and within the drum kit section, and Bingham conducted. One senior, Lyndon White Manghram III,[3] despite having profound hearing loss, cerebral palsy, and the inability to speak, performed an adapted improvisation with the ensemble. In this case, he created rhythm patterns on the drum kit while the Santa Fe College musicians improvised over his often intricate musical improvisations.

## Santa Fe College Adult Students with Disabilities Workshop

Bingham and DeVito were trying to fill a void between K–12 public school and postsecondary music opportunities when they adapted the Santa Fe College Adults with Disabilities course to include music workshops in the summer of 2013. The workshops aimed to provide an opportunity for an older group of individuals with disabilities— some alumni of Sidney Lanier and now in the disabilities program at Santa Fe College— with the basic fundamentals of making music in a group setting. In the first two-hour session, educators and students explored the "heartbeat" and similar basic fundamental rhythmic patterns using djembes and congas. The population included twenty individuals aged twenty to fifty years old (eight females and twelve males).

The workshop sought to teach as many different short rhythmic patterns as possible that would translate easily on a drum. The clinic was successful in that the teachers were able to reach individuals through participating in the medium of music. Three weeks later another clinic was offered, this time utilizing recorders and karaoke machines to help the students play along with familiar songs that they picked out themselves. The sessions were rewarding in that participants engaged in the thrill of music making, but the educators felt bereft because more could have been done to instill a real sense of camaraderie as well as musical growth, had they only been given more time to work.

Consequently, Bingham invited the adults with disabilities to play with his collegiate performing ensembles. The younger age group had already achieved success, so there was hope that they could create a similar ensemble to those at Sidney Lanier. Sadly, the governmental funding for the adult program was pulled. It wasn't until 2016 that some students from DeVito's class who had matriculated through his program were placed in what was left of the Adults with Disabilities class at Santa Fe College; they were ultimately invited to participate in the Rhythm and Blues Band ensemble in the Santa Fe Collegiate music program.

The Sidney Lanier students felt at home, as their past experiences allowed them to develop a bond with the other students in the program and gave them an outlet for their own need to perform. Although there are few of them (typically one or two students, sometimes three), the students from the collegiate disability program seem to enjoy the repartee and challenge of performing on djembes and congas, as well as adding percussion parts to the given tunes that the group is working on. The music material performed comes mainly from Motown musical selections, allowing the percussion section to be more evident than a jazz combo or big band, in which they could get lost among the larger number of participants.

One student who has consistently returned each semester has become a part of the group in every sense of the word. Indeed, he is part of the repartee of each rehearsal, asks questions about the musical form and the nuances of the rhythmic ostinato, and quips at others who don't seem to be "in it," who are not 100 percent committed to the group as he is. He finally had the courage to transition from rehearsal and participated in his first public concert last semester.

Receiving music preparation and performance opportunities at an earlier developmental age has yielded observable benefits in cognitive development, motor skill acuity, and enhanced social skills. Bingham and DeVito believe this could signify that the inclusive environments the students were part of, many from kindergarten to adulthood, helped the students to cross barriers, whether mental, physical, or emotional. "Assessment of the studies musical goals (improvised improvisation skills, musical blend and balance, rhythm skill acuity, plus the ability to communicate to the audience)," write Bingham and DeVito (2012), "were achieved by observing audience appeal of each performance and further analyzed by watching the video of the event" (p. 17).

Bingham indicates that the significance of inclusion of the Sidney Lanier students in the many clinics and performance opportunities is not a triumph in the actual presentation or who the presenters were, but one of continuation within the Santa Fe College program for the adult students to participate in once they have matriculated through this public school program.

A significant trend that Bingham noticed in the Sidney Lanier music program in every performance opportunity was that these students integrated themselves and relied heavily on one another, more so than did well-developed students without special needs when offered the same opportunities. Students with disabilities saw no limitations to their abilities to learn and progress; although some were withdrawn and introverted, one could not help but see and watch in amazement what students without basic physical muscle memory achieved time and time again in a performance medium. They refused to be intimidated in mediums that usually would exact a toll on normal, well-developed students.

What these students experienced is the sheer enjoyment of music making, as well as being there for each other. This fact is so fundamental to making music that it often gets lost in the theaters of adjudication, among the ratings and trophies. The Sidney Lanier students maintain a strong sense of togetherness that would be unlikely without a continued and sequential kindergarten-to-adulthood curriculum.

The underlying fundamental bond that holds this inclusive group together is need. They need each other to perform, to create a sense of unity as a band in spite of their physical, emotional, or cognitive limitations. They perform as one, all bringing to the table what they can and what they cannot do; they look to each other to help fill any void. This void sadly grows once a student leaves the confines of the learning center. Suddenly students are left without a sense of belonging; that is, unless there is a next level or tier for them to aspire to, such as the opportunities provided at Santa Fe College.

# Conclusion

How do we move beyond assessment for the purposes of evaluating teacher proficiency and student performance outcomes to instead consider assessment for understanding student musical experiences and preferences for the purpose of promoting lifelong musical engagement? This question began our discussion on qualitative assessment approaches for special learners. As shown in the three approaches to music inclusion discussed here, alternative forms of assessment in qualitative music education are best presented with alternative music experiences based on the interests, affective responses, and level of engagement of the students we serve. DeVito believes, after observing and documenting the results of this collaboration, that several observations can be made regarding assessment.

Notably, assessment is not just acknowledging proficiency at playing scales or reciting general information on a multiple-choice, end-of-year course exam. Assessing music teaching and learning is best when done qualitatively, when we take into account the interests of the students that lead to their engagement in a lesson, observe their affective responses, and accommodate our curriculum to afford students the skills and dispositions for lifelong musical learning.

DeVito believes there are two key reasons that current methods of assessment may lead to difficulty for students with disabilities in gaining access to middle and secondary school music programs. First, when assessment is connected to teacher evaluations based on end-of-year course exams, we run the risk of excluding students with special needs because of the effect this has on teachers' overall evaluation score. Second, audition-based public school performance ensembles in the United States can exclude students with disabilities from performing in ensembles. District-level marching and concert band assessments or "festivals" individually assess the school ensemble and make it easy to compare schools based on a single night, for which ensembles receive the "good, excellent, or superior" rankings typically used in these American events. Achieving a "streak" of straight superior ratings can unfortunately become the goal of these assessments, and the assessment rating of one ensemble may conveniently represent the entire school music program. The philosophical and qualitative assessment approaches discussed in this chapter demonstrate the authors' belief that assessing a music program should be based less on a single evening's performance or a standardized exam and more on individualized "customer service" to all learners through adaptation and accommodation within a diverse and inclusive curriculum.

Third, assessment should be meaningful; it should consider student preference in instrumentation; styles of music incorporated in the lessons; and a scope, pace, and sequencing of instruction that allows students to demonstrate their knowledge and mastery of the concepts taught in the class. DeVito believes this is vital for a fair assessment of student learning. Results of music assessment should have a direct application in the everyday lives of students outside of the school day.

Fourth, federally mandated IEPs contain useful diagnostic information that clarifies specific needs of exceptional learners. However, due to the emphasis on standardized and quantifiable data, which is increasing for music education as for other subjects, there is a specific emphasis on not utilizing the very document that indicates a student's greatest areas of need to be able to function in a school, a future workplace, and the community. IEPs identify the specific interests of the student, both academic and life goals; the transition services needed for accommodation beyond school; and the specific percentage of time that a student will be expected to exhibit specific skills during a school day. It makes complete sense that music education would look first to the IEP as the foundation for relating assessment of the curricular approach of music for lifelong learning to the greatest areas of need and interest of the student. In essence this collaboration between teachers and their students with disabilities relates to co-intentional education as described by Paulo Freire (2000): "A revolutionary leadership must accordingly practice co-intentional education ... as they attain this knowledge of reality through common reflection and action, they discover themselves as its permanent re-creators. In this way, the presence of the oppressed in their struggle for their liberation will be what it should be: not pseudo-participation, but common involvement" (p. 69).

## NOTES

1. These qualities are reflective of Universal Design for Learning, an approach to teaching that allows for all students to engage with material taught in a variety of educational settings (Hourigan, 2015).
2. The student's name is included here with permission.
3. The student's name is included here with permission.

## REFERENCES

Adamek, M. S., & Darrow, A. A. (2010). *Music in special education*. Silver Spring, MD: American Music Therapy Association.

Bingham, S., & DeVito, D. (2012). New pathways of community music inclusion: Multi-aged children with disabilities in college jazz ensembles. In D. D. Coffman (Ed.), *CMA XIII: Transitioning from historical foundations to 21st century global initiatives* (pp. 14–19). (Proceedings from the International Society for Music Education [ISME] 2012 seminar of the Commission for Community Music Activity.)

Bowman, W. (2009). Charting narrative territory. In M. S. Barrett & S. L. Stauffer (Eds.), *Narrative inquiry in music education: Troubling certainty* (pp. 211–22). Dordrecht, The Netherlands: Springer.

Choksy, L. (1981). *The Kodály context: Creating an environment for musical learning.* Englewood Cliffs, NJ: Prentice-Hall.

Choksy, L. (1988). *The Kodály method: Comprehensive music education from infant to adult* (2nd ed.). Englewood Cliffs, NJ: Prentice Hall.

Clay, S. (2009). Ideas for Kodály in the secondary classroom. *Kodály Envoy, 36*(1), 26–29.

Farmer, L. (2004). Narrative inquiry as assessment tool: A course case study. *Journal of Education for Library and Information Science Education, 45*(4), 34–35.

Freire, P. (2000). *Pedagogy of the oppressed.* New York: Continuum International Publishing Group.

Gallo, F. (2010). The Kodály concept in the secondary choral classroom: Increasing the use of Kodály-inspired techniques. *Kodály Envoy, 36*(3), 16–18.

Houlahan, M., & Tacka, P. (2015). *Kodály today: A cognitive approach to elementary music education.* New York: Oxford University Press.

Hourigan, R. (2015). Universal design for learning: Understandings for students with learning differences. In C. Conway (Ed.), *Musicianship-focused curriculum and assessment* (pp. 89–111). Chicago: GIA Publications.

Mazur, K. (2004). An introduction to inclusion in the music classroom. *General Music Today, 18*(1), 6–11.

National Research Council. (2001). *Knowing what students know: The science and design of educational assessment.* Washington, DC: National Academy Press.

Scott, S. J. (2008). Integrating inquiry-based (constructivist) music education with Kodály-inspired learning. *OAKE Envoy, 35*(1), 4–9.

Scott, S. J. (2012). Rethinking the roles of assessment in music education. *Music Educators Journal, 98*(3), 31–35. doi:10.1177/0027432111434742

Sinor, J. (1997). The ideas of Kodály in America. *Music Educators Journal, 83*(5), 37. doi:10.2307/3399007

Williams, M. (2016). Preference for popular and world music: A review of literature. *Update: Applications of Research in Music Education, 35*(3), 1–7. doi:10.1177/8755123316630349

# CHAPTER 13

# A MUSIC-CENTERED PERSPECTIVE ON MUSIC THERAPY ASSESSMENT

## JOHN A. CARPENTE AND KENNETH AIGEN

THE concepts of assessment, treatment, and evaluation have specific meanings in various therapeutic domains, including the practice of music therapy. In music therapy assessment, "a therapist collects and analyzes information about a client deemed necessary for planning and implementing an effective treatment program" (Bruscia, 1987, p. 13). *Treatment* is the process of working toward the goals or purposes behind the therapy. *Evaluation* is the process of determining the nature and degree of progress achieved toward the clinical goals.

Each of these components of therapy supports corresponding research topics. Assessment research examines aspects of clients including their challenges and problems, "their musical characteristics, their personal resources and experiences, and their therapeutic needs" (Bruscia, 2005, p. 81). Treatment research looks at interventions, models, the role of music and verbalization, the therapeutic relationship, and the overall process of therapy, in order to gain insight into what happens during courses of treatment. Research on evaluation considers the outcomes of therapy. It looks at areas such as the nature of therapeutic change in the client and the enhancement of the client's well-being or quality of life to determine the efficacy of the therapy.

A number of unspoken assumptions underlie the conventional, traditional view of these topics. Although, as Kenneth E. Bruscia (1987) observed thirty years ago, assessment can include searching for a client's "resources and potentials" (p. 13), in actual practice most therapists focus more on problems and deficits. An important contemporary publication that provides a strong antidote to this way of thinking is Randi Rolvsjord's (2010) exploration of resource-oriented music therapy, which includes as central elements empowerment philosophy, positive psychology, and putting into a central focus the process of building on client strengths. The existence of Rolvsjord's critique—and others like it—reflects the fact that the basic, defining components of music therapy are necessarily embedded within particular worldviews, value systems, and their corresponding models of practice. This observation may be surprising to some readers, as it could be assumed that as healthcare professionals, music therapists' primary focus—their clients' well-being—would be similar across different treatment models. However, in some ways music therapy is similar to education in the way that its core elements vary according to the practitioner's belief system.

Central areas of difference include the autonomy granted to clients and the nature of the therapeutic relationship, the relative importance of creative compared to more traditionally scientific considerations, and the relative importance and overall role of music in the process. Some models in music therapy stress the importance of activating both the client's and the therapist's musicality to produce the greatest benefit, while other approaches minimize these factors; some approaches build on the client's proclivity for musical experience and expression, seeing it as reflective of an inner drive to self-actualization, while others use musical motivations merely to induce other behaviors; and some approaches integrate progressive contemporary movements such as a resource orientation, empowerment philosophy, and neurodiversity theory, while others hew to the traditional medical model in which the client follows the dictates of the therapist as the authority figure.

The following section presents a brief overview of assessment in music therapy to provide a context in which the authors' views can be situated. We highlight the way in which assessment tools are embedded within the worldviews of particular treatment models. We then describe what we mean by music as a medium of experience in music therapy, how this view creates a context of musical goals in music therapy, and how it differs from the traditional notion of music therapy as a means for accomplishing nonmusical goals. We use this critique to highlight the elements that a music-based assessment tool should contain. The chapter concludes with a description of a tool that fits these characteristics, the Individual Music-Centered Assessment Profile for Neurodevelopmental Disorders (IMCAP-ND), which has received a fuller explication elsewhere (Carpente, 2013).

# AN OVERVIEW OF ASSESSMENT
# IN MUSIC THERAPY

Assessment is considered a vital part of music therapy and has been identified in the American Music Therapy Association Standards of Practice (AMTA, 2013) as the first step in providing effective treatment. During the assessment process, the client is observed and listened to while engaging in various musical experiences. The therapist formulates a clinical impression that contributes to formulating treatment goals based on these observations and interactions.

However, these clinical impressions are inextricably linked to the therapist's working practice model, with different models attributing vastly different levels of importance to the role of music and musical experiences. In order to develop a treatment plan, music therapists are faced with the task of choosing an assessment instrument that will guide them in ascribing meaning to the client's experience. But this treatment plan will inevitably be as much, or more, a reflection of the therapist's working model—and theoretical and pretheoretical assumptions—as of the needs and interests of the clients.

Moreover, in spite of repeated calls in the literature for universal assessment models, the facts of music therapy as a profession render this task both impossible and undesirable. Clinical applications of music therapy are extremely diverse and include psychotherapeutic music therapy, in which the focus is on addressing psychological functioning along with social behavior; rehabilitative music therapy, which focuses on the restoration of motor and cognitive skills lost to trauma, injury, or disease; community-oriented music therapy, which focuses on social integration and client empowerment; psychoeducational music therapy, which supports traditional learning processes; and medical music therapy, which can address the psychological and physical needs of clients facing various types of medical conditions, such as cancer, brain injuries, chronic pain, heart disease, Alzheimer's disease, and dementia. With such a wide array of focuses, it should be clear that no single assessment tool could—or should—be applicable to all of them.

In recent years considerable progress has been made in developing various types of music therapy assessments (Wheeler, 2013). Most music therapy assessment tools are comprised of general assessment categories that focus primarily on conventional health domains such as cognition, sensory functioning, motor activity, communication skills, and social engagement. A common feature of most assessment tools in music therapy is that they examine health domains independently and in isolation from one another. For example, cognitive functioning may be assessed first and not considered in the context of social-emotional functioning.

What may seem difficult to fathom, though, is the paucity of attention paid to the client's specifically musical experiences and expression. Generally, if music is listed as an assessment item, it is usually viewed independently from the other health domains. The client's musical preferences and/or musical skills might be examined based on prompting or directives and considered outside of the context of the therapeutic relationship. In the music-centered perspective, however, music is viewed as its own domain of health. Therefore, the client's ability to experience music making in a robust and deep relational manner with the therapist is at the core of the work. Hence, whereas the physical therapist works toward helping clients improve motor ability, and the speech therapist works toward helping people improve their speech, the music therapist focuses on helping clients engage with music.

The ability to make music can itself be viewed as an expression of health (Abrams, 2011). According to Brian Abrams (2011), when clients expand their capacities for musical experience, they have shifted something fundamental about their being. For example, children on the autism spectrum may find it difficult to engage in musical-play experiences that include a wide range of tempos and dynamics. They may only be able to maintain musical engagement and relatedness when the dynamics and tempo are fixed, thus limiting their music experience with the therapist. Therefore, the child's ability to experience music freely is limited in relation to expressiveness, communication, and relationship building.

The application of music is commonly used as a means to a nonmusical end, without consideration of musical process, social dimensions, relationship, and aesthetics. Music is considered merely as a motivational tool, a stimulus for certain behaviors, or a field for examining the plethora of nonmusical areas of human functioning rather than as an essential domain of functioning with intrinsic value, both in a diagnostic sense and in the sense of providing unique clinical benefits.

For example, music therapists assessing musical behaviors or skills may do so by asking or prompting a client to repeat a melodic rhythm on an instrument or to follow the therapist modeling the music behavior. This may serve the purpose of assessing the client's memory skills, ability to follow directions, and motor functions. It does not, however, consider the client's ability to intentionally engage, relate, and communicate musically to the musical-social cues and initiatives provided by the therapist. These procedures are based on a stimulus-response relationship as opposed to being centered on the experience of coactive relational musical play. In contrast, the music therapist assessing musical responses within a musical-relational context may provide music experiences focused on fostering interaction with the client in order to assess musical intra- and interpersonal capacities. This phenomenon is discussed further in the next section of this chapter.

There are many examples in the music therapy literature of assessment tools that focus on evaluating behaviors, musical skills, and musical preferences. The Individual Music Therapy Assessment Profile (IMTAP) (Baxter et al., 2007), used for a range of client groups from children to adults, is designed to assess eleven domain areas that deal with gross and fine motor skills, oral motor functioning, sensory processing, communication abilities, cognition, social functioning, emotional capacities, and musical skills. Each of the domains is assessed in an isolated manner while clients are asked to perform musical and nonmusical tasks. The Music Therapy Assessment Tool for Awareness in Disorders of Consciousness (MATADOC) (Magee, Siegert, Daveson, Lenton-Smith, & Taylor, 2014) is a validated and standardized measurement tool used with adults with disorders of consciousness and is designed to assess awareness levels of individuals with severe brain damage. The purpose of the MATADOC is to measure motor, communicative, arousal, auditory, and visual responses to music.

Music therapy assessments that are designed to measure educational objectives related to students performing specific nonmusical tasks in musical and nonmusical experiences include the Special Education Music Therapy Assessment Process (SEMTAP) (Coleman & Brunck, 2003) and Music Therapy Special Education Assessment Scale (MT-SEAS) (Bradfield, Carlenius, Gold, & White, 2007). SEMTAP is a criterion-based assessment tool designed for children in the school system with a current individual education plan (IEP) to determine if music therapy, as a related service, will help meet the student's educational goals as indicated in the IEP. An eligibility assessment tool, SEMTAP is designed to test a child's response to specific tasks that are linked to objectives listed in the IEP. The MT-SEAS is designed to be a supplement to SEMTAP. Although it assesses IEP goals and objectives, it also evaluates developmental skills within specific musical and nonmusical tasks.

Music therapy assessments that utilize music as a stimulus to target a specific nonmusical domain such as cognition include the Music-Based Attention Assessment (Jeong, 2013), which is designed to assess behaviors dealing with attention in patients living with traumatic brain injuries; the Music Attentiveness Screening Assessment (Waldon, Lesser, Weeden, & Messick, 2016), designed to assess the degree to which a child can attend to musical stimuli during medical procedures; the Computer-based Music Perception Assessment for Children (CMPAC) (Waldon & Wolfe, 2006), focused on evaluating musical preferences and responses within the context of nonmusical behaviors that deal with perception; and the Music-Based Evaluation of Cognitive Functioning (Lipe, 1995), which assesses cognitive abilities through various musical tasks. In addition, assessment tools designed to measure discrete components or behaviors of social communication, such as eye contact, include the Music Therapy Communication and Social Interaction Scale (MTCSI) (Bell, Perry, Peng, & Miller, 2014), Music Therapy Assessment for Severely Emotionally Disturbed Children (Layman et al., 2002), Assess the Quality of Relationship (AQR) (Schumacher & Calvet-Kruppa, 2007), and Assessment of Parenting Competencies (Jacobsen, 2012).

While all of these assessments view music independently from the other health domains and apply it as a means to a nonmusical end—or as a motivational tool to stimulate particular behaviors—the next group of assessment tools is music centered, in that the primary focus is music. These types of assessments work under the assumption that music experiences and the relationships that occur in them are meaningful to clients. Thus, music in music therapy is not just an organized sound experience, but rather a unique experience that involves specifically musical dynamics, relationships, and processes (Bruscia, 2014).

# RELATIONSHIP-BASED
# MUSIC-CENTERED ASSESSMENTS

The Improvisational Assessment Profile (IAP) is a music-centered assessment that emerged from a qualitative analysis of improvisational models in music therapy. It is designed to provide insight into the musical processes that occur in therapy (Bruscia, 1987). The IAPs provide the therapist with a group of scales that are focused on analyzing musical elements within the context of six profiles that deal with understanding the processes occurring in the music. The six profiles are autonomy, variability, integration, salience, tension, and congruence. Each includes specific criteria for analyzing improvisations and creating a continuum of five levels, ranging from one extreme to its opposite (Bruscia, 1987).

Paul Nordoff and Clive Robbins (2007) created assessment and diagnostic instruments that were designed to understand clients based on how they played during interactive musical-play experiences. Scale I, Child-Therapist Relationship in Coactive Musical Experience, was designed to describe the quality of the client-therapist musical relationship during musical activity. This tool includes an observational rating scale that assesses the qualities of the client's musical participation versus qualities of restiveness (Mahoney, 2010). Scale II, Musical Communicativeness, also developed by Nordoff and Robbins, is an observational rating scale developed to identify levels of musical communication during coactive musical play via instrument play, vocal play, and movement to music (Nordoff & Robbins, 2007). Scale III, Musicking: Forms of Activity, Stages and Qualities of Engagement, was created to assess and classify the complexity of musical form in client responses and the quality of engagement expressed in those responses. The observational rating scales provide classifications for how and what the client plays (instrumentally) and vocalizes with regard to the quality of engagement specific to rhythmic and melodic forms (Nordoff & Robbins, 2007; Bruscia, 1987). Finally, Thirteen Categories of Responses/The Tempo-Dynamics Schema, was designed to correlate or associate pathology with musical expression specific to the client's ability to engage in musical play with regard to tempo and dynamic range (Nordoff & Robbins, 2007). This music-centered assessment tool seeks to understand how clients relate musically and interpersonally to the therapist's improvisations while playing a drum, piano, and pitched percussion, and/or while vocalizing.

Kenneth Aigen's (1995) model, although not an assessment tool, is grounded in Nordoff-Robbins's music therapy and focuses on understanding the relationship between cognitive and affective processes in music therapy. The four-tiered model is based on the assumption that music experience is constructed through the integration of sensory, perceptual, cognitive, and affective processes. It provides the therapist with an understanding of how the client experiences music from basic concrete musical skills to the highest level of integration, which includes musical expression, affect, and thinking abstractly.

Joanne Loewy's (2000) music psychotherapy assessment involves a musical and verbal descriptive analysis within structured and improvisational musical play in order to determine the client's therapeutic needs in a musical-relationship-based context. Loewy's assessment examines thirteen areas of inquiry that are interconnected to address four main areas, within a music psychotherapy context: (1) relationship, (2) dynamics, (3) achievement, and (4) cognition.

# THE MEDIUM OF MUSIC AND ITS INTRINSIC VALUE IN MUSIC THERAPY

Conventional definitions consider music therapy to be the use of music to achieve nonmusical goals, thus distinguishing it from music education, music appreciation, and music performance. There are myriad goals, which vary according to the treatment milieu and the focus of the work in the sensory, cognitive, social, emotional, or motoric realms. Typical goals include increasing impulse control, enhancing social skills, increasing emotional expressiveness, resolving psychological conflicts, enhancing motor function, and improving cognitive functions such as increasing attention and memory. The rationale is that the clinical focus must be distinguishable from the musical activity for a particular use of music to be considered music therapy.

One problem with the conventional approach is that it renders the actual musical experience dispensable. The music becomes merely a tool to achieve some nonmusical goal. In contrast to this position, the goal of progressive, music-centered approaches to music therapy (Aigen, 2005) is the achievement of experiences and expressions specific and unique to music. In this view, the clinical and the musical are not separable. What is achieved through the music cannot be approached in any other way because musical experience and expression are the goals of therapy.

Two important, central notions underlie the music-based approach to treatment and assessment. First, musical experience and expression are considered inherently beneficial human activities that are legitimate ways to address the reasons for which people come to therapy. There is no denying that capacities such as impulse control, expressiveness, and social skills can increase from the musical engagement; however, benefits in these areas are considered secondary effects, not the primary locus of intervention.

Second, the fact that many music therapy clients are motivated primarily by a desire to make music is taken more seriously and recognized as a legitimate rationale for, and focus of, music therapy, rather than as merely a motivational factor for people to get the "real" therapy, typically located in the nonmusical areas of functioning. Whether we are considering an autistic child with an affinity for playing the piano, a group of adolescents with behavioral problems creating a rap song, or an elderly woman with Alzheimer's disease singing a song from her youth, in each case the client's primary motivation is to participate in music, not to achieve some nonmusical clinical goal. For such individuals the motivation behind the music making is no different from the motivations of people who make music in the nonclinical domain. What David Elliott and Marissa Silverman (2015; Elliott, 1995) call musicing can be the focus of music therapy.

When music is understood as an activity that enriches human lives in a unique and necessary way, music therapy can be considered a means of providing opportunities for musicing to people for whom special adaptations are necessary. The functions of music for disabled individuals or for those in need of therapy are the same as for other people. It is the means of achieving the musical state that comprises the music therapist's craft and differentiates music therapy from music performance or music education. In this view, music therapy involves the creating of special conditions in which musicking can happen for people who cannot create the conditions on their own, whether this is due to physical, cognitive, social, or emotional challenges. Thus, it is the means for achieving musicing that defines music therapy, not the presence of nonmusical, health-related goals.

In music-centered approaches to music therapy—such as that of Nordoff-Robbins's music therapy (Nordoff & Robbins, 2007)—the fundamental notion is that client limitations are reflected in the client's capacity for expressive, responsive, and engaged musicing. If a person can only play in one tempo or dynamic level, that person cannot have musical-emotional experiences that require other levels of tempo or dynamics or that require the use of a ritard, accelerando, diminuendo, or crescendo. The therapist works to expand the client's musical range of expression in order to help that client be able to experience all aspects of human emotional life.

This is why it is necessary to assess musical capacities such as tempo mobility, dynamic flexibility, and melodic and rhythmic complexity in music therapy assessment. These aspects of one's musical functioning are understood broadly as reflections of one's overall cognitive and affective relationship to the world and to oneself. Working on music is simultaneously working on one's inner life, as clients "order their being as they order their beating, realizing order and purpose in themselves as they find these qualities in the music" (Nordoff & Robbins, 2007, p. 53).

It is this musical self that is the core of the developing personality and that first integrates the cognitive, affective, and physical aspects of the being into a coherent, unified self. The musical self and musical skills are not seen as existing on the periphery of the self and then requiring absorption into the core of the person in order to be clinically beneficial. Instead, it is the musical self that exists at the core, and other areas of functioning and awareness radiate out from this center. By acting on a person's music, the therapist is directly engaged with the most central aspects of that person's being.

This notion speaks directly to the music-centered belief that musicing itself is an essential human activity that does not require generalization or translation into other areas in order to be a legitimate clinical focus. The development of the musical self becomes "an orientation point, a new center, around which a more developed personality can constellate itself" (Aigen, 1998, p. 144). The idea is not simply to alter behaviors but also to provide an alternative blueprint for the formation of a more functional, healthier personality structure. Musical experiences provide the template for the development of the newer and healthier self: "Much as the laws of DNA provide a plan for the structure of fully functioning physical bodies, aligning our naturally occurring propensities for emotional and cognitive development with the laws of music provides for fully functioning psychological beings" (p. 144).

# ELEMENTS OF A MUSIC-CENTERED ASSESSMENT TOOL

Human beings are affectively connected to others in everything we do. For infants and toddlers, human relationships are the context for learning skills involved in both basic communication and higher levels of thinking, such as symbolization and other forms of abstract thought (Greenspan & Thorndike, 1985; Rogers & Pennington, 1991; Stern,

2009; Trevarthen, 2011). The acquisition and development of all human motor, cognitive, language, and social functioning skills are led by the intentional effort to repeat desired emotional experiences. Thus, Greenspan and Shanker (2006) assert that functional skills are more meaningfully learned and assimilated across contexts when rooted in relational affect. Considered in this context, training a child to respond vocally to a series of cues or prompts does not necessarily represent the development of communication skills. We are not trained to talk; we develop the ability to communicate relationally.

In music therapy, the experience of making music with another person represents a living embodiment of relational affect. At the same time, it provides opportunities for assessing, accessing, and working through challenges that impede health across several domains. When clients are engaged in meaningful relational music-making experiences, they are simultaneously tapping into the physical, emotional, cognitive, and creative and expressive resources that are embodied in all domain areas. Thus, assessing how clients perceive, interpret, create, and play music with the therapist—as well as understanding the challenges that impede their ability to engage in robust relational music making—should be an important feature of all music therapy assessment tools, regardless of the treatment context for which they are developed.

When working in this manner, music is the primary domain and focus of the therapeutic experience. The musical process is the clinical process (Aigen, 2005) and is facilitated by the musical-interpersonal relationship between the client and therapist (Bruscia, 2014). Here, rather than viewing clients through the lens of conventional health domains in isolation from each other and independently from music, the therapist considers music and all of its social, dynamic, and aesthetic dimensions as the only domain area under assessment. Hence, just as a physical therapist works toward fostering a client's motor abilities, and a speech therapist focuses on helping clients develop speech skills, the music therapist works to help clients develop their capacities for musicality, musicianship, and musicing (or musicking, see Small, 1998).

Music-centered music therapy assessment, treatment, and evaluation are based on the concepts that music serves as the primary medium and agent for therapeutic change and that the experiences occurring are a reflection of the client's health (Aigen, 2005; Bruscia, 2014). So the task of the therapist is to help the client relate to and engage in the music, while understanding and assessing the various factors that may limit the depth of the client's music experience.

Thus, assessing and conceptualizing clients requires the music therapist to take into account all facets of their musical-social experiences. This involves the clinician focusing on how clients perceive, interpret, and create music, with the therapist as the first step in formulating a music therapy treatment plan (Carpente, 2013). It is therefore necessary to implement an assessment that considers how constitutional-maturational growth and interactive factors work together as clients progress through various musical-social-emotional levels.

# The Individual Music-Centered Assessment Profile for Neurodevelopmental Disorders (IMCAP-ND)

The IMCAP-ND is a musical-play-based assessment instrument that provides music therapists with a developmental, music-centered framework for understanding how clients perceive, interpret, and create music, with the therapist as the first step in formulating clinical goals and strategies for working with clients (Carpente, 2013, 2014). To that end, the IMCAP-ND uses musical-play experiences to examine core features of neurodevelopmental disorders that have an impact on communication, social interactions, the ability to experience and express affect, cognitive functioning, and sensory and motor processing.

There are two primary reasons this assessment tool is being highlighted in this chapter. First, it was developed specifically to assess clients whose diagnoses fit into the category of neurodevelopmental disorders, such as autism spectrum disorder (ASD), attention deficit hyperactivity disorder (ADHD), communication disorders, intellectual developmental disorder, and specific learning disorders. These disorders typically emerge in childhood and are most likely to be seen in the students engaged with by music educators. This makes the tool relevant to the primary reading audience of this chapter. Second, as noted previously, there is a paucity of assessment tools that focus extensively on musical concerns as opposed to nonmusical areas of functioning implicated in music. The IMCAP is the only music-based assessment to be developed in recent years that is both grounded in the original music-based assessments of Nordoff and Robbins (2007) and yet goes beyond those tools to establish connections to recognized treatment models outside of music therapy.

The IMCAP-ND provides music therapists with a way to assess clients in the manner most aligned with the very modality through which the work takes place: the music (Abrams, 2013). This music-centered assessment tool seeks to highlight the often difficult to describe, relational experiences embodied within the music making or musicing experience between client and therapist in a series of developmentally based, quantitative scales.

The IMCAP-ND does not isolate music into a separate domain; rather, music is understood and assessed as an experience and event of relational functioning. Thus, the IMCAP-ND situates music as the only domain area to be assessed within the context of relating and communicating. It provides not only musical procedures and protocols, but also a set of guiding principles for conducting the assessment process. In essence, it is a guide for doing quality music therapy and thus challenges the musical, interpersonal, and clinical integrity of the assessor's skills (Abrams, 2013).

Administering the IMCAP-ND requires the therapist to improvise music experiences based on the client's interests, music, and emotionality while targeting specific responses that are relevant to relating and communicating. Within the context of musical play, this observational tool examines musical-social-emotional abilities and cognition and perception skills, as well as overall responsiveness pertaining to musical preferences, perceptual efficiency, and self-regulation. Furthermore, it identifies and considers supportive interventions that are tailored to the client's specific target responses.

The IMCAP-ND is made up of three quantitative scales that evaluate the client's ability to engage in coactive musical play. Scale I, Musical Emotional Assessment Rating Scale (MEARS), evaluates musical-social-emotional capacities in musical play based on five developmentally sequenced areas: (1) musical attention, (2) musical affect, (3) adaptation to musical play, (4) musical engagement, and (5) musical interrelatedness. Scale II, Musical Cognitive/Perception Scale (MCPS), evaluates the client's ability to react, focus, recall, follow, and initiate five musical elements: (1) rhythm, (2) melody, (3) dynamic, (4) phrase, and (5) timbre. Scale III, Musical Responsiveness Scale (MRS), assesses client preferences, efficiency, and self-regulation in musical play.

Each of these areas is broken down into subcategories that identify its critical features. For instance, attention is composed of four subcategories assessing how the client attends to musical play: (a) focuses, (b) maintains, (c) shares, and (d) shifts. Each of these subcategories is rated on two dimensions: frequency of response and support. Frequency is scored according to a six-point scale that ranges from zero (does not exhibit response) to five (consistently exhibits response). The level of support reflects how much assistance was provided in order for the client to express a particular targeted response and is also based on a six-point scale from zero (not applicable due to functional incapacity) to five (no support needed as client independently exhibits response).

The aim of the MRS is to assess the overall preferences, perceptual efficiency, and self-regulatory abilities exhibited by the client throughout the session. Overall musical tendencies of the client at the different ranges of tempo, dynamics, pitch, and attack are rated on the same frequency scale as the MEARS and MCPS.

Scales I, II, and III work together to generate a musical profile for each client. Scales II (MCPS) and III (MRS) act as descriptors that indicate client musical tendencies, interests, preferences, and preferred media—that is, instruments, vocal, and/or movement—while engaged in coactive musical play. The data collected from scales II and III help to inform and guide the therapist's musical choices regarding elements and style in order to maximize the interaction of the musical experience. For example, to sustain musical relatedness, a client may require music experiences that are fast in tempo and loud in dynamic. When the music decreases in tempo and/or dynamics, the client may withdraw from the interaction. Other clients may require music that contains a fixed tempo in order to sustain engagement and might withdraw from play once the music changes in tempo. Hence, these musical descriptors, indicated in scales II and III, are clinically necessary for the therapist to understand and support the client's differences while providing experiences that help the client develop the capacities that will manifest in movement up the musical-social "ladder" of scale I (MEARS).

The IMCAP-ND was submitted to an inter-rater reliability analysis in order to empirically determine the degree to which two music therapists were consistent in their judgments of music therapy videos of thirty children with ASD. This was assessed using an inter-rater reliability statistic called "weighted kappa" (Landis & Koch, 1977). Results for MEARS indicated 98 percent of the forty-eight weighted kappa coefficients for the frequency and support ratings can be characterized as "almost perfect" using current interpretive standards for evaluating inter-rater reliability coefficients. Moreover, intra-class correlations between the two raters' frequency and support ratings aggregated in two MEARS summary scores exceeded 0.95. In addition, all of the weighted kappas (100 percent) for the subscales of this music therapy observational instrument, as well as the subscales of the MCPS and MRS, can be categorized as "almost perfect," that is, at the highest level of inter-rater reliability (Carpente & Gattino, 2016).

Currently the IMCAP-ND is being tested for predictive, concurrent, and convergent validity with children with ASD. The study involves two main components: (1) correlating IMCAP-ND with "gold standard" diagnostic and assessment instruments used to evaluate children with ASD and (2) comparing the IMCAP-ND's ability to distinguish between typically developing children and children diagnosed with ASD using "gold standard" instruments.

# Conclusion

The conventional conception of music therapy rests on the notion that music therapists must focus on the achievement of client goals in nonmusical areas in order to qualify their work as a bona fide form of music therapy. This is the primary reason that music therapy assessment largely focuses on nonmusical areas of functioning. However, this seemingly reasonable assumption is in conflict with important contemporary social trends.

First, it ignores the fact that engagement with music is increasingly being understood as an essential health resource, a basic aspect of identity creation, and an important component of quality of life. As such, it can be reasonably argued that there is a human right to music, a right that accrues to all people, whether or not they are disabled, traumatized, or experiencing any other type of exacerbated state of need. It is discriminatory if people with disabilities require the establishment of a nonmusical benefit from their musical engagement before social resources can be allocated to it, while other people are allowed to experience music's intrinsic value without being required to establish its benefits for nonmusical areas of functioning.

Thus, arguing that music therapy clients must demonstrate nonmusical areas of benefit in order to access music creates an artificial boundary between the seemingly abled and those with disabilities. Rather than establishing a professional foundation on the commonalities among people, the traditional view supports the marginalization of individuals with disabilities by claiming that the presence of their disability necessarily means that their engagement with music is somehow different from the engagement of others.

Many music therapy clients are motivated to participate in it not from a desire to achieve some extrinsic, nonmusical benefit, but because of what music specifically and uniquely provides. Music therapy assessment tools that look at nonmusical areas thus are looking away from the areas of engagement that clients themselves most want. Such tools are not based on the needs and desires of the primary stakeholders in the process. In contrast, music-centered assessment tools such as the IMCAP-ND reflect the fundamental desires and goals of clients, the people for whom the profession of music therapy exists.

# REFERENCES

Abrams, B. (2011). Understanding music as a temporal-aesthetic way of being: Implications for a general theory of music therapy. *The Arts in Psychotherapy, 38*(2), 114–19.

Abrams, B. (2013). Foreword. In J. A. Carpente (Ed.), *Individual music-centered assessment profile for neurodevelopmental disorders (IMCAP-ND): Clinical manual* (pp. x–xx). Baldwin, NY: Regina Publishers.

Aigen, K. (1995). Cognitive and affective processes in music therapy with individuals with developmental delays: A preliminary model for contemporary Nordoff-Robbins practice. *Music Therapy, 13*(1), 13–46.

Aigen, K. (1998). *Paths of development in Nordoff-Robbins music therapy.* Gilsum, NH: Barcelona.

Aigen, K. (2005). *Music-centered music therapy.* Gilsum, NH: Barcelona.

American Music Therapy Association (AMTA). (2013). *The standards of clinical practice.* Retrieved from http://www.musictherapy.org/about/standards/

Baxter, H., Berghofer, J., MacEwan, L., Nelson, J., Peters, K., & Roberts, P. (2007). *The individualized music therapy assessment profile: IMTAP.* Philadelphia: Jessica Kingsley.

Bell, A. P., Perry, R., Peng, M., & Miller, A. J. (2014). The music therapy communication and social interaction scale (MTCSI): Developing a new Nordoff-Robbins scale and examining interrater reliability. *Music Therapy Perspectives, 32*(1), 47–55.

Bradfield, C., Carlenius, J., Gold, C., & White, M. (2007). *MT-SEAS: Music therapy special education assessment scale manual (A supplement to the SEMTAP).* Grapevine, TX: Prelude Music Therapy.

Bruscia, K. E. (1987). *Improvisational models of music therapy.* Springfield, IL: Charles C. Thomas.

Bruscia, K. E. (2005). Research topics and questions in music therapy. In B. L. Wheeler (Ed.), *Music therapy research* (2nd ed., pp. 81–93). Gilsum, NH: Barcelona.

Bruscia, K. E. (2014). *Defining music therapy* (3rd ed.). University Park, IL: Barcelona.

Carpente, J. (2013). *Individual music-centered assessment profile for neurodevelopmental disorders (IMCAP-ND): Clinical manual.* Baldwin, NY: Regina.

Carpente, J. A. (2014). Individual Music-Centered Assessment Profile for Neurodevelopmental Disorders (IMCAP-ND): New developments in music-centered evaluation. *Music Therapy Perspectives, 32*(1), 56–60.

Carpente, J. A., & Gattino, G. (2018). Inter-rater reliability on the Individual Music-Centered Assessment Profile for Neurodevelopmental Disorders (IMCAP-ND) for autism spectrum disorder. *Nordic Journal of Music Therapy, 24*(4), 297–311.

Coleman, K. A., & Brunck. B. K. (2003). *SEMTAP: Special Education Music Therapy Assessment Process handbook* (2nd ed.). Grapevine, TX: Prelude Music Therapy.

Elliott, D. J. (1995). *Music matters: A new philosophy of music education.* New York: Oxford University Press.

Elliott, D. J., & Silverman, M. (2015). *Music matters: A philosophy of music education* (2nd ed.). New York: Oxford University Press.

Greenspan, S. I., & Shanker, S. (2006). *The first idea: How symbols, language, and intelligence evolved from our early primate ancestors to modern humans.* Cambridge, MA: Da Capo.

Greenspan, S. I., & Thorndike, N. T. (1985). *First feelings.* New York: Viking.

Jacobsen, S. L. (2012). Music therapy assessment and development of parental competences in families where children have experienced emotional neglect: An investigation of the reliability and validity of the tool, assessment of parenting competencies (APC). PhD Thesis: Aalborg University, Denmark. Retrieved from http://vbn.aau.dk/files/68298796/42798_jacobsen2012.pdf

Jeong, E. (2013). Psychometric validation of a music-based attention assessment: revised for patients with traumatic brain injury. *Journal of Music Therapy, 50*(2), 66–92.

Landis, J. R., & Koch, G. G. (1977). The measurement of observer agreement for categorical data. *Biometrics,* 159–74.

Layman, D. L., Hussey, D. L., & Laing, S. J. (2002). Music therapy assessment for severely emotionally disturbed children: A pilot study. *Journal of Music Therapy, 39*(2), 164–87.

Lipe, A. (1995). The use of music performance tasks in the assessment of cognitive functioning among older adults with dementia. *Journal of Music Therapy, 32*(3), 137–51.

Loewy, J. (2000). Music psychotherapy assessment. *Music Therapy Perspectives, 18*(1), 47–58.

Magee, W. L., Siegert, R. J., Daveson, B. A., Lenton-Smith, G., & Taylor, S. M. (2014). Music Therapy Assessment Tool for Awareness in Disorders of Consciousness (MATADOC): Standardisation of the principal subscale to assess awareness in patients with disorders of consciousness. *Neuropsychological Rehabilitation, 24*(1), 101–24.

Mahoney, J. F. (2010). Interrater agreement on the Nordoff-Robbins evaluation scale 1: Client-therapist relationship in musical activity. *Music and Medicine, 2*(1), 23–28.

Nordoff, P., & Robbins, C. (2007). *Creative music therapy: A guide to fostering clinical musicianship* (2nd ed., rev. & exp.). Gilsum, NH: Barcelona.

Rogers, S. J., & Pennington, B. F. (1991). A theoretical approach to the deficits in infantile autism. *Development and Psychopathology, 3*(2), 137–62.

Rolvsjord, R. (2010). *Resource-oriented music therapy in mental health care.* Gilsum, NH: Barcelona.

Schumacher, K., & Calvet-Kruppa, C. (2007). The AQR instrument (Assessment of the Quality of Relationship): An observational instrument to assess the quality of relationship. In T. Wosh & T. Wigram (Eds.), *Microanalysis in music therapy* (pp. 49–91). London: Jessica Kingsley.

Small, C. (1998). *Musicking: The meanings of performing and listening.* Hanover: University Press of New England.

Stern, D. N. (2009). *The first relationship: Infant and mother.* Boston: Harvard University Press.

Trevarthen, C. (2011). What is it like to be a person who knows nothing? Defining the active intersubjective mind of a newborn human being. *Infant and Child Development, 20*(1), 119–35.

Waldon, E. G., & Wolfe, D. E. (2006). Predictive utility of the computer-based music perception assessment for children (CMPAC). *Journal of Music Therapy, 43*(4), 356–71.

Waldon, E. G., Lesser, A., Weeden, L., & Messick, E. (2016). The Music Attentiveness Screening Assessment, Revised (MASA-R): A study of technical adequacy. *Journal of Music Therapy, 53*(1), 75–92.

Wheeler, B. (2013). Music therapy assessment. In *Feders' the art and science of evaluation in the arts therapies: How do you know what's working?* (pp. 344–82). Springfield, IL: Charles C. Thomas.

# CHAPTER 14

......................................................................

# A CASE FOR INTEGRATIVE ASSESSMENT FROM A FREIRIAN PERSPECTIVE

......................................................................

## FRANK ABRAHAMS

"ASSESSMENT" is an overarching term that may be conceptualized in many different ways. For example, Bernice McCarthy (2012) believes that assessment is "the process of gathering, describing, or quantifying information about performance" (p. 153). Martin Fautley and Richard Colwell (2012) add that the teacher "assigns value, describes the meaning of data and observations, synthesizes experiences, and the resulting judgments indicate the merit, worth, and significance of the educational venture" (p. 477). Antony John Kunnan (2004) delimits assessment to "all methods and approaches to testing and evaluation whether in research studies or educational contexts" (p. 1). Edward Asmus (1999) adds that assessment is authentic when the work students are assigned to do engages them in "real-world" tasks outside of the school building. Some scholars (e.g., Colwell, 2008; Fisher, 2008; Linn, 2000; McDonnell, 2005) rightfully claim that assessment ensures accountability. Others disagree (e.g., Resnick & Resnick, 1992; Linn, 2000; Nelson, 2014).

Unfortunately, assessment is not a universal practice in music education, particularly in the United States. Many music teachers argue that they do not have time to assess; that students, parents, and school administrators do not consider success in music seriously; and that student achievement in music classes is illustrated by level of participation, attitude, and behavior in class rather than content mastery, artistry, or proficiency as a musical person. Further, many music teachers conducting ensembles believe that their assessment should be the concert.

Assessment is generally divided into two categories: formative and summative. And although it might be argued that there is no such thing as "summative" assessment, as all assessments are "formative" in one way or another, I recognize both forms and argue for a third category that Ryan John and I have coined "integrative" assessment (see Abrahams & John, 2015, pp. 67–69).

Formative assessment is ongoing throughout the music lesson or ensemble rehearsal. It is informal when the teacher observes groups of students working together or assesses the quality of participation, for example, by monitoring the types and numbers of questions students ask. Formative assessment may include quizzes or written assignments from students throughout the duration of the learning episode. In the best-case scenario, teachers use the results of formative assessment to revise or redirect their lessons and rehearsals.

Summative assessment happens at the conclusion of the learning episode. It could be an examination at the end of a cycle of classes, a hearing in which students sing or play their parts in an ensemble piece just prior to the final performance, a recital or jury examination, or a demonstration of a finished product at the end of a unit of instruction. Nearly always, the summative assessment includes a grade—in other words, an evaluative measurement—that weighs heavily on the student's grade. While students may receive feedback from a summative assessment, often they do not have the opportunity to revise, resubmit, or repeat the work assessed. It is truly the end, and the teacher and students move on to the next topic or performance. A final examination or large paper is a summative assessment familiar to college and university students. Standardized tests are also summative assessments. In some teacher-evaluation models, a teacher is successful when her or his students can demonstrate the successful completion of a standardized test. Outcomes are connected to student grades and teacher performance.

In this chapter I argue for the efficacy of integrative assessment. Different from the types of assessment typically used in US schools, integrative assessment is based on the ideas of Paulo Freire, who argued that teaching and learning are a partnership between the teacher and student and that learning does not take place unless both teacher and student are changed (or transformed). Briefly, and for now, integrative assessment extends the concept of reflective practice by considering the ways in which students and the teacher change as a result of teaching and learning processes. Assessment should be ongoing and include students and their teachers together. This is a departure from a more traditional application of assessment, whereby the teacher assesses the student. In this view, assessment is something the teacher does *to* the student, not *with* the student. Instead, integrative assessment is something students and teachers engage in *with* each other.

Just as teaching and learning are intertwined, so assessments need to align to both teaching and learning. Formative and summative assessments tend to focus on student outcomes. Typically, teachers determine what "students should be able to know and do" prior to teaching; they assess—both during and after the lesson—whether or not students meet a specific learning objective. In such iterations, teachers assess students in relation to predetermined ends. Considering teaching and learning as a partnership between students and their teacher, integrative assessment focuses on the teacher and students together. Consistent with a Freirian view that "there can be no teaching without learning," suggesting that teachers also need to meet specific ends, integrative assessment strategies provide both formative and summative opportunities for the teacher to be self-reflective and assess her or his teaching performance and its impact on student learning. Adding this component to the general discussion of assessment links the student/teacher and teacher/student paradigms in positive ways. In fact, as Paulo Freire (1998) wrote, "critical reflection on practice is a requirement of the relationship between theory and practice. Otherwise theory becomes simply 'blah, blah, blah,' and practice, pure activism" (p. 30).

For example, after explaining the circle of fifths to her high school music theory students, watching their confused faces during the lesson, and reviewing their poor scores on homework and again on the test, Sarita sat quietly in her office and thought about what she might have done differently. She viewed video recordings of the lessons, something required for her school-based teacher evaluation, and watched them with a critical eye, looking for clues that might inform her future practice. Sarita examined the rubric she had developed to score the tests, looking for bias, and considered carefully the explanations she had given when she explained the circle of fifths. She re-read the chapter on the circle of fifths in the theory textbook, wondering if it was indeed clear. Then she invited any students who wished to meet with her to discuss together why the lesson did not meet Sarita's expectations. She thought they might have a perspective she had missed and ideas that would make the content more clear. As a result, and at the suggestion of a student, they worked together to design an interactive game for students to play on their smartphones that presented the information in ways that might be more consistent with the learning preferences of the students. In other words, she took the formative and summative data from the students, added her own analysis and interpretation of her own teaching performance, and integrated that with input from the students. Her goal was to make instruction better.

Considering this vignette, one sees examples of Freirian principles in action. Sarita opened herself to vulnerability by sharing the power to make changes with the students. Considering peer- and self-assessments, they made decisions together.

# A Freirian View of Assessment

Freire (1998) always connected teaching and learning. He believed that teachers and learners were partners in acquiring knowledge and skills and finding meaning in content:

> Whoever teaches learns in the act of teaching, and whoever learns teaches in the act of learning. . . . The more critically one exercises one's capacity for learning, the greater is one's capacity for constructing and developing what "epistemological curiosity" without which it is not possible to obtain a complete grasp of the object of our knowledge. (pp. 31–32)

Freire was outspoken on the issue of the "banking model" of teaching and learning. First discussed in *Pedagogy of the Oppressed* (1970) and developed further in *Pedagogy of Freedom* (1998) and *Education for a Critical Consciousness* (1973), Freire explained the banking model as a process whereby the teacher, who is all-knowing, deposits information into the mental bank accounts of the students, who know nothing. The students store the information until they are called upon to withdraw it for a test. And, as with a financial bank account, once the knowledge is withdrawn, it is spent or gone. The student then returns to the state of zero balance, as he or she was in the beginning, a blank slate.

Modern assessment practices, particularly summative assessments, place value on the quantity and quality of the content withdrawn, but do not consider that it is no longer in the memory of the student. If a goal of teaching and learning is to nurture a continuous transformation by which students and their teachers construct and reconstruct knowledge, formative and summative assessments fall short. According to Freire (1998), students who merely memorize information "fail to make concrete connections between what they have read and what is happening in the world" (p. 34). Integrative assessment connects to Freirian ideas in the ways that it accounts for change in students and their teacher. It is a collaborative assessment of how the teaching and learning shaped that change.

I use two key concepts of Freire's pedagogy to examine integrative assessment: critical consciousness, sometimes called "conscientization," and the ability to "read the word and the world."

# CRITICAL CONSCIOUSNESS

Freire (1973) considered critical consciousness the only true way of knowing. It results from a sense of connectedness with reality as a participant and not as an observer. He described this more fully:

> The critically transitive consciousness is characterized by depth in the interpretation of problems; by the substitution of causal principles for magical explanations; by the testing of one's "findings" and by openness to revision; by the attempt to avoid distortion when perceiving problems and to avoid pre-conceived notions when analyzing them; by refusing to transfer responsibility; by rejecting passive positions; by soundness of argumentation; by the practice of dialogue rather than polemics; by receptivity to the new for reasons beyond mere novelty and by the good sense not to reject the old just because it is old-by accepting what is valid in both old and new. (p. 18)

For music teachers, a goal is to bring musical experiences to children that connect to real-world problems, are meaningful to them, and connect to who they are. While this goal may be true of good teaching in general, when such encounters ignite the musical imagination, inspire musical creativity, and culminate in musical performances that help children see themselves as part of a world greater than themselves and where they are included as a unique and important component part, they are well on their way to the acquisition of a critical consciousness.

For assessment, critical consciousness means that the ways teachers evaluate themselves and their students and the ways the students evaluate themselves, each other, and the teacher are imbued with a commitment to meaning making and the improvement of all beyond the boundaries of the learning content. Acquiring a critical consciousness results from dialogue, which is both verbal and/or musical, and results in a co-construction of knowledge. It includes the responsibility to take action against the hegemonic practices in schooling, including assessment, and to repair and better the experiences of both students and their teachers inside and outside the school walls.

# READ THE WORD AND THE WORLD

In Brazil, Freire was a teacher of language literacy. Many of his ideas came from that domain. Reading the word and the world is one such concept. According to Freire, reading the word and the world could take place through powerful texts that addressed or portrayed concerns that affected the lives and self-perceptions of his students. He explained that it is every teacher's ethical duty "to intervene in challenging students to critically engage with their world so they can act upon it and on it" (Freire & Macedo, 1995, p. 10). Freire advocated talking with students about issues of social inequity and injustice to develop in them the disposition and habit of mind to learn and reflect about these problems, so that they can identify the issues that oppress them and decide to act on them (Shor, 1992). Pedagogy, for Freire, hopes to empower and encourage students to believe in their own power and voice.

For music education, the focus shifts from students learning about music to students doing music as composers, performers, and listeners. Music, as an art form, provides a window on culture and reflects the cultural capital, norms, and political agendas that are in place at the time of its creation. In popular and commercial music, the folk era concurrent with the Vietnam War documents musically the protests and the inequities of that time in US history. Benjamin Britten's *War Requiem* and John Adams's opera *Nixon in China* are examples from classical music. Musical theater pieces such as *Assassins* by Stephen Sondheim and *Rent* by Jonathan Larson emphasize social injustice in ways that the news reports on television and in the press fail to. And *Hamilton* by Lin-Manuel Miranda redefines the Broadway musical in a way that could not have been imagined a decade ago. The result of his merging hip-hop, rap, and traditional music theater song styles to explicate the biography of an American patriot connected contemporary audiences to American history in ways that were thought-provoking and riveting. These composers were able to "read the word and the world" in ways that were a catalyst for audiences to shape individual perspective, thus opening up the possibilities for audience transformation. It therefore seems reasonable to suggest that the music instruction that students encounter inside school should be rich with these same opportunities. In other words, students do not just learn about Mozart; they need to perform Mozart as Mozart intended, but also to re-envision Mozart's music in new, innovative, and creative ways.

Then they will see the cultural and historical implications of Mozart's contribution to the art form through lenses that refocus the traditional conceptions of his music in ways that they find relevant to their everyday lives.

## APPLYING FREIRIAN IDEAS TO ASSESSMENT

Freire (1998) believed that "there is no teaching without learning" (see chapter 2 of *Pedagogy of Freedom*). Ali Derakhshan, Saeed Rezaei, and Minoo Alemi (2011) concur and argue that "it is essential for both learners and teachers to be involved in and have control over the assessment methods, procedures and outcomes, as well as their underlying rationale" (p. 1). Tim McNamara (2001) states that "any deliberate, sustained and explicit reflection by teachers (and by learners) on the qualities of a learner's work can be thought of as a kind of assessment" (p. 343). To frame a Freirian view of assessment, I adapt characteristics of teaching and learning described by Dennie Wolf, Janet Bixby, John Glenn, and Howard Gardner (1991) and Menucha Birenbaum (1996) as cited in Brian Lynch (2001).

*Teaching and assessment practices should be integrated.* Freire always believed that teaching and learning were connected in powerful ways. When teaching and learning are unlinked, assessments become skewed and disadvantage many students who may know the content but are not able to defend that knowledge in the context of the assessment instrument. For example, although a learning episode may have been rich with musical activity, the assessment instrument for that musical engagement asks that students reflect on it through a written document. In that case, the ability of the student as a writer is privileged over the ability of the student as active music maker. In the musical ensemble, hearing students play their parts in band and orchestra or sing in choir, where students demonstrate an understanding of the style, affect, interpretation, and musical markings in the score by performing them with musicality and accuracy, is a much-preferred and more appropriate assessment over a paper-and-pencil, short-answer test on terms and markings. Having young children compose a song that includes both steps and skips, sing it for the teacher and the class, and then explain to the class where the steps and skips occur is more genuine than asking students to raise their hands when they hear a leap or circling the skips on a musical score. Thus the "musical event" can be both a musical event and an assessment of the preparation. Such an assessment, however, is not easy. The challenge, of course, is that some students can hide their level of understanding in the mass of a large ensemble.

As someone who prepares college students to be music teachers, I see many instances in which a student struggles to write a good lesson plan but teaches a wonderful music lesson. Watching the undergraduate preservice teacher in action, I can easily observe the enthusiasm on the part of the children; the energy from the teacher; the modeling of superb musicianship; the attention to timing, pace, classroom management; and so forth. I have watched enough preservice teachers in their internship placements to claim a degree of connoisseurship (see Eisner, 1994, pp. 215–216 for an explanation of educational connoisseurship) and to be confident that my assessment is accurate. In the United States, teacher performance is often assessed by means of the documentation that teachers supply to the evaluator and not by watching the teacher perform with students in the classroom.

*Students should be active participants in the process of developing assessment procedures, including the criteria and standards by which performances are judged.* Freire believed that children come to a learning experience with knowledge gleaned from their life experiences outside of school. He believed in honoring the children by encouraging teachers to use that knowledge as the springboard to new knowledge. He would agree with spending time talking with children, in dialogue, to engage them in the process of assessment. This gives students ownership of their own success, and this type of reciprocity is consistent with Freirian ideas.

*Both the process and the product of the assessment tasks should be evaluated.* Freire's goal was always to nurture a change in perception, an ability of the student to construct meaning and to be able to use perception and meaning making as a means to read the word and the world. For that to happen, process and product must both be present in the assessment. Looking at one without the other does not present a complete picture. For example, developing a rubric to assess the final product of a composition project could involve working in small groups to brainstorm ways that students might evaluate the final product with their teacher. An example of the connection of process and product is developing some criteria to watch a recent ensemble performance in which students participated, then engaging in substantive conversations, students with their teacher, to apply those criteria and unpack the process that produced the performance.

*Assessment results should usually be in the form of a qualitative profile rather than a single score or other quantification.* Freire recognized that education is a process that places the student at the center of the learning episode. Reducing teaching and learning to a numerical score and converting all student learning and teacher effectiveness to a grade or aggregate data dehumanizes the teaching and learning process and relegates the participants to objects rather than subjects. While numbers are important, one subscribing to a Freirian perspective would not privilege it over qualitative measures. I describe examples of those qualitative measures in upcoming sections of this chapter.

# A Case for Integrative Assessment in Music Education

For Freire, the ability to decode the written word provided a conduit through which his students learned to read the world, acquire a critical consciousness, become agentive, and realize empowerment. While his students were members of the subaltern (or, existing outside "power"), his ideology and methodology transfer easily to music education. Elsewhere, I have written extensively on critical pedagogy for music education, which adopts and applies principles of Freirian ideology to music teaching and learning (see Abrahams, 2005a, 2005b, 2007, 2014). Because the ability to decode written musical notation, which contributes to what music educators call music literacy, is at the heart of many music curricula and a goal of many music teachers, ideas from Freirian teaching are applicable. The activities in music classes that attend to reading musical notation provide a way for children to represent themselves in the world beyond school. They enable students to express themselves in original musical compositions, improvise, and perform on musical instruments. In simplest terms, all such activities focus on the development of musicianship and the building of what Janet Cape (2013) calls musical people. Teachers can easily measure the success of behavioral objectives so popular in these ways of teaching and apply such successes formatively or summatively. The children either can or cannot perform the tasks. Teachers can easily develop rubrics to frame formative and summative assessments, and scores can be totaled, quantified, and aggregated and can yield simple and complex statistics. But a musical education, especially one informed by Freirian teachings, considers more than the goals of musical literacy and the skills one acquires through engagements with school music. To embrace integrative assessment is to endorse a broad view of music in schools:

1. Music education is a discipline that empowers musicianship and in the process transforms both the students and their teacher. It is a field of study to enrich and change the knowings, understandings, and perceptions that students and teachers have as individuals and as members of society.
2. Music education in schools provides opportunities for teachers and students to interact in authentic musical experiences, which are acknowledged as important and meaningful to both of them. Music education is a domain in which students can hone important twenty-first-century skills, such as critical thinking, critical acting, critical feeling, collaboration, communication, creativity, and community.
3. A musical education nurtures a student's musical potential. Such potential includes musical imagination, musical intellect, musical creativity, and musical performance.
4. Music education in schools is a community of practice (Wenger, 2000) that provides a crosswalk to connect formal music learning inside school with informal music learning outside school. It provides a window into the cultural history of the past, records the cultural history of the present, and sets the foundation for a cultural history of the future. Most important, music education adds value to students' lives (adapted from Abrahams, 2014, pp. 45–47).

To assess progress and growth of both student and teacher in an environment that embraces these constructs requires more than formative and summative assessment instruments and measures.

# UNDERSTANDING INTEGRATIVE
# ASSESSMENT

While formative and summative assessments focus on student achievement, integrative assessment considers how teaching and learning prepare students and their teacher to "read the word and the world," as Freire (1970) advocated. It adds a transformative agenda to the discourse by adding a reflective practice on the part of both teacher and student. To reiterate Freire's words, "Critical reflection on practice is a requirement of the relationship between theory and practice. Otherwise theory becomes simply 'blah, blah, blah,' and practice, pure activism" (1998, p. 30). In this section I explain how the theories discussed previously can be applied, and in the next section I provide examples of integrative assessment in a high school choral ensemble, for a third-grade classroom music lesson, and as part of a classroom music lesson at the middle school.

Integrative assessment considers both theory and practice. For example, it answers questions such as how the learning contributed to the students' acquisition of a critical consciousness (Freire, 1973). That is, could the students make meaning of the content, achieve the skill competency, and glean from the learning encounters meaningful experiences that change the way that they think about themselves and themselves in the world? In what ways was the learning a catalyst for a change in perception? Was the learning deep and meaningful? Did it add value? Can the students name, reflect critically, make meaning, and act as musical people? Did the engagements the children and their teacher have foster the acquisition of critical consciousness, conscientization, and the ability to apply musical lenses to read the world? Rather than focusing on the students' success or failure, integrative assessment points students toward empowerment and musical agency.

Integrative assessment ensures trustworthiness. Together, teachers and students discuss connections that were made, comparisons of perceptions among and between students, and nonverbal representations of conceptual understandings such as a composition or arrangement or musical performance. Integrative assessment shows teachers the ways that their students "blend and adapt expert knowledge with their own" (McCarthy, 2000, p. 159).

It is curious to me that educators are keenly concerned with differentiation. In the United States, they attend professional development programs at which they are told to match teaching with the students' individual learning styles, to adapt instruction for students with learning challenges. Yet, and perhaps this is an overstatement, when it comes to assessment, one size is supposed to fit all.

If teachers believe that the goals of music education are to promote musical agency among students, empower musicianship as they journey to become musical people, and foster the acquisition of a critical consciousness, integrative assessment can help them know if students have learned what teachers intended to teach them. More important, it helps teachers see and reflect upon how the teaching and learning episode was a catalyst for a change in perception or worldview on the part of students and teacher. As teachers reflect, they ask and answer five questions (adapted from Abrahams & John, 2015, pp. 68–69) that frame integrative assessment:

1. In what ways did the instruction provide the information for the students to solve a musical problem and/or to answer an overarching essential or focusing question, posed by the teacher, that provided a rationale for the instruction?
2. In what ways did students' individual and collective performance represent their intentions and present their worldview in a coherent manner?
3. In what ways did the engagement with the instruction and instructional content nurture a change in perception on the part of the student? In what ways did it nurture a change in perception on the part of the teacher? By spending time with children as they engage in musical endeavors during music classes and engaging in feedback with them throughout and at the end, the teacher considers the following:
4. In what ways did engagement with the instruction and content present evidence of a transformational change in the perception or self-awareness of the student?
5. It what ways did it transform the teacher's perception and self-awareness?

## ENACTING INTEGRATIVE ASSESSMENT

The following examples provide answers to these questions. Each vignette shows how teachers include integrative assessment in their self-evaluation of their own teaching and the learning episodes that students experienced.

### High School Choir

Interested in the impact of informal music learning experiences on the singers in his high school choir, Dave divided the singers into octets and charged them with arranging a Christmas carol from a recording they found on the Internet (for a complete description of the study, see Abrahams, Rafaniello, Vodicka, Westawski, & Wilson, 2017). The goal was for students to apply what they had learned in the formal setting of their high school choral experience to an informal setting without intervention from their teacher. Another goal was for the students to learn the process of arranging a choral piece by figuring out, again on their own, a process to complete the assignment. How would they select the song? Who in the group would do what task? The students had to establish some criteria, a rubric if you will, for selecting an appropriate carol and then find examples on the Internet that they believed would be suitable. Did the song lend itself to a choral arrangement? What compromises would the group have to make to accommodate an SATB ensemble when the original was for a solo singer? Would they scribe, using dictation, any of the music from the original, or would they do the entire project "by ear"? Over a period of several weeks, they worked without intervention from their teacher to create the arrangements. The goal was to perform them in the December holiday concert. That performance was the summative assessment. Dave also had a rubric he had created to assess the final performance. In addition, and from a distance, Dave collected formative assessments, watching how the students worked together and listening to the unsolicited, informal comments students made to him before and after each session. He kept a journal throughout that contained memos, observations, and comments. He also scribed his own thoughts as the project progressed.

Integrative assessment happened when, after the concert, Dave met with the members of each group to process the experience. The students told Dave that they had a new respect for composers and arrangers, and Dave noticed that the students were more responsible when attending to all of the composer's markings on the musical score. They felt they had become better singers and more critical consumers. Outside of school, they listened to music with what they described as a "new set of ears." They paid attention to inner harmonies more deliberately and became aware of timbre and texture.

Dave also felt that he had changed. He acknowledged that he had underestimated his students' abilities to select appropriate repertoire and to learn music on their own. He also shared that they had chosen music he never would have considered but realized that he needed to consider in the future. Leaders in each group emerged, and some of them were surprises to Dave. He had never thought of them as leaders. Dave also made a decision, at the request of his students, that they repeat the project in the spring and perform their arrangements at the spring concert.

From the perspective of Freirian ideas, there was a transformation on the part of students and their teacher. In addition, that transformation informed the acquisition of a critical consciousness.

## Elementary School Classroom Music

When torrential rains flooded many parts of Texas during the spring of 2016, Loni challenged her third-grade general music class to develop a playlist of songs that might make the children who were most affected by the disaster feel some comfort and know that there were children in the United States who understood empathy, compassion, and social responsibility. Her lesson centered on making appropriate musical decisions. By the end of the lesson, students would be able to select music appropriate to a specific event. As a result of the lesson, they would show empathy for people in the community and acquire self-awareness of the devastation of a natural disaster. Students would experience taking action as a social responsibility and gain perspective on the power of music to produce an emotional response.

First she asked the children to share the ways that music was important to them. As predicted, the children mentioned how music made them happy or calmed them down or was what they danced to or what made a movie exciting to watch. Then she asked them to bring to class a recorded example of a musical selection that was particularly meaningful to them. Loni was surprised at the selections they chose. Some she knew, but many she did not. Some children selected rap and hip-hop. Others selected songs from the children's television shows they regularly watched. Some brought songs that their parents or grandparents sang to and with them. Still others brought songs from the Billboard list of top-10 hits. No one brought Mozart or Chopin or recordings by the Chicago Symphony or stars of the Metropolitan Opera. No one brought an example from the music Loni had taught them or that they had learned in prior years in school music classes. This was an eye-opening revelation to Loni. Somehow, the music Loni had taught did not seem important to her students.

After a discussion of the Texas floods and the stories children had seen on the news, Loni asked her students which of the songs they had brought to class might be appropriate for their playlist. She also asked each student to write a note to a child in Texas explaining why she or he chose it. Again, Loni learned something special about each student that she did not know. After they assembled their playlist, Loni asked the children what parts of the project were meaningful to them. They shared about social responsibility, empathy, and caring. Some children cried when they wrote their notes. Clearly, Loni and her students had changed. Loni realized that she was not as in touch with what her students listened to outside of the music class as she might be. She realized that there was a bridge she needed to build to connect "her" music with "their" music. Her students became more aware of the healing music could bring.

The playlist represented the summative assessment. Children demonstrated the ability to empathize and have self-perspective. These are two qualities Grant Wiggins and Jay McTighe (2005) include in their list of the facets of understanding. Each step of the project constituted the formative assessment. The changes that Loni observed in her students and the insights Loni gained during the project and acknowledged through her interactive dialogue with them constituted integrative assessment.

## Middle School Classroom Music

The United States celebrates the birthday of civil rights icon Martin Luther King Jr. (1929–1968). To honor King's memory and to provide a window to call attention to his accomplishments, Levi built a lesson around King's seminal speech "I Have a Dream" for his seventh-grade students. Levi began by asking the children about their dreams. He was surprised and impressed that students had dreams for themselves, their families, the country, and the world. Then they listened to a recording of King giving his famous speech. They talked about marginalization, oppression, racism, poverty, homelessness, and human rights, which were issues of concern to Freire as well. Next, working with the English teacher, the students wrote speeches about their dreams. When they returned to music class, Levi played some pieces that dealt with dreams from some of his favorite Broadway musicals. As a class, they listened to "The Impossible Dream" from *Man of*

*La Mancha*, "Soliloquy" from *Carousel*, and "Wheels of a Dream" from *Ragtime*. As a class, they sang "Tomorrow" from *Annie*. They also listened to "A Lincoln Portrait" by Aaron Copland. Then, working in small groups they took "Tomorrow" and added it as theme A in a "Dream Rondo" in which they integrated parts of their speeches, performed in rap style, as the B, C, and D sections. There was brief discourse about rondo form. For a school assembly, the class presented their "Dream Rondos."

Levi met the expectations of formative assessment at each point in the lesson by monitoring student engagement. For a summative assessment, he created a rubric for the final projects. After the performance, he asked the class again to think about their dreams. He processed the experience with the students, and that input provided additional summative assessment. But listening to the student comments after the performance and hearing how their dreams had changed as a result, Levi was also able to complete integrative assessment. He heard the students talk about how the project had changed them. Levi also thought about how the project had changed him and shared those thoughts with the students. He became acutely aware of the hopes and dreams of his students—something he would not normally have known. He discovered who the good writers were and who had difficulty expressing themselves on paper. He also saw students who had been reluctant to contribute in class be impressively creative—a side of them he had not known. His typical teacher-centered lessons did not provide such opportunities. In the end, Levi resolved to do more projects like the "Dream Rondo."

# Trustworthiness and Integrative Assessment

Integrative assessment is a qualitative measure. And like qualitative research, it has no generalizability and therefore no reliability (Yin, 2015). However, there is validity or trustworthiness that one can apply to integrative assessment. This is how one assesses the assessment. In the case of integrative assessment, trustworthiness is important to claim, because it demonstrates that what the teacher has found actually happened. This is not the case with other assessments. Assessment, when done well, aligns with instructional objectives and the teaching strategies that a teacher chooses to deliver the instruction. In addition, assessment, when done well, does maintain various degrees of validity. In what follows, I discuss some of those measures of validity.

Face validity and catalytic validity provide checks and balances that give credibility to integrative assessment. For instance, face validity ensures that the instruction provided the information students needed to meet the lesson objectives. It considers the lesson design to determine whether the assessment measures what it claims to measure (Creswell, 2003; Scott & Morrison, 2006). Dialogic validity (Wolcott, 1994; Herr & Anderson, 2014) includes the students' voices and accounts for the ways their individual and collective performances represent their intentions and present their worldview in a coherent manner. Dialogic validity is helpful for the teacher to consider how the outcomes of the instruction connected to the goals of the musical experience, as well as the broad view of schooling presented earlier in the chapter. The ways the engagement with the instruction and instructional content nurtured a change in perception on the part of the student and the teacher are verified through catalytic validity (Kincheloe, 1995; Gall, Gall, & Borg, 2007). Joe Kincheloe and Peter McLaren (2000) explain catalytic validity as the extent to which the learning episode affects and changes or transforms the student's view of the world; in integrative assessment, it ensures that the teacher and students work together for transformative change. This is of paramount importance when considering Freire's goals for education. Lather (1986) explains that catalytic validity "re-orients, focuses, and energizes participants to know reality in order to better transform it" (p. 67) in ways that Freire (1973) conceptualizes as conscientization, which is knowing reality in order to better transform it. Finally, self-reflexive validity is important because from a Freirian perspective, a goal of the learning episode is to transform and change the perception or self-awareness of the students and the teacher. Self-reflexive validity confirms how society has shaped the perceptions and beliefs of the participants and specifically how these perceptions and belief systems relate to the objectives of the learning episode (Saukko, 2005). In the instance of integrative assessment, one considers social discourses as they affect the learning episode, from both the students' and teacher's points of view.

*Face validity* is addressed by the question: In what ways did the instruction provide the information for the students to meet the learning goals for the lesson? In the choral class, instructions that the teacher gave to the students to set parameters and expectations for the project provided the information they needed to complete the task. For Loni's third-grade students, the opening of the learning episode in which children shared music that they found personally meaningful and the dialogue to explicate the devastations of a natural disaster set the students on course to complete the learning objectives. Connecting to a national holiday and introducing the "I Have a Dream" speech early in the learning episode provided context for the learning goals for the middle school students.

*Dialogic validity* was addressed by the ways that performance by the students represented their intentions and provided an opportunity for students to present a cohesive worldview. This was evident in each of the learning episodes. At the high school, original arrangements of the Christmas carols reflected student perceptions and understandings of style and genre. In the elementary school, the learning episode connected to an international concern for the devastations of global warming and the powerful ways that nature affects their lives. The impact of Martin Luther King Jr. on the forward movement of civil rights and the power of the spoken word, especially when enhanced by music as in the Copland listening example, combined to show the power of artistic expression. The students' final products showed a change in thinking and the ability to be critically reflective and creative. In all three learning episodes, students were able to demonstrate Freire's desire that students learn to "read the world."

*Catalytic validity* concerns the demonstration of a change of perception on the part of the students and also the teacher. This measure connects most closely to Freirian ideology and his desire for all to acquire a critical consciousness. By developing criteria for the selection of appropriate repertoire to arrange, the high school choral students had to examine their own biases and value system. They had to wrestle with the issue of whether their choice of music was "good," and if so if it was worthy of their time to arrange. The elementary school students had to think about the ways that music affects aesthetic and emotional responses. At the middle school, the music students saw connections between words and music and the power each has to enhance the other.

*Self-reflexive validity* considered the ways that engagement with the instruction and content presented evidence of a transformational change in the perception or self-awareness of the students and the teacher. Making choices was a centerpiece of the project for the elementary school children and for the high school choral singers. Self-expression through musical composition was at the heart of the middle school experience. In each instance, students were reflective. The teachers also shared that they learned things about their students as people, as musicians, as learners, and as citizens of the world that they did not know previously. (For a more complete discussion of validity, see Higgins & Abrahams, 2010.)

# CONCLUSION

According to Darrel Walters (2010), "To assess is to attach a value to something" (p. 3). Wiggins and McTighe (2005) suggest that when students can explain, interpret, apply, and analyze different perspectives, thus shaping their own, and then have empathy or can demonstrate self-knowledge, the teacher may claim that the students understand. Abrahams and Abrahams (2012) posit that when students can ask thoughtful and critical questions, summarize, predict, clarify, and connect learning to their own lives and their lived experiences, they demonstrate not only understanding, but also agency and the acquisition of the Freirian notions of a critical consciousness and the ability to "read the word and the world."

In the 1960s it was unlikely that issues of teacher evaluation and assessing student learning were concerns of Freire when he taught the Brazilian subaltern to read Portuguese. His primary concern was to teach his students to read so that they could vote, because the ability to read was a condition of voter eligibility. Nonetheless, just as in Freire's classroom, the oppressed, marginalized children, and children with learning challenges still populate many of the classrooms in the United States and throughout the world, and issues of race, ethnicity, and social class remain. Criticisms of assessment practices in the United States that they are not fair, do not connect to teaching and learning, and focus only on the students and their ability to demonstrate the acquisition of information for an assessment remain rampant. Adding integrative to formative and summative assessments closes the loop and presents a more complete picture of teaching and learning.

# References

Abrahams, F. (2005a). The application of critical pedagogy to music teaching and learning: A literature review. *Update: Applications of Research to Music Teaching, 23*(2), 12–22.

Abrahams, F. (2005b). Transforming classroom music instruction with ideas from critical pedagogy. *Music Educators Journal, 92*(1), 62–67.

Abrahams, F. (2007). Musicing Paulo Freire: A critical pedagogy for music education. In P. McLaren & J. L. Kincheloe (Eds.), *Critical pedagogy: Where are we now?* (pp. 223–38). New York: Peter Lang.

Abrahams, F. (2014). Starbucks doesn't sell hot cross buns: Embracing new priorities for pre-service music teacher preparation programs. In M. Kaschub & J. Smith (Eds.), *Promising practices in 21st century music teacher education* (pp. 41–60). New York: Oxford University Press.

Abrahams, F., & Abrahams, D. (2012). The impact of reciprocal teaching on the development of musical understanding in high school student members of performing ensembles: An action research. In K. Swanwick (Ed.), *Music education: Major themes in education* (Vol. 3, pp. 239–59). New York: Routledge.

Abrahams, F., & John, R. (2015). *Planning instruction in music: Writing objectives, assessments, and lesson plans to engage artistic processes.* Chicago: GIA.

Abrahams, F., Rafaniello, A., Vodicka, J., Westawski, D., & Wilson, J. (2017). Going green: The application of informal music learning strategies in high school choral ensembles. In F. Abrahams & P. D. Head (Eds.), *Oxford handbook of choral pedagogy* (pp. 65–86). New York: Oxford University Press.

Asmus, E. (1999). Music assessment concepts. *Music Educators Journal, 86*(2), 19–24.

Birenbaum, M. (1996). Assessment 2000: Towards a pluralistic approach to assessment. In M. Birenbaum & F. J. R. C. Duchy (Eds.), *Alternatives in assessment of achievements, learning processes, and prior knowledge* (pp. 3–29). Dordrecht, The Netherlands: Kluwer.

Cape, J. (2013). Student perceptions of the meaningfulness of high school guitar. *Visions of Research in Music Education, 23.* Retrieved from http://www-usr.rider.edu/~vrme/v23n1/visions/Cape_Meaningfulness_of_High_School_Guitar.pdf

Colwell, R. (2008). Assessment in an increasingly politicized, accountability driven educational environment. In T. S. Brophy (Ed.), *Assessment in music education: Integrating curriculum, theory, and practice; Proceedings of the 2007 Florida Symposium of Assessment in Music Education* (pp. 3–16). Chicago: GIA Publications.

Creswell, J. W. (2003). *Research design: Qualitative, quantitative, and mixed methods approaches* (2nd ed.). Thousand Oaks, CA: SAGE.

Derakhshan, A., Rezaei, S., & Alemi, M. (2011). Alternatives in assessment or alternatives to assessment: A solution or a quandary. *International Journal of English Linguistics, 1*(1). Retrieved from https://www.researchgate.net/profile/Minoo_Alemi/publication/228644491_Alternatives_in_Assessment_or_Alternatives_to_Assessment_A_Solution_or_a_Quandary/links/0c96051ecba830a12b000000/Alternatives-in-Assessment-or-Alternatives-to-Assessment-A-Solution-or-a-Quandary.pdf

Eisner, E. W. (1994). *The educational imagination: On the design and evaluation of school programs* (3rd ed.). Upper Saddle River, NJ: Prentice Hall.

Fautley, M., & Colwell, R. (2012). Assessment in the secondary music classroom. In G. E. McPherson & G. F. Welch (Eds.), *Oxford handbook of music education* (Vol. 1, pp. 478–94). New York: Oxford University Press.

Fisher, R. (2008). Debating assessment in music education. *Research & Issues in Music Education*, 6(1). Retrieved from https://ir.stthomas.edu/rime/vol6/iss1/4/

Freire, P. (1970). *Pedagogy of the oppressed.* M. B. Ramos (Trans.). New York: Continuum.

Freire, P. (1973). *Education for critical consciousness.* New York: Continuum.

Freire, P. (1998). *Pedagogy of freedom: Ethics, democracy and civic courage.* P. Clarke (Trans.). Lanham, MD: Rowman & Littlefield.

Freire, P., & Macedo, D. (1995). A dialogue: culture, language, and race. *Harvard Educational Review*, 65(3), 377–402.

Gall, M. D., Gall, J. P., & Borg, W. R. (2007). *Education research: An introduction* (8th ed.). Boston: Pearson.

Herr, K. G., & Anderson, G. L. (2014). *The action research dissertation: A guide for students and faculty* (2nd ed.). Thousand Oaks, CA: SAGE.

Higgins, L., & Abrahams, F. (2010). Making the grade: Preservice teachers and facilitators for school and community music programs. In T. Brophy (Ed.), *The practice of assessment in music education: Frameworks, models and designs* (pp. 485–96). Chicago: GIA.

Kincheloe, J. (1995). Meet me behind the curtain: The struggle for a critical postmodern action research. In P. L. McLaren & J. M. Ciarelli (Eds.), *Critical theory and education research* (pp. 71–90). Albany: State University of New York Press.

Kincheloe, J. L., & McLaren, P. L. (2000). Rethinking critical theory and qualitative research. In N. K. Denzin & Y. S. Lincoln (Eds.), *Handbook of qualitative research* (2nd ed., pp. 138–57). Thousand Oaks, CA: SAGE.

Kunnan, A. J. (2004). Regarding language assessment. *Language Assessment Quarterly*, 1(1), 1–4.

Lather, P. (1986). Issues of validity in openly ideological research: Between a rock and a soft place. *Interchange*, 17(4), 63–84.

Linn, R. L. (2000). Assessments and accountability. *Educational Researcher*, 29(2), 4–16. doi:10.3102/0013189X029002004

Lynch, B. (2001). Rethinking assessment from a critical perspective. *Language Testing*, 18(4), 351–72. doi:10.1177/026553220101800403

McCarthy, B. (2000). *About teaching: 4MAT in the classroom.* Wauconda, IL: AboutLearning.

McCarthy, B. (2012). *The learning cycle, the 21st century and millennial learners.* Wauconda, IL: AboutLearning.

McDonnell, L. M. (2005). Assessment and accountability from the policymaker's perspective. *Yearbook of the National Society for the Study of Education*, 104(2), 35–54.

McNamara, T. (2001). Language assessment as social practice: Challenges for research. *Language Testing*, 18(4), 332–49.

Nelson, C. B. (2014, November 24). Assessing assessment. *Inside Higher Ed.* Retrieved from https://www.insidehighered.com/views/2014/11/24/essay-criticizes-state-assessment-movement-higher-education

Resnick, L. B., & Resnick, D. P. (1992). Assessing the thinking curriculum: New tools for educational reform. In B. R. Gifford & M. C. O'Connor (Eds.), *Changing assessments: Alternative views of aptitude, achievement, and instruction* (pp. 37–75). Boston: Kluwer Academic Publishers.

Saukko, P. (2005). Methodologies for cultural studies: An integrative approach. In N. K. Denzin & Y. S. Lincoln (Eds.), *The Sage handbook of qualitative research* (3rd ed., pp. 343–56). Thousand Oaks, CA: SAGE.

Scott, D., & Morrison, M. (2006). *Key ideas in educational research.* New York: Continuum.

Shor, I. (1992). *Empowering education: Critical teaching for social change*. Chicago: University of Chicago Press.

Walters, D. (2010). *A concise guide to assessing skill and knowledge with music achievement as a model*. Chicago: GIA Publications.

Wenger, E. (2000). *Communities of practice: Learning, meaning, and identity*. Cambridge, UK: Cambridge University Press.

Wiggins, G., & McTighe, J. (2005). *Understanding by design* (2nd ed.). Alexandria, VA: ASCD.

Wolcott, H. F. (1994). *Transforming qualitative data: Description, analysis, and interpretation*. Thousand Oaks, CA: SAGE.

Wolf, D., Bixby, J., Glenn, J., & Gardner, H. (1991). To use their minds well: Investigating new forms of student assessment. *Review of Research in Education, 17,* 31–74. Retrieved from http://www.jstor.org/stable/1167329

Yin, R. K. (2015). *Qualitative research from start to finish* (2nd ed.). New York: Guilford Press.

# PART III

CREATIVITY

# CHAPTER 15

........................................................................

# CULTURAL IMPERIALISM AND THE ASSESSMENT OF CREATIVE WORK

........................................................................

### JUNIPER HILL

That music is coming from such a place deep within that it's not even referencing any particular thing besides who he is.... You won't be able to say, "ah, there's bebop and there's a bit of *mbaqanga* there and there's a bit of *marabi* there. There's township and there's *goema* there."... They just kind of whirl inside him and come out.... This comes out because this is who they are. It's like a tree being a tree. It doesn't think about being that particular thing. It's just the impact of environment. (Keith Tabisher)

In this interview excerpt[1] a music educator in South Africa explains how a teenager in his youth jazz ensemble automatically incorporates African jazz-pop and vernacular styles into his improvisations.

When developing musicians have experience with multiple music cultures—a situation that is increasingly the norm—their creative expressions will likely incorporate diverse stylistic elements that reflect their personal musical knowledge. Well-meaning instructors who wish to teach learners to master an idiom may give negative feedback[2] on work that goes beyond idiomatic conventions. Problems arise when such feedback is given or interpreted in a way that devalues the musical expressions of the individual and his or her cultural background. Such value judgments can inhibit the learner's future creative endeavors in other contexts and perpetuate social and cultural inequalities.

In this chapter I aim to raise awareness of how assessments of creative work[3] may contain implicit value judgments of other music cultures; how such value judgments may (often unintentionally) perpetuate racist, classist, or cultural imperialist biases; and how such biases may threaten the creative development of our students.

I write from the perspective of an ethnomusicologist who has spent many years researching how pedagogy and other cultural and social factors can enable or inhibit creative agency. I undertook extensive qualitative ethnographic field research in South

Africa, Finland, and the United States. In these field sites, I conducted in-depth personal interviews with over one hundred classical, jazz, and folk/traditional musicians, many of whom were instructors, students, or alumni of secondary or tertiary music education programs.[4] Their voices are prioritized in this essay, affording readers deeper insights into the lived experiences and perspectives of music learners and educators from diverse cultures.

# THE VALUE OF TRANSGRESSING IDIOMATIC BOUNDARIES

I begin by discussing some of the reasons for upholding or transgressing idiomatic conventions, because much assessment of developing musicians is based on the extent to which they and their work fulfill the ideals and conventions of a particular musical idiom and community, such conventions are often imbued with significant (if not always articulated) extramusical meanings, and much creativity poses a challenge to conventions.

All idioms have associated sets of conventions relating to style and performance practice. Maintaining these conventions serves multiple musical and social purposes. Musically, shared conventions provide common vocabulary, forms, frameworks, and inspiration—all of which facilitate collective participation, collaboration, and creative activities such as improvising, arranging, and composing. Shared conventions also provide expressive codes that aid communication and stimulate meaning and aesthetic pleasure for listeners. Socially, musical conventions may become imbued with extramusical associations and symbolism that provide a means of asserting ethnic identity and socioeconomic status, invoking religious or spiritual power, capitalizing on commercial potentials, and pursuing career pathways. Most readers are likely already aware of the professional, artistic, and social benefits for developing musicians of understanding, gaining proficiency in, and being able to uphold idiomatic conventions.

It is much less common for music educators and scholars to acknowledge the value in developing musicians having the permission, opportunity, and support to go beyond idiomatic conventions. Transgressing stylistic boundaries can be significant for multiple personal, artistic, and broader societal reasons. Leading creativity scholars, such as Margaret Boden (2004) and Mihaly Csikszentmihalyi (1996), assert the significance of transformative creativity for cultural innovation. The pedagogical benefits are numerous (some of which I have discussed in Hill, 2009, 2017, and 2018). Here I focus on the value of going beyond idiomatic conventions for the sake of (1) personal authenticity, (2) sociocultural identity, and (3) social equity.

Many musicians and music learners go beyond idiomatic boundaries because they need to do so to feel that their work is personally authentic. From the second half of the twentieth century, artists and audiences in Western societies have increasingly valued the ideal of personal authenticity, in which an artist honestly expresses her personal experiences, perspectives, and emotions in her creative work (see Weisethaunet & Lindberg, 2010; Hill & Bithell, 2014; Ronström, 2014).

For example, South African jazz singer Thando describes his creative music making thus: "This is who I am, this is my authenticity coming in." For Thando, being authentic includes an acknowledgment of his multicultural role models from home and abroad:

> I grew up in a very small semi rural kind of town in the Eastern Cape and I stayed in the township of the area.... In our [Xhosa] culture, story telling is always a song. So if you'd be going to bed or something, my grandma would tell us bed time stories, like she'd always sing me some songs and you remember these melodies and... she would make up new songs and just add things in.... They had a huge influence.... Growing up my mom took us to Sunday school every single Sunday... and I think that's where I started really singing.... My mom is a Presbyterian and she is also a singer, she leads songs in church. In the African churches that is like very open.... It was all the congregation singing... all in harmony and people improvise their own parts. So like you have many lead singers. Everyone's just going crazy. So it was very cool and responsive.... Those were my first singing experiences.... [Then] I was part of a choir at our school.... They have big choir competitions in South Africa... and I used to enter that quite a lot. I was very in to [European] opera and classical singing.... We [also] had a lot of African choral songs.... They had very traditional elements. Most of them are in vernacular in Xhosa or Zulu. Most of the harmonies [are] aurally put together.... There is a lot of freedom... because it's not written down, so the harmony changes to some extent, and we're able to add that to the compositions... [as well as] dance moves or an extra chorus or dynamics.... It's not like singing in a chorus of an opera where the dynamics are written out for you where everything is like very precise. It's more about the feeling of the moment and that's what I grew up doing quite a lot.... [These types of musical experiences] have been dismissed, but [in] coming to [a university music school], and even taking music seriously as a career, it is something that you are made aware of again. It's like, oh, wait a minute, this is my heritage. This is how I came to know music and this is my authenticity. This is what's influenced me as a musician.... It's been put in the back for quite a lot—African music, all of that—because the world is becoming very international in that a lot of European and American music has a huge influence in my country.... And going back to that [musical heritage] is so liberating, like, ah, wow. (Thando)

If musicians grow up and develop as artists in a cosmopolitan urban environment, or even in a postcolonial rural environment, they will often gain experience in multiple musical styles. With personal authenticity increasingly of greater value, these young musicians ask why they can't play music that is meaningful to them, that reflects the diversity of their own experiences.

Idiomatic conventions are seldom associated with music only; they can be deeply attached to sociocultural identity, as numerous ethnomusicologists and indeed scholars from all music disciplines have demonstrated (see, e.g., Stokes, 1997; MacDonald,

Hargreaves, & Miell, 2017). This is particularly true of folk and traditional musics, which remain deeply linked with ethnic, cultural, and national identities. This is a legacy of the romantic nationalist ideology initiated by eighteenth-century German philosopher Gottfried von Herder and his associates, who espoused the idea that folk music represents the "soul" of the folk (see Wilson, 1973). Classical music also has associations with identity, especially class identity within the Western world (see, e.g., Small, 1998). In the postcolonial world, Western classical music may carry connotations related to cultural imperialism. Jazz may be considered by some in the United States an African American classical music or an original American vernacular music. In South Africa jazz may carry other connotations, such as associations with the freedom and anti-apartheid movements (see Ansell, 2004; Ballantine, 2005; Kelley, 2012; Muller, 2013).

South African jazz composer Kyle Shepherd explains how the different musical elements he incorporates into his creative work are deeply connected to his identity:

We had a piano at home and I thought why don't I try?...I just started composing and I wasn't thinking that I'm composing in a style—that wasn't the thought process. It was just compositions. Whatever I was composing actually had a specific context...it was natural and it was personal....Stylistically I seemed to know without really having to think about it....The music I was composing was heavily influenced by the music from Cape Town....I grew up playing violin with some of the *klopse* [creole carnival troupes] and the Malay choirs....It's strong cultural music and so my contact with that obviously stays....Then with the African traditional music, I had many Xhosa friends and Zulu friends in the area that I grew up in, in the Cape Flats [townships]...and so when I hear that music it just never seems foreign. When I play other styles of music, like bebop, it takes more effort to play in the style...but when I play this traditional music or *goema* [creole carnival music], I don't have to think about it. It's just natural....[People are] influenced as much as they allow themselves to be....The racial thing unfortunately does come a lot in South Africa. Somebody made a big mistake once by asking me why I play with white musicians and I took total offense to that because we don't think about it like that. I think that time in South Africa is now over and we're trying to create this transformation within ourselves. And that's difficult because of our socio-political climate. We're making efforts....I think from my generation we don't really think about white musicians, black musicians, and coloured[5] musicians. We're all making music together....As a modern contemporary musician who is living now, we have all these influences and there's all these things that we listen to. It's not only jazz, it's not only classical music, it's not only traditional music, it's also contemporary music. And so I think the only way you ever are going to come out with that context we are taking about—the individual context—is if you take in all of that....Then when I'm composing I don't really think, "oh, I want to put this element now." It just starts coming out because I listen to quite a lot of music....[I was] music making in that [personal] context and making music in the context of being a South African, trying to assimilate all those elements to a point that it dissolves into something much bigger than it sounds. At that time, maybe five or six years ago, I was very much caught up in the South African identity within music, which was a necessary step. That's why I made a very conscientious effort to assimilate all of these traditional things that I grew up with. Where I am right now, I think that I'm playing more universal music....For me it's again just a personal music. (Kyle Shepherd)

As we can see, creating music that draws from multiple styles and that fits comfortably within no established idiom is not an abstract exercise, nor is it intentionally defiant for the sake of shock value, novelty, or antiestablishment aggression—potential motives that some other interviewees critiqued as distasteful or insincere. For Shepherd, it is a deeply personal creative process that confirms his multicultural heritage. His journey to realize his artistic vision developed intertwined with his journey to define his identity, first as a South African in the sociopolitical context of a nation actively embroiled in struggles to overcome and move beyond a racist and classist past (and present), and second as a more universally oriented human being.

These South African musicians present a moving argument, which is personal, artistic, and political, for playing across and beyond idiomatic boundaries. Similar arguments were made by musicians I interviewed in the United States and in Finland, especially ones who emphasized a desire for personal authenticity and the freedom to incorporate and express the diversity of one's life and musical experiences. Recently I have found Finnish contemporary folk musicians construing this desire as their artistic right, effectively displacing the formerly dominant nationalist preservationist ethos of much revived folk music (see Hill, 2014). Several musicians from different countries proposed leaving stylistic labels behind and simply calling their work "music."

If for some musicians transcending idioms is an assertion of individual identity, for others it is a means of bringing people together across social barriers. Adriaan Brand, the director of a community music program on a South African farm, shares some of his story:

I am an Afrikaans first-language speaker. Most people would view me looking like I do, speaking like I do...and would think I represent white people, white Afrikaans speakers, the oppressor. But that's not even [dark ironic laughter] the beginning of the story. I come from a family with a deeply traumatic history. Very much tied into the apartheid years....The woman I grew up with as my grandmother was my dad's step-mother, the woman who raised him....She was from a mixed family. Managed herself to do the very devaluing thing of trying for white then succeeding while half of her brothers and sisters did the same and did not, quote, succeed. So we had a secret family life, nightly visits. Really, really very heartbreaking sad story. People falling in love across what was then quite a tangible color line in terms of the law. And hiding their love, needing to hide it, abortions, pain, trauma, bitterness, forgiveness, love....But in the music, in the dancing there was no boundary. And I grew up as a musician in that context. I played with uncles and aunties, white and colored mixed. The music that we appreciate here is the music that I grew up with....Whenever we perform to an ethnically mixed audience of South Africans of various language speaking groups—even though the music is Afrikaans, the beat is South African, it's pan-South African, and the...melodic narrative, psalmodic harmonic and melodic progression...[is] indigenous at its center, open, major 1, 4, 5 chords...an open and transcendent harmony—that's where I see South Africans can experience a oneness that is real, as a nation, in our music, because we have internalized that so deeply. It's part of our soul. A so-called black gospel choir sings and I burst into tears and sing with them. Sometimes I can sing and sometimes I can't. It hits me too deeply, you know. So what is it that happens there? It's social healing, a sort of healing of the wounds created by that axe of segregation, the devaluing of it. And that devaluing is something I saw from a young age. I felt it with my family.

Brand shows us the social, personal, and political importance of acknowledging and valuing a mixed musical heritage. Embracing musical diversity thus can be a strong political statement and an attempt to realize a more utopian society that has moved beyond racialized strife.

Even though making music across idioms can be valuable on many personal, artistic, and social levels, idiomatic boundaries are frequently fiercely enforced.

# The Enforcement of Idiomatic Conventions

Within academia, academies, and schools, where idiomatic boundaries are so deeply entrenched, it is easy to take them for granted, and so it is worth pointing out that idiomatic conventions need to be actively enforced to be maintained, at least in our contemporary cosmopolitan societies. And such enforced maintenance can have a powerful influence on creative development.

Imagine a developing musician who grows up immersed in an environment in which he is only exposed to one musical idiom. His creative expressions would most likely conform inherently to idiomatic conventions, and there would not necessarily be any conflict between the conventions and his sense of personal authenticity and identity. Perhaps there are some isolated homogenous villages remaining in which this is the case. I interviewed a choral conductor-composer-educator who grew up in a rural village in South Africa, who described such a scenario to me:

Improvisation is in almost all the [black South African] cultures....For instance, this song is Tswana and within that specific kind of singing the Tswanas are able to do whatever they want....[JH: So there's an acceptable range of what you're allowed to do?] I wouldn't say allowed or expected to do. It's like you can't do what you don't know. So that's why it's something that becomes acceptable. It's just because everybody understands it, knows it. It's not a question of you can't or you can. It's just that you grew up listening to this, so you're confined by the knowledge that you have. It's not as though there are people who make rules. There are no rules....People just know what to do. (Sibusiso Njeza)

However, given the extent of urbanization, the sweep of colonialism and imperialism, the frequency of migration and travel, and the exponential growth of media access across the globe, I argue that this type of situation is the exception rather than the norm. For the millions of individuals around the world who have experience with multiple musical idioms, stylistic boundaries are not maintained naturally, in the sense that musicians are only nurtured in music from their one home idiom; rather, those boundaries must be actively enforced if they are to be maintained. When cosmopolitan young musicians improvise or compose what comes to them "naturally," they most likely draw upon their multiple musical influences—as exemplified in the quotations from Keith Tabisher and Kyle Shepherd—and so their creative work may be censored to fit idiomatic conventions.

The most effective policing of boundaries is achieved through formal assessment and informal feedback from instructors and other authority figures. As stated previously, I believe there is value in teaching developing musicians to understand, perform, and create within specific musical conventions. If the pedagogical goal is for a student to become proficient in a particular idiom, is it not appropriate for assessments to critique work that strays beyond the boundaries of the idiom? Yes and no. There is a big difference between explaining to learners how to achieve a result that fits into the conventions of a particular musical community and passing value judgments that assert that certain musical expressions are correct/incorrect, good/bad, beautiful/ugly, more/less valuable, and even honorable/shameful. Such judgments can be extremely inhibiting of creativity (for reasons explained further later in this chapter). They are often subtle and are unfortunately very common.

Here I share the experiences of musicians who received devaluing feedback on their creative work. South African composer Kyle Shepherd continues his story:

I'm very aware of the avenues in music that may not be creative....Without any offence to anyone, I think, unfortunately, teaching can often be counter-creative....When I came to this university, I was hearing other things in my head than what they were teaching....I was into [South African free jazz musician] Abdullah Ibrahim, into traditional music, into all these things and it was not endorsed here. So as a young seventeen-year-old or something, that leaves you in an incredibly vulnerable unsure kind of place. You just left school and you're entering this world, this life of some kind of independence, and then to have your ideas totally shot down is a disheartening thing...not in a sense that they drove a stake right through it but I was receptive enough to know that firstly they weren't encouraging it and subtly they were discouraging. It would be simple things, like when you sit down and play that way [the instructor] would say "yes, that's fine, but it's not really jazz." And so it becomes that argument again, that Wynton Marsalis–like very militarian type way of arguing what jazz is, and nationalizing it as…a purely American art form, which I think is presumptuous.…Always this power struggle and that's why I eventually had to leave.

As a young student, Shepherd did not have the authority to pursue an artistic vision that did not align with that of his instructors. He took an alternative pathway to receive legitimization and recognition (see Hill, 2018), and his work is now lauded by professors in the very institution where, according to Shepherd, others did not encourage him to pursue it.

Despite the current recognition of Shepherd's work, similar conflicts continue in jazz education in South Africa. Current vocal student Thando, who also has already been quoted, reveals how his instructor's feedback affected him:

Once you step out and you say "okay, this is what I think, this is me, this is my forte, this is who I am, this is my authenticity coming in," and a teacher, someone you look up to obviously, says they're not really keen on your arrangement, it's a bit disconcerting, disheartening.…I was like, "what do you mean?" I worked so hard, and because it was so personal, because I felt like it was something that was real to me…for a very long while [it made me more hesitant to really do my own personal interpretations]. You stick to the rubric…like getting things right for the certificate.…To a certain extent it paralyses your creativity for a while because you now think that your work is not good enough. And especially if you are a growing musician who's in an institution you look up to your teachers…they have a huge influence on your creativity and it changes your self-image and your perspective and what you think is okay. (Thando)

Similarly, in Finland academically trained jazz musicians such as Anja, quoted here, reported that instructors admonished them with critiques such as "that wasn't real jazz" when they incorporated vernacular styles into their music:

I thought that with my band I had found the music in my way and my style and my voice, and I felt really good. But then when I did the final concert [for my bachelor of music degree], the critiques I got were really quite negative, that I did something that wasn't real jazz.…The professor also said…"I know you can actually do jazz, why didn't you do it?"…Of course I felt terrible. (Anja)

Such feedback is not limited to jazz. For example, a black South African composer of art music was deflated by university-trained white composers who admonished him for not following the rules:

I've been writing music, composing music but because I haven't studied music.…I don't really understand music notation, but I'm trying. What is really discouraging me is when I talk to the people who know music they always make my score out to be like, "this is wrong, you can't do, you can't do that... you can't have this chord because it's dishonored. It doesn't sound nice. You can move from this to that." Then [I might think, aargh], anything as complicated as this thing is I can't do. (Dumile)

Feedback based on aesthetic value judgments—like that received by Kyle, Anja, Thando, and Dumile—can serve as a policing of the boundaries of acceptability for a given community and style. These types of feedback function as social and psychological punishment for not conforming to established norms and/or elite conventions (see Scheff, 1988; Hill, 2018).[6] Yet nonconformity is an essential component of creativity. Indeed, the most transformative types of creativity challenge our existing systems and rules of thought, as Boden (2004) demonstrates in the sciences and as the then revolutionary work of Bach, Beethoven, Stockhausen, Cage, Armstrong, Coltrane, Monk, Davis, the Beatles, and many others demonstrates in music. All these artists broke the aesthetic rules of the normative musical idiom of their upbringing. So to be creative in a transformative sense—which Csikszentmihalyi (1996) considers to be the only creativity of any value—entails running the risk of being told "that's not real jazz," "that's not a proper sound," "that's not a correct chord progression," or "you can't write scores like this."

Conventions of style and practice must be learned in order for musical idioms to be maintained. Yet the manner in which idiomatic boundaries are often enforced becomes a form of social pressure to conform that can significantly inhibit creativity. To be creative in spite of these messages requires a substantial amount of self-confidence and courage, which can be undermined by both actual and anticipated negative feedback. It also requires outside support and resources, to which not all music learners have access. I discuss the psychological impacts of negative feedback on creativity further later in the chapter, but first I address the cultural and social power dynamics of judging creative work.

# Cultural Value Judgments and Hidden Cultural Imperialism

The not uncommon experience of subtly delivered but powerfully felt idiomatic policing from well-meaning instructors results from a conflict of values and social positions. On the surface, the conflict appears to be between, on one side, a young musician's desire to develop personally meaningful and sociopolitically relevant artistry, and on the other side, an instructor's aim for learners to develop proficiency within a specific idiom and the means of being professionally successful. A deeper and somewhat less explicit conflict is the struggle for legitimacy of an oppressed culture versus a threat to the racially and economically unequal status quo.

This is how the policing and transgressing of idiomatic boundaries becomes political. Taking ethnic, national, class, and colonial/imperialist connotations into account, maintaining idiomatic boundaries may take on unintended (or at times intended) sinister implications related to racism, xenophobia, neocolonialism, or fascism. Attempts to maintain musical purity may be (mis)interpreted as attempts to maintain racial or ethnic purity.[7] Preserving classical music conventions may be a way of maintaining an elitist upper-class lifestyle or part of the strategy for those who do not enjoy such a lifestyle or have the status to strive for it.

It is not always easy to recognize the racism, classism, and cultural imperialism inherent in musical assessment, especially when they are subtle and couched in aesthetic terminology. Notice first that in all of the examples cited here, the creative work that was devalued had drawn on musical elements from oppressed cultures, including lower-class popular musics, African traditional musics, and African jazz. Second, look at the context: these assessments occurred in institutional settings in which curricula, funding, and even building allocation often indicate a prioritization of American and European art/academic music over non-Western and vernacular expressions. Finally, if we probe the attitudes of instructors and program leaders, prejudices may be revealed.

For example, the leading tertiary level jazz program in Cape Town (whose director and highest-ranking instructors are white) has been criticized for valuing American jazz over South African jazz. When I asked a senior white jazz professor about this apparent emphasis in their curriculum, he expressed the following opinion:

> It's nice to be able to play South African style and appreciate that, enjoy it. It's great fun, but that's just one part of jazz. I think people here actually try to make it more than it really is.... It's nice but it's—what it is, you know, I mean it's—you know, a lot of the so called "great players" were really not that great. I mean, they couldn't read, they couldn't play their instruments in tune, they were playing on bad equipment, they were uneducated. And it's not their fault, it was part of the state system, apartheid kept them down. They had to develop on their own and learn what they could in bits and pieces from wherever they could get it. I can say this very frankly, our students actually play a lot better than a lot of the so-called "greats." (Colin)

These criticisms reveal multiple underlying prejudices. For an academic musician to call an idiom nice, enjoyable, and fun is to dismiss it as not serious music. To criticize instrument quality and lack of education is classist—a type of classism that carries racist connotations (since economic inequality is racialized and racial stereotypes are often inferred from economic disadvantage; see Jost & Banaji, 1994, p. 12). To value notation reading over aural skills and the Western hegemonic intonation system over the pitch sensibilities of other cultures is ethnocentric and culturally imperialist. As a black South African jazz guitarist explains,

> Some people believe that South Africans—or Africans in general—play jazz differently: slightly "out of tune." But take it as the South African style. Pushing the notes is the way we sing. (Selaelo Selota cited in Ansell, 2005, p. 119)

Colin's reference to education might also refer to music theory training and the Western elite prioritization of harmonic complexity over other forms of musical sophistication. These Western ethnocentric/imperialist musical attitudes have a long history dating back to colonial times (for early examples, see Wallaschek, 1893). Colin's dismissive attitude also reveals his ignorance or disregard of many aspects of South African jazz, including the educational opportunities in black township art centers (such as Dorkier House and Fuba), the ethnic diversity of the musicians who developed it, and its tremendously rich variety of styles (as documented, e.g., by Ansell, 2005; Ballantine, 2012; Coplan, 2008; Muller, 2008; and Muller & Benjamin, 2011). It also reveals an American centrism. The majority of canonical American jazz musicians came from similar economically disadvantaged and informally trained backgrounds, but they are romantically considered geniuses who rose above the systemic racism they faced; it would seem that South African musicians, legends though they may be, do not qualify for genius status.

The white jazz music educators whom I interviewed in Cape Town do not appear to be explicitly racist. Many dedicate tremendous time and energy to educating nonwhite musicians, collaborate regularly with artists of multiple backgrounds, pride themselves on their previous anti-apartheid activities, and go to great lengths to distance themselves from the image of the racist white South African. Attitudes and prejudices vary from individual to individual, and it is likely that some students have been unlucky to work with instructors who are more prejudiced. However, it is also likely that instructors who consciously desire not to be prejudiced and intend to be egalitarian in their teaching have unconsciously and even against their will imbibed implicit ethnocentric, racist, and classist associations and attitudes. Indeed, given the prevalence of stereotyping in public discourse and the reality of social inequalities—in South Africa as well as in North America and Europe—it would be virtually impossible not to. In research on implicit social cognition, social psychologists have demonstrated that individuals ordinarily and unconsciously absorb stereotyping associations and attitudes from the culture around them that may contradict the individuals' explicit values (Jost & Banaji, 1994; Nosek, Hawkins, & Frazier, 2012).

The reader should keep in mind that these issues are relevant globally, even if they remain implicit or under the radar in some cultural settings. I have chosen more examples from South Africa because of their articulateness; sensitive issues of race, class, and social and political oppression tend to be more explicitly addressed in public discourse in South Africa than in North America or Europe. Since Cape Town's jazz scene is the most ethnically diverse and integrated of the nine case studies I researched, its stylistic boundaries and their social significance are the most contested—yet it is the very contestation of these boundaries that has fostered a great flourishing of creativity.

A major challenge facing instructors, critics, and musicians, then, is to become aware of and challenge how implicit biases influence our musical values and judgments. Blatantly prejudiced criticisms may be easier for students to dismiss. However, when musical assessments and curricular priorities founded in ethnocentrism, racism, classism, and cultural imperialism are disguised in an apparently neutral language of musical aesthetics, they become more powerful, insidious, and oppressive. Another challenge is to deliver feedback in a manner that is critically constructive without being personally or culturally destructive or devaluing. The ultimate challenge is to generate curricula and assessment practices that actively resist ethnocentrism, racism, classism, and cultural imperialism.

# The Far-Reaching Impacts
# of Devaluing Feedback

Whether based on underlying prejudices or not, feedback that is delivered or received in a devaluing and destructive way will in most cases inhibit creative development:

> When you have just negative feedback, it grows and grows. Then you have fear. And after that there can be some locks. Why are you so nervous, eh? Why can't you play so good anymore, eh? You can't find your technique or your creative ideas anymore. (Liisa, Finnish pianist and music educator)

Many of the musicians I interviewed had struggled with negative feedback that they had received from their instructors for incorporating musical elements that were not considered to be "honored," valued, worthy, or "real" according to their instructors' aesthetic and cultural value system. Here I define negative feedback as feedback that is delivered or interpreted in an overly critical, overly personal, or destructive manner— as opposed to constructively critical feedback, which helps a musician improve and develop without devaluing her person, work, artistic vision, or culture. Negative feedback can have long-lasting impacts far beyond the immediate assessment context. It can thwart creativity by leading to psychological and emotional struggles, musical problems, and adverse motivation to take fewer creative risks. Of the detrimental consequences of negative feedback that surfaced in my research, all appear to have stemmed from assessments given by authority figures, including teachers and examiners (especially in classical and jazz conservatory programs) as well as critics (whether of classical, jazz, or folk music).

I intertwine examples from distinct musical communities because the psychological impacts experienced by musicians from different cultures are more similar than different—a reminder of our common humanity irrespective of our ethnic, national, and musical identities. Note that in the following narratives, many musicians use the pronoun "you" instead of "I" when speaking about their own personal experiences; this creates distance so that situations can be discussed with less embarrassment or analyzed from a less personal perspective.

Negative feedback can be particularly powerful in influencing future behavior because many musicians find it difficult to separate their concept of self from their creative work. A Helsinkian jazz and folk singer reflects:

In situations where you have very strict rules then it's easier to separate, "ok, this is my work...it goes well or poorly or somewhere in between and that's it." But creativity is so much combined in the person that it's much more sensitive....If you sense that some person doesn't like what you do or is very critical about it...you feel like you are not accepted there....It feels like you are a bit locked...and you are not allowed to try all the limits....It's mainly from how you feel inside and how confident you feel about yourself that day. (Piia)

The highly personal nature of creative work makes it easier to internalize negative feedback, which can lead to intense self-criticism, a negative self-image, and in some cases depression. A Finnish violist elaborates:

If the teacher is criticizing you a lot for this, I think this is very dangerous. You can be really frightened of these mistakes, and also in music especially we can't separate ourselves and our personality from what we are doing. We can't just say "ok, it was just my playing." It's not just my playing, it is me. So it is a hit to me, or to the student, and then it is built into the student, and they start to criticize themselves in these very, very destructive ways, so that you're like in a roller coaster. If you succeed, you're good, as a person also, so then I can like myself, and then when I don't succeed, I'm down in the roller-coaster again, and now I'm a bad person and I don't like myself. It's a horrible way to be. I have been in that roller-coaster and so have almost all my students. (Sirpa)

Playing creatively is risky because of the potential impacts of anticipated feedback on one's emotional state and personal image. Sirpa continues:

I'm taking a risk of being myself in front of other people. That I will play in my own way...really from my full heart, means that you're very very emotional when playing. When you play like that most people like it very much...normally that touches them.... Then there are often a few people in the audience who criticize this and think this is ridiculous or too emotional or "oh, you can't play Brahms like this." So when you are very open it means that you're in a very sensitive mood, and then if someone would now come with some big boots and POW! jump on you like this mentally then this could hurt you very much. So it is a big risk. (Sirpa)

When past feedback is internalized individuals may become conditioned to fear future feedback (see Kenny, 2011). Such conditioning may have long-term impacts, as in the case of this middle-aged Finnish jazz musician who continues to be affected by experiences from his early twenties:

There were some teachers who were very critical and...at times it made me fearful and depressed. Made me feel like I was nothing and that I couldn't do anything right....[JH: How did you overcome that?] Well, I still haven't, I still haven't, you know....I found that very discouraging....That competitive attitude somehow has created this mind-set that whenever you play a solo you need to prove something. (Oskar)

Many musicians recounted feeling tremendous pressure to prove themselves, which is related to a desire for positive judgment from others. This pressure may be motivational. "Sometimes the anxiety may result in a surprisingly good performance," Oskar reflects, before adding, "but it's just not comfortable and, eh, I want to enjoy my life. I don't want to suffer." More commonly musicians experience the anticipation of feedback as emotionally disturbing, distracting from flow, leading to self-censorship, and stunting their willingness to take creative risks.

Such psychological pressure can be "distressing" when it "smothers and puts out the fire to want to play," in the words of a prominent Finnish folk composer (Ville). Musicians from multiple countries reported that negative feedback adversely affected their motivation to do original work. This adverse motivation not to take creative risks may be heightened when feedback is given on creative work connected to one's personal and cultural identity.

Psychologists Edward Deci and Richard Ryan (2002) propose a continuum of motivation, from external to highly internalized. At one end of the spectrum are completely external motivations, such as doing an activity purely to earn a degree or remuneration. Second are slightly internalized external motivators. These are self-esteem contingent, or dependent on the feedback and judgment of others, such as doing something for a good grade or review. Third are highly internalized motivators, which occur when an activity becomes linked to one's own sense of identity—in other words, making music in such a way that you perceive yourself to be a good or correct musician. This reflects an internalization of values. Fourth is intrinsic motivation, or doing an activity purely for the pleasure or satisfaction of doing it. Deci and Ryan found that the greater the degree of internalization, the more powerful, influential, and long-lasting the motivation. This model of motivation, known as self-determination theory, is often applied by educators and social workers to encourage positive, healthy, or otherwise socially desirable behavior. Here we can use this tool to help understand adverse motivators: the social pressures that encourage individuals to restrict their creativity. Following this model, direct punishment, such as failing an exam, would carry the least power to influence an individual's behavior; socially induced emotions, such as shame from negative feedback, would be somewhat influential; the anticipation of judgment from others, often experienced as anxiety, would be even more influential; and the most powerful influence would be the internalization of norms as values, often related to an individual's self-identity and self-perception. These adverse motivators operate in tension with individuals' intrinsic desire to be creative.

In real life, the pressures from strict exam and degree criteria, negative feedback, anticipation of feedback, and internalized values and self-image can have a powerful, and unfortunately often inhibitive, impact on creative development. For example, the South African jazz student Thando reports that instead of pursuing the personal authenticity and expressing the diverse musical influences that he enthusiastically described in his interview, "I've learned throughout the years to become almost like a carbon copy of the jazz singers that have passed." He reports that the feedback he received from his instructors "paralyzed" his creativity, and his diverse musical heritage has again been placed on the back burner.

# CHALLENGES AND RECOMMENDATIONS

Assessing creative work is often challenging, even more so in culturally diverse learning environments in which students and assessors may not hold the same musical values. In my field research, I unfortunately encountered numerous musicians who felt that their instructors had devalued their personal creative expressions, which in many cases reflected their diverse musical heritages. Such devaluing feedback can inhibit individual creative development, stifle innovation, and perpetuate sociocultural power imbalances.

I believe that in most cases this is not the instructors' intent. Indeed, many of us express value judgments without even being aware we are doing so. For example, I recently attended a composition workshop for music educators at which the instructor admonished our class to avoid the harmonic intervals of major and minor seconds, labeling these intervals "egregious sounding" and "bad crunchies." She was probably not aware that in many cultures in our world the beats created by close intervals are considered pleasing. Consonance and dissonance—like most aspects of musical aesthetics—are culturally relative cultural constructs. Participants had traveled from four continents to attend this intensive course. What if one of her students or her students' students came from a music culture where major seconds are common and considered pleasing, such as the Shop region of Bulgaria?[8] What if that Bulgarian student wanted to include major seconds in his improvisation or composition, just because such intervals came naturally to him? What would it do to that learner's self-esteem and motivation to take future creative risks if his teacher told him that the sounds he considered beautiful were ugly and should be avoided? Creative artists, especially learners, can be extraordinarily sensitive; even seemingly benign feedback can be interpreted in a very personal, negative way.

As music educators, I believe that we should aim to assess creative work in such a way that our critical feedback is not interpreted as devaluing anyone's personal identity or cultural heritage. There are no simple solutions, but I have a few strategies to propose that are drawn from the insights of the many musicians I interviewed.

The first challenge is to deliver critical feedback in a manner that is constructive and not negative. Drawing on musicians' experiences from multiple cultures, I identified five tactics that exemplify how critical assessment can be delivered in a manner supportive of creative development (see Hill, 2018). The first is to make the feedback clear, specific, and directed at particular aspects of the work—and not at the person—thereby raising awareness of specific items for future attention. The second key tactic is to use a conversational style with a mutual exchange of questioning and dialogue between the feedback giver and recipient, which can occur in informal chat sessions or in more structured environments and formal assessments (such as in Liz Lerman's critical response process; Lerman & Borstel, 2003). Heikki Laitinen explains how the Sibelius Academy Folk Music Department came to embrace a conversational approach in their exam board sessions following student recitals:

> At first we copied [our assessment method] directly from classical music and a long time went by before we noticed that…it leads to humiliation and subjugation.…So now what we do is first the student writes what he will do and what he aspires to in this examination, so that we don't discuss those types of things that he isn't even trying to do. And then after the examination the teacher speaks about what kind of project this has been. Then the student speaks and only after that is it the committee's turn.…The committee is instructed that it's preferable to ask questions than give answers.…Generally it's a conversation.… [The most effective conversations focus on these questions:] What kind of artist am I, how do I develop as an artist, how do I plan to develop, and can I do something so that I might advance further? What obstacles are there?…What should be done in my future study?

The third tactic is to choose the right time. "Feedback is generally too late when it comes after the examination," Heikki Laitinen points out. If critical feedback comes too early, however, it can smother the generation of raw ideas before they have a chance to be developed into something better. The fourth tactic is to establish a respectful and trusting relationship in which the recipient feels valued as a person regardless of how critical the feedback is. The fifth tactic is for assessors to acknowledge and recipients to be aware of the subjectivity and biases of the feedback.

A bigger challenge is to work toward giving feedback in both formal and informal assessment situations without passing value judgments. This involves self-reflection and conscientiousness on the part of assessors in terms of how we think of and label different elements of musical sound and style. What do we think of as good/bad, correct/wrong, beautiful/ugly? Common examples include intonation, timbre, harmony, timing, voicing, and complexity versus simplicity.[9] And how might the musical values of our students' cultures and subcultures be different? Here it would be helpful to become familiar with and learn to appreciate the styles, aesthetic preferences, and performance practices of diverse music cultures, especially those of our students and colleagues, including oral and informally learned music.[10]

In certain situations, teaching musical values may be a pedagogical aim, and this is where it is important to provide contextualization. It is worth explicitly articulating that what we think of as musical rules were developed to serve as explanatory guidelines for how to achieve a certain style. For example, "if you wish to compose or improvise music that fits in and sounds good to [nineteenth-century German romantic music or American bebop or South African gospel music] aficionados, these are the types of harmonic progressions and voicings that will help you achieve that." And it is especially important to explicitly articulate when creative work will be judged in part by how well it adheres to the rules or conventions of a particular style or idiom.

An even bigger challenge is to structure our curricula, assignments, and learning environments in such a way that they support creative work that challenges idiomatic conventions. This entails demonstrating that diverse musical expressions are valued by including them in our teaching content. It also entails providing space for both idiomatic and nonidiomatic creative development at both the exploratory and more finished stages. A good model is the Sibelius Academy Folk Music Department, which teaches improvisation and composition according to traditional models, offers exploratory free improvisation courses, and also requires a series of recitals, with the first two focusing on traditional styles and the third explicitly showcasing the student's "own" music (see Hill, 2018, 2009). In my own teaching (I developed a performance class called Creatively Courageous, informed by my creativity research), I have been striving to develop the assessment criteria for the final performances in conversation with the students based on their artistic visions.

In conclusion, I propose that by embracing musical stylistic hybridity we can help our students acknowledge, explore, and celebrate their diverse cultural heritages and experiences. And in these ways, perhaps we can take some small but meaningful steps to better support both individual creative development and social justice.

## INTERVIEWS CITED

Adriaan Brand. Personal interview. Franschhoek, South Africa. 2012.
Anja (pseudonym). Personal interview. Helsinki, Finland. 2012.
Colin (pseudonym). Personal interview. Cape Town, South Africa. 2012.
Eduard (pseudonym). Personal interview. Cape Town, South Africa. 2012.
Heikki Laitinen. Personal interview. Helsinki, Finland. 2008.
Jasper (pseudonym). Personal interview. Cape Town area, South Africa. 2012.
Keith Tabisher. Personal interview. Cape Town, South Africa. 2012.
Kyle Shepherd. Personal interview. Cape Town, South Africa. 2012.
Liisa (pseudonym). Personal interview. Helsinki, Finland. 2012.
Marlo (pseudonym). Personal interview. Cape Town, South Africa. 2012.
Sibusiso Njeza. Personal interview. Cape Town, South Africa. 2012.
Thando (pseudonym). Personal interview. Cape Town, South Africa. 2012.
Oskar (pseudonym). Personal interview. Helsinki, Finland. 2012.
Piia (pseudonym). Personal interview. Helsinki, Finland. 2012.
Sirpa (pseudonym). Personal interview. Helsinki, Finland. 2012.
Ville (pseudonym). Personal interview. Helsinki, Finland. 2008.

## NOTES

1. All interviews were conducted in person by the author. Full citation details are provided in the "Interviews Cited" section. Some interview excerpts are attributed to a first name only; this indicates a pseudonym.

2. I use "feedback" in a broad sense to encompass formal assessment, informal feedback, and any kind of judgment that is delivered, whether in writing, verbally, or nonverbally, to the creator/performer/learner.

3. I take a phenomenological or experiential approach to defining creative activities. In my extensive interviews with musicians from diverse cultures, I asked "What does creativity mean to you?" and "When do you feel most creative?" I identified six components that musicians regularly experience while perceiving themselves to be engaged in a creative activity: (1) generativity, (2) agency, (3) interaction, (4) nonconformity, (5) recycling, and (6) flow (see Hill, 2018). Creative agency entails having the permission and authority to make one's own decisions determining musical sound and meaning (see also Green, 2008, p. 103; Karlsen, 2011, p. 110).

4. I am grateful to the European Research Council, the Fulbright Program, and the Alexander von Humboldt Foundation for supporting this research. Much of the material presented in this chapter appears in greater detail and with broader contextualization in my book *Becoming Creative: Insights from Musicians in a Diverse World* (Hill, 2018).

5. The South African term "coloured" was a racial label used during apartheid, which remains a prominent yet problematic social identity encompassing English and Afrikaans speakers of Cape Malay, creole, and mixed heritages. For a more nuanced discussion of coloured identity and music, see Bruinders (2017) and Martin (1999, 2013).

6. According to sociologist Thomas Scheff, the socially induced emotions of pride and shame are part of a subtle and pervasive system of social sanctions that compel conformity to norms exterior to the self (Scheff, 1988, building on Goffman, 1967). We experience pride when we perceive positive judgment of our self by others; it is our reward for meeting the norms and expectations of others. We experience shame when we perceive negative judgment of our self by others. Low levels of shame are present though unacknowledged in most interpersonal interactions, while higher levels may be "so painful as to interfere with the fluent production of thought," contends Scheff (1988, p. 401). These painful emotions are punishment for not conforming. The decision not to conform always entails a risk of shame. The major distinguishing characteristic between those who choose to conform and those who choose not to conform is degree of self-esteem (pp. 404–5). A classic sociological study by Solomon Asch (1956) illustrated that among individuals who faced a majority that espoused a belief the individual knew to be wrong, those who did and those who did not have the courage to stand up for their beliefs both experienced shame. The difference was that those who stood up against the majority had higher self-esteem and better resources for coping with shame than those who did not (Scheff, 1988, pp. 402–5). This explains in part why self-esteem and courage are so important for creativity.

7. Though mostly implicit and often unintentional, efforts to restrict musical creativity in support of societal power structures are in some cases both intentional and explicit. For example, South Africa's apartheid-era Radio Bantu policies required musicians to perform styles that promoted the state's strategic divisions of race (Ansell, 2005).

8. Timothy Rice (2004) observes that "whether in two or three parts, the narrow pitch range of Shop songs creates an intensely dissonant effect, at least to most American listeners. However, when interviewed, the singers say the sound is 'pleasing' and 'smooth.' They regard their harmony as, in effect, consonant. The women appreciate the pleasurable aesthetic effect of the clash between the two or three close-together tones. They say that they are trying to make the harmony 'ring like a bell.' To produce this effect, the singers sit or stand close together, and those who 'follow' sing into the ears of the one who 'cries out.' This is a good example of a truism that ethnomusicologists have long known, namely that, the way

people understand and appreciate music, what they find beautiful or ugly, mellifluous or cacophonous, is a product of culture, not something universal" (pp. 31–33).

9. The early comparative musicologist Alexander Ellis did extensive comparative research on the intonation systems of different music cultures and determined that "the final conclusion is that the Musical Scale is not one, not 'natural,' nor even founded necessarily on the laws of the constitution of musical sound, so beautifully worked out by Helmholtz, but very diverse, very artificial, and very capricious" (Ellis, 1885, p. 526). See also Charles Keil and Steve Feld's (1994) discussion of "participatory discrepancies" in musical timing.

10. Communal, oral, and informal learning experiences are often undervalued. For example, the following interview excerpt exemplifies how such attitudes may be unconscientiously maintained by those in positions of authority, in this case a formally trained director of a community music program in an underprivileged area:

Juniper: What kind of musical backgrounds do program participants come in with?
Jasper: Nothing....
Juniper: But they must have some musical experiences, informal ones?
Jasper: Singing always, yeah. There have been people playing guitar.... They are very musical, musically talented. But when I say nothing, I apologize. I need to take that back. That is a sort of old-school assessment of musical technical training....... They have no music theory and no instrumental experience....... [But they have a strong sense of melody] and rhythm and also an indigenous way of harmonizing, a way of moving in parallel harmonies, and with a certain way of glissando. It's very, very traditional, very beautiful.

Such an automatic lack of respect or valuation of indigenous musical experience and intuitive musical knowledge is connected to the still pervasive attitude that European classical music is superior to both vernacular and non-European approaches to music making. These attitudes then become internalized by learners and can be held throughout their professional careers. For example, a Capetonian musician in his fifties who performs and teaches primarily in the idiom of jazz confessed, "I wouldn't call myself a jazz musician... because I didn't study jazz. I'm self taught in jazz" (Eduard). Another Capetonian musician who composes in the vernacular goema style told me that "getting those songs, I was not composing but just playing and writing out some harmonies and melodies" (Marlo).

# REFERENCES

Ansell, G. (2005). *Soweto blues: Jazz, popular music & politics in South Africa*. New York: Continuum.

Asch, S. (1956). Studies of independence and conformity: 1, a minority of one against a unanimous majority. *Psychological Monographs, 70*, 1–70.

Ballantine, C. (2005). Music and emancipation. In C. Luc (Ed.), *The world of South African music: A reader* (pp. 118–91). Newcastle, UK: Cambridge Scholars Press.

Ballantine, C. (2012). *Marabi nights: Jazz, "race" and society in early apartheid South Africa* (2nd ed.). Durbin: University of KwaZulu-Natal Press.

Boden, M. (2004). *The creative mind: Myths and mechanisms* (2nd ed.). New York: Routledge.

Bruinders, S. (2017). *Parading respectability: The cultural and moral aesthetics of the Christmas Bands Movement in the Western Cape, South Africa*. Grahamstown, South Africa: AHP Publications.

Coplan, D. B. (2008). *In township tonight! South Africa's black city music and theatre* (2nd ed.). Chicago: University of Chicago Press.

Csikszentmihalyi, M. (1996). *Creativity: Flow and the psychology of discovery and invention.* New York: Harper Perennial.

Deci, E., & Ryan, R. (2002). *Handbook of self-determination research.* Rochester, NY: University of Rochester Press.

Ellis, A. (1885). On the musical scales of various nations. *The Journal of the Society of Arts, 1688*, 526.

Goffman, E. (1967). *Interaction ritual.* New York: Anchor.

Green, L. (2008). *Music, informal learning and the school: The new classroom pedagogy.* Farnham, UK: Ashgate.

Hill, J. (2009). Rebellious pedagogy, ideological transformation, and creative freedom in Finnish contemporary folk music. *Ethnomusicology, 53*(1), 86–114.

Hill, J. (2014). Innovation and cultural activism through the re-imagined pasts of Finnish music revivals. In C. Bithell & J. Hill (Eds.), *The Oxford handbook of music revivals* (pp. 393–417). New York: Oxford University Press.

Hill, J. (2017). Incorporating improvisation into classical music performance. In J. Rink, H. Gaunt, & A. Williamon (Eds.), *Musicians in the making: Pathways to creative performance* (pp. 222–40). New York: Oxford University Press.

Hill, J. (2018). *Becoming creative: Insights from musicians in a diverse world.* New York: Oxford University Press.

Hill, J., & Bithell, C. (2014). An introduction to music revival as concept, cultural process, and medium of change. In C. Bithell & J. Hill (Eds.), *The Oxford handbook of music revivals* (pp. 3–42). New York: Oxford University Press.

Jost, J. T., & Banaji, M. R. (1994). The role of stereotyping in system-justification and the production of false consciousness. *British Journal of Social Psychology, 33*, 1–27.

Karlsen, S. (2011). Using musical agency as a lens: Researching music education from the angle of experience. *Research Studies in Music Education, 33*, 107–21.

Keil, C., & Feld, S. (1994). *Music grooves: Essays and dialogues.* Chicago: University of Chicago Press.

Kelley, R. (2012). *Africa speaks, America answers: Modern jazz in revolutionary times.* Cambridge, MA: Harvard University Press.

Kenny, D. (2011). *The psychology of music performance anxiety.* Oxford: Oxford University Press.

Lerman, L., & Borstel, J. (2003). *Liz Lerman's critical response process: A method for getting useful feedback on anything you make, from dance to dessert.* Takoma Park: Liz Lerman Dance Exchange.

MacDonald, R., Hargreaves, D. J., & Miell, D. (Eds.). (2017). *Handbook of musical identities.* New York: Oxford University Press.

Martin, D. C. (1999). *Coon carnival: New year in Cape Town.* Cape Town, South Africa: David Philip.

Martin, D. C. (2013). *Sounding the Cape: Music, identity and politics in South Africa.* Somerset West, South Africa: African Minds.

Muller, C. A. (2008). *Focus: Music of South Africa* (2nd ed.). New York: Routledge.

Muller, C. A. (2013). Spontaneity and black consciousness: South Africans imagining musical and political freedom in 1960s Europe. In B. Kutschke & B. Norton (Eds.), *Music and protest in 1968* (pp. 64–80). Cambridge, MA: Cambridge University Press.

Muller, C. A., & Benjamin, S. B. (2011). *Musical echoes: South African women thinking in jazz.* Durham, NC: Duke University Press.

Nosek, B. A., Hawkins, C. B., & Frazier, R. S. (2012). Implicit social cognition. In S. T. Fiske & C. Neil Macrae (Eds.), *The SAGE handbook of social cognition* (pp. 31–53). New York: Sage.

Rice, T. (2004). *Music in Bulgaria: Experiencing music, expressing culture.* New York: Oxford University Press.

Ronström, O. (2014). Traditional music, heritage music. In C. Bithell & J. Hill (Eds.), *The Oxford handbook of music revival* (pp. 43–59). New York: Oxford University Press.

Scheff, T. (1988). Shame and conformity: The deference-emotion system. *American Sociological Review, 53*(June), 395–406.

Small, C. (1998). *Musicking: The meanings of performing and listening.* Hanover: University Press of New England.

Stokes, M. (1997). *Ethnicity, identity and music: The musical construction of place.* London: Bloomsbury Academic.

Wallaschek, R. (1893). *Primitive music: Inquiry into the origin and development of music of savage tribes.* London: Longmans, Green, and Co. (Republished by BiblioLife).

Weisethaunet, H., & Lindberg, U. (2010). Authenticity revisited: The rock critic and the changing real. *Popular Music and Society, 33,* 4, 465–85.

Wilson, W. (1973). Herder, folklore, and romantic nationalism. *Journal of Popular Culture, 4,* 819–35.

## CHAPTER 16

.........................................................................................................

# ENTER THE
# FEEDBACK LOOP

*assessing music technology in music education
with personal bests*

.........................................................................................................

## ADAM PATRICK BELL

IN 2014, one year after the Boston marathon bombing, thirty-eight-year-old Mebrahtom
"Meb" Keflezighi, who had come to the United States as a refugee from Eritrea in 1987,
became the first American male since 1983 to win the Boston marathon. On its website,
the Boston Athletic Association (BAA), the group that organizes the race, posted the
following:

> Keflezighi, just two weeks shy of his 39th birthday, had turned back an armada of
> sub-2:06 thoroughbreds to take one of the sporting world's most prestigious titles.
> "I don't have a 2:04, 2:05," Keflezighi proffered with a smile, "but I've got the Boston
> Marathon title." (O'Brien, 2014, n.p.)

Meb achieved his ultimate goal, but leading up to the race many people assumed that
he was past his prime. Although he had won the silver medal in the 2004 Athens
Olympics marathon, as well as the New York City marathon in 2009, his bright career
seemed to be burning out, because a short time before Boston he ran his worst marathon
to date. Competitive running takes its toll on the body, and it seemed that Meb's injuries
had finally caught up with him.

In his column for *Runner's World*, published just hours after the race, Roger Robinson
(2014) reminded readers, "Never, as has been said so often, write off Meb." Robinson's
post-race commentary lauded Meb's victory as artistry and as a manifestation of ideal
running performance: "Keflezighi was giving us a display of sheer craft. It was like
watching a great artist at work, a marathon runner of consummate skill and mental
focus.... [T]his was above all a runner showing how a runner can get the best from himself.... Today, Meb Keflezighi was the ultimate runners' runner" (n.p.). To recreational

runners such as myself, Robinson's reference to Meb as the "ultimate runner's runner" is *the* unparalleled compliment. Regardless of how fast or slow we are, we all strive toward the same end: the personal best (PB). The beauty of the PB is that it is applicable to all, which explains why the term is deeply embedded in running culture, from amateurs like me to elites like Meb: "To me, 'running to win' doesn't mean getting first place, it means getting the best out of yourself" (Keflezighi, 2015, n.p.). Arguably, the arts and athletics are different animals altogether; still, music educators would do well to adopt the marathoner's "philosophy of the PB," which offers a means of guiding and assessing students' learning while we also nurture inclusive cultures of music making.

For the purpose of examining assessment in the context of music technology in/for music education, I begin with an examination of PB or "ipsative" assessment (Fautley, 2016) in the context of running culture. Following an explanation of "music technology," I turn to a discussion of theories of assessment, which provides a framework for suggesting ways of realizing learners' PBs. Central to this chapter is the concept of the feedback loop, a music technology analogy often employed by assessment scholars. Similar to how a guitarist creating swells of feedback with her amplifier will sway back and forth in proximity to the speaker cabinet based on embodied feelings of sound to sustain the feedback loop, the purpose of assessing music technology in music education should be to create feedback loops of sustained and meaningful learning. Two proposals I proffer are that peer feedback and self-feedback are synergistic strands of the feedback loop that learners must enter to experience an authentic and complex learning environment, and that summative assessment can and should be a natural outgrowth of formative assessment.

# The Runner's Rubric: The PB Mentality

> If you have given it your best while working toward your goal and been mentally strong in chasing that goal, you have to be satisfied, even if the outcome is short of your ultimate goal. As I like to say, you can reach for the stars, but it's not a bad thing if you land in a cloud.
>
> —Meb (Keflezighi & Douglas, 2015, p. 10)

In 2013 I ran "against" Meb in the New York City Marathon and placed well behind him, trotting across the finish line in 11,865th place. I was not the least bit concerned about how I finished relative to others. In a sea of over 50,000 runners, you do not feel you are running against everyone around you; you feel you are running *with* them. Runners understand that we all must run our own respective races, meaning that we need to pace and push ourselves at the right moments. Even two runners who finish with nearly identical times may run very different races, with their paces ebbing and flowing as needed, until they surge or stumble to the finish line. When a fellow runner asks you how your race went, the topic of the PB is bound to surface in the conversation. A PB is understood to be a great victory. In this sense, everyone can win.

Why is the PB so sacred to runners? Because the act of running reminds us that we are not all built to run like Meb. Ectomorphs, mesomorphs, endomorphs, or whatever-morphs, we, as members of the human species, are wonderfully diverse; we do not possess equal abilities in all activities. Whether we are running to reduce our blood pressure, clear our heads, make friends, raise funding and awareness for a cause we care about, or simply because it is a way of being—whatever the reason—the vast majority of the running community assesses itself by the PB standard. According to Meb, the PB has four pillars. PBs must

1. have personal meaning;
2. be specific;
3. be challenging, but realistic; and
4. have a time element (Keflezighi & Douglas, 2015).

Further, this four-pronged plan must be supported by accountability, which entails making these goals explicit and sharing them with others. The PB pursuer must understand that commitment is what makes such a plan plausible to execute. Commitment in this regard is an act of faith or risk-taking because runners do not know for certain that they can attain their PBs. In Meb's view, a missed goal is a learning experience and should not be cause for disappointment: "Commitment is the sign that you welcome the test. When you live like that, even if you fall short of your goal, you've passed the test" (Keflezighi & Douglas, 2015, p. 9). Meb's PB philosophy and plan is supported by research in the field of sports psychology; goal setting has been found to have a strong effect on athletes' performances (Burton & Weiss, 2008). Based on their review of related literature on goal setting in sports, John Kremer, Aidan Moran, and Graham Walker (2011) emphasize the importance of focusing on process and performance goals such as the PB as opposed to outcome goals because the latter are often beyond the control of the athlete. They conclude: "Rather than imploring his client to 'Show me the money,' Jerry Maguire may have been better imploring him to 'Show me the process!'" (n.p.).

The PB standard ought to be employed when we evaluate music making with music technologies in educational contexts. We ought to create and cultivate a learning culture in which we value wherever students are in their respective music-making journeys. We recognize the degree of previous experience they have with music-making technologies, if any at all, and build on them; we recognize that access to music-making technologies can be a barrier, so we strive to obtain access for the marginalized in this regard. In short, we recognize that the playing field is not even and act on this by doing our utmost to make the experience of participating both accessible and sustainable.

D. Royce Sadler (2005) argues convincingly that assessments that rely on relative standards (such as the PB model) are problematic because, ultimately, learners should assess themselves based on the standards of professional practice to be prepared for real-world occupations. Striving to adhere to the standards of a professional practice and PBs are not necessarily incompatible models of assessment (it is possible that an individual's PB could meet the standards of a professional practice), but evaluating novice and intermediate learners using the professional standards of music technologists is analogous to expecting a recreational runner like me to lace up for the Boston marathon and keep up with the elites. Such a PB would be challenging, but far from realistic. An ethical educator cannot in good conscience chart a course that cannot be completed. This perspective does not dismiss PBs, nor does it serve as a scapegoat to subvert them. In the case of assessing music technology in music education, we can strive toward proficiency and professional practices, but the more immediate need is to nurture the confidence to continue, and assessment plays a critical role in this respect.

In the realm of running, newcomers are congratulated by their seasoned peers for making their first strides and continually encouraged as they progress, espousing the mentality that runners never stop, they just take breaks. Runners also understand the context of their respective conditions and adjust their PB expectations of themselves accordingly: some courses are more difficult than others, some days the wind is at your back, some days you feel better than others, and so on. And finally, runners know, often from experience, that it takes time to work up to a new challenge. One cannot roll out of bed one day and run the Boston marathon the next; preparation over a span of years is necessary to even attempt such a feat. When runners talk to each other about PBs, they can appreciate the contexts of their accomplishments. A PB is not simply a number to compare to another. It is a deeply contextualized and highly personalized evaluation of a performance, and a performance that is very much ongoing.

How might such a conception of assessment be applied to evaluating music technology in music education? I propose that we embrace a PB mentality modeled after the runner's rubric. That is, we set specific goals with personal meaning that are challenging, but realistic, and can be accomplished within the allotted time we have to attempt these tasks. We will commit to our goals by being accountable to ourselves and our peers, novices and experts alike. To support these aims, we will need to integrate mechanisms to assess our learning processes much like runners do to evaluate their training. While runners have GPS watches, heart rate monitors, pedometers, and other biodata measurement tools to aid in the process of assessing their development, gauging the learning process with music technology requires more nuanced, qualitative methods of detection. These methods, which for the moment can be generalized as *feedback,* demand the continual attention of both the learner and instructor to conceptualize assessment *as* learning. While the PB can quite easily be conceived of as a form of self-assessment, it can and should encompass much more. The PB is not merely a self-check of whether or not a strong effort has been put forth. Rather, in the context of assessing learning, the PB is meant to be a sustainable model of assessment, one that can be used to assess both current and future learning (Boud, 2000). This entails not only self-assessment, but also the assessment by peers both informally and formally, through formative and summative assessment processes. If we commit to an iterative process of assessment *as* learning, one in which we start but don't stop, then we will have entered the feedback loop. The feedback loop is where the learner should dwell because it's authentic to real-world musical practice. If we want educational contexts to prepare learners for the realities of being lifelong music makers, we need pedagogies and assessment practices that mirror them. We need to enter the feedback loop.

# ENTER THE FEEDBACK LOOP

It seems appropriate that a technological analogy—the loop—serve as a guiding principle for evaluating the use of music technology in or as music education because iteration is a foundational concept in many musical practices dependent on electronic music technologies. Consider the following examples: a hip-hop DJ alternates playing an identical breakbeat on two turntables to create a continuous loop for breakdancing; an electronic musician using the digital audio workstation Ableton Live on her laptop triggers a pre-programmed drum loop so she can improvise a bass line to accompany it; a cellist uses a looping pedal in a concert to build a polyphonic texture, making one string player sound like four; and a live musical coder uses the program Sonic Pi to create an ostinato with a few quick keystrokes, typing the command "loop do."

In practice, making music with music technologies often entails entering into a circular mentality of being in a loop; future musical actions are contingent on the feedback, or lack thereof, received from musical actions performed during previous iterations. Paul Black and Dylan Wiliam (1998) explain the electronic origins that the feedback analogy is derived from: "Originally, feedback was used to describe an arrangement in electrical and electronic circuits whereby information about the level of an 'output' signal (specifically the gap between the actual level of the output signal and some defined 'reference' level) was fed back into one of the system's inputs. Where the effect of this was to reduce the gap, it was called negative feedback, and where the effect of the feedback was to increase the gap, it was called 'positive feedback'" (p. 47). Based on this description of the feedback phenomenon, Black and Wiliam propose that a feedback system has four elements:

1. data on the actual level of some measurable attribute;
2. data on the reference level of that attribute;
3. a mechanism for comparing the two levels and generating information about the gap between the two levels; and
4. a mechanism by which the information can be used to alter the gap (p. 48).

This model reinforces the earlier writings of Arkalgud Ramaprasad (1983) and Sadler (1989), who both make clear that the learner must go beyond being able to recognize that a gap exists and take action to alter it, thus demonstrating that the feedback loop has been completed. This concept can be applied to evaluating our learning with music technologies. Self-reflection and feedback from peers, educators, and community members are critical components in each iteration of the feedback loop. This flexible approach to evaluation—tethered to the PB standard—strives to accommodate a wide spectrum of abilities and previous experiences as it relates to using music technologies, while also honoring the unique learning dispositions of each individual. Ultimately, the aim of this approach is to construct a context in which learners of all levels and abilities can engage in meaningful experiences with music technology while providing a framework to evaluate the quality of the learning that has taken place from multiple perspectives.

In the rest of this chapter I provide an example of the feedback loop assessment model used in practice to support the realization of student PBs and contextualize it within the literature on assessment. While my example is taken from a learning context in higher education, the principles of assessment are applicable to a broad spectrum of music education environments that support learners of diverse ages and abilities with varying levels of experience using music technologies. As a primer for this discussion, it is necessary to first provide a clear definition of "music technology" in the context of this chapter on assessment.

# ASSESSING INSTRUMENTS: MUSIC-MAKING TECHNOLOGY (MMT)

In the field of music education, "music technology" is understood to be many different things to many different people. Using this broad conception of music technology requires a vast range of practices pertaining to music education that could potentially be subjected to assessment of some kind. In the context of music education, time spent together with learners in the classroom, community, or elsewhere under the guise of "music technology" ought to privilege music-making activities above other applications of technology to music. As a means to delimit this discussion to technologies used for making music, I employ the term *music-making technology* (MMT). This small but significant lexical alteration makes it clear that the purpose of the technology employed is to make music. It is critical for the music educator to understand that MMTs are musical instruments. A failure to grasp this reality will have deleterious effects on music education by setting up a hierarchical, two-tiered value system in which "musical instruments" are perceived to be at one level and "music technology" a rung above or below. The reality of the music-making world is that people use instruments to make music; some of these instruments are older than others, some instruments "power on," and some do not. As George Odam (2004) states succinctly: "Traditional musical instruments themselves are, after all, merely older technology" (p. 132). This mindset will help us avoid common pitfalls when talking about music technology, such as lauding it as a democratic solution simply because apps are relatively inexpensive compared to other instruments (the same could be argued for the recorder), or at the other end of the spectrum, lambasting music technology because anyone can push a button (the same could be said for the harpsichord).

Misunderstood, "music technology" can be a damning term for swaths of musicians, depicting what they do as mostly mechanized or automated. As I have discussed elsewhere (Bell, 2015), such a view of music technology fails to recognize the complexities of the relationship between a person and his or her instrument. The ability to discern what is being done when a person plays an instrument will have direct repercussions on assessment. Consider the case of the hip-hop DJ to illustrate the issues surrounding the social process of validating what counts as a musical instrument. When hip-hop turntablism broke into the mainstream, perhaps best represented by the performance of GrandMixer DXT (formerly GrandMixer D.ST) in Herbie Hancock's "Rockit" at the 1983 Grammys, the issue of whether or not a hip-hop DJ was a musician was questioned by many, including DXT himself. In an interview with Bill Brewster and Frank Broughton (2010), who asked, "When did you first feel like musician rather than a DJ?," DXT responded: "Took me a while. You know when I really felt it. . . . When Quincy [Jones] said . . . 'it's incredible' " (p. 222). Having a musician of Jones's stature offer feedback exemplifies the critical role of the greater community of musicians in fostering the development of fragile and vulnerable new musical communities. Music educators must keep open minds about what counts as a musical instrument, recognize the musicality required to design and play new instruments, and be the first to champion and support them. For example, if we see smartphones as simple instruments because we know how to make phone calls or send text messages with the same devices, we're *simply failing* to discern what constitutes the music-making process.

Looping back to the case of hip-hop music, the same could be said of the difference between the ability to play a record and *play*ing records. Justin A. Williams (2013) affirms that the "overt use of preexisting material to new ends" is fundamental to hip-hop culture and aesthetics (p. 1). Failure to grasp this precept of hip-hop culture would preclude the ability to discern the musicianship of the hip-hop DJ and its predecessors in sample-based hip-hop. Joseph Glenn Schloss (2014) reasons: "If you believe that musicians should make their own sounds, then hip-hop is not music, but, by the same token, if you believe that artists should make their own paint, then painting is not art. The conclusion, in both cases, is based on a preexisting and arbitrary assumption" (p. 23). If music educators can understand an instrument from the perspective of the culture from which it comes, they can understand the musicianship associated with it. Impasses occur when we attempt to bridge our cultural conceptions of instrumentality directly to another and encounter dissimilarities that we cannot reconcile. This principle of understanding can be extended to different generations, subcultures, and cohorts within a society. Those of us leading music-learning experiences need to be conscious of the fact that "it is not simply through the actions of musicians that a new instrument comes to be; it is a community of listeners that renders the verdict" (Katz, 2012, p. 63). When we approach new MMTs with the learners we guide, we need to be ever conscious of our presuppositions about what constitutes technology versus an instrument. Further, we would be wise to endeavor to glean the perspectives of the very people in the process of transitioning technologies to instruments.

Assessing instruments should be the first line of assessment in a music education negotiating MMTs. MMTs are not a solution for music education, such as a way to update seemingly ailing practices. Rather, they are a part of an ongoing evolution of people developing new ways to make music; MMTs should be seen as part of a continuum. Referred to generally, MMTs are genre-less, but in music education they tend to be associated with the music-making practices of newer genres. In and of itself, using instruments of the twenty-first century to play music in the style of contemporary genres is not problematic, but we need to be mindful that we can look in both directions along the historical continuum of musics. We can use new instruments to play older musics and vice versa. Ideally, MMTs in the learning environment would not be presented as a special topic—an adjunct or abstracted activity—but would be integral instruments in everyday music making. Assessing instruments is a social process, one in which learners and their respective guides (teachers, instructors, tutors, etc.) should participate collaboratively. When we, like DXT, can see that we are more than machine operators and instead identify as musicians, we can consider the music-making experience itself and how the learning therein would optimally be assessed.

# Design as Assessment

Assessing the learning that takes place with MMTs begins with the designs of the learning experiences, which are typically coordinated and controlled, at least to some extent, by the educator. As the individual responsible for designing and facilitating the learning experience, the educator is cast in the role of assessment architect. Each decision the educator makes about how to structure a music-making experience is implicitly etched into the blueprint of assessment. For example, consider the following hypothetical scenario: a music teacher designs a lesson in which students must work by themselves and create a hip-hop beat on their iPads using GarageBand "by the end of class." By design, certain skills are privileged in this lesson, namely the ability to work independently and quickly, be familiar with beat-making conventions in hip-hop and able to emulate them, and be proficient with an iPad and GarageBand. By design, the aforementioned list of skills is *what* will be assessed. Whether or not this is a good design depends on the learning goals that have been established. In designing and guiding learning experiences, educators need to be ever conscious of the (mis)alignment of what is done in the learning experience and what is assessed. John B. Biggs and Catherine Tang (2011) promote the concept of "constructive alignment," in which the educator creates a learning environment wherein assessment directly corresponds to what is intended to be learned (p. 97). In constructive alignment, assessment is ushered in with the groundwork of planning.

What makes for a solid foundation on which to commence the construction of learning with MMTs? Even if ever so slightly, each learner's ground floor is a different level, and these differing points of reference from which assessment will be gauged need to be *assessed*. As confusing as this may seem in principle, in practice the educator need only engage in dialogues with learners to assess their abilities and aspirations with MMTs and to begin framing learning experiences. Assessing the ambitions of learners will reveal their perceptions of standards and how they relate to them. Following are the questions that need to be posed to learners:

1. Where are we?
2. Where do we want to go?
3. How can we get there?

Employing the feedback loop analogy, Sadler (1989) summarizes that "the learner has to (a) possess a concept of the standard (or goal, or reference level) being aimed for, (b) compare the actual (or current) level of performance with the standard, and (c) engage in appropriate action which leads to some closure of the gap" (p. 121). To aid learners in entering the feedback loop and staying active once in it, Peter Knight (2007) proposes that educators need to create "complex learning environments" that emulate professional life, as described by Hubert L. Dreyfus and Stuart E. Dreyfus (2005). Complex learning environments entail

1. valued and feasible goals;
2. role variety and stretch—opportunities to engage with others on routine and challenging work;
3. social interaction and challenge through working with diverse people on a variety of tasks, always with the provision that collaboration has benefits;
4. time for metacognitive activity, including working with others to get feedback, feedforward, and legitimation; and
5. an extensive view of workplace effectiveness, including an appreciation of the emotional and interpersonal faces of professional being and doing (Knight, 2007, p. 80).

Paralleling complex learning environments, assessment would then be invoked by

1. directing attention to opportunities and goals that are valued by the program;
2. encouraging social interactions, especially academic ones among students;
3. supporting metacognition;
4. consolidating an extensive view of learning;
5. helping students pace their activities;
6. evoking feedback and feedforward; and
7. supporting public representations of achievement (Knight, 2007, p. 81).

What might a complex learning environment integrating constructive alignment look like when applied to music-making experiences with MMTs? We need designs that demand feedback (or what Knight terms "feedforward") to assist learners as they strive for PBs within their own respective feedback loops, and we need to model these designs on authentic practice to derive standards that inform assessment criteria. To exemplify a practical implication of this theory, let us consider an authentic music-making practice replete with MMTs: that used to produce the vast majority of content on contemporary hits radio (CHR), as detailed by John Seabrook (2015) in *The Song Machine*.

## SIMULATING THE "SONG MACHINE": AUTHENTIC ASSESSMENT IN THE ABSENCE OF AN EXPERT

Digital audio workstations (DAWs)—a generic term encompassing software programs used for playing, recording, editing, sequencing, mixing, and many other acts of producing music—are the primary instruments employed in the production of music for CHR. DAWs are somewhat amorphous in that the ways in which they are played are as varied as the people that play them. Like a Matryoshka doll, DAWs contain layers of complexity; they are instruments that contain other instruments. This design is a result of being modeled (at least initially) on the analog recording studio, in which different signal processing devices were linked to comprise a single entity: "the studio." Thus, when the concept of "using the studio as a musical instrument" is invoked (Moorefield, 2010, p. 19), it refers to the playing of a meta-instrument, requiring in tandem an assortment of skills to play it. Because DAWs are software packages, the hardware used to host them varies and includes desktop and laptop computers, smartphones, and tablets. Further, some DAWs are cloud-based applications that run in a web browser, which means that any device with Wi-Fi capability could potentially become an instrument. The DAW is the locus of CHR production; therefore, learners aspiring to make music in the vein of CHR must do so with a DAW. DAW designs are derived largely from audio engineering equipment and practices of the analog recording era (Bell, Hein, & Ratcliffe, 2015). As a result, to play a DAW, a track-and-hook producer must be able to execute actions traditionally associated with audio engineering to achieve "innovation in sound," a hallmark of pop music creation (Warner, 2003). Seabrook (2015) describes the DAW-dependent music-making process he calls "track-and-hook": "By the mid-2000s the track-and-hook approach to songwriting—in which a track maker/producer, who is responsible for the beats, the chord progression, and the instrumentation, collaborates with a hook writer/topliner, who writes the melodies—had become the standard method by which popular songs are written" (p. 200). The pedagogical benefit of simulating the song machine is that learners are immersed in a complex learning environment, a real-world practice in which playing MMTs is learned and assessed in context. Learners *learn by doing*, consistent with Seymour Papert's constructivist pedagogy "constructionism" (1993), but they also *assess by doing*. In a complex learning environment the two processes of learning and assessing are symbiotic; they cannot be parsed out from each other—to do so would sever the feedback loop. In this hands-on approach, tech-dependent sound-shaping concepts such as compressor ratios, delay times, ASDR (attack, sustain, decay, release) envelopes, equalization curves, and so on are experienced as integral to making music rather than dissociated acts designated to the domain of sound engineering. The novice's workflow in learning to play a DAW in this approach may meander but not aimlessly; each mouse click is made with intent as the path to a specific sound is sought.

In Seabrook's depiction of how the song machine works, he reports that in each stage of the track-and-hook process assessment is often rapid, almost reactionary. For example, producers working in the first phase of track-and-hook will abandon a song mid-process after much time and effort has been devoted to it because they reach a point where they intuitively know it will not measure up to their standards. The criteria to define these standards are often veiled as tacit knowledge. While the producers cannot fully articulate their reasoning, they know on a seemingly instinctual level whether or not the music they are making will meet the standards of their industry.

This case presents several issues for the educator to navigate with regard to assessment. First, can the enigmatic elements of "latent criteria" (Sadler, 1983) be made explicit for the learner? Ideally, "the aim is to work towards ultimate submergence of many of the routine criteria once they are so obviously taken for granted that they need no longer be stated explicitly" (Sadler, 1989, p. 134). In reality, making manifest the multifarious musical actions in the track-and-hook production approach using DAWs is not possible. The tacit can be transferred from one person to another (as is often the case in an apprenticeship), but not necessarily stated and serialized to produce a prescribed pedagogy. Michael Polanyi (1966) summarizes this view: "*[W]e can know more than we can tell*" (p. 4; italics added). Further, while stylistic commonalities exist across CHR, there is no singular compositional code for CHR to be cracked. On the surface, CHR may at first seem simple (e.g., basic rhythms, rudimentary chord progressions, predictable song structures), but its production—its calling card—is complex: "While the development of those elements traditionally associated with creativity in music—melodic, harmonic, rhythmic, and structural manipulation/innovation—often may be derivative in pop recordings, the ways in which technology is used are often highly innovative. The result is a vast body of work characterized by variety and startling innovation in sound and sound manipulation" (Warner, 2003, p. 18). Seabrook's three-step track-and-hook formula is more like a basic ingredient list than a recipe, akin to divulging that an apple pie is made with flour, butter, sugar, and apples. An account of the artistry is absent. The experienced baker knows that a single tablespoon of water can create a considerably different consistency in the crust, from cadaverous to crispy. Similarly, making a beat is a nuanced feat; a track-and-hook producer can nudge an equalizer knob ever so nimbly to add the psychoacoustic phenomenon of heaviness to the bass drum or tweak the timing of the snare hits to humanize a machine-made groove. In sum, much of what occurs in the production process of CHR is so subtle that it goes undetected by a seasoned journalist such as Seabrook, let alone by a casual listener. And yet, as Timothy Warner (2003) reports, the idiosyncrasies of pop production are elemental in authentic professional practice. In the absence of an expert, how can an educator inexperienced with these practices be expected to facilitate assessment of them?

Traditionally, the craft of audio engineering was taught and assessed in an apprenticeship-style model in which "the expert shows the apprentice how to do a task, watches as the apprentice practices portions of the task, and then turns over more and more responsibility until the apprentice is proficient enough to accomplish the task independently" (Collins, Brown, & Holum, 1991, p. 2). In an apprenticeship, the expert does not provide a series of instructions to the apprentice based on a self-reflective distillation of her working processes; rather, she initiates the transfer of her tacit knowing by modeling the target skill set, and the apprentice emulates her. The expert scaffolds the learning experience by providing whatever support is needed, but her goal is to withdraw this support to give more responsibility to the apprentice over time. Formative assessment occurs throughout this process as the apprentice continually seeks feedback from the expert and the "diverse range of people that we learn from at work" (Boud & Middleton, 2003, p. 201). In reality, the likelihood of tracking down and securing a commitment from Max Martin or Stargate to visit a classroom and serve as an expert mentor is next to nil. The major disadvantage of a learning environment in which there are no experts—such as a classroom in which a teacher wants to mimic the song machine with her students, but she has little experience with MMTs—is that the opportunities for tacit transfer are limited. Accessing and asking experts in the greater community to participate in the assessment process is one possible solution to this problem, but in the event that experts are in short supply, assessment among the amateurs can still have significant value.

The gap between identifying an authentic model utilizing MMTs, such as the song machine, and being able to emulate it in an educational setting without the expertise of a professional from the field, can be vast, but it can be bridged. Histories of music production reveal that learning by trial and error is an oft-utilized approach, to the point that it is traditional (Bell, 2014). In the absence of an expert mentor, learning is likely to be less efficient but can still be authentic in terms of real-world practice, and it can be productive when guided by quality peer feedback and self-feedback.

## PEER FEEDBACK

Simulating the song machine imposes certain structures on the learning experience, and thereby assessment. To mirror what's done in the real world of CHR, learners must organize themselves into small production crews or teams to create backing tracks consisting of beats and chord progressions on which the hooks/toplines (melodies) will be based. To facilitate this task, groups must collaboratively identify standards (i.e., CHR exemplars) and the criteria that comprise them, plan their course of action, articulate what they know for each other, and give constructive feedback (Falchikov, 2007, p. 138). First, a group must sift for standards from which to derive assessment criteria. Such a task demands reflection, dialogue, and questioning consistent with professional practice, all of which are components of assessment. Learners must start by listening to potential exemplars and come to a consensus on the style(s) they want to pursue. For example, they may choose to examine the work of Dr. Dre and Dr. Luke and seek to strike a balance between their respective hip-hop and pop production approaches.

Once exemplars have been selected, groups can identify criteria within them that they want to emulate and commence working toward them. This could be a particular vocal or instrumental sound, a distinct texture or timbre, or a more global quality such as a groove or a perceived sense of width or depth in the mix. Identifying criteria will lead to questioning how they were realized in professional practice and an ensuing pursuit to chart a similar course toward those ends. Message boards, video tutorials, and online articles are combed for any bit of helpful "how-to" information that might lead a group toward their established goals. Immersed in this process, learners experience assessment as learning because they are confronted with having to make judgments about the quality of learning resources they encounter. Ultimately they are assessing to what degree their learning objectives are being assisted by the resources available to them.

Learner-selected standards serve as a baseline from which a group can assess itself (Boud & Falchikov, 2007). Groups may "divide and conquer" a task, assigning roles such as beat maker or topliner, consistent with the song machine, or they may choose to work side by side in each successive stage. Nevertheless, in the process of collaboration, students produce and respond to each other's concurrent or intrinsic feedback (Nicol & Macfarlane-Dick, 2006). Informal peer feedback moments, typified by questions such as "Hey, can you listen to this and tell me what you think?," are representative of what one would find in a professional environment. Collaborators cannot be dismissive in giving their feedback, because they could risk upsetting the working relationship within a group and ostracizing themselves. Through this process, group members quickly learn both the complexity and the delicacy that are essential in articulating the quality of a peer's work. In this act of forming and delivering judgments, learners grapple with what Sadler (1989) calls "fuzzy criteria," which "are characterized by a continuous gradation from one state to another" (p. 124). As opposed to "sharp criteria," wherein the distinctions between one state and another are clearly bounded, assessing fuzzy criteria requires sound understanding of the context of the artistic practice. Together, peer groups can assess the degree to which they have achieved their aims by continually referencing the criteria of their selected standards and then adjust accordingly. This iterative process hinges on "recursive feedback" (Falchikov, 2001), in which, through multiple meetings, the peer group revisits and revises their work.

In these differing degrees of peer-provided feedback, there are numerous parallels to the types of assessment that would occur in a traditional apprenticeship. Most important, what remains is a fixation on standards and their criteria and the promotion of a culture that craves critique in the interest of improvement—not only accepting peer opinions, but seeking them, too (Kvale, 2007). In Seabrook's *The Song Machine* (2015) there are no explicit rubrics or formulas for success, only trends prone to shifts that producers continually navigate together. By modeling this reality replete with fuzzy criteria in the learning environment, learners are inserted into a similar feedback loop that they would find themselves in if they were to saunter into one of the studios chronicled in *The Song Machine.*

To meld Meb's PB philosophy with Sadler's (2005) standards-based strategy of assessment, the professionally based PB should be espoused to encourage learners to strive toward real-world practice principles while retaining a realistic outlook and attainable achievements within a bounded amount of time. Ideally, learners will continue to seek out peer feedback as they progress toward their PBs well after the structured learning experience has ended.

# REFLEXIVE AND REFLECTIVE
# SELF-FEEDBACK

Self-feedback, which is an oxymoron, is not a term typically used by assessment scholars, who alternatively tend to employ the descriptors "reflection" (e.g., Carnell & Lodge, 2002; Dreyfus & Dreyfus, 2005) or "self-monitoring" (e.g., Boud, 1995; Boud & Falchikov, 2007; Sadler, 1989, 1998, 2005). However, self-feedback is an apt descriptor for what occurs reflexively in the act of music making and can serve as an apt analogy for assessment. Musicians make subtle but complex adjustments while playing their instruments as they perform. For example, Tiger Roholt (2014) convincingly argues that a drummer must embody a groove to feel it, pushing or pulling respectively ahead or behind a beat in immeasurable ways that elude analytical theories. With each hit on the drum kit a sound is produced, and the drummer's successive actions are contingent on the previous ones. Playing a DAW is no exception to this line of thinking. Each action in the music-making process becomes a point of reference for later actions. Even in the case in which the musician decides to "undo" an action in the DAW environment, it still influences future actions, which become part of the mental map of the territory previously explored and surveyed.

While these reflexive actions of self-feedback occur in the moment, reflective actions of self-feedback entail consciously attending to assessing what has been done and what needs to be done in due course. Optimally, learning experiences enable and empower learners to transition from participating in self-assessment *activities* to harnessing self-assessment *abilities* (Tan, 2007). Like the producers profiled in *The Song Machine*, educators should aspire to foster in learners the ability to make accurate snap assessments about the quality of their work. But the ability to assess must be nurtured, which requires training and practice to develop (Falchikov, 2005). To this end, in my own teaching in higher education I require my students to keep learning (b)logs (the "b" is silent) to monitor and assess their learning, following the criteria of "thick description" prescribed by Norman Denzin (2001): "The thick description has the following features: (A) it gives the context of an action, (B) it states the intentions and meanings that organize the action, (C) it traces the evolution and development of the action, and (D) it presents the action as a text that can be interpreted. A thin description simply reports facts, independent of intentions or the circumstances that surround action" (p. 153). Attended to frequently and consistently, the learning (b)log serves as an evidence trail to trace one's own path of learning. The learning (b)log should indicate what was done, how it was done, where it was done, when it was done, and with whom, if anyone, it was done. Why something was done should attend to the notion of standards discussed in the previous section.

Lebler (2006) discusses the incorporation of self-feedback in the bachelor of popular music (BPM) program at Griffith University in Australia, describing a similar approach in which students must keep a journal to assess their work, which includes, "a description of their recording projects for the semester, a rationale for what they have chosen to do, critical reflection on the outcome and more general reflection on the learning they have experienced during the semester" (p. 45). As the project proceeds to the culminating stage of submitting recordings to a panel of peers for evaluation, "they also mark themselves using the same criteria as the assessment panels will use later in the process, importantly acting as their own first markers" (Lebler & Weston, 2015, p. 127). Like the learning (b)log, the journals used in the BPM at Griffith University serve not only as a means to aid learners in developing their abilities to assess themselves, but also to contextualize the work that will be evaluated by others in the learning community, such as peers and instructors.

Self-feedback is a loop made up of reflexive and reflective processes. It is tempting to deduce that the reflective process will directly inform the betterment of reflexive processes "in which criteria are translated for the student's benefit from latent to manifest and back to latent again" (Sadler, 1989, p. 134), but "if such formalization of tacit knowing were possible, it would convert all arts into mathematically prescribed operations, and thus destroy them as works of art" (Polanyi, 1969, p. 164). Reflection cannot completely unpack "reflexion" because it is disembodied from the moment of action. Haridimos Tsoukas (2005) explains why this is the case and is worth quoting at length on this point:

> By focusing on particulars after a particular action has been performed, we are not focusing on them as they bear on the original focus of action, for their meaning is necessarily derived from their connection to that focus. When we focus on particulars we do so in a new context of action which itself is underlain by a new set of subsidiary particulars. Thus, the idea that somehow one can focus on a set of particulars and convert them into explicit knowledge is unsustainable... Tacit knowledge cannot be "captured," "translated," or "converted," but only displayed—manifested—in what we do. New knowledge comes about not when the tacit becomes explicit, but when our skilled performance—our praxis—is punctuated in new ways through social interaction. (p. 158)

The implication stemming from Tsoukas's explanation of the nature of tacit knowledge is that reflective self-feedback is limited in what it can make explicit (or "manifest," to use Sadler's terminology). However, this does not imply that attempting to make the latent manifest is a fully futile act. Polanyi (1969) recognized that formalizing tacit knowing "expands the powers of the mind" and "opens up new paths of intuition," but he cautioned that "any attempt to gain complete control of thought by explicit rules is self-contradictory, systematically misleading, and culturally destructive" (p. 156). The pragmatic takeaway is that through reflection we can tease out some understanding of the reflexive, which has value in aiding the learning and assessment processes, but we must be mindful that any prescribed pedagogy for the arts will always be incomplete. Completeness comes through transferring the tacit *as is*, without being made manifest; the answer to the age-old question of how to do something is embedded in the question itself: do something. As circular as this concept may seem, it is central to the apprenticeship model.

Learners are capable of acquiring new skills independently, largely through a process of trial and error, which demands self-feedback in the form of reflexive and reflective assessments. By referencing the criteria of a standard, which provides clear goals, learners can progress toward a PB independently, staying within their own personalized feedback loop of assessment. Steinar Kvale (2007) posits that assessment in relation to a model "may be so obvious that assessment from others is superfluous" (p. 59). A learner can simulate the song machine independently, playing all of the instruments within the DAW herself to create backing tracks and then, later, adding the hooks, but this would circumvent a key step of authentic practice: peer collaboration and its associated assessments. Further, the efficiency of the song machine can be increased with a more complex design. On the one hand, by introducing peers into the feedback loop, a more complicated system of learning is created; on the other hand, the depth, scope, rate, quality, complexity, applicability, and individual and collective level of learning can be enhanced (Hounsell, 2007, p. 101). While much learning and assessment can be facilitated by self-feedback alone, it can never rival or replace the values that arise in/from peer feedback. The two must be taken in tandem to effectively set up and sustain a feedback loop that is PB oriented and anchored to authentic practice with MMTs.

# No Finish Line: Running
## to the Summit-ive

Simulating the song machine is but one example of modeling a complex learning environment that uses MMTs in a context of authentic practice. While it is by no means comprehensive in its uses of MMTs, as is the case with any practice that plays MMTs, it illustrates that in an authentic practice, formative assessment (peer feedback and self-feedback) is enmeshed in acts of music making. Because music-making practices with MMTs vary from context to context, so too will the manifestation and use of assessment. There cannot be a singular approach to assessing MMT practices, only guiding principles to which learners and educators alike must be sensitive. Those in search of a formula to assess MMT practices will not find one in authentic practice.

The point of entering the feedback loop is not to leave it. A traditional approach to summative assessment would suggest that some prescribed task serve as a point of exit from the feedback loop, a final test in one form or another in which the learner can showcase progress or mastery. But as Ronald Barnett (2007) points out, the summative task need not be mutually exclusive of the formative; in fact, the summative should be an outgrowth of the formative. In this way of conceptualizing the summative, distinctions between summative and formative become blurred. In the example of simulating the song machine, a series of formative assessments brings learners to the doorway of summative assessment. This process is akin to the runner building up endurance over time to be able to complete a desired distance or course. Whereas "summative" is derived from summation, the final judgment, or *summit-ive*, infers a journey upward to a peak experience, a PB. Reaching the peak is a celebration, something to be relished, not reviled. The summit-ive experience should embody the ethos of race day, in which runners are cheered on toward their PBs. If summit-ive assessment replaced summative assessment, learners "would be fired up, tackling their assessments with relish, hurling themselves forward into the fray" (Barnett, 2007, p. 40).

Authentic learning environments are complex and therefore so are their associated systems of assessment. For the music educator aiming to replicate real-world music-making practices with MMTs, an acceptance of the reality of complexity is a prerequisite. Regardless of the practice that involves playing MMTs, as disparate as they may seem, the guiding principle of authentic assessment for educators and learners alike must be the standards of the practice. These standards are situated; they exist within a context that must be appreciated and understood in order to be implemented authentically. From these standards stem the criteria that educators and learners can look to for frames of reference. But we must be mindful of Meb's advice and temper our expectations with an honest accounting of our current experiences and abilities to settle on PBs that are both challenging and realistic. To support the realization of learners' respective PBs, educators need to usher learners into the feedback loop. Nestled in layers of peer feedback and self-feedback, learners awash in formative assessment experience *assessment as learning*, which not only serves to benefit their current learning but also prepares them for future learning. By learning how to assess one's self and peers, and how to receive assessment, the learner is positioned to ascend to the summit-ive and succeed in doing so. So, what's an A? 4.0? Honors? Summa cum laude? In the case of playing MMTs, you tell me. What's your PB?

## References

Barnett, R. (2007). Assessment in higher education: An impossible mission? In D. Boud & N. Falchikov (Eds.), *Rethinking assessment for higher education: Learning for the longer term* (pp. 29–40). London: Routledge.

Bell, A. P. (2014). Trial-by-fire: A case study of the musician-engineer hybrid role in the home studio. *Journal of Music, Technology & Education, 7*(3), 295–312. doi:10.1386/jmte.7.3.295_1

Bell, A. P. (2015). Can we afford these affordances? GarageBand and the double-edged sword of the digital audio workstation. *Action, Criticism, and Theory for Music Education, 14*(1), 44–65. Retrieved from http://act.maydaygroup.org/articles/Bell14_1.pdf

Bell, A. P., Hein, E., & Ratcliffe, J. (2015). Beyond skeuomorphism: The evolution of music production software user interface metaphors. *Journal on the Art of Record Production, 9.* Retrieved from http://arpjournal.com/beyond-skeuomorphism-the-evolution-of-music-production-software-user-interface-metaphors-2/

Biggs, J., & Tang, C. (2011). *Teaching for quality learning in university: What the student does* (4th ed.). Berkshire, UK: Open University Press.

Black, P., & Wiliam, D. (1998). Assessment and classroom learning. *Assessment in Education, 5*(1), 7–74.

Boud, D. (1995). *Enhancing learning through self-assessment.* London: Kogan Page.

Boud, D. (2000). Sustainable assessment: Rethinking for the learning society. *Studies in Continuing Education, 22*(2), 151–67.

Boud, D., & Falchikov, N. (2007). Developing assessment for informing judgment. In D. Boud & N. Falchikov (Eds.), *Rethinking assessment in higher education* (pp. 181–97). New York: Routledge.

Boud, D., & Middleton, H. (2003). Learning from others at work: Communities of practice and informal learning. *Journal of Workplace Learning, 15*(5), 194–202.

Brewster, B., & Broughton, F. (2010). *The record players: DJ revolutionaries.* New York: Black Cat.

Burton, D., & Weiss, C. (2008). The fundamental goal concept: The path to process and performance success. In T. Horn (Ed.), *Advances in sport psychology* (3rd ed., pp. 339–75). Leeds, UK: Human Kinetics.

Carnell, E., & Lodge, C. (2002). *Supporting effective learning.* London: Paul Chapman.

Collins, A., Brown, J. S., & Holum, A. (1991). Cognitive apprenticeship: Making thinking visible. *American Educator, 15*(3), 6–11.

Denzin, N. K. (2001). *Interpretive interactionism* (2nd ed.). Thousand Oaks, CA: SAGE.

Dreyfus, H. L., & Dreyfus, S. E. (2005). Peripheral vision: Expertise in real world contexts. *Organization Studies, 26*(5), 779–92.

Falchikov, N. (2001). *Learning together: Peer tutoring in higher education.* New York: Routledge.

Falchikov, N. (2005). *Improving assessment through student involvement.* New York: Routledge

Falchikov, N. (2007). The place of peers in learning and assessment. In D. Boud & N. Falchikov (Eds.), *Rethinking assessment in higher education* (pp. 128–43). New York: Routledge.

Fautley, M. (2016). Music education assessment and social justice: Resisting hegemony through formative assessment. In C. Benedict, P. Schmidt, G. Spruce, & P. Woodford (Eds.), *The Oxford handbook of social justice and music education* (pp. 513–24). New York: Oxford University Press.

Hounsell, D. (2007). Towards more sustainable feedback to students. In D. Boud & N. Falchikov (Eds.), *Rethinking assessment in higher education* (pp. 101–13). New York: Routledge.

Katz, M. (2012). *Groove music: The art and culture of the hip-hop DJ.* New York: Oxford University Press.

Keflezighi, M. (2015, October 29). The finish line. *The Players Tribune.* Retrieved from http://www.theplayerstribune.com/meb-keflezighi-marathon-running/

Keflezighi, M., & Douglas, S. (2015). *Meb for mortals.* New York: Rodale.

Knight, P. (2007). Grading, classifying, and future learning. In D. Boud & N. Falchikov (Eds.), *Rethinking assessment in higher education* (pp. 72–86). New York: Routledge.

Kremer, J. M., Moran, A., & Walker, G. (2011). *Key concepts in sports psychology. SAGE key concepts series.* London: SAGE.

Kvale, S. (2007). Contradictions of assessment for learning in institutions of higher learning. In D. Boud & N. Falchikov (Eds.), *Rethinking assessment in higher education* (pp. 57–71). New York: Routledge.

Lebler, D. (2006). The master-less studio: An autonomous education community. *Journal of Learning Design, 1*(3), 41–50.

Lebler, D., & Weston, D. (2015). Staying in sync: Keeping popular music pedagogy relevant to an evolving music industry. *IASPM@Journal*, 5(1), 124–38.

Moorefield, V. (2010). *The producer as composer: Shaping the sounds of popular music* (Rev. ed.). Cambridge, MA: MIT Press.

Nicol, D. J., & Macfarlane-Dick, D. (2006). Formative assessment and self-regulated learning: A model and seven principles of good feedback practice. *Studies in Higher Education*, 31(2), 199–218.

O'Brien, J. (2014). *Meb Keflezighi (USA) becomes first American male champion since 1983.* Boston Athletic Association. Retrieved from http://www.baa.org/races/boston-marathon/results-commentary/2014-boston-marathon/2014-mens-race-recap.aspx

Odam, G. (2004). Music education in the Aquarian age: A transatlantic perspective (or "how do you make horses thirsty?"). In C. Rodriguez (Ed.), *Bridging the gap: Popular music and music education* (pp. 127–39). Reston, VA: MENC, the National Association for Music Education.

Papert, S. (1993). *The children's machine: Rethinking school in the age of the computer.* New York: Basic Books.

Polanyi, M. (1966). *The tacit dimension.* New York: Doubleday.

Polanyi, M. (1969). *Knowing and being: Essays by Michael Polanyi.* M. Grene (Ed.). Chicago: University of Chicago Press.

Ramaprasad, A. (1983). On the definition of feedback. *Behavioral Science*, 28(1), 4–13.

Robinson, R. (2014, April 21). Meb wins the Boston Marathon: Keflezighi first American male to win since 1983. *Runner's World.* Retrieved from http://www.runnersworld.com/newswire/meb-wins-the-boston-marathon

Roholt, T. (2014). *Groove: A phenomenology of rhythmic nuance.* New York: Bloomsbury.

Sadler, D. R. (1983). Evaluation and the improvement of academic learning. *Journal of Higher Education*, 54(1), 60–79.

Sadler, D. R. (1989). Formative assessment and the design of instructional systems. *Instructional Science*, 18(2), 119–44.

Sadler, D. R. (1998). Formative assessment: Revisiting the territory. *Assessment in Education*, 5(1), 77–84.

Sadler, D. R. (2005). Interpretations of criteria-based assessment and grading in higher education. *Assessment & Evaluation in Higher Education*, 30(2), 175–94.

Schloss, J. G. (2014). *Making beats: The art of sample-based hip-hop* (Rev. ed.). Middletown, CT: Wesleyan University Press.

Seabrook, J. (2015). *The song machine: Inside the hit factory.* New York: Norton.

Tan, K. (2007). Conceptions of self-assessment: What is needed for long-term learning? In D. Boud & N. Falchikov (Eds.), *Rethinking assessment in higher education* (pp. 114–27). New York: Routledge.

Tsoukas, H. (2005). *Complex knowledge: Studies in organizational epistemology.* New York: Oxford University Press.

Warner, T. (2003). *Pop music—technology and creativity: Trevor Horn and the digital revolution.* Aldershot, UK: Ashgate.

Williams, J. A. (2013). *Rhymin' and stealin': Musical borrowing in hip-hop.* Ann Arbor: University of Michigan Press.

CHAPTER 17

........................................................................

# IMPROVISATION, ENACTION, AND SELF-ASSESSMENT

........................................................................

## DYLAN VAN DER SCHYFF

EVERY human culture engages in activities that people recognize as musical. And in various ways, such behavior is often characterized by spontaneous acts of sound making. While these "improvised" expressions occur within melodic, rhythmic, sonic, harmonic, and social frameworks that evolve culturally, they also vitalize traditional practices keeping the music (and the culture) alive. Through improvisation the practitioner may explore his or her embeddedness in a given milieu, while simultaneously making unique contributions to the living enactment and transformation of that same sociocultural environment. And sometimes this may involve making radical breaks from established practice and ways of thinking and doing (Bailey, 1993; Borgo, 2007; Elliott, 1996; Lewis, 2004). Indeed, there is a strong sense in which improvisation may be seen as a meeting place for the present and the ancestral, the individual and the group, tradition and innovation. In many ways the phenomenon of musical improvisation may also be understood to reflect the adaptive and relational nature of human meaning and world making more generally. As Lee Higgins and Roger Mantie (2013) note, "improvisation is a distinctive way of being in and through music that reflects the fact that the act of living is largely improvisatory" (p. 38). This insight is echoed by thinkers such as Vijay Iyer (Miller & Iyer, 2010) and Stephan Nachmanovitch (1990), who argue that there is no essential difference between human experience and improvisation, and George E. Lewis (2009a), who suggests that the human condition *is* the condition of improvisation.

However, although improvisation is central to most musicking (Small, 1998)—and may be an important characteristic of human cognition—it has been essentially eliminated from Western classical music practice[1] and largely ignored in scholarship (Nettl, 1974). Keith Sawyer (2007) notes that although improvisation was common in European art music well into the nineteenth century, the current musical culture in Western countries—one in which a highly skilled instrumentalist may be completely incapable of improvising—is historically and culturally unique. Today, in Western cultures, improvisation is almost completely absent from the high art tradition and, consequently, is almost completely absent from the music education curriculum.

As a result, improvisation now "enjoys the curious distinction of being both the most widely practiced of musical activities and the least acknowledged and understood" (Bailey, 1993, p. ix).

This situation is beginning to change, however, and a growing number of scholars are exploring musical improvisation from a range of philosophical, psychological, historical, and cultural perspectives (Born, Lewis, & Straw, 2017; Heble & Caines, 2014; Lewis & Piekut, 2016). Likewise, critically minded thinkers in music education have begun to develop approaches that place improvisation at the core of the curriculum (Sawyer, 2007; Heble & Laver, 2016; Hickey, 2009). In doing so they argue that as a situated practice that embraces adaptivity, contingency, and the unexpected, improvisation challenges many standard ways of thinking about knowledge construction, meaning making, and cognition in general (Kanellopoulos, 2011). Indeed, it is often said that musical improvisation cannot be taught (see Borgo, 2005; Hickey, 2009). Nevertheless, people do learn how to do it. And most often such learning occurs collaboratively and outside of predetermined formal methods or institutional contexts (Green, 2008; Wright & Kanellopoulos, 2010). It follows, then, that a nonreductive and open-ended exploration of improvisation may reveal new perspectives on teaching, learning, and assessment that could have profound implications for the future of education, musical or otherwise (Sawyer, 2007).

With such concerns in mind, this chapter develops a number of threads drawn from pedagogical theory and embodied cognition in an attempt to contribute to a better understanding of the meaning of improvisation for music education. I begin by considering a number of pedagogical perspectives on improvisation and examine the challenges they pose to taken-for-granted assumptions about teaching and assessment. Drawing on these ideas, I then develop the aforementioned insight regarding the deep continuity among improvisation, life, and cognition. Here I consider improvisation in the context of an alternative but increasingly influential *enactive* approach to mind (Varela, Thompson, & Rosch, 1991; Stewart, Gapenne, & Di Paolo, 2010; Thompson, 2007)—a perspective that I suggest allows us to explore the primacy of improvisation in a way not available through standard information-processing models of cognition. Following this, I consider how the "4E" model associated with enactivism (which sees living cognition as essentially *embodied, embedded, enactive,* and *extended*) may provide a useful framework for developing self-reflective and collaborative ways of exploring and assessing improvisational experiences in music education. I conclude by offering suggestions for improvisational practice and assessment in pedagogical settings drawn from a number of existing musical communities and my own experience as a performer and educator.

I should make it clear that my goal is *not* to offer some kind of repeatable or fixed method for the assessment of improvisation in music. Rather, through a critical exploration of what improvisation entails I hope to draw out a general theoretical orientation that might aid educators and students in developing approaches that are relevant to their lives, goals, and shared experiences. As a result, I will not focus solely on assessment, but will also explore issues related to pedagogy and praxis.

# IMPROVISATION AND MUSIC EDUCATION

In recent decades a range of thinkers have begun to critically examine taken-for-granted attitudes about music and music education. For example, while the score and the composer continue to hold privileged places in Western music culture, this is increasingly problematized in association with a number of cultural and historical developments. These include, among other things, the rise of romantic notions of the elite composer-genius, the concert hall and the institutionalization of the classical cannon, mechanical reproduction and commodification, and the bureaucratic-capitalist cultural environment that characterizes modern life (DeNora, 1986; Goehr, 1992; Small, 1998; van der Schyff, 2015b). Some scholars have suggested that the dominant Eurocentric view of what "serious" music entails has exerted a colonizing (Bradley, 2012) influence on music education around the world—one that often obscures the rich improvisational characteristics of indigenous musical traditions in favor of the "gold standard" offered by the classical canon (Imada, 2012; Nettl, 1974, 1998).

According to many writers, this perspective downplays the importance of situated and creative activities associated with nonclassical music—that is, playing by ear, improvisation, and the creation of original music (Rodriguez, 2004; Creech et al., 2008). As such, it does not encourage the development of unique ensembles and approaches to music-making that reflect the day-to-day lives of individuals, social groups, and indigenous or marginalized cultures. Therefore it is claimed that the standard focus on the reproduction and analysis of Western musical works tends to leave little space for the development of personhood, as well as the expression and exploration of difference and diversity that is so crucial for understanding and navigating the complex, heterogeneous world we live in in the twenty-first century (Elliott & Silverman, 2015).

Notably, in recent years there has been a growing call for the (re)introduction of improvisation—not only for music education, but also for pedagogical theory and practice more generally (Campbell, 2009). For example, Sawyer (2003, 2006, 2007) sees the focus on "the composition" as a residue of industrial era thinking, in which, as with other aspects of life and work, the modes of production became isolated from each other. This, Sawyer (2007) argues, led to a situation in the musical domain in which performance and composition became two separate activities: "Where the creation of new music is almost exclusively associated with composers; and where a performers' primary role is to execute those compositions. In this division of labor, instrumentalists do not need to be capable of creating new music, nor do they need the correspondingly deeper conceptual understanding of music that underlies composition. [...] In our culture's stereotypical view, we do not think their creativity is of the same order as the composer who generates the score." Here, Sawyer (2003, 2007) develops comparisons with the "decontextualized and compartmentalized" industrial era approach to education, in which students are simply trained to memorize and reproduce existing knowledge, and they study and are tested essentially in isolation. Furthermore, Sawyer (2007) argues that we need to leave this "production line" approach behind as it tends to isolate and instrumentalize teachers and students, affording little practice in developing "the deeper conceptual understanding[s] and adaptive expertise that allow them to generate new knowledge."

To meet the latter concern, Sawyer (2006, 2007) draws on research associated with learning science, outlining four key and overlapping cognitive-pedagogical goals that reflect the creative possibilities of the human mind. These involve the development of *deep conceptual understanding*, in which facts and techniques are not simply learned for their own sake, but rather are explored within complex and evolving conceptual frameworks. Related to this is the advancement of *integrated* knowledge, which highlights the relational nature of knowledge building, in which understanding does not result from the possession of "compartmentalized knowledge," but rather emerges from the way knowledge is integrated in practice. Central to this process is the notion of *adaptive expertise*, which involves developing the ability to draw on previous experiences and skills in ways that are flexible, that adapt appropriately to the contingent demands of the moment. Finally, Sawyer (2007) considers the importance of *collaborative skills*, in which "unlike the hierarchical corporation of old, where everyone's job description was quite specific, the boundaries between each team member are fluid, and many tasks require the simultaneous and joint contributions of multiple experts to be successfully accomplished."

Importantly, these four pedagogical goals are also necessary requirements of effective musical improvisation. Indeed, improvising musicians must *understand, integrate*, and *adapt* a wide range of skills and knowledge. And often this is done in *collaborative* environments (Azzara, 2002; Monson, 1996; MacDonald, Wilson, & Miell, 2011)—where outcomes are not pre-given, unforeseen challenges continually emerge and are met in various ways, and working relationships between people are not rigidly defined. Similarly, as Sawyer (2006, 2007) points out, the new environments for general education proposed by learning science explicitly embrace an improvisational attitude: "They place students in loosely structured environments, where they work together in a relatively unstructured, improvisational fashion. [...] In these learning environments, different student groups can develop different solutions to the same problem, which is exactly what you would expect if they were truly given the freedom to improvise" (2007).

In brief, it is argued that involving students in collaborative improvisational activities may help them not only develop new ways of engaging with music, but also open ways of thinking, doing, and being that are relevant across a range of domains. Here it is also important to note that such perspectives do not necessarily imply that the study and practice of classical music should be done away with. Rather, it is suggested that this field (and the composition and interpretation of notated music more generally) may be critically resituated within a richer understanding of what human musicality and creativity entails (Lawrence, 1978; Sawyer, 2007).[2]

# TEACHING AND THE QUESTION
# OF "IMPROVISATION"

While there has indeed been a growing recognition of the importance of improvisation in music education in recent decades, the question of just how it should be introduced and developed continues to be debated. Some authors assert that while improvisation is important, the chief focus should remain on composition (Paynter, 1992). Others argue that improvisation should come first in music education, and that it should remain at the core of the music curriculum, with part reading and score analysis taking on an important but secondary role only later on in the educational process (Hickey, 2009; Sawyer, 2007). Perhaps more problematically, a growing number of writers suggest that by and large, the way improvisation is currently understood and practiced in music education does not always embrace the full possibilities of what it entails, and thus current curricula may not be able to meet the kinds of cognitive-creative potentials outlined here (Hickey, 2009).

To better understand such concerns, it may be useful to consider the shifting pedagogical attitudes toward improvisation that have developed over the last century. For example, some of the earliest research and literature on improvisation and music education in the United States emerged in the early and middle twentieth century (Coleman, 1922, 1927a, 1927b, 1939; Moorhead & Pond, 1941/1978). These early studies embrace an open (and interdisciplinary) approach, in which pupils are free to develop their relationships to various instruments and each other in ways that are not strictly prescribed. As Gladys Evelyn Moorhead and Donald Pond (1941/1978) note: "To produce his own music a young child's first need, we find, is freedom—freedom to move about in pursuit of his own interests and purposes, and freedom to make the sounds appropriate to them" (p. 33). This research remained relatively marginalized, however, and it was not until the 1970s that "improvisation as a real learning outcome in American schools first appeared [...] mostly in the form of jazz improvisation, as jazz was beginning to be accepted as a legitimate music ensemble in public schools" (Hickey, 2009, p. 289; see also MENC, 1974). But this new approach to improvisation was not based in the free processes of discovery that characterized earlier research. Instead, improvisation is understood here as consisting of a set of (objective) skills, which are first to be acquired by the teacher and then passed on in a systematic fashion to students (e.g., Konowitz, 1973; Lasker, 1971; see also Pressing, 1988).

Generally speaking, these approaches tend to follow a linear schema, wherein the learner moves from one stage to the next in a controlled fashion. Often this begins with embellishing (or completing) existing melodies and musical phrases. This is followed by exposure to patterns (e.g., the licks or riffs that may be played over certain harmonic cadences), which students become adept at deploying in stylistically appropriate ways (e.g., Aebersold, 2000; Azzara & Grunow, 2003; Baker, 1988; Coker, 1997; Gordon, 2003a). Such skills are then applied to solving larger musical problems (e.g., improvising through longer and more complex harmonic forms), which may be supplemented by transcriptions and imitating by ear. More open ways of improvising—if they are considered at all—are generally introduced (i.e., permitted) only once such skills have been acquired. Many jazz methods proceed in this way. Early music education approaches (e.g., Orff-Schulwerk) that claim to teach improvisation use similar linear frameworks to provide students with the appropriate "building blocks" to proceed through clearly defined stages of learning and assessment (see Abril, 2013).

Of course the assertion here is *not* that such technical forms of training are valueless. Learning to navigate musical compositions and genres—and understanding the theoretical frameworks (e.g., tonal harmony) by which they are constructed and analyzed—is extremely important. And practicing within defined parameters can help with the development of instrumental control and ensemble awareness. However, critics argue that improvisation involves much more than this (Borgo, 2005, 2007; Elliott, 1996; Hickey, 2009; Lewis, 2007). Indeed, it is suggested that the focus on a standardized and technically driven music improvisation pedagogy ignores the informal, exploratory, or "free" processes of discovery, collaboration, and adaptation that result in new situated forms of knowing and doing. It only asks students to understand preexisting knowledge and methods and (re)produce musical "products" that are deemed to be functional (or "correct") within such pre-given frameworks. As such, it is often assumed that students are necessarily subordinate to these frameworks and that their development must therefore be controlled—that is, that they are incapable of improvising "correctly" without supervised interventions. The possibility is rarely entertained that, given the appropriate environment and encouragement, students could (and will) adapt and transform such frameworks (and the skill sets and understandings that characterize them) and thus collectively develop new approaches (their own ways of musicking) that resonate with and express their individual and shared experiences in unique and sometimes unexpected ways. Researchers who explore "informal learning" have shown that it is just these kinds of collaborative and socially relevant processes—that is, the adaptive acquisition and development of skill and understanding through situated praxis—that characterize creative musical activity outside of formal contexts (Green, 2002, 2008; Musical Futures, 2008; O'Neill, 2014; Price, 2006; Wright & Kanellopoulos, 2010).

In brief, it is argued that the "technicist" (Regelski, 2002) orientation of much formal music education tends to impose a reduced understanding of improvisation, which is assumed to consist of a set of "carefully prescribed technique[s] centered around tonal harmony and regular rhythms, but is devoid of both context and freedom" (Hickey, 2009, p. 290). In many ways this orientation reflects the same trends toward standardization associated with Sawyer's (2003, 2007) critique of industrial age thinking, in which the possibilities of human creativity and understanding are curtailed. Not surprisingly, however, this approach does make assessment a relatively straightforward affair, whereby a student's progress may be mapped against a list of externally imposed criteria (i.e., technical requirements).[3]

# IMPROVISATION AND THE QUESTION OF "TEACHING"

I mentioned previously that the technical and product-driven approach to music education is often out of touch with how students frequently engage with music outside of school environments (Green, 2008). Equally problematic is the observation that the emerging pedagogy of improvisation in the last three decades of the twentieth century essentially ignored the living forms of improvisation that are actually occurring in the world at large—for example, the remarkable developments in jazz and free improvisation (Bailey, 1993; Berliner, 1994; Hickey, 2009, 2015; Lewis, 2007)—and how such developments intersect with cultural and critical perspectives, as well as a range of new technologies (Borgo, 2014; Borgo & Kaiser, 2010; Born, Lewis, & Straw, 2017). For example, most often large ensembles (big bands) dominate jazz education, in which improvisation fills out areas within a composition. However, such improvisations are almost always subservient to the framework imposed by the composer/arranger and generally involve sedimented hierarchies within the ensemble that interact in highly prescribed ways (e.g., soloist-rhythm section).[4] Moreover, as Michael Szekely (2012) argues, all of this reflects a trend toward codification, institutionalization, and commodification of the "language" of jazz, wherein the insistence that jazz should somehow be understood as "America's classical music" has resulted in a range of problematic assumptions. Thus, while there are many important skills that may be developed in more codified contexts, the resulting musical products often have little to do with the lives of the students who perform them, and the processes involved resonate only superficially with the collaborative and often highly idiosyncratic ways jazz musicians actually go about creating the music they do.

Along these lines, a number of writers discuss improvisation not in terms of products or outcomes, but rather as an activity to be pursued for its own sake,[5] often exploring the relevance of "free" or "nonidiomatic" improvisation for education (Borgo, 2007; Kanellopoulos, 2011; Wright & Kanellopoulos, 2010). As Jacques Attali argues, free improvisation is "NOT undertaken for its exchange or use value. It is undertaken solely for the pleasure of the person who does it. [...] Such activity involves a radical rejection of the specialized roles (composer, performer, audience) that dominated all previous music" (1985/2006, p. 135). As Derek Bailey (1993) remarks, "Diversity is its most consistent characteristic. It has no stylistic or idiomatic commitment. It has no prescribed idiomatic sound. The characteristics of freely improvised music are established only by the sonic-musical identity of the person or persons playing it" (p. 83). Following these insights, Maude Hickey (2009) points out that "free improvisation is a form of improvisation that is ultimately the most open, non-rules bound, most learner directed, and, consequently, the least (if ever) approached in schools. It is not a free-for-all approach, as it requires attentive and sensitive listening to the environment and others involved. However, it is an improvisation that *cannot* be taught in the traditional sense, but experienced, facilitated, coached, and stimulated. [...] There is no right way to do it, and the process often requires more attention than the product" (p. 249). Indeed, because free improvisation highlights process, diversity, and the unique evolving relationships enacted between situated musical agents and their environments, it does not fit neatly into the standardized practices and prescribed outcomes that often characterize music curricula and assessment. Thus, as Ruth Wright and Panagiotis Kanellopoulos (2010) point out, "Improvisation becomes a means for unsettling dominant conceptions of music learning and for engaging with informal learning practices. Improvisation not only offers a way of active engagement with music, but also is situated [...] in an epistemology that does not regard knowledge as 'an accurate representation of a pre- existing reality' (Biesta & Osberg, 2007, p. 16) but emphasizes the situatedness of knowledge construction as a form of creative socio-cultural praxis" (p. 82).

With such concerns in mind, a number of writers argue that improvisation, in its fullest sense, should not be understood as something to be inculcated, but rather as a kind of fundamental "disposition" that is to be nurtured and cultivated. This resonates with the insights mentioned previously regarding the improvisatory nature of life itself (more on this shortly). I suggest, therefore, that it should be this "improvisational disposition" that is initially recognized in music education so that students may develop a strong sense of their own creative potentials as self-making beings (Hickey, 2009). In other words, I argue that free improvising should be introduced first and encouraged throughout students' development. In this way, when technical and genre-specific concepts, practices, and cultural models are introduced to students, they may be encountered from the outset not as prescriptive, but rather as tools and possibilities for creative engagement with the (musical) worlds they co-enact.

This all leads back to the suggestion articulated by Hickey (2009): namely, that true improvisation may not be "teachable" within the rather narrow didactic (or "industrial") understanding of what education involves. Indeed, embracing this deeper understanding of improvisation in pedagogical contexts demands a new and more complex understanding of the relationship between teachers and students, one that looks beyond rigid hierarchies and predetermined outcomes. Here the teacher must become more than simply a source of information, facts, and skills. Rather, he or she takes on the status of a facilitator and collaborator, providing the "scaffolding" (Lajoie, 2005; see also Elliott, 1995, pp. 278–80) for fertile creative environments to emerge and grow, in which students are encouraged to think critically, creatively, and collaboratively. From this perspective, teaching involves knowing when to play an active role and when to stand back and let the students take charge of their own learning, when to introduce a new cultural model or a conceptual/technical challenge, and when to let students explore without intervention (Green, 2008; Wright & Kanellopoulos, 2010).

Of course, this all demands a good deal of critical reflection, creativity, adaptive flexibility, and the ability to engage with the needs of students (Laroche & Kaddouch, 2015;

O'Neill, 2010; Silverman, 2012). Indeed, to be effective, teachers cannot simply teach by rote; they must develop the ability to integrate and adapt their knowledge to the contingent demands and opportunities that arise in a given situation and perhaps even engage in the kinds of "subversive" teaching that looks outside of the standard curriculum (Elliott & Silverman, 2015). Put simply, this means that teachers must actually embody the kinds of adaptive, creative, and collaborative learning that improvisation involves, so that by example they may reveal the kinds of processes they hope to encourage in their students.

I return to these concerns later in this chapter to explore possibilities for assessment and praxis. First, however, I further develop this idea of *improvisation as a disposition*, wherein "the act of living itself is largely improvisatory" (Higgins & Mantie, 2013). Here I examine how emerging embodied or "enactive" approaches to cognition (Stewart et al., 2010; Thompson, 2007; Varela et al., 1991) may offer support for this insight and thus help to inform and ground new ways of thinking about improvisation, learning, and assessment.

# COGNITION AND IMPROVISATION

Until recently, our understanding of how the mind works was framed largely by a standard "information-processing" or "cognitivist" approach to cognition (Pinker, 2009). Put very simply, this approach understands the mind as analogous to a computing machine, in which "mind" is the software to the brain's hardware (Damasio, 1994). Here cognition is confined to nonconscious information processing *in the head*; it is understood to occur in a mechanistic or rule-based fashion that begins with the *input* of sense data and proceeds hierarchically through the development of evermore complex *representations*. This results, finally, in *outputs*—responses, behaviors, and "knowledge"—that correspond with a pre-given "world out there." In this view, we have no direct access to the world; our "experience" is of the representations (or "mental content") formed in the brain. Thus our "knowledge" of the world may be "assessed" in terms of the degree to which our mental content and resulting behaviors (outputs) correspond with a supposedly preexisting reality (see Varela et al., 1991). It is also important to note that this approach does not see the body as playing a significant role in cognition as such; it simply provides the necessary biological scaffolding, "where brain and body are related but only in the sense that the former cannot survive without the life support of the latter" (Damasio, 1994, p. 48).

In many ways, this orientation has informed and reinforced the ways we think about and do music and education in the industrial and postindustrial eras. As a number of critical pedagogues have discussed, many modern approaches to education adopt a mechanistic or, indeed, a "banking" approach to education (Freire, 2000; Giroux, 2011). Again, this involves a rather depersonalized and mechanical input-output understanding of human cognition in which students are trained to perform and think (and are assessed) according to standardized practices and outcomes; as a result, the critical and creative potentials of teachers and students (and performers and listeners) are downplayed (see Kincheloe, 2003, 2008; van der Schyff, Schiavio, & Elliott, 2016).

The cognitivist perspective has increasingly drawn criticism from thinkers across a range of disciplines who argue that it tends to reduce human cognition to an abstract "in-the-skull" problem-solving process that largely ignores the exploratory, embodied, and creative nature of perception (Clarke, 2005; Kincheloe, 2003). These concerns are central to the interdisciplinary research program known as *enactivism*, which by contrast explores the mind as a fundamentally situated, embodied, and ecological phenomenon.[6] The enactive approach does not reduce cognition to the representational recovery of a pre-given environment. Nor does it first understand the mind in mechanistic or computational terms. Rather, it explores cognition as originating in the basic biological processes of life itself—in the ways even the simplest organisms move, interact, and thus actively shape the environments they inhabit. Put simply, the enactive perspective sees mind and world (organism and environment) not as a fixed duality, but rather as continually co-arising in an *improvised* way—like "a path laid down in walking"[7] (Varela et al., 1991). As such, it may help us to understand the deep continuity between cognition and improvisation and thus better account for (and lend support to) the conception of improvisation as disposition introduced in this chapter.

## Cognition as Embodied, Embedded, Enactive, Extended, and . . . Improvised

Despite its broad interests and its openness to being integrated—most notably as a theoretical framework—within a range of research programs (see Stewart et al., 2010), enactivism can be defined, broadly speaking, in two ways. First, it may be approached according to the basic qualities it identifies as characterizing cognition. Recently, these have been referred to as the "4Es," which describe the mind as fundamentally:

- **Embodied**: mind is an embodied phenomenon involving a deep relationship between action and perception (neural + extra-neural factors).
- **Embedded**: mind is situated within a contingent milieu.
- **Enactive**: mind involves a process of bringing forth or "enacting" a meaningful world.
- **Extended**: mind cannot be reduced to "in-the-skull" processes, but rather includes an "extended" cognitive ecology involving objects, technologies, sociocultural engagements, and other agents (organic + inorganic factors).

Second, the enactive perspective may also be distinguished by three overlapping principles that explain the quartet of characteristics just mentioned. The first of these, *autopoiesis*, describes how a living creature self-organizes its own existence in conjunction with the environment it emerges from and that sustains it, how it actively develops viable relationships within the contingent constraints and affordances of the given milieu it is *embedded* within according (most fundamentally) to its biological requirements. Importantly, living organisms are not seen as mere responders. Rather, they actively "reach out" to their environment to "seek out" and *enact* a world that is relevant to their continued well-being (Thompson, 2007). This involves an ongoing recursive or "circular" process of embodied interactivity and adaptivity that occurs, most primordially, through affectively motivated action as perception (Colombetti, 2014; Nöe, 2006; Schiavio, van der Schyff, Cespedes-Guevara, & Reybrouck, 2016).

Such *embodied* processes are central to the second principle, *sense making*, which concerns the active ways living creatures disclose unique worlds of meaning that are informed and transformed by their interactions with every kind of otherness they encounter (Ihde, 1977; van der Schyff, 2015b). Indeed, while an organism may be differentiated by the bounded metabolic, self-regulative processes associated with the living body and its "inner" milieu, the same organism (if it is to remain a living individual) must also simultaneously maintain the dynamic organism-environment interactivity that allows it to make sense of its world in relation to its intrinsic needs. Thus, living cognition, mind, "identity," and "self" are necessarily *relational* and thus *extended* phenomena at the most primordial levels (McGann, De Jaegher, & Di Paolo, 2013; Weber & Varela, 2002).

This brings us to the third principle, *autonomy*, which describes how an organism's world and the "meanings" that arise from it are not externally imposed, but emerge through unique histories of interactivity with the environment (Di Paolo, 2005). This is to say that unlike computing machines—which require external entities (i.e., humans) to provide inputs and give meaning to their outputs—living cognitive systems *actively* and *autonomously* participate in the construction of their own lifeworlds (Varela et al., 1991). An important further consequence of this is that "information," "knowledge," and "meaning" can no longer be reduced to pre-given features of an external environment. Rather, they are seen as *ontogenic*—that is, as growing from the relevant relationships and valences that emerge as a *dynamic organism-environment system* constitutes a lifeworld (Oyama, 2000; Thompson, 2007). Along these lines, Varela and colleagues (1991) write that living cognition is based in the adaptive and embodied learning processes that enable not simply knowledge of "this" or "that," but rather "knowing how to negotiate our way through a world that is not fixed and pre-given but that is continually shaped by the types of actions in which we engage" (p. 144). With such insights in mind, I suggest that there is a very strong sense in which the enactive perspective reveals living cognition to be fundamentally improvisational.[8]

In recent years the enactive approach has been developed across a range of human activity and experience, including the field of social cognition. This has resulted in interesting new dimensions to the enactive perspective, including the notions of *participatory sense making* and *relational autonomy* (De Jaegher, 2013; De Jaegher & Di Paolo, 2007). These concepts have been advanced, for example, in the context of the prelinguistic and embodied modes of communication and understanding that occur between infants and primary caregivers. Importantly, such basic social activity is no longer understood simply in terms of imitation or "hardwired" responses. Rather, infants are observed to play active roles in shaping the relationship by developing a repertoire of utterances and bodily movements that facilitate the enactment of a unique shared ecology of meaning (Krueger, 2013; Reddy, Markova, & Wallot, 2013; Service, 1984). Again, this may be understood as continuous with the adaptive and improvisational character of living cognition more generally. It also expresses the relational conception of autonomy just mentioned, wherein "the self" cannot be reduced to some kind of fixed status, but rather is seen as an ongoing 4E process of (improvised) social and cultural enaction.

Moreover, a growing number of scholars are exploring the importance of musicality for such fundamental intersubjective forms of self and world making, including the primary forms of communicative movement and sound making just discussed (Krueger, 2014; Trevarthern, 2002; van der Schyff, 2015a). Indeed, musicality, broadly understood, is increasingly seen not simply as a cultural (pleasure) technology (Pinker, 2009), but rather as a "primordial, empathic, and embodied sense-making capacity that plays a central role in how we enact the personal and socio-cultural worlds we inhabit" (van der Schyff et al., 2016, p. 83). From this perspective improvisation and musicality go hand in hand as essential aspects of the human mind.

## IMPROVISATION AND ASSESSMENT

As I discussed at the outset of the chapter, musical improvisation often occurs within social and cultural contexts (Azzara, 2002; Hickey, 2002). Such contexts are characterized, with varying degrees of specificity, by certain historically enacted ways of doing and knowing—culturally sedimented techniques and understandings that allow a given music to be identified with a place, time, or social milieu. With this in mind, there are certain aspects of improvisation that can be seen as correlating with existing standards and that can be assessed more or less "objectively."[9] For example, within current modes of improvisation *training*, a teacher can assess knowledge of a given scale by asking a student to improvise a melody with it and by deducting a mark for every wrong note played. Likewise, the teacher could "test" a student's ability to play by ear by asking him or her to repeat melodic, harmonic, and rhythmic passages that are played or by getting the student to "outline" a set of chord changes, choosing from a given set of genre-based patterns and scales.

These examples are relatively easy to assess and reflect current modes of training that characterize improvisation pedagogy. However, as I have noted, we must be careful not to let our understanding of music, education, and assessment be limited to those aspects that are simply in line with "national music standards" or reductionist and/or false concepts of what improvisation and assessment entail. In other words, I argue that while such technical forms of learning and assessment are important, they need to be decentered and take their place as one aspect of more open-ended, adaptive, and collaborative learning environments that embrace the concept of improvisation as disposition. But what new approaches to assessment might accompany the richer models of cognition, improvisation, and music education I have explored here? And what kinds of activities might be associated with them? What we are looking for, of course, is not simply another "method." Rather, what is needed is an open-ended framework for thought and action that may be developed by teachers and students as an ongoing project.

As I discuss next, a 4E cognition approach offers a way of decentering the "isolationist," "technically driven," and externally imposed forms of assessment associated with "industrial thinking" (see Sawyer, 2007). From this perspective "self-assessment" involves developing a deepened awareness of the reciprocity of the personal *and* collective processes that contribute to the development of a unique musical-cognitive ecology. Here "self" may refer both to the individual and to the shared reflective capacities of the ensemble or class as a whole. As such, this framework may better suit the kinds of contingent, collaborative, and open-ended forms of self-assessment that more complete improvisation pedagogy requires.

# 4Es and an I . . . or Improvisation as Self-Assessment

I suggest that if the 4Es can be used to describe the fundamentally improvisatory nature of living minds, characteristics of the 4E model can also be used to guide an approach to assessment and praxis that applies the concept of improvisation as disposition. While such forms of assessment will not exclude the technical or skills-based aspects of music making, they will necessarily be more concerned with reflecting and fostering the kinds of creative potentials and collaborative environments described previously (Sawyer, 2007; van der Schyff et al., 2016). This will involve encouraging students to be attentive to and reflect on how relationships form and develop with the people (ensemble mates), things (instruments), and places that constitute their reality; how their "selves" extend into the environment and play a role in constituting the lives of others; and how their sense of musical identity is continuously transformed through the activities of their peers. This reflects the relational conception of autonomy that I explored previously—one that goes far beyond the Enlightenment notion of "a lone individual merely extending [his or her] cognitive reach" (Urban, 2014, p. 4) toward a vision of selfhood as a communal project (Benson, 2001).

Of course, such processes cannot be assessed simplistically and objectively, but rather require an open, cooperative dialogical approach that involves shared processes of action and critical reflection. Praxis and assessment should be understood as continuously guiding one another in a reciprocal fashion that reflects the biocognitive principles of autopoiesis and participatory sense making. From this perspective, "goals" and "outcomes" are not simply pre-given criteria, but possibilities that emerge from the needs, desires, and relevant self-assessments of the individual and group as they evolve dynamically. Thus, while the best way to begin improvisation in educational contexts may be, as Lewis suggests (see Borgo, 2005), to simply "throw" students directly into doing it, teachers must also be able to help students begin to critically examine and share the experiences that result and through such forms of self-assessment help students recognize the problems they wish to overcome, as well as open new possibilities to be developed.

With this in mind, students may be encouraged to engage in open-ended explorations of their relationship with their instrument(s) and to bring their discoveries to the ensemble. This will necessarily involve self-assessing the deeply embodied aspects of improvisation and instrumental practice (Berkowitz, 2010; Iyer, 2002, 2008). It will also include examining how the "resistance of the instrument" (Cochrane, 2013) plays a role in shaping the kinds of music one makes, as well as exploring the kinds of complex dynamics and embodied feedback loops that occur among the performer, instrument, acoustic environment, and other performers (Biasutti & Frezza, 2009; Borgo, 2005; Pressing, 1998; Walton, Richardson, Langland-Hassan, & Chemero, 2015).[10]

Central to such reflective processes will be developing in-the-moment assessments of shifting bodily-instrument-environment relationships and a growing awareness of the kinds of cross-modal, emotional-affective, self-regulatory, and "flow" experiences that characterize and motivate the improvising process (Csikszentmihalyi & Rich, 1997; Johnson, 2007; McPherson, Lopez-Gonzalez, Rankin, & Limb, 2014; Wopereis, Stoyanov, Kirschner, & Van Merriënboer, 2013). Here the development of a "phenomenological attitude" will also be important (see Schiavio, this volume; van der Schyff, 2016). Indeed, as a number of authors have demonstrated, phenomenology offers a coherent means of analyzing and discussing first-person experience and is thus highly useful in musical contexts (Clifton, 1983; Ferrera, 1984, 1991; Ihde, 1976; Krueger, 2011; Roholt, 2014; Sudnow, 1978). Along these lines, the introduction of mindful awareness and meditation, as well as aspects of the Alexander technique, may also be very useful in developing such direct, embodied forms of self-assessment (Biswas, 2012; Sarath, 2013; van der Schyff, 2015a).

Teachers should also recognize that students do not come to musical improvisation as detached and decontextualized onlookers, as "blank slates." Rather, they are already embedded within a milieu that has developed historically. However, as previously discussed, the enactive perspective does not conceptualize the cognitive activity of people as simply determined by their environments; –rather, we actively shape the cognitive ecologies we inhabit, and mind and world stand in a circular, co-emergent relationship to each other (Varela et al., 1991). Therefore, students and teachers should also be encouraged to critically examine the social, cultural, and gendered worlds they participate in, as well as the musical-sonic spaces they "live through," and to reach out to the worlds of others through empathy, action, and imagination (Greene, 1995; Silverman, 2012). In this way, students may gain a better understanding of the world in which they find themselves. In doing so, key aspects may be "put into play," forming material for improvisations and the enactment of new relationships.

Such processes are likely to highlight the autonomous activities of individuals in the critical assessment of the (musical) worlds they inhabit and enact. At the same time, they will also encourage participants to embrace the collaborative possibilities of the ensemble. At advanced levels, this will involve (1) developing highly nuanced understandings of, and the ability to deconstruct, a wide range of existing musical practices, styles and techniques; (2) advancing deeper understandings of the relational nature of sound,[11] movement, and space (Ihde, 1977); (3) developing ways of musicking that are unique to the individual and group; and (4) gaining the ability to reflect and (collaboratively) self-assess across multiple timescales (e.g., reflecting *in* action and reflecting *on* action; Schön, 1983).

With all of this in mind, a 4E framework for individual and collaborative forms of self-assessment asks students and teachers to consider questions such as the following:

- **Embodied:** What new instrumental challenges have emerged and what new body-instrument relationships and understandings have developed in the process of meeting them?
- **Embedded:** How have our musical activities explored and developed our understandings of the broader physical, sonic, historical, social, cultural, and gendered world(s) we live in as individuals and social groups? What roles does the sociocultural environment play in shaping the ways we improvise?
- **Enactive:** What new meanings have we opened up through our music making? What new relationships have emerged? And how have they transformed the ways we engage with the world musically, sonically, socially, emotionally, and so on?
- **Extended:** In what ways have my creative possibilities been enhanced or made possible through my interactions with coperformers, technologies, and other non-organic ecological factors? And how have I helped to facilitate the creative development of others?

As I have suggested, the 4Es may be juxtaposed with the four-part criteria that Sawyer (2007) lays out (see previous discussion) in relation to learning science. In this way, a 4E approach may offer ways for students and teachers to collectively assess to what degree their activities have met such potentials and what new levels of understanding and activity have emerged as possible goals. And of course, these categories may also provide a starting place for more explicitly critical forms of assessment—that is, recognizing what kinds of behaviors and conditions might hinder creative development.

Again, such understandings can only be properly developed, discussed, and assessed through the kinds of active, adaptive, and integrative praxis associated with a critically engaged approach to improvisation—that is, where practice and self-assessment become part of the same ongoing process. Indeed, the focus here is not simply on the products of training, but rather on assessing the process of creative development as it happens in an ongoing way (Dewey, 1997; Tarasti, 1993). And so, for example, while students might indeed be asked to self-assess a performance they have given according to various criteria, many of these criteria will have emerged through the reflective-creative processes of the students themselves. Here, assessment is framed less by externally driven standards and more by issues relevant to the development of the class (ensemble) itself as an autonomous, self-making system in its own right.[12]

The kinds of collaborative reflective processes a 4E improvisation pedagogy requires may also draw on (and help develop) the distinction between "authentic" and "inauthentic" forms of assessment—that is, the critical and reflective (self)assessment that is concerned with creative, contextual, and process-based learning, as opposed to the depersonalized, isolationist, and technically driven approaches associated with objectivist or standardized forms of assessment (see Weil, 2001). Importantly, a range of possibilities already exists for such "authentic" or "formative" types of assessment, including, for example, "folio-based" approaches. Here reflections and ideas, teacher-student and student-student interviews, descriptions and critiques of class activities, practice diaries, listening-viewing logs, performance reviews, the results of collaborative and self-directed research projects, and more may be collected and used to further enhance class dialogue (Elliott & Silverman, 2015; Gardner, 1991). And indeed, such materials could be organized and discussed according to the 4E framework presented here. Moreover, thanks to developments in digital technology such "process folios" may also be easily supplemented with video and audio recordings.[13] Likewise, previously difficult to acquire documentary films and performance footage of improvising musicians are now readily available online. These offer a range of real-world examples for students to consider. In this way, the process folio itself may be understood as a kind of bricolage (Kincheloe & Berry, 2004)—a creative and critical pedagogical project in which material and ideas are collected, organized, and expressed in various ways that contribute to the development of the student and the class or ensemble.

## CONCLUSION: TOWARD PRAXIS

While the enactive approach to improvisation explained here does not offer a fixed method of assessment, it nevertheless resonates with a rich pool of existing knowledge that informs possibilities for integrating creative practice, reflection, and self-assessment. Indeed, this orientation aligns most closely with ongoing research and theory associated with critical, "post-formal," and praxial approaches to education (Bowman, 2004; Kincheloe, Steinberg, & Villaverde, 1999; Kincheloe, 2003; Elliott & Silverman, 2015). It also encourages teachers and students to reach out to experienced improvisers, and to improvising communities and cultures, to explore living, real-world models (Bailey, 1993; Berliner, 1994; Borgo, 2007; Lewis, 2009a; Monson, 1996).[14] In the process, a wide range of possibilities may be discovered that are closely connected with the many concerns and insights discussed in this chapter.

Consider, for example, the free jazz and free improvisation movements that developed in the 1960s in America and Europe, respectively. Both produced a range of unique ensembles, performers, and creative communities, and both were in many ways politically charged. Free jazz strove to spiritually transform an oppressive and racist society in the United States (Monson, 2007), and free improvisation took on, among other things, the bourgeois capitalist-consumerist culture that characterized postwar European society (Borgo, 2005; Lewis, 2004, 2007). Many of the artists involved in both movements developed highly original approaches to their instruments, as well as ensembles that expanded understandings of what "music" can entail. Today, a range of texts, recordings, and films document these artists. These will be useful to students and educators in reflecting on their own relationships to music and culture (Bailey, 1993; Corbett, 2016; Lewis, 2009b; Litweiler, 1990; Toop, 2016; Watson, 2013; Whitehead, 2000; Stevens, 1984).

Excellent examples of communities of improvisers are Chicago's Association for the Advancement of Creative Musicians (AACM) and St. Louis's Black Artists Group (BAG) (see Lewis, 2009b). These organizations emerged to support important but highly marginalized communities of African American improvising musicians and to encourage creative musical practices that reflect the lived experiences and creative possibilities associated with black culture more generally. Importantly, in these communities the idea of culture and the individual identities that constitute it are not seen as pre-given, and the kinds of musical activities that these artists engage in are not strictly prescribed. Rather, culture and identity involve fluid, improvised processes in which various musical, mythological, historical, social, and sonic relationships are deconstructed and reconstructed. Individuals are encouraged to develop their own approaches to music making, which continually draw on, inform, and transform both the ensembles and the broader cultures they participate in.

Readers may wish to explore the Art Ensemble of Chicago (the AACM's "flagship" ensemble) and the ways it integrates and adapts "Great Black Music, Ancient to Future," as well as the members' individual perspectives on sound making and musical form. Another important example may be found in the music of the "Downtown" scene that emerged in New York City in the 1980s. These musicians explored a range of new approaches that often involved improvising with genre itself. Here, otherwise disparate types of music were juxtaposed, and musicians from diverse backgrounds were thrown into performances together. One important development of this community is the "game pieces" and improvised "conductions" associated with John Zorn (2004) and Butch Morris (Monga, 2012), respectively.[15]

Communities of creative musicians such as these offer useful models for those wishing to gain a better understanding of what improvising praxis entails in living contexts (see also Stevens, 2007). In the course of my career as an improvising musician, I have been fortunate to work with and learn from such artists. And in my teaching I have developed a number of activities and approaches informed by these experiences. For example, a "game piece" like Zorn's "Cobra" offers an excellent framework for exploring basic aspects of improvisation in pedagogical contexts. Put very simply, the game consists of a series of "prompts"—open frameworks for improvising within certain parameters that include memory, different ensemble groupings, dynamics, and so on. The ensemble members are required to develop their own strategies and material for effectively engaging with such prompts, which are initiated in various ways by the ensemble itself through a system of hand gestures (Brackett, 2008). While the complete game is very complex, it can be simplified for beginning improvisers. Moreover, "Cobra" does not require specific instrumentation or knowledge of a specific style of music; all instruments and backgrounds are welcome. Most important is that the game is enjoyable, and it affords a coherent but nevertheless open framework for participants to explore and discuss basic aspects of improvisation.[16]

Another activity involves a process I sometimes call "modular composition." It is inspired by the range of improvising communities discussed previously and was developed collaboratively with improvising ensembles in Europe and Vancouver, Canada. It involves getting participants to research and bring to the ensemble (among other things) forms, melodies, chord structures, rhythms, field recordings, new and old technologies, other media, new instrumental techniques, and sound-making possibilities, as well as concepts derived from their listening and reading. The material is then developed and given forms by the ensemble through an improvisational, exploratory process in which it is integrated, juxtaposed, and adapted in various ways (bricolage). This can result in fixed forms, wherein the musicians eventually improvise within and against an overarching structure they have developed collectively, or it can involve a mobile form, in which the various materials and ideas are cued and structured by the ensemble members in real time and in accordance with the flow of the music. The way such collaborative processes develop over time (i.e., through experimentation, negotiation, self-assessment, and the adaptive development of techniques and embodied understandings) can lead to distinct ensemble approaches and the enactment of strong musical identities and extended musical communities.

The wide range of concerns, ideas, and possibilities I have discussed in this chapter are intended to inspire richer and more open-ended approaches to improvisation pedagogy, curriculum, and assessment. In the end, however, it is up to educators themselves to engage in the kinds of ongoing critical reflection that will help them decide how to develop and address these issues in praxis. With this in mind, I hope that in the years to come a diverse range of new accounts will emerge about how improvisation may be implemented and assessed in pedagogical contexts. Moreover, it will be very interesting to see how such accounts align with the growing body of theory and research that explores the musical mind as an embodied, enactive, or 4E phenomenon (Borgo, 2005; Krueger, 2011a, 2011b, 2014; Matyja & Schiavio, 2013; Reybrouck, 2001, 2005, 2006; Schiavio et al., 2016; Silverman, 2012; van der Schyff, 2015a, 2015b).

Finally, although free improvisation remains a marginalized practice, it has nevertheless spread around the globe. Today most urban centers have an improvised music scene, where artists from diverse backgrounds collaborate and develop new approaches to music and sound making. Likewise, many contemporary communities are constituted by a range of indigenous and immigrant subcultures that engage in more traditional forms of musical improvisation. So if they are willing to search, educators and students may find substantial living resources of improvised music(s) in creative musical communities close to home.

## Acknowledgments

Many thanks to Andrea Schiavio, Susan O'Neill, and David Borgo for their helpful comments on early drafts of this chapter. This work was supported by the Social Sciences and Humanities Research Council of Canada.

## Notes

1. It should be noted that improvisational practice remains an important part of organ performance and pedagogy.
2. While several studies have explored how the two processes differ (Sarath, 1996; Azzara, 2002), it has been suggested that composition and improvisation should no longer be understood as opposites, but rather as mutually reinforcing aspects of the creative musical process (Biasutti, 2015; Marsh, 1995; Sessions, 1941). Indeed, in Swanwick and Tillman's (1986) studies of how young children "compose" music, improvisation and composition are essentially indistinguishable. And likewise, as Burnard (2000) writes, "our aim as music educators should be to facilitate a form of music education that focuses on genuine experiences of children *being* improvisers and composers rather than acting out a pre-defined model" (p. 21).
3. See, for example, the K–4 improvisation assessment strategy in MENC (1996, p. 39; also in Hickey, 2009).
4. Such codifying tendencies have also dominated small group pedagogy. As Bailey (1993) writes of bebop: "The mechanics of this particular style—its somewhat stylistic rigidity, its susceptibility to formulated method - created a field day for the educators. [...] It has proved to be one style of improvising which can be easily taught" (p. 49).
5. Perhaps a loose distinction should be made here between "free improvisation" as an open-ended pedagogical approach and "free improvisation" as a specific musical movement that developed in Europe in the mid-twentieth century.
6. In the course of its development, enactivism has produced a number of schools of thought, with each positing contrasting perspectives that originate in a shared group of basic principles (Hutto & Myin, 2012). As space does not permit a full treatment of each of these perspectives, the brief outline I offer here draws mostly on the original *autopoietic* approach introduced in the early 1990s by Varela et al. (1991), and that has recently been updated by Evan Thompson (2007) and others (see Stewart et al., 2010).
7. As Varela et al. (1991) elaborate: "There is always a next step for the system in its perceptually guided action [...] the actions of the system are always directed toward situations that have yet to become actual. Thus cognition as embodied action both poses the problems and specifies those paths that must be tread or laid down for their solution" (p. 205).
8. For an interesting supporting discussion that considers musical improvisation in the context of the enactive biological principles discussed here, see Walton, Richardson, & Chemero (2014).
9. However, it is important to understand that such normative or institutionalized ways of thinking and doing also emerge from historical processes of human enactment and thus need not be understood as entirely fixed (De Jaegher, 2013).
10. Developments in musical semiotics may also offer useful ways of exploring and discussing how communication develops in such contexts. Here a range of recent research has drawn

on embodied-enactive cognition and dynamical systems theory to explain how sonic, kinesthetic, and ecological factors contribute to the enactment of meaningful signals in improvising ensembles (Iyer, 2002, 2004, 2008; Reybrouck, 2001, 2005; Sawyer, 1996; Walton et al., 2014). Although some of this literature involves complex terminology and detailed empirical studies, it is certainly not beyond the ability of a dedicated educator to draw out and introduce the key areas of inquiry for use in collaborative assessment.

11.  Here the introduction of sound studies into the music curriculum becomes important (Sterne, 2012). R. M. Schafer's (1986, 1994) writings on music education and soundscape studies offer an excellent starting place.

12.  By now it should be apparent that from a 4E perspective distinctions between reflection and self-assessment necessarily become less clearly defined. Reflection is sometimes associated with the goal of "knowing," while the goal of self-assessment is "growing." The former involves "a personal process that can deepen one's understanding of self and can lead to significant discoveries or insight," while the latter is often understood as "a process that involves establishing strengths, improvements, and insights based on predetermined performance criteria" (see Desjarlais & Smith, 2011, p. 3). However, because the conception of improvisation discussed here goes beyond such "predetermined criteria," a 4E understanding of what self-assessment entails will necessarily involve an overlapping or reciprocal relationship with critical reflection and with the creative praxis of the larger musical ecology.

13.  For an interesting approach to the analysis of recordings of free improvisation, see Canonne and Garnier (2012).

14.  Readers are especially encouraged to explore the four-part documentary series *On The Edge*, hosted by improvising guitarist Derek Bailey and presented by Channel 4 (UK).

15.  Of course there is also a range of possibilities for exploring improvisation across a range of non-Western traditions (Nettl, 1974; Nettl & Russell, 1998).

16.  Elsewhere (van der Schyff, 2013) I discuss a rehearsal and performance of "Cobra" in detail and briefly consider my experience developing it in an educational context.

# REFERENCES

Abril, C. (2013). Critical issues in Orff Schulwerk. In C. Wang (Ed.), *Orff Schulwerk: Reflections and directions* (pp. 11–24). Chicago: GIA Publications.

Aebersold, J. (2000). *The II/V7/I progression*. Vol. 3, *A new approach to jazz improvisation*. New Albany, IN: Jamey Aebersold.

Attali, J. (1985/2006). *Noise: The political economy of music*. Minneapolis: University of Minnesota Press.

Azzara, C. D. (2002). Improvisation. In R. Colwell & C. Richardson (Eds.), *New handbook of research in music teaching and learning* (pp. 171–87). Oxford: Oxford University Press.

Azzara, C. D., & Grunow, R. F. (2003). *Developing musicianship through improvisation*. Chicago: GIA Publications.

Bailey, D. (1993). *Improvisation: Its nature and practice in music*. New York: DaCapo Press.

Baker, D. (1988). *Jazz improvisation: A comprehensive method for all musicians*. Van Nuys, CA: Alfred Publishing.

Benson, C. (2001). *The cultural psychology of self: Place, morality, and art in human worlds*. London: Routledge.

Berkowitz, A. (2010). *The improvising mind*. Oxford: Oxford University Press.

Berliner, P. (1994). *Thinking jazz: The infinite art of improvisation*. Chicago: University of Chicago Press.

Biasutti, M. (2015). Pedagogical applications of cognitive research on musical improvisation. *Frontiers in Psychology, 6*, 614. doi:10.3389/fpsyg.2015.00614

Biasutti, M., & Frezza, L. (2009). The dimensions of music improvisation. *Creativity Research Journal, 21*(2–3), 232–42.

Biesta, G., & Osberg, D. (2007). Beyond re/presentation: A case for updating the epistemology of schooling. *Interchange, 38*(1), 15–29.

Biswas, A. (2011). The music of what happens: Mind meditation and music as movement. In D. Clarke & E. Clarke (Eds.), *Music and consciousness: Philosophical, psychological, and cultural perspectives* (pp. 95–110). Oxford: Oxford University Press.

Borgo, D. (2005). *Sync or swarm: Improvising music in a complex age*. New York: Continuum.

Borgo, D. (2007). Free jazz in the classroom: An ecological approach to music education. *Jazz Perspectives, 1*(1), 61–88.

Borgo, D. (2014). Ghost in the music, or the perspective of an improvising ant. In G. E. Lewis & B. Piekut (Eds.), *The Oxford handbook of critical improvisation studies* (Vol. 1) [Online]. New York: Oxford University Press.

Borgo, D., & Kaiser, J. (2010, July 1–3). Configurin(g) KaiBorg: Interactivity, ideology, and agency in electro-acoustic improvised music. *Proceedings of the International Conference Beyond the Centres: Musical Avant-Gardes Since 1950*. Thessaloniki, Greece. http://btc.web.auth.gr/

Born, G., Lewis, E., & Straw, W. (Eds.). (2017). *Improvisation and social aesthetics*. Durham, NC: Duke University Press.

Bowman, W. (2004). Cognition and the body: Perspectives from music education. In L. Bresler (Ed.), *Knowing bodies, moving minds: Toward embodied teaching and learning* (pp. 29–50). Dordrecht, The Netherlands: Kluwer Academic Press.

Brackett, J. (2008). *John Zorn: Tradition and transgression*. Bloomington: Indiana University Press.

Bradley, D. (2012). Good for what, good for whom? Decolonizing music education philosophies. In W. Bowman & A. L. Frega (Eds.), *The handbook of philosophy in music education* (pp. 409–33). New York: Oxford University Press.

Burnard, P. (2000). How children ascribe meaning to improvisation and composition: Rethinking pedagogy in music education. *Music Education Research, 2*(1), 7–23.

Campbell, P. S. (2009). Learning to improvise music, improvising to learn. In G. Solis & B. Nettl (Eds.), *Musical improvisation: Art, education, and society* (pp. 119–42). Urbana: University of Illinois Press.

Canonne, C., & Garnier, N. B. (2012). Cognition and segmentation in collective free improvisation: An exploratory study. *Proceedings of the 12th International Conference on Music Perception and Cognition and 8th Triennial Conference of the European Society for the Cognitive Sciences of Music*, 197–204, http://icmpc-escom2012.web.auth.gr.

Clarke, E. F. (2005). *Ways of listening: An ecological approach to the perception of musical meaning*. Oxford: Oxford University Press.

Clifton, T. (1983). *Music as heard: A study in applied phenomenology*. New Haven, CT: Yale University Press.

Cochrane, T. (2013). On the resistance of the instrument. In T. Cochrane, B. Fantini, & K. R. Scherer (Eds.), *The emotional power of music: Multidisciplinary perspectives on musical arousal, expression and social control* (pp. 75–84). Oxford: Oxford University Press.

Coker, J. (1997). *Elements of the jazz language for the developing improviser*. Miami, FL: Alfred Publishing.

Coleman, S. N. (1922). *Creative music for children: A plan of training based on the natural evolution of music, including the making and playing of instruments, dancing–singing–poetry*. New York: G. P. Putnam's sons.

Coleman, S. N. (1927a). *Creative music for schools: Suggestions to teachers to be used in connection with first steps in playing and composing*. New York: The John Day Company.

Coleman, S. N. (1927b). *First steps in playing and composing: A music book for children*. New York: The Lincoln School.

Coleman, S. N. (1939). *Creative music in the home: Music, stories, how to make instruments, how to play them, and many tunes to play*. New York: The John Day Company.

Colombetti, G. (2014). *The feeling body: Affective science meets the enactive mind*. Cambridge, MA: MIT Press.

Corbett, J. (2016). *A listener's guide to free improvisation*. Chicago: University of Chicago Press.

Creech, A., Papageorgi, I., Duffy, C., Morton, F., Hadden, E., Potter, J., . . . Welch, G. (2008). Investigating musical performance: Commonality and diversity among classical and non-classical musicians. *Music Education Research, 10*(2), 215–34.

Csikszentmihalyi, M., & Rich, G. (1997). Musical improvisation: A systems approach. In K. R. Sawyer (Ed.), *Creativity in performance* (pp. 43–66). Greenwich, CT: Ablex.

Damasio, A. (1994). *Descartes' error: Emotion, reason, and the human brain*. New York: Putnam.

De Jaegher, H. (2013). Rigid and fluid interactions with institutions. *Cognitive Systems Research, 25–26*(0), 19–25.

De Jaegher, H., & Di Paolo, E. A. (2007). Participatory sense-making: An enactive approach to social cognition. *Phenomenology and the Cognitive Sciences, 6*(4), 485–507.

DeNora, T. (1986). How is extra-musical meaning possible? Music as a place and space for "work." *Sociological Theory, 4*(1), 84–94.

Desjarlais, M., & Smith, P. (2011). A comparative analysis of refection and self-assessment. *International Journal of Process Education, 3*(1), 3–18.

Dewey, J. (1997). *Democracy and education*. New York: Simon & Schuster.

Di Paolo, E. A. (2005). Autopoiesis, adaptivity, teleology, agency. *Phenomenology and the Cognitive Sciences, 4*(4), 429–52.

Elliott, D. J. (1995). *Music matters: A new philosophy of music education*. New York: Oxford University Press.

Elliott, D. J. (1996). Improvisation and jazz: Implications for international practice, *International Journal of Music Education, 26*(1), 3–13.

Elliott, D. J., & Silverman, M. (2015). *Music matters: A philosophy of music education* (2nd ed.). New York: Oxford University Press.

Ferrara, L. (1984). Phenomenology as a tool for musical analysis. *Musical Quarterly, 70*(3), 355–73.

Ferrara, L. (1991). *Philosophy and the analysis of music: Bridges to musical sound, form and reference*. Westport, CT: Greenwood Press.

Freire, P. (2000). *Pedagogy of the oppressed* (30th anniv. ed.). New York: Bloomsbury Academic.

Gardner, H. (1991). *The unschooled mind: How children think and how schools should teach*. New York: Basic Books.

Giroux, H. (2011). *On critical pedagogy*. New York: Continuum.

Goehr, L. (1992). *The imaginary museum of musical works: An essay in the philosophy of music*. Oxford: Clarendon Press.

Gordon, E. E. (2003a). *Improvisation in the music classroom. Sequential learning.* Chicago: GIA Publications.

Gordon, E. E. (2003b). *Learning sequences in music: Skill, content, and patterns; A music learning theory.* Chicago: GIA Publications, Inc.

Green, L. (2002). *How popular musicians learn: A way ahead for music education.* London: Ashgate.

Green, L. (2008). *Music, informal learning and the school: A new classroom pedagogy.* London: Ashgate.

Greene, M. (1995). *Releasing the imagination.* San Francisco, CA: Jossey-Bass.

Heble, A., & Caines, R. (Eds.). (2014). *The improvisation studies reader: Spontaneous acts.* London: Routledge.

Heble, A., & Laver, M. (Eds.). (2016). *Improvisation and music education: Beyond the classroom.* London: Routledge.

Hickey, M. (2002). Creativity research in music, visual art, theatre and dance. In R. Colwell & C. Richardson (Eds.), *The new handbook of research on music teaching and learning* (pp. 398–415). New York: Oxford University Press.

Hickey, M. (2009). Can improvisation be "taught"? A call for free improvisation in our schools. *International Journal of Music Education, 27*(4), 285–99.

Hickey, M. (2015). Learning from the experts: A study of free-improvisation in university settings. *Journal of Research in Music Education, 62*(4), 425–45.

Higgins, L., & Mantie, R. (2013). Improvisation as ability, culture, and experience. *Music, Educators Journal, 100*(2), 38–44.

Hutto, D., & Myin, E. (2012). *Radicalizing enactivism: Basic minds without content.* Cambridge, MA: MIT Press.

Imada, T. (2012). The grain of the music: Does music education "mean" something in Japan? In W. Bowman & L. Frega (Eds.), *The Oxford handbook of philosophy in music education* (pp. 147–62). Oxford: Oxford University Press.

Ihde, D. (1976). *Listening and voice: A phenomenology of sound.* Athens: Ohio University Press.

Ihde, D. (1977). *Experimental phenomenology: An introduction.* New York: G. P. Putnam's Sons.

Iyer, V. (2002). Embodied mind, situated cognition, and expressive microtiming in African-American music. *Music Perception, 19*(3), 387–414.

Iyer, V. (2004). Exploding the narrative in jazz improvisation. In R. G. O'Meally, B. H. Edwards, & F. J. Griffin (Eds.), *Uptown conversation: The new jazz studies* (pp. 393–403). New York: Columbia University Press.

Iyer, V. (2008). On improvisation, temporality, and embodied experience. In P. Miller (Ed.), *Sound unbound* (pp. 273–93). Cambridge, MA: MIT Press.

Johnson, M. (2007). *The meaning of the body: Aesthetics of human understanding.* Chicago: University of Chicago Press.

Kanellopoulos, P. A. (2011). Freedom and responsibility: The aesthetics of free musical improvisation and its educational implications—a view from Bakhtin. *Philosophy of Music Education Review, 19*(2), 113–35.

Kincheloe, J. L. (2003). Critical ontology: Visions of selfhood and curriculum. *Journal of Curriculum Theorizing, 19*(1), 47–64.

Kincheloe, J. L. (2008). *Knowledge and critical pedagogy: An introduction.* London: Springer.

Kincheloe, J. L., & Berry, K. (2004). *Rigour and complexity in educational research: Conceptualizing the bricolage.* New York: Open University Press.

Kincheloe, J. L., Steinberg, S., & Villaverde, L. (1999). *Rethinking intelligence: Confronting psychological assumptions about teaching and learning.* New York: Routledge.

Konowitz, B. (1973). *Music improvisation as a classroom method: A new approach to teaching music.* New York: Alfred Publishing.

Krueger, J. (2011a). Doing things with music. *Phenomenology and the Cognitive Sciences, 10*(1), 1–22.

Krueger, J. (2011b). Enacting musical content. In R. Manzotti (Ed.), *Situated aesthetics: Art beyond the skin* (pp. 63–85). Exeter, UK: Imprint Academic.

Krueger, J. (2013). Empathy, enaction, and shared musical experience. In T. Cochrane, B. Fantini, & K. Scherer (Eds.), *The emotional power of music: Multidisciplinary perspectives on musical expression, arousal, and social control* (pp. 177–96). Oxford: Oxford University Press.

Krueger, J. (2014). Affordances and the musically extended mind. *Frontiers in Psychology, 4,* 1003. doi:10.3389/fpsyg.2013.01003

Lajoie, S. (2005). Extending the scaffolding metaphor. *Instructional Science, 33*(5–6), 541–57.

Laroche, J., & Kaddouch, I. (2015). Spontaneous preferences and core tastes: embodied musical personality and dynamics of interaction in a pedagogical method of improvisation. *Frontiers in Psychology, 6,* 522. doi:10.3389/fpsyg.2015.00522

Lasker, H. (1971). *Teaching creative music in secondary schools.* Boston: Allyn and Bacon.

Lawrence, I. (1978). *Composers and the nature of music education.* London: Scolar Press.

Lewis, G. E. (2004). Improvised music after 1950: Afrological and Eurological perspectives. In D. Fischlin & A. Heble (Eds.), *The other side of nowhere: Jazz, improvisation, and communities in dialogue* (pp. 131–62). Middletown, CT: Wesleyan University Press.

Lewis, G. E. (2007). Improvisation and pedagogy: Background and focus of inquiry. *Critical Studies in Improvisation, 3*(2), 1–5. Retrieved from http://www.criticalimprov.com/article/view/412/659

Lewis, G. E. (2009a). *The condition of improvisation.* Keynote address, International Society for Improvised Music, Santa Cruz, New Mexico.

Lewis, G. E. (2009b). *A power stronger than itself: The AACM and American experimental music.* Chicago: University of Chicago Press.

Lewis, G. E., & Piekut, B. (2016). *The Oxford handbook of critical improvisation studies* (Vol. 1). Oxford: Oxford University Press.

Litweiler, J. (1990). *The freedom principle: Jazz after 1958.* New York: Da Capo Press.

MacDonald, R., Wilson, G., & Miell, D. (2011). Improvisation as a creative process within contemporary music. In D. Hargreaves, D. Miell, & R. MacDonald (Eds.), *Musical imaginations: Multidisciplinary perspectives on creativity, performance and perception* (pp. 242–56). Oxford: Oxford University Press.

Marsh, K. (1995). Children's singing games: composition in the playground. *Research Studies in Music Education, 8*(2), 80–93.

Matyja, J., & Schiavio, A. (2013). Enactive music cognition. *Constructivist Foundations, 8,* 351–57.

McGann, M., De Jaegher, H., & Di Paolo, E. (2013). Enaction and psychology. *Review of General Psychology, 17*(2), 203–9.

McPherson, M. J., Lopez-Gonzalez, M., Rankin, S. K., & Limb, C. J. (2014). The role of emotion in musical improvisation: An analysis of structural features. *PLoS ONE, 9,* e105144. doi:10.1371/journal.pone.0105144

MENC, National Commission on Instruction. (1974). *The school music program: Description & standards.* Reston, VA: MENC.

Miller, D., & Iyer, V. (2010). Improvising digital culture: A conversation. *Critical Studies in Improvisation, 5*(1), 1–10.

Monga, V. (Producer & Director). (2012). *Black February: Music is an open door* [Motion picture]. United States: Studio unavailable.

Monson, I. (1996). *Saying something: Jazz improvisation and interaction.* Chicago: University of Chicago Press.

Monson, I. (2007). *Freedom sounds: Civil rights call out to jazz and Africa.* New York: Oxford University Press.

Moorhead, G. E., & Pond, D. (1941/1978). *Music for young children.* Santa Barbara, CA: Pillsbury Foundation for the Advancement of Music Education. (Reprint from the 1941–1951 editions.)

Musical Futures. (2008). *Musical Futures curriculum.* Retrieved from http://www.musicalfutures.org.uk/mfInWords.html

Nachmanovitch, S. (1990). *Free play: Improvisation in life and art.* New York: Tarcher/Perigee.

Nettl, B. (1974). Thoughts on improvisation: A comparative approach. *Musical Quarterly, 60*(1), 1–19.

Nettl, B. (1998). Introduction. In B. Nettl (Ed.), *In the course of performance* (pp. 1–26). Chicago: University of Chicago Press.

Nettl, B., & Russell, M. (Eds.). (1998). *In the course of performance: Studies in the world of musical improvisation.* Chicago: University of Chicago Press.

Nöe, A. (2006). *Action in perception.* Cambridge, MA: MIT Press.

O'Neill, S. A. (2010). On becoming a music learner: Understanding relationships that foster growth. *Canadian Music Educator, 51*(3), 26–28.

O'Neill, S. A. (2014). Mind the gap: Transforming music engagement through learner-centered informal music learning. *The Recorder: Journal of the Ontario Music Educators' Association, 56*(2), 18–22.

Oyama, S. (2000). *The ontogeny of information* (2nd ed.). Durham, NC: Duke University Press.

Paynter, J. (1992). *Sound and structure.* New York: Cambridge University Press.

Pinker, S. (2009). *How the mind works.* New York: Norton.

Pressing, J. (1988). Improvisations, methods and models. In J. Sloboda (Ed.), *Generative processes in music* (pp. 129–78). New York: Clarendon Press.

Pressing, J. (1998). Psychological constraints on improvisational expertise and skill. In B. Nettl (Ed.), *In the course of performance* (pp. 47–67). Chicago: University of Chicago Press.

Price, D. (2006). *Personalizing music learning.* London: Paul Hamlyn Foundation.

Reddy, V., Markova, G., & Wallot, S. (2013). Anticipatory adjustments to being picked up in infancy. *PLoS ONE, 8*(6), 1–9.

Regelski, T. A. (2002). On "methodolatry" and music teaching as critical and reflective praxis. *Philosophy of Music Education Review, 10*(2), 102–23.

Reybrouck, M. (2001). Biological roots of musical epistemology: Functional cycles, umwelt, and enactive listening. *Semiotica, 134*(1–4), 599–633.

Reybrouck, M. (2005). A biosemiotic and ecological approach to music cognition: event perception between auditory listening and cognitive economy. *Axiomathes, 15*(2), 229–66.

Reybrouck, M. (2006). Music cognition and the bodily approach: Musical instruments as tools for musical semantics. *Contemporary Music Review, 25*(1/2), 59–68.

Rodriguez, C. X. (2004). Popular music in music education: Toward a new conception of musicality. In C. X. Rodriguez (Ed.), *Bridging the gap: Popular music and music education* (pp. 13–28). Carlos Reston, VA: MENC.

Roholt, T. C. (2014). *Groove: A phenomenology of rhythmic nuance*. New York: Bloomsbury.

Sarath, E. W. (1996). A new look at improvisation. *Journal of Music Theory, 40*, 1–38.

Sarath, E. W. (2013). *Improvisation, creativity, and consciousness: Jazz as integral template for music, education, and society*. Albany: State University of New York Press.

Sawyer, K. R. (1996). The semiotics of improvisation: The pragmatics of musical and verbal performance. *Semiotica, 108*(3–4), 269–306.

Sawyer, K. R. (2003). *Group creativity: Music, theater, collaboration*. Mahwah, NJ: Erlbaum.

Sawyer, K. R. (Ed.). (2006). *The Cambridge handbook of the learning sciences*. New York: Cambridge University Press.

Sawyer, K. R. (2007). Improvisation and teaching. *Critical Studies in Improvisation, 2*(2). Retrieved from http://www.criticalimprov.com/article/view/380/626

Schafer, R. M. (1986). *The thinking ear: Complete writings on music education*. Bancroft, ON: Arcana Editions.

Schafer, R. M. (1994). *The soundscape: Our sonic environment and the tuning of the world*. Rochester, VT: Destiny Books.

Schiavio, A., van der Schyff, D., Cespedes-Guevara, J., & Reybrouck, M. (2016). Enacting musical emotions: Enaction, dynamic systems and the embodied mind. *Phenomenology and the Cognitive Sciences, 16*(5), 785–809. doi:10.1007/s11097-016-9477-8

Schön, D. A. (1983*). The reflective practitioner: How professionals think in action*. London: Temple Smith.

Service, V. (1984). Maternal styles and communicative development. In A. Lock & E. Fisher (Eds.), *Language development* (pp. 132–40). London: Croom Elm.

Sessions, R. (1941). The composer and his message. In A. Centeno (Ed.), *The intent of the artist* (pp. 101–34). Princeton, NJ: Princeton University Press.

Silverman, M. (2012). Virtue ethics, care ethics, and "the good life of teaching." *Action, Criticism, and Theory for Music Education, 11*(2), 96–122.

Szekely, M. (2012). Musical education: From identity to becoming. In W. D. Bowman & A. L. Frega (Eds.), *The Oxford handbook of philosophy in music education* (pp. 163–79). New York: Oxford University Press.

Small, C. (1998). *Musicking: The meaning of performing and listening*. Middletown, CT: Wesleyan University Press.

Sterne, J. (2012). *The sound studies reader*. New York: Routledge.

Stevens, J. (2007). *Search and reflect: A music workshop handbook*. Middlesex, UK: Rockschool.

Stewart, J., Gapenne, O., & Di Paolo, E. A. (Eds.). (2010). *Enaction: Toward a new paradigm for cognitive science*. Cambridge, MA: MIT Press.

Sudnow, D. (1978). *Ways of the hand: The organization of improvised conduct*. Cambridge, MA: Harvard University Press.

Swanwick, K., & Tillman, J. (1986). The sequence of musical development: A study of children's compositions. *British Journal of Music Education, 3*, 305–39.

Tarasti, E. (1993). From *Mastersingers* to Bororo Indians: On the semiosis of improvisation. In T. Bram (Ed.), *Proceedings from the Congress on Improvisation* (pp. 62–81). Lucerne, Switzerland.

Thompson, E. (2007). *Mind in life: Biology, phenomenology and the sciences of mind*. Cambridge, MA: Harvard University Press.

Toop, D. (2016). *Into the maelstrom: Music, improvisation and the dream of freedom*. New York: Bloomsbury.

Trevarthen, C. (2002). Origins of musical identity: Evidence from infancy for musical social awareness. In R. A. R. MacDonald, D. J. Hargreaves, & D. Miell (Eds.), *Musical identities* (pp. 21–38). Oxford: Oxford University Press.

Urban, P. (2014). Toward an expansion of an enactive ethics with the help of care ethics. *Frontiers in Psychology, 5*, 1–3. doi:10.3389/fpsyg.2014.01354

van der Schyff, D. (2013). The free improvisation game: Performing John Zorn's "Cobra". *The Journal of Research in Music Performance* (Spring, 2013). https://ejournals.lib.vt.edu/JRMP/article/view/726.

van der Schyff, D. (2015a). Music as a manifestation of life: Exploring enactivism and the "Eastern perspective" for music education. *Frontiers in Psychology, 6*, 345. doi:10.3389/fpsyg.2015.00345

van der Schyff, D. (2015b). Praxial music education and the ontological perspective: An enactivist response to *Music Matters 2*. *Action, Criticism and Theory for Music Education, 14*(3), 75–105.

van der Schyff, D. (2016). From Necker cubes to polyrhythms: Fostering a phenomenological attitude in music education. *Phenomenology and Practice, 10*(1), 4–24.

van der Schyff, D., Schiavio, A., & Elliott, D. J. (2016). Critical ontology for an enactive music pedagogy. *Action, Theory and Criticism for Music Education, 15*(5), 81–121.

Varela, F. J., Thompson, E., & Rosch, E. (1991). *The embodied mind: Cognitive science and human experience*. Cambridge, MA: MIT Press.

Walton, A., Richardson, M. J., & Chemero, A. (2014). Self-organization and semiosis in jazz improvisation. *International Journal of Signs and Semiotic Systems, 3*(2), 12–25.

Walton, A., Richardson, M. J., Langland-Hassan, P., & Chemero, A. (2015). Improvisation and the self-organization of multiple musical bodies. *Frontiers in Psychology, 1*(6). doi:10.3389/fpsyg.2015.00313

Watson, B. (2013). *Derek Bailey and the story of free improvisation*. London: Verso.

Weber, A., & Varela, F. J. (2002). Life after Kant: Natural purposes and the autopoietic foundations of biological individuality. *Phenomenology and the Cognitive Sciences, 1*(2), 97–125.

Weil, D. (2001). Whose world, which economic classes, and what standards? In J. L. Kincheloe & D. K. Weil (Eds.), *Standards and schooling in the United States: An encyclopedia* (Vol. 1, pp. 505–33). Denver, CO: ABC-CLIO.

Whitehead, K. (2000). *New Dutch swing*. New York: Billboard Books.

Wopereis, I. G. J. H., Stoyanov, S., Kirschner, P. A., & Van Merriënboer, J. J. G. (2013). What makes a good musical improviser? An expert view on improvisational expertise. *Psychomusicology, 23*, 222–35. doi:10.1037/pmu0000021

Wright, R., & Kanellopoulos, P. A. (2010). Informal music learning, improvisation and teacher education. *British Journal of Music Education, 27*, 71–87.

Zorn, J. (2004). The game pieces. In C. Cox & D. Warner (Eds.), *Audio culture: Readings in modern music* (pp. 196–200). New York: Continuum.

# CHAPTER 18

# PHILOSOPHY OF ASSESSMENT IN POPULAR MUSIC EDUCATION

### BRYAN POWELL AND GARETH DYLAN SMITH

WHILE "popular music education" (PME) clearly has much in common with both popular music and music education, there is enough that is discrete or at least uniquely interesting about PME that it warrants its own focus within a handbook such as this (Smith, Moir, Brennan, Rambarran, & Kirkman, 2017). Much that is in other chapters will of course be relevant to this chapter and its audience, and likely the converse will also be true. In this chapter, however, we outline issues relating to the philosophy of assessment in music education as they pertain specifically to PME contexts. The chapter outlines the expanding presence of PME programs and poses important questions pertaining to philosophy of assessment in PME. We also discuss the relationships among music education, higher education, and popular music as commoditized product(s), as well as the context for and a set of (sub)cultural practices, and look through the lens(es) of authenticity, before exploring canon and repertoire in PME. We highlight examples of assessment practices in particular PME contexts and the ideologies and philosophies that consciously or unconsciously undergird these. We then present a model of assessment called "negotiated assessment" (Kleiman, 2009, p. 2), which we propose as one possible broad, inclusive approach to establishing a philosophy of assessment for popular music education. This chapter does not interrogate practices so much as it probes the values and rationales (often tacit or implied) by which they are supported. As such, the chapter has an axiological focus (Jorgensen, 2006, p. 186).

As identified by Gareth Dylan Smith, Zack Moir, Matt Brennan, Shara Rambarran, and Phil Kirkman (2017) and Bryan Powell, Andrew Krikun, and Joseph Pignato (2015), there has recently been a proliferation of activity around PME, including numerous conferences, the establishment in 2010 of the Association for Popular Music Education (Powell et al., 2015), and publication of a special issue of *IASPM@ Journal* (Green, Lebler, & Till, 2015), the *Routledge Research Companion to Popular Music Education* (Smith et al., 2017), and the Bloomsbury Handbook of Popular Music Education

(Moir, Powell, & Smith, 2019). Programs in popular music are increasingly prevalent in higher education, especially at the undergraduate level (Cloonan & Hustedt, 2012; Parkinson & Smith, 2015; Reinhert, 2018), and popular music has a growing presence in schools in many countries (Smith et al., 2017). These developments, along with the establishment of the International Society for Music Education's Special Interest Group for Popular Music Education (ISME PME SIG) in 2014 and, in the United States, the recently formed National Association for Music Education's Popular Music Education Special Research Interest Group (NAfME PME SRIG), have helped PME reach the point where it deserves recognition as its own field or subfield (Smith et al., 2017).

As noted elsewhere (Mantie, 2013; Smith & Powell, 2017; Till, 2017), "popular music education" is comprised of two broad constituencies: a community of scholars and practitioners in higher education who prepare undergraduate and graduate students for the professional popular music marketplace (higher popular music education, hereafter, HPME), and a contingent of school music teachers whose jobs it is to prepare young people for lives in and beyond compulsory education, including, potentially, in music, for "professional" or leisure purposes. In US contexts, PME often refers to the use of popular music instruments and repertoire in K–12 settings; internationally, the term PME tends to apply to vocational education for students for whom a career in the (popular) music ecosystem is the goal (Smith & Powell, 2017).

# Popular Music Teaching
# and Learning

Tremendously diverse constituencies converge around nebulous notions of popular music. Popular music includes music that is widely consumed by a large portion of the population (Rodriguez, 2004) while at the same time including decidedly "unpopular" music (Kirschner, 1998; Smith, 2016). There is also much divergence about the nature of popular music within HPME. For instance, some focus on industry preparedness (Jones, 2017; Morrow, Gilfillan, Barkat, & Sakinofsky, 2017; Sylvester & O'Reilly, 2017) and entrepreneurship, others on commitment to issues of social justice for graduates (Parkinson & Smith, 2015; Smith, 2015a, 2015b; Whiteley, 2013). For those working in K–12 schools and teacher preparation programs, there is also a strong social justice agenda, usually concerned with democratizing access to music-making experiences (Allsup, 2008; Kratus, 2007; Williams & Randles, 2017) and to culturally relevant, meaningful music making (Elliott, Silverman, & Bowman, 2016; Smith, Gramm, & Wagner, 2018). There is a risk that democracy and/or personal agency are assumed outcomes for all participants when popular music is used in classroom settings, but the error in making such assumptions is becoming increasingly clear: music that is "popular" does not necessarily mean music that resonates equally, or even at all, among diverse cohorts of students (Christophersen & Gullberg, 2017; Hebert, Abramo, & Smith, 2017; Kallio, 2017b), nor does the incorporation of popular music necessarily democratize pedagogical approaches (Green, 2002, 2008).

# CANONIZATION OF POPULAR
# MUSIC IN EDUCATION

Popular education music programs have a tendency to create musical canons of "good" and "acceptable" popular music. "Good" popular music is less easily quantifiable than, for instance, quality Western classical music. In popular music, the qualities of artistry that might lead to canonization are as diverse as the artists themselves; these qualities can include lyrics (Bob Dylan), unsurpassable iconic status (Beatles), and virtuoso jazz crossovers (Snarky Puppy). The most successful commercially popular music operates as subcultural identifier, the most successful societally resonates as zeitgeist artifacts, and "underground" popular music (also intrinsically *un*popular) attracts fan-based community as much as it exhibits "musical" criteria (Kirschner, 1998; Smith, 2016). Motti Regev (2002) cited the canonization of a specific body and style of music that stands in the collective memory of consumers and musicians as the "great artworks" or "masterpieces" of popular music. Regev warned that these "canons are produced and erected by interested parties" and have been constructed by a particular group of professionalized fans who are mostly male (p. 255). The emergence and construction of a popular music canon has generated an artistic hierarchy in the field of popular music studies that is synergistic to the Western classical music hierarchies that have limited traditional music education programs. Green (2002) discussed the tendency to create musical canons even inside popular music:

> Precisely by virtue of its entrance into education and the concomitant production of a scholarly literature, popular music develops canons within itself, often based on assumptions that it lays claim to universal, complex, original, or autonomous properties. In this way, it conjoins rather than dismantles the same evaluative axes upon which classical canons are built.    (p. 269)

As a result of the canonization of PME, popular music in the classroom frequently defaults to Anglo-American guitar-based pop-rock music; this aesthetic, moreover, is a characteristic of the homogenization of music(s) the world over, identified by Regev (2002) as the "pop-rockization of music," whereby musics of all nations and traditions default to a sound that has converged around "vanilla" easy listening (to some). This sound is characterized by, usually, 4/4 time signature; a "backbeat";[1] simple chordal and formal structures; limited note range; and predictability with narrow parameters of key, tonality, and rhythm. Although this "sound" incorporates elements beyond what may be familiar in the vast breadth of styles and substyles in what some term "pop-rock," Regev's point nevertheless holds water as far as highlighting that a sort of generic global music has emerged in recent decades: the music is largely, virtually (or even precisely) identical in elevators, hotel lobbies, shopping malls, and TV commercials around the world. The popular music written and performed in music colleges in the United States, Europe, Southeast Asia, and Australia is often characterized by broadly this sound: one that becomes increasingly reified and normalized through the symbiotic processes of commodification and establishment of classic repertoire in college curricula and through incorporation in "official" histories via college courses and textbooks (Covach & Flory, 2015; Dougan, 2017). The tendency toward canonization in K–12 settings can lead to an experience that is less student-centered than intended. If repertoire selection in K–12 PME ensembles tends to focus on guitar-based rock music, then the musical identities of the students, especially in urban environments, might not be validated, and the aims of diversity and inclusion might be lost (Kallio, 2017a).

# Authenticity and Aims

In order to interrogate assessment in PME, it is first necessary to consider the diverse aims and aspirations of those working in PME contexts. While we would not wish to codify a list of prescribed PME aims and thereby risk limiting the scope, purpose, or impact of PME, certain aims are apparent. In HPME these include commercial success, personally meaningful artistic expression, building community, and identity realization. In K–12 schools, PME often more directly addresses issues of equity, diversity, and inclusion, in addition to the aspirations of HPME. Popular music is functional in that it serves society, and the entertainment industries, in particular ways (Tagg, 2012). Appreciation of and engagement in popular music is not limited to those with a prior experience of formal music education, but it is instead appreciated by the populace (Adorno, 2001; DeNora, 2000, 2016; Frith, 1981). To assume, however, that popular music is intended for consumption by a mass market, or indeed any market at all, risks misconstruing its purpose and function. Those who play popular music as primarily a leisure activity (i.e., the vast majority of people doing it worldwide) do so because they like to and because they feel committed to doing so (Ferrarese, 2016; Smith & Gillett, 2015; Mantie & Smith, 2016). Often the music making serves a cathartic purpose; the doing is the whole point of it. How does one assess this? Why might one even attempt to do so? Whether one assesses or not, one risks imposing false or irrelevant criteria on music and musicians. As previously mentioned, the expanded presence of popular music in schools, both in K–12 and postsecondary contexts, makes it necessary for music educators to receive guidance on what and how to assess PME. This understanding of PME assessment is especially difficult for music teachers who lack prior experience playing or otherwise creating popular music. This dearth of personal experience in making popular music is compounded by the fact that preservice music education preparation programs in the United States often fail to include popular music instruction in any coursework (Hebert, 2011). Only 0.54 percent of instructional time in higher education has been devoted to popular music (Wang & Humphreys, 2009), although this has increased in recent years, for example with the inclusion of modern band initiatives (Byo, 2018; Powell & Burstein, 2017; Williams & Randles, 2017).

An examination of assessment practices and aims in PME might usefully center around notions of authenticity. But to whom are we being authentic? The student? The institution? Assessment boards? The popular music ecosystem? If the goal of vocationally focused PME programs is to prepare students for careers in the music ecosystem, then assessment practices that limit creativity, establish PME canons, or attempt to codify performance practices are at odds with these established outcomes. Likewise, it can be argued that for nonvocationally focused PME programs, the aims of equity, diversity, inclusion, community, and identity realization are not readily bolstered by the presence of structured assessment. Some of the best, most (sub)culturally successful popular music experiences may not look so successful when decontextualized; for instance, an experientially tremendous punk or rap performance might not stand up under the light of more traditional music education assessment frameworks. It is thus vital to bear in mind the breadth and eclecticism encapsulated by PME, and that a philosophy of assessment must reflect and account for these in order to stand a chance of being "authentic."

The core value of popular music in school music education contexts arguably resides in personal meaning, values, and identity for the people making and listening to it (D'Amore & Smith, 2016; Green, 2002; Powell, 2011). As such, much of popular music's essence derives from the fact that it is dynamic, evolving, fleeting, and relentlessly current. Western European classical music, on the other hand, is supposed to be timeless, to be able to exist for its own sake, to be abstracted, decontextualized; therein resides its timeless value. While this view has been challenged in postmodernist literature (e.g., Elliott, 1995; Elliott & Silverman, 2014; McClary, 1991; Small, 1977), it still persists as a powerful ideology in contemporary Western societies, perhaps particularly among policymakers and other influential figures (Department for Business, Innovation and Skills, 2016; Froehlich & Smith, 2017; Scruton, 2016). For popular music, however, such reification *removes*, *misplaces*, or *denies* all it is worth.

In order to better understand how, or indeed whether, we need to assess students in PME programs, we must examine concepts of authenticity and what our desired learning outcomes are. Once we do this, perhaps we can better understand how we might be able to assess for those outcomes. Colwell (2006) observed that "assessment has become one of the more important issues in education, and now education outweighs almost all other domestic social issues" (p. 199). It is generally accepted and expected that students' music performance will and should be assessed in educational settings. As music educators, we need reference points, for as Estelle Jorgensen (1997) reminds music educators, "many rules govern particular musics. Each must be understood in its own terms" (p. 35).

Gary Spruce (1996, p. 169) notes the perceived inherent difficulties in assessment in the arts in general, as educators navigate the terrain between restrictive attempts at objectivity and claims that artistic endeavor is unassessable. The tendency in music education assessment is to establish rubrics and grading structures to measure a student's adherence to an assignment. Such an approach, however, may be antithetical to the nature or aims of learning (in) music. Lucy Green (2000), for instance, observes that "many musical qualities will always escape any system of either evaluation or assessment" (p. 103). According to Richard Bentley (1966), "attempts to apply...measurements in the aesthetic sphere are particularly open to challenge, and this is even more so in music" (p. 17). This is a perennial issue across subjects and disciplines in education and resonates among scholars in music education. David J. Elliott (1987), for example, notes that "there has been considerable argument over appropriate methods of assessment. At the centre of these arguments is whether or not it is possible to assess work in the arts in an objective way" (p. 157). Later in this chapter we explore a model of assessment in which objectivity is not explored as an end.

Keith Swanwick (1998) suggests that assessments might even counteract effects of good teaching, asserting that "unlike the richer conversations that characterize teaching, the ultimately formal assessment statement is likely to be cryptic: perhaps a brief statement, a number, a grade or degree classification. It is here that judgments can be most hotly disputed" (p. 73). If, as previously suggested, PME (particularly in school settings) is concerned with democratizing experiences of and access to musicking opportunities, the intentions behind and effects of assessment in PME need to be considered very seriously. As Ivan Illich (1973) suggests, schooling itself, and assessment in particular, may be deleterious to the process of learning.

# Issues with Assessment
# of Popular Music in Education

The increased prevalence of HPME programs[2] has led examination boards in the United Kingdom to try to fit these programs into the requirements for other liberal arts degrees. For instance, Parkinson and Smith (2015) point to the substantial dissertations that students on popular music performance programs are required to write in order to hit subject and level benchmarks set by the Quality Assurance Agency that monitors standards in UK higher education (QAA, 2008, pp. 24–27). Parkinson and Smith (2015) argue that while there is surely an educational benefit of having students engage in undergraduate dissertation (senior thesis) research, this requirement seems to bear little connection to students' aspirations to engage authentically as performers in the popular music ecosystem.

Pivoting to performance assessment in PME, established rubrics for music performance that are appropriate for Western European classical music are unsuited to the assessment of students in a PME program. Martin Fautley (2015), writing about school music contexts, describes the problematic example of assessing music thought to be "other" when he posits that assessing dhol drummers using criteria or rubrics that were designed for an orchestral player would inevitably lead the dhol drummers to retreat from "school music" when they realize that their performances are not valued in and by the dominant assessment culture. Spruce (2001) warns that the manner in which musical achievement is defined and assessed "inevitably articulates a set of philosophical and political [principles] about the nature and purpose of learning, the subject being assessed, and the relationship between the school and society" (p. 118). According to Fautley (2015), these philosophical assessment principles result in a "concomitant stratification of assessment practices that render otherwise valid forms of musical expression as becoming inadmissible for assessment purposes" (p. 517). Similarly, Smith (2017) discusses the limited and limiting picture of musicality painted by musical aptitude models and tests, citing their focus on very young people's ability to discern and articulate intervals, "frequently involving a piano or another middle-class instrument from antiquity with the timbre of which most are likely unfamiliar" (p. 266). Smith also points out that while there may be nothing inherently wrong with measuring a child's ability to differentiate pitches played on eighteenth-century keyboard instruments, "it is misleading and unjust to characterize performance on such tests as indicators of capacity or deficiency in musical aptitude or ability" (p. 266).

## ASSESSMENT IN CREATIVE MUSIC MAKING

As noted previously, PME covers a variety of contexts, from K–12 to higher education, from vocational-focused programs to approaches focused on leisure and social/emotional ends. Songwriting and other more creative aspects of popular music, such as producing and working collaboratively in creative ensembles, are arguably where there is the most common ground among these constituencies. Students both in schools and in higher education find meaning in writing and expressing themselves. These activities, while popular with students of all ages and increasingly common in curricula from middle school to graduate programs (Bennett, 2017; Kratus, 2016), are notoriously tough to measure and assess (Scott, 2017); when the value, meaning, and quality are so deeply personal, evaluation by a third party can seem inappropriate, unhelpful, or even absurd (Smith, 2011, p. 43). It can be difficult to reconcile work in and on the creative process with necessarily measurable outcomes expressed through evaluation criteria and with poorly understood notions of creativity and the creative process in popular music and songwriting contexts (Scott, 2017; Smith, 2017). Many systems of assessment in music education pass judgment on an artifact rather than making an assessment of learning. Popular music educators are thus confronted with the truism that "meeting the grading criteria don't mean the criteria meet the grade" (Smith, 2011, p. 43), and "much of what is important is not easy to 'count'; not everything that we can count easily is important" (Michelli & Jacobowitz, 2015, p. 37).

With much music making in PME (especially in schools, pre–higher education) emerging from informal learning practices (Folkestad, 2006; Green, 2002; Stålhammar, 2003) and from the widespread availability of increasingly affordable and capable hardware and software technology (Bell, 2015, 2016), it is difficult to justify holding to regimented assessment strategies, program aims, or course titles for more than a few months or perhaps a couple of years at a time. In Western classical music, by contrast, the function and purpose of composition and the composer are comparatively more static.

In practices common in popular music, it is often unclear where or even if boundaries exist among composition, improvisation, performance, and production. While songs enjoy primacy of position in popular music, production, composition, and performance can even become conflated with songwriting. The overlap for musicians in these areas of practice led to naming one module (course) in an undergraduate program in the United Kingdom Production, Songwriting, and Composition, yet according to one's interpretation, most of the courses in that degree program (BA in creative musicianship) could have been titled that way (ICMP, n.d.). As Zack Moir and Haftor Medbøe (2015) and Shara Rambarran (2016) explain, popular musicians will often combine all of these activities when performing live on stage, especially when working alone or collaboratively to make music using a computer, often combined with using conventional instruments and/or voices. It can be difficult, and arguably of little value, to determine whether or in what proportions to assess (or even to differentiate among) performance, improvisation, or composition, considering the multiple creativities at play (Bruford, 2019).

The terminology to which many educators are accustomed is outdated and outmoded. In order to keep up with musicians' "real-world" practices, some music colleges in the United Kingdom, for example, have gone from offering one undergraduate degree in popular music performance in 2010 to providing full three-year undergraduate programs in creative musicianship (with a focus on collaborative and individual creation of original music), songwriting (with a similar focus, but emphasizing the art of the song), and creative music production (focusing on fluency with digital audio workstations, or DAWs and recording studios) (e.g., Institute of Contemporary Music Performance). With this program denoted as specifically focusing on "creative music production," one wonders what is implicitly so noncreative about other types of production, a field that Pamela Burnard (2012, p. 43) finds worthy of its own particular type of "production creativity." The notion of the music producer is so unanimously and comprehensively misunderstood by almost all in the music industry and the public that the term is almost meaningless; only fifty years ago, a producer would hire musicians, control a budget, and be a project manager, whereas today a producer frequently writes, records, arranges, engineers, and performs (on) popular music products (Askerøi & Viervoll, 2017).

# THE ROLE OF STUDENTS IN PME ASSESSMENT

As popular music educators seek to engage students in the decision-making processes of instrument and repertoire selection, so too should they include the students in assessment practices. Don Lebler (2007) argues that "it is necessary for students to do much that has previously been teachers' business, setting the direction of work and at least participating in its assessment" (p. 207). Lebler also states that assessment practices influence the nature of student learning, and students should be actively involved in their own assessment, rather than only being those on whom assessment is conducted. As a result of students engaging in self-assessment, they will develop an increased awareness of the learning process and enhanced transferability of skills. Too often the process of assessment relies on the students trying to guess what the teacher is looking for, rather than having assessment serve as a meaningful part of the learning experience (McLaughlin & Simpson, 2004).

In assessment practices, it is vital that the assessment activities align with the learning outcomes intended for the activity being assessed (Partti, Westerlund, & Lebler, 2015). The following section presents a model for assessment that prioritizes student input in determining assessment criteria and how those criteria are valued before the start of the project. In so doing, this model allows for differentiated assessment that is unique for each student.

## Negotiated Assessment

Paul Kleiman (2009) sets out a model of assessment that was tried and tested over several years in a cross-disciplinary undergraduate degree at the Liverpool Institute for Performing Arts. The model embraces the concept of "negotiated assessment" (Kleiman, 2009, p. 2), which encompasses the aims and aspirations of PME in a range of school and higher education contexts. "Negotiated assessment" is a specific instance of formative assessment in which the assessor and the individual being assessed are expected to interact by exchanging views (Verberg, Tigelaar, & Verloop, 2015). Kleiman's negotiated assessment approach is built on four ideas (Kleiman, 2009, p. 2):

- Students engaged in creative practice will be working not only at different levels but also in different ways, and the products they create will be different, as will the processes and methods utilized.
- Assessment should operate as and be perceived to be an integral part of the learning process rather than "bolted-on" to the end of that process.
- The form, content, and implementation of the assessment process should be commensurable with the discourse and practices of the field.
- The word "assessment" derives from the Latin *ad sedere*, which means "to sit down together," so students should become agents in their own assessment rather than objects of assessment.

For application of these ideas, six fields of activity were identified by the team who developed the negotiated assessment model (Kleiman, 2009, p. 2):

- Presentation/production: the finished product presented to an audience
- Process: the journey that led to the product
- Idea: the ideas that informed both the process and the product
- Technical: the quality and utility of the technical features of the product and the skills with which they were assembled and/or operated

- Documentation: research, design, planning, evaluation, and so forth
- Interview: the students' ability to articulate their understanding, utilization, and application and use of any of the preceding fields

Through working with their teachers, students negotiate where the balance (percentage) of assessment of their work lies among the six fields; the balance can and should shift from assignment to assignment. This flexibility in assessment design allows students and teachers/assessors to focus on developing the skills, experience, and expertise deemed most relevant to given "fields" in particular contexts. By moving away from a codified assessment of creative output and toward an approach that allows a teacher and student to prioritize different elements of the process over others, the music education field can also move away from a "one-size-fits-all" approach to music education assessment. Sadler (2009) warns that "if a way forward is to be found by focusing again on holistic methods, traditional approaches are not up to the task" (p. 174).

This approach to assessment is democratizing in that students, with their teachers, design their own assessment models as applied to their own work. Kleiman (2009) demonstrates one application of this approach in describing a student who is "quite consciously and determinedly 'taking a creative risk'" and can negotiate with the tutor(s) the altering of assessment weighting for each of the fields so that the "assessment emphasis placed less on presentation/production and more on process, idea, and documentation" (p. 3). While replacing the imposition of a top-down model from teacher to student and empowering learners and assessors more as equals in the process of learning, negotiated assessment is aimed at empowering students to "own" their learning journeys, taking greater responsibility for outcomes and the work toward them. Negotiated assessment may provide a lens through which to imagine, and a toolkit with which to create, assessment practices for PME that align with the diversity of practices, practitioners, and perspectives in the field. Embracing diversity in education (through assessment) allows for greater diversity of music making and thus for more conceptions of personal success in music, thereby hopefully increasing agency and joy in the world. In reference to diverse populations, and equally applicable to music-learning practices and attendant negotiated assessment activities, Randall Allsup (2016) asserts that "diversity, understood through the production and arousal of differences, enlarges our capacity to look at the world as though it could be otherwise" (p. 127)

# CHALLENGES FOR INCORPORATING NEGOTIATED ASSESSMENT

While the incorporation of negotiated assessment into formative and summative assessment activity democratizes assessment practice, it is not without its challenges. Cristal Verberg, Dineke Tigelaar, and Nico Verloop (2015) argue that negotiated assessment offers little to guidance teachers in understanding and developing reflective skills among their own students as students reflect on various aspects of the assessment process. Vergerg, Tigelaar, and Verloop also point out that descriptions of the fields of activity to be negotiated, such as the six fields listed in this chapter, provide insight into what the negotiations may be about, but not into the actual negotiation process. They argue that "knowing more about the negotiation process within the context of formative assessment for teachers can also further our understanding of formative assessment in general, and negotiated formative assessment in particular" (p. 139).

Another challenge with negotiated assessment is the potential for disagreement in the negotiating process between the teacher and the student. By definition, negotiation is an interpersonal communication process that involves engaging in discussion to reach an agreement with a positive outcome for both parties (Thompson, 2006). It is possible then for the process of negotiated assessment to lead to disagreements that can be viewed negatively by student and teacher. In many school cultures teachers have been found to regard disagreement as conflict and conflict as a problem rather than an opportunity for learning (Hargreaves, 2001).

In Kleiman's approach to negotiated assessment, the students are able to provide input on how each field of activity is valued, but not on the fields of activity themselves. It is probable that music projects such as songwriting would necessitate different activities and would thus require different fields of assessment. If negotiated assessment serves to democratize the assessment processes by incorporating the input of the students, then this input should, we argue, include which fields of activity are being assessed. This further complicates the assessment process because different students might wish to negotiate different fields of assessment for respective projects, leading to the possibility of a teacher having one project with different fields of assessment, all weighted differently, for each student.

# CONCLUSION

This chapter has detailed the expanded presence of PME programs, as well as some of the challenges faced when examining issues of authenticity, canonization, and the assessment of creative and re-creative work in PME. Through conceptualization and application of one model of negotiated assessment (Kleiman, 2009, p. 2), we hope popular music educators might find ways to break free of the limited and limiting assessment philosophies and attendant practices that have defined and delimited possibilities in music education assessment. Through negotiated assessment, the potentiality of collaborative and democratized elements of formative assessment, or "assessment *for* learning" (Fautley, 2015, p. 513), comes into focus. When educators conceptualize aims and processes of PME assessment in this way, students become "agents in their own assessment rather than objects of assessment" (Kleiman, 2009, p. 2). Through this approach, meaningful, *authentic* formative assessment can develop as a process that "involves teacher and student in dialogue about the music produced" (Fautley, 2016, p. 514).

Kleiman's flexible model of negotiated assessment also provides the opportunity for student and teacher to develop "local standards of merit" (Gracyk, 2007, p. 4) and music learning environments in which the "critical discernment of quality becomes a key aspect of learning" (Sadler, 2009, p. 176). An approach to PME that incorporates differentiated and democratized assessment practices will provide a means for embracing diversity—of students, skill levels, and student outcomes—within and beyond the classroom and institutionalized PME spaces (Hebert, Abramo, & Smith, 2017). Assessment in PME must be responsive to the context, skill level, and desired outcomes of students, in negotiation with professional educators. As such, assessment procedures used must aim to address the nuances of particular musical contexts and should afford expert music educators and their students autonomy to prioritize the relevant fields of activity within students' work.

## Notes

1. "Backbeat" is the term used to describe the emphasis on beats two and four that is typical to songs in popular music styles (songs are almost always in 4/4 or 12/8 time). The backbeat is normally played on a snare drum or equivalent-sounding instrument/sample, sometimes also emphasized by staccato notes or chords on, for example, electric guitar.
2. The following institutions, among others, are home to HPME programs: British and Irish Modern Music Institute, University of Southern California, University of Miami, Berklee College of Music, Griffith University, Royal Northern College of Music, Edinburgh Napier University, Loyola University, and William Patterson University.

## References

Adorno, T. W. (2001). *The culture industry: Selected essays on mass culture.* New York: Psychology Press.

Allsup, R. E. (2008). Creating an educational framework for popular music in public schools: Anticipating the second-wave. *Visions of Research in Music Education, 12*(1), 1–12.

Allsup, R. E. (2016). *Remixing the classroom: Toward an open philosophy of music education.* Bloomington: Indiana University Press.

Askerøi, E., & Viervoll, A. (2017). Teaching studio production in an academic institution. In G. D. Smith, Z. Moir, M. Brennan, S. Rambarran, & P. Kirkman (Eds.), *The Routledge research companion to popular music education* (pp. 231–42). Abingdon, UK: Routledge.

Bell, A. P. (2015). DAW democracy? The dearth of diversity in "Playing the Studio." *Journal of Music, Technology & Education, 8*(2), 129–46.

Bell, A. P. (2016). DIY recreational recording as music making. In R. Mantie & G. D. Smith (Eds.), *The Oxford handbook of music making and leisure* (pp. 81–98). New York: Oxford University Press.

Bennett, T. (2017). *Learning the music business: Evaluating the vocational turn in music industry education.* London: UK Music.

Bentley, A. (1966). *Musical ability in children and its measurement.* Windsor: NFER.

Bruford, W. (2019). Learning experiences of expert Western drummers: A view from cultural psychology. In Z. Moir, B. Powell, & G. D. Smith (Eds.), *Practices and perspectives in popular music education* (pp. 83–100). London: Bloomsbury.

Burnard, P. (2012). *Musical creativities in practice*. Oxford: Oxford University Press.

Byo, J. L. (2018). "Modern band" as school music: A case study. *International Journal of Music Education, 36*(2), 259–69.

Christophersen, C., & Gullberg, A. (2017). Popular music education, participation and democracy: Some Nordic perspectives. In G. D. Smith, Z. Moir, M. Brennan, S. Rambarran, & P. Kirkman (Eds.), *The Routledge research companion to popular music education* (pp. 425–37). Abingdon, UK: Routledge.

Cloonan, M., & Hulstedt, L. (2012). *Taking notes: A mapping of HE popular music and an investigation into the teaching of theory and analysis*. York, UK: The Higher Education Academy.

Colwell, R. (2006). Assessment's potential in music education. In R. Colwell (Ed.), *The new handbook of research on music teaching and learning* (pp. 1128–58). Reston, VA: The National Association for Music Education.

Covach, J., & Flory, A. (2015). *What's that sound? An introduction to rock and its history*. New York: W. W. Norton & Co. Inc.

D'Amore, A., & Smith, G. D. (2016). Aspiring to music making as leisure through the musical futures classroom. In R. Mantie & G. D. Smith (Eds.), *The Oxford handbook of music making and leisure* (pp. 61–80). New York: Oxford University Press.

DeNora, T. (2000). *Music in everyday life*. Cambridge, UK: Cambridge University Press.

Department for Business, Innovation and Skills. (2016). *Success as knowledge economy: Teaching excellence, social mobility and student choice*. London: Department for Business, Innovation and Skills.

DeNora, T. (2016). *Music asylums: Wellbeing through music in everyday life*. New York: Routledge.

Dougan, J. (2017). Don't know much about history—and we don't care! Teaching punk rock history. In G. D. Smith, M. D., & T. Parkinson (Eds.), *Punk pedagogies in practice* (pp. 91–108). New York: Routledge.

Elliott, D. J. (1987). Assessing musical performance. *British Journal of Music Education, 4*(2), 157–84.

Elliott, D. J. (1995). *Music matters: A new philosophy of music education*. New York Oxford University Press.

Elliott, D. J., & Silverman, M. (2014). *Music matters: A new philosophy of music education, second edition*. New York: Oxford University Press.

Elliott, D. J., Silverman, M., & Bowman, W. (2016). Artistic citizenship: Introduction, aims, and overview. In D. J. Elliott, M. Silverman, & W. Bowman (Eds.) *Artistic citizenship: Artistry, social responsibility, and ethical praxis* (pp. 3–21). New York: Oxford University Press.

Fautley, M. (2015). Music education assessment and social justice: Resisting hegemony through formative assessment. In C. B., P. Schmidt, G. Spruce, & P. Woodford (Eds.), *The Oxford handbook of social justice in music education* (pp. 513–24). New York: Oxford University Press.

Ferrarese, M. (2016). *Banana punk rock trails: A Euro-fool's metal punk journey in Malaysia, Borneo and Indonesia*. Selangoar, Malaysia: Strategic Information and Research Development Centre.

Folkestad, G. (2006). Formal and informal learning situations or practices vs formal and informal ways of learning. *British Journal of Music Education, 23*(2), 135–45.

Frith, S. (1981). *Sound effects: Youth, leisure, and the politics of rock 'n' roll*. New York: Pantheon Books.

Froehlich, H. C., & Smith, G. D. (2017). *Sociology for music teachers: Practical applications*. New York: Routledge.

Gracyk, T. (2007). *Listening to popular music, or, How I learned to stop worrying and love Led Zeppelin*. Ann Arbor: University of Michigan Press.

Green, L. (2000). On the evaluation and assessment of music as a media art. In R. Sinker & J. Sefton-Green (Eds.), *Evaluation issues in media arts production* (pp. 89–106). London: Routledge.

Green, L. (2002). *How popular musicians learn: A way ahead for music education*. London: Ashgate Publishing, Ltd.

Green, L. (2008). *Music, informal learning and the school: A new classroom pedagogy*. London: Ashgate Publishing, Ltd.

Green, L., Lebler, D., & Till, R. (2015). Editors' introduction to Popular music in education [Special issue]. *IASPM@ Journal, 5*(1), 1–3.

Hargreaves, A. (2001). The emotional geographies of teachers' relations with colleagues. *International Journal of Educational Research, 35*(5), 503–27.

Hebert, D. G. (2011). Originality and institutionalization: Factors engendering resistance to popular music pedagogy in the USA. *Music Education Research International, 5*, 12–21.

Hebert, D. G., Abramo, J., & Smith, G. D. (2017). Epistemological and sociological issues in popular music education. In G. D. Smith, Z. Moir, M. Brennan, S. Rambarran, & P. Kirkman (Eds.), *Routledge research companion to popular music education* (pp. 451–78). Abingdon, UK: Routledge.

Illich, I. (1973). *Deschooling society*. Harmondsworth, Middlesex, UK: Penguin.

Institute of Contemporary Music Performance (ICMP). (n.d.) *Find a course*. Retrieved from http://icmp.ac.uk/study-at-icmp/find-a-course.

Jones, M. (2017). Addressing the neoliberal employability agenda in higher education at a time of music-industrial turbulence. In G. D. Smith, Z. Moir, M. Brennan, S. Rambarran, & P. Kirkman (Eds.), *The Routledge research companion to popular music education* (pp. 341–54). Abingdon, UK: Routledge.

Jorgensen, E. (2006). On philosophical method. In R. Colwell (Ed.), *MENC handbook of research methodologies* (pp. 176–98). New York: Oxford University Press.

Jorgensen, E. R. (1997). *In search of music education*. Chicago: University of Illinois Press.

Kallio, A. A. (2017a). Popular "problems": Deviantization and teachers' curation of popular music. *International Journal of Music Education, 33*(5), 319–32.

Kallio, A. A. (2017b). Give violence a chance: Emancipation and escape in/from school music education. In G. D. Smith, M. Dines, & T. Parkinson (Eds.), *Punk pedagogies: Music, culture and learning* (pp. 156–72). New York: Routledge.

Kirschner, T. (1998). Studying rock: Towards a materialist ethnography. In T. Swiss, J. Sloop, & A. Herman (Eds.), *Mapping the beat: Popular music and contemporary theory* (pp. 247–68). Oxford: Blackwell.

Kleiman, P. (2009). *Negotiating assessment: An approach to assessing practical work, including assessment criteria*. Retrieved from https://www.heacademy.ac.uk/system/files/negotiating-assessment.pdf

Kratus, J. (2007). Music education at the tipping point. *Music Educators Journal, 94*(2), 42–48.

Kratus, J. (2016). Songwriting: A new direction for secondary music education. *Music Educators Journal, 102*(3), 60–65.

Lebler, D. (2007). Student-as-master? Reflections on a learning innovation in popular music pedagogy. *International Journal of Music Education, 25*(3), 205–21.

Mantie, R. (2013). A comparison of "popular music pedagogy" discourses. *Journal of Research in Music Education, 61*(3), 334–52.

Mantie, R., & Smith, G. D. (2016). Grasping the jellyfish of music making and leisure. In R. Mantie & G. D. Smith (Eds.), *The Oxford handbook of music making and leisure* (pp. 3–12). New York: Oxford University Press.

McClary, S. (1991). *Feminine endings: Music, gender, and sexuality*. Minneapolis: University of Minnesota Press.

McLaughlin, P., & Simpson, N. (2004). Peer assessment in first year university: How the students feel. *Studies in Educational Evaluation, 30*(2), 135–49.

Michelli, N. M., & Jacobowitz, T. (2015). Why do we educate in a democracy? In L. DeLorenzo (Eds.), *Giving voice to democracy in music education: Diversity and social justice in the classroom* (pp. 36–50). New York: Routledge.

Moir, Z., & Medbøe, H. (2015). Reframing popular music as performance-centered practice. *Journal of Music, Technology, & Education, 8*(2), 147–61.

Moir, Z., Powell, B., & Smith, G. D. (Eds.) (2019). The Bloomsbury Handbook of Popular Music Education: Perspectives and Practices. London: Bloomsbury.

Morrow, G., Gilfillan, E., Barkat, I., & Sakinofsky, P. (2017). Popular music entrepreneurship in higher education: Facilitating group creativity and spin-off formation through internship programmes. In G. D. Smith, Z. Moir, M. Brennan, S. Rambarran, & P. Kirkman (Eds.), *The Routledge research companion to popular music education* (pp. 328–40). Abingdon, UK: Routledge.

Parkinson, T., & Smith, G. D. (2015). Towards an epistemology of authenticity in higher popular music education. *Action, Criticism & Theory for Music Education, 14*(1), 93–127.

Partti, H., Westerlund, H., & Lebler, D. (2015). Participatory assessment and the construction of professional identity in folk and popular music programs in Finnish and Australian music universities. *International Journal of Music Education, 33*(4), 476–90.

Powell, B., & Burstein, S. (2017). Popular music and modern band principles. In G. D. Smith, Z. Moir, M. Brennan, S. Rambarran, & P. Kirkman (Eds.), *The Routledge research companion to popular music education* (pp. 243–54). Farnham, UK: Ashgate.

Powell, B., Krikun, A., & Pignato, J. M. (2015). "Something's happening here!": Popular music education in the United States. *IASPM@ Journal, 5*(1), 4–22.

Powell, B. J. (2011). *Popular music ensembles in post-secondary contexts: A case study of two college music ensembles* (Unpublished doctoral dissertation). Boston University.

Quality Assurance Agency. 2008. Subject benchmarks for music. Available at: http://www.qaa.ac.uk/Publications/InformationAndGuidance/Documents/Music08.pdf. [Accessed January 18, 2014].

Rambarran, S. (2016). "Feel good" with gorillaz and "reject false icons." In S. Whiteley & S. Rambarran (Eds.), *The Oxford handbook of music and virtuality* (pp. 148–70). Oxford: Oxford University Press.

Regev, M. (2002). The "pop-rockization" of popular music. In D. Hesmondhalgh & K. Negus (Eds.), *Studies in popular music* (pp. 251–64). New York: Oxford University Press.

Reinhert, K. (2018). *Developing popular music programs in higher education: Exploring possibilities* (Unpublished doctoral dissertation). University of Miami.

Rodriguez, C. X. (2004). Popular music in music education: Toward a new conception of musicality. In C. X. Rodriguez (Ed.), *Bridging the gap: Popular music and music education* (pp. 13–28). Reston, VA: MENC—The National Association for Music Education.

Sadler, D. R. (2009). Indeterminacy in the use of preset criteria for assessment and grading. *Assessment & Evaluation in Higher Education, 34*(2), 159–79.

Scott, J. C. (2017). Advanced songwriting pedagogy and creative block. In G. D. Smith, Z. Moir, M. Brennan, S. Rambarran, & P. Kirkman (Eds.), *The Routledge research companion to popular music education* (pp. 190–202). Abingdon, UK: Routledge.

Scruton, R., 2016. *Understanding music: Philosophy and interpretation.* London: Bloomsbury Publishing.

Small, C. (1977). *Music–society–education: A radical examination of the prophetic function of music in Western, Eastern and African cultures with its impact on society and its use in education.*New York: Schirmer.

Smith, G. D. (2011). Freedom to versus freedom from: Frameworks and flexibility in assessment on an edexcel BTEC level 3 diploma popular music performance program. *Music Education Research International, 5*, 34–45.

Smith, G. D. (2015a). Neoliberalism and symbolic violence in higher music education. In L. DeLorenzo (Ed.), *Giving voice to democracy: Diversity and social justice in the music classroom* (pp. 65–84). New York: Routledge.

Smith, G. D. (2015b). Masculine domination and intersecting fields in private-sector popular music performance education in the U.K. In P. Burnard Y. Hofstander, & J. Söderman (Eds.), *Bourdieu and the Sociology of Music and Music Education* (pp. 61–79). Farnham: Ashgate.

Smith, G. D. (2016). (Un)popular music making and eudaimonia. In R. Mantie & G. D. Smith (Eds.), *The Oxford handbook of music making and leisure* (pp. 151–70). New York: Oxford University Press.

Smith, G. D. (2017). Becoming musical with popular music. In F. Abrahams & R. John (Eds.), *Becoming musical* (pp. 263–80). Carlsbad, CA: GIA.

Smith, G. D., & Gillett, A. (2015). Creativities, innovation, and networks in garage punk rock: A case study of the Eruptörs. *Artivate: A Journal of Entrepreneurship in the Arts, 4*(1), 9–24.

Smith, G. D., Gramm, W., & Wagner, K. (2018). Music education for social change in the United States: Towards artistic citizenship through Little Kids Rock. *International Journal of Pedagogy, Innovation and New Technologies, 5*(2), 11–21.

Smith, G. D., & Powell, B. (2017). Welcome to the journal. *Journal of Popular Music Education, 1*(1), 3–7.

Smith, G. D., Moir, Z., Brennan, M., Rambarran, S., & Kirkman, P. (2017). Popular music education (r)evolution. In G. D. Smith, Z. Moir, M. Brennan, S. Rambarran, & P. Kirkman (Eds.), *The Routledge research companion to popular music education* (pp. 5–13). Abingdon, UK: Routledge.

Spruce, G. (1996). Assessment in the arts: Issues of objectivity. In G. Spruce (Ed.), *Teaching music,* (pp. 168–84). London: Routledge and the Open University.

Spruce, G. (2001). Music assessment and the hegemony of musical heritage. *Issues in music teaching,* 118–30.

Stålhammar, B. (2003). Music teaching and young people's own musical experience. *Music Education Research, 5*(1), 61–68.

Swanwick, K. (1998). The perils and possibilities of assessment. *Research Studies in Music Education, 10*(1), 1–11.

Sylvester, R., & O'Reilly, D. (2017). Remixing popular music marketing education. In G. D. Smith, Z. Moir, M. Brennan, S. Rambarran, & P. Kirkman (Eds.), *The Routledge research companion to popular music education,* (pp. 298–312). Abingdon, UK: Routledge.

Tagg, P. (2012). *Music's meanings: A modern musicology for non-musos.* New York & Huddersfield: Mass Media's Scholar's Press.

Thompson, L. L. (Ed.). (2006). *Negotiation theory and research.* New York and Hove, UK: Psychology Press.

Till, R. (2017). Popular music education: A step into the light. In G. D. Smith, Z. Moir, M. Brennan, S. Rambarran, & P. Kirkman (Eds.), *The Routledge research companion to popular music education* (pp. 14–30). Abingdon, UK: Routledge.

Verberg, C. P., Tigelaar, D. E., & Verloop, N. (2015). Negotiated assessment and teacher learning: an in-depth exploration. *Teaching and Teacher Education, 49,* 138–48.

Wang, J. C., & Humphreys, J. T. (2009). Multicultural and popular music content in an American music teacher education program. *International Journal of Music Education, 27,* 19–36. doi:10.1177/0255761408099062

Whiteley, S. (2013). *Women and popular music: Sexuality, identity and subjectivity.* London: Routledge.

Williams, D. A., & Randles, C. (2017). Curricular change in music teacher education in the United States. In G. D. Smith, Z. Moir, M. Brennan, S. Rambarran, & P. Kirkman (Eds.), *The Routledge research companion to popular music education* (pp. 46–59). Abingdon, UK: Routledge.

# CHAPTER 19

# "HE SINGS WITH RHYTHM; HE IS FROM INDIA"

*children's drawings and the music classroom*

## ROGER MANTIE AND BEATRIZ ILARI

How do we display what we have learned? What forms can we trust? What modes are legitimate? How shall we know?

—Elliot Eisner

IF assessment is taken as a process aimed at ascertaining abilities and understandings, particularly in relation to instructional intent, one reads into common music assessment practices in American P–12 schooling a belief that the *what* of assessment primarily consists of performing ability and perceptual-conceptual understanding of the "elements" of music: pitch, rhythm, form, and so forth. The *how* of assessment follows from the *what* and is almost always framed in terms of the degree to which students achieve a predetermined goal. For example, the "Singing Performance Scoring Form" of the second-grade general music "performing strand" of the Model Cornerstone Assessments of the US National Core Arts Standards is to be used to assess a recorded version of a student's singing performance. The form contains rubric statements such as: *Pitches are mostly accurate, but contain errors that detract from the overall performance* and *Rhythm is generally accurate. Any errors do not detract from the overall performance.* In the "responding strand" of the Model Cornerstone Assessments one finds the following: *Teacher tells students to create locomotive or non-locomotive movements that show the musical element of tempo in "Peer Gynt: In the Hall of the Mountain King."* Students are to be video recorded, verbally questioned, and then assessed on the basis of a rubric containing statements such as: *Movements accurately represented tempo, dynamic changes, and texture in the music* and *Used appropriate musical vocabulary to describe the musical elements*. (It is unclear to us what kinds of movements might "accurately" represent tempo, dynamic changes, and texture, but we leave that challenge to others.)

In this chapter we offer another view of music assessment, one predicated on a belief that the *what* of assessment in P–12 music education could and should include understandings and attitudes about music and culture not typically ascertainable through commonly used music assessment practices, and that the *how* of assessment should include diagnostic forms that go beyond ascertaining that students have "got it right." The use of student-produced images is a way music educators might develop understandings of children's learning beyond performing ability and perceptual-conceptual understanding of the elements of music. To be clear, we make no claims in the name of novelty here. The theoretical grounds for using children's drawings emerged over the course of the twentieth century, arguably reaching its peak in the 1980s, but educationalists and other researchers continue to explore the ways in which they may be used with various populations and for various purposes (e.g., Fargas-Malet & Dillenburguer, 2014; Hair, 1993; Kerchner, 2000; Southcott & Coisatis, 2015).

Despite being present in other fields, including education more broadly, using student-produced images for diagnostic purposes (i.e., as a window into children's thinking) has been rare in music education, except for its use as a tool intended to aid the development of notation fluency, a practice that dates back to at least the 1980s (e.g., Bamberger, 1982; Davidson & Scripp, 1988; Upitis, 1990). The use of drawings and invented, graphic representations of sounds (see Davidson, Scripp, & Welsh, 1988) in teaching and learning contexts often precedes the introduction of Western staff notation, which probably explains why its use tends to be associated with the early years and with general music (Ilari, 2004). As a pedagogical tool, drawings have been used as a way to help children remain focused and quiet while listening to music or as a means for children to represent specific musical elements (e.g., melodic contour, rhythmic patterns) or characters or a plot in programmatic music, such as in the story of Peter and the Wolf (see Moore, 2013). Less common among music educators is the use of drawings as a tool to gain deeper understandings of a child's meaning making or as a window onto broader patterns of cultural assumptions.

In this chapter we argue that children's drawings take advantage of multimodality to expose rich additional insights music educators might use to further inform instruction. Through the use of six vignettes we present various ways that children's drawings might be used to expose and discern (i.e., assess) children's thinking, understandings, and attitudes about music and culture—aspects we consider important to a broader conception of music education that isn't predicated on right/wrong thinking. We begin the chapter with a short exposition on multimodality and then discuss various methodological and philosophical issues related to the use of children's drawings for assessment purposes. For example: What do drawings expose about children's thinking about music and culture? Are drawings art or research? Do we recognize and respect children's drawings as authentic expression or merely as products of immature or incomplete development? What concerns might be considered when using children's drawings as a form of assessment in the music classroom?

# MULTIMODALITY

The historic emphasis on the "three Rs" in schooling may have a reasoned basis for the development of literacy and numeracy competencies. The exclusive emphasis on just language and numbers, however, risks an impoverished view of the human capacity for symbolic and structural meaning making (Gardner, 1982, 1993) and results in the marginalization of other forms of symbolic representation, such as those central to the arts. When considered either as an integration of the senses or as a form of expanded literacy, there is arguably much to be gained from a "multimodal" approach to learning and teaching. One thinks, for example, of how music and movement are, in many examples around the world complementary if not indistinguishable. And while performative and nonperformative modes are not necessarily commensurate with music and movement, this does not rule out the potential for insights to be drawn from the intersection and overlap of multiple modes of symbolic and representational engagement. Drawing on Dyson (1986), Angela Anning and Kathy Ring (2004) suggest that children do not distinguish drawing and writing early on (p. 5). Indeed, one finds in an 1892 volume edited by G. Stanley Hall an article by Earl Barnes (1892) entitled, "A Study of Children's Drawings," in which he asserts, "Pictures are for a young child simply a language. He [sic] makes pictures not to exactly imitate something, nor to produce an aesthetic feeling, but to convey an idea. Picture making is picture writing" (p. 460).

Howard Gardner (1980) suggests that by the age of five children often mix and match expressive media at will: "The child sings as he draws, dances as he sings, tells stories while at play in the bathtub or in the backyard. . . . [C]hildren move readily and even eagerly from one form to another, combine the forms, and play them off one against another" (p. 99). Niklas Pramling and Cecilia Wallerstedt (2009) go so far as to employ the concept of synesthesia to describe "ways of communicating and making sense through combining tools of different sense modalities" (p. 136). It is children's ease with various "languages of childhood" that leads Susan Young and Joanna Glover (1998) to advocate the use of gestures, visual symbols, syllables, words, and notation as an aid to "bringing children to a level of more conscious understanding" (p. 92).

The "value added" created by combining modalities perhaps helps to explain why those who advocate drawing techniques also encourage talking and/or writing as a complementary process (e.g., Angell, Alexander, & Hunt, 2015; Mitchell, Theron, Stuart,

Smith, & Campbell, 2011; Freeman & Mathison, 2009), a suggestion echoed in music education by Barrett (2001, 2002), who noted the importance of the verbalizations that accompanied children's music notation efforts. It is thus not just the drawings or visual representations themselves that are important in assessment, but what children write and say about their drawings. The primary value in drawing is that it opens up expressive and representational possibilities not afforded by traditional means such as writing or, in the music class, performance alone.

## Children's Drawings and Assessment

[F]or children, drawing is representative of many things—development, personality, emotions, interpersonal relationships, and cultural and social influences.

—Malchiodi (1998, p. xii)

Humans represent their lifeworlds in many ways. They write letters to create words on paper (as we are doing); paint pictures to illustrate ideas, concepts, and emotions; draw maps of geographical areas; and notate the sounds of the music that they hear. Cultural groups the world over emphasize these different modes of representation, which are reiterated and reproduced by formal education (Pramling, 2009). Human beings are the only species capable of producing and interpreting images that are based on something as simple as a single trace (Gardner, 1994). If adults do not perceive themselves as "artists," however, they do not draw. Children, on the contrary, are known to draw, regardless of culture, ethnicity, schooling experiences, and artistic training (Mitchell et al., 2011).

Gardner (1980) speculates that it is likely children have always drawn (though not always with paper and today's array of pencils, markers, and crayons). Sonia Grubits (2003) argues that drawing is actually ubiquitous to childhood. For those concerned with education and upbringing, the human proclivity to express and represent visually from an early age raises many issues, not least being why children draw and what they derive from the experience. Children's drawings also present something of a dilemma for educators: Are these creations best understood as artistic/aesthetic artifacts or as some sort of developmental byproduct? There is in some cases very little aesthetic difference between a drawing produced by an adult and one produced by a child. Thus, asks Gardner (1980), "must we therefore conclude that the child of five, six, or seven is a young artist," or do the child's works represent something quite different to her or him? (pp. 99–100).

Gardner's question highlights problems of intentionality and purpose. Analyzing the meaning or merit of an unsolicited drawing a child has produced is quite different from analyzing the response of the child to a drawing prompt or evaluating the child's drawing ability in relation to guidance. The child who draws independently as a playful activity may have no artistic intent yet produce an image with admirable aesthetic qualities (see boxes 19.1 and 19.2). This same child may have artistic intent when asked to produce a particular image, yet fail to produce anything as artistically recognizable, and this same child may show signs of improvement (i.e., learning) when guided by a knowledgeable other, irrespective of the artistic merits of her or his creation. The meaning of the process and product for the drawer, in other words, should not be confused as isomorphic with the meaning of the process and product for the caregiver, educator, or therapist.

---

**BOX 19.1 VIGNETTE 1: ON A TRAIN WITH PIERRE SCHAEFFER**

In a small rural school in Antonina, southern Brazil, two student teachers in music are delivering a short lesson on electroacoustic music to classes of approximately twenty to twenty-five children from varied age groups. They ask children to listen attentively to the 2'50" piece "Etude aux chemins du fer" by Pierre Schaeffer and then visually represent on paper what they hear. As the children listen, images begin to emerge. The children ask to listen to the music again in order to "finish their drawings." Once the children consider their drawings done, the student teachers go around the room and ask children to explain them. An animated discussion follows, and the students' work is collected. The student teachers repeat the successful experience in three other classes and collect more drawings. Later, when the student teachers examine the drawings, some interesting patterns begin to appear. There are drawings of aliens, trains, monsters, houses, trees, and human figures. Some drawings also include words (e.g., "train running away," "fear," "fast," "clap clap") and onomatopoeias such as "piuí-tchi-tchi [pi u'wi: 'ʧi 'ʧi]⁴," "la la la."⁵ Others attempt to trace the course of sound. Twelve-year-old Aldinei (see figure 19.1) and eight-year-old Mario (see figure 19.2) represent what they perceived and imagined as they listened to Pierre Schaeffer's music.

While there was no deliberate intent on the part of the student teachers to assess anything specific, it was clear from the drawings that music served as an important source of inspiration for artistic creation. Drawing in response to music was, in this case, a playful activity that was aimed at keeping children on task. The created artifacts, however, provided unanticipated insights into the children's conceptualized worlds.

---

**BOX 19.2 VIGNETTE 2: THE TRAIN WINDOW**

In Curitiba, Brazil, the student teachers from vignette 1 repeat the electroacoustic music drawing experience with a group of children from the local university's early childhood music education program. João, a four-year-old boy, uses a black crayon to draw (see figure 19.3). When asked about what he drew, he is quick to offer: "This is the train window." This is a typical case in which the child's voice is imperative for the adult to understand the intentions behind the drawing.

**FIGURE 19.1** Drawing made in response to electroacoustic music by twelve-year-old Brazilian boy

8 Arryson Antonio Schumarest
Leopoldino

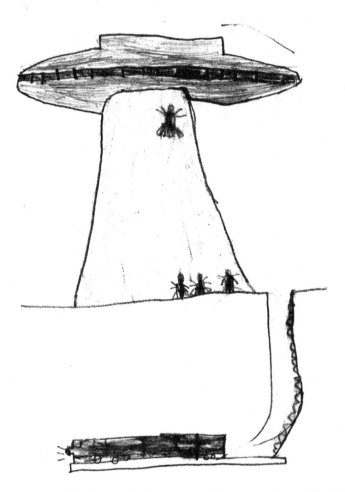

**FIGURE 19.2** Drawing made in response to electroacoustic music by eight-year-old Brazilian boy

FIGURE 19.3 Drawing by a four-year-old Brazilian boy made in response to electroacoustic music

# DRAWINGS AS WINDOWS INTO CHILDREN'S MINDS

Arguably, human creative expression has always intrigued and fascinated. Beginning in the late 1800s this fascination began to take on scientific aspects. Psychiatrists, for example, began making connections between mental illness and the drawings of those diagnosed as mentally ill, with the drawings serving as a confirmation of the diagnosis (Malchiodi, 1998).[1] Carl Jung apparently asked patients to draw (Malchiodi, 1998), continuing a tradition of using art as a means for connecting to the unconscious or the emotional world of the patient (Freeman & Mathison, 2009). In line with the emerging "child study" movement, scientific interest in the drawings of children also dates from the late 1800s, with Cooke's 1885 early stage theory and Ricci's 1887 publication of drawings by Italian children being perhaps the earliest examples (Malchiodi, 1998, p. 3). These nineteenth-century examples were extended by many, but perhaps none in as detailed a manner as Rhoda Kellogg, who created a classification and taxonomy of artistic development based on analyzing hundreds of thousands of child drawings from around the world. In a similar vein, Viktor Lowenfeld's (1947) *Creative and Mental Growth* provides an elaborate stage theory of drawing development by correlating children's drawings to specific facets of intellectual growth (Freeman & Mathison, 2009, p. 111).

The limitation of naturalistic study of completed drawings is that it fails to account for the conditions and circumstances that give rise to drawings. Early interventions, known in psychology as "projective tests," were used to evaluate and assess cognitive development. As Malchiodi (1998) summarizes, projective drawing "was thought to offer an alternative to self-expression that words alone could not" (p. 5). Perhaps the most famous example of projective drawing is Florence Goodenough's (1926) Draw-a-Man test. The more complete or realistic the image produced (scored on fifty-one items), the more intellectually mature the child was presumed to be. Importantly, but often overlooked, Goodenough also suggested that the test revealed aspects of personality. Variations of this test, such as Buck's (1948, 1966) House-Tree-Person test, Machover's (1949) Draw-a-Person test, and the more recent Draw-an-Engineer or Draw-a-Scientist test (the latter developed on the basis of the work of Margaret Mead and Rhoda Metraux) continue to be used today to examine children's attitudes and knowledge (see Ganesh, 2011).

The idea that projective drawing tests might help to determine personality and identify sociocultural influences was (and is) certainly attractive to those with an interest in generating data about children. As Gardner (1980) cautions, however, "while [the Draw-a-Man test] may well serve certain clinical and assessment purposes, it exists in fundamental tension with artistic criteria" (p. 150). A similar criticism has been leveled against stage theories of drawing, which, as Anning and Ring (2004) point out, are premised on deficit where exacting representation is the goal. Such viewpoints helped to inspire psychologist Rudolf Arnheim to propose a more art-based view of drawing that stresses the equal importance of aesthetics and cognition (see Malchiodi, 1998, p. 10).

The foregoing introduction to the use of children's drawings highlights several issues for the music teacher, who as an arts educator no doubt appreciates the artistic aspects of children's drawings. For researchers like Howard Gardner, children's drawings are important for what we might learn about creativity and the arts as distinct ways of knowing. For those music teachers also concerned with educating "the whole child" (for a discussion see Suárez-Orozco, Sattin-Bajaj, & Suárez-Orozco, 2010), the potential for using drawing techniques to elicit social and cultural understandings that may not be evident from music performance or the elements of music is likewise important. With an eye toward viewing assessment as a form of research (i.e., data gathering and analysis), we turn now to how drawing methods have been used by researchers.

# DRAWING AS METHOD

The use of drawings as windows into the lifeworlds of children is far from new. Clinical psychologists and therapists alike have used drawings to gain insight into children's thinking, emotions, and experiences, particularly in situations where verbal language proves to be inefficient (e.g., Mitchell et al., 2011; Thomson, 2008). In educational settings, however, drawings are often positioned in an "artistic" realm. Schools that use portfolios to assess student learning tend to position drawings as representations of children's creativity (often loosely defined), but rarely as evidence of their thinking, emotions, and conceptions about the world. As Maureen Kendrick and Roberta Mackay (2004) have convincingly argued, while there is some acknowledgment of children's knowledge as a social construction and of children as competent users of multiple forms of representation, the politics of how the former is represented is particularly challenging in classrooms of today. In Kendrick and Mackay's words, "a major pedagogical challenge is to help children transform what they know into modes of representation that allow for a full range of human experience" (p. 109).

The use of drawings as a form of systematic research is growing. Early theorizing (e.g., Gardner, 1980) has resulted in new theories (e.g., Quaglia, Longobardi, Iotti, & Prino, 2015) and empirical projects (e.g., Aradau & Hill, 2013; Elkoshi, 2015) in multiple fields. Melissa Freeman and Sandra Mathison (2009), for example, document the use of drawing in many nontherapeutic investigations in domains, including education: for example, elementary students' experiences of reading and writing in school, students of all ages reacting to taking state standardized tests, and children drawing images of teachers.[2] Drawing has been shown to be effective when working with all children but can be especially effective when dealing with special populations such as street youth, who might otherwise not open up or be able to articulate the same way in language (Malindi & Theron, 2011), or children living in areas marked by war and political turmoil (Aradau & Hill, 2013; Fargas-Mallet & Dilleburger, 2014). Based on her involvement with large-scale cross-cultural research projects, Leonore Loeb Adler (1982) points out that drawings, "as a projective technique, provide children with a good opportunity not only to reflect their personal feelings and their attitudes toward people and situations, but also to express the group values that are prevalent within their cultural environment" (p. 96; see also Golomb, 1992). As McNiff (1981) explains, art "becomes a means through which the child can communicate about those phenomena which are too complex to describe verbally, but which are being perceived and integrated into a child's organization of reality" (as cited in Freeman & Mathison, 2009, p. 112).

# DRAWING AND MUSIC EDUCATION RESEARCH

Using drawings as a window into children's thinking, understandings, and attitudes about music and culture can expose important socialized beliefs that go well beyond performing abilities, notation, and the elements. While such use of drawings is arguably not new (e.g., Hair, 1993; Kerchner, 2000), it has never been a priority for developmental music researchers. This is surprising, given the pervasive use of drawings and graphic representations—sometimes called listening maps or guides—in music classrooms (e.g., Moore, 2013; Szot, 2006). Some recent works, however, are picking up from where others have left off, offering many important insights into children's meaning making in and through music. Some of these studies utilize musical prompts, whereas others use verbal prompts to elicit preexisting understandings. Ann Colley, Gerry Mulhern, Sarah Relton, and Suzana Shafi (2008), for example, inquired whether there were gendered associations of musicians during middle childhood. Similar to the Draw-an-Engineer or Draw-a-Scientist tests, the researchers asked British children (ages seven to eleven) to draw a musician and then had each individual describe her or his representation. The researchers found some consistent gendered associations, particularly where older girls were concerned. When asked to draw a musician, older girls tended to draw male figures more often than younger girls or boys from all age groups. In addition, there was a predominance of stereotypical masculine instruments such as drums or guitar in the drawings. The authors interpreted these findings as evidence that by age ten or eleven, girls have already internalized the "male domination of public musical performance" (p. 474).

Based on an earlier work by Kleinen and Schmitt (1991, cited in Alexandra Kertz-Welzel, 2012) that examined five thousand drawings of German children, Kertz-Welzel (2012) collected and analyzed drawings by students (ages ten to thirteen) at a high school in the southwestern part of Germany. Students were instructed to draw pictures freely to the verbal prompt "Me and Music." Some students drew instruments, rehearsal and performance scenes, or images of their favorite singers or bands. Others focused on the functions of music in their own lives, including emotional responses and imaginary events and places. Kertz-Welzel's findings did not differ substantially from those of Kleinen and Schmitt twenty years earlier, suggesting a high degree of cultural stability, at least within the German context in which the studies took place. Kertz-Welzel did not mention gender issues.

Similar to Kertz-Welzel's study, Jane Southcott and Wei Coisatis (2015) investigated drawings by Australian fourth graders (ages nine to ten) in response to a verbal "Music and Me" prompt. As in Colley et al. (2008), gendered associations emerged in children's drawings. These included more representations of solitary music making in the form of listening to music through iPods and "boom boxes" outside of schools. Girls often drew themselves making music with others and engaging in performances, including school-based recitals. Southcott and Coisatis interpreted the collected drawings in light of a continuum of different degrees of engagement of the self with music. At one end of the continuum is "me immersed in music," and at the other end, "music but no me."

To some music educators, gendered meanings might be considered outside the purview of music education. If music education is conceptualized solely on the basis of disembodied musical elements devoid of social meaning, then music assessment can rightly ignore social aspects of human existence. If, on the other hand, music education accepts its participation in the social construction of our world, children's understandings and assumptions of gender, race, class, sexuality, culture, and so on should figure prominently among our educational concerns, as many socially minded scholars in music and music education have been arguing in recent decades (e.g., Benedict, Schmidt, Spruce, & Woodford, 2015; Bradley, 2006; Gould, Countryman, & Stewart, 2009; Hesmondalgh, 2013).

The problem of how music, culture, and sociality intersect is, of course, exceedingly complex. To cite but one example related to children's drawings, Rivka Elkoshi (2015) examined drawings by Israeli children (kindergartners to third graders) in response to Claude Debussy's "Jimbo's Lullaby" from *Children's Corner*. Three types of representations emerged from her work: *associative responses* with metaphorical interpretations; *formal responses* or references to musical elements such as pitch, timbre, and so forth; and *compound responses*, which included a combination of both. The use of purely associative responses was found to decrease over the course of development, with older children showing more formal and compound responses. In light of earlier studies, Elkoshi interpreted these findings as evidence that different types of tasks elicit different responses from students. Elkoshi also speculated that verbal tasks may lead to formal responses concerning musical structures, whereas audio-graphic tasks (e.g., invented notations and drawing in response to music) elicit more associative responses. In another study, Peter DeVries (2011) videotaped and examined the relationship between musicking (Small, 1998) and images drawn by his eight-year-old son. Interestingly, the child's everyday musical experiences, preferences, and lifeworld that were captured by and co-interpreted in the drawings bore little to no association with school music education. These studies all suggest that drawing to prompts, be they verbal or musical, can provide windows into children's lifeworlds: cognitions, embodiments, beliefs, and values. One such example is described in box 19.3

### BOX 19.3  VIGNETTE 3: LA NEGRITA ANCUA

At an elite music conservatory in Mexico City, a class with fifteen children aged nine and ten listens to recordings of three different songs from Senegal, Peru, and India sung by six- to nine-year-old individuals. The students are asked to represent the child singers and to write down what country or area they think the music comes from. After each drawing is complete, the children are invited to speak about their representations. The children do "show and tell" of their drawings and ideas related to the listening experiences on a separate day.

Upon hearing the Senegalese song, Pedro begins to draw (figure 19.4). He imagines the child singer as a nine-year-old girl "negrita" (term of endearment for a black girl) named Ancua (hank'a, meaning popcorn in the Quechua language indigenous to South America). She speaks Haitian, has dark skin, and comes from Nigeria. Pedro also imagines Ancua living in an old house. It is clear from this representation that the drawing exposes learned associations with social, cultural, and ethnic groups, assumptions about and attitudes toward various groups and their lifestyles, and various social and cultural values. Importantly, the intent to assess children's meaning making in music, as suggested by the teacher's instruction at the beginning of the activity, led to a more focused listening experience.

la niña tiene 9 años y se xama ancua abla aytiano es negrita y es nigeriana vive en una casa blesa

FIGURE 19.4 Drawing made in response to a Senegalese song ("Fatou you") by a nine-year-old Mexican boy

## DEVELOPMENTAL, SOCIOCULTURAL, AND CROSS-CULTURAL ISSUES

In the main, the use of children's drawings continues to reflect developmental and stage theories of the twentieth century. According to Gardner (1980), the "prerepresentational child" (p. 46) begins making marks (i.e., scribbles) during the second year of life. At some point during the third to fifth years of life a "pivotal moment" occurs: "The child for the first time produces a recognizable depiction of *some thing* in the world" (p. 11; emphasis in original). That is, drawing evolves from what might be called (at least to adults) "pure expression" to intentional representation. This representation, which begins with a period in which the expressive and representative intersect, gradually gives way in the early school years, suggests Gardner, to "a single-minded determination to achieve photographic realism in drawing" (p. 11). In his appraisal, drawings by eight- and nine-year-olds become strikingly different from those drawn at younger ages, featuring "a kind of precision, a concern for detail, [and] a command of geometrical form which are lacking in the attempts by younger artists" (p. 143). Gunther Kress and Theo van Leeuwen (2006) point out that children in the early years of schooling are frequently encouraged to draw, but that these drawings are not usually "corrected" in the same way as children's written language because they are viewed as self-expression rather than communication: "something which the children can do already, spontaneously, rather than as something they have to be taught" (p. 14). Gardner's developmental sequence clearly emphasizes this expressive, artistic side of drawing. Other stage theorists, however, emphasize connections between intellectual development and creative development. Lowenfeld (1947; Lowenfeld & Brittain, 1982), for example, has detailed six stages of growth: scribbling, pre-schematic, schematic, dawning realism, pseudo-realism, and period of decision. Box 19.4 illustrates how developmental, sociocultural and cross-cultural issues may emerge through children's drawings.

An important question raised by stage theories is the extent to which development in drawing is or should be intentionally impacted by adults. Frank Cizek's work in the 1930s, for example, celebrated child art and admonished those who would taint children with adult expectations. Such a view contrasts sharply with that of Maria Montessori (1917/1964), who considered children incapable of meaningful expression and rejected Rousseauian notions of child innocence and unfettered development. For Montessori, it is the proper role of the teacher to nurture the child's developing command of visual representation and expression. Building on the work of Kress (1997), Pramling (2009) suggests that the shift toward literalism in drawing reflects not only the influence of schooling, but also the child's growing awareness that "representations cannot be arbitrary" if they are to serve a communicative as well as expressive purpose (p. 278). Such a view aligns well with that of Lev Vygotsky (1978), who suggests that children begin to master the symbolic meaning of drawing around the age of seven, "and that

---

**BOX 19.4 VIGNETTE 4: DRAWING "GUANTANAMERA"**

Vanessa and Luciana, four-year-old students in an early childhood music program in Curitiba, Brazil, were asked to represent "Guantanamera," a well-known Cuban song. A human figure and an image that resembles a flower can be identified in the drawing produced by Vanessa (see figure 19.5) among several unidentifiable traces. In Luciana's drawing (see figure 19.6), a geometric figure is perhaps the only identifiable element. While hints of intentionality can be seen in Vanessa's work, this is less clear in Luciana's case, which could be understood as "pure expression."

FIGURE 19.5 Drawing made by a four-year-old Brazilian girl in response to a Cuban patriotic song ("Guantanamera")

drawing can serve as a cultural tool, in the same way as signs and language, for the mediation and transmission of experience" (Greene & Hogan, 2005, pp. 261–62).

For Vygotsky, development is both a biological and sociocultural process: "Every function in the child's cultural development appears twice: first, on the social level, and later, on the individual level; first, between people (interpsychological), and then inside the child (intrapsychological)" (1978, p. 57). It stands, then, that drawing, as a process of not only performance but also conception, should function as an index of cultural values. The conclusions here are mixed, however. Ganesh (2011) points out that eliciting drawings of the human figure as a cognitive assessment tool was based on culture-free assumptions that have ultimately proven problematic (p. 216). The work of Margaret Mead and others in the fields of cultural anthropology and visual sociology have drawn attention to cultural variations that trouble the purported universality of certain theories of developmental psychology. Alexander Alland's work, for example, challenges the universal classification schemes of Rhoda Kellogg. Rather than a window on the person, drawings may be better viewed as "a window on culture itself" (Freeman & Mathison, 2009, p. 111).

FIGURE 19.6 Drawing made by a four-year-old Brazilian girl in response to a Cuban patriotic song ("Guantanamera")

---

### BOX 19.5 VIGNETTE 5: ON LATIN LANGUAGES, CHICKENS, AND RHYTHMS

In the same conservatory in Mexico City described in vignette 3, ten-year-old Marcelo "guesses" (incorrectly) that the Peruvian song, although sung in a somewhat "close" language, is not in Spanish. He states, "His language is like Portuguese. He is ten years old. Maybe the accent could be Italian? Perhaps [the child singer] lives in Italy" (see figure 19.7).

In Los Angeles, a six-year-old cellist in a Suzuki music program draws what she hears in "Chicken Rhythm" by Slim Gaillard. Elizabeth's drawing (see figure 19.8) depicts her attention to the lyrics of the song ("the chicken") and musical timbres (piano and "horn," as she calls it). The "box" that the chicken is holding is, in Elizabeth's words, "a bag of chips," a reference to "Potato Chips," the next song on the CD, indicating her preexisting familiarity with the musical material.

Although they live many miles apart from one another, both Marcelo and Elizabeth drew human figures to represent the music that they heard. While this was intuitive for the Peruvian song, sung by a solo voice, it was perhaps less so for the jazz piece, performed by a small jazz group. Despite age differences between Marcelo and Elizabeth, both human figures display characteristics that have been common to drawings of children found across the world, such as elongated arms and feet "set apart" (see Gardner, 1980). Even if both children were being trained in the Western "art" music tradition, there were clear differences in the drawings in terms of what to represent. While Marcelo focused on linguistic markers found in the music, Elizabeth concentrated on musical timbres. Taken together, these two drawings show the pervasiveness of enculturation in and through music in children's lives.

That social and cultural processes play a part in child development is not to imply a lack of consistency or homogeneity among children. Gardner (1980) claims that "children within specific cultures tend to draw in formally similar ways" (p. 160). Beyond this observation there are sometimes surprising cross-cultural similarities that raise further questions about the role of development in children's drawings. The work of L. L. Adler from the 1960s through the 1980s, for example, suggests curious global commonalities. In numerous studies she conducted in which children were instructed to draw a fruit tree, the majority drew an apple tree—even in countries where apple trees did not grow (see Adler, 1982). The propensity for drawing an apple tree increased with the age of the child, regardless of country. Building on the work of Wayne Dennis (1966), Adler (1982) theorized that drawings tend to reflect either a *value orientation*, in which drawings reflect culturally desirable or socially acceptable qualities (helping to explain the apple tree, a supposedly desirable fruit regardless of culture), or a *familiarity orientation*, in which drawings reflect direct experience or knowledge of the environment. According to Dennis, value takes priority over familiarity. As the works of Adler (1982) and Dennis (1966) are by now quite old, one wonders how the effects of globalization, particularly via the Internet, have come to impact notions of value and familiarity, a question brought to light in vignette 5 (see box 19.5).

**FIGURE 19.7** Drawing made in response to a Peruvian song ("Cholita") by a ten-year-old Mexican boy

FIGURE 19.8 Drawing made in response to a jazz tune ("Chicken Rhythm") by a six-year-old American girl

## VOICE

An issue closely connected to developmental theories is the degree to which intervention is viewed paternalistically. There is a fine line between "scaffolding" and imposition. Schooling very often militates against genuine recognition of children's voices and perspectives (Griffin, 2009). Pat Thomson (2008) notes that "despite the evidence that connections between age and the capacity to take responsibility are culturally constructed, we more often than not see children and young people as persons whose views are completely 'immature' and not to be taken seriously" (p. 1). In research, children are often thought to be "unreliable as informants" due to their "lack of maturity and rationality" (see Freeman & Mathison, 2009, p. 5). Johnson (2008) echoes this sentiment, admonishing that there is an abundance of research "which assumes that children are incompetent, treats them as incompetent and which then produces findings which confirm that incompetence" (p. 78).

The term *voice* often refers to the capacity to speak and to be heard. In addition to the assessment potential afforded by multimodality, the use of children's drawings, when used carefully, represents an important ethical stance. Because drawings tend to be regarded as personal expression, regardless of the age of the drawer, they are rarely faulted as "wrong" in the way that spelling, grammar, mathematics, and even musical performance so often are. As a result, drawings are a distinctive means of "giving voice" to children. The use of "draw and tell," for example, is not just encouraged as a methodological technique. It "allow[s] the drawer to give voice to what the drawing was intended to convey" (Mitchell et al., 2011, p. 25).

The concept of voice is much more involved than we can do justice to here. For our purposes we draw attention to Haw's (2008) summary of values central to voice advocates. Voice (1) privileges experience as the basis of the understanding of an individual or an issue or activity; (2) favors excluded, silenced, or subordinate voices over dominant voices; (3) is inclusive and recognizes proliferation of different voices; and (4) is linked to activism, participation, and empowerment (p. 203). As an assessment practice, children's drawings hold the potential to embody all four of these values to the extent that they validate the subjective values and understandings of all children in a classroom and resist policy imperatives that demand conformity, compliance, and standardization based on right/wrong thinking.

## MEANING AND INTERPRETATION

> Music is meaningful in some ways that some language cannot be, but it shares in the general embodiment of meaning that underlies all forms of symbolic expression, including gesture, body language, ritual, spoken words, visual communication, and so on.
>
> —Johnson and Larson (2003, p. 81)

One of music's many charms—and frustrations—is its semantic ambiguity. Ian Cross and Elizabeth Tolbert (2009) have argued, for example, that although music may have significance, "by comparison with language it is very difficult to say what it is that music refers to, or indeed, whether music refers to anything else at all" (p. 24). Attempts at understanding the semantics of music have been made for some time, with contrasting theories and viewpoints. One such viewpoint rests on the idea that musical meanings are inextricably linked to the social and cultural circumstances in which they arise (Cross & Tolbert, 2009). Music serves varied social and personal functions (Merriam, 1964) for different cultural groups, including symbolic representation (Langer, 1957; Goodman, 1976). Clayton (2009) goes as far as to call music an "efficient semiotic medium" (p. 41) that emphasizes issues of identity and alterity, body motion, and interactions between the self and other.

Musical meanings may emerge in at least four different ways. First, they can result from an association with environmental sounds such as bird songs or car horns. Laurel Trainor and Sandra Trehub (1992) suggest that imitation can be perceived without prior knowledge of a musical system. This is not the case for musical association that arises through the second way musical meanings emerge, metaphors, which require some knowledge of (or at least familiarity with) the musical style or genre in question. A metaphor, as Susanne Langer (1957) put it, "is simply the principle of saying one thing and meaning another, and expecting to be understood to mean the other" (p. 23). Metaphors are not merely linguistic devices, but rather important modes of representation and thought (Lakoff & Johnson, 1980). An example in music is given by Lawrence Zbikowski (1998), who explains that the characterization of musical pitches as high and low is actually metaphorical. In his words, "behind these linguistic expressions is the conceptual metaphor *pitch relationships are relationships in vertical space*, which maps spatial orientations such as *up-down* onto the pitch continuum" (p. 3). A third way in which musical meaning can arise is through cultural conventions. Take, for example, a child who grows up listening exclusively to Western tonal music. While it may not be difficult for her to derive meaning from a piece based on tonality, tempo, or character or through simple priming (e.g., a slower minor melody heard as sad), the same may not be true in the case of music that is based on a different system, like an Indian raga. Finally, a fourth way meanings emerge is through indexical association, such as when couples choose a song as an icon of their relationship (i.e., "they are playing our song"). In the case of children, the most interesting of all four associations is perhaps the metaphorical one (Sloboda, 1985).

Drawings, at least those with representational intent, present something of a middle ground between language and music where interpretation and meaning are concerned, insofar as there are at least allusions to some kind of referents identifiable by most viewers. This is not to suggest that the meaning or interpretation of a drawing is uncomplicated, however. Catherine Angell, Jo Alexander, and Jane A. Hunt (2015) write of the "thorny issue of analysis" with children's drawings (p. 22); similarly, Thomson (2008) writes of "the image and its capacities for deception" (p. 9). As researchers point out, the "content" or meaning of a drawing is dependent on many factors, not least of which are the theoretical orientation of the viewer and the conditions of production.

Claudia Mitchell, Linda Theron, Ann Smith, and Jean Stuart (2011) ask of the drawing, "[I]s it art or is it research?" (p. 3). When used as an assessment tool, the answer to this question is clearly a form of the latter. To be of value to the educator, the meaning and interpretation of drawings must account for more than simply the image itself. As Rose (2001) explains, "visual images do not exist in a vacuum, and looking at them 'for what they are' neglects the ways in which they are produced and interpreted through particular social practices" (p. 37). Or, as Mitchell et al. (2011) put it: "The picture does not tell a story ... it comes with a story" (p. 33; ellipses in original). Clearly a drawing created by a child at home just for the pleasure of drawing should be regarded differently from a drawing created in response to an assignment from the school art teacher, which should be regarded differently from the kind of projective test prompts employed by psychologists. Context matters—by which is meant not just the here and now, but the composite history that has influenced and informed a particular drawing (see box 19.6). What we are suggesting, then, is that music educators avail themselves of the opportunity to better grasp the lifeworlds of children through the use of children's drawings in order to inform instruction that addresses, for example, underdeveloped social and cultural assumptions.

---

**BOX 19.6 VIGNETTE 6: "HE SINGS WITH RHYTHM; HE IS FROM INDIA"**

Juan, a ten-year-old conservatory student from Mexico City, and Felipe, a thirteen-year-old choralist from Curitiba, Brazil, were faced with the same challenge of imagining the origin and characteristics of the singer of a traditional Carnatic song. Both boys identified the song as being from India, yet their representations were markedly different. Juan described the singer as a twelve-year-old boy named Artemio: "He sings with rhythm; he is from India" (figure 19.9). Felipe imagined the singer as someone who was surrounded by chickens and other animals. He also imagined the singer spoke a language that used a different alphabet (the symbols coming out of the mouth in figure 19.10). Felipe explained in the post-drawing debriefing session that the singer is a poor person who lives a sad life, indicated by the shape with an arrow pointing to the words "represents misery."

Both representations tell different stories of how these two students perceive and represent the music they have heard. Their social and cultural imaginaries are at work and likely align with associations and stereotypes learned through their upbringing and the surrounding culture.

FIGURE 19.9 Drawing made in response to a Carnatic song ("Chante traditionnel") by a 12-year-old Mexican boy

FIGURE 19.10 Drawing made in response to a Carnatic song ("Chante traditionnel") by a thirteen-year-old Brazilian boy

# NARRATIVES OF MEANING

Following Banks (2001), Freeman and Mathison (2009) describe data as having *internal* and *external narratives* of meaning, the former referring to the content of an image, the latter to the social context in which the data were created. Consistent with the advice of other researchers, Freeman and Mathison suggest that interpretation and meaning is generally aided by soliciting the verbal commentaries of participants on their drawings.[3] For the music educator, drawings can help identify *emotional*, *associative*, and *concrete* meanings children may derive in and through music (internal narratives), supporting Elliott and Silverman's (2015) claim that a goal of music learning and teaching is "to encourage students to experience and discuss the emotions they might feel and attach to musical-visual, musical-tactile, musical-social, and musical-movement experiences" (p. 331). Through the use of children's writing and talking about their drawings, music educators can better understand the ways musical meanings have arisen in an individual or a group (external narratives).

The well-known image examples of rabbit/duck, old woman/young lady, and hourglass/two faces demonstrate that viewer/audience perspective and gestalt influence interpretation. In the case of assessment, asking children about their drawings helps to clarify the meaning intended by the representation. To be of greatest value, then, assessment needs to account for processes of production. Images are not neutral or inert. They are constructed through a process of *selection* (i.e., content), *processing* (i.e., aesthetic judgments), and *editing* (i.e., presentation and dissemination) (Thomson, 2008, p. 10). As Kress and van Leeuwen (2006) explain further, "signs are never arbitrary, and 'motivation' should be formulated in relation to the sign-maker and the context in which the sign is produced, and not in isolation from the act of producing analogies and classifications" (p. 8).

# CRITICISMS AND CONCERNS

None of what we have presented here is meant to imply that drawing for diagnostic purposes is without its critics. Angell, Alexander, and Hunt (2015), for example, describe the "lively debate" in the research community between those who regard drawing as merely an aid to communication and those who regard it as a valid means of identifying a child's "real" beliefs (p. 18). In their review of literature, the authors point out how some researchers regard children's drawings as simply reflecting dominant discourses, while others highlight the value of the technique for exposing children's understandings of dominant discourses (p. 21). As our concerns lie with assessment rather than research *qua* research, it would seem that distinctions between a child's "real" beliefs and a child's understanding of dominant discourses are moot if the data generated serve the purpose of informing subsequent instruction. Nevertheless, the problem of interpretation remains, as Eliot Eisner (1997) acknowledges: "What will count as misinterpretation?... One peril of ambiguity is the Rorschach syndrome: Everyone confers his or her own idiosyncratic meaning to the data. No consensus is possible. The data mean whatever anyone wants them to mean; or worse, no one knows what they mean" (p. 9). Angell, Alexander, and Hunt (2015) observe that generally few, if any, children decline to participate in drawing research. Greene and Hogan (2005), however, point out that, not unlike with any other medium of expression, children need to be comfortable with the drawing task. While Gardner (1980) may be correct that virtually all children draw, this should not be confused with believing that all children love to draw equally. Whether as research or as assessment, drawing serves best in situations where it is part of regular activities and not an exception. Greene and Hogan argue that drawing may "suffer from diffuseness" when children are unclear of what is being asked, or they may "passively resist revealing personal material" if a relationship of trust has not been established (p. 265). In an assessment context, one similarly imagines that children may attempt to "game" the process if they feel a "correct answer" is being sought (as is often the case in school teaching-learning contexts).

To be of greatest value as a data-generating method, drawing is thought to serve best when the conditions of its production are taken into account. Most researchers today caution against interpreting or analyzing drawings without having witnessed their creation (Freeman & Mathison, 2009, p. 159)—something Mitchell et al. (2011) describe, in educational settings, as "kidwatching" (p. 32). In their study of children aged three to five, Coates and Coates (2006), for example, noted the importance of observing children's "narrative accompaniment" to drawings, which varied considerably from child to child and provided valuable data for making sense of the drawings. Finally, Leitch (2008) advises that drawing methods are "best undertaken by those researchers who have strong empathic and interpersonal understanding, and who have been exposed themselves to the use of the arts" (p. 55).

# EPISTEMOLOGIES OF THE CRAYON

> Subject-produced drawings have the potential, when used with care and rigor, to serve as useful descriptive and analytical tools. As a descriptive tool, subject- produced drawings can be used to elicit individuals' understandings of a specific idea or construct. As an analytical tool, subject-produced drawings can be used to compare an individual's changes over time.
>
> —Ganesh (2011, pp. 238–39)

Departing from the notion of children as "being in the world" rather than "in the process of becoming" (James & Prout, 1997), we have offered rationales for and examples of using drawings as a form of assessment in music classrooms in order to go beyond the "innocence" of assessment based primarily if not exclusively on right/wrong performing ability and knowledge of musical elements. Drawing in response to musical experiences has enormous potential because it exposes underlying social and cultural beliefs and assumptions that children and adults alike might have about music and music making. Meaning making in each drawing presented in the vignettes in this chapter was affected by a complex web of relationships among children's experiences and dispositions, the musical pieces, developmental issues (i.e., ability and motivation to draw, vocabulary), and the adult's input. Through drawing, children had opportunities to express themselves and to voice their own perceptions, belief systems, and ways of being in the world, often in ways not possible through musical performance or spoken/written language.

Each multimodal "drawing to music" experience that took place in Brazil, Mexico, or the United States was distinctive in terms of children's behaviors and engagement. Some children listened quietly and attentively to the music. Others engaged with music in a more kinesthetic way—by means of body motions in response to rhythmic or melodic features, by mimicking singers and instrumentalists, and by laughing or making commentaries to themselves or peers. These experiences are consistent not only with the idea of individual differences in human approaches to music, but also with the notion of music as a complex phenomenon that is embodied, multimodal, and related to cultural, social, and emotional spheres. Regardless of their technical abilities, drawings give voice to children to tell stories of who they are, what they know, and how they perceive the world and the people around them. They are valuable modes of representation of knowledge that shed light on individual and sociocultural understandings. More than that, the act of representing ideas and thoughts through artistic means such as drawings provides fertile ground for the emergence and discovery of new ideas and thoughts (Eisner, 2002).

Kendrick and McKay (2004) argue that "[schools] often fail to recognize the alternative modes of representing knowledge available in the culture. There is an urgent need for including in school curricula multimodal representations which allow for the expression of a much fuller range of human emotion and experience, and which acknowledge the limits of language" (p. 111). We wholeheartedly agree, and hope that more music educators will avail themselves of the opportunity to utilize "picture writing" as a legitimate language of childhood in order to inform their instruction in ways that better account for the existing lifeworlds of children.

## NOTES

1. Hans Prinzhorn's book, *Artistry of the Mentally Ill* (Original edition was 1922) was based on five thousand pictures taken from the 1920s onwards.
2. Examples abound. See Theron, Mitchell, Smith, and Stuart (2011) and Thomson (2008).
3. Mitchell, Theron, Smith, and Jean (2011) are even more insistent: "Never assume you are experts on what [children's] drawings mean; ask them!" (p. 4).
4. In Brazil, "piuí-tchi-tchi" is an onomatopeia that is commonly used to represent a moving train.
5. "La la la" is often used to represent singing.

## REFERENCES

Adler, L. L. (1982). *Cross-cultural research at issue*. New York: Academic Press.

Angell, C., Alexander, J., & Hunt, J. A. (2015). "Draw, write and tell": A literature review and methodological development on the "draw and write" research method. *Journal of Early Childhood Research*, 13(1), 17–28.

Anning, A., & Ring, K. (2004). *Making sense of children's drawings*. Maidenhead, UK: Open University Press.

Aradau, C., & Hill, A. (2013). The politics of drawing: Children, evidence, and the Darfur conflict. *International Political Sociology*, 7, 368–87.

Bamberger, J. (1982). Revisiting children's drawings of simple rhythms: A function for reflection in action. In S. Strauss & E. Stavy (Eds.), *U-shaped behavioral growth* (pp. 191–226). New York: Academic Pres.

Barnes, E. (1892). A study of children's drawings. In G. S. Hall. (Ed.), *The pedagogical seminary* (pp. 455–63.). Worcester, MA: J. H. Orpha.

Barrett, M. (2001). Constructing a view of children's meaning-making as notators: A case-study of a five-year-old's descriptions and explanations of invented notations. *Research Studies in Music Education*, 16(1), 33–45.

Barrett, M. (2002). Invented notations and mediated memory: A case-study of two children's use of invented notations. *Bulletin of the Council for Research in Music Education*, 153/154, 55–62.

Benedict, C., Schmidt, P. K., Spruce, G., & Woodford, P. (Eds.). (2015). *The Oxford handbook of social justice in music education*. New York: Oxford University Press.

Bradley, D. (2006). Music education, multiculturalism, and anti-racism—Can we talk? *Action, Criticism, and Theory for Music Education*, 5(2). Retrieved from http://maydaygroup.org/ACT/v52n/Bradley5_2.pdf

Clayton, M. (2009). The social and personal functions of music in cross-cultural perspective. In S. Hallam, I. Cross, & M. Thaut (Eds.), *The Oxford handbook of music psychology* (pp. 35–44). Oxford: Oxford University Press.

Coates, E., & Coates, A. (2006). Young children talking and drawing. *International Journal of Early Years Education*, 14(3), 221–41.

Colley, A., Mulhern, G., Relton, S., & Shafi, S. (2008). Exploring children's stereotypes through drawings: The case of musical performance. *Social Development*, 18(2), 464–77.

Cross, I., & Tolbert, E. (2009). Music and meaning. In S. Hallam, I. Cross, & M. Thaut (Eds.), *The Oxford handbook of music psychology* (pp. 24–34). Oxford: Oxford University Press.

Davidson, L. & Scripp, L. (1988). Young children's musical representations: Windows on music cognition. In J. A. Sloboda (Ed.), *Generative processes in music: The psychology of performance, improvisation and composition* (pp. 192–230). Oxford: Clarendon Press.

Davidson, L., Scripp, L., & Welsh, P. (1988). "Happy birthday": Evidence for conflicts of perceptual knowledge and conceptual understanding. *Journal of Aesthetic Education*, 22, 65–74.

DeVries, P. (2011). An 8-year-old's engagement with preferred music: A case study. *Research Studies in Music Education*, 33(2), 161–77. doi:10.1177/1321103X11424195

Dyson, A. H. (1986). Transitions and tensions: Interrelationship between drawing, talking, abd dictating of young children. *Research in the Teaching of English*, 20, 379–409.

Eisner, E. (1997). The promise and perils of alternative forms of data representation. *Educational Researcher*, 26(6), 4–10.

Eisner, E. (2002). *The arts and the creation of mind*. New Haven, CT: Yale University Press.

Elkoshi, R. (2015). Children's invented notations and verbal responses to a piano work by Claude Debussy. *Music Education Research*, 17(2), 179–200. doi:10.1080/14613808.2014.930116

Elliott, D. J., & Silverman, M. (2015). *Music matters: A philosophy of music education*. New York: Oxford University Press.

Fargas-Malet, M., & Dillenburguer, K. (2014). Children drawing their own conclusions: Children's perceptions of a "postconflict" society. *Peace and Conflict: Journal of Peace Psychology*, 20(2), 135–49. doi:10.1037/pac0000029

Freeman, M., & Mathison, S. (2009). *Researching children's experiences*. New York: Guilford Press.

Ganesh, T. G. (2011). Children-produced drawings. In E. Margolis & L. Pauwels (Eds.), *The SAGE handbook of visual research methods* (pp. 214–41). Los Angeles: SAGE.

Gardner, H. (1980). *Artful scribbles: The significance of children's drawings*. New York: Basic Books.

Gardner, H. (1982). *Art, mind, and brain: A cognitive approach to creativity*. New York: Basic Books.

Gardner, H. (1993). *Multiple intelligences: The theory in practice*. New York: Basic Books.

Gardner, H. (1994). *The arts and human development: A psychological study of the artistic process*. New York: Basic Books.

Golomb, C. (1992). *The child's creation of the pictorial world*. Los Angeles: University of California Press.

Goodenough, F. L. (1926). *Measurement of intelligence by drawings*. Yonkers-on Hudson, NY: World Book Company.

Goodman, N. (1976). *Languages of art: An approach to a theory of symbols* (2nd ed.). Indianapolis, IN: Hackett.

Gould, E., Countryman, J., & Stewart, L. R. (Eds.). (2009). *Exploring social justice: How music education might matter.* Toronto: Canadian Music Educators' Association.

Greene, S., & Hogan, D. (2005). *Researching children's experiences: Methods and approaches.* London and Thousand Oaks, CA: SAGE.

Griffin, S. M. (2009). Listening to children's music perspectives: In-and out-of-school thoughts. *Research Studies in Music Education, 31*(2), 161–77.

Grubits, S. (2003). A casa: Cultura e sociedade na expressão do desenho infantil [The house: Culture and society in the expression of children's drawings]. *Psicologia em Estudo, 8,* 97–105.

Hair, H. I. (1993). Children's descriptions and representations of music. *Bulletin of the Council for Research in Music Education, 119,* 41–48.

Haw, K. (2008). "Voice" and video: Seen, heard and listened to? In P. Thomson (Ed.), *Doing visual research with children and young people* (pp. 192–207). London and New York: Routledge.

Hesmondalgh, D. (2013). *Why music matters.* Chichester, West Sussex, UK: Blackwell Publishing.

Ilari, B. (2004). Aspectos da cognição musical implícitos em representações inventadas e desenhos de crianças e adultos [Aspects of music cognition implicit in invented representations and drawings by children and adults]. *Revista da Associação Portuguesa de Educação Musical—Lisboa, Portugal, 118,* 27–43.

James, A., & Prout, A. (1997). *Constructing and reconstructing childhood: Contemporary issues in the sociological study of childhood* (2nd ed.). London: Routledge.

Johnson, K. (2008). Teaching children to use visual research methods. In P. Thomson (Ed.), *Doing visual research with children and young people* (pp. 77–94). London and New York: Routledge.

Johnson, M., & Larson, S. (2003). Something in the way she moves: Metaphors of musical motion. *Metaphor & Symbol, 18*(2), 63–84.

Kendrick, M., & McKay, R. (2004). Drawings as an alternative way of understanding young children's constructions of literacy. *Journal of Early Childhood Literacy, 4*(1), 109–28. doi:10.1177/1468798404041458

Kerchner, J. (2000). Children's verbal, visual, and kinesthetic responses: Insights into the music listening experience. *Bulletin of the Council for Research in Music Education, 146,* 31–50.

Kertz-Welzel, A. (2012). Children's and adolescents' musical needs and music education in Germany. In P. S. Campbell & T. Wiggins (Eds.), *Oxford handbook of children's musical cultures* (pp. 371–86). Oxford and New York: Oxford University Press.

Kleinen, G., & Schmitt, R. (1991). *Musik verbindet: Musikalische Lebenswelten auf Schüllerbildern.* Essen, Germany: Blaue Eule.

Kress, G. R., & Van Leeuwen, T. (2006). *Reading images: The grammar of visual design* (2nd ed.). London: Routledge.

Lakoff, G., & Johnson, M. (1980). *Metaphors we live by.* Chicago: University of Chicago Press.

Langer, S. K. (1957). *Philosophy in a new key: A study in the symbolism of reason, rite, and art* (3rd ed.). Cambridge, MA: Harvard University Press.

Leitch, R. (2008). Creatively researching children's narratives through images and drawings. In P. Thomson (Ed.), *Doing visual research with children and young people* (pp. 37–58). London and New York: Routledge.

Lowenfeld, V. (1947). *Creative and mental growth: A textbook on art education.* New York: Macmillan.

Lowenfeld, V., & Brittain, W. L. (1982). *Creative and mental growth* (7th ed.). New York: Macmillan Co.

Malchiodi, C. A. (1998). *Understanding children's drawings.* New York: Guilford Press.

Malindi, M., & Theron, L. (2011). Drawing on strengths: Images of ecological contributions to male street youth resilience. In L. Theron, C. Mitchell, A. Smith, & J. Stuart (Eds.), *Picturing research: Drawing as visual methodology* (pp. 105–18). Boston: Sense Publishers.

Merriam, A. (1964). *The anthropology of music.* Evanston, IL: Northwestern University Press.

Mitchell, C., Theron, L., Smith, A., & Jean, S. (2011). Picturing research: An introduction. In L. Theron, C. Mitchell, A. Smith, & J. Stuart (Eds.), *Picturing research: Drawing as visual methodology* (pp. 1–18). Boston: Sense Publishers.

Mitchell, C., Theron, L., Stuart, J., Smith, A., & Campbell, Z. (2011). Drawing as research method. In L. Theron, C. Mitchell, A. Smith, & J. Stuart (Eds.), *Picturing research: Drawing as visual methodology* (pp. 19–36). Boston: Sense Publishers.

Moore, P. (2013). Listening guides draw students closer to music: Visual depictions of sounds, rhythms, and musical events can keep kids engaged and expose deeper meanings. *Teaching Music, 20*(6), 65–66.

Pramling, N. (2009). External representation and the architecture of music: Children inventing and speaking about notations. *British Journal of Music Education, 26*(3), 273–91. doi:10.1017/S0265051709990106

Pramling, N., & Wallerstedt, C. (2009). Making musical sense: The multimodal nature of clarifying musical listening. *Music Education Research,11*(2),135–51. doi:10.1080/14613800902924433

Quaglia, R., Longobardi, C., Iotti, N., & Prino, L. E. (2015). A new theory on children's drawings: Analyzing the role of emotion and movement in graphical development. *Infant Behavior & Development, 39*, 81–91. doi:10.1016/j.infbeh.2015.02.009

Rose, G. (2001). *Visual methodologies: An introduction to the interpretation of visual materials.* London and Thousand Oaks, CA: SAGE.

Sloboda, J. A. (1985). *The musical mind: The cognitive psychology of music.* Oxford: Oxford University Press.

Southcott, J., & Coisatis, W. (2015). Drawing "music and me": Children's images of musical engagement. *Australian Journal of Music Education, 2,* 78–90.

Suárez-Orozco, M., Sattin-Bajaj, C., & Suárez-Orozco, C. (2010). Introduction: Architectures of care. In M. Suárez-Orozco & C. Sattin-Bajaj (Eds.), *Educating the whole child for the whole world: The Ross School model and education for the global area* (pp. 1–24). New York: New York University Press.

Szot, J. (2006). Music makers: Strings—An idea for creative and artistic listening lesson. *Canadian Music Educator, 47*(3), 37–38.

Theron, L., Mitchell, C., Smith, A., & Stuart, J. (Eds.). (2011). *Picturing research: Drawing as visual methodology.* Boston: Sense Publishers.

Thomson, P. (Ed.). (2008). *Doing visual research with children and young people.* London: Routledge.

Trainor, L. J., & Trehub, S. E. (1992). The development of referential meaning in music. *Music Perception, 9,* 455–70.

Upitis, R. (1990). Children's invented notations of familiar and unfamiliar melodies. *Psychomusicology, 9,* 89–106.

Vygotsky, L. S. (1978). *Mind in society: The development of higher psychological processes.* Cambridge, UK: Harvard University Press.

Young, S., & Glover, J. (1998). *Music in the early years.* London and Bristol, PA: Falmer Press.

Zbikowski, L. M. (1998). Metaphor and musical theory: Reflections from cognitive sciences. *Music Theory Online: A Journal of the Society for Music Theory, 4*(1). Retrieved from http://www.mtosmt.org/issues/mto.98.4.1/mto.98.4.1.zbikowski.html

# PART IV

........................................................

# INTERNATIONAL PERSPECTIVES

........................................................

....................................................................................

# CHAPTER 20

# THE ASSESSMENT OF CLASSROOM MUSIC IN THE LOWER SECONDARY SCHOOL: THE ENGLISH EXPERIENCE

....................................................................................

## MARTIN FAUTLEY

THE case of assessment of classroom music in the lower secondary school is especially interesting when viewed through the lenses of the topics of this current handbook, namely the philosophical and qualitative. There are many lessons to be drawn from the English experience, which makes this more than a simple discussion of regional issues; it has ramifications for the consideration of assessment in generalist class music in many jurisdictions, wherever in the world such educational activity is taking place. To describe why this is the case, we first need to understand the form and nature of classroom music education in England.

Music education in England in the lower secondary school (for pupils eleven to fourteen years old) has been a compulsory subject in the state-mandated National Curriculum (NC) since its launch in 1988, and has had to be taught and learned by all pupils in maintained (state) secondary schools. This stage of education in the lower secondary school is known as Key Stage 3 (KS3) in local usage. What counts as a state school has become much broader in recent years, with the introduction of what are locally termed academies and free schools; academies are schools set up independently of local governmental control and often grouped in autonomous multi-academy trusts (MATs), and free schools are in many ways similar to the charter schools movement in the United States, where interested parties can set up and run schools. Both of these school types receive central government funding, but neither is compelled to follow the NC, which is compulsory in other state schools. In practice, the vast majority of all state-funded schools in England *do* follow the National Curriculum, even if in a diluted or arm's-length form.

Important for an international audience to understand, and quite unlike the situation that exists in many other countries, is that in England there is a school inspection body, which operates at arm's-length from the government, known as the Office for Standards in Education, or Ofsted. Ofsted inspects schools on behalf of the government and publicly reports its findings (Cullingford, 1999). Ofsted inspects and reports on schools under four headings:

- Achievement of pupils
- Quality of teaching
- Behavior and safety of pupils
- Leadership and management

Using these four headings, a grade for "overall effectiveness" is then produced, for which Ofsted uses a four-point grading system:

Grade 1 Outstanding
Grade 2 Good
Grade 3 Requires improvement
Grade 4 Inadequate (Ofsted, 2018)

Teachers' and school leaders' fear of Ofsted inspections cannot be overemphasized. There have even been cases of head teachers committing suicide after a poor Ofsted report (see Adams, 2015). Indeed, such are the systemic requirements that many school management teams spend much of their learning strategy planning time asking themselves if Ofsted would like what they are planning rather than the more context-specific and possibly useful question: Would this be good for the learners in our school?

# MUSIC EDUCATION IN THE NATIONAL CURRICULUM

Music teaching and learning according to the NC in England takes the form of a generalist music education, which is organized around three main aspects: listening, performing, and composing (Finney, 2011; Pitts, 2000). These also need some clarification for an international audience. Performing is not usually instrument specific, in the sense of an extended series of lessons on an orchestral or band instrument, although it can be. What normally occurs is that performing takes place using classroom instruments, such as tuned or untuned percussion, as well as keyboards, guitars, ukuleles, and so forth. Some schools offer classroom band lessons, and some use "musical futures"

(Green, 2008; Musical Futures, n.d.) lessons in which all children learn using popular styles. This breadth of provision is similarly matched by the composing strand. This is not necessarily composing using staff notation, although it can be; it is composing directly into sound and can include songwriting, experimental music, or any style and form the teacher deems appropriate. Listening is concomitantly eclectic. There is no specified repertoire in the NC; no styles and genres are delineated, and instead learners are required to

> build on their previous knowledge and skills through performing, composing and listening. They should develop their vocal and/or instrumental fluency, accuracy and expressiveness; and understand musical structures, styles, genres and traditions, identifying the expressive use of musical dimensions. They should listen with increasing discrimination and awareness to inform their practice as musicians. They should use technologies appropriately and appreciate and understand a wide range of musical contexts and styles.   (DfE, 2013)

Alongside the NC there was also an assessment regime that consisted of a series of *level statements*, which were statutory for all schools until the requirement was removed in 2014. As was standard for all NC subjects in the school curriculum, there were eight of these level statements, plus one for what was termed *excellent performance* (not in the musical sense, but performance in terms of learner attainment), with the requirement that by the time they reached the end of the lower secondary school, normally at age fourteen, pupils would be awarded one of these level statements to summarize their attainment. The typical expectation for the average fourteen-year-old pupil at this stage was to attain level 5, the statement for which reads as follows: "Pupils identify and explore musical devices and how music reflects time, place and culture. They perform significant parts from memory and from notations, with awareness of their own contribution such as leading others, taking a solo part or providing rhythmic support. They improvise melodic and rhythmic material within given structures, use a variety of notations, and compose music for different occasions using appropriate musical devices. They analyse and compare musical features. They evaluate how venue, occasion and purpose affect the way music is created, performed, and heard. They refine and improve their work" (QCA, 2007, p. 186).

With the content-light curriculum discussed here, it follows that specifying assessment topics is problematic, so it can be clearly seen that the level 5 statement (the others are similar in construction) is holistic in nature and encompasses attainment in the three areas of composing, listening, and performing. What this meant in practice is that teachers employed these statements in a "best-fit" fashion (Fautley, 2010, 2012), weighing up judgments about what aspects of individual pupils' work they would be taking into account in order to award them their final level statements at the end of the course (Sainsbury & Sizmur, 1998). This sounds relatively uncontentious, if somewhat nebulous in application. It is indeed the case that application was somewhat nebulous, and what happened as a result is an interesting case study in manipulation and interference.

# THE USE OF ASSESSMENT LEVELS IN
# THE NATIONAL CURRICULUM

The level statements, as exemplified in the level 5 statement, were originally intended to be used once only, at the end of a specific period of study in music (Bray, 2002). However, what came to be standard procedure was for schools to employ these levels far more frequently, initially every term and then latterly almost on a lesson-by-lesson basis. Indeed, so prevalent was the use of these levels that they were expected to be known and used by all of the pupils in their various subjects at all times throughout their schooling. However, what schools found was that the levels themselves were far too coarse-grained to be of much use in demonstrating these smaller degrees of progress. In order to address this problem, many schools subdivided the level statements into smaller units. Although there was no nationally established protocol for this procedure, by means of what Jerome Bruner (1996) might have referred to as a "folk-pedagogy," the custom and practice became widespread of schools subdividing these into three levels, normally labeled a–c, with "a" representing secure attainment, "b" meaning that the standard had been appropriately met, and "c" meaning that the level had only just about been achieved.

Given that the level statements are holistic and somewhat nonspecific in terms of content requirements, the upshot was that these subdivided levels became increasingly idiosyncratic and varied significantly from school to school. Some schools rewrote the level statements in such a way that they became quite far removed from the original intention. Indeed, Ofsted (2009) commented on this: "In one lesson seen, for example, students were told: 'Level 3: clap a 3 beat ostinato; Level 4: maintain a 4 bar ostinato; Level 5: compose an ostinato.' This demonstrated a significant misunderstanding of the expectations inherent in the level descriptions" (p. 31). Ofsted (2009) also reported on the use of subdivided levels, observing that they "did not take account of the National Curriculum guidance about progress within levels being seen in terms of increasing confidence, ownership and independence and so they ended up being based on arbitrary degrees of competence in separate and specific components of music" (p. 32). With Ofsted making such pejorative statements about the use of these levels, it seems remarkable that their use continued, and yet it did.

With different rewritten level statements in place in each school, the ready comparison of pupil attainment from one school to another became increasingly difficult, if not impossible in some cases, as not only had the level statements been reduced and distorted so as to become unrecognizable regarding the original intentions, but they had also been subjected to tailoring to match specific projects. In other words, subdivided level statements for a performing piece of work, as in the case of the ostinato-based assessment observed by Ofsted described here, could be very different for a keyboard unit of work, where statements could be found such as the following, observed by the author in one school:

Level 3: play melody with one finger
Level 4: play melody with two fingers
Level 5: play melody with more than two fingers

This example duplicates the issues observed by Ofsted but places the level statements in a completely different sphere of reference. Contrast "play with more than two fingers" or "maintain a 4 bar ostinato" with the holistic complexity of the level 5 statement, and the reductio ad absurdum nature of many of these homemade rewritten level statements can be clearly observed (Fowler, 2008).

Indeed, so problematic did the use of subdivided level statements become that the chief Ofsted inspector for music was moved to write that "using levels and sub levels to try to prove pupils' ongoing progress in music doesn't work, as Ofsted has pointed out many times. It is usually superficial, time wasting and neither reliable nor valid. It is most certainly not any kind of 'Ofsted requirement.' To be absolutely clear, our inspectors do not expect to see it. There are no, and never were, sub levels in music anyway, for good reason" (Hammerton, 2014). This is important for the thematic focus of this handbook, as qualitative assessment in music education classes has been the norm for many years, but—and this is a big caveat—this has gone hand in hand with the placing of numerical values on these qualitative judgments once they have been made. This creates a number of issues:

1. It implies a positivist, quantitative stance that is at odds with the often qualitative assessment data-gathering techniques employed.
2. These pseudo-positivist conversions are then taken to be both valid *and* reliable and are treated accordingly.
3. The pseudo-positivist conversions are then used to "track" progress made by children and young people, in ways that may not always be appropriate or valid.

To discuss further why these issues might matter, we need to consider the ways in which the assessment of musical endeavor actually takes place "on the ground," as it were, in the music classroom in the English secondary school.

## CLASSROOM PRACTICES AND PHILOSOPHIES

We have already seen how music is taught in a generalist way in England. In the 2007 iteration of the NC, the following was noted about the nature and purpose of music education:

> Music education encourages active involvement in different forms of music-making, both individual and communal, helping to develop a sense of group identity and togetherness. Music can influence students' development in and out of the academy

by fostering personal development and maturity, creating a sense of achievement and self-worth, and increasing their ability to work with others in a group context.

Music learning develops students' critical skills: their ability to listen, to appreciate a wide variety of music, and to make judgements about musical quality. It also increases self-discipline, creativity, aesthetic sensitivity and fulfilment.

(QCA, 2007, p. 179)

These are the values that lie behind classroom music in England. The types of knowledge that this approach espouses were delineated by Chris Philpott (2016):

Knowledge about music: This might be referred to as factual knowledge, that is, factual knowledge about composers, about style, about theory, about musical concepts.

Knowledge how: how to play an instrument, how to distinguish between sounds, perceptual know-how (e.g. to recognize a drone), knowing how to present a piece to an audience, knowing how to read and write music, knowing how to make music sound in a particular way.

Knowledge of music: by direct acquaintance.    (pp. 33–34)

These types of knowledge are not rooted in a single musical instrument performance modality; neither are they specified by ensemble type, such as band or orchestra. They are not defined by style and genre; no specific composers, performers, works, or pieces of music are mentioned in the NC documentation. Neither are pedagogies or pedagogic traditions suggested; so, for example, it is entirely possible to construct schemes of work based on the music of Queen, or of William Byrd, or on stylistic types ranging from Pavans and Galliards to thrash metal guitar. Some schools concentrate heavily on composing music, some on performing, while others prefer to focus on listening and historical knowledge. But what they all have in common is that the three pillars of musical knowledge types—listening, composing, and performing—will all, to a greater or lesser degree, be taught in some quantity. This breadth in ranges of approach is left to the discretion of the individual teacher and management team, should they wish to be involved, in each school separately.

By way of illustration, the range of subjects taught in the lower secondary school to pupils between eleven and fourteen years of age can be seen in the "Top Thirty" music curriculum topics taught in London schools, as described in a 2016 report: "Latin American Music; Medieval Music; Minimalism; Keyboard skills; Renaissance Music; Form and Structure; Ground Bass; Instruments of the orchestra; Samba; Graphic score; Hip Hop; Musical Futures; Adverts; Stomp; African Drumming; Viennese Waltz; Programme Music; Pop and Rock; Ukulele; Reggae and Caribbean; Singing; Pitch, Scales, Modes; Indian Music; Song-writing; Music Tech; Jazz; Film Music; Music Concrete; Gamelan; Blues" (Fautley, 2016, p. 25). This list of topics (and remember these were only the top thirty topics) shows the breadth, range, and scope of curricular areas covered. From this breadth, it is reasonable to assume that no single-item-response, pencil- and paper-based assessment could hope to cover all of the work done by all these pupils.

In a similar vein, philosophical decisions regarding approaches to content and pedagogy can vary hugely among schools. For example, many schools follow David J. Elliott's (1995) notion of a praxial music education, and their curricula consist of approaches that could be recognized as following Elliott's (1995) four typologies:

- Music is a human endeavor.
- Music is never a matter of musical works alone.
- Making music includes moving, dancing, worshipping, as well as musicking and listening.
- Musical sounds can be made for a variety of purposes and functions across cultures (p. 129).

These two philosophical approaches, those outlined by Philpott and Elliott, are important to the ways in which music is taught and learned and, important for our present discussion, assessed. What this variety means is that there is no simple and straight-forward progression to be observed across what might be considered otherwise unitary music curriculum constructs such as performing; instead there are always many other things going on at the same time. One of the ramifications of this situation is that teachers are not only the architects of their own curriculum content, they are also architects of the style, form, range, approach, utility, and substance of any assessments that they pro-duce. Certainly there will be specific school requirements in terms of frequency and reporting arrangements, but the substance of any assessment undertaken will be at the will (some might say whim!) of the individual classroom teacher.

# FORMATIVE ASSESSMENT IN THE ENGLISH CONTEXT

Given this complexity, it useful at this juncture to outline the types of assessment activity undertaken by teachers in the classroom and to describe and discuss what takes place during such assessments. Highly significant in the English context, and differing sub-stantially in many ways from American understandings of the term, is the notion of "formative assessment," also known as assessment for learning, or AfL. In the English usage, following the work of the Assessment Reform Group (Assessment Reform Group, 1999, 2002) and Paul Black and Dylan Wiliam (Black, 1993, 1995; Black, Harrison, Lee, Marshall, & Wiliam, 2003a, 2003b; Black & Wiliam, 1998), the term is used to mean

- observing pupils—this includes listening to how they describe their work and their reasoning;
- questioning, using open questions, phrased to invite pupils to explore their ideas and reasoning;

- setting tasks in a way that requires pupils to use certain skills or apply ideas;
- asking pupils to communicate their thinking through drawings, artifacts, actions, role play, concept mapping, and writing; and
- discussing words and how they are being used (Assessment Reform Group, 1999, p. 8).

This situates AfL at the heart of the teaching and learning process, and it is this usage that is understood by teachers of all subjects in England. It does, however, put this meaning somewhat at odds with the understanding of formative assessment in other jurisdictions, particularly the United States, as Dylan Wiliam (2004) observes:

> In the United States, the term "formative assessment" is often used to describe assessments that are used to provide information on the likely performance of students on state-mandated tests—a usage that might better be described as "early-warning summative." In other contexts it is used to describe any feedback given to students, no matter what use is made of it, such as telling students which items they got correct and incorrect (sometimes called "knowledge of results"). These kinds of usages suggest that the distinction between "formative" and "summative" applies to the assessments themselves, but since the same assessment can be used both formatively and summatively, it follows that these terms cannot describe assessment themselves, but are really describing the use to which the resulting outcomes are put.   (p. 4)

Wiliam makes an important distinction here, in that it is not so much the assessment typologies that are different, but rather the uses to which the resultant assessment is put. This is a point to which I return later. In England, the use of formative assessment according to the understanding described here is well embedded in classroom practice. Indeed, in national governmentally produced training materials for teachers of all subjects, a music lesson was chosen to show formative assessment in action (DfES, 2002).

# SUMMATIVE ASSESSMENT IN THE ENGLISH CONTEXT

In contrast with the situation regarding formative assessment, summative assessment in music is characterized in the English nomenclature as being *teacher assessment*, often abbreviated as TA. It is important to note that this does not mean assessment or evaluation *of* teachers, but instead refers to assessment activities undertaken *by* teachers to generate assessment data on the learners in their charge. There are no widespread externally set assessments, tasks, or tests for music in the lower secondary school. In this regard, teachers design all summative assessment activity for their own use only. Neither is there very much by way of interschool standardization or moderation; again, it is left to the discretion of individual schools to manage this aspect of their work. Although we lack in-depth national research data on TA, we do know anecdotally and from small-scale research (e.g., Fautley & Savage, 2011; Soundhub, n.d.; Hampshire, n.d.) that the majority of teacher summative assessment undertaken in lower secondary school music lessons is criterion referenced. Usually this involves a range of criteria against which pupil learning outcomes are marked and graded. Such statements take a variety of forms. Sometimes they are statements against which teachers can assess attainment, such as the following (Daubney & Fautley, 2014, p. 7):

- Experiment with voice, sounds, technology and instruments in creative ways and to explore new techniques.
- Maintain a strong sense of pulse and recognize when going out of time.
- Demonstrate increasing confidence, expression, skill, and level of musicality through taking different roles in performance and rehearsal.
- Maintain an independent part in a group when singing or playing.
- Use a variety of musical devices, timbres, textures, techniques etc. when creating and making music.

Assessment criterion statements such as these are normally intended to be graded using a three- or five-point scale. Scoring is achieved by allocating a numeric grade to each level and adding up the grades from a series of such assessments to provide an overall score.

Another form of assessment criterion statement commonly met is the "I can" version, in which pupils situate themselves upon a scale, sometimes with help and prompting from the teacher. Examples of this sort of statement follow (Ofsted, 2012c, p. 37):

Level 3.6: I can decide how I am going to use the elements of music in my composition.
Level 4.0: I can compose appropriate music that accompanies my story.
Level 4.2: I can use the elements of music when composing to create an effect.
Level 4.4: I can compose short ideas to represent different parts.
Level 5.0: I can use more than one element at the same time to create an effect.

There are a number of things to note about these exemplar criterion statements:

1. They provide a numeric outcome based on a qualitative grading decision made by the teacher and/or the pupil.
2. The grade awarded is treated as being statistically sound.
3. The scored outcome is then used as a summative grade for tracking and monitoring purposes.

These three observations can be isomorphically mapped onto the three issues described previously in this chapter:

| | |
|---|---|
| It implies a positivist, quantitative stance that is at odds with the often qualitative assessment data-gathering techniques employed. | They provide a numeric outcome based on a qualitative grading decision made by the teacher and/or the pupil. |
| These pseudo-positivist conversions are then taken to be both valid *and* reliable and are treated accordingly. | The grade awarded is treated as being statistically sound. |
| Said pseudo-positivist conversions are then used to "track" progress made by children and young people, in ways that may not be appropriate. | The scored outcome is then used as a summative grade for tracking and monitoring purposes. |

However, the English assessment context is not alone in moving from judgements to scores. After all, in music we are well used to taking qualitative judgments and turning them into scored grades, and we then work with the scoring alone. This, however, is a different order of problem, in that we are not clear on either the reliability or the validity of the grades awarded. At this point it is useful to bear in mind the observation made by Caroline Gipps (1994) that "assessment is not an exact science, and we must stop presenting it as such" (p. 167).

# ATTAINMENT AND PROGRESSION

What is of potentially greater interest than the issues of pseudo-positive assessment just discussed, which are likely to be common across a range of international contexts and practices, is that a highly significant qualitative shift in assessment practice has taken place in the English context of school music lessons: the move from considering the assessment of *attainment* to the assessment of *progress*. These are two significant words in the English assessment lexicon, and we need to fully understand what is meant by them. Whatever assessment, marking, and grading system is being employed, the terminology used is that these will be assessments of "attainment." Attainment has a very specific meaning in the English context of marks, grades, or levels, which a pupil has been awarded in terms of results from assessments. Contrast this with "achievement," which includes an element of progress. Ofsted (2012b) normally uses these words in a very precise way and looks at "pupils' academic achievement over time, taking attainment and progress into account" (p. 8), with judgments about achievement being based on "pupils' attainment in relation to national standards and compared to all schools, based on data over the last three years, noting particularly any evidence of performance significantly above or below national averages, and inspection evidence of current pupils' attainment" (Ofsted, 2012a, p. 6).

Progress can be thought of in simple terms as the speed at which pupils transition through whatever attainment grading system is being employed. The term "rapid progress" contains a speed judgment within it, as does its opposite, "slow progress." In 2014 Ofsted wrote to all schools in England, saying that it would be looking closely at pupil work to determine what progress the pupils had been making. This links back to an earlier utterance on this subject, in which Ofsted (2012b) had said that it would be "observing learning over time…scrutiny of pupils' work, with particular attention given to…pupils' effort and success in completing their work and the progress they make over a period of time" (p. 35). What this means in schools is that progress has become a major focus for music teachers. School leadership teams (SLTs) have in many cases become focused on being able to *prove* that progress has taken place should the Ofsted inspector call. In order to try to demonstrate that progress is being made, and at the right speed, many schools have invested time and money in complicated attainment tracking systems, known as "flightpaths," which show progression, often represented on a graph as a series of straight lines for different cohorts of pupils. Each of these flightpaths is usually ability based, in the sense that the trajectories are derived from pupil attainment scores in mathematics and English.

This close focus on progress means that teachers have in many cases become overly concerned with matters of speed of attainment. What tends not to happen very much is that progress is conceptualized as operating on two separate axes simultaneously, those of *breadth* and *depth*, and so breadth of curriculum coverage receives the greatest attention, often at the expense of depth. The way that this is expressed in school curriculum materials is that many lower secondary school schemes of work resemble what might be thought of as a "Cook's tour" of aspects of world music, along with key milestones from Western art music and selected other genres. The way that these are normally organized is that each topic area is scheduled to be taught for half a term, which amounts to about six weeks. This means that in the average Key Stage 3 course lasting for three academic years, eighteen such topics could be taught. Constructing a learning program of any eighteen topics from the list of the top thirty quoted previously shows that any such music curriculum would be, at the very least, eclectic.

There is, however, a further complication that needs to be investigated here, and that is that the flightpath charts normally show linear progress. This means that assessment grades given to pupils need to constantly be an improvement over previous ones, as otherwise teachers will be deemed to be failing their pupils. This places an artificially distorting element in qualitative assessment, as the effect of these diktats from SLTs means that pupils can *only* be given marks, grades, or levels that are higher than their previous ones, whatever the topic and whatever the engagement and attainment of the learners. This has the unforeseen consequence of placing unwarranted constraints upon curriculum design, as what this means in practice is that teachers need to plan their individual programs of study so that topics with the potential to be less engaging are placed nearer the beginning of the course, so that dips in attainment—and therefore dips in progress—do not occur. Clearly, from any meaningful view of assessment this is nonsense. Pupils cannot attain in a linearly higher manner in topics, whatever the flightpath says. This means that in a school with a highly engaging unit on, say, songwriting, followed by a potentially less engaging unit on the Viennese waltz, to choose two from the London top thirty list, teachers *cannot* give any pupils a lower attainment grade for the latter, as their professionalism may well be called into question.

The joint effect of a relentless focus on attainment at all costs to please what schools think of as the requirements of Ofsted—although Ofsted (2016) has published a document describing many such activities as myths—and the strictures of purchased attainment- and progress-tracking software packages has had the net result that assessment of attainment in England at KS3 can be thought of as being neither particularly reliable nor valid. Indeed, its sole purpose seems to be to avoid undesirable consequences; this is rather like medical staff being more concerned to avoid litigation than to treat the patient! Assessment made under these circumstances cannot be thought of as true assessment of pupil attainment; instead, it has become a paper exercise whose main purpose is compliance with what has come to be called the performativity agenda. Performativity, as Stephen J. Ball (2003) observes,

> is a technology, a culture and a mode of regulation that employs judgments, comparisons and displays as means of incentive, control, attrition and change—based on rewards and sanctions (both material and symbolic). The performances (of individual subjects or organizations) serve as measures of productivity or output, or displays of "quality," or "moments" of promotion or inspection. As such they stand for, encapsulate or represent the worth, quality or value of an individual or organization within a field of judgment....Typically, at least in the UK, these struggles are currently highly individualized as teachers, as ethical subjects, find their values challenged or displaced by the terrors of performativity.   (p. 216)

Assessment of attainment and assessment of progress have become sites of "terror" in English music classrooms, as teachers struggle, on the one hand, to teach logical and developmental programs of study, and on the other, to fulfill the complex demands of an accountability regime that does not recognize the unique nature of music as a mode of knowing and being, but instead constrains it to fit onto a linear trajectory of constant improvement.

# Conclusions

One of the key roles of summative assessment, not just in music but in any discipline, ought to be that it provides useful and informative material for learners and teachers. As Wynne Harlen (2007) observes: "There are two main purposes for assessing students: to inform decisions about learning experiences and to report on what has been achieved" (p. 15). It will be immediately apparent from this admittedly brief discussion of assessment practices in English music classes that neither of these functions is likely to be adequately fulfilled by contemporary customs and practices. Instead, the relentless pursuit of progression data—which, when examined closely, turn out to be no such thing—prevents any meaningful discussion of either attainment or progress being made. The notion of having to "prove" progression against a straight line drawn by statistical software that has no basis in the sonic art of music has prevented classroom music teachers being able to make any form of sensibly differentiated judgments about the progress that their pupils have *really* been making while musicking. It does not help inform either teachers or learners about what steps they need to take next in developing learning. Instead we have a situation in which formative and summative uses and purposes of assessment have become increasingly detached from each other, such that many teachers are now relying more heavily on their own formative assessment judgments, which they make as the class is in progress, to help, as Harlen (2007) observed, "inform decisions about learning experiences" (p. 15). Teachers increasingly see the provision of summative assessment grades as something the performativity juggernaut requires but that contains no real meaning for them or their pupils.

There are clearly lessons for an international audience to be drawn from these English experiences, regarding the real philosophical purposes of assessment in music education not being drowned out by the need for ever-increasing accountability measures and the need for qualitative assessment techniques to be truly assessments of *quality*—of music making, musical learning, and musicianship—rather than being simply numbers used to create a large stick with which to beat teachers. Sadly, in what the Finnish education writer Pasi Sahlberg (2014) has called the global educational reform movement (GERM), assessment issues are likely to spread across continents: "GERM assumes that external performance standards, describing what teachers should teach and what students should do and learn, lead to better learning for all" (p. 150).

It is to be hoped that music educators and their associated administrative regimes around the world will wake up to these issues before it becomes too late for action. Music education already occupies a precarious position in many jurisdictions. It would be sad for its inherent creativity to be stifled by the requirements of statisticians and management consultants, rather than having had a chance to flourish and to make a very real difference to the lives of children and young people, who we know are touched by what music as a subject and a practice has to offer them.

# REFERENCES

Adams, R. (2015, November 20). *Guardian, The*. Headteacher killed herself after Ofsted downgrade, inquest hears. Retrieved from https://www.theguardian.com/uk-news/2015/nov/20/headteacher-killed-herself-after-ofsted-downgrade-inquest

Assessment Reform Group. (1999). *Assessment for learning: Beyond the black box*. Cambridge, UK: University of Cambridge School of Education.

Assessment Reform Group. (2002). *Assessment for learning: 10 principles*. London: ARG. Retrieved from http://k1.ioe.ac.uk/tlrp/arg/publications.html.

Ball, S. J. (2003). The teacher's soul and the terrors of performativity. *Journal of Education Policy, 18*(2), 215–28.

Black, P. (1993). Formative and summative assessment by teachers. *Studies in Science Education, 21*, 49–97.

Black, P. (1995). Can teachers use assessment to improve learning. *British Journal of Curriculum and Assessment, 5*(2), 7–11.

Black, P., Harrison, C., Lee, C., Marshall, B., & Wiliam, D. (2003a). *Assessment for learning: Putting it into practice.* Maidenhead, UK: Open University Press.

Black, P., Harrison, C., Lee, C., Marshall, B., & Wiliam, D. (2003b). The nature and value of formative assessment for learning. *Improving Schools, 6*(3), 7–22.

Black, P., & Wiliam, D. (1998). *Inside the black box: Raising standards through classroom assessment.* London: School of Education, King's College.

Bray, D. (2002). Assessment in music education. In G. Spruce (Ed.), *Aspects of teaching secondary music* (pp. 79–93). London: RoutledgeFalmer.

Bruner, J. (1996). *The culture of education.* Cambridge, MA: Harvard University Press.

Cullingford, C. (Ed.) (1999). *An inspector calls: Ofsted and its effect on school standards.* London: Kogan Page.

Daubney, A., & Fautley, M. (2014). *The national curriculum for music: An assessment and progression framework.* London: The Incorporated Society of Musicians.

DfE. (2013). *Music programmes of study: Key stage 3.* Retrieved from https://www.gov.uk/government/uploads/system/uploads/attachment_data/file/239088/SECONDARY_national_curriculum_-_Music.pdf

DfES. (2002). *Training materials for the foundation subjects.* London: DfES.

Elliott, D. J. (1995). *Music matters: A new philosophy of music education.* New York: Oxford University Press.

Fautley, M. (2010). *Assessment in music education.* Oxford: Oxford University Press.

Fautley, M. (2012). Assessment issues within National Curriculum music in the lower secondary school in England. In T. S. Brophy & A. Lehmann-Wermser (Eds.), *Proceedings of the Third International Symposium on Assessment in Music Education* (pp. 153–64). Chicago: GIA Publications.

Fautley, M. (2016). *Teach through music evaluation report.* London: Trinity Laban Conservatoire of Music and Dance.

Fautley, M., & Savage, J. (2011). Assessment of composing in the lower secondary school in the English National Curriculum. *British Journal of Music Education, 28*(1), 51–67.

Finney, J. (2011). *Music education in England, 1950–2010: The child-centred progressive tradition.* Farnham, UK: Ashgate.

Fowler, A. (2008). Assessment—A view from the classroom. *NAME (National Association of Music Educators, UK) Journal, 23*, 10–12.

Gipps, C. (1994). *Beyond testing: Towards a theory of educational assessment.* London: Falmer Press.

Green, L. (2008). *Music, informal learning and the school: A new classroom pedagogy.* Aldershot, UK: Ashgate.

Hammerton, R. (2014). Music in schools: Where words finish, music begins [Web log post]. TES Ofsted Resources. Retrieved from https://www.tes.com/blogs/ofsted/music-schools-where-words-finish-music-begins

Hampshire. (n.d.). *Assessing KS3 music: An introduction.* Retrieved from http://www3.hants.gov.uk/education/hms/hms-schools/hms-secondary/hms-nat-curr-music-at-ks3/hms-assessing-ks3-music.htm

Harlen, W. (2007). *Assessment of learning.* London: SAGE.

Musical Futures. (n.d.). Home page. Retrieved from https://www.musicalfutures.org

Ofsted. (2009). *Making more of music.* London: Ofsted.

Ofsted. (2012a). *The evaluation schedule for schools 2012*. London: Oftsed.

Ofsted. (2012b). *The framework for school inspection from January 2012*. London: Oftsed.

Ofsted. (2012c). *Music in schools: Wider still, and wider*. Manchester, UK: Ofsted.

Ofsted. (2014). *Letter to schools from HMCI: July 2014*. Retrieved from https://assets.publishing. service.gov.uk/government/uploads/system/uploads/attachment_data/file/750098/Letter_ to_schools_from_HMCI_20-_20July_2014-archived.doc

Ofsted. (2016). *Ofsted insepctions myths*. Retrieved from https://www.gov.uk/government/ publications/school-inspection-handbook-from-september-2015/ofsted-inspections- mythbusting

Ofsted. (2018). *School Inspections A guide for parents*. Retrieved from https://assets.publishing. service.gov.uk/government/uploads/system/uploads/attachment_data/file/720519/School_ inspections_-_a_guide_for_parents-v2.docx

Philpott, C. (2016). The what, how and where of musical learning and development. In C. Cooke, K. Evans, & C. Philpott (Eds.), *Learning to teach music in the secondary school* (3rd ed., pp. 32–51). London: Routledge.

Pitts, S. (2000). *A century of change in music education*. Aldershot, UK: Ashgate.

QCA. (2007). *Music: Programme of study for key stage 3*. Retrieved from http://media.education. gov.uk/assets/files/pdf/m/music2007programmeofstudyforkeystage3.pdf

Sahlberg, P. (2014). *Finnish lessons 2.0: What can the world learn from educational change in Finland?* New York: Teachers College Press.

Sainsbury, M., & Sizmur, S. (1998). Level descriptions in the National Curriculum: What kind of criterion referencing is this? *Oxford Review of Education*, 24(2), 181–93.

Soundhub. (n.d.). *Assessing Musical Learning and Progression at Key Stage 3*. Retrieved from https://www.kent-music.com/app/uploads/Module-5-Website-and-Email-version.pdf

Wiliam, D. (2004). *Keeping learning on track: Integrating assessment with instruction*. Invited address to the 30th annual conference of the International Association for Educational Assessment (IAEA), Philadelphia.

CHAPTER 21

..........

# IMAGINING
# ENDS-NOT-YET-IN-VIEW

*The ethics of assessment as valuation*
*in Nepali music education*

..........

DANIELLE SHANNON TREACY,
VILMA TIMONEN, ALEXIS ANJA KALLIO,
AND IMAN BIKRAM SHAH

ALTHOUGH diversity and change are by no means conditions exclusive to the present, global economic instabilities, mass migration, political turbulence, the accessibility of and speed at which information is produced and shared, and developments in media and technology have characterized the contemporary world as one of uncertainty and intensified encounters with difference. Amid such sociocultural complexity and fast-paced change, music education policy and practice are required to contend with various and at times conflicting musical and cultural values and understandings. Thus curriculum, teaching and learning practices, and related assessment practices are of ethical concern. Indeed, as argued in this chapter, assessment can play a key role in framing knowledge and pedagogical approaches in music education and can therefore be understood as partially constituting the process of legitimation. It is therefore important to broaden our understandings of assessment beyond processes and practices used to monitor, measure, and give feedback on student learning and related processes of evaluation such as assigning a mark or grade.

In this chapter we discuss assessment in music education in the context of Nepal. The inquiry framing this chapter became crucial during our research and collaborative work developing music teacher education there.[1] Adopted by the Ministry of Education in 2010, the Nepali music education curriculum guides music teaching and learning in 77 national districts for 126 caste/ethnic groups, with 123 languages spoken as mother tongues (including indigenous sign languages), and representing 10 religious groups (Government of Nepal, 2012), all within a rapidly globalizing society. In the absence of formal, government-recognized music teacher education, representatives of the Nepal

Music Center—the music institute that lobbied the government to introduce music into the curriculum and later built that curriculum—approached the Sibelius Academy and proposed collaboration. During the resulting collaboration, we repeatedly encountered tensions between the justifications for including formal music education in schooling and assessment as a form of legitimation driving education in Nepal. For example, assessment frequently arose during early interviews with school administrators as part of Treacy's ethnographic work in 2014, even though no questions about assessment were asked. Similarly, questions of organizing student and program assessment became central during Shah and Timonen's collaborative work designing a music education program for advanced level students at the Nepal Music Center, Kathmandu.

In light of these early observations, we were compelled to engage in collaborative "critical work" (Kuntz, 2015, p. 25). This work begins with an anticolonial stance (Patel, 2014) and combines *educational* (Pole & Morrison, 2003) and *collaborative* (Lassiter, 2005) *ethnography* with *appreciative inquiry* (see, e.g., Cooperrider, Whitney, & Stavros, 2005). This chapter is supported by Nepali curriculum documents and assessment policy for general education and interviews conducted with school administrators and musician-teachers[2] working in the Kathmandu Valley. Leaning on pragmatist philosopher John Dewey's *Theory of Valuation*, we analyze the institutional visions framing music education in Nepali schools. In particular, we consider these visions in relation to Dewey's notion of the *continuum of ends-means* (LW13[3]:226–36)–the "temporal continuum of activities in which each successive stage is equally end and means" (LW13:234). Thus, instead of viewing these visions as ends-in-themselves, we use Dewey to focus ethical deliberations on the relationships between means and ends in learning processes and thereby the quality of student experience. We then apply sociocultural anthropologist Arjun Appadurai's theories of the *imagination* (1996) and the *capacity to aspire* (2004)—"the social and cultural capacity to plan, hope, desire, and achieve socially valuable goals" (Appadurai, 2006, p. 176)—to highlight the need to envision unforeseen assessment practices and thereby a more ethical engagement with intensifying diversity and fast-paced social change.

# IMPLEMENTATION OF THE STUDY

Although music has long been a part of the Nepali primary school curriculum (grades 1–5, students six to eleven years old) through the subject social studies under "creative and performance art," it was only introduced into the lower secondary and secondary school curricula (grades 6–8, students twelve to fourteen years old; grades 9–10, students fifteen to sixteen years old) in 2010. While these music curricula have been prepared and approved for implementation since 2011, there are currently no schools teaching them, partly because music is just one of many subjects from which the school can choose only one, and this subject is then taken by all students. Consequently, music is competing with subjects such as computer science and health and physical education. As of the writing of this chapter, an elective music curriculum for high school (grades 11–12, students seventeen to eighteen years old) has been approved and adopted but not widely implemented. Thus, curricula development and assessment strategies for music continue to be in their formative stages.

The material for this chapter includes translations (from Nepali to English) of the following government policy documents[4]:

- The National Curriculum Framework for School Education in Nepal 2007, published by the Government of Nepal Curriculum Development Centre.
- The Nepali Music Curriculum for grades 1–5 (2011, currently approved and adopted as the primary school music subject under the local subject curriculum, by the Nepal Ministry of Education, but not yet implemented).
- The Nepali Music Curriculum for grades 6–8 (2011, currently approved and implemented as a possible optional subject by the Nepal Ministry of Education).
- The Nepali Music as an Elective Curriculum for grades 9–10 (2011, awaiting official approval by the Nepal Ministry of Education).

Supporting these policy documents are thirteen interviews conducted by the first author in 2014 and guided by appreciative inquiry (see, e.g., Cooperrider et al., 2005). Six interviews were held with seven school administrators, such as principals or directors, from six private schools in the Kathmandu Valley, who are largely responsible for deciding which subjects are offered by the school and for curricular implementation. The primary intent of administrator interviews was to inquire into the general background of the schools, including the overarching visions and the place of music in the broader curriculum. As already mentioned, no questions were asked about assessment. In addition, seven interviews were conducted with private school musician-teachers. As government schools[5] rarely employ music teachers, and music as a curricular subject is in its infancy throughout the country, private school musician-teachers were seen to offer important insights into music teaching and learning practices in schools. Musician-teacher interviews were guided by the appreciative inquiry generic questions (see Cooperrider et al., 2005, p. 25; Watkins, Mohr, & Kelly, 2011, pp. 155–56) with the addition of questions on the themes of diversity, repertoire selection, assessment, and the school-specific song practice, assessment having been added for the purposes of this particular inquiry. All interviewees were contacted and selected through the Nepal Music Center's network of schools known to offer music as a curricular subject or extracurricular activity. Interviews with administrators were in English, while musician-teachers were encouraged to speak Nepali, with an interpreter present for all interviews. The thirty- to one hundred-minute, audio-recorded interviews were transcribed and translated into English as needed. Excerpts of the transcripts related to this chapter were then shared with all coauthors.

The material was interpreted in collaboration with all coauthors and at various levels. These levels include the contexts of Nepal and other diversifying societies more generally, our experiences from our own individual research projects, and thinking with theory

(Jackson & Mazzei, 2012). Faced with the tensions between the justifications of music in schooling and assessment as legitimation, we first asked: What institutional visions frame the valuation of music education in Nepali schools? This led us to identify four visions: the desire to create socially unifying practices, moving from traditional to progressive education, including public performances in schooling, and achieving success in externally administered examinations. Extending this exploration, we then engaged in "productive critique" (Kuntz, 2015, p. 109), striving toward "ethically laden creative alternatives to normative rationalities and normalizing practices" (p. 25). This second stage of inquiry was guided by the question: How might these visions be explored and reframed through ethical deliberations on the quality of student experience and against the fast-changing sociocultural climate of Nepal?

## ASSESSMENT IN THE NEPALI CURRICULUM

Public education is relatively young in Nepal, with public schooling having been prohibited by the Rana rulers as a deliberate method of control. Not until the Shah kings regained power in 1951 was education expanded to the masses, not only as a means of modernization and economic and social development, but also to promote loyalty to the nation-state and the one-party system of government (Skinner & Holland, 2009). Nepal already had a long history of social stratification (along the lines of gender, caste, ethnicity, and race) (Manandhar, 2009, p. vii), so the elevation of "the King, Hinduism, and the Nepali language as the basis of national cohesion" (Shields & Rappleye, 2008, p. 268) only served to uphold stratification and hegemony. Later, despite the 1990 constitution declaring Nepal to be multiethnic, secular, and democratic, persisting discrimination and inequality led to a decade-long civil war (1996–2006). In light of this history, the restoration of peace in 2006 and the publication of the National Curriculum Framework for School Education in Nepal in 2007 may appear to outsiders to coincide; however, in recent decades foreign actors, such as the international donor community, have had a powerful influence in shaping educational policy (Shields & Rappleye, 2008). Indeed, Pramod Bhatta (2009) asserts that changes to educational policy in Nepal are often in "response to the conditions put by the aid agencies supporting educational reforms" (p. 152). One example of the "politics of donor interests" (Shields & Rappleye, 2008, p. 271) in Nepal's assessment policy is the reflection of both the international donor countries that value continuous assessment and those that value standardized testing, the result being that both have been adopted to satisfy the respective donors.

The National Curriculum Framework for School Education in Nepal (Government of Nepal, 2007) is "the main document of school education" and "presents the vision, policy and guidelines of school level education" (p. 55). This document defines student assessment as "the process of gathering, interpreting, recording and analyzing data, using information and obtaining feedback for re-planning educational programmes" (p. 26) and varies assessment according to grade level. Grades 1–7 outline a school-based continuous assessment system (CAS), meaning that teachers should "encourage the students to learn by giving due attention to customized teaching or an individual approach" (Music Curriculum 1–5, p. 13) in order to "assess the expected learning outcomes, behavioral change, attitudes, competency, skill and the application of feedback for teaching and learning activities" (Government of Nepal, 2007, p. 47). In addition, assessment strategies suggested in the National Curriculum Framework include class, project, and community work; unit and achievement tests; observation; and formative and innovative work (p. 46).

Students in general education in Nepal are also assessed through standardized external examinations. At the time of study, the "resource centers" that facilitate government-school policy communication and serve to aid teachers with content knowledge, pedagogical training, and collecting local school demographic information for relevant authorities also coordinated an external examination at the end of grade 5. In addition, there were summative district-level, standardized examinations at the end of grade 8 and national, standardized examinations at the end of grade 10 (the School Leaving Certificate [SLC]), as well as at the end of grade 12 for those students who continued to higher secondary school.[6]

These assessment strategies evaluate students by assigning a letter grade, provide certificates of achievement, and facilitate the progression from one year-level to the next. The National Curriculum Framework (Government of Nepal, 2007), however, raises ethical concerns that assessment has "not been developed as an integral part of teaching learning activities nor has it been tied up with student's intellectual level, interest, pace, and needs" (pp. 26–27). Rather, the focus on standardized external examinations has been seen as a way to respond to various international interests and involvement and also to establish equal standards throughout the country—to "maintain the quality of [the] education" system (p. 47).

The Nepali Music Curriculum is divided into grades 1–5, 6–8, and 9–10. Each curriculum document outlines specific assessment strategies, including descriptions of recommended processes, activities, and methods for tracking student progress and assigning grades. Similar to the overall school curriculum, in grades 1–5 the focus of music classes is on learning by doing, evaluated through formative assessment "aimed at improving the level of students' learning" (Music Curriculum 1–5, p. 18). More standardized approaches to assessment in music are introduced in the curricula for grades 6–8 and 9–10. Assessment can thus be seen to play an increasingly important role in school music education as students progress through the grade system; indeed, the "grading system can be considered as one of the most vital factors in terms of teaching" (Music Curriculum 6–8, p. 10; Music Curriculum 9–10, p. 14). This acknowledgment recalls David Boud's (1995) assertion that while "students can, with difficulty, escape from the effects of poor teaching, they cannot (by definition if they want to graduate) escape the effects of poor assessment" (p. 35). Indeed, assessment defines not only *what* is to be learned but *how* students go about that learning (see, e.g., Boud, 1995). As such, one way of considering how assessment in Nepali music education might be developed in a way that ethically engages with intensifying diversity and fast-paced social change is to reflect on the underlying values framing music education in Nepal, the values that assess what is taught and how; for this, we turn to John Dewey.

# VALUATION IN AND OF MUSIC
# EDUCATION IN NEPAL

In his pragmatist *Theory of Valuation* (LW13), John Dewey asserts that "valuations are constant phenomena of human behavior" (LW13:241). Indeed, "all deliberate, all planned human conduct, personal and collective, seems to be influenced, if not controlled, by estimates of value or worth of ends to be attained" (LW13:192), the only exceptions being blind, unreflective impulses and mechanical routines and habits. The difference between impulses and desires then, according to Dewey, is "the presence in desire of an end-in-view, of objects *as* foreseen consequences" (LW13:217; emphasis in original). Dewey asserts: "This is the origin and nature of 'goals' of action. They are ways of defining and deepening the meaning of activity. Having an end or aim is thus a characteristic of *present* activity. It is the means by which an activity becomes adapted when otherwise it would be blind and disorderly, or by which it gets meaning when otherwise it would be mechanical. In a strict sense an end-in-view is a *means* in present action; present action is not a means to a remote end" (MW14:156; emphasis in original). Thus, ends-in-view are not fixed but created in action, a kind of mediating end, as ends that are too distant cannot function as guides in action. Dewey further asserts that valuation is the result of ongoing critical inquiry, through which ends-in-view arise and are revised through continual reflection upon past experiences and valuation of means. He illustrates how this process takes place through "careful observation of differences found between desired and proposed ends (ends-*in-view*) and attained ends or actual consequences. Agreement between what is wanted and anticipated and what is actually obtained confirms the selection of conditions which operate as means to the desired end; discrepancies, which are experienced as frustrations and defeats, lead to an inquiry to discover the causes of failure" (LW13:218; emphasis in original). Importantly, this process is "capable of rectification and development" (LW13:241).

Reading the school curricula documents and interview transcripts with Dewey's *Theory of Valuation*, we identified four interrelated visions framing the valuation of music education in Nepali schools:

- The desire to create socially unifying practices,
- Moving from traditional to progressive education,
- Including public performances in schooling, and
- Achieving success in externally administered examinations.

We here illustrate how these visions are in tension with each other, with assessment practices often obstructing the capability of schools, administrators, and teachers to realize other aims.

## "Woven from Hundreds of Flowers, We Are One Garland"

The first of the identified visions framing the valuation of music education in Nepali schools was a desire to create socially unifying practices amid intense sociocultural diversity. With its long history of social stratification and recent civil war, Nepal is characterized as a post-conflict nation in which "social exclusion, inclusion, and inclusive democracy" (Bhattachan, 2009, p. 12) are now highlighted as key concerns for all. These concerns can be seen for example in the garden discourse that opens the new national anthem (adopted in 2007): "Woven from hundreds of flowers, we are one garland that's Nepali." This perceived need to counter hundreds of years of divisive policies and practices also constructs unity and cohesion as an aim of general education in Nepal, with music education being evaluated as a potential means to this end. This valuation of music and music education can also be seen in our material on various levels. At the level of government policy, the Nepali Music Curricula for grades 1–5, 6–8, and 9–10, for example, reflect an explicit desire to build national unity through the inclusion of patriotic songs and a common repertoire of class (year-level) songs for government schools:

> Subject matter: Grade 1
> Singing:
> ...Practice of children's songs, class songs,[7] the national anthem and patriotic songs.
>
> (Music Curriculum 1–5, p. 7)

In enacting such curricular objectives and constructing assessment strategies, however, teachers are also required to engage in valuations, for example through repertoire selections, balancing more or less specified iterations of the local through the inclusion of music and dance from particular communities, for instance; and the global, through the inclusion of "western[8] music" and "western musical terminologies" (Music Curriculum 6–8, p. 2).

School administrators interviewed as part of this research also expressed a desire to create unifying practices and values within their schools, often evaluating music and music education as a means to this end. Some administrators described practices that had been created to engage with issues of diversity and to educate for mutual respect and solidarity. One such practice was the school-specific song (Treacy & Westerlund, in press), which sometimes echoed the botanical metaphor in the national anthem that was said to be related to the need to cultivate a sense of belongingness in the school community (Administrator 6[9]). In justifying his school's music program, one administrator explained, "Nepal is a garden of so many ethnic groups.... And each ethnic group, has their own culture, they have their own costumes, traditions, folk-songs, folk-dance and all" (Administrator 3). As such, learning songs or dances from different Nepali ethnic groups was evaluated by the school as a means to "get the taste of" and "learn to respect other cultures... [to] really enrich the students" because "in the music, you see the whole history of a particular ethnic group... it is an identity of a culture" (Administrator 3).

# To "Prepare Students for Life and Not for Examinations"

The second of the identified visions framing the valuation of music education in Nepali schools was what administrators described as "progressive" (Administrator 2) or "contemporary" (Administrator 6) education. This vision involved institutional desires to "break away from the traditional means of teaching and learning" and become "more student-focused" (Administrator 6). Making this shift was valued not only at the institutional level, but also at the policy level. Indeed, the National Curriculum Framework (Government of Nepal, 2007) poses it as a contemporary challenge for schools and teachers: "Teaching and learning activities are conducted on the basis of textbooks designed in accordance with the curriculum developed at the central level. Aspects such as grade teaching, multi grade teaching, subject teaching, community work and project work have not been given due importance. The teaching and learning environment has [thus been] more instruction oriented rather than learning oriented" (p. 21). As such, teaching approaches that prioritized student participation and agency were seen as a remedy to the traditional, teacher-centered pedagogies of the past.

Interviewed administrators described valuing music education as a means for their schools to make this shift toward "more and more child-centric" (Administrator 3) teaching and learning. An important means to this end was perceived to be the widening of the focus of education in their institutions from only educating students academically to "developing life-skills . . . [as schools] should prepare students for life and not for examinations" (Administrator 2). Indeed, one administrator explained the importance of helping students identify and build their "potential" and valued the music lessons in his school as "a platform to explore what they believed they couldn't do" (Administrator 2). Music was also valued by administrators as a means of developing students' creativity, confidence, curiosity, and collaboration as well as fostering their abilities to focus and be patient. These views can be seen to align with the national objective for general education to "help foster inherent talents and the possibility of personality development of each individual" (Government of Nepal, 2007, p. 31). Music was also evaluated as important for "break[ing] the monotony" of the long school days, helping to energize and motivate students (Administrator 3), and simply as a "meaningful" use of students' free time (Administrator 2).

# The Pressure to Perform

The third vision identified as framing the valuation of music education in Nepali schools was including public performances in schooling, a common value of music education practices in many parts of the world. Performance features in every grade level of the Music Curricula. For instance, the curricular objectives for students in grades 1–5 direct teachers to ensure that students have the opportunity to "take part with interest in different musical programs" (p. 4),[10] while for grades 6–8 it is stated: "Student work should always be practice-based, and students should have opportunities to demonstrate whatever has been learned in the classroom via various concerts, programs, classroom activities, and also at home" (p. 9). As such, performance is often constructed as an assessment of sorts, an opportunity for students to present the fruits of many hours spent rehearsing on their own or together. However, it can also serve as a means of, and justification for, dividing students into categories of more or less capable. As one musician-teacher noted: "The skilled students are allowed to play in the orchestra and perform during the parents' day concert. The unskilled students are not" (Teacher 6). However, this same teacher noted that performances should not be the *only* goals for teaching and learning, as he explained: "Some music teachers are not very good. They use the rote routine to teach the students…for a long period. During competitions, the students come first or second, but if they are given different notations the students cannot play" (Teacher 6). One of the administrators expressed wholly different values in terms of performances, explaining that they were not necessarily opportunities to display the most talented students, but rather for all students to participate in community celebrations, "On parents' day we make sure that every child is on the stage" (Administrator 3). Thus, to ensure this in a school of over two thousand students, they have moved to grade-specific, rather than entire school, parents' days. This more participatory approach, however, does not necessarily do away with the evaluative role that performances might assume.

Many musician-teachers noted that more than an assessment of student skills, performances served as a public assessment of their work as teachers and of the standards or values of the school more generally. Performances were seen to "prove my teaching skills" (Teacher 7) or provide "publicity…and positive things about [the school]" (Administrator 6). Performances were also experienced negatively by teachers who felt that they could not "teach [students] anything else but prepare them for the event" (Teacher 7). As an administrator reflected, this also impeded student learning: "A lot of schools are not really, really imparting good music education.… [I]t's always centered either around the program or some show or event" (Administrator 6). Regardless of the impact on pedagogy and learning, the pressure to perform was felt as a need to legitimize the place of music in many schools. Indeed, one teacher lamented that "if there are no [performances], the priority given to music is very minimal" (Teacher 2).

## The "Iron Gate"

The fourth and arguably most important vision framing the valuation of music education in Nepali schools was achieving success in the externally administered examination, the SLC. The "Iron Gate" of the SLC is seen to determine students' access to further education and work opportunities and thus their future socioeconomic well-being. Similar to public performances, SLC examination results also serve as an assessment of the school's reputation (Mathema & Bista, 2006) in wider society, and it is common to see posters adorning schools' walls featuring the photos and results of their high-achieving students. Consequently, teaching and learning in the final years of general education, grades 9 and 10, are almost exclusively focused on rote learning the content that will be examined. As an optional subject—meaning that it is elective for the *school* but then taken by *all* students—schools may choose to offer music as one of the SLC exam subjects; however, this is extremely rare. As such, music—and any other subject not examined by the SLC—does not get taught in grades 9 and 10.

Interviewed school administrators described how the SLC limited their school's ability to provide the kind of education to which they aspired: "The curriculum, the syllabus, lesson planning, exams, all the activities that we do are all based around the SLC, which we have no control over. So even though we try to break away from the traditional means of teaching and learning, at the end of the day the students have to appear for the SLC exams, so that's something we have to keep in mind whilst we are sort of using a more modern approach of teaching and learning" (Administrator 6). Furthermore, school administrators expressed concern that the SLC limited students' agency with regard to what they can study: "There is no choice for them, I'm so sorry for our students, for our country's system" (Administrator 4). The SLC did not only frame curricular choices, however. As a result of the SLC pressures, students and schools often discontinue extracurricular music programs in order to encourage students to concentrate exclusively on the studies legitimized by the SLC. This was summarized by one administrator as "now it's time to stop playing the guitars, it's time to stop playing football. All you've got to do is study" (Administrator 6). Parental expectations were also seen as a major pressure for both schools and students. With parents having gone through the same SLC process, one administrator expressed difficulty in "convinc[ing] the parents that academics are not the only important thing." He said, "It is not only that if you score high marks you will be successful in life.... Yet it is very difficult to convince the parents that marks are not important. They are important, but they are not *the* important thing" (Administrator 3). Thus, for students attending private schools, administrators felt "compelled to satisfy the parents because they are the ones who are investing money for their children's education" (Administrator 4).

# IMAGINING BEYOND FIXED ENDS

In the previous section we identified four visions that frame the valuation of music education in Nepali schools. We now extend the interpretation, considering these four visions through the work of John Dewey to imagine students' ends-in-view and Arjun Appadurai to imagine the unforeseen.

## Imagining Students' Ends-in-View

Our exploration indicated that the assessment practices of public performances and the SLC were often seen by interviewees as obstructing not only the potential of music education to realize a wider range of desired ends, but its very inclusion in schools. If we explore this challenge with Dewey's theory of means and ends, it could be that rather than these assessment practices being framed as ends-in-view—that is, as "means to future ends" (LW13:229)—they are framed as ends-in-themselves. Dewey asserts that

> nothing happens which is *final* in the sense that it is not part of an ongoing stream of events.... [T]he distinction between ends and means is temporal and relational. Every condition that has to be brought into existence in order to serve as means is, *in that connection*, an object of desire and an end-in-view, while the end actually reached is a means to future ends as well as a test of valuations previously made. Since the end attained is a condition of further existential occurrences, it must be appraised as a potential obstacle and potential resource.
>
> (LW13:229; emphasis in original)

As such, Dewey warns of the risk that "the only problems arising concern the best means for attaining [ends-in-themselves]" (LW13:229). Alternatively, if these assessment practices have been framed as ends-in-view, they have been evaluated as *the* most important ends-in-view. Dewey's notion of the continuum of means-ends—whereby actions are interconnected and an end achieved is also a means to future ends, while the ultimate end may remain unknown—is thus useful for considering these assessment practices in terms of student experience. Leaning on Dewey, Heidi Westerlund (2002) states that "music in education is a mixture of the actual and potential" (p. 187) and that music students evaluate ends from multiple perspectives: "The learner will evaluate the value of his or her learning experiences in relation to his or her personal life which includes past and future events, whether educational or not. In this process, every good and meaningful experience is suggesting some consequences on the life goals of the individual" (2008, p. 87). Thus, understanding assessment practices, such as public performances and SLCs, as fixed ends or ends-in-themselves, without considering the means or how the end could become a means in the means-ends continuum, is an ethical problem, as assessment practices as fixed ends may hinder, rather than become the means to, further learning.

The opportunity to participate and exercise "voice" through public performance may be seen as a matter of ethical and democratic concern. When public performances serve as the primary form of assessment for music students and music teachers and as an assessment of the schools themselves, the focus of teaching and learning may be more on achieving a predetermined standard of "excellence" rather than on the experiences of students. Westerlund (2008) has emphasized that questions of valuation in music education are questions of the means—or the "hows"—of music education and therefore argues for the importance of the quality of the learners' experiences over musical outcomes such as public performances only. She suggests that from the student's perspective, good public performances may risk remaining ends-in-themselves, rather than ends-in-view to continued engagements with music making, if the learning process, the means, fails to support the creation of sufficiently positive experiences. Indeed, "the costs of music studies can even become intolerable prohibiting the final enjoyment of what should be enjoyable by its very nature" (Westerlund, 2008, p. 85). Moreover, when "quality" public performances function as ends-in-themselves—without considering how they might serve as an end-in-view for all students—exclusionary practices may be justified through the selection of students who are "most talented" or "most proficient," leaving the participatory requirement of democracy unfulfilled. In other words, music education becomes only for the select few, and not for all. Thus, the valuation of music performances in Nepali music education may serve not only as a "potential resource" but also as a "potential obstacle" (Dewey, LW13:229) for democratic action. In democratizing the performance aspect of music teaching and learning, we need to imagine beyond those ends that construct music as product and instead consider how performances could function as qualitatively good ends-in-view in the students' lives. As claimed by David J. Elliott (1995) among others, if music is not a *thing*, but a social action, the focus of music education ought to be on the process of *doing* music. As such, assessment should not be an evaluation *of* the performance itself, but of the preparation *for* it—or perhaps even more important, of students' experiences of both the preparation for and the performance itself. Similarly, with performance serving as an assessment of the teacher or the school, *what* is being assessed, rather than the teacher's ability to select and nurture "talent" or display technical proficiency, could be the ability to enact democratic ideals of inclusion and participation. As mentioned in the National Curriculum Framework, performances could illustrate an institution's, a teacher's, or students' engagement with "social equality and justice...to help create an inclusive society" (Government of Nepal, 2007, p. 31).

The processes or products of music making in schools that *are* valued in Nepali music education are closely linked to the legitimation of the subject as a whole, with assessment determining what is deemed important for young people to study and to what ends. Success in the SLC plays a key role as "part of a selective tradition, someone's selection, some group's vision of legitimate knowledge" (Apple, 1996, p. 22). As what is assessed is deemed valuable, music's absence from all but a very few school's SLC offerings serves to maintain the stigmatized place of music as a subject worth studying and a career worth pursuing more broadly (Treacy, in press; Treacy, Thapa, & Neupane, in press). Although the SLC may be viewed by schools and parents, and even by students, as an end-in-view to success in life, its position as *the* most important end-in-view and the externally fixed nature of this "Iron Gate," which fails to take into account student diversity and student choice, cause students to pay "too high a price in effort and in sacrifice of other ends" (LW13:228). However, the SLC is not implemented unquestioningly and has been subject to "critical examination of the relation of means and ends" (LW13:230), as illustrated through our interviews and reports such as the extensive *Study on Student Performance in SLC* (Mathema & Bista, 2006). Still, the abandonment of elective courses and hobbies not subject to the scrutiny of standardized tests, when combined with the enormous pressures placed on students to focus and achieve academic excellence, continues to come at a high price associated with assessment as an end in and of itself. As one administrator explained: "There is this huge stress on children which I firmly believe should not be there. I personally don't believe in this examination system where everything you learn throughout the year is just dumped into one [examination] paper. It's not a judge of what you've learned" (Administrator 6). As such, it is imperative to imagine beyond success in standardized examinations if assessment is to ethically work for, and not against, such curricular ideals as producing "healthy citizens" (Government of Nepal, 2007, p. 42) and inclusive education, where "inclusive education means to understand and respect others, respond to educational needs and include the experiences, interests and values of children of all strata" (p. 34).

## Imagining the Unforeseen

In addition to the need to consider student experience in questions of assessment in Nepali schooling, the four previously identified visions also highlight how questions of assessment are entangled with the need for schools to contend with the rapid pace of societal change. As such, we propose that in navigating multiple, fast-changing, and at times opposing interests and values, the most established ends and related foreseen consequences may not be sufficient for engaging in the level of critical inquiry required in the Nepali context. Indeed, we have already shown how a fixed understanding of assessment places constraints on schools and administrators striving to contend with this change. Therefore, we argue that envisioning an ethically engaged future of assessment, and school music education in Nepal more broadly, requires *imagination* and the *capacity to aspire*. Appadurai (1996) asserts that "lives today are as much acts of projection and imagination as they are enactments of known scripts or predictable outcomes" (p. 61). Moreover, he contends that the capacity to aspire is an essential social and cultural capacity that supports the exploration of "alternative futures" (Appadurai, 2004, p. 69) and "guarantees an ethical and psychological anchor, a horizon of credible hopes" (pp. 81–82). This is especially important in Nepal, a post-conflict nation with many diverse communities and social groups working toward equality and democracy while engaging with ever-increasing globalization. Appadurai (2004) states: "The capacity to aspire provides an ethical horizon within which more concrete capabilities can be given meaning, substance, and sustainability. Conversely, the exercise and nurture of these capabilities verifies and authorizes the capacity to aspire and moves it away from wishful thinking to thoughtful wishing" (p. 82). Such "thoughtful wishing" may offer one means by which assessment in Nepali schools could potentially be part of, and enact, more democratic processes. In suggesting that administrators and teachers need to imagine beyond what is foreseeable, we return to the first two visions: the desire to create socially unifying practices and moving from traditional to progressive education.

Recalling the garland metaphor in the opening of the Nepali National Anthem, different cultures are described as individual, unchanging, separate flowers to be woven together. As such, creating unity through multiculturalism, as an end-in-itself in Nepali music education, is not simply a descriptive term but is used to connote a "social ideal; a policy of support for exchange among different groups of people to enrich all while respecting and preserving the integrity of each" (Elliott, 1990, p. 151). However, this ideal raises questions about the feasibility and also the ethics of maintaining distinctions between caste/ethnic groups as part of the guiding paradigm of music education. Moreover, the preservation of difference as an end-in-itself, or taken as an end-in-view in education toward a multicultural society, is symptomatic of what Dewey (LW4) refers to as a "Quest for Certainty." This is further complicated by the "fluidities of transnational," and transcultural, "communication" that frame culture as "an arena for conscious choice, justification, and representation" (Appadurai, 1996, p. 44). As such, Nepali society cannot be adequately represented by a garland, but is rather a society in which "the appearance of a people as a coherent ethnic group reflects a group's particular historical relationship with the state more than its cultural distinctiveness" (Hangen, 2010, p. 27) and "as much variation exists within groups that share an ethnic label as exists between groups with different names" (p. 27). Indeed, Susan I. Hangen (2010) asserts that identities in Nepal are constantly "in flux" (p. 27), reflecting "the political efforts of various sociocultural groups to renegotiate their identities and their place in the state" (p. 28). Cultural identity, also as expressed in and through music, is not static, with "[discrete] but clear and lasting boundaries between 'this' culture and 'that' culture" (Gaztambide-Fernández, 2012, p. 44), but an altogether more complex experience. Accordingly, framing music education and its assessment strategies with the vision of a Nepali garland of sociocultural unity risks archiving musics or values as cultural artifacts, rather than constructing practices that engage with musics as dynamic and changing social activities. Thus, assessment may face challenges in relating to *musicing* as something we *do* and something we already *are* (Elliott, 1989, 1995), especially if *who we are* is understood as not fixed, but rather an ongoing process of *becoming*. Preserving cultural difference is also of ethical concern, particularly in a highly stratified society like Nepal. While the caste system is officially illegal, it is far from obsolete and has left a heavy hangover of inequity and injustice. *Whose* criteria then determine success in Nepali school music education? *Whose* music is deemed legitimate and valuable? *Whose* approaches to teaching and learning ought to inform the development of teacher education? Rather than perpetuating systems of inequity through multicultural policy, if "culture is a dialogue between aspirations and sedimented traditions" (Appadurai, 2004, p. 84), there is an ethical imperative to "bring the future back in" (p. 84). Through this, teachers might imagine a more equitable, socially just music education and society at large, consistent with curriculum directives to "help create an inclusive society by focusing upon equality between different races, castes, religions, languages, cultures, and regions... [and to foster students' awareness of]...human rights, social norms and values, and feel responsible for the nation and its people" (Music Curriculum 1–5, p. 2).

Envisioning schooling as more than preparation to pass examinations aligns with pragmatist ideas and ideals of education as more than inculcating students with a priori knowledge or skills. However, conceptualizing teaching and learning as *preparation for life* risks isolating the school from life itself. Education structured in isolation from society contrasts with the Deweyan understanding of the school as reproducing "within itself, [the] typical conditions of social life" (MW4:272), whereby school classrooms are already, and always, a microcosm of society, albeit in a critical mode (Allsup & Westerlund, 2012; Westerlund, 2002). This discourse of preparation also permeates the values outlined in the National Educational Objectives (Government of Nepal, 2007), which state that schools should "help prepare citizens with good conduct and morals for a healthy social and collective lifestyle...help prepare productive and skilled citizens...develop and prepare human resources to build the nation [through the] modernization of society....Prepare citizens respectful to nation, nationality, democracy" (p. 31). Here too the implication is that schools are detached from "real life," preparing students until they are qualified to participate in society, rather than seeing schools as "workplaces, as sites of identity formation, as places that make particular knowledge and culture legitimate, as arenas of mobilization and learning of tactics, and so much more" (Apple, 2013, p. 158). Furthermore, in a rapidly changing society such as Nepal, what it is exactly that school should prepare students for is uncertain, as the foreseeable future changes on an almost daily basis. Thus, progressive music education may be better understood not as preparing students for participation in a democratic society, but as already democratic in and of itself. In this way, music education may be envisioned as an experimental site "to exercise 'voice,' to debate, contest, and oppose vital directions for collective social life as they wish, not only because this is virtually a definition of inclusion and participation in any democracy" (Appadurai, 2004, p. 66).

## TOWARD AN ETHICALLY ENGAGED FUTURE OF ASSESSMENT

In this chapter we have illustrated how the visions guiding music education in Nepal may not afford teachers and students the capacity to ethically navigate the conditions of intensifying diversity and fast-paced social change. In imagining beyond fixed ends, and therefore anticipating the unforeseeable, assessment—as both processes of valuation and specific assessment practices—is intricately and inextricably entwined, whether the teacher acknowledges this or not, with the ethical dimensions of teaching and learning. The uncertainty about what "personal, social and national challenges" (Government of Nepal, 2007, p. 32) the twenty-first century will bring for young people in Nepal, however, means that assessment cannot be "traditional," relegating culture to archives and determining students' future possibilities on the basis of a single exam. Rather than assessment serving as an "Iron Gate" or end-in-itself, we propose that it ought to be re-envisioned as integral to enacting the democratic ideals of participation and equality. This is not so much a way to insure young people against the challenges the future holds, but more a means of enabling confident, agential, and meaningful engagements with uncertainty. This requires, from the students themselves, the ability to form ends-in-view and in this way aspire to change their own lives and society. Through this, students are enabled "not only [to] adapt [themselves] to the changes that are going on, but [to] have power to shape and direct them" (MW 4:271). Through this inquiry, we have argued that this requires the imagination and the capacity to aspire.

Importantly, teacher education may be one appropriate arena for this work, which we suggest requires a shift to positioning teachers as critical inquirers rather than as transmitters of knowledge, only responsible for the implementation of a prescribed curriculum. This follows Appadurai's (2013) argument for "research as a human right" (p. 269), as a way to develop "the capacity to systematically increase the horizons of one's current knowledge, in relation to some task, goal or aspiration" (Appadurai, 2006, p. 176). However, as the goals and aspirations are *not-yet-in-view*, the teacher must engage in constant reflection—looking both backward and forward in a reflexive circling and deliberation of what role assessment plays in evaluating and enabling learning. This "thoughtful wishing" (Appadurai, 2004, p. 82) can thus engage the imagination in a continual process of shaping and reshaping values, assessment practices, and other practices in the classroom, through creative small steps: ends-in-view rather than fixed ends that function as ends-in-themselves.

In sum, developing the capacity to aspire, and by extension the capacity to inquire, is crucial for envisioning an ethical future for and through assessment and school music education more broadly. As such it is important that we understand assessment as dynamic, allowing space for the imagination and capacity to aspire. Although administrators interviewed in this study acknowledged the need for such a dynamic understanding, they described the problematic nature of fixed assessment practices that place constraints on the school and teachers from engaging their imagination in terms of ends-in-view and ends-not-yet-in-view. The capacities to aspire and inquire can support music teachers and students as they engage with the existing and increasing diversity of contemporary societies such as Nepal and rapid societal change and reflect upon the inclusive and exclusive processes of assessment that frame *whose* ends and ends-in-view count, when, how, and what for. Thus, imagining ends-not-yet-in-view in music education offers a means of ethically engaging with values different to one's own and enacting the democratic ideals of participation, equality, and the capacity to aspire for all.

## ACKNOWLEDGMENTS

The authors would like to thank the interviewees for sharing their perspectives and experiences as part of this research, *dhanyabaad!* We would also like to thank the Nepal Music Center for their continued support and the doctoral community at the Sibelius Academy, University of the Arts Helsinki, for comments and guidance in refining this text.

**Funding**: This publication has been undertaken as part of the project Global Visions through Mobilizing Networks: Co-developing Intercultural Music Teacher Education in Nepal, Finland, and Israel, funded by the Academy of Finland (project no. 286162) in 2015–2019.

# Notes

1. The Global Visions project engages music educators and researchers in three institutions (the Sibelius Academy, University of the Arts Helsinki, in Finland; the Nepal Music Center, in Kathmandu, Nepal; and Levinsky College of Education, in Tel Aviv and Jerusalem, Israel) in collaboration with the overarching goal to envision how future teachers may be equipped with the necessary skills and understandings to work within increasingly diverse environments.

2. We use the term "musician-teachers" to refer to musicians who are employed to teach music by private schools, music institutes, and private individuals. In the absence of formal music teacher qualifications, they are usually hired on the basis of artistic merit rather than demonstrated pedagogical competence.

3. References to John Dewey in this chapter appear as MW (middle works) or LW (later works) followed by the volume number, a colon, and the page numbers. The edited volumes are listed in the references as Dewey (1977), Dewey (1983), Dewey (1984), and Dewey (1988).

4. It should be noted that citations to The National Curriculum Framework for School Education in Nepal refer to the page numbers in the original Nepali document, and citations to the music curricula refer to the page numbers in the final Nepali document submitted to the Ministry of Education.

5. The term "government school" is used in Nepal to refer to state-funded and -mandated school education.

6. Since this inquiry, the external standardized examination system has changed. The grade 5 examination has been discontinued, the grade 8 examination is now a school-level examination, the grade 10 SLC examination has been changed to the Secondary Education Examination (SEE), and the grade 12 examination is now the National Board Examination (NBE). These changes were made as part of the amendment to the Education Act, and implementation was begun during the 2016–2017 school year.

7. Class songs refer to songs in national textbooks published by the Ministry of Education. Each grade level has specific class songs.

8. In countering the hegemonic centrality of the western world and the Othering of the majority world—within which this research is located—we do not capitalize the "west" as a conscious and political decision.

9. Although not an ideal means of referring to specific individuals, as names in Nepal are closely tied to caste/ethnic identity, we have opted to use numbers to identify interviewees rather than assign pseudonyms.

10. "Programs" in the Nepali context refers to organized performances such as those during school open days and other events.

# References

Allsup, R. E., & Westerlund, H. (2012). Methods and situational ethics in music education. *Action, Criticism, and Theory for Music Education*, 11, 124–48.

Appadurai, A. (1996). *Modernity at large: Cultural dimensions of globalization*. Minneapolis and London: University of Minnesota Press.

Appadurai, A. (2004). The capacity to aspire: Culture and the terms of recognition. In V. Rao & M. Walton (Eds.), *Culture and public action* (pp. 59–84). Stanford, CA: Stanford University Press.

Appadurai, A. (2006). The right to research. *Globalisation, Societies and Education, 4*(2), 167–77. doi:10.1080/14767720600750696

Appadurai, A. (2013). *The future as cultural fact: Essays on the global condition*. London: Verso.

Apple, M. W. (1996). *Cultural politics and education*. New York: Teachers College Press.

Apple, M. W. (2013). *Can education change society?* New York: Routledge.

Bhatta, P. (2009). Improving schools through decentralization: Observations from Nepal's primary education. In P. Bhatta (Ed.), *Education in Nepal: Problems, reforms and social change* (pp. 151–86). Kathmandu, Nepal: Martin Chautari.

Bhattachan, K. B. (2009). Discourse on social exclusion and inclusion in Nepal: Old wine in a new bottle. In *Identity & society: Social exclusion and inclusion in Nepal* (pp. 11–43). Kathmandu, Nepal: Mandala.

Boud, D. (1995). Assessment and learning: Contradictory or complementary? In P. Knight (Ed.), *Assessment for learning in higher education* (pp. 35–48). London: Kogan Page.

Cooperrider, D. L., Whitney, D., & Stavros, J. M. (2005). *Appreciative inquiry handbook: For leaders of change* (2nd ed.). Brunswick, OH: Crown Custom Publishing.

Dewey, J. (1977). *The middle works: 1899–1924* (MW). Vol. 4 of *The collected works of John Dewey 1882–1953*. J. A. Boydston (Ed.). Carbondale: Southern Illinois University Press.

Dewey, J. (1983). *The middle works: 1899–1924* (MW). Vol. 14 of *The collected works of John Dewey 1882–1953*. J. A. Boydston (Ed.). Carbondale: Southern Illinois University Press.

Dewey, J. (1984). *The later works: 1925–1953* (LW). Vol. 4 of *The collected works of John Dewey 1882–1953*. J. A. Boydston (Ed.). Carbondale: Southern Illinois University Press.

Dewey, J. (1988). *The later works: 1925–1953* (LW). Vol. 13 of *The collected works of John Dewey 1882–1953*. J. A. Boydston (Ed.). Carbondale: Southern Illinois University Press.

Elliott, D. J. (1989). Key concepts in multicultural music education. *International Journal of Music Education, 13*(1), 11–18.

Elliott, D. J. (1990). Music as culture: Toward a multicultural concept of music education. *Journal of Aesthetic Education, 24*(1), 147–66.

Elliott, D. J. (1995). *Music matters: A new philosophy*. New York: Oxford University Press.

Gaztambide-Fernández, R. A. (2012). Decolonization and the pedagogy of solidarity. *Decolonization: Indigeneity, Education & Society, 1*(1), 41–67.

Government of Nepal. (2007). *National curriculum framework for school education in Nepal*. Bhaktapur, Nepal. Retrieved from http://www.moe.gov.np/assets/uploads/files/National-Curriculum-Framework-2007-English.pdf

Government of Nepal. (2012). *National population and housing census 2011 (national report)*. Retrieved from http://unstats.un.org/unsd/demographic/sources/census/wphc/Nepal/Nepal-Census-2011-Vol1.pdf

Hangen, S. I. (2010). *The rise of ethnic politics in Nepal: Democracy in the margins*. London: Routledge.

Jackson, A. Y., & Mazzei, L. A. (2012). *Thinking with theory in qualitative research: Viewing data across multiple perspectives*. London: Routledge.

Kuntz, A. M. (2015). *The responsible methodologist: Inquiry, truth-telling, and social justice*. London: Routledge.

Lassiter, L. E. (2005). *The Chicago guide to collaborative ethnography*. Chicago: The University of Chicago Press.

Manandhar, M. D. (2009). Preface. In *Identity & society: Social exclusion and inclusion in Nepal* (pp. vii–viii). Kantipath, Kathmandu, Nepal: Mandala.

Mathema, K. B., & Bista, M. B. (2006). *Study on student performance in SLC*. Kathmandu, Nepal: Ministry of Education and Sports Education Sector Advisory Team. Retrieved from http://www.moe.gov.np/assets/uploads/files/SLC_Report_Main_English.pdf

Patel, L. (2014). Counting coloniality in educational research: From ownership to answerability. *Educational Studies, 50*(4), 357–77.

Pole, C., & Morrison, M. (2003). *Ethnography for education*. Berkshire, UK: Open University Press.

Shields, R., & Rappleye, J. (2008). Uneven terrain: Educational policy and equity in Nepal. *Asia Pacific Journal of Education, 28*(3), 265–76. doi:10.1080/02188790802270237

Skinner, D., & Holland, D. (2009). Schools and the cultural production of the educated person in a Nepalese hill community. In P. Bhatta (Ed.), *Education in Nepal: Problems, reforms and social change* (pp. 295–332). Kathmandu, Nepal: Martin Chautari.

Treacy, D. S. (in press). "Because I'm a girl": Troubling shared visions for music education. *Research Studies in Music Education.*

Treacy, D. S., Thapa, S., & Neupane, S. K. (in press). "Where the social stigma has been overcome": The politics of professional legitimation in Nepali music education. In A. A. Kallio, S. Karlsen, K. Marsh, E. Saether, & H. Westerlund (Eds.), *The politics of diversity in music education.*

Treacy, D. S., & Westerlund, H. (in press). Shaping imagined communities through music: Lessons from the *school song* practice in Nepal. *International Journal of Music Education.*

Watkins, J. M., Mohr, B., & Kelly, R. (2011). *Appreciative inquiry: Change at the speed of imagination* (2nd ed.). San Francisco, CA: Pfeiffer/Wiley.

Westerlund, H. (2002). *Bridging experience, action and culture in music education* (Doctoral dissertation). Helsinki, Finland: Studia Musica 16. Sibelius Academy.

Westerlund, H. (2008). Justifying music education: A view from the here-and-now value experience. *Philosophy of Music Education Review, 16*(1), 79–95.

# CHAPTER 22

CREATING CARING
MICRO-ASSESSMENT
CULTURES IN
SOUTH AFRICA

JANELIZE VAN DER MERWE

IN this chapter I explore the concept of micro-assessment cultures in music education through the lens of care ethics (Gilligan, 2011; Held, 2015; Noddings, 2013; Silverman, 2012). I do so by discussing macro- and micro-assessment cultures in South African schools in terms of the Independent Examinations Board's (IEB) Subject Assessment Guidelines (SAGs). In South Africa, private and public schools are governed by different curricula. In what follows I draw on my experience with the curriculum for the IEB to provide examples and discussions of macro- and micro-assessment culture in the grades 10 to 12 music classroom, focusing on the three topics described in the SAGs: music performance and improvisation, music literacy, and general music knowledge and analysis.

Music education in South Africa faces many challenges. Despite the inclusion of indigenous African music, along with jazz and Western art music, in the curriculum, a view that Western music performance and literacy is the pinnacle of musicianship remains entrenched in many schools (Drummond, 2014). This is reflected in the outcomes assessed in the grade 12 written portfolio, in which candidates are expected to compose a musical work (providing a score using staff notation) and submit an example of four-part harmony, adhering to the rules of Western harmony (IEB, 2014). There is also a challenge regarding assessing performances that do not adhere to the criteria set for Western art music. I had a candidate at an IEB school in Johannesburg who wanted to perform her grade 12 examination on the African marimba. Upon asking the chief examiner about the guidelines in such a case, I was informed that a candidate could only be examined if the examiner were provided with scores of the work in staff notation. This case points to a mismatch between the praxis of South African marimba music and the process of the practical examination (Elliott & Silverman, 2015). It serves as one example of the ways in which I felt constrained by assessment policy in music education in South Africa. The beliefs, tools, and practices informing assessment in music education in South Africa pose many challenges for music educators practicing their craft from within the transformative paradigm (Mertens, 2008).

Thus, this discussion is a tentative attempt at planting seeds of caring micro-assessment cultures in South African music education. Joan Tronto (2013) inspired me to begin this dialogue by stating that practices informed by alternative ethical frameworks necessarily are tentative. She further states that a practice driven by an ethic of care "does not mean that every caring need will be met or that controversy, conflict, and disagreement will disappear. It may mean, however, that people in institutions and in public discourse about caring will become more adept at thinking about caring" (Tronto, 2013, p. 168). I hope to further the dialogue about caring in music education and in assessment in music education that I first encountered in the works of Marissa Silverman (2012) and David Elliott (2012).

I first provide a brief overview of care ethics and explore assessment for learning through the lens of care ethics. As noted previously, I use this philosophical underpinning to discuss assessment as care in the IEB grades 10 to 12 music curriculum in South Africa.

# Macro-Assessment Culture in South Africa

What are we talking about when we say that we need to rethink the kind of assessment culture we are creating in music education? I interrogate this question by first considering what an assessment culture is. Next I consider what happens when we adopt a cultural practice in assessment. Finally, I offer a vision for a caring assessment culture.

Linda Allal (2016, p. 260) defines an assessment culture as "a socially transmitted body of beliefs, practices, and tools that are found throughout an education system." This definition describes a macro level that guides assessment practices at a broader, systemic level. Allal (2016, p. 260) differentiates between macro-assessment and micro-assessment cultures by stating that a micro-assessment culture is "the contextualized beliefs, practices, and tools that are socially constructed by the actors in each classroom . . . and in each school."

## Beliefs That Inform the Macro-assessment Culture in South African Music Education

Unpacking and (re)membering (Boyce-Tillman, 2007) South African music education deserves far greater attention than I am able to provide in this chapter. However, this section provides the bird's-eye view necessary to understand the need for caring micro-assessment cultures in South African music education.

## Eurocentrism

Susan Harrop-Allin and Cynthia Kros (2014) accentuate the entrenched Eurocentric beliefs and assumptions that dominate macro-assessment culture in South African music education in their analysis of the intermediate phase curriculum (grades 4–6). I assert that similar beliefs dominate the macro-assessment culture in the further education and training phase (grades 10–12).

This is clearly visible in the reference to the Cambridge International IGCSE and Trinity College assessment tools in the assessment rubrics teachers are expected to use throughout the learner's schooling (IEB, 2014). Similarly, the graded examinations of the Associated Board of the Royal Schools of Music, Trinity College and the South African equivalent, Unisa, are used as a benchmark to judge the quality of practical examinations. Candidates may present a program that does not adhere to examination board canons, but as I learned from personal experience, this program should still adhere to the confines of literate music praxes by providing a detailed score for the external examiner to use.

These beliefs are further mirrored in the weight given to the externally set and evaluated final grade 12 examination. The internal assessments are worth 25 percent of the score and are moderated externally, while the external assessments are worth 75 percent. Furthermore, there is a complete disregard for communal sharing as a valid form of assessment (Bagley, 2010) and joint ownership of knowledge creation in forcing students to sign declarations that their work is independent. This reflects a strong belief in rugged individualism and a disregard for the importance of communitarian value systems such as Ubuntu (Swanson, 2015; Chuwa, 2014). Continuing to use standardized, externally evaluated assessments directly contradicts calls to indigenize and decolonize education (Hickling-Hudson & Ahiquist, 2003; Nichol, 2011).

## Managerialism

Current macro systems in education focus on summative assessment (testing) that could undermine the cultivation of caring micro-assessment cultures (e.g., Elliott & Silverman, 2015; Allsup, 2016). The beliefs that inform the macro-assessment culture in South African music education are no exception to this situation. The core role of summative assessment in South African music education is grounded in beliefs about education and assessment that value the latter as a tool to measure accountability (Birenbaum, 2016). Allsup and Westerlund (2012) discuss the ways in which teachers have increasingly been viewed as incapable of regulating themselves and their own teaching practices. This is evident in the macro-assessment culture in South African music education in the prescriptive nature of assessment tools and practices and the emphasis on external evaluation through externally set examinations. The table for conversion of practical examination marks serves as one such example. This table prescribes for teachers (and examiners) how practical marks (using the Assessment of Practical Performance rubric) should be adapted, based on the difficulty of pieces performed. In turn, difficulty is further managed and prescribed in the SAGs as a program consisting of three pieces, two of which are at least grade 5 standard and one at least grade 6.

Within this environment assessment is used as a tool to keep teachers accountable for their students' learning. Learning here is defined in quantifiable ways: as skills that can be measured and traded. Assessment also serves to keep students accountable by prescribing what they are supposed to learn, when they are supposed to learn it, and how they are supposed to learn. The need to measure and ensure that everyone is being held accountable leads to a macro-assessment culture that emphasizes standardization (Birenbaum, 2016).

## Tools and Practices Informing Macro-Assessment Culture in South African Music Education

In formal music education in South Africa the tools and practices informing macro-assessment culture are the school-based assessments, written portfolio, and the final written and practical examination.

### School-Based Assessment

School-based assessments consist of three tasks that assess music performance and improvisation (topic one) according to the outcomes listed in the SAGs. The first task requires candidates to improvise stylistically, employing Western, indigenous, or contemporary scales. The scales included here are the major, minor, pentatonic, blues, and modes. Assessment also requires candidates to improvise a short accompaniment to a prescribed melody as well as variations on a given melody. Candidates are assessed according to a rubric adapted from the National Association for Music Education Performance Standards for Music (USA), the Associated Board of the Royal Schools of Music's Jazz examination (UK), and the Regina Public Schools (Canada). This assessment rubric is another indication of the macro-assessment culture, which subjugates local knowledge (such as the use of indigenous scales and styles).

The second task used to assess topic one is a performance of the same program to be performed at the final examination, under the same (or similar) circumstances, and adhering to the same quality measures (as determined by the grades 5, 6, 7, and 8 syllabi of the examination boards in question). This practice does not adhere to the principles of authentic assessment (Villarroel et al., 2017). Placing candidates in a situation in which they have to perform a piece in front of an examiner sitting behind a desk while following staff notation extremely closely is very removed from the principles of authentic assessment (Villarroel et al., 2017). Beyond the shortcomings of a practical examination such as this, candidates may also feel violated by such assessment settings. The feeling of violation may be greater for candidates who are newly inducted into the examination rituals of Western art music (Nichol, 2011).

The third task assessed for topic one is ensemble or group performance. This is the only task for which the candidate is placed in a communal setting, although many school ensembles remain far from being egalitarian (Elliott & Silverman, 2015). The distinct power hierarchy embedded in traditional school ensembles such as school choirs and school orchestras may impede candidates' ability to meet assessment criteria, which includes the opportunity to make performance suggestions. In my experience in South African music education, marimba bands serve as a distinct contradiction to the implicit power hierarchy. Although these bands present a more democratic ensemble experience for candidates, I have experienced many cases in which music students in IEB schools have been discouraged from participating in these bands, as they are seen to be inferior to school choirs and orchestras. This situation is further complicated by the facts that candidates are required to participate in an ensemble on their first instrument, which is usually a Western instrument, and that the requirements for sheet music (preferably staff notation) at the final practical examination exclude many aural music praxes.

## *The Written Portfolio*

In the written portfolio, work from all three topics is covered: music performance and improvisation, music literacy, and general music knowledge and analysis. The task assigned to candidates for topic one is to write program notes for their examination pieces. To assess candidates' music literacy (topic two), they are evaluated on their ability to compose a piece using software to notate a score and show examples of four-part harmony and melody writing. Once again, the assessment criteria are taken from the Cambridge International IGCSE. Criteria for the composition assignment include assumptions about the use of tonality and structure in music that once again point to a heavily Eurocentric macro-assessment culture.

The melody-writing assessment criteria, as well as the criteria for four-part harmony, are based on assumptions about tonality that require candidates to adhere to the conventions of Western tonal music. In the melody-writing rubric there is reference to formulaic writing in the category for students who attain a mark of 40–49 percent. In my experience as a teacher in the IEB system and a moderator during cluster meetings,[1] assessment criteria and teaching practice do not align in this instance. Teachers often teach students to write melodies using strict formulas. This is in part because of the criteria set for students, requiring them to write 16-bar melodies without lyrics, or alternatively, 12-bar melodies with lyrics. These two structures are often interpreted by teachers as consisting of 4-bar phrases. It is also very common for teachers to prescribe the kinds of cadences each phrase should have and to teach students to set harmonic frameworks to superimpose on their melodies. These teaching practices clearly contradict the assessment criteria, but this contradiction is often ignored during the assessment and moderation process.

Topic three, general music knowledge and analysis, is assessed by means of long essays containing both superficial musicological and theoretical analysis of some of the set works. This task relies heavily on verbal musical thinking and knowing (Elliott & Silverman, 2015). Candidates are encouraged to analyze notated and recorded musics and to pay attention to their historical contexts. Furthermore, the musical elements are suggested as a backbone for the analysis.

## *The Final Written and Practical Examination*

The final examination is externally set and evaluated and serves as the ultimate objective for all training from grade 10 to grade 12 The examination consists of two written papers, a performance examination, and an aural assessment.

The practical exam takes place under strict, controlled conditions, with timetables set externally. Although the SAGs state that the examination is viewed as a performance, the mere practice of providing a score to be followed or playing in an empty room to an audience of two (both of whom are taking notes throughout the performance) does not equate to an authentic performance. This is even more true when musics that involve different audience-performer relations, such as jazz, rock or pop, and South African traditional and urban musics, are presented as part of the examination.

The examination also includes sight-reading. During preparation time the candidate is not allowed to try out any passages. This raises the question of to what extent the sight-reading assessment is designed to test performance abilities and to what extent it is merely an exercise in decoding symbols (staff notation in this instance).

The aural assessment tests candidates' ability to sing or play back a four-bar melody, clap back a 4-bar rhythm, sight-sing, identify cadences, and identify the meter. Beyond accuracy, prompt and intuitive response forms part of the assessment criteria. Once again, there is very little intuition about the practice or the assessment tools used for this assessment.

There are few times, outside of the artificial settings of examinations and auditions for tertiary education, when a musician would be required to perform these tasks in isolation, with so little musical context surrounding the performance. For example, during sight-singing assessment, candidates are provided with a tonic chord, after which they are required to sing a passage of seemingly randomly selected semibreves bearing no resemblance to actual, idiomatic melodies in any particular style.

The written examinations ask questions concerning music literacy and general music knowledge. Although some sociocultural aspects of the prescribed works are included— and there have been advances in including South African musics in the syllabus (such as *Meadowlands* and the musical *King Kong*)—assessment still requires formalist knowledge at the expense of musical understanding (e.g., the writing of scales in semibreves, exercises in compositional techniques without musical contexts, and mere repetition of learned analyses).

This contrasts with an ethic of care, in which the emphasis is on contextualizing our practice to ensure that the needs of the "one-caring" as well as the "cared-for" are met (Noddings, 2013). Given the macro-assessment culture in South African music education, it is easy to understand how teachers might feel helpless. Although it is beyond the purview of most classroom music teachers to change the macro-assessment culture, every teacher is an agent in creating a unique micro-assessment culture. Therefore, it is imperative for teachers to consider the ways in which we may be instrumental in creating caring micro-assessment cultures in South African music education.

# CREATING CARING MICRO-ASSESSMENT CULTURES IN SOUTH AFRICAN MUSIC EDUCATION

Given the strongly regulated macro-assessment culture in South African music education, teachers may feel disempowered. However, when we examine the micro level of assessment culture, as music educators we can find many freedoms, even within confining, test-driven macro-assessment culture. As mentioned previously, micro-assessment culture refers to the assumptions, beliefs, and practices that characterize local interactions. In music education, these assessment cultures shape the particular approaches we employ when teaching new material, the kinds of goals we set for our students, the ways in which we assess, and how we adapt our practices based on the feedback we receive. In this section I project a possible caring micro-assessment culture in South African music education (particularly in schools that follow the IEB examinations) by suggesting foundations for caring beliefs, tools, and practices.

## Beliefs Informing a Caring Micro-Assessment Culture

Through the lens of an ethic of care micro-assessment cultures should be informed by caring practices, caring dispositions, and a respect for teachers and learners as multi-faceted persons.

### An Ethic of Care

Feminist scholars have found various dominant moral theories inadequate. Although there is no universal feminist moral theory, the work undertaken under the broader umbrella of "an ethic of care" addresses many of the feminist critiques of dominant moral theories. Several leading feminist scholars have asked questions about our normative assumptions about morality. Carol Gilligan's (1982) book *In a Different Voice* questioned the legitimacy of normative moral theory by exploring the moral development of women. Nel Noddings (1984, p. 7) asks: "Why care about caring?" Her book, *Caring: A Feminine Approach to Ethics and Moral Education*, has contributed greatly to our understanding of caring as a framework for moral education. Tronto (1993, pp. 2–3) asks: "What would it mean in late twentieth century American society to take seriously, as part of our definition of a good society, the values of caring—attentiveness, responsibility, nurturance, compassion, meeting others' needs?"

Although it is impossible to lay out a definitive ethic of care (such an enterprise would go directly against the values of care), there are some ideas that most care ethicists agree on. In general, there is consensus that the practice of caring has been stigmatized in a patriarchal and neoliberal context. If we are to inform our own practices through care, we need to destigmatize the gendered stereotypes of care, dependency, and vulnerability (Gouws & van Zyl, 2015). Moving beyond gender stereotypical care, we need to acknowledge that interdependency is not a sign of weakness, but rather an integral part of our ontological makeup as human beings (Held, 2006).

Our relational nature, as human beings, means that care cannot be defined merely as goods to be traded (Held, 2006). This argument highlights a shortcoming in our current system that views education as a commodity. In this model, a teacher "cares" by providing inputs (such as lessons and feedback), which directly lead to certain outputs (such as high scores on an examination). Using market criteria to evaluate our caring practices will inevitably lead to alienation of both the "one-caring" (Noddings, 2013, p. 30) and the "cared-for" (p. 59). In the example just mentioned, the teacher may not feel satisfied within her teaching practice, since she is merely delivering the tools to meet the criteria of a high-stakes examination, instead of engaging artistically and emotionally with the student to grow together as members of a caring musical community. The student, on the other hand, may feel demotivated by certain assessment practices. Furthermore, viewing care as a commodity creates a problem of scarcity, which does not exist within the context of an ethic of care as practice, disposition, and relation (Tronto, 2013).

We should also make a distinction between "caring-about" and "caring-for" (Noddings, 2015, p. 75). I can "care-about" access to music education in South Africa without actually "caring-for" the students who are affected by it, even though I might find it unsettling that many students in South Africa do not have access to music education. In other words, I "care-about" the issue of access to music education in South Africa. Going one step further, I could donate to a community music school, thereby taking action to address the problem, but still fail to "care-for" the students. "Caring-for" would require interaction with people, engaging in a relationship with them, and becoming responsive to their needs. Noddings (2013, p. xiv) defines "caring-for" as "an encounter or set of encounters characterized by direct attention and response. It requires the establishment of a caring relation, person-to-person contact of some sort." Therefore, if I "care-for" students who are unable to access music education, I will volunteer at a community music school and give lessons for free, while truly engaging in meaningful dialogue with these students to better understand their needs.

To further explore the definition of care, I explore what it means to be a person within the framework of an ethic of care. Thereafter I look at the concept of care through the lens of care as a practice and as a disposition.

## Defining Care as a Practice

As highlighted in the previous section, care is not something that we can trade in the same way that we trade goods. Rather, it is a human activity and needs to be engaged with on a consistent basis (Tronto, 2013). By engaging in the practice of care, members of a community promote particular values. For members of a community to engage in the practice of care, it is necessary that they care enough about this practice to take action. Care as a social practice is situated within a specific environment.

Once again I use the example of a music teacher in her classroom. Suppose she is teaching composition to grade 10 learners. For her to engage in the practice of care she first needs to be in a particular kind of trusting relationship with her students; she is unable to practice care without them graciously allowing her to care for them. Second, she needs to take caring actions in this particular setting. She might ask students what genre they would like to compose in, thereby asking them to express their experiences and needs, as opposed to assuming that she knows what their musical needs are.

## Defining Care as a Disposition

When we define caring as a disposition, we are looking for the values that might make a person caring. From this point of view, engaging in an activity of care (such as teaching music) is not enough. We also need to have a certain attitude that accompanies this activity (Held, 2007). It is possible to take action as a music teacher but fail to do this with care. For example, it is possible for me to teach a student a bassoon sonata by going through a series of lessons and all the steps of teaching. I point out where the student should adapt her embouchure, I provide insight into interpretation, and I ensure that the student develops all the required performance skills. However, if we view caring as a disposition, we realize that merely *acting as though we care is not sufficient*. Instead, we need to *act with an attitude (or a disposition) for care*. Tronto (2013) provides the following criteria to judge whether a disposition is caring: attentiveness, responsibility, competence, responsiveness, and solidarity and trust.

Attentiveness refers to the ability to pay attention to the particulars of each unique situation (Held, 2006). When I am attentive to the needs of my students, I recognize that even within the same class or ensemble, they may have different needs. Attentiveness allows me to be open to the possibility that the needs that I assume they have may be different from their actual needs.

When I move away from the distance "caring-about" allows for, toward the face-to-face encounters that are required when "caring-for" another person, I have to take responsibility for the moral character of that caring interaction (Noddings, 2013). When I place myself in a concrete situation and decide what to do based on the particulars of that situation, I take responsibility as "one-caring" (Noddings, 2013). When we evaluate the role that responsibility plays in caring, we need to be aware that should we become overwhelmed by the amount of responsibility a situation requires, we will become fatigued and unable to "care-for" our students and musical communities effectively (Noddings, 2013).

At this point it is important to distinguish between altruism and care. Caring is not characterized by a sacrifice of the self (selflessness or altruism), but rather by "selffulness" (Silverman, 2012, p. 114): "It is imperative for teachers, parents, and students who care about themselves and education to focus on personal and public caring, happiness, and joy. When someone is cared for, she is loved." In this sense, caring and being cared for are not mutually exclusive because we become simultaneously capable of fulfilling the roles of the "one-caring" and the "cared-for." Therefore, when we become overwhelmed by the responsibility of care, we need to question who is being deemed "compliant to care" and who is being exempted from the responsibility to care (Tronto, 2013, p. 140). We see this fatigue in many teachers, when the responsibility to care is thrust on only one individual, thereby robbing her of the joy of care.

Competence in care ethics may refer to possessing either the necessary skills and knowledge to care or the capability to care. A music educator needs to be in control of certain skills and sets of knowledge to be able to care for her students. For example, if she is not an accomplished performer, she cannot teach her students the skills and under-standings needed to perform well. Beyond this, however, there are other competencies that she must possess to care effectively. Competence within the framework of care therefore refers to skills but also encompasses "a global mastery of conditions in one's personal or professional environment and, indirectly, to the desire for such mastery" (Noddings, 2013, p. 62).

## Personhood, Autonomy, and Care Ethics

An ethic of care assumes that we are ontologically relational. What does this mean? This statement assumes that we are, at least in part, constituted through our social relations. Therefore, a person—from the viewpoint of an ethic of care—is an "embodied nexus of relations" (Held, 2006, p. 49).

Elliott and Silverman (2015, p. 158) refer to a person as "greater *than the sum of his or her unified dimensions* [emphasis in original], which are always in a continuous, fluid, and contingent state of becoming." This means that our relational existence begins within the self, in whom there are constant and ever-changing relationships between conscious and subconscious states. These processes involve the body, the mind, and the brain in processes resulting in the formation and reformation of identity. Through interdependent relationships among these (and many more) processes, we bring our world into existence (Elliott & Silverman, 2015). On a broader level, we are interrelationally dependent on our interactions with our specific social contexts, working up from the micro systems to the macro systems that characterize our social worlds (Bronfenbrenner, 1994).

Some conceptions of care ethics view our interrelational nature through the lens of the caring dyad: the relationship between the "one-caring" and the "cared-for" (Noddings, 2013). Other theorists assert that we need to transcend the dyadic concept of caring relations to include macro systems (Tronto, 2013). To further discuss person-hood in care ethics, I now explore the dyadic relationship between the "one-caring" and the "cared-for" as it translates into interactive regulation in South African music education.

## Practices and Tools That Inform a Caring Micro-Assessment Culture

The practices and tools that inform a caring micro-assessment culture are informed by a process of interactive regulation. The process of interactive regulation helps teachers and students to build meaningful relationships during assessment and informs assessment as a relational practice.

## Interactive Regulation

As transformative practitioners, music educators are constantly reflecting on the particular approaches we employ when teaching new material, the goals we set for our students, the ways we assess those goals, and how we adapt our practices based on feedback. This process is called *regulation*. Considering the types of regulation we employ may help us create a caring micro-assessment culture. The first step in this process should be to question the power relations that our assessment cultures create (Birenbaum, 2016). A macro-assessment culture that focuses on accountability and standardization implies a hierarchical power relation, allowing the student little to no say in determining learning goals or how to go about achieving them. This is clear in the many strict guidelines for assessment in the SAGs. We should instead strive to view assessment's goal as creating a nurturing environment for teaching and learning (Birenbaum, 2016), in which both the teacher and the students are working toward human flourishing (Noddings, 2003; Silverman, 2012). This approach to regulation emphasizes the aims of assessment as teaching and learning through the creation of an "interactional dialogue" (Birenbaum, 2016), in which both the teacher and the student contribute to learning goals, determine how they will go about achieving them, and evaluate their progress toward achieving them.

Allal (2016) differentiates among three types of regulation: (1) retroactive regulation, in which the teacher decides whether learning outcomes were achieved through formative assessments; (2) proactive regulation, in which the teacher plans future teaching and learning activities based on the feedback gained through assessment; and (3) interactive regulation, in which the next steps in the teaching and learning process are determined by interaction between the teacher and the student, as well as interaction with the learning environment. When a music educator engages in retroactive regulation, she may be practicing care as virtue. She may be defined as a caring person, but her assessment practices are not aimed at identifying and helping her students meet their needs. This might be a teacher who knows the tools and practices employed in the SAGs, but who continues to remain uncritical toward the beliefs underpinning these assessment practices and tools. She is caring in that she helps her students to meet the assessment criteria and supports them through the formal external examination by adhering to the guidelines and conducting school-based assessments in a manner that mirrors the formal external examination.

During proactive regulation, a music educator may be practicing care but be focused on the students' assumed needs, since there is little to no interaction between her and them in mapping their path forward. Interactive regulation, on the other hand, implies caring as a relational practice, since the teacher is building a caring relationship with the student through an "interactional dialogue" (Birenbaum, 2016), which aims to identify and meet the student's expressed needs. To some extent this form of caring is embodied in the inclusion of three streams for performance in the SAGs. By including the indigenous African stream and the jazz stream, many teachers are trying to meet assumed needs, yet their students' voices remain unheard. To some extent, because the content of the curriculum has changed, we assume that we are changing the process and tools of assessment, but because we remain uncritical toward beliefs and hierarchies, the micro-assessment culture does not become fully caring. A caring micro-assessment culture needs to encourage a fully fledged egalitarian dialogue between students and their teacher. Therefore, a micro-assessment culture, informed by interactive regulation, holds the promise of creating assessment practices based on building relationships and meeting students' expressed needs. Such assessment practices may lead to assessment as caring.

### Assessment as a Relational Practice

As discussed in the previous section, interactive regulation takes relationships as the basis of assessment practice. This means that all phases of the assessment practice are guided by the relationships we build. Through a relational lens, I now focus on the phases of the assessment practice and the three levels of regulation. This discussion takes interactive regulation as the basis for a caring assessment culture.

The assessment process that I refer to largely concerns the practice of formative assessment (or assessment for learning). It focuses on employing assessment as a tool to promote teaching and learning. This may be contrasted with summative assessment, in which the goal is usually to certify or report on the learning that has already taken place (Andrade & Brockhart, 2016). Admittedly, this clear-cut distinction may be simplistic, but it serves my purpose because I am advocating for more emphasis on formative assessment (in which micro-assessment cultures can develop more freely), as opposed to a music education assessment culture that emphasizes summative assessment (in which macro-assessment cultures are dominant).

Andrade and Brockhart (2016) view the formative assessment process as consisting of three interrelated stages: goal setting, progress monitoring, and revision and adjustment. During the first phase, it is important for teachers and students to engage in dialogue to clearly identify their goals (Andrade & Brookhart, 2016). I assert that if we are to engage in assessment as care, then during this stage the student's voice needs to be heard. The student needs to feel safe and supported in order to express her needs clearly. To be able to interact with students' needs and to identify instances in which there may be assumed needs (prescribed by the genre of music or the discipline) that the students are not yet aware of, the teacher also needs to feel confident in the caring relationship she has built with her students. This dialogue will serve to make learning goals clear through a caring interaction in which both the "one-caring" and the "cared-for" are able to express their opinions.

During the second phase, the dialogue needs to be extended to monitor progress toward the goal (Andrade & Brookhart, 2016). Through the creation of a caring relationship during the first phase, it becomes possible for both the student and the teacher to clearly express their thoughts about the processes involved. This phase also includes dialogues about the kinds of product-based assessments employed. Thus, the student is guided through learning processes in a way that makes her feel empowered, since she is able to contribute to the choice of assessment instrument and the reflective practice.

During the third phase, the student and teacher move the dialogue to a metacognitive level (Andrade & Brookhart, 2016). As I see it, this stage is where caring truly becomes evident. During the first two phases the teacher and student interact to determine which goals they are working toward and how they are progressing toward reaching those goals. In the third stage, the student becomes empowered because she is taught how to reflect on the learning process and enabled to identify the adjustments needed to reach her goals in future. These three stages of assessment are then repeated, working toward greater depth and finer distinctions. Through this process the student becomes empowered not only to function as the "cared-for" (relying on the teacher to fulfill her musical needs), but also to become the "one-caring" (by becoming autonomous and being able to help others meet their musical needs).

Although the entire process is guided by the caring dyad (student and teacher), understanding assessment as a relational practice implies understanding that there are different levels of relationships simultaneously at work during assessment. Menucha Birenbaum (2016) identifies three levels that have an impact on assessment: the relationship between the student and the learning environment, the teacher-student relationship, and the student-peer relationship. The elements in these relationships are never inde-

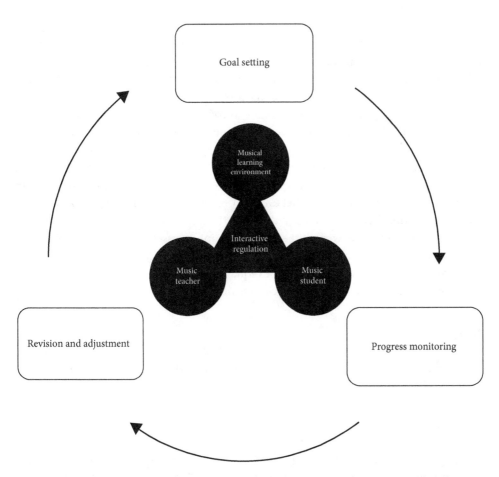

FIGURE 22.1 A relational practice model for assessment as caring in music education

pendent from each other and therefore, in a learning environment characterized by an ethic of care, they interact to create nine reciprocal relationships. Because the directedness of the relationship matters, each of the elements and/or agents within the environment may engage in a unique relationship with each of the others. Since there are three agents (the teacher, the learner, and the peers) and one element (the learning environment), there is the possibility for nine distinct relationships and a unique set of nine relationships form the viewpoint of each learner in the learning environment. Together, these relationships also affect and are affected by the three stages of the cyclical assessment process. When all of these relationships work together toward the promotion of "self-fulness" (Silverman, 2012), assessment can function as an act of caring. Figure 22.1 illustrates a relational practice model for assessment as caring in music education.

# CONCLUSION

This chapter has explored the macro-assessment culture in South African music education and reflected on cultivating a caring micro-assessment culture. I have examined caring in the context of music education as a virtue and a relational practice. Viewing caring as a relational practice emphasizes the interconnected nature of the one caring and the cared-for. Realizing this, it is impossible to continue practicing assessment in ways that damage this relationship. While it remains important to critique the macro-assessment culture in South African music education, many teachers functioning within the transformative paradigm may feel weighed down by the great task ahead of them. It is undoubtedly important to transform the macro-assessment culture in South African music education to be caring, but I believe that this work can begin by individual teachers transforming the micro-assessment cultures in their own classes into caring, nurturing spaces. At the micro level we find the freedom to infuse assessment culture in our own classrooms with an ethic of care. This assessment culture views assessment as a relational process, in which all parties have an equal voice. These voices engage in a dialogue to regulate the three phases of the cyclical assessment process.

## NOTE

1. Moderation cluster meetings are district level meetings at which teachers moderate portfolios collectively.

## REFERENCES

Allal, L. (2016). The co-regulation of student learning in an assessment for learning culture. In D. Laveault & L. Allal (Eds.), *Assessment for learning: Meeting the challenge* (pp. 259–92). Cham, Switzerland: Springer.

Allsup, R. E. (2016). *Remixing the classroom: Toward an open philosophy of music education.* Bloomington: Indiana University Press.

Allsup, R. E., & Westerlund, H. (2012). Methods and situational ethics in music education. *Action, Criticism, and Theory for Music Education, 11*(1), 124–48. Retrieved from http://act.maydaygroup.org/articles/Allsup Westerlund11_1.pdf

Andrade, H., & Brookhart, S. M. (2016). The role of classroom assessment in supporting self-regulated learning. In D. Laveault & L. Allal (Eds.), *Assessment for learning: Meeting the challenge* (pp. 293–309). Cham, Switzerland: Springer.

Bagley, S. S. (2010). Students, teachers and alternative assessment in secondary school: Relational models theory (RMT) in the field of education. *The Australian Educational Researcher, 37*(1), 83–106.

Birenbaum, M. (2016). Assessment culture versus testing culture: The impact on assessment for learning. In D. Laveault & L. Allal (Eds.), *Assessment for learning: Meeting the challenge of implementation* (pp. 275–92). Cham, Switzerland: Springer.

Boyce-Tillman, J. (2007). Spirituality in the musical experience. In L. Bresler (Ed.), *International handbook of research in arts education* (pp. 1405–24). Dordrecht: Springer.

Bronfenbrenner, U. (1994). Ecological models of human development. In *International Encyclopedia of Education* (2nd ed., Vol. 3). Oxford: Elsevier. (Reprinted in *Readings on the development of children,* 2nd ed., pp. 37–43, by M. Gauvian & M. Cole (Eds.), 1993, New York: Freeman).

Chuwa, L. T. (2014). *African indigenous ethics in global bioethics: Interpreting Ubuntu.* New York: Springer.

Drummond, U. (2014). *Music education in South African Schools after apartheid: Teacher perceptions of Western and African music* (Doctoral dissertation). Glasgow University, Ireland. Retrieved from http://theses.gla.ac.uk/6298/1/2014DrummondEdD.pdf

Elliott, D. J. (2012). Music education as/for artistic citizenship. *Music Educators Journal.* September, 21–27.

Elliott, D. J., & Silverman, M. (2015). *Music matters: A philosophy of music education* (2nd ed.). New York: Oxford University Press.

Gilligan, C. (1982). *In a different voice.* Cambridge: Harvard University Press.

Gilligan, C. (2011). *Joining the resistance.* Cambridge: Polity.

Gouws, A., & van Zyl, M. (2015). Towards a feminist ethics of ubuntu. In D. Engster & M. Hammington (Eds.), *Care ethics and political theory* (pp. 166–86). New York: Oxford University Press.

Harrop-Allin, S., & Kros, C. (2014). The C major scale as index of "back to basics" in South African education: A critique of the curriculum assessment policy statement. *Southern African Review of Education, 20*(1), 70–89.

Held, V. (2006). *The ethics of care: Personal, political, and global.* New York: Oxford University Press.

Held, V. (2007). The ethics of care. In D. Copp (Ed.), *The Oxford handbook of ethical theory* (pp. 538–66). New York: Oxford University Press.

Held, V. (2015). Care and justice, still. In D. Engster & M. Hamington (Eds.), *Care ethics and political theory* (pp. 20–35). New York: Oxford University Press.

Hickling-Hudson, A., & Ahlquist, R. (2003). Contesting the curriculum in the schooling of indigenous children in Australia and the USA: From Eurocentrism to culturally powerful pedagogies. *Comparative Education Review, 47,* 64–89.

Independent Examinations Board. (2014). *Music.* Retrieved from https://www.ieb.co.za/pages/subjectassessmentguidelineslibrary

Mertens, D. M. (2008). *Transformative research and evaluation*. New York: Guilford.

Nichol, R. M. (2011). *Growing up indigenous: Developing effective pedagogy for education and development*. Boston: Sense.

Noddings, N. (1984). *Caring, a feminine approach to ethics & moral education*. Berkeley: University of California Press.

Noddings, N. (2003). *Happiness in education*. Cambridge, UK: Cambridge University Press.

Noddings, N. (2013). *Caring: A relational approach to ethics and moral education*. Berkley, CA: University of California.

Noddings, N. (2015). Care ethics and "caring" organizations. In D. Engster & M. Hamington (Eds.), *Care ethics and political theory* (pp. 73–85). New York: Oxford University Press.

Silverman, M. (2012). Virtue ethics, care ethics, and "the good life of teaching." *Action, Criticism, and Theory for Music Education, 11*(2), 96–122. Retrieved from http://act.maydaygroup.org/articles/Silverman11_2.pdf.

Swanson, D. M. (2015). Ubuntu, indigeneity, and an ethic for decolonizing global citizenship. In A. A. Abdi et al. (Eds.), *Decolonizing global citizenship education* (pp. 27–38). Boston: Sense.

Tronto, J. C. (1993). *Moral boundaries: A political argument for an ethic of care*. New York: Routledge.

Tronto, J. C. (2013). *Caring democracy: Markets, equality, and justice*. New York: Oxford University Press.

Villarroel, V., Bloxham, S., Bruna, D., Bruna, C., & Herrera-Seda, C. (2017). Authentic assessment: creating a blueprint for course design. *Assessment & Evaluation in Higher Education, 43*(5), 840–54.

# CHAPTER 23

# ASSESSMENT AND THE DILEMMAS OF A MULTI-IDEOLOGICAL CURRICULUM

## *the case of Norway*

### SIDSEL KARLSEN AND GEIR JOHANSEN

FORMAL curricula, such as the documents constituting the national curricula for the primary and lower secondary schools in England or the Nordic countries, come into existence via multifaceted processes and may consist of various parts created at different times and under shifting political and ideological circumstances. Despite these often conglomerate births, curricula are ultimately expected to function as instruments that provide coherent guidelines for school teaching and learning. Teachers will also hope to find tools here for systematic formulation of criteria, which will lead to reliable and valid acts and processes of assessment. This, however, may not always be the case.

In this chapter we take the present Norwegian formal curriculum situation as a point of departure for exploring how a multi-ideological curriculum impacts the processes of assessment in one particular school subject, namely music. Music is a compulsory subject in Norwegian schools, from year 1 through year 10. It is allotted a total of 368 sixty-minute teaching hours: 285 for years 1–7 and 83 for years 8-10 (Norwegian Directorate for Education and Training, 2006b). While summative assessment during the first seven years is typically given as an oral or written statement, the assessment procedures for lower secondary school require a graded evaluation.

Regarding the overall compulsory school system in Norway,[1] the national primary and secondary school curriculum consists of two interdependent but separately written parts, implemented in 1993 and 2006, respectively. The older Core Curriculum (Norwegian Ministry of Church, Education and Research, 1993) summarizes and elaborates on the Norwegian Education Act and provides guidelines for the broader aims of education as well as for the cultural, moral, and scholarly foundations on which primary and secondary education and training should be built. Examining this particular part from an educational ideology point of view, one could say that it is clearly marked by the humanist *Bildung* tradition and by progressive education ideas, emphasizing holistic development of the well-rounded child, adolescent, and adult as the primary goal. The second and newer part of the curriculum, named Knowledge Promotion (Norwegian Directorate for Education and Training, 2006a), is comprised of individual subject curricula (or syllabi) for all school subjects, both compulsory and elective. As an example, the music subject curriculum for years 1–10 is a six-page document, in which the first page is dedicated to describing the overarching objectives of the subject and the latter five pages to giving an overview of the main subject areas, the basic skills of the subject, and a detailed list of "competence aims"[2] (Norwegian Directorate for Education and Training, 2006b, p. 4) to be reached at years 2, 4, 7, and 10. Ideologically, the first page of this subject curriculum mirrors the values expressed in the 1993 Core Curriculum, while the latter part, which entered the system much later, is clearly an operationalization of a positivist-oriented, ends-means approach to music education.

This chapter examines the apparent multi-ideological split of the Norwegian music curriculum and explores implications for assessment. Our questions follow a twofold interest, namely: What are the consequences of the ends-means related objectives and assessment criteria shaping the music subject? What other assessment criteria and procedures could be used that might align better with the humanist *Bildung* and the progressive education foundations of the curriculum? Pursuing these interests, we first elaborate on the educational ideologies found within the two-part Norwegian curriculum and their consequences as expressed through actual curricular texts. Second, we look at the dilemmas that the current ideological split causes when using the music subject curriculum as an instrument for acts of assessment and discuss ways to better solve the challenges of assessing students' performances and achievements in the music subject in the Norwegian compulsory school system of today.

# EDUCATIONAL IDEOLOGIES AND THE NORWEGIAN CURRICULUM

## *Bildung* and Ideas of Progressive Education

The philosophies of *Bildung* and progressive education have had a great influence on Norwegian public schooling during most of the twentieth and into the twenty-first centuries. Arising during the Enlightenment and articulated by philosophers such as Kant, Goethe, Schiller, Hegel, and Humboldt, the *Bildung* philosophy addresses human growth and development from birth to death, entailing all the processes at work in socialization and enculturation of individuals. Within this comprehensive notion of developing the whole person during the entire human life span, formal schooling is regarded as a central part, guided by some particular *Bildung* philosophy-based characteristics. At the core lies the vision, or *Bildungsideal*, of the emancipated, self-determined, but socially responsible human being. This means that humans take part, deliberately and actively, in their own *Bildung* processes. This includes the maturation of individuals through aesthetic experiences and the development of a democratic society aiming for "the utopian guiding concept" (Klafki, 2000b, p. 94) of peoples, nations, and cultures living together in peace. In order to enhance students' development in this direction, it is vital that schooling be centered around a well-defined and well-selected curriculum content, preserving and renewing cultural heritage. In other words, the content should possess high *Bildungs*-value.

Several *Bildung* priorities of schooling resonate with the principles of the North American pedagogical movement of progressive education, such as the focus on development of social skills, social responsibility, and democracy (Dewey, 1921); aesthetic experiences (Dewey, 1934); lifelong learning; and individual and social development, helping children become not only good learners but also good people and citizens. In addition, progressive education highlights principles and priorities that are less visible in, but still in resonance with, *Bildung* educational theory. This includes the principles of problem solving and critical thinking, along with group work and collaborative learning. Peer teaching and learning that is situated in a caring community—with less focus on behavior than on underlying motives, values, and reasons—is vital, and so is attention to the emotional, artistic, and creative aspects of human development, as opposed to education based on testing and business-oriented, cost-benefit principles. Hence, learning is a matter of constructing ideas rather than passively absorbing information or practicing skills, and it requires students' and teachers' active participation at every stage of the process. One last category of progressive education principles, which might appear to be more tangential to the *Bildung* educational theory of the mid-twentieth century (Klafki, 2000a) than the others, is the emphasis on experiential learning and project-based education (Kilpatrick, 1918). This entails a focus on thematic units according to how children learn, rather than a strict division of school subjects, along with the organizing of teaching and learning around problems, projects, and questions emphasizing interdisciplinarity rather than around lists of facts and skills presented as belonging to separate disciplines.

## The Norwegian Core Curriculum

As stated previously, both the *Bildung* philosophies and the ideas of progressive education have had a long-standing impact on the Norwegian system of public schooling. As such, the Core Curriculum of 1993 (Norwegian Ministry of Church, Education and Research, 1993) represented mainly a continuation and strengthening of ideals already well known and implemented by most parties in education. The curriculum's overarching *Bildungsideal* is described by the term "the integrated human being," entailing the ability to take charge of oneself and one's own life as well as "the vigor and will to stand by others" (p. 5). It presents a holistic perspective on human beings and society, a view that is clearly in line with both the *Bildung* focus on the totality of the socialization processes and the progressive education ideal of students becoming good people, not only good learners.

An overarching and clearly *Bildung*-related priority of the curriculum is that schooling must provide a multifaceted and well-rounded general education. To achieve this, the educational content must constitute a careful selection of subject matter and working methods, which should also "uphold and renew our cultural heritage" (p. 7). This is seen as a precondition for the evolution of the whole personality and for developing manifold interpersonal relationships. Priorities pointing to progressive education as well as *Bildung* philosophies highlight the reciprocal relationship between individualism and social responsibility. Moreover, the curriculum maintains that schooling should foster equality between the sexes and among people with different cultural heritage and groups with differing modes of life, as well as solidarity with those whose skills differ from those of the majority.

In the field of arts education, *Bildung* and progressive education priorities complement each other, as previously discussed. In the Core Curriculum (Norwegian Ministry of Church, Education and Research, 1993) these concerns are expressed by pointing out that students should develop "an appreciation for beauty" as well as experience how "confrontation with creative art can wrench us out of our habitual modes of thought and break with conventional wisdom and customary modes" (p. 13). Education must hence "sharpen the [students'] senses for the experiential aspects of every subject" (p. 14), including music and the arts. Here, the *Bildung* priority of enhancing existential experiences (Varkøy, 2010) meets priorities clearly related to John Dewey's (1934) ideas of artworks as both "esthetic— that is, framed for enjoyed receptive perception" (p. 49) and sites for *undergoing*, the surrender or "adequate yielding of the self" (p. 55) in order to be able to "*take* in" (p. 55) the deeper experiential and existential aspects that the work of art invites.

Progressive education influences can also be found in an evident priority of creativity and an outspoken attentiveness to the value of the child and the child's perspective. Moreover, emphasized priorities of intrinsic motivation, good working habits, and preparation for working and social life add to this picture. The curriculum also forwards working forms pointing to project methods and suggests problem solving as a way to "test one's explanations by examination of sources, experimentation, or observation" (Norwegian Ministry of Church, Education and Research, 1993, p. 14). To this belong also the priorities of group work and collaborative learning. Finally, the school should constitute "an active source of energy and culture for the local community, and promote contact with local services and industry" (p. 34).

# A Positivist Ends-Means Approach to Education

The so-called ends-means curriculum model was first developed in the United States by Ralph W. Tyler (1949) to provide teachers with a practical tool that would help them plan, conduct, and assess their own teaching and their students' learning more rationally and effectively. Tyler formulated four basic questions that in his opinion should underlie all curricula, syllabi, and teaching plans: (1) What educational purposes should the school seek to attain? (2) How can learning experiences be selected that are likely to be useful in attaining these objectives? (3) How can learning experiences be organized for effective instruction? and (4) How can the effectiveness of learning experiences be evaluated? As is apparent from these questions, unlike in the *Bildung* tradition or in the philosophy of progressive education, in the ends-means approach it is the particular ends—the subject-related objectives—that form the point of departure for choice of content, teaching methods, and assessment or evaluation. The ends also give directions for the order of decisions. In other words, relevant ends are what one should first agree upon in education; all other decisions are subordinate and should be made at a later stage. This is not to say that methods are unimportant in this line of curricular thinking. Methods—and choosing the right ones—are crucial for reaching the goals and for ensuring that the knowledge and skills that should be acquired are learned in the right way. As such, the ends-means curriculum model can be understood as heavily influenced by positivist natural science thinking, in that it conveys a view of teaching and learning implying that it is desirable, and also possible, to uncover indisputable connections among educational ends, content, methods, teaching material, and assessment. In other words, by making the right choices in this respect, each teacher should be able to predict the learning outcomes that the students will derive from her teaching. Hence, according to this view, learning can, and should, be governed and controlled.

In Norway, Tyler's model has been further developed and made fit for use in the educational system by adding ideas from the field of business and leadership, first coined as "management by objectives" or "management by results" (Drucker, 1954; Odiorne, 1965). According to these management principles, those in positions of leadership define the overarching goals. In addition, the leadership assesses the results; however, the concretization of goals into sub-goals and working objectives should be left to the staff members. Translated to the world of education, this was first used as a leadership model for the total enterprise of schooling but soon developed into a model for governing teaching more specifically. However, instead of only the overarching goals being decided at the top level, as was the idea in the original "management by objectives" model, from the early 1990s the management—in this case the Norwegian Ministry of Church, Education and Research—intervened and made decisions on all goal and objective levels, formulating detailed and object-specific curricula and syllabi (Hanken & Johansen, 2013, p. 211). The ends-means control of learning was hence moved from the teacher to the state level. This tendency has been reinforced in Norwegian education ever since.

## The Knowledge Promotion Curriculum

As mentioned previously, the second and newer part of the Norwegian curriculum, named Knowledge Promotion, was implemented in 2006 (Norwegian Directorate for

Education and Training, 2006a). Preceding this implementation a number of events contributed to major changes being made to the Norwegian educational system. First of all, when the results from the first PISA test initiated by the Organisation for Economic Co-operation and Development (OECD) arrived in 2000, this led to a heated public debate about the quality of Norwegian schools (see Bergesen, 2006; Elstad & Sivesind, 2010) because Norwegian students achieved only average scores. Consequently, leading politicians identified the need for school reform. Second, white papers were written (Norwegian Ministry of Education and Research, 2002, 2003), laying the groundwork for a national quality assessment framework and curriculum reform, which were then implemented. As part of this quality framework, since 2004 national assessment tests have been conducted annually to measure students' achievement in reading, mathematics, and English. Third, also in 2004 a new state directorate was formed—the Norwegian Directorate for Education and Training—which oversees the entire Norwegian educational system and "has the overall responsibility for supervising kindergarten, education and the governance of the education sector, as well as the implementation of Acts of Parliament and regulations" (Norwegian Directorate for Education and Training, 2005). The national curricula are managed by this directorate, as are all forms of assessment conducted on the national level. Hence, when the Knowledge Promotion curriculum was implemented, a comprehensive nationwide system for governing teaching as well as controlling and measuring students' learning and educational outcomes was already in place.

The Knowledge Promotion curriculum consists of two parts. Part one is the Quality Framework, which provides guidelines for the general principles of education (Norwegian Directorate for Education and Training, 2006c). Part two is the detailed subject curricula for all teaching subjects offered in Norwegian schools, both mandatory and electives. All subject curricula follow the format outlined in the introduction to this chapter, describing the overarching objectives of the subject in question and its main areas and basic skills, as well as giving an overview of the teaching hours allotted through years 1–10. In addition, all curricula have detailed lists of objectives to be reached at years 2, 4, 7, and 10. While the Quality Framework's principles can be said to be tied ideologically to the Core Curriculum, the overall design of the subject curricula leans toward an ends-means ideological connection. Adding to this, the curriculum implementation was followed by an enhanced focus on assessment through a national program, launched by the Norwegian Directorate for Education and Training, called Assessment for Learning (Norwegian Directorate for Education and Training, 2010). This initiative was a novelty in Norwegian education. Through the Assessment for Learning program, teachers are given detailed guidelines and principles for how to perform formative and summative assessment in "just and relevant" ways, and they have access to resources that explicate how assessment should be done. Some larger municipalities have even prepared their own supervisory material, showing teachers in detail how assessment could, or should, be executed in each subject (see, e.g., Municipality of Oslo Education Authority, 2009). Hence, due to the 2006 curriculum reform and its preceding and subsequent related initiatives and events, the focus on "the ends" and how to reach them is currently a major feature of the Norwegian educational system, not only on the level of the individual teacher, as Tyler (1949) prescribed, but also on municipality and state levels, to an extent that surpasses anything hitherto experienced in public education in Norway.

## The Norwegian Music Subject Curriculum for Years 1–10

As mentioned in the introduction to this chapter, the first page of the Norwegian music subject curriculum for years 1–10—the page on which the long-range objectives of the subject are described—mirrors the values expressed in the 1993 Core Curriculum to a large extent. The idea of creating an integrated and good human being with a well-developed personality is touched upon in the first paragraph, and music is positioned as central to such development: "Music embraces, expresses and presents moods, thoughts and emotions relating to all aspects of what it is to be a human being. Thus music is a source of self-awareness and interpersonal relations across time, place and culture" (Norwegian Directorate for Education and Training, 2006b, p. 1). The social responsibility and manifold aspects of interrelationships are emphasized, among other things, by pointing to music's "important role in adapted teaching in the inclusive school" (p. 1); the potential when engaging with music for experiencing and developing "perception, empathy, expression and participation" (p. 1); and "the tolerance and respect for the cultures of others" (p. 1) that can be gained by engaging with a variety of musical expressions. The upholding and renewal of cultural heritage is also mentioned, among other things by stating that music has the ability to promote "a sense of belonging in one's own culture with awareness of one's cultural heritage" (p. 1). This is seen as especially important for developing one's identity in a multicultural society. Furthermore, the existential dimensions of music as an art form are emphasized, more so in this than in former curricula (see Varkøy, 2010), by describing the act of listening to music as "an unpredictable experience... [that can be] understood as both an aesthetic perception and existential experience" (p. 1). Finally, the value of children and children's culture is addressed by stating that the musical background and outside-of-school acquired competence of the students "should be used in the subject when this is reasonable" (p. 1). All in all, then, this opening page relates heavily to *Bildung* and progressive education ideals.

This cannot be said, however, about the sections in which the objectives of the subject are described. Despite the fact that the Knowledge Promotion music curriculum can be viewed as more "open" than some of its predecessors—in terms of not giving any directions for specific content, methods of instruction, or procedures for assessment—the pointed and rather narrowly defined objectives, together with the 2006 curriculum reform's surrounding assessment documents and programs (discussed previously), make it even more ends-means oriented than previous curricula. Most objectives are formulated so that they can be measured in a quite accurate manner. For example, after year 2, the student should be able to "use his/her voice in a varied manner with different strengths and pitches" (p. 4) as well as "talk about the sound, melody, rhythm, dynamics and tempo of music" (p. 6). Likewise, after year 10, students should master using "the basic elements of music, symbols for figures and chord progressions when playing an instrument" and recognizing and naming "various instruments and ensembles from various genres" (p. 7). As such, the objectives form good points of departure for governing and controlling learning, since they are quite easily perceived as ends that can be connected to specific teaching content and methods and also assessed in the "just" (and measurable) ways required by the Assessment for Learning program. If in doubt, teachers can always consult the more detailed assessment guidelines (see Municipality of Oslo Education Authority, 2009) for additional information on how to go about operationalizing and assessing the subject curriculum objectives in a "correct" manner approved by the educational authorities.

# THE MULTI-IDEOLOGICALLY SPLIT CURRICULUM

As should be evident from both the chapter introduction and the previous descriptions of its various underpinnings and parts, the Norwegian national curriculum, viewed as a totality, clearly demonstrates a split in ideology between the 1993 Core Curriculum and the 2006 Knowledge Promotion reform. Even within the individual subject curricula or syllabi, this split can be detected, as is evident from the previous description of the music subject curriculum. Unpacking this split even further, before exploring its consequences for and the dilemmas of assessment, in this section we dig briefly into the larger philosophical traditions resonating with the educational ideologies already outlined. This means looking into their main ontological and epistemological understandings, asking big questions such as What characterizes the human being?, What counts as knowledge?, How does learning occur?, and What should be the role of the teacher?

The Norwegian Core Curriculum is mainly based on humanist educational philosophy and ideology. As previously outlined, its basic view of the human being is holistic, and it is clearly inspired by *Bildung* theory. Along with this, one can trace influences from the German Gestalt theory, which suggests that human experiences or actions cannot be adequately described as a sum of smaller, independent events. This again resonates with influences of North American progressive philosophy (Dewey, 1921, 1934; Kilpatrick, 1918) and humanist psychology (Allport, 1961; Maslow, 1954; Rogers, 1970). In addition to being holistic, the view of the human being in the Core Curriculum is characterized by the vision of the emancipated, self-determined, but socially responsible human, aiming at self-actualization and with inner motivation as her or his strongest drive. Furthermore, the epistemological understandings of the Core Curriculum are designated by viewing knowledge as multifaceted, including explicit as well as tacit dimensions. Teachers and students in collaboration construct knowledge, preferably in holistic settings such as project-related group work, in which the participants aim to find solutions to specific problems. Learning is best promoted by practical work and problem solving and is guided by the ideal of the learner possessing great amounts of internal motivation. Moreover, the curriculum's views on knowledge and learning are mainly philosophically based, and less interest is shown in the need for establishing empirical evidence for supporting their worth and validity. With respect to the role of the teacher, the Core Curriculum reflects the central European and Nordic notion of a *Lehrplan* (e.g., Westbury, 2000)—that is, a document describing all sides of schooling by which teachers are guaranteed professional autonomy, since subject content "can only become educative as it is interpreted and given life by teachers" (p. 17). Consequently, and as a counter to neoliberal currents, the teacher is expected to demonstrate significant agency in interpreting and analyzing the formal curriculum in order to select relevant strategies for enhancing student learning. This of course presupposes that teachers are acquainted with a comprehensive repertoire of teaching strategies and methodologies rather than having expert knowledge of one particular method.

The Knowledge Promotion reform, on the other hand, seems guided by positivist and neopositivist philosophies. Showing connections to behaviorist notions of the human being, the view is atomistic, seeing human experiences or actions as the sum of smaller, separately experienced, but still somehow interconnected events. Moreover, it is built on the positivist notion that we cannot know anything beyond what we can observe, leading to a heavy emphasis on behavior and the behaviorist notion of human drive by external motivation caused by stimuli and responses. The epistemological understandings of the Knowledge Promotion part of the curriculum are designated by knowledge as being primarily epistemic, observable, and possible to describe in behavioral terms. Learning is viewed as regulated by stimulus-response processes, requiring that students should always have the aim of a lesson presented for them before they start working. Also, learning is guided by external motivation factors, such as grades and taxonomic scales of targets or standards to reach. The positivist and neopositivist bases lead to priority being given to empirical evidence. This can be seen through the educational authorities' trust in testing, meta-studies of empirical research (Hattie, 2009), and international rankings such as PISA (OECD, n.d.) and TIMSS (TIMSS & PIRLS International Study Center, 2015), and in how this trust seems to have formed the main point of departure for redesigning the entire system of public schooling in Norway, given that this was initiated as a direct consequence of the PISA results received in 2000. The conceptions of a formal curriculum, as found in the detailed subject curricula of the Knowledge Promotion reform, entail Tylerist ideals of defining and describing the exact and expected experiences of the students along with the North American notion of national standards. Therefore, the subject curricula are designed according to a hierarchical ideal, by defining objectives and goals. Likewise, according to business-life-inspired ends-means ideals, they allot teachers the possibility to select the relevant subject content and working forms in order to reach the goals. Following this line of thought, the subject curricula are seen as something being implemented by teachers "just as a system's business officials are expected to implement a system's accounting procedures" (Westbury, 2000, p. 17). Demonstrating how the Tyler rationale and curricula based on its ideals function to disempower teachers, the teacher role under the Knowledge Promotion reform becomes that of a technical executor. The corresponding notion of expertise is mainly focused on formulating behavioral goals for lectures and enhancing student learning by reinforcing strategies and constructing relevant taxonomies.[3] Ultimately, students' outcomes and performances are assessed according to the taxonomy levels. As a consequence, teacher thinking and planning should follow a hierarchical model, within which the subject curricula objectives and goals always come first and the connections between these categories and the assessment criteria are paramount. In the Knowledge Promotion reform, the priority of objectives and assessment is also heavily strengthened by means of the particular assessment regulations following the subsequent implementation of the Assessment for Learning program and the specific and often local guidelines for assessment available for each subject. Ideologically, this *seemingly* aligns (see more on this later in the chapter) with empirical studies on assessment, such as those of Paul Black and Dylan Wiliam (1998) and those reported by John Hattie (2009), highlighting the benefits of assessment in enhancing the quality of student learning.

# DILEMMAS OF ASSESSMENT INHERENT IN THE NORWEGIAN MUSIC SUBJECT CURRICULUM

The multi-ideological split of the Norwegian curriculum has significant consequences for music as a school subject, and these are manifested in several dilemmas. To a large extent, these dilemmas connect explicitly with the ways in which the priorities of the Core Curriculum and the Knowledge Promotion curriculum meet in the music subject syllabus. However, the coexistence of different ideologies also reveals dilemmas of assessment on a more general basis, indirectly affecting the subject of music.

Priorities and visions in the first part of the music curriculum hold that music "embraces, expresses and presents moods, thoughts and emotions relating to all aspects of what it is to be a human being" (Norwegian Directorate for Education and Training, 2006b, p. 1). This creates a dilemma of *qualitative* versus *quantitative* ideals of assessment. In particular, this comes to the fore when related to the ideal of describing assessment criteria in accurate, behavioral terms related to a number of taxonomy levels of achievement. It is self-evident that these priorities and visions cannot be operationalized in behavioral terms unless their very substance is lost. On the contrary, they would require qualitative, connoisseurship-based assessment strategies (Eisner, 1985). Even if music teachers have extended experiences with such qualitative strategies, there is currently not much room for implementing them unless the teachers oppose the prevailing system.

Dilemmas between the qualitative priorities of the first part of the music curriculum and the precise, behavioral objective descriptions of the second part also reveal a dilemma of *holistic* versus *atomistic* assessment. This can be seen by considering objectives such as "the student should be able to talk about the sound, melody, rhythm, dynamics and tempo of music" (Norwegian Directorate for Education and Training, 2006b, p. 6). Here, the holistic ideal of developing comprehensive musical competence through music making, composition, and listening (p. 2) is reduced to an atomistic, single-dimensional notion of talking about music as the sole indicator of musical perception and experience. The music teachers' assignment is then to operationalize this goal into assessment criteria on three different taxonomic levels (see note 3), and by no means to evaluate whether this is a good way of defining, say, music appreciation outcomes.

By forming good points of departure for practicing the ends-means ideology of assessment for control, the objectives of the music curriculum also reveal a dilemma between *assessment for control* and *assessment as a tool for supervision*. Compared with *Bildung* and progressive education ideals of assessment, the latter entails a more (for these ideologies) suitable formative view on assessment, wherein the students' potential for further growth is regarded as equally important as their present performances. Hence, embedded in the former dilemma is a related one, namely that of *formative* (supervision) versus *summative* (control) assessment priorities. Moreover, the dilemma between supervision and control assessment principles can also be detected in the confusion about their effects, which seems to exist among educational authorities as well as music teachers. This confusion is caused by the authorities' attention to data from empirical studies that suggest that assessment is perhaps the most effective factor in helping students learn (Black & William, 1998; Hattie, 2009). This attention stems from rather simplified and neopositivist beliefs in the prescriptive potential of empirical research, beliefs well fitted for neoliberal ways of conceiving of education. What was overlooked by the authorities however, was that the research in question mainly supported and promoted the supervision perspective, or the formative sides of assessment. This again caused confusion about the principles and laid the groundwork for a summative way of practicing formative assessment[4] that caused the supervising assessment ideals in music to disappear.

When the Assessment for Learning program (Norwegian Directorate for Education and Training, 2010) was introduced, a dilemma of *assessment as an integrated* versus *dominant category* was revealed. Drawing the attention away from the *Bildung* and progressive education ideal of assessment as a tacit, integrated category of music teaching and learning, the program strengthened the function of assessment as *the* paramount educational category as well as the ends-means principle of measurability and precise, objective descriptions. To some extent, this also caused an ends-means ideological internal imbalance between the role of the objectives of a subject and its actual assessment criteria, for example as formulated through the three-part taxonomies mentioned previously, resulting in the assessment criteria attaining the strongest guiding force and function.

In general, the implementation of the Knowledge Promotion curriculum in 2006 and the 2010 Assessment for Learning program, as well as the formulation and publication of the municipal assessment guidelines, have caused the ends-means ideology to achieve a stronger-than-ever grip on Norwegian education, both more broadly and in individual subjects specifically, music being no exception in this regard. This has also changed the teacher role by strengthening the top-down guidance—the "management" aspect—of this ideology and has reduced the teachers' agency and perceived autonomy. In a recent study on music teachers' assessment practices, John Vinge (2014; see also Almqvist, Vinge, Väkevä, & Zandén, 2017) concludes that teachers use assessment as "didactic strategies for self-defence" (Vinge, 2014, p. 321). What is implied here is that the concrete tools that the teachers have for making summative assessment make them feel "safe." On the one hand, they can justify music as a "real" subject, in which the required measurability and reliability can be attained. Hence, they can defend themselves (and their subject) against educational authorities on all levels. On the other hand, by having "enough" (read: many) points of assessment for each student, music teachers can justify their own grading and prove its relevance and fairness. This works as a defense against angry parents and potential lawsuits in cases where students claim unjust assessment outcomes. In our view, the teachers' perceived necessity for self-defense strategies points to a change from professional autonomy to a notion of teachers as business officials (Westbury, 2000), needing to justify and prove that they have effectuated what they have been told to do by the authorities. The phenomenon also reveals that assessment strategies that seem to function well for the teachers may not be working equally well for their students with respect to the possibilities for the latter to reach objectives and goals. In particular, this concerns reaching the long-range objectives of the curriculum.

When seen together, the assessment dilemmas we have described also influence the students' experienced curriculum (Goodlad, Klein, & Tye, 1979), including its hidden dimensions (Jackson, 1968). What students actually learn about what music *is* would prove to have quite different characteristics growing out of the ideology of the Core Curriculum versus the Knowledge Promotion reform. On the one hand, if music teaching and learning is based on the Core Curriculum along with the first part of the music syllabus, students may learn that music is a subject wherein performance, participation, meaning, appreciation, and aural-motoric human abilities and qualities work together in developing a comprehensive understanding of music per se as well as of its multifarious cultural and societal aspects. On the other hand, if music teaching and learning is based on the Knowledge Promotion reform and its corresponding parts of the music curriculum, students may learn that music is a measurable and theoretical subject, with a component of technically oriented instrument playing, wherein, for example, the number of chords one can play on the guitar (e.g., Vinge, 2014, p. 224) is valued far beyond musical expression and artistic interpretation. As is evident from the foregoing, we hold that along with the implementation of the Knowledge Promotion reform and its related curriculum parts, programs, and guidelines, the focus has slid from the former way of perceiving the music subject to the latter. Consequently, through an extensive emphasis on the measurable aspects of evaluation, the day-to-day teaching practices of music have changed in ways that have made assessment outbalance the overall objectives with respect to impact. Thus, during the past ten years we have seen a shift from *assessment-based* to *assessment-governed* music education in Norway.

# IF *BILDUNG* AND PROGRESSIVE EDUCATION
## RULED THE WORLD

So, what would be a better solution to music assessment in Norway? As the reader may already have gathered, our sympathy—ideologically—does not lie with the current positivist and neopositivist assessment paradigm that seems to have taken over the Norwegian educational system during the past decade. As musicians, music educators, music teacher educators, and music education researchers, our educational-ideological standpoint is much closer to the *Bildung* and progressive education ideals expressed in the older part of the Norwegian curriculum. Within these latter traditions—and perhaps especially *Bildung*—assessment of the formative kind is seen as an integrated part of teaching, something that teachers should always conduct as part of their everyday work. However, this educational ideology does not come with a ready-made assessment program, campaign, or package. Rather, constant assessment—or vigilant attention to the progression of students—is a self-evident action of good teachers. As Dewey (1904/2008) reminds us, a teacher should develop the mental habit of looking "upon the internal, not upon the external; [a habit] which sees that the important function of the teacher is direction of the mental movement of the student" (p. 793), and certainly not the incessant collection of numeric evidence of the student's performance. This direction of mental movement—or facilitation of student *learning*, to use a more common word—requires careful and thoughtful formative assessment and feedback from the teacher's side in order to enhance student growth. This way of conducting assessment also strongly resonates with the assessment practices already inbuilt in most traditions of music learning and teaching, in which the teacher's whole being—her verbal comments, eye movements, and body language—will always contain real-time and constantly updated information to students about what works, what could be improved, and how to make this happen. In what follows, we briefly outline an alternative to the current way of assessing the music subject in Norway, one that we believe resonates better with the *Bildung* and progressive education ideals expressed in the curriculum as well as with the long-standing practices and traditions of assessment in the subject of music as such.

The foundations for our alternative lie in the North American curriculum theory and more specifically in the writings of Michael Scriven (1973), Robert Stake (1967), and Eliot Eisner (1967, 1969). Criticizing Tyler's notion and practice of objectives together with the development of taxonomies after World War II as well as the test development of the 1960s (see Pinar, Reynolds, Slattery, & Taubman, 1995), they introduced principles of curriculum evaluation such as the conceptual split between formative and summative assessment and the notion of expressive objectives. They also questioned the potential of formulating objectives in behavioral terms and spoke up for holistic assessment, capturing more than the sum of a row of taxonomically sorted achievements. Warning against the dangers of viewing education "with a microscope rather than with a panoramic viewfinder" (Stake, 1967), they introduced the notion of goal-free evaluation (Scriven, 1973), in which assessment should be carried out by evaluators without particular knowledge of the stated objectives or goals. Thereby assessment attends to all the consequences of the curriculum, not just "those intended by those writing objectives" (Pinar et al., 1995, p. 734).

Concerning music as a school subject, establishing such a basis would redirect our assessment principles and procedures in ways that would take music seriously to a much larger extent than it is within the present system of assessment. We would be able to pay increased attention to the processes and worthiness of formative assessment (Scriven, 1973) in music, providing space for developing this kind of assessment practice without solely focusing its function on future, summative connections. This might allot teachers and students more freedom in choosing what music to work with and how to work with it compared with the strong, implicit governance of the present system that is effectuated by the assessment criteria and the restrictions of their use. Or, to quote Keith Swanwick (1999), it would allow us to "[teach] music musically" (p. iii). Moreover, we could reformulate the objectives and assessment principles of the music subject in order to arrive at expressive objectives (Eisner, 1967, 1969), "written metaphorically and not behaviourally or operationally" (Pinar et al., 1995, p. 734), describing students' musical development, participation in projects, attitudes toward unknown music cultures, and ability of musical expression, to mention some relevant priorities. Among these objectives would be some worthy of pursuing regardless of how well they are achieved (p. 734), because they are important for developing the subject in certain directions. Following such priorities might also revitalize music's own assessment traditions, embedded in Eisner's notions of connoisseurship and the artist as an evaluator (Eisner, 1985).

In Norway, and perhaps elsewhere, the positivist and neopositivist turn of assessment philosophy has hampered the further development of the qualitative curriculum and assessment philosophy as well as its practice in music, which in fact was given much attention in earlier curricula. Furthermore, with respect to curriculum coherence—or to our introductory comments about curricula being expected to function as points of departure for providing coherent guidelines for education—the case of Norway is a lost one, since our current formal curriculum is inherently incoherent, ideologically speaking. What we can hope and strive for, however, is a better and more thoughtful balance between the priorities emphasized by its different foundational traditions and philosophies, perhaps especially in the area of assessment. Thus, it is time that we recognize the shortcomings of the present and assessment-governed system and initiate the development of an assessment philosophy that will give the music subject, our students, and ourselves a better future.

## NOTES

1. Schooling in Norway is compulsory for years 1–10 (primary and lower secondary school). All students have the right to attend years 11–13 (upper secondary school), but this is not compulsory by law. Although the curriculum being used as a point of departure for this chapter spans primary, secondary, and adult education, we are primarily concerned with the part covering compulsory schooling.

2. In the English version of the Norwegian music subject curriculum, the word *kompetansemål* (which is used in the version available in Norwegian) is translated as "competence aims." However, a more accurate translation would be "objectives," denoting the more detailed goals that students should meet during their education. Hence, hereafter when referring to *kompetansemål*, we use "objectives."

3. Whether or not actual grades should be given, it is customary in most primary and lower secondary schools in Norway to operationalize the subject curricula objectives into the tax-onomic levels of low, medium, and high goal achievement. At the lower secondary stage, these levels are again connected to actual grades on a scale from 1 to 6. Such practices are not described in the actual curricular texts but have come to constitute a significant part of teachers' work of operationalizing these texts into local strategies for assessment.

4. Typically, during the school year students will be given many smaller tasks, which will be assessed individually. Instead of using these tasks as checkpoints for formative supervisory assessment, all tasks will be graded in a summative way, and then those grades will be added up toward a final, summative assessment at the end of the year.

# REFERENCES

Allport, G. (1961). *Pattern and growth in personality* (2nd ed.). New York: Holt, Rinehart & Winston.

Almqvist, C. F., Vinge, J., Väkevä, L., & Zandén, O. (2017). Assessment *as* learning in music education: The risk of "criteria compliance" replacing "learning" in the Scandinavian countries. *Music Education Research*, 39(1), 3–18.

Bergesen, H. O. (2006). *Kampen om kunnskapsskolen* [The battle about the school of knowledge]. Oslo: Universitetsforlaget.

Black, P., & Wiliam, D. (1998). *Inside the black box: Raising standards through classroom assessment*. London: GL Assessment.

Dewey, J. (1904/2008). The relation of theory to practice in education. In M. Cochran-Smith, S. Feiman-Nemser, D. J. McIntyre, & K. E. Demers (Eds.), *Handbook of research on teacher education: Enduring questions in changing contexts* (3rd ed., pp. 787–98). New York: Routledge.

Dewey, J. (1921). *Democracy and education: An introduction to the philosophy of education*. New York: Macmillan.

Dewey, J. (1934). *Art as experience*. New York: Capricorn Books.

Drucker, P. F. (1954). *The practice of management*. New York: Harper & Row.

Eisner, E. W. (1967). Educational objectives: Help or hindrance. *School Review*, 75, 250–60.

Eisner, E. W. (1969). Instructional and expressive objectives: Their formulation and use in curriculum. In W. Popham, E. W. Eisner, H. Sullivan, & L. Tyler (Eds.), *Instructional objectives* (pp. 1–31). A.E.R.A Monograph Series on Curriculum Evaluation: No. 3. Chicago: Rand McNally.

Eisner, E. W. (1985). *The art of educational evaluation: A personal view*. London and Philadelphia, PA: The Falmer Press.

Elstad, E., & Sivesind, K. (Eds.). (2010). *PISA—sannheten om skolen?* [PISA—the truth about the school?]. Oslo: Universitetsforlaget.

Goodlad, J., Klein, F., & Tye, K. (1979). *Curriculum inquiry: The study of curriculum practice*. New York: McGraw-Hill.

Hanken, I. M., & Johansen, G. (2013). *Musikkundervisningens didaktikk* [The *Didaktik* of music education]. Oslo: Cappelen Damm Akademisk Forlag.

Hattie, J. (2009). *Visible learning*. New York: Routledge.

Jackson, P. (1968). *Life in classrooms*. New York: Holt, Rinehart & Winston.

Kilpatrick, W. H. (1918). *The project method*. New York: Teachers College Record.

Klafki, W. (2000a). *Didaktik* analysis as the core of preparation of instruction. In I. Westbury, S. Hopmann, & K. Riquarts (Eds.), *Teaching as a reflective practice: The German* Didaktik *tradition* (pp. 139–59). London: Erlbaum.

Klafki, W. (2000b). The significance of classical theories of *Bildung* for a contemporary concept of *Allgemeinbildung*. In I. Westbury, S. Hopmann, & K. Riquarts (Eds.), *Teaching as a reflective practice: The German* Didaktik *tradition* (pp. 85–107). London: Erlbaum.

Maslow, A. (1954). *Motivation and personality*. New York: Harper and Row.

Municipality of Oslo Education Authority. (2009). *Vurdering i musikk på ungdomstrinnet: Veileder* [Assessment in music at the lower secondary school level: A guide]. Retrieved from http://www.musikkpedagogikk.no/sfiles/9/33/2/file/veileder-vurdering-i-musikk.pdf

Norwegian Directorate for Education and Training. (2005). *Norwegian Directorate for Education and Training*. Retrieved from http://www.udir.no/Stottemeny/English/Norwegian-Directorate-for-Education-and-Training/

Norwegian Directorate for Education and Training. (2006a). *Knowledge promotion—Kunnskapsløftet*. Retrieved from http://www.udir.no/Stottemeny/English/Curriculum-in-English/_english/Knowledge-promotion—Kunnskapsloftet/

Norwegian Directorate for Education and Training. (2006b). *Music subject curriculum*. Retrieved from http://www.udir.no/Stottemeny/English/Curriculum-in-English/Curricula-in-English/

Norwegian Directorate for Education and Training. (2006c). *The quality framework*. Retrieved from http://www.udir.no/globalassets/upload/larerplaner/fastsatte_lareplaner_for_kunnskapsloeftet/prinsipper_lko6_eng.pdf

Norwegian Directorate for Education and Training. (2010). *Vurdering for læring* [Assessment for learning]. Retrieved from http://www.udir.no/Vurdering-for-laring/

Norwegian Ministry of Church, Education and Research. (1993). *Core curriculum for primary, secondary and adult education in Norway*. Retrieved from http://www.udir.no/globalassets/upload/larerplaner/generell_del/5/core_curriculum_english.pdf

Norwegian Ministry of Education and Research. (2002). *Førsteklasses fra første klasse: Forslag til rammeverk for et nasjonalt kvalitetsvurderingssystem av norsk grunnopplæring* [First-class from first class: Outline of a framework for a national quality assurance system for Norwegian compulsory education]. Retrieved from https://www.regjeringen.no/no/dokumenter/nou-2002-10/id145378/?ch=1&q=

Norwegian Ministry of Education and Research. (2003). *I første rekke: Forsterket kvalitet i en grunnopplæring for alle* [First and foremost: Strengthened quality in compulsory education for all]. Retrieved from https://www.regjeringen.no/no/dokumenter/nou-2003-16/id147077/

Odiorne, G. S. (1965). *Management by objectives: A system of managerial leadership*. New York: Pitman Publishing Corp.

Organisation for Economic Co-operation and Development (OECD). (n.d.). *About PISA*. Retrieved from http://www.oecd.org/pisa/aboutpisa/

Pinar, W. F., Reynolds, W. M., Slattery, P., & Tauberman, P. M. (1995). *Understanding curriculum: An introduction to the study of historical and contemporary curriculum discourses. Studies in the Postmodern Theory of Education: Vol. 17*. New York: Peter Lang.

Rogers, C. (1970). *Freedom to learn*. Toledo, OH: Merrill.

Scriven, M. (1973). Goal-free evaluation. In E. House (Ed.), *School evaluation: The politics and the process* (pp. 319–28). Berkley, CA: McCutchan.

Stake, R. (1967). The countenance of educational evaluation. *Teachers College Record, 68*, 523–40.

Swanwick, K. (1999). *Teaching music musically*. London: Routledge.

TIMSS & PIRLS International Study Center. (2015). *Latest publications from TIMSS and PIRLS*. Retrieved from http://timssandpirls.bc.edu/

Tyler, R. W. (1949). *Basic principles of curriculum and instruction*. Chicago: University of Chicago Press.

Varkøy, Ø. (2010). Musikkopplevelse som eksistensiell erfaring [Musical experience as existential experience]. In G. Salvesen & J. H. Sætre (Eds.), *Allmenn musikkundervisning* (pp. 23–38). Oslo: Gyldendal Akademisk Forlag.

Vinge, J. (2014). *Vurdering i musikkfag: En deskriptiv, analytisk studie av musikklæreres vurderingspraksis i ungdomsskolen* [Assessment in the music subject: A descriptive-analytic study of music teachers' assessment practices in the lower secondary school]. (Unpublished doctoral dissertation). Norwegian Academy of Music, Oslo.

Westbury, I. (2000). Teaching as a reflective practice: What might *Didaktik* teach curriculum? In I. Westbury, S. Hopmann, & K. Riquarts (Eds.), *Teaching as a reflective practice: The German* Didaktik *tradition* (pp. 15–39). Mahwah, NJ: Erlbaum.

CHAPTER 24

...................................................................................

# BUILDING A CULTURE OF ETHICAL, COMPARABLE, AUTHENTIC ASSESSMENT

*music education in queensland*

...................................................................................

ANDREW REID AND JULIE BALLANTYNE

ASSESSMENT within music education is called on to shift and change as global and educational priorities and challenges shift and change (Broadfoot, 2009, p. ix). Appropriate responses to such forces are often best viewed and evaluated retrospectively. In this vein, the recent experiences of music assessment in Queensland are discussed in an effort to share the evolving response to problems faced by other complex, large-scale music curriculum and assessment systems and to provoke discussion about assessment in school music education. This reflection on the story of Queensland's experience in senior secondary school music over the past twenty years aims to provide a unique example of music's place in the growing discourse on complex interactions among standards-based assessment, curriculum design, teacher autonomy, education communities and system-level structures. Through designing quality syllabi and developing supportive systemic mechanisms, Queensland demonstrated an innovative, evolving approach to building a culture of ethical, comparable, authentic assessment in music. The writers aim to share Queensland's recent experiences, not as a critique, but as a narrative and description of the evolution of music assessment within a specific Australian context, one that has aspired to build inclusive and diverse music assessment opportunities in a climate of increasing conservative influence on educational policy and systems. The subject music, of course, does not exist in a vacuum, and this is not a complete story, as its evolution and influences continue.

This chapter first introduces the recent past context of Queensland, Australia, and explains its system of externally moderated, school-based assessment, which has been in place for approximately forty years. This is followed by an explanation of how Queensland's music curriculum and assessment approach developed over time within that system, including specific reference to evolving syllabus frameworks, and the experiences involved in designing and aligning music curriculum and assessment using dimensions, objectives, and standards. The chapter then details approaches that were used to develop music assessment strategies, procedures, and instruments within a school-based moderation environment and related experiences of both developing teachers as assessors, and building music assessment cultures and communities. The chapter concludes by provoking the reader to consider implications for other contexts.

# Queensland, Australia

Queensland is the second largest state in Australia. It covers an area of 1.85 million square kilometers and has a population of approximately five million. Queensland is home to many Aboriginal peoples and Torres Strait Islander peoples, who were and are the first musicians of this state. Their songs, art, stories, and dances tell of times past and of today. Queensland's peoples and cultures are as varied as its immense environment, living in large urban cities, rural and remote settings, and coastal and island communities, with diverse cultural identities, heritages, and histories. This diversity of Queensland's peoples, their pasts, and their collective current and future cultures, multiple narratives, and varying perspectives is a key richness and challenge that has shaped the development of music curriculum and assessment in Queensland.

Each year approximately fifty thousand students complete senior schooling, and Queensland's population is growing. Secondary schooling is compulsory to year 10, and completion rates to year 12 are high. Schools are administered by government, religious, independent, and other bodies, and the Queensland Curriculum and Assessment Authority (QCAA) provides curriculum, assessment, and certification to all sectors. Senior music is one subject within the suite of subjects offered to students. Students elect approximately six subjects to make up their two-year senior course of study (ages sixteen to seventeen), and approximately twenty-two thousand have completed year 12 music over the last ten years. Queensland has a long history of state-funded specialist music education for every child in primary classroom settings, alongside complementary instrumental music programs.

# Externally Moderated, School-Based Assessment in Queensland

In an instructional video produced for the assessment authority, Gordon Stobart commented that "Queensland has something that is really remarkable—a system of high-stakes assessment in which the teachers are at the center. That school-based assessment is trusted as a way of arriving at a reliable decision about student achievement" (QCAA, 2015a, p. 1).

In Queensland, a standards-based approach to senior music has been implemented through a system of externally moderated, school-based assessment since the 1970s. This system will be replaced by 2020 with a system combining internal and external assessments. Across the state, a professional culture and community has been in place to support and assist schools in meeting requirements of the syllabus and to moderate school-based decisions about student achievement. Within this context, teachers have played several vital roles. They have developed their own programs, devised and implemented assessments, and made judgments about students within their classes against set criteria and qualitative music standards describing the full range of context-specific student achievements. The moderation system has engaged panels of experienced music teachers coordinated and trained by the central state authority to review and discuss schools' decision-making in relation to mandated conditions and standards (QCAA, 2015b, 2015c). Schools have developed and implemented internal structures to facilitate the system, coordinated by principals, heads of curriculum, and teachers. The system has been characterized as a partnership between schools and the assessment authority, and detailed manuals have provided consistent policies, protocols, procedures, and guidelines (see Appendix A: Definitions).

The process of moderation has been key to the system producing results that "stand up" to scrutiny in a high-stakes assessment environment. As seen in figure 24.1, moderation has been a staged process, which initially involved periodic subject syllabus development and revision. From this document, each school generated a school-specific work program outlining its approach, which was reviewed and approved by the central body, the assessment authority. The process then progressed for each cohort through the year 11 and 12 courses.

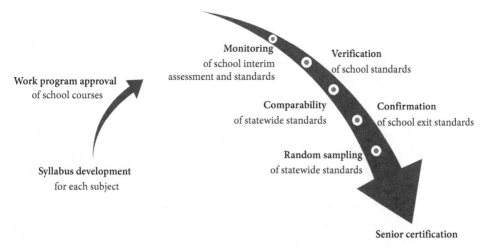

FIGURE 24.1 Queensland's system of externally moderated, school-based assessment

Approximately halfway through the course, trained district review panels of teachers moderated school samples demonstrating schools' capacity to develop effective assessment instruments and make interim judgments. In music, sample portfolios included assessment instruments and student responses: written, digital, and audiovisual materials. Information was collated centrally by the assessment authority to guide training, professional development, and state reports.

Prior to course completion, trained review panels of teachers met to moderate samples and provide advice to schools about judgments of student achievement in course objectives, against syllabus standards, and in awarding levels of achievement. In music, sample portfolios included assessment instruments and responses: written, digital, and audiovisual materials.

Following this, school submissions of sample portfolios were sent to trained state review panels to compare the extent to which judgments across the state were comparable to each other and to the syllabus standards, and to inform state reports. In music, information was gained about developments and patterns across the state in assessment task design, application of standards, and changes in students' musical styles and genres of expression.

Detailed checking processes ensured that data for student achievement and placement were correct and that moderation processes had been followed.

A stratified random sample of student portfolios would be undertaken in nominated subjects to consider the question: How consistently do teachers around Queensland apply standards in determining students' levels of achievement in Authority subjects? Senior music was last randomly sampled in 2014.

The system's foundation of teacher professional learning communities has been vital to creating a culture of ongoing professional development in assessment (Black & Wiliam, 2007). Such learning communities (Wenger, McDermott, & Snyder, 2002) assist teachers to develop shared understandings and practices around music assessment, enabling them to become more effective as teachers and assessors through their shared experiences.

Over time these learning communities have facilitated regular, robust professional dialogues about how curriculum, teaching, learning, assessment, and standards contribute to better music assessment practices. They are characterized by a community of people with relationships based on making change through music education in their individual schools and professional networks. While the assessment authority is charged with the task of quality, valid, authentic, reliable, and equitable outcomes through a formalized large-scale structure, teachers have consistently recognized additional professional development benefits, their professional growth, and personal connections made across the geographically, demographically, culturally, and musically diverse state. As Carol Myford claimed in a keynote address : "When people ask me who is at the cutting edge, my first response is "look down under."... On re-reading a 1985 account of Queensland's externally moderated school-based assessment, I remember thinking how truly revolutionary it was in its scope. Upon my second reading and taking into consideration the political realities of the late 1990s...I find it even more remarkable.

My reaction to this program has moved up at least two notches on the excitement scale" (cited in Matters, 2006).

## ALIGNING MUSIC CURRICULUM AND ASSESSMENT: DIMENSIONS, OBJECTIVES, AND STANDARDS

Alignment among dimensions, objectives, and standards has been a key feature of the assessment system in Queensland. The framework allows for diverse and individual demonstrations of music knowledge and skills, while maintaining a consistent benchmark for teachers, students, and review panels. The use of "uniform criteria and standards across the state allows for a variety of approach in assessment and helps to achieve comparability without destroying the autonomy of the school" (Sadler, cited in Bell, Allen, & Brennan, 1986/2011, p. 59). In the Queensland context, this alignment does not denote "standardization" of assessments, and this distinction is vital. Rather, the opposite has been the aim: a robust structural basis upon which to support the widest and most inclusive individual expressions of Queensland's musical voices, cultures, histories, perspectives, and identities through providing ample points of differentiation in how the standards may be met. The intent of these structures has been to enable Queensland's growing cultural richness of diverse young musical "voices" to be heard and assessed equitably across the spectrum of contexts.

Alongside structural considerations, a key cultural feature of assessment development in Queensland has been the ownership and engagement felt by teachers and the feedback loop built into the process of moderation (see previous discussion). The following section details the ways that the syllabus has developed and changed over time as a result of teacher and student experiences, predominantly observed through the moderation process. By viewing the evolution of key concepts and processes, it is possible to see how Queensland's assessment culture and community has been crucial to the development of this curriculum and assessment structure.

## DEVELOPING QUEENSLAND'S MUSIC CURRICULUM AND ASSESSMENT

Queensland music students in the senior years of schooling (years 11 and 12) have over the past twenty years been taught by teachers following a series of syllabi: the 1995, 2004, and 2013 versions of a document designed to guide pedagogy and to detail assessment requirements across the state. The 1995 syllabus was revised in 2004 and implemented in

2006. This document was revised in 2013 and implemented in 2014. The ways that these syllabi have developed and the impetus for the revisions are discussed in detail in the following section. While it is acknowledged that no syllabus document is perfect, by describing the development of this syllabus through its current iteration, it is hoped that insights may be provided for others facing similar challenges in the development of music assessment systems.

Underlying the Queensland senior music syllabi of 1995, 2004, and 2013 has been an articulated (and diagrammatically represented) conceptual framework. This framework provided the internal structure for all curriculum and assessment. The diagrammatic representation in figure 24.2 shows the progression of complexity of music syllabi over time. The 1995 diagram with "Repertoire" at the core and a simple relationship representation of three dimensions and learning experiences developed into a more complex set of contributing factors in the 2004 syllabus framework focusing on "Audiation," adapted from the work of Edwin Gordon. The developing complexity of this refinement is evident in the 2013 construct with "Musicianship" at the core, reflecting the complex interrelationships among the component parts and that each part of the music curriculum jigsaw contributes singularly and collectively to the whole. For these reasons, figure 24.2 demonstrates a move toward musicianship cognition, recognition of complexity, provision for diversity, and an increasingly robust framework to support flexible implementation and assessment.

While there are many aims of any course in music, arguably the most fundamental common goal is to develop engaged musicianship. Musicianship is at the core of all learning in the 2013 senior music syllabus, and establishing its meaning frames all discussion, although it is not separately assessed. The 2013 syllabus states that "all learning in Senior Music leads to developing students' musicianship, i.e. the unique set of knowledge, understanding, skills, attitudes and dispositions that allows students to engage in all forms of music making and music interaction. Music is sound, and any experience of

|  1995  |  2004  |  2013  |
|---|---|---|

| Taken from Queensland Board of Senior Secondary School Studies: Senior Music Syllabus 1995 | Taken from Queensland Studies Authority Senior Music Syllabus 2004 | Taken from Queensland Studies Authority Senior Music Syllabus 2013 |

FIGURE 24.2

music is essentially and fundamentally aural. Students develop their inner hearing, music skills, techniques and artistry when they have opportunities to use their imagination, creativity, personal and social skills in music making" (QSA, 2013, Introduction).

Differentiation in music assessment is made possible when essential pillars of "what students know" form the structural foundations, applicable to the widest range of contexts. The introduction of elements of music in the 2004 revision as a structuring device provided clarity for music curriculum and assessment in Queensland. This equipped teachers with a common reference point for pedagogy, assessment, and moderation. It provided a through-line for the content around which processes, cognitions, and practices could revolve, as well as internal stability to the syllabus and flexibility in resultant teaching, learning, and assessment. With this content basis for curriculum, teaching and learning, and assessment, structural frameworks for organizing connections became more complex, able to cover increasingly diverse needs such as established and evolving cultural identities and considerations, creativities, and notions of rigor.

Statewide moderation reports from 2005–2015 noted significant improvement in teacher-devised and -implemented assessment as well as associated improvement in student responses (QCAA, 2005–2015). Teachers indicated that the elements of music emphasis in the 2004 syllabus gave them a common language with which to approach the subject of music, something that they had worked hard to figure out but had not previously codified. The list of elements of music is not prescriptive or exhaustive, and it was arrived at to establish a terminology for learning in, through, and about music that was applicable to the broadest range of contexts, styles, and genres. These factors, as well as the caveat that it is not exhaustive, resulted in the list's being retained and refined in the 2013 revision (see Appendix B: Elements).

When establishing "what students can do," differentiation in music assessment is made possible by designing essential dimensions and objectives that are clear and unambiguous and applicable to the widest range of contexts. The 2013 syllabus defined dimensions and objectives as being "the salient properties or characteristics of distinctive learning for this subject. The dimensions are described through their objectives and it is these that schools are required to teach and that students should have the opportunity to learn. The objectives describe what students should know and be able to do by the end of the course of study.... Schools must assess how well students have achieved the objectives. The standards have a direct relationship with the objectives, and are described in the same dimensions as the objectives" (QSA, 2013, p. 2). While the entire course may be seen as an iterative process of developing engaged musicianship through distinct but interrelated dimensions of *Composition, Musicology,* and *Performance,*[1] explanation of individual dimensions using a number of objectives may be seen as an internal process, which may be iterative and nonsequential or step by step. This flexibility was necessary in music curriculum, where dimensions are complex processes; it allowed for various pedagogical methodologies and approaches that teachers wish to use, as well as catering for student differentiation and varied assessment.

A change took place between the 2004 and 2013 syllabi in the structure of dimensions and objectives. This involved an increased consistency of structure across all syllabi.

In music, a shift from a single statement about each dimension (*Composition*, *Musicology*, *Performance*) to a more refined explanation of separate but interrelated objectives within each dimension had several implications for assessment. First, it provided clarity for teachers in understanding the salient properties and characteristics of the dimension, improving their ability to plan and develop assessment tasks. Second, it proposed an effective scaffold within which students may respond. A process for working may be inferred, but not required; while some student musicians arrive at creative processes of composition and performance in an entirely holistic way, this provides scope to organize and manage their assessment responses. Third, it offered a framework for developing assessment standards to support teacher decision-making, as each objective within the dimension may be expressed for its own complexity or challenge in the associated standards.

The three dimensions in the syllabi—*Composition*, *Musicology*, and *Performance*— provide the foundations for all assessment strategies and have changed over time, in line with assessment requirements, and the articulated role of musicianship. Regarding *Composition*, the 2013 syllabus states:

> The dimension Composition involves the creation of music by combining music elements and concepts (see Section 3.2.1) in a range of contexts, styles and genres (see Section 3.1.3). It entails innovation through exploring and experimenting with sound to synthesize and express personal music ideas and enhance musicianship in Musicology and Performance. In Senior Music, students are expected to be able to:
> - select and apply music elements and concepts in the creation of their own works
> - demonstrate composition techniques in the creation of their own works
> - synthesize and communicate music ideas and stylistic characteristics to create their own works.   (QSA, 2013, p. 2)

The internal iterative process established in *Composition* objectives demonstrates how clarity can support differentiated compositional teaching, learning, and assessment while ensuring comparable creative student work. This structure does not dictate specific context, style, or genre; rather, it provides a flexible approach to allow schools to explore and assess all types of music and creative composition. Students are able to select, manipulate, and express using skills, techniques, and devices relevant to the particular genre they choose to compose in, inclusive of their own and others' cultural and musical heritages, histories, and identities.

In syllabus revisions of *Composition*, increased inclusivity of these characteristics was the key factor in providing equity, particularly in terms of building upon Western traditional forms and in creativities of increasingly diverse Queensland cultures of the present and into the future. This catered to a rise in musical fusions and enabled the move from twentieth-century constructs of school composition to more progressive notions of compositional expression. Developments in the 2004 and 2013 syllabi emphasized manipulating musical elements and compositional devices to convey context, style, and genre. Arguably, this allowed for students to authentically express their own creative voices.

It was noted in reports that there was an increasing variety of styles and genres in *Composition* and formats of presentation (QCAA, 2005–2015). Teachers' own pedagogical approaches to compositional teaching were catered for, and provision was made for students' aesthetics and personal tastes. In this way, creating music was given a flexible and fluid structure, while providing enough framing to be practical.

Technological advances impacted assessment in this dimension over time and influenced the development of the syllabus framing of *Composition*. As students and teachers gained greater access to and proficiency in quality digital music technologies, developments in teaching techniques and discourses related to composition changed also. There has been increasing complexity in student responses and musical success in creative work. Teachers have stated that the reason for this is mainly twofold. First, the immediacy of aural response by students when composing using digital technologies meant that they made more rapid and authentically aural decisions in self-editing and structuring music, which pleased them aurally, not just theoretically. For some, the "pen had come to sing." Second, fast editing techniques using digital music technologies enabled an increase in the scope of compositions, as students were able to structure larger-scale works in more manageable ways. For some, the ability to document the intentions of their music ideas was the key feature; removing the need to assess notation meant that those styles and genres that for cultural, historical, and ethnic reasons are more authentically documented using recorded sound rather than a score could be presented alongside the same objectives and standards as notated scores.

Regarding *Musicology*, the 2013 syllabus states: "The dimension Musicology involves the study of music in social, historical and cultural contexts. It entails researching, analyzing and evaluating repertoire and other music sources, in a range of contexts, styles and genres, to synthesize and express a music viewpoint, and enhance musicianship in Composition and Performance" (pp. 2–3). The *Musicology* dimension has seen significant change in the course of the revisions of the syllabus, alongside broader developments in critical thinking, problem solving, literacy policy, and inquiry learning. In earlier syllabus iterations, the dimension was labeled "*Listening*," and assessment emphasized repertoire knowledge and application through visual analysis of scores, aural analysis of recordings, and aural skills. At that time, internal school-based examinations were implemented for all three of these areas, resulting in a heavier emphasis on this dimension than on *Composition*. Subcriteria were used to structure and assess students' knowledge, application, and communication, which were further classified into detailed subsets. In the 2004 revision, greater emphasis in assessment was placed on cognitive processing of musical information, holistically using visual and/or aural stimulus in order to make meaning. The dimension was labeled "*Analyzing repertoire*" and required students to deconstruct and evaluate interrelationships among elements and context, style and genre with justification. The 2013 iteration provided a more robust internal framework of musical problem solving through identification, analysis and evaluation, justification, synthesis, and communication. Of significant importance was inclusion in tasks of a personal or individual "viewpoint" for students to arrive at, to serve as a reference or concrete position, rather than comparing or contrasting various works or ideas for a preordained, stated purpose.

Whereas assessment emphasis had previously been on students' ability to read scores and listen to works, additional emphasis was placed on working with the techniques and tools of a musicologist. Therefore, students were expected to perceive and interpret; analyze; evaluate and determine; and synthesize, justify, and communicate using elements and concepts, repertoire and music sources. In so doing, they could explore individual ways to express their findings, viewpoints, and music ideas. This flexible framework allowed for increasingly broad contexts, styles, and genres, while still providing a robust platform for measuring achievement in the analytical dimension.

Successive state panel reports indicated that teachers required support in this dimension, as understandings of analysis, synthesis, and justification developed over time and worked with models of inquiry-based learning found in other subject areas (QCAA, 2005–2015).

Deeper statewide understandings of assessment in deconstruction and evaluation within the 2004 syllabus evolved to more complex processes of analysis, synthesis, evaluation, and justifying a viewpoint in the 2013 document. A key priority of professional development was authentic analysis and evaluation of both task design and student responses.

Regarding *Performance*, the 2013 syllabus states: "The dimension Performance involves the interpretation of music elements and concepts through playing, singing and/or conducting in context. It entails communicating music to audiences through the synthesis of music ideas, stylistic characteristics and practices, while enhancing musicianship in Composition and Musicology" (p. 3). As notions of what constitutes performance developed over time, the framework of dimensions, objectives, and standards provided a comprehensive structure for allowing differentiation among students while maintaining comparable standards. *Performance* has seen the greatest diversity in student and teacher aptitudes, ability, aesthetics, preferences, cultural heritages, identities, and backgrounds, which influence the ways teachers and students learn, teach, express and experience, and assess music. There is a wide variety of school resourcing required for performance across any school district, and differences in a state the size of Queensland are immense.

The 1995 syllabus emphasized assessment of students' literacy, technique, and interpretation in numerous separate tasks for singing and playing in large and small ensembles, conducting, and sight-reading. The 2004 revision reduced this to a holistic approach of interpreting music ideas to an audience through one *Performance* assessment task in any context, style, and genre that best revealed students' abilities. Further development in the 2013 syllabus involved a combination of these constructs, reflecting positive aspects of the 1995 approach and flexibilities of the 2004 approach.

To ensure equity, diversity, and inclusivity in assessment, no stipulated lists of repertoire were provided in the syllabi. Advice was added to syllabi about considerations for selection of repertoire, supporting teacher and student identity and autonomy, and ensuring that the complexity of repertoire allowed students opportunities to demonstrate standards for *Performance* and provided realistic challenge in technique.

The following sections detail how the Queensland assessment frameworks have been implemented through building a culture and community of music teachers.

# Developing Standards
# for Assessing Music

> There are qualities that we can recognize as *musical* wherever they appear.
> Can we identify these qualities? If we can then we are on the way towards
> declaring our criteria for musical assessment, towards putting our cards
> on the table. The task is challenging. What are we looking for?
>
> —Swanwick (1999, p. 74)

In responding to challenges similar to those identified by Keith Swanwick, the
Queensland Curriculum and Assessment Authority has since 1995 provided standard
descriptors to cater to issues of equity and comparability across diverse musical contexts. This does not mean that assessment has been "standardized"; rather, standards
descriptors have been developed to be applied to the vast, evolving, and complex
cultural and musical landscape of Queensland's music students and teachers. These
standards have had a direct relationship to each corresponding dimension and its objectives and have qualitatively described variance on a five-point scale at more thorough,
sophisticated, or nuanced levels, or at less than adequate range. Using the alignment
approach, a key principle in devising standards has been to replicate the statement of the
objectives as the C or satisfactory standard statement, then describe discernible differences across a five-point scale of variance (see Appendix C: Standards (*Composition*)).

# Developing Music Assessment
# Strategies, Procedures, and
# Instruments in a School-Based
# Moderation Environment

Paul Black and Dylan Wiliam (2007) recognize the effectiveness of the Queensland
system in providing valid, reliable, and authentic assessment results: "A [third] method
is the use of group moderation meetings, as described for Queensland. The experience
there, following the detailed guidelines, shows how teachers' assessments, even with a
range and variety of assessment events, can achieve higher reliability than external tests
and can also help achieve higher standards of validity in that the contexts for assessment
reflect those of the learning experience, and resemble the contexts of future application
of learning more closely than the context of the examination room" (p. 41). To build
assessment capacity, professional development and training centered on five main characteristics of effective assessment instruments: a clear and unambiguous task statement,
an indication of the dimensions and objectives that are being assessed in the task, clearly

stated associated conditions under which the assessment is to be completed, guidelines for the parameters within which students should work, and assessment standards to be used to measure achievement. A balance between those aspects that are mandated and those that are flexible was provided to teachers by the syllabi, and sample assessment tasks provided on centralized digital platforms built teachers' assessment knowledge, skill, and capacity.

This approach and structure were implemented with the goal of increasing validity, reliability, and authenticity in assessment and supported teachers and students in tailoring the requirements of music assessment to their individual school settings and the ways that music manifests within their schools and communities. With these underpinnings, students' demonstration of their achievement may be diverse in context, style, genre, and format, but the assessment structure caters for statewide difference. Clear articulation of these messages ensured comparable reference points within and across the state.

## DEVELOPING TEACHERS AS ASSESSORS

In Queensland's externally moderated, school-based experience of senior music, aiming to ensure valid, reliable, and comparable assessment decisions has relied on building teachers' understanding of how to make various kinds of judgments. A progressively higher level of consistency and comparability in statewide judgments across the life span of each syllabus was noted when teachers made an on-balance judgment about the range of evidence in individual portfolios compared to the syllabus standards. Building teacher assessment capacity focused on making a judgment in two ways. First was making judgments about an individual student response by looking for evidence to match characteristics and qualities within student work to syllabus standards descriptors, then making an on-balance judgment about the overall match within the assessment task response to a particular standard. Second, professional development focused on making larger-scale judgments over the course of study by considering students' portfolios of various assessment work that demonstrates their achievements in the full range of dimensions and objectives of the syllabus. Requirements stipulated in syllabi guided statewide consistency of these portfolios while allowing for the individual nature of student responses and portfolios to vary. Provisions for variety in assessment techniques and modes were detailed in all syllabus versions, reinforcing the construct of rigor in flexible contexts.

## BUILDING MUSIC ASSESSMENT
## CULTURES AND COMMUNITIES

Teachers' engagement in the moderation process, as musicians, pedagogues, assessors, and panelists, arguably gave them agency and mobility within the assessment culture and community of music. This was especially the case for those involved beyond the school level, as members of moderation panels, committees, and reference groups. Access to and participation in the moderation process, from the "chalk-face" to the "panel meeting" and "syllabus design," facilitated a sense of collegiality, common understanding, and room for difference and created an arena for capacity building and development. Developing this culture of assessment in music within the Queensland moderation system has required developing teachers' assessment expertise, agency, and community.

The success of strategies in ensuring consistent comparability in assessment was noted in the 2011 review conducted by the Australasian Curriculum, Assessment and Certification Authority (ACACA). Specific commendations were made for Queensland's assessment authority documentation and the strong training, support, and monitoring of panelists at all levels: school, region, and state. "The Queensland system rests on the expertise and commitment of the panelists (who conduct moderation meetings) and it is clear that QSA (QCAA) recognizes and supports the need to maintain a high level of expertise among its panelists" (Marion, Peck, & Raymond, 2011, p. 4).

In music, when teachers were provided an opportunity to encounter samples from outside their own musical, cultural, and teaching experience through structured discussions and analysis, they developed perspectives on how different contexts, styles, and genres fit within broad frameworks. The comparison of samples against explicit standards, in a collegial environment, "sharpens teacher judgment and builds knowledge and expertise about assessment more successfully than any other process" (Maxwell, 2004, p. 7). In addition, greater variety of student responses was seen as teachers developed theoretical and practical knowledge of a broader range of musical possibilities in assessment (QCAA, 2005–2015).

The alignment story of dimensions, objectives, and standards provided the clearest narrative structure for delivery of these messages in statewide training of review panelists and professional development of teachers. Implementing this model required common clarity of understanding and consistency of messaging. This was achieved through strategic, structured dialogue, and detailed supporting materials. Primary reference points for messages were music syllabi and documentation of moderation processes. Panelists were trained to match evidence to the standards, to find evidence to support schools' judgments. They did not re-mark work, but commented on the extent to which there was or was not a match. This understanding developed in Queensland via what may be described as an ongoing communication and feedback loop about music assessment, incorporating the spectrum of diverse cultural identities and perspectives across the state through evolving discourse, both formal and informal.

# Conclusion

Exploring Queensland's experiences reveals the intricate, organic interplay between evolving discipline and process ontologies and epistemologies of music assessment. The developing assessment framework and processes discussed demonstrate reconciliatory transitions between largely rationalist and constructivist philosophical approaches.

Fashioned from enacted and engaged social theory and theory of practice, Queensland's unique experiences may provide perspectives for others who face challenges in large-scale music assessment systems. The story and discussion of our unique context has enabled the development of some provocations that we continue to grapple with, and which similarly may be considered in all such systems:

1) How do we ensure that music assessment is conceptualized, devised, and implemented to address complex interactions among curriculum and assessment design, teacher autonomy, education communities, and system-level structures?

2) How can systems and structures be put in place to nurture cultures and communities of practice that sustainably ensure shared quality, consistency, and effectiveness, and also ensure successful, significant paradigm shifts?

3) To what extent do existing large-scale music assessment developments take into consideration the real contexts of students and teachers, providing strong support and development and a sense of belonging to a community and culture of practice? How can this be improved?

4) How effective is music curriculum and assessment design in recognizing and responding to increasing student identity and culture, differentiation, and musical diversity while aiming for valid, comparable outputs at micro and macro levels? How can curriculum and assessment design ensure an appropriate response to patterns and progress over time in educational assessment design, musicianship, and cultural priorities?

We are by no means at the end of this story; the education priorities and challenges continue to shift and change around us, and we continue to be challenged by our own provocations in providing the best possible music assessment for future students. Indeed, as stated previously, Queensland's system of externally moderated, school-based assessment is to be replaced by 2020 with a system combining internal and external assessments, resulting in a reconsideration and reshaping of this narrative as it rapidly progresses in new ways. As we consider these issues, we reflect on what we have learned in the pursuit of building a culture of ethical, comparable, authentic music assessment.

In order to build an assessment system that is *ethical*, music educators and assessors must challenge contexts for learning and measurement and move to value increased inclusivity. We must question what assessment structures, cultures, beliefs, and practices can enhance diversity in musics, for teachers and learners, and support them in their individual and collective musical journeys. An *ethical* assessment system must aim to engage and promote cultural diversity, inclusion, and respect as fundamentals.

In order to build a system that is *comparable*, music assessors must acknowledge and cater to the qualities and attributes of an ever-widening range of music and musicians, maintaining integrity of musicianship as a core value. The characteristics of dimensions and standards need to be commonly understood by those who have to interpret their meaning in a variety of contexts, particularly students and teachers, building musical individuality, agency, creativity, competence, and confidence. A *comparable* music assessment system must aim to achieve valid and reliable outputs at the micro and macro levels while fully accommodating diversity.

Finally, in order to build a system that is *authentic*, music assessors need to be clear about what and how they are assessing. We must build and participate in effective, respectful, informed, and understanding communities and cultures of practice to share this information in meaningful ways. An *authentic* music assessment system must aim to align stated objectives and associated standards clearly and unambiguously, while emphasizing that an inclusive concept of musicianship is central.

## APPENDIX A

# DEFINITIONS (FROM QCAA, 2014)

A syllabus is a document that prescribes the curriculum for a course of study for schools and includes standards of learning and of assessment.

A standard of learning is a statement of what students are expected to know and do by the end of key junctures of schooling (outcomes or objectives) and of the scope of that learning (core content or subject matter).

A standard of assessment is a fixed reference point used to describe how well students have achieved the outcomes, objectives, or essential learnings in syllabi. The standards of assessment are derived by groups of teachers and subject experts describing the actual differences in examples of student work.

A standards descriptor is a statement (or list of statements) that succinctly conveys the required quality of, or features in, student work necessary to be awarded a particular standard of achievement.

## APPENDIX B

# ELEMENTS OF MUSIC (FROM QSA, 2013)

- duration—the relative lengths of sounds and silences in music
- expressive devices—ways of influencing mood and character of music
- pitch—the relative frequency of sound
  - melody—the horizontal arrangement of sound
  - harmony—the vertical arrangement of sound
  - tonality—the organization of pitches that establishes tonal relationships
- structure—the form and design of music
- texture—the density of sound
- timbre—the characteristic quality of sound sources, or tone color

# APPENDIX C

## STANDARDS (*COMPOSITION*) (FROM QSA, 2013, P. 22)

| | Standard A | Standard B | Standard C | Standard D | Standard E |
|---|---|---|---|---|---|
| *Composition* | The student work has the following characteristics: | The student work has the following characteristics: | The student work has the following characteristics: | The student work has the following characteristics: | The student work has the following characteristics: |
| | consistent and proficient selection and application of music elements and concepts in the creation of their own works | effective selection and application of music elements and concepts in the creation of their own works | selection and application of music elements and concepts in the creation of their own works | variable selection and application of music elements and concepts in their own works | selection and application of some music elements and concepts in their own works |
| | skillful manipulation of compositional techniques in the creation of cohesive and well-structured music | manipulation of compositional techniques in the creation of cohesive music | demonstration of compositional techniques in the creation of their own works | use of basic compositional techniques to develop works of variable quality | use of rudimentary compositional techniques to produce partial works |
| | discerning synthesis and convincing expression of music ideas and stylistic characteristics integral to the creation of their own works | effective synthesis and expression of music ideas and stylistic characteristics that support the creation of their own works | synthesis and communication of music ideas and stylistic characteristics to create their own works | presentation of music ideas and stylistic characteristics in their own works | use of music ideas in their own works |

# NOTE

1. Throughout the chapter, where *Composition*, *Performance*, *Musicology*, *Analyzing repertoire*, and *Listening* are capitalized and in italics, they refer to the dimensions of syllabus documents, while more generic uses of these terms appear in lowercase roman script.

# REFERENCES

Bell, E., Allen, R., & Brennan, P. (1986/2011). *Review of school-based assessment (ROSBA).* (Discussion papers). The State of Queensland (Queensland Board of Senior Secondary School Studies). (Queensland Studies Authority; reformatted 2011).

Black, P., & Wiliam, D. (2007). Large-scale assessment systems: Design principles drawn from international comparisons. *Measurement: Interdisciplinary Research and Perspectives, 5*(1), 1–53.

Broadfoot, P. (2009). *Signs of Change: Assessment Past, Present and Future.* In C. Wyatt-Smith & J. J. Cumming (Eds.), *Educational assessment in the 21st century: Connecting theory and practice.* Dordrecht, The Netherlands: Springer, pp. i–xi.

Marion, S. F., Peck, B., & Raymond, J. (2011). *Year-to-year comparability of results in Queensland Studies Authority senior secondary courses that include school-based moderated assessments: An ACACA sponsored review.* Australasian Curriculum, Assessment and Certification Authority (ACACA).

Matters, G., (2006). *A report to the Queensland Studies Authority: Assessment practices in Queensland senior science syllabuses.* Australian Council for Educational Research.

Maxwell, G. S. (2004, March). *Progressive assessment for learning and certification: Some lessons from school-based assessment in Queensland.* Paper presented at the Third Conference of the Association of Commonwealth Examination and Assessment Boards, Redefining the Roles of Educational Assessment, Nadi, Fiji.

Myford, C. M. (1999). *Assessment for accountability vs. assessment to improve teaching and learning: Are they two different animals?* Paper presented at the Australasian Curriculum, Assessment and Certification Authority (ACACA) Conference, Perth.

QCAA (2005–2015). *State Review Panel report—Music.* The State of Queensland (Queensland Curriculum and Assessment Authority).

QCAA. (2014, July). *Assessment glossary.* The State of Queensland (Queensland Curriculum and Assessment Authority).

QCAA. (2015a, April). *Assessment: From the syllabus to the classroom.* Transcript of video (Part 1). The State of Queensland (Queensland Curriculum and Assessment Authority).

QCAA. (2015b, June). *Moderation handbook for Authority subjects.* The State of Queensland (Queensland Curriculum and Assessment Authority).

QCAA. (2015c, July). *The A–Z of senior moderation.* The State of Queensland (Queensland Curriculum and Assessment Authority).

QSA. (2004). *Senior music syllabus.* The State of Queensland (Queensland Studies Authority).

QSA. (2013). *Music senior syllabus.* The State of Queensland (Queensland Studies Authority).

Swanwick, K. (1999). *Teaching music musically.* London: Routledge.

Wenger, E., McDermott, R., & Snyder, W. (2002). *Cultivating communities of practice.* Boston: Harvard Business School Press.

# CHAPTER 25

······················································································

# MUSIC AS *BILDNING*

*the impracticability of assessment within
the scandinavian educational tradition*

······················································································

## JOHAN SÖDERMAN

DURING recent decades there has been an increased focus on standardized assessment procedures through testing and grades in compulsory school systems of most (Western) countries. As a result of this focus, an instrumental understanding of teaching, learning, and education has been established in the common discourse. Simplified, this instrumental view can in part be considered to constitute the "teaching for the test" culture, leading only to superficial knowledge rather than a changed understanding of oneself and the world.

Sweden has a tradition of advocating holistic ideals of education and learning, which connects with the Swedish model of democracy, in which voluntary self-learning of the general public is an essential part. This tradition is called *bildning* (*Bildung* in German) and developed in the early nineteenth century when Sweden was still a poor, nonindustrialized, Scandinavian, farmer society undergoing a large-scale wave of emigration to the United States. Over the course of decades one-quarter of the Swedish population left the country, which at that time was characterized by major inequality within the population. A major portion of the Swedish people had minor, even close to no, opportunities for social mobility. The still undeveloped form of democracy at this point created a need for education for the people of the masses in order for them to be able to take part in society. Therefore, the people themselves started to organize through social movements and through these movements came to found their own educational institutions in what is called *folkbildning* (popular adult education). In the Swedish context, the prefix "folk" (people in English) indicates a focus on *bildning* of the masses, in contrast to the more elitist traditional education system. In *Light from the North*, Joseph K. Hart (1927) described how he was inspired by the Scandinavian folk high schools and through them saw a future for American education. Hart was especially fascinated with the lack of instrumental curriculum and grades and with the focus on students' self-motivation.

The educational ideals of *folkbildning* were in turn inspired by thinkers such as John Dewey. Bernt Gustavsson (1991) states that *folkbildning* is a free and lifelong process of self-education in which each individual uses his or her own individual potential for his or her personal empowerment. W. E. B. Du Bois (1903/1999) had similar thoughts about self-education. Accordingly, he was strongly convinced that people would be able to attain empowerment and emancipation through self-education. Furthermore, Gustavsson (1991) argues that *folkbildning* is embedded in the meeting of the individual's own experience with the collective experience. Since its beginnings, *folkbildning* has had a double nature. As much as *folkbildning* has been claimed to be a changing, radical force in society, it has also emerged as a conservative community force used to reinforce traditional, bourgeois values.

On the one hand, during the last hundred years *folkbildning* has promoted the belief that people can achieve emancipation and empowerment through education. Staffan Larsson (1995) writes: "Groups who at various times challenged elites of society have used folkbildning as a way towards knowledge" (p. 41). Of course this can be considered a radical educational ideal: working to empower people with the overall aim to change society (Rydbeck, 1995). On the other hand, *folkbildning* has been used to discipline people: the same people it claims to work to empower. Old habits and the "bad taste" of the people should be replaced with more proper ones (Ambjörnsson, 1988; Elias, 1989). The relation between these two different purposes within the concept of *folkbildning* is called *the double feature of folkbildning* (e.g., Söderman, 2011; Brändström, Söderman, & Thorgersen, 2012).

In the early 1900s the emergence of Swedish study associations and folk high schools led to *folkbildning* being institutionalized. With this long tradition of egalitarian ambitions in educational politics, the question arises of whether it is at all possible to adapt assessment components to education, or they stand in contradiction to the very ideals of *bildning* that permeate Swedish society. The aim of this chapter is to discuss how standardized assessment strategies contradict the ideals of *bildning*. The chapter unfolds in the following manner. First I examine the definition and essence of the concept of *bildning* and its history. After that is a conceptual analysis of *bildning*, after which I review the educational tradition of *folkbildning*. In the next section I examine musical *(folk)bildning* and its holistic educational ideals. The following section presents the context of Swedish music education. In the final section I discuss *bildning* and neoliberal educational politics, which may be regarded as a cul-de-sac.

## What Is *Bildning*? Historical Matters

The concept of *bildning* has attracted more attention in recent years in a Scandinavian context. Björn Wiman (2013) even talks about a renaissance for *folkbildning* and notes that *bildning* nowadays holds high societal relevance. The concept of *bildning* originated in educational discussions in the late 1700s regarding individual liberation and can be considered to have started with Immanuel Kant's Enlightenment ideals of human emancipation, which emanated from thoughts about every person being her own worst enemy. Kant claimed that the importance of every human is released from her own imagined chains. In Sweden in the 1800s, the concept of *bildning* was discussed in various societal contexts but became particularly significant for the three classical Swedish social movements: temperance, revivalist, and labor. *Bildning* can be seen as specifically directed toward the poor and unprivileged. Representatives of the social movements wanted these people to engage in their movements in order to develop good manners, become educated, and act in a more proper way.

From the 1800s to the present day, discussions about the interpretation of the *bildning* concept have continuously recurred. Advocates for holistic *bildning* ideals have repeatedly directed criticism at the formal school system and its cramming culture ("teaching for the test") and elitist ideals and have claimed that learning, through a *bildning* perspective, should be characterized by the enjoyable, motivational, and voluntary aspects of learning and lead citizens to a state of emancipation. Advocates for a more traditional viewpoint on learning, however, claim *bildning* is the natural result of education.

Anders Burman and Per Sundgren (2010) argue that despite disagreements over how the concept of *bildning* can be understood, its proponents have always seen *bildning* as a counterbalance to the views of advocates of contemporary school systems. The proponents of *bildning* always perceive the traditional education system as too mechanical, instrumental, and utilitarian. *Bildning* has often been contrasted with formal education/schooling (in Swedish *utbildning*), the latter having a beginning and an end, which stands in contrast to *bildning*, a learning process continuing from cradle to grave. Early Swedish *bildning* advocates of the nineteenth century, such as Hans Larsson and Ellen Key, were in their time highly critical of the contemporary cramming/teaching for the test school culture. Instead they endorsed ideals of self-education in which voluntary and enjoyable learning should be the focus for growth of individuals and eventually lead them to become emancipated citizens.

Interestingly, Larsson and Key considered arts education as the alternative to the more mechanical and instrumental teaching culture of academic school subjects. In artistic disciplines, such as music, there are knowledge elements that constitute the very essence of *bildning*. *Bildning* and artistic disciplines are both focused on creativity and creative learning processes and offer individuals alternative ways of expression to what is common in more traditional areas of knowledge. Sven Eric Liedman (2012), one of the most prominent *bildning* proponents in Sweden, claims aesthetic subjects are necessary in Swedish schools. He criticizes the tendency to one-sidedly emphasize traditional and instrumental learning methods and school subjects.

## *BILDNING*: CONCEPTUAL ANALYSIS

The Swedish word *bildning* suggests both "form" and "picture": both "shape" and "to foreshadow" (Gustavsson, 1996). *Bildning* involves aspects of free human development, as well as of human formation. Within this lies a double feature: a bottom-up approach, in which the human forms herself (collectively and individually), and a top-down approach, in which someone (often from the bourgeois environment) educates (*bildar* in Swedish) citizens of a lower societal class. This dual role of *bildning* is shared with the Greek concept of *paideia*, which indicates the all-around development of humans' intellectual, artistic, and physical capacity. In this process there will also be individuals who transmit knowledge from an agreed cultural canon to the *bildning* process that they are undergoing. Focusing on both content and process then becomes of importance, or the concept of *bildning* will lose its significance (Varkøy & Söderman, 2013).

The classical concept of *bildning* is historical and therefore may not always relate directly to the social perceptions, changes, and cultural conditions of our time. *Bildning* can be seen both as a constantly relevant educational concept and representing historical educational ideals that are out of date in our time. An individual described as being *bildad* is usually regarded as cultured or cultivated. *Bildning* in this sense directly parallels the thoughts of Dewey in his classical work *How We Think* (1910), in which a clear difference is marked between the state of having information and the state of being intellectually educated. The intellectually educated man is formed through what Dewey calls the training of Mind, which is a process that leads to cultivation.

The *bildning* process takes time, rarely generates any swift economic dividends, and therefore does not always harmonize with the educational principles of our time, which promote "efficiency" in the "knowledge society" leading to a state of constant "employability." However, a closer look at the *bildning* philosophy portrays beliefs about knowledge and learning as being a relationship between the colloquial and the new, unknown, and unfamiliar.

The individual is perceived as breaking away from the mundane, to venture out into the unknown and thereby gain new experiences. The journey is therefore a central metaphor in the concept of *bildning*. As manifested in Johann Wolfgang von Goethe's classic Bildungsroman *Wilhelm Meister's Journeyman Years*, the hero leaves home to go out into the world, only to come back rich in experience and knowledge. In this context *bildning* can be considered a steady process, without a preset purpose and without formal ending. *Bildning* has no goal beyond itself, or to put it in Dewey's words: "The purpose of education is education." While traditional formal education has a clear beginning and a predestined ending, *bildning* is a timeless process, truly lifelong. It has an intrinsic value and is critical of the "useful knowledge" represented in traditional education settings. "There is nothing as useful as useless knowledge"; this phrase is commonly articulated by *bildning* advocates of the Swedish *folkbildning* tradition, which is related to the fact that no one can really tell what knowledge will be needed in the future. Undoubtedly *bildning* contributes both to the democratic development of society and to personal growth toward global citizenship (Gustavsson, 1991). Knowledge that constitutes the concept of *bildning* contributes to creating greater tolerance, openness, and an expanded framework of understanding in society and, therefore plays an important role in the development of democracy in global citizenship.

# THE *FOLKBILDNING* TRADITION

In the compound word and concept *folkbildning* (popular adult education in an English-speaking context), emancipatory functions and voluntary, informal learning processes are the focus. The word "folk" (people in English) indicates *bildning* of the masses, in contrast to the more elitist formal education system that was available only to the elite minority of the population. Through the emergence of study associations and folk high schools (intended for adults past the age of eighteen) in the 1900s, *folkbildning* in Sweden became institutionalized (however, Swedish folk high schools, which sprang out of the Swedish institutionalized *folkbildning* tradition, still do not test or grade their students). Hart (1927) was inspired by Scandinavian folk high schools and through them saw a future for American education.

In contemporary Sweden, folk high schools are considered an equal alternative to formal education, which is still regarded as more instrumental and elitist. Over the course of time, *folkbildning* has been linked to democratic development in Sweden. An educated and enlightened population is considered key for a blossoming democracy that enables as many as possible to participate in democratic discussions and congregations. Former Swedish prime minister Olof Palme allegedly once said that Sweden should become a democracy based on study circles in which people would be given the opportunity to discuss complex topics with each other. *Folkbildning* should lead individuals to develop from the state of simply expressing their superficial views to the state of *bildning*, which includes gaining insights about the complexity of existence.

Since *folkbildning* can be regarded as civic education, the enjoyable and self-selected aspects of learning are considered preconditions for the start of every individual *bildning* journey. Educational and learning motifs related to aspects of employability and "useful knowledge" can therefore be seen to stand in direct opposition to what constitutes genuine learning. Even within a higher education context, the stress on self-selected and enjoyable learning is regarded as significant because higher education is directly linked to Swedish democracy and the development of the country as a "knowledge nation." The stress on the self-selected and enjoyable as preconditions for education relates to holistic educational ideals that have the voluntary and emancipatory as core aspects. *Folkbildning* and the classical Swedish social movements are thus tightly intertwined, and for these movements, music has always been central (Göransson, 2010).

The musically talented Joel Häggström was raised within the revivalist movement in Sweden, but he immigrated to America when he was a teenager. Shortly after arriving in the United States in the first years of the twentieth century, Häggström became involved with the American labor movement, for which he used his musical skills to write songs with radical liberation lyrics. Years later he became known, even to an international audience, by the name Joe Hill. His songs, and his particular way of using music as a vehicle to convey social and political messages, were very effective. Even in our time, his songs have been performed by artists such as Bruce Springsteen, Billy Bragg, and Pete Seeger, and his work was also a source of inspiration for artists such as Bob Dylan and John Lennon.

In contemporary Sweden, many young people with foreign backgrounds use hip-hop music in a similar way and can thus also be understood as part of the *folkbildning* tradition (Snell & Söderman, 2014). Bengt Göransson (2010) writes that people have flocked to social movements, such as the revivalist movement, simply because of their musical elements. Sture Brändström, Johan Söderman, and Ketil Thorgersen (2012) write about musical *folkbildning*. For over a hundred years, people in Sweden have learned music through study associations, in folk high schools, and in social movements. Today there is an extensive musical infrastructure within *folkbildning* in Sweden. It consists of local/community music halls run by various study associations, as well as high-level music education programs, such as the jazz music education program at the folk high school of Skurup (e.g., Nylander, 2014). The musical branch of *folkbildning* has clearly contributed to what is usually described by international media as the "Swedish music miracle," and it has led to Sweden becoming a leading international country, competing with the United States and the United Kingdom (among others) in exporting popular music.

# MUSICAL (*FOLK*)*BILDNING*: APPROACHING HOLISTIC EDUCATIONAL IDEALS

What is the core of musical *bildning*? Since *bildning* can be described as a process leading to enlightenment, rather than simply expressing views and opinions, musical *bildning* can be regarded as a process aiming to enable people to reach musical insights about previously known music, as well as insights about unknown music. Therefore, music education in the municipal school system should not be obsequious or populist and only engage students in music they already know. Instead, music education in K–9 schools should strive to incorporate aspects of musical *bildning*. From a *bildning* musical learning perspective, the role of teachers is to inspire and guide students through a complex musical universe in which unknown musical worlds are yet to be explored.

From this standpoint, teachers can also be seen to "open the doors" to unknown worlds of knowledge. In contrast, focusing only on what is already known, such as the current popular music and hit lists, risks being too one-sided to lead to deep musical knowledge and understanding. Theodor Adorno (1976) argued that jazz music is "rhythmically obedient" and that the classical music tradition stands for eternal values, as well as a built-in resistance to capitalism and commercialism. Adorno came to this conclusion during a time when jazz was part of the popular music culture that was just starting its foray into contemporary new media such as sound recordings and films. Today, even jazz is an unknown music world for many young people. To gain musical insights valued as part of musical *bildning*, students should thus be introduced to music of historical value.

Music can in many ways be regarded as a liberating force. When people engage in music making, it can lead to empowerment, a fact well known by most music educators. In the classic book *The Souls of Black Folk*, Du Bois (1903/1999) describes the distinct role of music among African Americans. Du Bois wrote that because African American slaves were denied traditional schooling and therefore remained illiterate, music became one of the few channels that enabled them to communicate with each other and the outside world.

Du Bois's own life can also be regarded as a classic narrative of a "journey of *bildning*." He was born in 1868 and was one of the first African Americans to gain a doctoral degree. He first developed his interest in the German theory of *bildning* when he was staying in Germany as an exchange student during the Bismarck era (1890s). When he returned to the United States, with slavery only a few decades behind in the civic memory, he participated in public discussions regarding the organization of education for African Americans. In opposition to his African American critics, Du Bois argued for a more holistic view of education, as opposed to a narrow focus on vocational schools for African Americans, which critics believed was the key to prevent the state of mass unemployment that was dominant at that time. Du Bois argued that a narrow concept of education linked to employability and vocational schools could very well be a dead end for African American society. He claimed that with only low-quality and narrow educational opportunities, African Americans would remain part of the underclass, and American society would remain socially preserved, resulting in even smaller opportunities for social mobility for African Americans.

Based on his education and his own personal experiences, Du Bois argued for what can be understood as traditional values of "journeys of *bildning*," claiming that class mobility was made possible through the study of the arts and humanities, and that these would lead the way for African Americans to gain social influence and eventually (an unthinkable scenario at the end of the 1800s) an African American president. Du Bois was *the* advocate for holistic educational ideals in America. He believed that *bildning* would lead marginalized people to empowerment, a strengthened collective self-esteem, and a greater impact on society.

Applying the thoughts of Du Bois to contemporary Sweden, which has become increasingly segregated by social and economic gaps—despite the fact that population numbers are on the rise—*bildning* of, for example, classical music could generate cultural capital and social empowerment for those who are now marginalized. Western classical music is typically considered "high culture" and therefore related to cultural capital. Horace Engdahl (2006) suggests that high culture is the new subculture, which operates in the margins of cultural institutions. Popular culture is dominant in Sweden, and hierarchies of values, such as the "high" and "low," can also be found within popular culture. Engdahl proposes that there is a need to start processes of *folkbildning* for Western classical music. This must of course be understood within a Swedish context, in which higher music education departments have been drained of Western classical music. In an American context, the relation could therefore very well be the opposite, and popular music could be used to lead the way toward musical *bildning*.

# SWEDISH MUSIC EDUCATION

In the late 1960s the Swedish music education system went through significant changes. In order to better reflect current popular music, the new curriculum at this time took a clear step away from the previously one-sided use of Western classical music that had dominated school music programs prior to these reforms. Instead, music teachers were now encouraged to use music that was popular among youths outside of school as part of their curricula. With further revisions to curricula in 1980, 1994, and 2000, the current form of music education in the compulsory school has become dominated by classroom singing and instrument playing in pop and rock bands.

Several studies have criticized the strong focus on popular music in the Swedish music curriculum. Over the last few decades this focus has led Swedish students to learn music history almost exclusively as rock and pop music history from the 1950s onward (Ericsson & Lindgren, 2010; Georgii-Hemming & Westvall, 2010). Annika Falthin (2015) quotes a music teacher who claims that the only content that should qualify as part of contemporary music education in Sweden is classic rock composition (guitar, bass, drums, keyboards), which is easy to play. Classical music, contemporary classical music, folk music, and even latter-day hip-hop music may therefore be considered forms of musical craftsmanship that are too advanced and consequently not suitable as part of music education in Swedish schools.

Such a view of music education is in direct opposition to the concept of *bildning*. People who have devoted much time and effort to learning to play music are well aware of its liberating force. To acquire musical skills, such as learning to play an instrument at high level, takes time. For example, El Sistema has developed in multicultural neighborhoods in Sweden and has been well received in the nation, and it could contribute to the regrowth of classical music. The research of Cecilia Hultberg (2000) has shown the importance of having knowledge of musical genres in order to be able to play classical music through notation. Even though pop and rock styles dominate music education in primary schools, students in general still lack knowledge and understanding of the music they perform. And not all teachers have the necessary knowledge to teach students important aspects of music related to musical genres, including rock music. For instance, Claes Ericsson and Monica Lindgren (2010) highlight how the central message of Pink Floyd's famous school-critical song, "Another Brick in the Wall" was completely ignored in Swedish music education, where a teacher taught students to play the song in a way that reproduced the very school tradition that the song criticizes.

In educational discussions about the concept of *bildning* in the 1800s, there was a fear that "half-*bildning*" would emerge in relation to issues concerning an accelerated and widespread expansion of the educational system (e.g., Burman & Sundgren, 2012). Also, *bildning* advocates argued that "taught prejudices" could be more dangerous than "prejudices gained," and that ignorance thrived in contexts lacking *bildning*. Nowadays, the higher education system in Sweden is sometimes described as a factory-oriented mass education system that provides too little time for teacher-led classes and student reflection. The debate of the 1800s could therefore be seen as again relevant in the Swedish educational context, leading to the question of whether or not *bildning* can actually exist within increasingly formalized professional educational programs, such as the Swedish mass teacher education program (e.g., Sundgren, 2008).

Music teacher education in music schools, however, holds a special position in the higher education system, and it could very well be in the forefront when it comes to *bildning* for music teacher students. It may even lead them to eventually become *folkbildning* teachers, who are definitely needed to contribute to a more cohesive society. Indeed, it is important to be vigilant in regard to populist elements in music education and to place greater emphasis on music as a means of opening doors to the as yet unknown. Music teachers advocating this *bildning* tradition of opening doors to new musical worlds for their students will definitely be needed in the future.

# Bildning and Neoliberal Educational Politics: A Cul-de-Sac

The international trend of increased testing has influenced the Swedish school system to the extent that the national pedagogical legacy of *bildning* risks falling into oblivion (Kamens & McNeeley, 2010). However, music could be regarded as just the radical force needed when it comes to motivating marginalized students with nonacademic backgrounds in urban areas. For these students, music can support their voluntary, self-educational learning processes. The emancipatory force that lies in music, and that has been the foundation of the Swedish *folkbildning* tradition—which has contributed to the transformation of Sweden from an undeveloped farmer society to a modern postindustrial nation—runs the risk of being lost if music as an official school subject loses its *bildning* core.

Music as a school subject is mandatory in the Swedish K–9 school system, and students are therefore graded on music the same way as in other academic subjects. Although the very essence of music may be considered the very core of the concept of *bildning*, there are good arguments for why it should not be assessed and graded at all. However, an increased focus on assessment has recently begun to develop in relation to music (Zandén & Thorgersen, 2015). An instrumental perspective on music as simply a school subject among others connects to an understanding of music as useful or beneficial in relation to learning in general, a perspective that stands in opposition to a position in which arts and music are valued for their own sake.

According to historical advocates for the *folkbildning* tradition, music cannot be assessed in the same way as academic subjects. This chapter points out that music itself is *bildning* oriented and thus plays a part in liberation processes of the individual. Sociological aspects of music education should therefore be part of music teaching, for example, in relation to dilemmas of social inequality and increased gaps between rich and poor in the Western world. Terms such as "gentrification" and "segregation" can be dissected within a music educational setting (e.g., musical gentrification, Dyndahl, 2015). Through this process, students may be able to discover their own social reality and take power over their own lives.

Hip-hop is a good example of how music can describe today's diverging contemporary society (Snell & Söderman, 2014). Present-day American debates about the lack of diversity in music education have recently become a focus. It is being argued that music education must reflect the multicultural society of today (e.g., Kelly-McHale, 2016). The contemporary Swedish school system has chosen to go down the instrumental path in regard to assessment, that is, "teaching for the test culture." Because of this, schools do not meet the needs, thoughts, and concerns of their students. This leads back to the school culture of the early 1900s, when marginalized people took power over their own learning processes through the *folkbildning* tradition of the social movements of that time.

The unaccompanied refugees who come to Europe today are the same age Joe Hill was when he emigrated to the United States at the beginning of the last century. For Joe Hill, music became the ticket into a new context, political engagement, and a role in American society. For the young, unaccompanied immigrants who are new members of European society today, music could also make a great difference. Music, just as for Joe Hill more than one hundred years ago, still matters as a tool for empowerment. Drawing on aspects of *folkbildning*, the question is: Is it even possible to apply assessment to music in K–9-schools?

Hip-hop and rap have raised questions that have not been answered in the schools: Why are our neighborhoods stigmatized? How should the increasing class divisions between different parts of the urban landscape be understood? Does society have to consist of winners and losers? And why did we, of all people, end up in these poor areas? Young people's search for answers to these questions is intertwined with their aesthetic practices as one dimension of their identity work. The aesthetical practices in youth cultures can be seen as a new language that the young develop in order to handle their inner and outer worlds; accordingly, it is important to respect cultural expressions in youth culture. According to Söderman (2011), hip-hop can be seen as an expression of contemporary *folkbildning*.

Michael Apple (2014) states that Western educational policy is influenced by neoliberal ideology. He questions how this ideology has developed into the hegemonic discourse of our time. It is time for music educators to revolt against the "teaching for test culture" and other neoliberal, instrumental educational experiments. Music educators must stand up for holistic educational ideals that constitute the essence of music education and that have been advocated by thinkers such as Dewey, Du Bois, and Paulo Freire, as well as through the Swedish *bildning* tradition. It has to be made clear that the instrumental path is a cul-de-sac for music education.

## REFERENCES

Adorno, T. (1976). *Inledning till musiksociologi: 12 teoretiska föreläsningar*. Kristianstad: Bo Cavefors Bokförlag.
Ambjörnsson, R. (1988). *Den skötsamme arbetaren: Idéer och ideal i ett norrländskt sågverkssamhälle 1880–1930*. Stockholm: Carlsson.

Apple, M. W. (2014). *Official knowledge: Democratic education in a conservative age.* New York: Routledge.

Brändström, S., & Söderman, J., & Thorgersen, K. (2012). The double feature of musical folkbildning: Three Swedish examples. *British Journal of Music Education, 29*(1), 65–74.

Burman, A., & Sundgren, P. (2010). *Bildning: Texter från Esaias Tegnér till Sven-Eric Liedman.* Göteborg: Bokförlaget Daidalos.

Du Bois, W. E. B. (1903/1999). *The souls of black folk.* New York: Oxford University Press.

Dyndahl, P. (2015). Academisation as activism? Some paradoxes. *Finnish Journal of Music Education, 18*(2), 20–32.

Elias, N. (1989). *Sedernas historia.* Stockholm: Atlantis.

Engdahl, H. (2006, April 2). Högkultur som subkultur. I *Sydsvenskan.* Retrieved from: https://www.sydsvenskan.se/2006-04-01/horace-engdahl-hogkultur-som-subkultur

Ericsson, C., & Lindgren, M. (2010). *Musikklassrummet i blickfånget: Vardagskultur, identitet, styrning och kunskapsbildning.* Halmstad: Högskolan i Halmstad.

Falthin, A. (2015). *Meningserbjudanden och val: En studie om musicerande i musikundervisning på högstadiet* (Unpublished dissertations). Royal College of Music, Stockholm.

Georgii-Hemming, E., & Westvall, M. (2010). Music education—a personal matter? Examining the current discourses of music education in Sweden. *British Journal of Music Education, 27*(1), 21–33.

Gustavsson, B. (1991). *Bildningens väg: Tre bildningsideal i svensk arbetarrörelse 1880–1930.* Stockholm: Wahlström & Widstrand.

Gustavsson, B. (1996). *Bildning i vår tid: Om bildningens möjligheter och villkor i det moderna samhället.* Stockholm: Wahlström & Widstrand.

Göransson, B. (2010). *Tankar om politik.* Falun: Ersatz.

Hart, J. K. (1927). *Light from the north: The Danish folk high schools; their meanings for America.* New York: Henry Holt & Co.

Hultberg, C. (2000). *The printed score as a mediator of musical meaning: Approaches to music notation in Western tonal tradition.* Malmö: Musikhögskolan i Malmö, Lunds universitet.

Kamens, D. H., & McNeely, C. L. (2010). Globalization and the growth of international educational testing and national assessment. *Comparative Education Review, 54*(1), 5–25.

Larsson, S. (1995). *Folkbildningen och vuxenpedagogiken.* In B. Bergstedt & S. Larsson (Red.), *Om folkbildningens innebörder* (pp. 35–57) . Norrköping: Mimer.

Liedman, S. E. (2012). *Hets! En bok om skolan.* Stockholm: Albert Bonniers förlag.

McHale, K. J. (2016). Why music education needs to incorporate more diversity. *The Conversation.* Retrieved from https://theconversation.com/why-music-education-needs-to-incorporate-more-diversity-53789

Nylander, E. (2014). *Skolning i jazz: Värde, selektion och studiekarriär vid folkhögskolornas musiklinjer.* Linköping: Linköping Studies in Behavioral Science, Linköping University.

Rydbeck, K. (1995). Den svenska folkbildningshistorien från 1800-talets början till 1900-talets mitt. Ett panorama. In E. Öhrström (Red.), *Musiken, folket och bildningen* (pp. 13–34). Linköping: Mimer.

Snell, K., & Söderman, J. (2014). *Hip-hop within and without the academy.* New York: Lexington Books.

Söderman, J. (2011). Folkbildning through hip-hop: How the ideals of three rappers parallel a Scandinavian educational tradition. *Music Education Research, 13*(2), 211–25.

Sundgren, G. (2008). *Bildning och pedagogik.* Report from Stockholm University.

Varkøy, Ø., & Söderman, J. (2014). *Musik för alla—filosofiska och didaktiska perspektiv kring musik, bildning och skola.* Lund: Studentlitteratur.

Wiman, B. (2013, June 30). Också i Almedalen får ordet bildning en renässans. *DN*. Retrieved from: https://www.dn.se/kultur-noje/bjorn-wiman-ocksa-i-almedalen-far-ordet-bildning-en-renassans/

Zandén, O., & Thorgersen, C. F. (2015). Teaching for learning or teaching for documentation? Music teachers' perspectives on a Swedish curriculum reform. *British Journal of Music Education, 32*(1), 37–50.

# CHAPTER 26

# NONREGULATED ASSESSMENT IN MUSIC EDUCATION

## an urban Iranian outlook

NASIM NIKNAFS

The natural world is filled with examples of species that operate in a collective fashion that defies the top-down or centralized chain of command.

—David Borgo

MUSIC education in Iran is not centralized, officially established, regulated, or standardized. Rather, it is unbounded, multidimensional, homegrown, and subjective and impassioned. Due to years of unpredictable regulations on cultural production after the 1979 revolution, music education in Iran, especially in the urban framework, was not a public and/or systematic endeavor. Young people, and the public in general, benefited from educational deregulation because they could create their own ways of learning and making music. They circumvented discordant situations by learning music from one another in local and private spaces. This musical and educational freedom allowed them to *live in and through music making*. Thus, and irrespective of the content of the music, acts of music making and learning became political. Music was a medium for the expression of people's everyday feelings of frustration, happiness, sadness, and encouragement.

Accordingly, the public became even more passionate about music. However, and regardless of musical genres, the number of public performances was minimal from the early days of the revolution through the late 1990s. Afterward young people filled each and every public space of music, stood in long lines to purchase tickets, and participated in collaborative and at times subversive approaches to learning music. Playing, singing, and learning music through enculturation is a common activity in private gatherings among most Iranians. In short, "the very intention of abolishing music in [Iranian] public life unexpectedly led to [the] increasing practice of music within the family circle by the younger generation of all social classes" (Youssefzadeh, 2000, p. 38).

In his seminal work on musical values in Iranian society, Bruno Nettl (1980) remarks that "one aspect of the musical culture of [Iran] can be analyzed and explained as a particular kind of symbol of Iranian society and its values" (p. 129). This aspect is improvisation, which is deeply rooted in Iranian traditional music. Thus, music teaching and learning in Iran is profoundly improvisatory. Despite directives and regulations on the production of music, young people have adapted, improvised, and created new ways to learn and make their music.

This chapter addresses the philosophical underpinnings of Iran's grassroots music education movement, parallel to its societal values, whose agents are active; are technologically savvy; and use the elements of self-regulation, improvisation, peer learning, trial and error, and overall formative assessment (Fautley & Colwell, 2012) to learn and evaluate their music.

This examination of assessment in urban Iranian music education stems from Iran's deeply structured history of Persian art music. Even though it "rests on a complex and highly detailed theoretical system" (Naqvi, 2012, p. 181)—and is part of the psyche of the Iranian populace in general—"its concern [is] for developing performative freedom and fluency grounded in intuitive awareness of deep structure" (Naqvi, 2012, p. 181). This framework works only when it operates intuitively and holistically, not sequentially and atomistically (Schippers, 2010, pp. 65–75).

This chapter suggests that the field of music education should take a "slightly outside perspective" (Lundström, 2012, p. 652) and a proactive approach toward assessment, rather than a reactionary approach to music teaching and learning in which assessment becomes an end goal, instead of an embodied approach within the larger learning process itself. From this perspective, the centerpiece of music education is not "music schooling," because this is only one way—and a contested way—of conceptualizing and carrying out music teaching and learning. As Håkan Lundström (2012) notes:

> When the perspective with which an object is looked at is changed, the positions and relations between its parts will change—the way the picture in a kaleidoscope changes when it is turned around, even though the parts that make up the picture are the same. Some parts that seem peripheral in the original perspective may stand out as central in the new perspective, and the other way around.   (p. 655)

Although it is not ideal that the Iranian state government does not officially support music education, this situation has a silver lining. Indeed, I suggest that music education in many nations would benefit from escaping "official" government recognition (however tepid or enthusiastic) and policies (however slapdash or careful) and concomitant restrictions on music education that require formal assessments.

My aim in this chapter is to provide a perspective on assessment in music education—stemming from my Iranian background—that is decentralized, eschews standardized practices, and is carried out locally.

# Music Teaching and Learning in Iran
## after the 1979 Revolution

For some years after the Iranian 1979 revolution,[1] and intersecting with the eight years of the Iran-Iraq War (1980–1988)—the last and longest conventional trench war known internationally—performing music in public was only permitted for "revolutionary songs" (*Soroodhaaye Enqelabi*), which existed to boost the newly established Islamic government and to "repair" the nation's war-torn psyche in efforts to create a united national consciousness. In terms of music education, when music was related to popular music, Western classical, or dance music, music teaching and learning was considered illegal. Hence, "concerts in homes and private teaching at homes became common" (master *tar* player Alizadeh, cited in Nooshin, 2005a, p. 241). Laudan Nooshin (2005a) remarks that the war years saw difficult tensions between the religious and national identity of the Iranians. On the one hand, the newly shaped government wanted to fit cultural production into an Islamic structure, which proved to be a difficult task. On the other hand, years of modernization policies—or better said, "Westernization"—by the shah before the 1979 revolution had created a skeptical and weary population that saw anything Western as a symbol of elitism, which did not relate to the majority of the public. Therefore, "the profound contradictions in cultural policy during the [1980s] were partly the result of a government trying to impose a hegemonic Islamic identity on a people intensely aware of, and unwilling to forfeit, their pre-Islamic heritage," which was deeply rooted in music and poetry (Nooshin, 2005a, p. 236).

By the early years of the 1990s, purchasing and selling instruments was permitted again, as long as they were not used for "illicit purposes" (Youssefzadeh, 2000). Teaching, learning, and performing Persian art music and Persian folk music regained their status among officialdom after the war years "to encourage [their] preservation, as [they were] considered an important facet of Iranian ethnic identity" (Miller, cited in Naqvi, 2012, p. 183). Ameneh Youssefzadeh (2000) linked this ethnic identity with national identity, inseparable from politics (During, cited in Youssefzadeh, 2000, p. 42).

Western classical music, in contrast, occupied a precarious position, associated as it was with the concept of "Western toxification" (*Tahajom-e Farhangi*), a sign of Western ideologies and influences. In the Iranian context, Western music was linked to and deeply rooted in historical Western, colonial practices, which the authorities would not and could not accept at the time. Prior to 2000, teaching and learning Western classical music most often occurred in private studios. At the university level, if one sought to pass admission auditions to study Western classical music, she or he had to have a certain level of proficiency on a Persian instrument. Thus, public performances of Western music were rare, and audience members stood in long lines, sometimes for days, to purchase tickets for these concerts. After the election of President Mohammad Khatami in 1997, Western classical music was more widely accepted by the authorities, which led to an increase in the number of public performances.

The state of popular music was even more insecure. In the 1960s and 1970s a wave of popular musicians emerged. They combined "existing urban popular styles and used Persian lyrics and Iranian melodies and rhythms, [and they] also drew heavily from conventions of Western pop music images, fashion and instruments" (Nooshin, 2005a, p. 234). This music, again, represented Western toxification and colonial agendas. It was never broadcast by government-sponsored radio and televisions after the revolution, and it was never officially taught, but rather learned through unofficial channels. It was not until the reform era that popular music gained some official prominence.

# REFORM ERA (1997–2005)

The landslide victory of Mohammad Khatami as president in 1997 launched the reform era. Part of Khatami's presidency campaign involved initiating *goftogoo-ye-tamaddonha* (the dialogue between civilizations). A deeply cultural campaign, rather than an economic or a political one, made Khatami the torchbearer of cultural evolution in Iran after almost twenty years of limited access to cultural production—specifically music. The new regulations, though at times still unpredictable, allowed the Iranian public to use more public spaces for artistic production. Music halls and art galleries opened their doors to many public performances of all kinds of music, such as traditional Persian music, Persian folk music, Western classical music, and—to many people's surprise—alternative pop and rock music (but with strict regulations). Sales of all kinds of instruments increased, as did the number of cultural centers that offered music lessons.

During the reform era (Semati, 2008, p. 4), or as Nooshin (2005a) calls it, the "Cultural Thaw," the relaxation of control over the production of music, regardless of genre, content, or learning and teaching approaches, allowed for other kinds of musicianship to come to fruition. For example, the Khatami government announced the official launch of Performance of World Instruments in certain universities. It was the first time since 1979 that learning and teaching Western classical music became officially sanctioned. Although it was never illegal, it had always occupied a liminal space (Nooshin, 2005a). In 1998 Seda o Sima, the national radio and television broadcasting agency, sanctioned a style of Iranian pop reminiscent of prerevolutionary Iranian pop called the "new pop" (*Pop-e-Jadid*; Nooshin, 2005a). As Nooshin (2005a) remarks: "Stylistically this new pop shared a great deal with other kinds of Iranian pop, which were officially illegal" (p. 247). Known as *pop-e-Los Angelesi* (Los Angeles pop)—for years this was the epitome of underground Iranian wedding and dance party music—this kind of music was created by Iranian expatriates, some of them well known in the prerevolutionary era, and was smuggled across borders or sold on the black market.

In addition to performers in these genres of pop music, rock musicians, who were creating and practicing their music mostly in apartment basements and behind closed doors, appeared overground (Nooshin, 2008). During the war years Western rock bands and popular musicians—such as Eloy, Deep Purple, Led Zeppelin, Iron Maiden, Metallica, Pink Floyd, Michael Jackson, Madonna, Duran Duran, and Depeche

Mode—gained prominence among Iranian youth groups, partly due to the latters' discontent with the continuous tensions of religious-national identity in Iran. All of these kinds of music were consumed through unofficial channels of satellite TV and the black market. Thus, neophyte Iranian rock musicians, who at the time were mostly male, middle class, educated, and technologically savvy, created music that was considered to be alternative, rock, punk, or metal, and their subgenres. Not having rock role models in Iran at the time (Robertson, 2012), these youngsters started their music by using the "soundscapes" they developed during their early years and gradually refining their sounds by adding Persian lyrics, local issues, and struggles, later refining their instrumentation. They thrived under the peculiar and inconsistent permissions and freedoms granted by the authorities, most notably *vezarat-e-ershad-o-farhang-e-eslami* (the Ministry of Cultural and Islamic Guidance). The unpredictability of the authorities' decisions on album permissions and performance approvals caused these musicians to feel constantly apprehensive, yet as a result they became creative and resourceful. "Because they faced such opposition, concerts that did take place became symbolic events and were often used as an arena for challenging imposed limits in a way not always possible on commercial recordings" (Nooshin, 2005a, p. 248).

Furthermore, aligned with the lifting of some controls over kinds of musicianship, ways of music teaching and learning also flourished in the country. For one of the most prominent *tar* masters in Iran, "playing and teaching music itself became a kind of resistance and a way of maintaining identity" (Alizadeh, cited in Nooshin, 2005a, p. 241). Also, as Alizadeh notes: "Limitations which were placed on learning music increased the number of people wanting to learn. When the municipal authorities of Tehran opened cultural centers (*farhangsara*) all over the city, they started music classes. Now it is really not an exaggeration to say that in every family someone plays an instrument" (p. 246).

# RESURGENCE OF FUNDAMENTALISM

In 2005, after the two terms of Khatami and looser regulations on cultural and artistic production, Mahmoud Ahmadinejad assumed office. His new presidential cultural policies, which looked back to the war years, contradicted Khatami's. Rock musicians retreated to unofficial spaces, the number of musical lessons in cultural centers diminished, the quality of teaching music at universities plummeted, and regulations on the production of music became severe. During the two terms of Ahmadinejad's presidency, the second starting with a turbulent uproar of mass demonstrations in 2009, authorities reduced the number of public performances again. The quantity of album permits for rock musicians dropped significantly. These musicians, who had enjoyed eight years of quasi-freedom, either retreated underground (occasionally creating and performing their music) and became unofficial again or left the country. Music departments changed direction and scope, and cultural centers reduced music lessons and public performances of Western classical and alternative musics. For eight years, musical efforts became precarious and received greater government scrutiny.

Nevertheless, certain genres of music emerged during this time. For example, in a change in the Iranian eulogy (*Maddahi*), in which orators performed mostly mournful songs of the Shia Imams, religious beat boxers would stand beside orators and create an intense rhythmic cycle while performing their narrations.[2] Also, Persian hip-hop emerged forcefully among Iranian urban male and female youth in unofficial spaces, thereby subverting government scrutiny.

During the Ahmadinejad years, music faced severe prohibitions, experienced troubling conditions in promotion, and was manipulated in many ways by the authorities. Nevertheless, even during the harsh cultural and political years of Ahmadinejad, music had a central place in Iranians' lives.

# And Now

Currently—since the election of President Hassan Rouhani, another reformist—the number of performances of most genres of music is reasonably high. Finding it profitable, the authorities decreased restrictions on public performances, and musicians of all walks of life have more opportunities to showcase their music to the public. However, these regulations are inconsistent and have created "some blatant contradictions and some interesting opportunities for subversion" (Nooshin, 2005a, p. 246). Female vocalists in all genres of music are still officially banned from solo performances, but some doors have opened for them to minimally try their solos in public. In 2013 the Iranian public enjoyed the first production since 1979 of Puccini's comic opera *Gianni Schicchi*, and female singers relished their roles in the opera.[3] After watching the opera, Alizadeh said: "I had a sense of pride, not only me but all those who were in the hall. I didn't feel the time go by. Maybe I wouldn't have enjoyed this opera as much if I had seen it in Italy" (cited in PressTV, 2013).

As I write this chapter, music is to some extent celebrated in Iran once again. Oddly, though, while musical instruments cannot be shown on television, the silhouettes of actors and actresses playing an instrument in television series can be televised. And while music is still not considered an official subject in public schools, some private schools have introduced it into their curricula. In addition, the number of music institutes has risen dramatically. Altogether, music education in Iran and its assessment is a local and personal phenomenon.

# The Position of Iranian Music Education in the Field at Large

There is a sense of urgency concerning the contextualization of the term "assessment" in Iranian music education, as the term music education has different connotations from that of the Global-North Centric approach (Niknafs, 2018). Indeed, the music education literature contains very few discussions of music education in a Middle Eastern country such as Iran, which has no centralized and systematic approach to music teaching and learning. More generally, Persian music and music education are either dismissed or hidden under the amorphous term "world music." To some, it is useful to know about Persian music, but not necessary to learn it.

Even though ethnomusicologists know a great deal about Persian art music (During, Mirabdolbahi, & Safvat, 1991; Farhat, 1991; Miller, 1999; Nettl, 1978), this knowledge is not embedded in teaching and learning practices in school curricula, especially in the northwest regions of the world. Rather, it is "tokenized" (Hess, 2015) and dealt with as an external object—something to be touched upon for its exotic sounds alone. Further, Persian music cannot be bracketed simplistically, as a form of Middle Eastern traditional art music. As in many other regions of the world, in Iran music making and learning is vibrant, diverse, dynamic, and abundant. Therefore, if we are to understand Iranian music education and its assessment, we must recognize the multidimensionality of Iranian music and Iranians' ways of interacting with it.

One often reads about how *schools* in North America, Australia, northern European countries, and Southeast Asian countries apply assessment in/to music education (Beston, 2004; Fautley & Savage, 2008; Holmes, Gokturk, Aguilar, & Chen, 2010). But beyond the boundaries of school, music is often carried out through informal learning or community music. Sometimes the term "assessment" implies that there is a strict border between *learning*, considered to happen mainly outside of schools,[4] and *teaching*, deemed to occur mostly within the walls of schools. Assessment is still a rarity when applied to school programs in local or national contexts that do not follow and are not controlled by standardized forms of musicianship in band, choir, and orchestra. In short, a dichotomy exists between the concept of assessment in schools and evaluation outside of schools. Echoing Lundström (2012), despite an increase in attention to informal learning situations in research and practice, "still there is a difference between extending a field of practice or research from the inside and applying a totally outside perspective to the whole field" (p. 656). It is the "totally outside perspective" within the assessment of Iranian music education that I turn to now, which might shed some light or add another perspective on the whole field.

# ANALYSIS OF ASSESSMENT IN URBAN IRANIAN MUSIC TEACHING AND LEARNING

Here I offer not an alternative perspective, but rather a combination of perspectives on the concept of assessment in music education. I begin by reflecting on some characteristic features of assessment in urban Iranian music teaching and learning that relate well to Bo Nilsson and Göran Folkestad's (2005) ecocultural perspective. This perspective/framework consists of four elements: (a) James J. Gibson's (1979) concept of affordances, (b) orality, (c) theories of play, and (d) theories of chance (Nilsson &

Folkestad, 2005, p. 23). Although this framework has been applied to children's musical creativity, and although it did not emerge from the Iranian context, the important point here is that its "theoretical points of departure emerge in an ecocultural perspective, in which learning, improvisation and creativity are seen as taking place within everyday activities, and a basic human function" (Nilsson & Folkestad, 2005, p. 24). Overall, assessment in urban Iranian music education can be categorized as follows:

1. do-it-yourself (DIY) and do-it-with-others (DIWO) assessment,
2. interactive and decentralized assessment,
3. local anarchism, and
4. lifestyle assessment.

How do former underground and official rock musicians[5] learn and practice their music? Because these practices occur outside the walls of schools, assessment in this context pertains predominantly to musicians' lifestyles and urban living, processes of renegotiating governmental and nongovernmental channels, and actions that are afforded to them (Gibson, 1977). I argue that the interplay among what is afforded to these musicians and what they create generates unique, full-bodied, holistic, local assessments. DIY and DIWO assessment provides good examples of what I mean.

# DIY (DO-IT-YOURSELF) AND DIWO (DO-IT-WITH-OTHERS) ASSESSMENT

Formative assessment—with specific adaptations—is at the heart of DIY and DIWO. Formative assessment in Iran is "concerned with taking learning forward.... True formative assessment is a process"; [I]t is dynamic, part of the learning encounter that involves feedback, [and] is reactive to the learning situation (Fautley & Colwell, 2012, p. 481). It empowers students' ability to teach themselves what they need to learn.

However, some discrepancies exist between "traditional" formative assessment and DIY and DIWO assessment. In formative assessment, the role of the teacher is paramount, even in an informal learning situation. This role focuses on helping "the learners with understanding what it is they wish to achieve, and then trying to remove barriers that prevent them from achieving it. This entails knowing what the learners wish to achieve" (Fautley & Colwell, 2012, p. 492). Furthermore, formative assessment is reactionary to the learning situation; that is, teachers react to the learning impediment and adapt their teaching to encourage better learning.

But in DIY and DIWO assessment, there is no role for teachers. The line between a professional (teacher) and amateur (student) musician is blurred. "A DIY practice expands definitions of what is deemed musical, incorporates new kinds of subject matter, and takes seriously the efforts of musicians who might in other schema be considered amateur" (Cogan, cited in Przybylski & Niknafs, 2015, p. 109). DIY and DIWO also enjoy a proactive approach to music learning rather than a reactive one.

During the years after the 1979 revolution, unofficial musicians in Iran had almost no opportunities to create, rehearse, and perform their music in public. Deemed to be either influenced by the West, Satanic music, or alien worshipping (*biganeh-parasti*), the kinds of music these musicians created were banned from public spaces. Reading from the ecocultural perspective of Gibson (1979), this situation was the musical option "offered to the individual by the environment" (Nilsson & Folkestad, 2005, p. 23). That is, because these musicians were not able to openly make and learn their music, they sought out and found grassroots ways of circumventing the unpredictable regulations impeding performances of their music. They used basements or rooftops for their rehearsals, and they communicated with gallery owners and rich philanthropists who were willing to risk providing spaces for their musical performances or publishing their music online through social media.

As a proactive approach to music learning and assessment, DIY and DIWO assessment was and is a holistic musical culture practice. In this sense, music learning is not detached from the life of these musicians; rather, it is a form of enculturation that is embedded in everyday life.

Moreover, these musicians could not have sustained their musical practices without each other's help, hence DIWO. In a sense, "DIWO processes encourage participants to learn how to identify resources as well as how to provide assistance to others. At their best, DIWO music communities begin by inviting members to act as band members, cooperating on the process of music making. They then encourage [beginners] to learn how to incorporate the expertise of [advanced musicians] as mentors within their creations. Finally, DIWO fosters a sense of mastery within [learners], inviting them to offer useful feedback to peers" (Przybylski & Niknafs, 2015, p. 113).

DIY and DIWO assessments were and are the only ways to approach this kind of musicianship in urban Iran. Although the circumstances are not always ideal, it is valuable to have expert musicians/teachers be directly involved during students' learning, so that they can provide ongoing constructive advice. Often the need for continuous constructive assessment is overlooked in the formal rhetoric of assessment. Assessment is often conceived of as something that happens *after the fact*—thereby simplifying music lessons so students can meet predetermined goals (another way of *reacting* to the situation). But as Sennet says: "Getting better at using tools comes to us, in part, when the tools challenge us, and this challenge often occurs just because the tools are not fit-for-purpose.... [T]he challenge can be met by adapting the form of a tool, or improvising with it as it is, using it in ways it was not meant for" (cited in Bell, 2015, p. 195).

In the Iranian situation, musicians learn their music and live their music through trial and error; they probe pathways that are not meant to be challenged, yet they challenge them, thereby confronting the status quo, and often emerge successfully. In practical terms, they manage to find performance venues, acquire album permits, and discover overground rehearsal locations. They turn opportunities into realities without any guarantee of success. They are proactive rather than reactive, without the guidance of music teachers at schools. Echoing Bronwen Robertson (2012): "Many of Tehran's unofficial rock musicians have had limited musical training, particularly in contemporary music styles. They teach each other how to play and they learn technical aspects and song writing skills from DVD-footage and music videos of their favourite artists. Practice rooms also double as teaching rooms.... With very few outlets for official music training in the styles that unofficial musicians enjoy, these young men empower each other and build on the communal knowledge of the scene by teaching new recruits" (p. 70).

# INTERACTIVE AND DECENTRALIZED ASSESSMENT

According to Martin Fautley and Richard Colwell (2012), "in many national contexts, a summative assessment is what is meant when assessment is being discussed" (p. 480), and it is a common practice in "accountability contexts" (p. 481), in which a grade or a value judgment is granted to represent the proficiency of the learner for a specific task, or a course, a semester, a degree level, and so forth. This kind of assessment represents an understanding of where the learner stands according to an ability in a particular subject. In the context of urban Iran, summative assessment does not have, nor can it have, a place in music education because music is not "acceptable" as an official public school subject. Thus, national studies do not contain any data on this topic. In contrast, all kinds of music—such as Persian art and folk music, Western classical, jazz, rock, hiphop, and many other genres—are vigorously practiced, learned, and performed. So why and how is music "assessed?"

To respond to this question, one must look at Persian art music as a representation of Iranian society (Nettl, 1980). According to Hormoz Farhat (1991), Persian art music is "monophonic; it employs a range of sound generally not exceeding two and a half octaves; it is fundamentally soloistic but not virtuosic; and it lacks grandeur and dramatic power. But it is fundamentally rich in modal variety, in melodic subtlety, and is highly personal and intimate" (p. x). Arguably, Persian art music aligns well with a decentralized theory of assessment because this music is intimate and improvisatory at its core. In this music, a "sync or swarm" (Borgo, 2005) approach operates smoothly. Because Persian art music lacks grandeur, it does not need a top-down, systematic approach to assessment. Rather, learners need to acquire necessary "soundscapes" by painstakingly practicing and memorizing the *radif*—melodic patterns that have been preserved orally over centuries. The art of improvisation within this music comes into play when a learner understands its explicit and implicit governing rules and its subtle melodic changes, then adapts them to his or her own desires and moods based on any given situation.

I suggest that this approach to music learning mirrors Iranians' lives during the repressive years after the constitutional revolution in 1905, insofar as the public had to improvise their way out of, and adapt to, new and/or unpredictable regulations of all kinds. Hence, subtle acts of resistance/subversion emerged in everyday life. Notably, the current situation of assessment in urban Iranian music education seems to follow the same path. Persian art music is soloistic, with each musician having a voice in the production of the music, yet it is not a virtuosic voice because musicians do not seek perfection, the highest musical skills possible, or showmanship. Rather, their music making manifests itself as an interactive relationship with other musicians present in the particular locality where they are creating music. Therefore, depending on each musical event, based on a specific time, place, and space, musicians (amateur or professional) "assess" musical situations. In this context, a decentralized, situated, "space and place" form of assessment comes into play.

Referring to Lev Vygotsky's theory of language, Nilsson and Folkestad (2005) state that orality, the second element of their proposed ecocultural framework, "constitutes an important part of a situated perspective in order to understand music, musical practice and musical creativity" (p. 24). The practice of Persian art music is based largely on oral and aural practices and consists of

> a repertoire—termed the *radif*—rooted in a deeply elaborate system of organization that guides the performing musicians....What is distinctive about Persian art music's instructional practice, however, is not its aural basis (a basis shared by many musical practices) but rather the complete absence of theoretical discussion in instruction. That is, the apprentice is expected to absorb the *radif* without any explicit instructional reference to theory, even though the organizing principles of the *radif* structure each performance to a great degree. This highly theoretical system is taught and learned *as if* it is not theoretically structured.    (Naqvi, 2012, pp. 185–86)

Considering orality as a part of Persian art music that represents an aspect of Iranian society in general, one can recognize the similarity between musicianship in Persian art music and its contemporary urban counterpart. Music teaching and learning in urban Iran are highly structured, in that musicians have deeply absorbed the sociopolitical norms of society, such as the framework and regulations of *Vezarat-e-ershad*—that is, the unceasing capriciousness of the authorities in their decision-making. Musicians are actively resourceful, imaginative, and practical in finding homegrown ways to reciprocally adapt their music making to the volatile changes in these regulations. As one musician in Robertson's (2012) research mentioned: "We never had anything close to us to critique, and so we learnt everything ourselves. You know, you're asking who our teachers were, but in reality teachers didn't exist" (p. 72).

Nonetheless, these affordances were found by and given to musicians regardless of their disinclination toward such conditions. Through an instinctive (Naqvi, 2012) approach, musicians constantly negotiated and interacted with the requirements of their environment and their own self-developed musical needs. Through these dynamic exchanges, one can define assessment in urban Iranian music as a decentralized interaction with the environment and ever-new musical challenges that are intuitive, intimate, and grassroots.

# LOCAL ANARCHISM

When the first generation of rock musicians in Iran emerged during the presidency of Khatami, they did not have any local role models in the genres of music they wanted to pursue (Nooshin, 2008; B. Omrani, personal communication, December 28, 2015; Robertson, 2012): "In every society there are certain and specific roles that have accompanying typecasts. Western societies have pre-conceived ideas about what a 'rocker' should look like or how they should act, but in Iran there is no local typecast for the 'rocker.' This is why a great deal of the scenes' musical and stylistic influence has been drawn in from the outside" (Robertson, 2012, p. 80). Most music these musicians were creating followed Western-origin genres such as rock 'n' roll, punk, progressive rock, and metal. Most often the lyrics to their music were either written in English or used the cherished poetries of Hafez, Mowlana (Rumi), and Saadi. Instrumentation was also similar to that of their Western counterparts: electric guitar, electric bass, keyboard, and drums. It took some years before these musicians finally found their voices and identities by adding Persian vocal techniques, fusing Persian *dastagâhs* into their Western modalities, and creating lyrics inspired by their locales: love themes; societal dilemmas such as traffic, air pollution, and rent; international stereotypes of their generation; and local politics (Nooshin, 2008). "While the musical language of Iranian rock is indeed predominantly Western, it should be noted that some bands do draw on more localized sounds. For some, the rejection of nationalistic determination of aesthetics has led to what might be called a 'placeless music.'... In such cases, the Persian lyrics and vocal style and timbre are often the only 'codes' of belonging, that which gives the music a sense of place" (Nooshin, 2008, p. 77).

During these years musicians had the opportunity to play underground, overground (Nooshin, 2005b, 2008), and abroad to flirt with ideas of Westernization, and local identities metamorphosed into fluid identities; an amalgamation of ethnic, national, secular, and religious identities (Nooshin, 2005a); and exoticization. At present, members of at least one generation of Iranian rock musicians have lived their musical careers traveling between Iran and abroad: musicians such as Raam, initially from Hypernova; Behzad Khiavchi, initially from Sarakhs (Fern); and now B-Band. They have become pioneers in their own right, whom younger bands emulate and then evolve from (B. Omrani, personal communication, December 28, 2015).

Because musicians did not have systematic guidelines or music teachers who were savvy in alternative scenes, they have become creative and self-reliant, seeking the help of the community of like-minded people in their localities to sustain their music-making practices. Their practices change constantly, based on any given moment and situation. In these conditions, securing a universal model of assessment for the country is futile and not pragmatic, as each neighborhood, city, or region has its own evolving musical rules to meet the needs of the local authorities and musicians. This status is quite similar to an anarchic community, or what Borgo (2005) called a complex system: "As opposed to systems that may simply be complicated, complex systems exhibit the possibility for adaptation and emergence by being open to energy influxes from outside the system and through their own highly interconnected nature. Their dynamics are hard to predict but not entirely random. They can exhibit regularities, but these regularities are difficult to describe briefly and impossible to describe over time with absolute precision" (p. 62). Naqvi (2012) also mentions that Persian art music is highly structured but intuitive in nature. Precisely because music making in Iran follows the rules of a complex system, its assessment should also follow the rules of this system because, as Judith Suissa (2012) points out regarding the vital facet of the anarchistic situation, "the belief that the exact form which the future society will take can never be determined in advance; the creation of the harmonious, free society is a constant, dynamic process of self-improvement, spontaneous organization and free experimentation" (p. 13).

Assessment in urban Iranian music education cannot be standardized. I argue that it should not be standardized. By allowing each locality to have its own voices of music making, similar to Persian art music, assessment becomes a diverse, intimate, organic, and grassroots approach to evaluating not only the quality of music being practiced but also the surrounding conditions. In this way, assessment spontaneously intertwines with musical practices in a natural way. It becomes part of musical practices, rather than an external force gauging musical situations and levels. This anarchistic situation has broader implications for education in general, especially in places such as Iran, where school music does not have any place: "These concern both the policy level (i.e., questions about educational provision and control), the content level (i.e., questions about the curriculum and the underlying values and aims of the educational process) and what could be understood as the meta level (i.e., questions about the moral justification of education *per se*)" (Suissa, 2012, p. 16).

A blessing in disguise, since music is not a subject in schools, is that authorities cannot take a coercive approach toward education in music—a situation one may witness in many school music contexts globally. Rather, an "anti-hierarchy, in the sense that all centralized, top-down structures are to be regarded with suspicion, and small communities favored as basic units of social organization" (Suissa, 2012, p. 62), would be the core value of such assessment in music.

# LIFESTYLE ASSESSMENT

According to Nilsson and Folkestad's (2005) ecocultural framework, theories of play and chance play remarkable roles in understanding one's musical practices and creativities: "Play is something we do for its own sake. It is free, separate, uncertain, unproductive, 'make believe' and yet governed by rules. Play with a lower degree of order is, according to Caillois (1961), associated with diversion, turbulence and improvisation, whilst play with a higher degree of order is associated with effort, patience, skill and ingenuity" (p. 24). One reason that defining and dissecting components of assessment in the urban

Iranian situation is challenging is the role of music in Iranian people's lives. Music is an embedded part of their lives (Naqvi, 2012) and does not necessarily serve any external purpose. Thus far I have addressed descriptive elements of assessment in the Iranian urban situation. In the following section these aforementioned elements resolve into the concept of lifestyle.

The four components of effort, patience, skill, and ingenuity in higher order play are indeed entrenched in Iranian youth's music-making habits and lifestyles (Nilsson & Folkestad, 2005). These elements are also crucial parts of their musical creativity, which are ingrained in theories of free improvisation, chance, and uncertainty, referencing unpredictable regulations of the authorities. Nevertheless, some elements can delineate and complement categories of assessment in this context: resistance, acts of survival, confidence, collectivity, and participatory music making (Turino, 2008), which manifest in theories of play and chance.

The unpredictability of authorities' regulations on cultural production over the years have made the practice of rock music in Iran an act of resistance. Nooshin (2005a), in discussing the role of pop music in the 1980s in Iran, notes: "While the government promoted discourses of local resistance against Western global hegemony, certain aspects of Western culture were used as a means of resisting the government-imposed hegemony.... The songs themselves were not particularly subversive or challenging, but by banning this music, the post-1979 government effectively gave pop music its subversive power" (p. 243).

Acts of music making, teaching, and learning became subversive and acts of resistance. These musicians evolved the uncertain situations into a flourishing improvisatory musical practice. What was supposed to be a disadvantage was transformed into an opportunity. The musicians used the element of surprise to their benefit, adding a certain collective character to their music making. "What remains steadfast is the scene's inherent collectivity [that] stands up for the community as a whole as it challenges societal norms, governmental policy, and outsider opinion" (Robertson, 2012, p. 80). The thought of facing potential dangers and getting into trouble with the authorities made these musicians' performances and music making exciting and ever more meaningful. Similarly, these situations made the act of music teaching and learning, and consequently its assessment, exhilarating and interesting. The constant fear of the authorities (who maintained a somber aspect) turned into a playful and not-taken-seriously situation. Nevertheless, musicians went beyond merely playful events and performed acts of survival. As Abbas Milani (2012) notes: "The [Persian] culture's knack for survival, for bending with prevailing winds and waiting for the occasion to rise again" (p. 114) directly manifests itself in its musical practices.

The concept of play as a form of regulated improvisation enjoys a certain collectivity and participation by all the involved parties. Related to the nature of improvisatory musics, Borgo's (2005) remarks are useful in viewing urban Iranian music teaching and learning: "An important goal of improvised music [scenes] appears to be ensemble self-organization so that critical levels of complexity, responsiveness, and surprise can be reached and maintained over the course of an extended performance [or musical event]" (p. 81). Negotiating musico-political moments over the years has created resilient and confident musicians who have collective ownership over their music making. Echoing Nooshin (2005a): "Musicians have become skillful at finding creative ways of working around restrictions, subtly pushing at boundaries without appearing to contest them openly and thus averting a reaction from the authorities" (p. 246). Musical assessment operates in the urban Iranian music education scene; it is dynamic and constantly pushes the boundaries.

# Concluding Remarks

Without official state-sanctioned, public music education, Iranian youth follow a self-organized and anarchistic path of music making. Youth expertly negotiate between the act of music making and the unpredictable situations they face daily. They become creative in finding new ways to propagate their music and learn the rules of their profession. Meanings attached to assessment in these circumstances become redefined and overshadow the quality of music that is being created. Assessment becomes a local activism that countervails the top-down model of assessment.

Through constant possibilizations (Goldman, 2004, p. 2), benefiting from the malfunctions stemming from societal contradictions, these musicians have created decentralized and improvisatory music-learning events that are ever changing. Musical assessment in this context is a collective, transformative, and creative act, similar to its (i.e., urban Iranian) music performative art form: an embodied experience in which the space of learning becomes the interplay between self-transformation and possibility for growth. These musicians become fully immersed in the act of music learning, which prepares them to take risks, improvise, and experiment with a multitude of ideas and actions in close association with their surrounding communities. Assessment in this context is DIY and DIWO, interactive and decentralized, locally situated, and part of their lifestyle.

## Notes

1. For a thorough understanding of the situation of music in Iran after the 1979 revolution, see Niknafs (2016), Nooshin (2005a), and Youssefzadeh (2000).
2. Couched by the religious rituals, these beat boxers create their music without any legal consequence.
3. For more details on the realization of this opera and the singing of female soloists, please refer to Tehran Bureau (2014).
4. See, for example, de Oliveira (2000) for assessment outside of schools.
5. For a complete understanding of labeling these musicians, see Nooshin (2005b, 2008) and Robertson (2012).

## REFERENCES

Bell, A. P. (2015). Can we afford these affordances? GarageBand and the double-edged sword of the digital audio workstation. *Action, Criticism, & Theory for Music Education, 14*(1), 44–65.

Beston, P. (2004). Senior student composition: An investigation of criteria used in assessments by New South Wales secondary school music teachers. *Research Studies in Music Education, 22*, 28–41. doi:10.1177/1321103X040220010401

Borgo, D. (2005). *Sync or swarm: Improvising music in a complex age.* New York: Continuum.

Caillois, R. (1961). *Play and games.* Translated from French by Meyer Barash (1961). New York: The Free Press.

de Oliveira, A. (2000). Street kids in Brazil and the concept of teaching structures. *International Journal of Music Education, 35*, 29–34. doi:10.1177/025576140003500111

During, J., Mirabdolbahi, Z., & Safvat, D. (1991). *The art of Persian music.* Washington, DC: Mage.

Farhat, H. (1991). *The dastgah concept in Persian music.* Cambridge, UK: Cambridge University Press.

Fautley, M., & Colwell, R. (2012). Assessment in the secondary music classroom. In G. E. McPherson & G. F. Welch (Eds.), *The Oxford handbook of music education* (Vol. 1, pp. 477–93). New York: Oxford University Press. doi:10.1093/oxfordhb/9780199730810.013.0029

Fautley, M., & Savage, J. (2008). *Assessment for learning and teaching in secondary schools.* Exeter, UK: Learning Matters.

Gibson, J. J. (1977). The theory of affordances. In R. E. Shaw & J. Bransford Hillsdale (Eds.), *Perceiving, acting, and knowing* (pp. 127–43). Hoboken, NJ: Lawrence Erlbaum.

Gibson, J. J. (1979). *The ecological approach to visual perception.* Boston, MA: Houghton Mifflin.

Goldman, E. (2004). *The modern drama.* Whitefish, MT: Kessinger.

Hess, J. (2015). Decolonizing music education: Moving beyond tokenism. *International Journal of Music Education, 33*, 336–47. doi:10.1177/0255761415581283

Holmes, A. V., Gokturk, D., Aguilar, B. E., & Chen, J. J. (2010). Assessment "over the ocean"— Outside the US. In T. S. Brophy (Ed.), *The practice of assessment in music education: Frameworks, models, and designs* (pp. 95–102). Chicago: GIA.

Lundström, H. (2012). Music education from a slightly outside perspective. In G. E. McPherson & G. F. Welch (Eds.), *The Oxford handbook of music education* (Vol. 1, pp. 652–57). New York: Oxford University Press. doi:10.1093/oxfordhb/9780199730810.013.0029

Milani, A. (2012). *The shah.* New York: Palgrave Macmillan.

Miller, L. (1999). *Music and song in Persia.* Salt Lake City: University of Utah Press.

Naqvi, E. (2012). Teaching practices in Persian art music. In W. Bowman & A. Frega (Eds.), *The Oxford handbook of philosophy in music education* (pp. 180–91). New York: Oxford University Press.

Nettl, B. (1978). Classical music in Tehran: The process of change. In B. Nettl (Ed.), *Eight urban musical cultures* (pp. 146–85). Chicago: University of Illinois Press.

Nettl, B. (1980). Musical values and social values: Symbols in Iran. *Asian Music, 12*(1), 129–48. doi:10.2307/833800

Niknafs, N. (2016). In a box: A narrative of a/n (under)grounded Iranian musician. *Music Education Research, 18*(4), 351–63.

Niknafs, N. (2018). Tehran's epistemic heterotopia: Resisting music education. *Philosophy of Music Education Review, 26* (2), 155–75.

Nilsson, B., & Folkestad, G. (2005). Children's practice of computer-based composition. *Music Education Research, 7*, 21–37. doi:10.1080/14613800500042042

Nooshin, L. (2005a). Subversion and countersubversion: Power, control, and meaning in the new Iranian pop music. In A. J. Randall (Ed.), *Music, power and politics* (pp. 231–72). New York: Routledge.

Nooshin, L. (2005b). Underground, overground: Rock music and youth discourses in Iran. *Iranian Studies, 38*, 463–94. doi:10.1080/00210860500300820

Nooshin, L. (2008). The language of rock: Iranian youth, popular music and Iranian identity. In M. Semati (Ed.), *Media, culture and society in Iran: Living with globalization and the Islamic Republic* (pp. 69–93). Abingdon, UK: Routledge.

PressTV. (2013, August 30). *First opera in Iran in decades.* Retrieved from https://www.youtube.com/watch?v=BtNAxu9jlug

Przybylski, L., & Niknafs, N. (2015). Teaching and learning popular music in higher education through interdisciplinary collaboration: Practice what you preach. *IASPM@Journal, 5*(1), 100–123. doi:10.5429/2079-3871(2015)v5i1.7en

Robertson, B. (2012). *Reverberations of dissent: Identity and expression in Iran's music scene.* London: Continuum.

Schippers, H. (2010). *Facing the music: Shaping music education from a global perspective.* New York: Oxford University Press.

Semati, M. (2008). Living with globalization and the Islamic state: An introduction to media, culture, and society in Iran. In M. Semati (Ed.), *Media, culture and society in Iran: Living with globalization and the Islamic state* (pp. 1–13). Abingdon, UK: Routledge.

Suissa, J. (2012). *Anarchism and education: A philosophical perspective.* Abingdon, UK: Routledge.

Tehran Bureau. (2014, August 29). *Alone again, naturally: Women singing in Iran.* Retrieved from https://www.theguardian.com/world/iran-blog/2014/aug/29/women-singing-islamic-republic-iran

Turino, T. (2008). *Music as social life: The politics of participation.* Chicago: University of Chicago Press.

Youssefzadeh, A. (2000). The situation of music in Iran since the revolution: The role of official organizations. *British Journal of Ethnomusicology, 9*(2), 35–61.

# CHAPTER 27

·········································································

# INTERNATIONAL PERSPECTIVES ON ASSESSMENT IN MUSIC EDUCATION

·········································································

## ALEXANDRA KERTZ-WELZEL

ASSESSMENT happens daily in many classrooms around the world. Often it is a natural part of music learning, offering opportunities for evaluating achievement and improving learning. Even though it can sometimes interfere with the flow of music making or the joy of inventing new sounds, it is part of our classroom routines. However, it looks different in different countries: Australian high school students evaluate, in dialogue with their teacher and each other, the compositions they create; seventh graders in Switzerland work on a self-evaluation regarding the improvement of their singing skills during the previous three months; at the end of a learning sequence, students in a Swedish high school perform for the teacher their favorite pop songs, individually and together; third graders in a German elementary school solve a riddle about Mozart's life; and young people in an Austrian middle school present their portfolios containing introductions to pieces for an upcoming school recital. These and other kinds of assessment happen daily around the world. Assessment usually affects all subjects that are part of the public school curriculum, even though in artistic subjects such as music education, assessment can be challenging.

The variety of assessment tools just presented illustrates the richness of music education worldwide. In times of increased globalization and internationalization, when international student assessments such as the Program for International Student Assessment (PISA)[1] try to redefine education as a project of the global community, it is crucial to look at the global diversity of assessment practices. This includes above all the educational background of prominent educational ideas, such as *Ubuntu* in Africa (Enslin & Horsthemke, 2004), *Ren* in China (Li & Ni, 2015), and *Bildung* in Germany. Investigating assessment in music education from an international perspective can facilitate an understanding of the global music education community as a diverse yet united community that offers many opportunities to learn from each other (Kertz-Welzel, 2018).

This chapter presents international perspectives on assessment in music education. In analyzing significant aspects of assessment in selected countries, the importance of educational ideals and goals becomes obvious. This leads to a broader understanding of how successful practices in some countries work and could be utilized to improve assessment practices elsewhere. At the core of these considerations is the idea of fostering students as self-determined and mature individuals—as proposed in the German notion of *Bildung*—who are involved in the assessment practices in partnership with their teachers. Assessment is particularly meaningful for young people when they participate in it and when it is related to their own musical worlds, supporting their personal and musical development.

The chapter begins with considerations of the global music education community in view of assessment. The second section focuses on selected aspects of international assessment methods, first investigating the significance of educational ideals and goals and then scrutinizing assessment policies and practices regarding creativity in music. The final part summarizes the value of international perspectives on assessment in music education and envisions utilizing selected assessment strategies to improve music education internationally.

# International Music Education and Assessment

In many countries, music education is part of the public school curriculum. While there are national differences in music education systems and approaches, there are many international commonalities. They indicate that we are a global music education community. Marie McCarthy (2012) states that music educators internationally "are united by a common purpose: to engage children and youth in music and to develop their artistic life and their humanity" (p. 40). Thus, music educators around the world share the same motivations and intentions, no matter how music education is carried out in their respective countries. McCarthy (2012) characterizes the richness of the diverse yet united international community as "the global tapestry of music education" (p. 57). This indicates that music educators worldwide are not only part of this multifaceted global community, but also can make valuable contributions to the international music education discourse, using the specific perspectives of their national music education systems. Only if we share our knowledge and skills will music education globally be improved. This certainly involves assessment as one of the most contested areas of music education worldwide.

# International Perspectives

When investigating the nature of assessment in different countries and music education systems, there are various challenges. One is that assessment practices are always connected to a specific system of education and music education, including a curriculum. Investigations solely focusing on assessment might therefore be in danger of being fragmentary. A much broader perspective is necessary, considering various aspects of a particular music education system. This can, for instance, involve significant educational ideals and goals (e.g., *Bildung*), the most common music education approach in a specific country (e.g., general or performance-based music education), music education's status as mandatory or elective, or the kind of music favored (e.g., Western European art music, popular music). This educational context helps in understanding more thoroughly why assessment is happening in a specific way in a particular country.

But aside from the general problem of focusing on a single aspect of music education, there is another aspect often overlooked in international music education: language. Due to the international hegemony of Anglo-American music education, English is used as the international language in music education. While a common language is certainly important to facilitate communication, using English terminology implies that we all mean the same, even though non-native English speakers use English words as translations that may not always fit the meaning of the original words they had in mind (Kertz-Welzel, 2016). The English term "assessment," for example, has been translated into German in numerous ways, such as *Bewertung*, *Beurteilung*, and *Einschaetzung*.[2] The most appropriate term in German music education for the English understanding of assessment would be *Leistungsbewertung*. This German concept refers to evaluating students' learning progress or success, resulting in the assigning of grades. This meaning of assessment is slightly different from what the term assessment describes in an international context. However, since assessment does not play as significant a role in German music education as it does in other countries due to German educational traditions and approaches to music education, the German vocabulary for assessment is rather limited. A differentiation between summative and formative assessment certainly happens in everyday practice, such as evaluating the learning achievement at the end of a learning sequence or evaluating progress during the learning process. But the terminological differentiation in German is not as distinct or in all aspects comparable to the differentiation in Anglo-American music education. Therefore, it is important to refer to the general educational context and to take issues of language and terminology into account when discussing specific aspects of international music education such as assessment.

There are certainly many factors that have an impact on the assessment culture in different countries, such as the sociocultural context, the connection of school music to students' musical cultures, and the respective definitions of musical learning and knowledge. While it might never be possible to thoroughly analyze all issues, considering at least some of them facilitates gaining a better understanding of what assessment means in music education worldwide and what we could learn from each other (Holmes, Goektuerk, Aguilar, & Chen, 2010). Overall, international perspectives on assessment broaden the individual point of view and help to envision new ways of thinking and acting in music education.

## The Meaning of Assessment

Assessment happens daily, in obvious or implicit ways, informing music educators about their students' learning progress and the success of their teaching. Assessment can be complex or simple, written or oral, formative or summative; it can occur through auditions, portfolios (digital, analog, multimedia), structured response protocols, rubric-based scoring procedures, informal observations, reflections and self-reflections, or peer response. This diversity of assessment practices exemplifies that assessment is concerned with gathering information about various dimensions of learners' development to make the best instructional decisions (Airasian & Russel, 2007). It is a way of monitoring and summarizing learning progress. For Regina Murphy (2013), "the most important purpose of assessment in music is to enable the child to make progress over time" (p. 142). Assessment helps music teachers make appropriate instructional decisions.

Sandra Stauffer (2008) suggests a framework for discussing assessment policies and practices globally, highlighting certain aspects. First, assessment might be closely linked to accountability, maybe even be equal to it. Students should demonstrate that they have reached specific curricular goals and that teachers have taught in an appropriate way. Assessment aims at students' and teachers' performances, because both are accountable for what is going on in classrooms. Second, assessment serves many functions that might change according to time and circumstances. It can be focused on teachers, students, or schools. It can be conducted according to specific guidelines or standards, whether national, regional, or local. It can be concentrated on different aspects such as competencies in music technology, performance ability, or creativity. Third, assessment is part of the daily routine of music teaching and learning, in the same way that performers evaluate the music they make while practicing. This means that it is a natural part of learning processes. Fourth, at its best, assessment helps students develop musical knowledge and skills, including musicianship. Assessment is a way to indicate what competencies need to be improved, perhaps in a dialogue with the music teacher or peers. It can support individual musical development, regardless of country and circumstances.

However, assessment is also a contested area and a complex endeavor, regardless of the country and the system of music education it is bound to. It raises many questions. These may concern the misuse of assessment as related to issues of power, for instance through the wrong assessment tools being used to demonstrate to students that they are incompetent and might never be able to reach the intended goals. This danger of assessment could be addressed through questions facilitating a better understanding of assessment, such as: Who decides what is assessed? How is it assessed? By whom is it assessed? The answers to these questions vary, depending on national, regional, or local guidelines. Most often, curricular documents or policies are points of reference for assessment. But despite these documents, the reality in music classrooms world-wide depends on the individual implementation of them and personal relationships between students and music teachers.

Aside from the aspects previously mentioned, there are more general challenges to assessment in international music education, such as music's nature as art or social action, the subjectivity of musical experiences, the diversity of musical cultures and competencies, and issues of talent. For the sake of having simple evaluation criteria, sometimes the varieties of musical competencies, knowledge, and skills are reduced to mere factual knowledge, such as mastering the labeling of major or minor chords, knowing the most important works of Beethoven, or identifying the characteristics of the blues. But despite the challenges, assessment is an important part of music teaching and learning. Harold Abeles, Charles Hoffer, and Robert Klotman (1995) summarize:

> There is a need to determine students' achievement and to gather feedback about the effectiveness of the teaching and instructional materials, as well as to identify areas in which students may need additional instruction. To be effective, teachers must assess to determine what their students have learned. Without this informa-tion, teachers do not have ways of improving their own teaching or identifying and helping students who need additional assistance.    (p. 303)

This statement underlines the various functions of effective assessment strategies. From this point of view, assessment is indispensable because it helps improve instruction and learning. It is an important form of feedback for both teachers and students. Certainly the effectiveness and meaningfulness of assessment depend on the way it is utilized and how the information gathered is interpreted. These activities vary internationally.

# INTERNATIONAL PERSPECTIVES

Educational systems are complex and the result of particular historical and political developments. While it is not possible to capture their multifaceted nature completely, it is possible to get an impression of some aspects, particularly of those that might be use-ful for the international music education community.

## The Power of Educational Ideals

Assessment and evaluation have never played significant roles in German music educa-tion, even though music is a mandatory subject in public schools, most often until the ninth or tenth grade. There are various reasons for this, the most important being the notion of *Bildung* as the main goal of German education in general and music education in particular.

*Bildung* has in international music education always been a "secret" term, difficult to understand, although there have been various attempts at explication (Kertz-Welzel, 2004; Nielsen, 2007; Varkøy, 2010; Heimonen, 2015). While there is no literal translation into English, *Bildung* is similar to what the English term "education" represents, but it also means more. It aims at educating mature and self-determined people, at the development of character, knowledge, and abilities in terms of formation or cultivation. Anglo-American concepts such as liberal education (Lovlie & Standish, 2002) and critical pedagogy (Gur-Ze'ev, 2002) capture at least some aspects of its meaning.

The notion of *Bildung* that is still common today was developed at the end of the eighteenth century. As a result of the Enlightenment, people's destiny was no longer determined by church doctrines. There was no metaphysical security anymore, and everybody was free to choose his or her own destiny. Without the support of a common meaning of life, self-cultivation and formation became crucial tasks. *Bildung* , as Jan Masschelein and Norbert Ricken (2003) state, is "the endless voyage of the individual towards himself/herself as part of an ideal humanity" (p. 140). It is the journey a person undertakes to find herself and to unfold her inner potential. How can somebody achieve *Bildung*? Through her own efforts and the help of teachers. In its original meaning, as developed by Wilhelm von Humboldt (1767–1835), *Bildung* was connected to neohumanist educational theory, favoring an ideal image of humanity that could best be fostered through specific lesson content such as ancient Latin or Greek literature and philosophy.[3] Even though the preferred content facilitating *Bildung* has changed over time, schooling's main goal of shaping mature and self-determined young people has remained the same. Music education plays an important role in this process.

*Bildung* in music as the main goal of German music education aims at two different things: becoming mature and self-determined through transformative musical experiences and acquiring specific musical knowledge and skills. The notion of *Bildung* unites musical and nonmusical goals, not differentiating between students' personal growth and acquiring specific musical competencies. However, there is no unified notion about what exactly *Bildung* in music means. Wilfred Gruhn (1999) asserts that *Bildung* in music particularly describes the ability to experience music musically, to feel or understand it appropriately, and to express its meaning in various ways. Stefan Orgass (1999) emphasizes that *Bildung* particularly happens when music becomes meaningful to people, helping them to understand it more deeply while performing or talking about it. Kaiser (1998) underlines that *Bildung* concerns individual musical identities, learning how to use music responsibly and to make informed musical choices. For Christian Rolle (1999), *Bildung* in music particularly happens when people have intense and transformative musical experiences through music making.

If the goal of *Bildung* in music is self-determined, artistically experienced, and creative individuals, this cannot be easily assessed. This explains why assessment has not played an important role in German music education. However, the general function of assessment is usually determined in political documents such as the Bavarian School Laws (Bayerische Staatskanzlei, 2016). These state that teachers in Bavarian schools are bound to regularly assess their students' achievements in written, oral, or practical ways. The kind of assessment and the frequency depend on the type of school, the grade, and the subject, giving teachers considerable scope, particularly in music education. Usually a state curriculum suggests a specific number and type of assessment for music education. Music teachers are for the most part free to choose the appropriate kind of assessment, as well as when to assess. But eventually they must give students a specific grade in music education, which appears on their two annual report cards. The general curriculum for elementary schools in Bavaria (Staatsinstitut fuer Schulqualitaet und Bildungsforschung, n.d.) states that assessment should not only function as an evaluation of performance, but also be connected to acknowledgment and personal relationships between teachers and students, according to the notion of *Bildung*. It should not just be a tool for measuring achievement, but also be related to a general personal feedback culture: "Students are interested in learning and accomplishments. An atmosphere of acknowledgement and appreciation and the feeling of being competent and of being able to accomplish something by themselves strengthens students' self- confidence and keeps their motivation alive."[4]

Assessment should be part of a personal learning partnership between students and teachers, facilitating a supportive learning atmosphere. It is based on the belief that young people enjoy being successful. Therefore, assessment should not just be about assigning a grade, but rather support young people's motivation to learn. A positive feedback culture in terms of carefully evaluating and supporting individual learning processes should be the preferred kind of assessment in view of the notion of *Bildung*. This includes appreciating effort and achievement, regardless of whether there are current limits to a child's capacity. Even though the reality in German music classrooms might not always live up to this ideal, *Bildung* represents the framework for understanding what assessment means in German music education.

But what does assessment in German music education look like? In some regards, it might not be so different from what happens in other countries. There are written tests, oral examinations, student presentations, and auditions. Tests often evaluate knowledge about easy-to-check musical facts in music theory and history such as intervals, chords, or the sonata form. Auditions can take the form of the old-fashioned but still common singing solo in front of the class or performing on an instrument, which students have often learned primarily through private tuition because general music education is the common approach in German schools. Presentations about specific topics, such as popular singers, bands, or genres such as hip-hop, are commonplace. But more innovative methods of assessment are also used, which often aim at relating music education in schools to the musical culture of young people. These kinds of assessment might take the form of learning diaries, individual feedback, self-assessment, monitoring of learning progress, or learning contracts between students and teachers. German music educators are mostly free to create the appropriate kind of assessment for their students in relation to the notion of *Bildung* and respective learning objectives, competencies, or standards as suggested in a state curriculum. The fact that the typical approach in German music education is general music education also plays a role in assessment.

But even though the notion of *Bildung* and the characteristics of the German school system might support unique aspects of the assessment culture, there are also challenges, which are similar to those in other countries. Reducing lesson content to what can easily be assessed (Stauffer, 2008), focusing on assigning grades rather than creating a positive feedback culture, and having lack of clarity regarding the assessment criteria (Schaefer-Lembeck, 2008) may be global assessment commonalities. Research on assessment in German music education raises additional issues, such as the function and design of questions in written tests and their relatedness to students' musical worlds (Niessen, 2008), the meaning of the standards movement for assessment (Lehmann-Wermser, 2008), and the use of problem-based learning to further link the goals of music education in schools and students' individual musical lives (Orgass, 2008). The ability to discuss music and argue about it, questioning and explaining why somebody likes a song or why one composition might be better than another, is also a goal for German music education, which can be assessed with specific tasks (Rolle, 2008).

The music project Voice Training (Stimm:*Bildung* ), conducted at the Anne-Frank-Gesamtschule in Dueren, Germany, exemplifies the role *Bildung* can play in assessment in terms of self-assessment as part of constructing individual ways of learning (Geuen, 2008).[5] The project's first goal is to improve students' singing; they should get to know their own voices and develop vocal self-awareness and confidence. The second goal is knowing music of various times and cultures, including music theory and the ability to improvise in respective styles. Third, students should help develop their choir's specific sound and memorize a decent number of choral works. Finally, through meeting the goals previously mentioned, students should generally improve their self-confidence, social competence, voice, body awareness, and ability to concentrate (Geuen, 2008, p. 4). A specific lesson structure supporting students in designing their individualized learning pathways helps them achieve these goals. Teachers first introduce new voice exercises and practice them with students; later, students oversee the practicing, choosing the exercises and giving advice for further improvement.[6] Delegating responsibility to students also shapes the kind of assessment. Students receive a questionnaire on which they can evaluate their own learning progress. They assess their competencies in such areas as "Getting to know music from various times and cultures," "Knowing notation," "Development of musical memory," "Singing high pitches," "Knowledge about how the voice works," and "Keeping the right tempo." Students mark how they think they are doing ("I am able to do that," "I need to practice that," "I am so far not sufficiently familiar with that," "I do not like practicing this song") (Geuen, 2008, p. 65). These questionnaires can be related to specific songs or voice exercises, such as imitating a fly by humming. Instead of regular questionnaires, students can also keep a learning diary, documenting daily what they have learned, what they liked, what they have done particularly well, and what they still need to practice.[7] The lesson content is organized in various small units, with tests evaluating whether somebody needs further assistance or can move on to the advanced unit. Individual work and group activities alternate, giving students freedom but also offering support at each stage of the learning process.

The general success of this project underlines the fact that assessment is particularly effective when students are involved in the process of evaluation. If they recognize what they know and what they still need to learn, they are motivated to improve their knowledge and abilities. Agency returns to the students and empowers them. Being in charge of one's own learning and formation, at least to a certain degree, is a significant dimension of *Bildung*.

From a global perspective, *Bildung* is just one example of the impact educational ideas can have on assessment in music education. There are many other interesting international points of view regarding assessment, particularly related to creativity.

## Assessing Musical Creativity Internationally

Developing creativity is an important goal for music education in many countries. However, the meaning of creativity and its assessment vary internationally, depending on particular school and music education systems, educational policies, and music teacher education programs. Generally, there is a broad understanding of creativity internationally, related not only to composing or improvisation, but also to various kinds of musical activities such as listening or performing, including digital musicianship (Burnard, 2012; Hennessey & Amabile, 1999).

In their chapter about international perspectives on assessing creativity in music, Samuel Leong and his colleagues (2012) examine evaluation practices in the United Kingdom, Australia, and Hong Kong. Their emphasis is particularly on comparing exemplary assessment tasks. What is striking at first is the fact that the assessment tasks are not so different in the countries investigated:[8] Composition and improvisation seem to be identified as particular fields for creativity. For example, in a British primary school, creativity was fostered through composing a piece that musically depicted somebody jogging. This task was assigned after the children (ages ten and eleven) had listened to a composition based on the same theme (Leong, Burnard, Jeanneret, Leung, & Waugh, 2012, p. 394). Students were expected to use untuned percussion instruments to create an appropriate sonic exploration. Assessment was primarily carried out by the teachers, who used the original description of the task as assessment criteria. In another example from an Australian primary school, students (ages eleven and twelve) were asked to compose a short piece exemplifying the theme "Under African Skies," using fitting sounds and instruments found through the GarageBand software. This was assigned as group work, as was the case in the British example, and the teacher provided feedback and assessment regarding the activities, particularly related to the originality of sound and specific African features (Leong et al., 2012, p. 397). The description of the tasks functioned as a guideline for assessment and thereby helped students to understand what was expected of them. In another example, in primary schools in Hong Kong groups of six to eleven students were free to choose various kinds of performances they wanted to present, thereby demonstrating their creativity. Creativity was thought to be particularly related to the choice of what was performed on stage and the performance style. Originality and confidence were important success criteria (Leong et al., 2012, p. 400). In secondary schools in Hong Kong, students were supposed to musically illustrate a story, thereby demonstrating their ability to choose appropriate instruments and to design sounds in a way exemplifying the respective story. In addition to the musical goals, social skills as demonstrated in successful group work were also a factor indicating success (Leong et al., 2012, p. 402).

What is striking regarding the meaning of creativity in these three countries is, first, that composing and improvising are the foremost musical activities demonstrating creativity, although creativity can be related to various kinds of musical engagements. This could indicate a rather narrow understanding of what creativity is, which could be broadened, for instance, by recent research (Burnard, 2012). Second, the assessment criteria might address not only creativity, but many more aspects. Criteria such as "improvise with specific Indian features" or "demonstration of cooperative skills" are rather "loose parameters, with which students can structure their work, and around which the work will be assessed" (Leong et al., 2012, p. 403). These criteria are not at all specific to creativity. While this could be problematic, these criteria indicate that musical creativity might be complex and cannot be reduced completely to some distinct criteria. In the end, it might not be so much the well-defined criteria that define what good assessment is, but rather the partnership between students and teachers. If assessment utilizes various kinds of formative and summative approaches in a meaningful way, music education can foster students' creativity and support their musical and individual development in ways that are similar to what *Bildung* implies.

In German music education and in the context of *Bildung*, creativity is related to various musical activities such as listening, composing and improvising, or arguing about music. A typical example of creative activities would be composing a musical piece for paper and stones (Stoeger, 2006). First, fifth-grade students try out various sounds with paper and stones, experimenting with different kinds of musical structure, including trying out processes of creating phases of tension and release. Then students start to create a piece of music, having twenty minutes for accomplishing this group work. These rules are set as guidelines for the composition: "(1) The piece should be interesting. (2) Remember the piece, so that you are able to repeat it. (3) All sounds need to be planned in advance and performed according to your agreements about the organization of the piece. (4) At least at one point, there needs to be a longer break" (Stoeger, 2006, p. 6). These rules served not only as guidelines for creating and performing the music, but also as assessment criteria. In addition to teachers and peers providing permanent feedback during the group work, after the performance there was extra time for additional evaluation, self-assessment, and discussions. Evaluating the performances was a significant part of the learning process. It helped students to listen thoroughly and to make informed musical judgments. The ability to talk and argue about music, personal choices, and musical judgments is a significant part of the German concept of *Bildung* in music (Rolle, 2008). This connects music education in schools with students' musical worlds and makes it more meaningful for their individual musical lives.

The examples from the United Kingdom, Australia, Hong Kong, and Germany show that creativity is often understood as improvising and composing, and that assessing these forms of music making is varied and complex. However, how students' creativity is assessed depends not only on sound assessment criteria, but also on preparing teachers appropriately, as Jane Cheung-Yung and her colleagues (2008, p. 98) point out regarding Hong Kong. Music teachers need to know what creative musical activities are, how they can facilitate them in their classrooms, and how they can best be assessed. When music teachers learn more about creativity and the way it can be evaluated, they can utilize assessment in a more meaningful way. Jay McPherson (2008, p. 136) points out that in New South Wales (Australia), support for teachers is crucial for implementing new assessment policies in creativity, for instance regarding students taking part in the assessment process.

In transforming assessment practices internationally toward being more meaningful for students, teacher education and music education policies are important points of reference (Kertz-Welzel, 2017). New policies need to be developed. But they are only useful if implemented by administrators and teachers who have the competencies and the resources to do so. International perspectives on assessment can certainly help in developing new ideas for improving assessment practices, even though the global dominance of Anglo-American music education and tendencies toward homogenization and standardization might present a challenge (Kertz-Welzel, 2018).

# CONCLUSION

The examples from different countries presented here indicate that there are commonalities and differences regarding assessment in music education around the world. The educational systems, the general assessment culture, the history of music education, and the particular approaches to and overall goals of education play significant roles in understanding the nature and values of assessment. In particular, educational ideas specific to a certain country such as *Bildung* are paramount. They underline something we often tend to overlook: everyday practices, including assessment, are based on various philosophical assumptions, regardless of whether these assumptions include a specific image of humanity, the meaning of education, or a special notion of music. Indeed, international perspectives help us pinpoint often-overlooked aspects of music education, thereby underlining the significance of philosophical perspectives for various kinds of daily routines in music education classrooms. Perhaps the significance of *Bildung* for German music education and the vision of educating mature and self-determined people who feel responsible for the welfare of society and its people could be inspiring for international music education—as can many more educational ideals such as the African *Ubuntu* and the Chinese *Ren*.

Recent publications in music education emphasize the longing for new visions in music education, trying to implement social justice (Benedict, Schmidt, Spruce, & Woodford, 2015), arguing for artistic citizenship (Elliott, Silverman, & Bowman, 2016), and presenting a general call for humanistic education (UNESCO, 2015). In international student assessments, the global standards movement, and various attempts at measuring students' achievements, the humane dimension of education is often lost. Perhaps *Bildung*, as one example among many other possibilities, can help broaden our horizons for the philosophical foundations of what we do as music teachers. It is not only about designing the best methods of assessment, but rather about facilitating learning partnerships, personal encounters, acknowledgment, and appreciation. Music education is successful if it empowers students and teachers to develop their potential and to make valuable contributions to the welfare of society and its people. Assessment could play an important role in this process, as underlined by Martin Fautley (2015) concerning social justice.

Assessment—when approached from an international perspective, including philosophical foundations and a vision of a just society—can be a powerful tool for much-needed transformations in music education. Murphy's (2013) statement could serve as an inspiration: "Undertaken effectively, assessment can bring a shared vision of teaching, learning and creativity in the school, generate high expectations for learners and teachers alike, and enable all to move forward consistently towards higher goals and fulfillment in music learning" (p. 141). Fleshed out according to the respective music education contexts of various countries, and thereby supporting our visions of a humane society, Murphy's insight may be internationally applicable. It could inspire more successful assessment policies and practices in music education worldwide.

## Notes

1. For more information, see Program for International Student Assessment (PISA) at http://www.oecd.org/pisa/
2. Dict.cc, retrieved from http://www.dict.cc/?s=assessment
3. For further information about Humboldt's educational ideas, see Hohendorf, G. (1993). Wilhelm von Humboldt (1767-1835). *Prospects: The quarterly review of comparative education,* 23(3–4) (pp. 613-623). Retrieved from http://www.ibe.unesco.org/sites/default/files/humbolde.PDF
4. Translated by Alexandra Kertz-Welzel.
5. This is a ninety-minute project in music education on a weekly basis, in addition to the regular weekly general music lesson in grades 5 and 6.
6. Students are only in charge of vocal exercises. Leading rehearsals is the job of the music teachers.
7. The learning progress and success are documented in portfolios. Certificates that are used for the biannual reports summarize the students' learning development.
8. A reason for this similarity might be that Australia and Hong Kong are former British colonies and share some educational traditions.

# REFERENCES

Abeles, H. F., Hoffer, C. R., & Klotmann, R. H. (1995). *Foundations of music education* (2nd ed.). New York: Schirmer.

Airasian, P. W., & Russel, M. (2007). *Classroom assessment: concepts and applications* (6th ed.) New York: McGraw-Hill.

Bayerische Staatskanzlei. (2016). *Bayerisches Gesetz ueber das Erziehungs- und Unterrichtswesen (BayEUG)*. Retrieved from http://www.gesetze-bayern.de/Content/Document/BayEUG

Benedict, C., Schmidt, P., Spruce, G., & Woodford, P. (2015). *The Oxford handbook of social justice in music education*. New York: Oxford University Press.

Burnard, P. (2012). *Musical creativities in practice*. Oxford: Oxford University Press.

Cheung-Yung, J. W. Y., Cham-Lai, E. S. C., & Mak, C. W. C. (2008). The impact of music education policy on creative music-making in the school curriculum. In C. C. Leung, L. C. R. Yip, & T. Imada (Eds.), *Music education policy and implementation: International perspectives* (pp. 97–110). Hirosaki: Hirosaki University Press.

Elliott, D. J., Silverman, M., & Bowman, W. (Eds.). (2016). *Artistic citizenship: Artistry, social responsibility and ethical praxis*. New York: Oxford University Press.

Enslin, P., & Horsthemke, K. (2004). Can Ubuntu provide a model for citizenship education in African democracies? *Comparative Education, 40*(4), 545–58.

Fautley, M. (2015). Music education assessment and social justice. In C. Benedict, P. Schmidt, G. Spruce, & P. Woodford (Eds.), *The Oxford handbook of social justice in music education* (pp. 513–24). New York: Oxford University Press.

Geuen, H. (2008). "Das kann ich schon!"—Leistungbewusstsein als Element individueller Lernweggestaltung im Musikunterricht. In H.-U. Schaefer-Lembeck (Ed.), *Leistung im Musikunterricht* (pp. 55–69). Muenchen: Allitera Verlag.

Gruhn, W. (1999). Wie entsteht musikalische Bildung? Von den Chancen und Schwierigkeiten des Musikunterrichts heute. *Musik und Aesthetik, 3*(12), 52–65.

Gur-Ze'ev, I. (2002). Bildung and critical theory in the face of postmodern education. *Journal of Philosophy of Education, 36*(3), 391–408.

Heimonen, M. (2015). Bildung and music education. *Philosophy of Music Education Review, 22*(2), 188–208.

Hennessy, B. A., & Amabile, T. M. (1999). Consensual assessment. In M. A. Runco, & S. R. Pritzker (Eds.), *Encyclopedia of creativity* (Vol. 1, pp. 248–60). Millbrae: California Academic Press.

Hohendorf, G. (1993). Wilhelm von Humboldt (1767–1835). *Prospects: The quarterly review of comparative education, 23*(3–4), 613–23. Retrieved from http://www.ibe.unesco.org/sites/default/files/humbolde.PDF

Holmes, A. V., Goektuerk, D., Aguilar, B. E., & Chen, J.-J. (2010). Assessment "over the ocean"—outside of the U.S. In T. S. Brophy (Ed.), *The practice of assessment in music education. Frameworks, models and designs* (pp. 94–102). Chicago: GIA Publications.

Kaiser, H.-J. (1998). Zur Bedeutung von Musik und musikalischer Bildung. In H.-J. Kaiser (Ed.), *Aesthetische Theorie und musikpaedagogische Theoriebildung* (pp. 98–114). Mainz: Schott.

Kertz-Welzel, A. (2004). Didaktik of music: A German concept and its comparison to American music pedagogy. *International Journal of Music Education (Practice), 22*(3), 277–86.

Kertz-Welzel, A. (2016). Sociological implications of English as an international language in music education. *Action, Criticism & Theory for Music Education, 15*(3), 53–66. Retrieved from http://act.maydaygroup.org/articles/KertzWelzel15_3.pdf

Kertz-Welzel, A. (2017). Revisiting Bildung and its meaning for international music education. In P. Schmidt & R. Colwell (Eds.), *The Oxford handbook of music education policy* (pp. 107–21). New York: Oxford University Press.

Kertz-Welzel, A. (2018). *Globalizing music education: A framework.* Bloomington: Indiana University Press.

Lehmann-Wermser, A. (2008). Kompetenzorientiert Musik unterrichten? In H.-U. Schaefer-Lembeck (Ed.), *Leistung im Musikunterricht* (pp. 112–33). Muenchen: Allitera Verlag.

Leong, S., Burnard, P., Jeanneret, N., Leung, B. W., & Waugh, C. (2012). Assessing creativity in music: International perspectives and practices. In G. McPherson & G. Welsh (Eds.), *The Oxford handbook of music education* (Vol. 2, pp. 389–407). New York: Oxford University Press.

Li, J., & Ni, M. (2015). Renewing the Confucian tradition: Kindness and respect in children's everyday schooling. In: P. L. Thomas (Ed.), *Pedagogies of kindness and respect: On the lives and education of children* (pp. 69–80). New York: Peter Lang.

Lovlie, L., & Standish, P. (2002). Bildung and the idea of a liberal education. *Journal of Philosophy of Education, 36*(3), 317–40.

Masschelein, J., & Ricken, N. (2003). Do we (still) need the concept of Bildung? *Educational Philosophy and Theory, 35*(2), 139–54.

McCarthy, M. (2012). International perspectives. In G. McPherson & G. Welch (Eds.), *The Oxford handbook of music education* (Vol. 1, pp. 40–62). New York: Oxford University Press.

McPherson, J. (2008). Assessment for learning in the New South Wales music years 7–10 syllabus: An approach to promote best practice. In C. C. Leung, L. C. R. Yip, & T. Imada (Eds.), *Music education policy and implementation: International perspectives* (pp. 131–40). Hirosaki: Hirosaki University Press.

Murphy, R. (2013). Assessing creatively. In P. Burnard, & R. Murphy (Eds.), *Teaching music creatively* (pp. 141–52). New York: Routledge.

Nielsen, Frede V. (2007). Music (and arts) education from the point of view of Didaktik and Bildung. In L. Bresler (Ed.), *International handbook of research in arts education* (pp. 265–86). Dordrecht: Springer.

Niessen, A. (2008). Leistungsmessung oder individuelle Foerderung? Zur Funktion und Gestaltung von Aufgaben im Musikunterricht. In H.-U. Schaefer-Lembeck (Ed.), *Leistung im Musikunterricht* (pp. 134–52). Muenchen: Allitera Verlag.

Orgass, S. (1999). Musikalische Bildung als soziale Kategorie—Musikunterricht als bildungsrelevante Praxis. *Musik und Bildung, 6,* 10–15.

Orgass, S. (2008). "Entwicklung von Problemloesekompetenzen" als schlechte Trivialisierung der Aufgabe des Musikunterrichts: Ueberlegungen zu einem musikpaedagogischen Leistungsbegriff. In H.-U. Schaefer-Lembeck (Ed.), *Leistung im Musikunterricht* (pp. 153–225). Muenchen: Allitera Verlag.

Rolle, C. (1999). *Musikalisch-aesthetische Bildung.* Kassel: Bosse.

Rolle, C. (2008). Argumentationsfaehigkeit: Eine zentrale Dimension musikalischer Kompetenz? In H.-U. Schaefer-Lembeck (Ed.), *Leistung im Musikunterricht* (pp. 70–100). Muenchen: Allitera Verlag.

Schaefer-Lembeck, H.-U. (2008). Einleitung. In H.-U. Schaefer-Lembeck (Ed.), *Leistung im Musikunterricht* (pp. 11–14). Muenchen: Allitera Verlag.

Staatsinstitut fuer Schulqualitaet und Bildungsforschung Muenchen. (n.d.). *LehrplanPLUS fuer Bayerische Grundschulen*. Retrieved from http://www.lehrplanplus.bayern.de/*Bildung*s-und-erziehungsauftrag/grundschule

Stauffer, S. L. (2008). Points of intersection and the problems of agency and place in assessment and creativity in music. In C. C. Leung, L. C. R. Yip, & T. Imada (Eds.), *Music education policy and implementation: international perspectives* (pp. 166–70). Hirosaki: Hirosaki University Press.

Stoeger, C. (2006). Leistungsbeurteilung im Musikunterricht. *AfS-Magazin*, *22*, 4–9. Retrieved from https://www.afs-musik.de/files/Magazin/Nr.%2022%20November%202006/AfS Mag22_02_Stoeger.pdf

UNESCO Publications. (2015). *Rethinking education: Towards a global common good*. Retrieved from http://unesdoc.unesco.org/images/0023/002325/232555e.pdf

Varkøy, Ø (2010). The concept of "Bildung." *Philosophy of Music Education Review*, *18*(1), 85–96.

# INDEX

.........................

*Note*: Page numbers followed by *b, f,* and *t* indicate boxes, figures, and tables, respectively.

Bavaria 519
beat boxers 500
Beatz to Da Streetz (B2DS) 35
behaviorism 110
Bennett, Randy Elliot 90–91
Bentley, Richard 351–52
Betasamosake Simpson, Leanne 43
Bhatta, Pramod 414
Biesta, G. 55
big data 140
Biggs, John B. 168–69, 306
*bildning (Bildung)*
    conceptual analysis 485–86
    and *folkbildning* tradition 487–88 (see also
        *folkbildning*)
    in German music education 518–24
    and holistic educational ideals 488–89
    and neoliberal educational politics 491–92
    and Norwegian Core Curriculum
        449–50, 454
    origins 448–49
    origins and history 484–85
    in Scandinavian educational
        tradition 483–92
    and Swedish music education 490–91
Bingham, Steven 237–38
Birenbaum, Menucha 443–44
Birge, Edward Bailey 195
Black, Paul 303, 475
Black Artists Group (BAG) 335
black market 499
Blommaert, Jan 87
body awareness, as habit of mind 213
Booth, Barbara 188
Booth, E. 206
border crossers 97n4
Borgo, David 495, 506–9
Boston Athletic Association (BAA) 299
Boston marathon 299–300
Boud, David 415
Boulez, Pierre 131
Bowman, Wayne 233
Brand, Adriaan 281–82
Brändström, Sture 488
Breunig, Mary 91–92
bricolage 97n4
Broadfoot, Patricia 84

Brookhart, S. M. 442
Brooks, N. 110
Bruscia, Kenneth E. 243
B2DS (Beatz to Da Streetz) 35
Buber, Martin 62m
Burman, Anders 485
Burnard, Pam 54–55, 337n2, 354
business, education as 7–8. *See also*
        neoliberalism

# C

Caillois, Roger 507
calculability 189–90, 197
Cambridge International IGCSE 433, 435
Campbell's Law 161
Canada, indigenous education in 43
canonization 16, 349–50
capitalism
    economic utility and discipline 41
    and musical norms 40
    and subjectification 37–38
    *See also* neoliberalism
care ethics
    and assessment as relational
        practice 442–44
    basics 437–38
    care as a disposition 439–40
    care as a practice 438–39
    interactive regulation 441–42
    and interrelationships 440
    macro-assessment culture vs. 435
    and micro-assessment cultures in South
        African music education 431–32, 437–44
    practices/tools informing a caring
        micro-assessment culture 440–44
*Caring: A Feminine Approach to Ethics and
    Moral Education* (Noddings) 437
caring-about, caring-for vs. 438
Carlson, Kenneth 11–13
catalytic validity 270, 271
causality, correlation vs. 5–6
Chawla-Duggan, Rita 101
Chen-Edmund, Jian-Jun 232, 234–35
Cheung-Yung, Jane 523
"Chicken Rhythm" 380b, 382, 382f
*Children's Corner* (Debussy) 376
choir, integrative assessment for 266–67